DICTIONARY OF
DEMOGRAPHY

DICTIONARY OF DEMOGRAPHY

TERMS, CONCEPTS, AND INSTITUTIONS

A–M

WILLIAM PETERSEN
AND
RENEE PETERSEN

with the collaboration of an
International Panel of Demographers

GREENWOOD PRESS
New York • Westport, Connecticut • London

Library of Congress Cataloging in Publication Data

Petersen, William.
  Dictionary of demography, terms, concepts, and
institutions.

  Bibliography: p.
  Includes index.
  Contents: v. 1. A–M —— v. 2. N–Z.

  1. Demography—Dictionaries—Polyglot. 2. Diction-
aries, Polyglot. I. Petersen, Renee. II. Title.
HB849.2.P47 1986   304.6′03   83-12571
ISBN 0-313-24134-1 (lib. bdg. : set : alk paper)
ISBN 0-313-25141-X (lib. bdg. : v. 1 : alk paper)
ISBN 0-313-25142-8 (lib. bdg. : v. 2 : alk paper)

Library of Congress Catalog Card Number: 83-12571

ISBN 0-313-24134-1 (set)
ISBN 0-313-25141-X (v. 1)
ISBN 0-313-25142-8 (v. 2)

First published in 1986

Greenwood Press, Inc.
88 Post Road West
Westport, Connecticut 06881

Printed in the United States of America

The paper used in this book complies with the
Permanent Paper Standard issued by the National
Information Standards Organization (Z39.48-1984).

10 9 8 7 6 5 4 3 2 1

Contents

Collaborators

The international range of this work was possible only with the full and conscientious cooperation of the collaborators, whom we thank most cordially. In some cases the entries on persons of other countries were drafted from sources in the United States and then corrected, amended, and brought up to date by demographers personally acquainted with the work in each area. Many of the collaborators wrote drafts of entries themselves and suggested persons to be included or deleted. The major compensation for this task has been the knowledge that we were all contributing to a reference work that will be of use in the discipline.

Thanks are due also to librarians especially at the University of California, Santa Cruz, and at the University of California, Berkeley; Stanford University; and Hoover Institution Library, Stanford.

Some of the collaborators advised on one of the languages into which the demographic terms were translated in the multilingual glossary or on countries' demographic institutions, both of which are in the companion volumes, *Dictionary of Demography: Biographies*, and *Multilingual Glossary*. All collaborators except those marked with a double asterisk are also included in the regular alphabetical listing, in *Biographies*, which provides more details on their professional careers and writings.

John S. Aird, Chief, Foreign Demographic Analysis Division, U.S. Bureau of the Census, Washington, D.C.
China (PRC): biographies

Barbara A. Anderson, Department of Sociology, University of Michigan, Ann Arbor
Russian glossary

Eduardo E. Arriaga, Special Assistant for International Demographic Methods, International Demographic Data Center, U.S. Bureau of the Census, Washington, D.C.
Spanish glossary; Latin American demographic institutions and biographies

Mikhail S. Bernstam, Fellow, Hoover Institution on War, Revolution, and Peace, Stanford, California

Russian glossary; U.S.S.R.: demographic institutions and biographies; Soviet society

W. D. Borrie, Executive Director, Academy of the Social Sciences in Australia, Canberra, Australia

Australia and New Zealand: demographic institutions and biographies

Salustiano del Campo, Department of Sociology, University of Madrid, Madrid, Spain

Spain: demographic institutions and biographies

Emilio Casetti, Department of Geography, Ohio State University, Columbus, Ohio

Italian glossary

S. Chandrasekhar, Editor, *Population Review*, La Jolla, California

India: demographic institutions and biographies

Jean-Claude Chasteland, Assistant Director, U.N. Population Division, New York, N.Y.

Iran: demographic institutions and biographies

**Wen-shun Chi, a research linguist at the Center for Chinese Studies, University of California, Berkeley, has translated a large number of programmatic statements of the Chinese government, which were published by the University of California Press, Berkeley: *Readings in Chinese Communist Documents* (3rd ed.; 1968); *Readings in Chinese Communist Ideology* (1968); and *Readings in the Chinese Communist Cultural Revolution* (1971). He is also the author of a *Chinese-English Dictionary of Contemporary Usage* (Berkeley: University of California Press, 1977), and is completing a work on the ideology underlying China's programs of social reconstruction.

Chinese glossary

Lee-Jay Cho, President, East-West Center, Honolulu, Hawaii

South Korea: demographic institutions and biographies

Halûk Cillov, Director, Institute of Statistics, University of Istanbul, Turkey

Turkey, demographic institutions and biographies

Carlo Corsini, Professor of Demography in the Statistics Department, University of Florence, Florence, Italy

Italy: demographic institutions and biographies

Ståle Dyrvik, History Institue, University of Bergen, Bergen, Norway

Norway: demographic institutions and biographies

Juan C. Elizaga, Director, Latin American Demographic Center (CELADE), Santiago, Chile, until his retirement in 1979

Latin American demographic institutions and biographies

Gustav Feichtinger, Professor of Statistics, Vienna University of Technology, and Director, Institute of Demography, Austrian Academy of Sciences, Vienna, Austria

Austria: demographic institutions and biographies

Murray Feshbach, Center for Population Research, Georgetown University, Washington, D.C.

Russian glossary; U.S.S.R.: demographic institutions and biographies

Gunnar Fougstedt, now retired, was at the Swedich School of Economics, Helsinki, and Chairman, Swedish Population Association in Finland

Finland: demographic institutions and biographies

Tomas Frejka, Associate, Center for Population Studies, Population Council, New York, N.Y.

Czechoslovakia: demographic institutions and biographies

Eugene Grebenik, Office of Population Censuses and Surveys, London, and Editor, *Population Studies*, London, England

United Kingdom: demographic institutions and biographies

Jack Harewood, Director, Institute of Social and Economic Research, University of the West Indies, St. Augustine, Trinidad

English-speaking Caribbean area: demographic institutions and biographies

Hans Harmsen, until his retirement in 1968 Professor of Hygiene and Preventive Medicine, University of Hamburg; president, German Academy of Demography

West Germany: demographic institutions and biographies

Jacques Henripin, Professor of Demography, University of Montreal, Montreal, Canada

French Canada: demographic institutions and biographies

Erland Hofsten, Professor of Statistics, University of Stockholm, Stockholm, Sweden

Sweden: demographic institutions and biographies

Kurt Horstmann, now retired, was with the Federal Statistical Office, Wiesbaden, West Germany

West Germany: demographic institutions and biographies

Nathan Keyfitz, until his retirement in 1983 Professor of Sociology jointly at Harvard University, Cambridge, Mass., and Ohio State University, Columbus, Ohio

mathematical demography; Canada: demographic institutions and biographies

András Klinger, Chief, Population Statistics Department, Central Statistical Office, Budapest, Hungary

Hungary: demographic institutions and biographies

**Shigeru Kojima, a native of Japan, earned his doctorate in 1984 from the Department of Sociology, University of California, Berkeley. His interests center on social demography and the sociology of work and occupations.

Japanese glossary; Japan: demographic institutions and biographies

**Hilja Kukk is a reference librarian at the Hoover Institution on War, Revolution, and Peace, Stanford, California

Russian glossary; U.S.S.R.: biographies

Massimo Livi Bacci, Professor of Demography, University of Florence, Florence, Italy

Italian glossary

Francis C. Madigan, S.J., Director, Research Institute for Mindanao Culture, Xavier University, Cagayan de Oro City, Philippines

Philippines: demographic institutions and biographies

Kurt B. Mayer, now retired, was Professor of Sociology, University of Bern, Bern, Switzerland

Switzerland: demographic institutions and biographies

D. Peter Mazur, Professor Sociology, Western Washington University, Bellingham, Washington

Poland: demographic institutions and biographies

Robert J. McIntyre, Department of Economics, Bates College, Lewiston, Maine

Bulgaria: demographic institutions and biographies

Geoffrey McNicoll, Deputy Director, Center for Policy Studies, Population Council, New York, N.Y.

Indonesia: demographic institutions and biographies

Walter Mertens, Advisor on Demographic Research and Training, U.N. Development Program in China, Peking, China; subsequently visiting scholar at the Center for Population Studies, Harvard University, Cambridge, Massachusetts

China (PRC): demographic institutions

Henrik Mørkeberg, sociologist at the Danish National Institue of Social Research, Copenhagen, Denmark

Denmark: demographic institutions and biographies

Helmut V. Muhsam, Professor of Demography and Statistics, Hebrew University of Jerusalem, Jerusalem, Israel

Israel: demographic institutions and biographies

Charles B. Nam, Professor of Sociology and Director, Center for the Study of Population, Florida State University, Tallahassee, Florida

General review

Joaquim Nazareth, Chairman, Department of Sociology, New University of Lisbon, Lisbon, Portugal

Portugal: demographic institutions and biographies

Patrick O. Ohadike, Special Assistant to the Executive Secretary, U.N. Economic Commission for Africa (ECA), Addis Ababa, Ethiopia

Black Africa: demographic institutions and biographies

Roland Pressat, demographer at the National Institute of Demographic Studies (INED), Paris, and the University of Paris, Paris, France

France: demographic institutions and biographies

Ferdinand J. C. M. Rath, chief technical advisor to the Bureau of Population and Employment Policies, International Labor Organization, in Guatemala; formerly Director, U.N. Demographic Center (CEDOR) in Bucharest, Romania

Romania: demographic institutions and biographies

Georges Sabagh, Department of Sociology, University of California, Los Angeles, California

Arab countries: demographic institutions and biographies

Jan L. Sadie, Bureau of Economic Research, University of Stellenbosch, Stellenbosch, South Africa

South Africa: demographic institutions and biographies

Nafis Sadik, Assistant Executive Director, U.N. Fund for Population Activities, New York, N.Y.

Pakistan and Bangladesh: demographic institutions and biographies

Sagaza Haruo, Professor of Sociology, Waseda University, Tokyo, Japan

Japanese glossary; Japan: demographic institutions and biographies

Saw Swee-Hock, Department of Economics and Statistics, National University of Singapore, Singapore

Malaysia, Singapore, and Hong Kong: demographic institutions and biographies

George S. Siampos, Director, Population Division, National Statistical Service of Greece, Athens, Greece

Greece: demographic institutions and biographies

T. H. Sun, Director, Taiwan Provincial Institute of Family Planning, Taichung, Taiwan

Taiwan (ROC): demographic institutions and biographies

Riad B. Tabbarah, Resident Representative, U.N. Development Program, Tunis, Tunisia

Arab countries: demographic institutions and biographies

Arumugam Thavarajah, Director, Policy and Evaluation Division, U.N. Fund for Population Activities, New York, N.Y.

Sri Lanka: demographic institutions and biographies

Ralph Thomlinson, Professor of Sociology, California State University, Los Angeles, California

Thailand: demographic institutions and biographies

Philip van Praag, now retired in the Netherlands, was at the Free University of Brussels (Dutch-language) and President, Belgian Demographic Society

Belgium and the Netherlands: demographic institutions and biographies

Joseph Velikonja, Department of Geography, University of Washington, Seattle, Washington

Yugoslavia: demographic institutions and biographies

Brendan Walsh, Department of Political Economy, University College, Dublin, Ireland

Ireland: demographic institutions

Hilde Wander, now retired, was an economic demographer at the Kiel Institute of World Economics, Kiel, West Germany

German glossary; West Germany: demographic institutions and biographies

**Florence L. Yuan has been since 1956 a research assistant in the Foreign Demographic Analysis Division, U.S. Bureau of the Census, Washington, D.C. She has prepared numerous translations of key Chinese statements on population policy and has compiled bibliographies on China's population and regional economic development. Most recently she has completed a Chinese-English glossary of demographic terms.

Chinese glossary

Introduction

A "dictionary" of "demography" is not a very precise designation, for these terms can signify many things. The format adopted here is in fact a compromise among several possible alternatives.[1] If, for example, readers want to know what a *general fertility rate* is, they need only look for that term in its regular alphabetical place—the best arrangement in that simple case. If they want also to compare the general fertility rate with other *fertility measures, the cross-reference indicated by an asterisk tells them where to proceed. And then, if they want to get a better idea of the entity or process that these various rates measure, they are directed to the long entry on *fertility. Or, vice versa, they might begin with the most general discussion and then work down to those details about which they want information. Proceeding in either direction, readers can be guided quickly to the desired place in the volume by the very full index.

In short, all the 1,484 entries are in a single alphabetical order. Some are no more than a line or two in length, others are essays of some depth. The range of the work is indicated briefly by a list of the book's components:

Vocabulary: the special terms of demography and related disciplines defined and illustrated.

Demographic and related institutions: a brief description of all important research, promotional, or teaching institutions throughout the world, including national statistical bureaus.

Countries: a discussion of factors influencing population trends in the largest nations, as well as in some of the smaller ones of especial interest or importance in this context.

References: works where more information can be found about particular topics.

Index: a complete cross-reference to every notation of a person, country, or main topic of demography.

---

[1] A somewhat longer statement of the theme expounded in this introduction is given in William Petersen, "Thoughts on Writing a Dictionary of Demography," *Population and Development Review*, 9 (1983), 677-687.

Each of these features is discussed at greater length in this introduction. Biographies of 3,363 analysts of population, past and present, the world over, are given in the companion volume, *Dictionary of Demography: Biographies*. Cross-references to persons in that volume are marked with daggers.

Vocabulary.   Paul †Vincent, a member of the team that developed the first of the multilingual demographic dictionaries sponsored by the United Nations, wrote an interesting article on his experience.[2] Much of his paper pertained to difficulties in translating technical terms, but much also to the less obvious but more pervasive blocks to an acceptable definition of the field and an appropriate presentation of its main terms and concepts. Several decades later, when Roland †Pressat finished his dictionary of demography, he wrote a similar appraisal of his experience.[3] In both cases these seasoned and competent demographers found that they had to rethink matters that they might have assumed they already knew. One recurrent dilemma, as Vincent put it, was whether to define demography in a "restrictive" or "extensive" manner. In arguing for the second alternative, he asked the reader to imagine the reaction of someone who, "in order to translate a work *on demography* had to resort to a whole series of technical dictionaries—sociological, juridical, medical, economic, etc.—after having vainly searched in his 'demographic' dictionary for terms currently used in demography." In order really to satisfy Vincent's imagined reader, we found it would be necessary—just in relation to morbidity and mortality, for example—to define such terms as "asepsis," "cancer," "death," "epidemiology," "injury," "suicide," "war," and so on. And to define many of such terms is hardly adequate. We all know what is meant by "suicide," and the interesting question is rather how many self-inflicted deaths get included in the statistics, and particularly whether the proportion of suicides disguised as accidental or natural deaths varies from one social category to another.

Pressat noted that sometimes the same word had been coined several times with different meanings. For example, in 1901 a Belgian demographer named Gustaaf †Cauderlier used *fecundability in a sense that did not survive; then, in 1924, the Italian demographer Corrado †Gini gave the word its current meaning. Pressat chose, undoubtedly correctly, to forgo historical completeness and restrict his definitions to the usages present-day readers would generally want to know. Some archaic usages also of English words are embedded in famous historical works (*population in the sense of "growth in numbers" appears in the U.S. Declaration of Independence), but except for such occasional instances, we agree, obsolescent meanings are better left out.

[2]Paul Vincent, "Conception d'un Dictionnaire Démographique," *Population*, 8 (1953), 103-120. See also *Multilingual Demographic Dictionary: English Section*, Population Studies of the U.N., no. 29 (New York, 1958).

[3]Roland Pressat, "Le Vocabulaire de la Démographie," *Population*, 35 (1980), 850-859; *Dictionnaire de Démographie* (Paris: Presses Universitaires de France, 1979).

We had to make more difficult decisions about what H. W. Fowler in his *Dictionary of Modern English Usage* called "sturdy indefensibles"—usages that should never have been adopted but are too widespread to be attacked success-fully. Persons aged 20-24, for instance, comprise a category—not a group, which implies a degree of conscious coherence; but the standard term *age group, however unfortunate, is irremovable. The more recent *natural fertility has all the ambiguity of "nature" in any sense; it does *not* mean, as some might suppose, the fertility of beings living outside a cultural setting. As Pressat illustrated at length, even such routine technical terms as *rate and *ratio are not used entirely consistently. And in some cases words that demographers define precisely can be confused with looser usages. For example, *longevity is defined in a general dictionary simply as "long duration of life" or "length of life"; generally demographers use it to mean the maximum life span attainable. Or, the distinction between *fecundity and *fertility, crucial in a demographic analysis, is seldom maintained when physicians use the words.

An alphabetical list of words with their meanings and sometimes their etymol-ogies makes up the core of this book's vocabulary: such terms as *cohort and *demographic transition and such distinctions as between immigration and in-migration (see *migration, international, and *migration, internal). Included also are words whose meanings might seem obvious—*birth and *death, for instance, which are defined more precisely in a medical-legal context than in everyday usage. In fact, however, the special vocabulary of demography is not very large, and the problem is often not the meaning of terms but rather the validity of theses associated with them. The fertility of the United States or of less developed countries is much discussed, and often the problem is not the word but the relative worth of opposed arguments. Is the *rhythm method an ineffective means of contraception? (It depends on which rhythm method is used.) Is *zero pop-ulation growth a desirable goal in the United States? (Yes and no, for it would bring some benefits at some costs.) Is the extensive effort to reduce the birth rate of *less developed countries succeeding? (Yes in some, possibly in others, almost certainly not in still others.) As such questions suggest, the ideological debate is often between antagonists both of whom are partly wrong, and the first defense against their half-true statements is more knowledge. In their discussion of fertility, what account do they take of how it interacts with the population's *age structure? Are their data well based or, on the contrary, the sometimes unduly positive reports of those who have used up one research grant and would like another? No general reference work could respond to such detailed queries, but the list of readings included with each of the major items affords the possibility of following the arguments on both sides.

Demography can be understood in either of two senses. *Formal *demography* means the study of how *fertility, *mortality, and age structure interact and, more routinely, the application of techniques appropriate to the gathering, col-lating, statistical analysis, and presentation of population data. What can be designated in contrast as *population analysis* is the systematic study of population trends and phenomena in relation to their social setting. A special problem arises in specifying the vocabulary associated with "the determinants and consequences of population trends," as the larger context of demography was called in a well known publication of the United Nations. We need move only a short way into this broader population analysis to find ourselves crossing one discipline boundary after another—biology as it relates to conception and, birth, nutrition, and the causes of death; medicine and public health at least in their overall features; geography, human ecology, and city planning as they concern migration and the spatial distribution of population and the relation of people to their physical environment; those portions of sociology and anthropology pertaining to public opinions, ethnicity, urbanism, forms of the family and their relation to fertility and family planning; the new subdiscipline of development economics and other branches of economics that pertain to the labor force, human capital, and demographic variables; archeology and history as they relate to the past growth of humankind.

This staggering scope does not reflect an idiosyncratic view of the discipline. If we take as one indication of demography's dimensions the topics of inquiry in United States censuses and population surveys, we find most of the same subjects: for example, marital status and the number of children desired and borne; race, nationality, language(s) spoken, and citizenship; rural, urban, or metropolitan residence; occupation, income, whether employed, and various related facts; years of schooling; whether a veteran or a military pensioner; whether suffering from an acute or chronic disease; and so on. Moreover, interpretations of the data baldly tabulated in census volumes sometimes use additional special terms in relating population figures to other trends. Some interesting new developments, such as historical demography or population anthropology, transcend census data by definition and with another extension of the professional vocabulary that some analysts of population phenomena use. The bibliographic journal *Population Index*, which is another convenient measure of the discipline's compass, also ranges very far from the narrow concerns of demography in a more restricted sense.

Where to draw the line between items included in the vocabulary and those excluded had to be decided again and again, and the decisions have erred, intentionally, on the generous side. Our overall principle has been that a term must be related in some way to population analysis and that the definition or description, though including generalities when these seemed appropriate, should concentrate on that relation. The entry on each of the disciplines associated with demography, for instance, expounds its main characteristics but especially its particular relevance to the study of population. The articles on many of the world's major cultures (*African society, *Soviet society, etc.) concentrate on the specific determinants in that setting of fertility, mortality, and migration. Such discussions of larger topics are supplemented by more concise ones of narrower terms; for example, the articles on *Jews and *Judaism summarize what is known about the relation between being Jewish and population processes; and such ancillary terms as *ghetto and *holocaust are also defined and exemplifed.

Countries and Demographic Institutions.   Entries on 161 countries are of three types. The broad discussions of topics like *India sometimes pertain to particular nations, including seven of the world's largest. However, it would serve no purpose in such a work as this to discuss the factors related to population in, for instance, each Muslim country; and the common characteristics are noted under *Islam. Eight other countries that are discussed individually, such as *Israel and *Taiwan, are of small size and slight power; but their population characteristics or history are especially interesting. On the other hand, there is no entry for the United States or American Society, for many of the terms and concepts are illustrated with examples from that country.

In another type of entry, all the world's significant demographic institutions are listed and briefly described under the name of the country in which they are located. These items were drafted or corrected by the book's collaborators, in each case a demographer personally familiar with population research in the country or region. In the special case of the United States, academic institutions are grouped under the heading *United States: Universities and Related Associations, and government bureaus under *United States: Federal Agencies or *United States: State and Local Demographic Centers; private nonacademic organizations concerned with population matters are in their regular alphabetical order.

Many countries, of course, have no research or teaching unit in demography, but all do have some sort of statistical unit that gathers and publishes whatever population data are made available. For such nations the entry gives at least the name and address of the agency, as well as the title(s) of its principal serial publication(s).

International demographic institutions are in one sense of fundamental importance, for a meaningful comparison can be made across cultures or time periods only if the data are gathered and classified by categories defined in the same way. In the past international professional societies, particularly the *International Statistical Institute, were instrumental in setting universal standards, and when these could not be achieved, it noted the differences remaining in national practices. Over the century or more that demographers, biostatisticians, epidemiologists, and others have struggled to construct an adequate base for international statistics, the main impediment has been national sentiment. For population data can reveal much to critics or adversaries—potential military weakness, a gross inequity in the distribution of income, a lack in the number or quality of medical facilities, and so on. The *United Nations, which by a wide margin is currently the largest and most cited international agency, also reflects in many of its activities and publications this conflict between transnational objectivity and a pervasive and seemingly growing nationalist sensitivity.

The entries on international agencies describe their functions and activities and also, when it seems appropriate, the efficiency with which they work.

References. The scope of this work has meant that much of it derives from other sources; indeed, one of the important uses of the book is to direct the reader to that source where additional information on a particular topic can be found. The reference work(s) with which almost every one of the entries ends represent(s) the end point of much research. A list of the works cited in abbreviated form is given on pages 1015–1016.

   The accuracy of the items in this book, thus, must sometimes depend on how accurate the sources are—and that many of them are disappointingly inaccurate became apparent when we checked one source against another. Indeed, the collaboration of the considerable number of experts has eliminated many of the errors or omissions to be found in print, but it would be fanciful to suppose that our great effort to avoid mistakes of fact or interpretation has been entirely successful. If those who use the book would note errors and write to the publisher, their kindness in helping correct subsequent printings will be much appreciated.

Index. The usefulness of a work like this depends largely on how easy it is to find precisely the information one wants. In the main body of the text, the many cross-references, indicated by asterisks, lead from one article to what may be another pertinent one. Cross-references to our *Dictionary of Demography: Biographies* are indicated by daggers. With an alphabetical ordering of the items, an index would be almost nugatory if it did no more than replicate the same list. Instead, the very full index notes every mention of every person or major topic. In other words, the considerable amount of variegated information is organized in such a way as to make quickly available any bit that is being sought. The main listing for Thailand, as an example, includes only a brief notation on demographic institutions in that country; but under Thailand in the index the reader will be directed to every item where its population is mentioned.

DICTIONARY OF
DEMOGRAPHY

A

aborigines, the population native to a country, are in many cases alien to the urban core included in demographic statistics. Thus, several South American countries have deliberately excluded from their counts the "Indian jungle population"; New Guinea and other Pacific areas have omitted the "indigenous population"; several southern African states have failed to count either all "Africans" (the term used in South Africa to designate blacks) or those lacking any meaningful contact with industrial society; and the United States, until 1890, left out *American Indians not taxed. In many instances, moreover, general theses pertaining to fertility, mortality, and so on do not apply to a primitive population, the rubric under which many aborigines fit. If the cultural distance between them and the other sectors of the population becomes smaller, those previously designated as aborigines may be included in counts as an ethnic group, but typically with a vague and somewhat erratic delineation. See also *population, primitive.

abortifacient, a drug or substance used to induce an *abortion.

abortion, the premature expulsion of the fruit of a conception from the uterus. An abortion may be spontaneous or induced; if the latter, it may be therapeutic or brought about as a substitute for contraception. According to some authorities' guesses, it is the most widely used method of controlling fertility in the world today, in spite of its ambivalent status in ethical norms and many legal codes (cf. Tietze, 1983).

Western tradition is not consistent on the issue. Jewish law permitted an abortion to save the mother's life, but not otherwise (Greenberg, 1976). Among Greek philosophers, both †Plato and †Aristotle accepted abortion as licit under certain conditions, but the Hippocratic oath, which all physicians swear still today, includes the pledge that they will not give a woman an abortive remedy. Roman law did not define the fetus as human, and some early Church fathers followed this interpretation, while others held that the embryo acquired a soul at the moment of conception. †Augustine, however, differentiated between a "formed" and "nonformed" fetus, holding that an abortion of the latter does not constitute murder; similarly, Thomas †Aquinas taught that life begins at the moment of "quickening," or the first recognizable movements of the fetus, which take place between the sixteenth and eighteenth weeks following conception. This differentiation between an abortion early and late in pregnancy was embodied in canon law and thus influenced English common law and some American legislation (see also *Humanae Vitae). A distinction is made also in medical terminology: the development from a fertilized *ovum between one week after conception to the end of the second month is called an "embryo"; the subsequent *fetus is called "viable" if it can live outside the uterus; an abortion is called "early" before twenty-two weeks of gestation.

Indicative data suggest that abortions were very common in the nineteenth century (Sauer, 1974, 1978). The large body of writings on the probable number of abortions performed when they were illegal has not resulted in any degree of consensus (see, e.g., the exchange between James, 1971, and Goodhart, 1973). Whatever figures one deduced had important political implications, since they indicated that abortion was either an aberrant behavior of a relatively small number or, alternatively, a surreptitious means of fertility control by many otherwise law-abiding women and physicians. Broader grounds for legal abortions have recently been instituted in France, West Germany, and (most remarkably) Italy, for example, as well as in such less developed countries as India, Singapore, and Tunisia, among others. In 1973, thus, when in *Roe* v. *Wade* the U.S. Supreme Court substantially curtailed the power of the states to limit a woman's right to an abortion, it was going along with an international trend (see also *privacy; *Soviet society).

The legalization of abortion has everywhere intensified political conflict over the issue. In the United States the major organizations supporting and opposing legal abortion are, respectively, the National Abortion Rights Action League (NARAL) and the National Right to Life Committee (NRLC). NARAL members are typically young, white, urban, college-educated, non-Catholic women. Of NRLC members about 70 percent are Catholics; and generally all the members deem religion to be important to them, in contrast to the more or less secularist members of NARAL. The two memberships differ significantly also on such related questions as sex education in the schools, premarital sex, homosexuality, sterilization, and the proposed Equal Rights Amendment to the U.S. Constitution (Granberg, 1981). Neither view—that any adolescent or woman should have access to abortion on demand or that abortion is morally equivalent to murder—reflects the majority point of view in the United States (Blake, 1977, 1981); and the issue is troublesome for politicians of both major parties.

Whether legalization has resulted in an increased number of abortions, as one might reasonably expect, depends on which of the disputed figures one uses as the pre-legal base. Many who support the right to abortion as a backup to contraception that has failed would not like to see it become a substitute. Analyses in several countries—Denmark (Somers, 1977) and England (Brewer, 1977),

Abortions, United States, 1974-1980

Year	Abortions (thousands)	Abortions per 1,000 Women Aged 15-44	Pregnancies Terminated by Abortion (percent)	Repeat Abortions (percent)
1974	899	19.3	22.0	15.2
1977	1,317	26.4	28.6	26.6
1978	1,410	27.7	29.2	29.5
1979	1,498	28.8	29.6	31.7
1980	1,554	29.3	30.0	33.0

for instance—do not show consistent results, probably because many repeat abortions are not so reported (Potter and Ford, 1976; see also Tietze and Jain, 1978). The effect on fertility is also ambiguous; in California, legalization did not slow the growth even of illegitimate births (Sklar and Berkov, 1973). Since abortions became legal in the United States, their number has increased greatly, particularly in the first years (Henshaw and O'Reilly, 1983). This increase has reflected not only legal and, in many cases, free medical services, but also cultural factors inhibiting the use of contraceptives (Francome and Francome, 1979).

In operations performed in industrial countries safety has increased considerably with the better facilities and personnel used in legal abortions, as well as by the wide adoption of new methods. The once standard procedures of *saline solution or dilatation and curettage have been largely replaced for first-trimester abortions by *suction curettage. Later in the pregnancy, however, the more complicated technique known as *dilatation and evacuation is required. In the United States the women's death rate in recent years has been 1.4 per 100,000 abortions performed. The situation is sharply different in less developed countries, particularly those where abortion is illegal. Deaths are estimated to be in the range of 50 to 100 per 100,000 operations, or one woman for every 1,000 to 2,000 illegal abortions performed. Women who do not die often suffer more or less serious complications (Liskin, 1980).

Undoubtedly Japan is the best place to test whether abortions are intrinsically injurious to a woman's health—that is, apart from the conditions that prevail when they are illegal. Under a law passed in 1948-49, the state has provided abortions at very low prices in several hundred clinics throughout the country. Trained physicians have performed aseptic operations and prescribed penicillin for every patient; but operations have been permitted up to the seventh month of pregnancy rather than before the end of the first trimester, as doctors generally consider preferable or mandatory. Inconclusive evidence suggests that one or two abortions under such conditions are not typically harmful, but several more may be; and some Japanese physicians and other authorities have recommended that the major emphasis in the state clinics be shifted to contraception, sterilization, or both.

Form Approved
OMB No. 68R 1901

U.S. STANDARD

REPORT OF INDUCED TERMINATION OF PREGNANCY

TYPE OR PRINT IN PERMANENT INK

SEE HANDBOOK FOR INSTRUCTIONS

FACILITY - NAME (If not hospital or clinic, give address)

CITY, TOWN OR LOCATION OF PREGNANCY TERMINATION

COUNTY OF PREGNANCY TERMINATION

STATE FILE NUMBER

1a.

1b.

1c.

PATIENT IDENTIFICATION

AGE OF PATIENT

MARRIED? (Check)
☐ YES ☐ NO

DATE OF PREGNANCY TERMINATION (Month, Day, Year)

2a.

2b.

2c.

3.

RESIDENCE—STATE

COUNTY

CITY, TOWN OR LOCATION

INSIDE CITY LIMITS (Check)
☐ YES ☐ NO

4a.

4b.

4c.

4d.

RACE (Check)
☐ White
☐ Black
☐ American Indian
☐ Other, Specify

EDUCATION (Specify only highest grade completed)

Elementary or Secondary (0-12)

College (1-4 or 5+)

PREVIOUS PREGNANCIES (Complete each section)

LIVE BIRTHS

Now living
Number ____
7a. None ☐

Now dead
Number ____
7b. None ☐

OTHER TERMINATIONS

Spontaneous
Number ____
7c. None ☐

Induced
Number ____
7d. None ☐

5.

6.

TYPE OF TERMINATION PROCEDURES

8a PROCEDURE THAT TERMINATED PREGNANCY

(CHECK ONLY ONE)

☐ - - - - - - - SUCTION CURETTAGE - - - - - - -

☐ - - - - - - - SHARP CURETTAGE - - - - - - -

☐ - - - - INTRA–UTERINE SALINE INSTILLATION - - - -

☐ - - INTRA–UTERINE PROSTAGLANDIN INSTILLATION - -

☐ - - - - - - - HYSTEROTOMY - - - - - - -

☐ - - - - - - - HYSTERECTOMY - - - - - - -

☐ - - - - - - - OTHER (Specify) _____

8b. ADDITIONAL PROCEDURES USED FOR THIS TERMINATION, IF ANY

(CHECK ALL THAT APPLY)

☐
☐
☐
☐
☐
☐
☐

9. COMPLICATIONS OF PREGNANCY TERMINATION

(CHECK ALL THAT APPLY)

☐ NONE
☐ HEMORRHAGE
☐ INFECTION
☐ UTERINE PERFORATION
☐ CERVICAL LACERATION
☐ RETAINED PRODUCTS
☐ OTHER (Specify)

DATE LAST NORMAL MENSES BEGAN (Month, Day, Year)

10.

PHYSICIAN'S ESTIMATE OF GESTATION

11. _____ Weeks

NAME OF ATTENDING PHYSICIAN (Type or print)

12.

NAME OF PERSON COMPLETING REPORT (Type or print)

13.

DEPARTMENT OF HEALTH, EDUCATION, AND WELFARE—PUBLIC HEALTH SERVICE—NATIONAL CENTER FOR HEALTH STATISTICS
1978 REVISION

In the United States basic data on abortions are reported on a standard form entitled ''Report of Induced Termination of Pregnancy'' and then compiled by the National Center for Health Statistics into totals for the country. Abortions are classified as legal or illegal (also termed criminal or clandestine), as induced or spontaneous (also called miscarriages), and as therapeutic or contraceptive. Several measures are used to indicate the relative number of induced abortions. An *abortion rate*, the number of abortions in a year per 1,000 in the base population, may be related to the total population, the women of reproductive ages, married women, or another denominator, as in the comparable series of *fertility measures. In an *abortion ratio*, the number of abortions is related to the number of live births or to the live births plus the abortions. Similarly, deaths are measured by the *abortion mortality rate*, the number of deaths attributed to abortion per 100,000 females in the fecund age range, and the *abortion mortality ratio*, the number of deaths attributed to abortion per 100,000 abortions performed (also known as the death-to-case rate). One other index frequently used by analysts is the *prevalence rate*, or the percentage (or other proportion) of women who have had one or more abortions at any time during their lifetime.

REFERENCES: Judith Blake, ''The Supreme Court's Abortion Decision and Public Opinion in the United States,'' *Population and Development Review*, 3 (1977), 45-62; ''Negativism, Equivocation, and Wobbly Assent: Public 'Support' for the Prochoice Platform on Abortion,'' *Demography*, 18 (1981), 309-320. Colin Brewer, ''Third Time Unlucky: A Study of [English] Women Who Have Three or More Legal Abortions,'' *Journal of Biosocial Science*, 9 (1977), 99-105. Caroline Francome and Colin Francome, ''Towards an Understanding of the American Abortion Rate,'' *Journal of Biosocial Science*, 11 (1979), 303-313. C. B. Goodhart, ''On the Incidence of Illegal Abortion,'' *Population Studies*, 27 (1973), 207-233. Donald Granberg, ''The Abortion Activists,'' *Family Planning Perspectives*, 13 (1981), 157-163. Blu Greenberg, ''Abortion: A Challenge to Halakhah,'' *Judaism*, 25 (1976), 201-208. Stanley K. Henshaw and Kevin O'Reilly, ''Characteristics of Abortion Patients in the United States, 1979 and 1980,'' *Family Planning Perspectives*, 15 (1983), 5–16. William H. James, ''The Incidence of Illegal Abortions.'' *Population Studies*, 25 (1971), 327-330. Laurie S. Liskin, ''Complications of Abortion in Developing Countries,'' Population Information Program, Johns Hopkins University, *Population Reports*, Ser. F, no. 7 (1980). Vera Plaskon, ''Abortion: Medical Techniques,'' in *International Encyclopedia of Population*, 1, 8-11. Robert G. Potter and Kathleen Ford, ''Repeat Abortion,'' *Demography*, 13 (1976), 65-82. R. Sauer, ''Attitudes to Abortion in America, 1800-1973,'' *Population Studies*, 28 (1974), 53-67; ''Infanticide and Abortion in Nineteenth-Century Britain,'' *Population Studies*, 32 (1978), 81-93. June Sklar and Beth Berkov, ''The Effects of Legal Abortion on Legitimate and Illegitimate Birth Rates,'' *Studies in Family Planning*, 4 (1973), 281-292. Ronald L. Somers, ''Repeat Abortion in Denmark,'' *Studies in Family Planning*, 9 (1977), 142-147. Christopher Tietze, ''Induced Abortion,'' *Reports on Population/Family Planning*, no. 14 Supplement (1977); *Induced Abortion: A World View, 1983* (New York: Population Council, 1983). Tietze and Anrudh K. Jain, ''The Mathematics of Repeat Abortion: Explaining the Increase,'' *Studies in Family Planning*, 9 (1978), 294-299.

absenteeism, the habitual failure to report for work, is measured with a variety of indexes (Mikalachki and Gandz, 1979). It is often a serious problem, especially in less developed countries. Peasants work on a schedule set by the seasons and the sun, and it takes them a generation or two to adapt fully to the clock. Moreover, many of those who take industrial jobs retain some links to the traditional sector and leave whenever their assistance is needed, for example, on a family plot. Since the level of skill is generally low, some employers see little reason to develop a fixed labor supply. According to the sparse research in industrial countries, absenteeism is greater among low-paid workers and those who do arduous work, in large as compared to small firms, among the young rather than the old, and among single rather than married men (cf. International Social Security Association, 1981). In the United States, the 1970 and 1980 censuses (with a somewhat different wording of the questions) supplemented the monthly reports by the Bureau of Labor Statistics with questions on absenteeism and *employment. A respondent temporarily absent from his job or business during the week prior to the census was asked whether the reason was a layoff, illness, vacation, bad weather, a labor dispute, or another cause. Obviously the list may represent excuses rather than underlying factors, and a mere compilation does little to explain the phenomenon.

REFERENCES: International Social Security Association, *Absenteeism and Social Security* (Geneva, 1981). A. Mikalachki and J. Gandz, "Measuring Absenteeism," *Industrial Relations* (Quebec), 34 (1979), 516-545.

abstinence, voluntary forbearance from the customary gratification of sensual appetites. In a demographic context, it usually pertains to the forgoing of sexual intercourse, what †Malthus termed moral restraint.

REFERENCE: I. O. Orubuloye, *Abstinence as a Method of Birth Control: Fertility and Childspacing Practices among Rural Yoruba Women of Nigeria* (Canberra: Department of Demography, Australian National University, 1981).

acceptance, a term used by administrators of birth-control programs to designate a common criterion of a successful effort. As generally calculated, an acceptance rate is defined as the number who took the contraceptives proffered to them, and presumably used them for the first time, per thousand of the population to which they were offered. These acceptors are contrasted with nonacceptors, who rejected the means because they were already practicing birth control or because they did not want to, or because of some other motive. There are three reasons why an acceptance rate may not be an accurate indicator of how well a program to reduce fertility is working. (1) Some accept the contraceptives with no intention of using them. (2) Some, who were using contraceptives before the program, shift to those made available to acceptors more cheaply or even gratis. (3) Some who take the contraceptives use them ineffectively or only for a short period, so that the reduction in their fertility is negligible.

access, or accessibility, denotes a physical means of approach to a particular area, as by an "access road." Whether food shortages develop into general famines depends in large part on how isolated various regions are and thus how difficult it is to bring in supplies from the outside. Such raw materials as minerals or forests, on the other hand, are described as "accessible" if they can be usefully exploited. Administrators of health or *family-planning programs use the term "access to services" to indicate potential clients' physical, psychological, financial, and moral ability to use the facilities presumably available to them.

accession rate, the net annual increase in the stationary labor force per 1,000 in the stationary population, after allowing for the retirement or mortality of workers during the year. It can be derived from a table of working life, an adaptation of the *life table to an analysis of the *work force. See also *population, stationary.

accidents, literally chance happenings, are restricted in the context of demography to events that can result in injury or death. Happenings that are seemingly unintentional, unexpected, or at least partly unavoidable can often be analyzed in the aggregate to show recurrent patterns and thus probable causes and meliorative measures (Haddon et al., 1964; Iskrant and Joliet, 1968). Children, of course, are especially susceptible and their mortality from accidents is often analyzed separately (e.g., Marcusson and Oehmisch, 1977). Not surprisingly, each important advance in technology has been associated with at least a temporary rise in accidents related to power machinery, for example, or to automobiles— or even, in the United States during the late 1970s as a reflection of a fad rather than an invention, to bicycles. The long-term trend in Western countries can be exemplified by the partial statistics on deaths from accidents available for France from 1826 on (Chesnais, 1974). In the middle of the nineteenth century the main category of deaths was drownings. Then mortality associated with mechanical, steam, or electrical power increased, leveled off, and finally declined sharply except for the special category of automobile accidents, now the principal cause of death among children and young adults in both France and other industrial countries.

According to recent United States data, accidents have ranked fourth among causes of death (U.S. National Center for Health Statistics, 1980; cf. Preston, 1974). But the three causes of death that have ranked higher—cardiovascular diseases, cancers, and strokes—generally affect persons of relatively advanced ages; and in the typical year of 1978, accidents ranked first among those aged 1–44, contrasted with fourth for those aged 45-64, and seventh for those aged 65 and over. By "accidents" is meant especially motor-vehicle accidents, in spite of great improvements in such engineering factors as the design of automobiles, the construction of roads, and the regulation of traffic (cf. Ellis, 1977). Apart from such obvious factors as drunken driving, assessing the relative importance of human characteristics is difficult because of the slight relevance of the statistics. As collected by either the police or insurance companies, the data reflect the narrow interests of those institutions, and the concept of responsibility that underlies these sets of records has been eroded by laws permitting no-fault insurance. A better understanding of what social factors contribute to motor-vehicle accidents would have to start, in fact, from collecting statistics specifically related to that question (Moynihan, 1966). A short step in this direction has been taken by the U.S. National Transportation Safety Board, a federal agency established in 1974. It maintains what it terms "go-teams," presumably always ready to proceed to the site of a serious accident and make an independent investigation on the spot. From its annual reports, it is evident that the board concentrates on airplane accidents and, among those involving automobiles, on those with multiple deaths (U.S. National Transportation Safety Board, 1980).

Probably the ethnic minority in the United States with the highest mortality from accidents is *American Indians, especially children and old people. During a typical year's observation of the Navajo, there were 4,803 accidents resulting in injury, equivalent to an *incidence rate of 43.9 per 1,000 population. The crude death rate from accidents was 104.2, contrasted with 58 for the general population (Brown et al., 1970).

REFERENCES: R. Chris Brown, Bak S. Gurunanjappa, Rodney J. Hawk, and Delphine Bitsuie, "The Epidemiology of Accidents among the Navajo," *Public Health Reports*, 85 (1970), 881-888. Jean-Claude Chesnais, "La Mortalité par Accidents en France depuis 1826," *Population*, 29 (1974), 1097-1136. P. M. Ellis, "Motor Vehicle Mortality Reductions since the Energy Crisis," *Journal of Risk and Insurance*, 44 (1977), 373-381. William Haddon, Jr., Edward A. Suchman, and David Klein, *Accident Research: Methods and Approaches* (New York: Harper & Row, 1964). Albert P. Iskrant and Paul V. Joliet, *Accidents and Homicide* (Cambridge, Mass.: Harvard University Press, 1968). Hildegard Marcusson and Wilhelm Oehmisch, "Accident Mortality in Childhood in Selected Countries of Different Continents, 1950-1971," *World Health Statistics Report*, 30 (1977), 57-92. Daniel P. Moynihan, "The War against the Automobile," *Public Interest*, no. 3 (1966), 10-26. Samuel H. Preston, "Demographic and Social Consequences of Various Causes of Death in the United States," *Social Biology*, 21 (1974), 144-162. U.S. National Center for Health Statistics, "Final Mortality Statistics, 1978," *Monthly Vital Statistics Report*, 29:6, Supplement (September 17, 1980). U.S. National Transportation Safety Board, *Annual Report to Congress, 1979* (Washington, D.C., 1980).

accommodation, any adjustment that tends to reduce conflict. In a schema still used by many analysts, the American sociologists Robert E. †Park and Ernest W. †Burgess designated accommodation as one of the sequences of four processes through which groups go when they come into social or cultural contact—namely, *competition, conflict, accommodation, and *assimilation.

REFERENCE: Robert E. Park and Ernest W. Burgess, *Introduction to the Science of Sociology* (Chicago: University of Chicago Press, 1921).

accouchement, French for childbirth, once a common euphemism. Note also *accoucheur* for obstetrician, *accoucheuse* for midwife.

acculturation comprises, according to a study initiated by the *Social Science Research Council, "those phenomena which result when groups of individuals having different cultures come into continuous first-hand contact, with subsequent changes in the original cultural patterns of either or both groups" (Redfield et al., 1936). This is essentially what British anthropologists mean by "culture contact." Among social demographers who have written about migration, acculturation is sometimes used as a generic term similar to *assimilation, sometimes as a more specific denotation of changes in language, religion, and other cultural variables.

REFERENCE: Robert Redfield, Ralph Linton, and Melville J. Herskovits, "Outline for the Study of Acculturation," *American Anthropology*, N.S. 38 (1936), 149-152.

accuracy, the relative closeness of an estimate or observation to the true value, to be distinguished from *precision, the relative dispersion of observations or estimates from some central value, whether or not this is taken to be the "true" one.

action-research, the combination into one operation of efforts to right a social wrong and to understand its causes. Such a merger, however, contradicts the conventional norms set for each of the two components. According to the scientific canon, research should take place in a context rendered as neutral as possible, and in particular the outcome that the researcher hopes for should not be allowed to affect the findings. It is ordinarily expected, moreover, that no public policy should be instituted before research has indicated what its effects are likely to be. The principal reason that on occasion these guidelines have been ignored is that the urgency of a social problem supposedly demands that the two processes be collapsed into one. An additional reason may be the difficulty of conducting research before meliorative measures are taken. According to the principal population officer of the U.S. Agency for International Development (AID), "Because the extent of availability of family-planning information and means is usually a dominant determinant . . . [of] reproductive behavior, no reliable studies nor judgments of additional measures which may ultimately be needed to achieve the desired rate of population increase can be made *in advance* of the extension of family-planning services" (Ravenholt, 1968). However true this may be, even after the fact it is extraordinarily difficult to trace a causal chain through an intricate social complex; and the task is not easier if it is carried out by someone supervising *family-planning programs and, quite naturally, anxious that they be proved successful. One reason that "the great debate on population policy" (Berelson, 1975) has not been resolved is that the protagonists have started from incompatible premises, but another significant factor is that research embedded in action programs has been too biased to resolve any of the issues (cf. Mauldin and Berelson, 1978; Petersen, 1981).

REFERENCES: Bernard Berelson, *The Great Debate on Population Policy: An Instructive Entertainment* (New York: Population Council, 1975). W. Parker Mauldin and Berelson, "Conditions of Fertility Decline in Developing Countries, 1965-75," *Studies in Family Planning*, 9 (May, 1978), 89-147. William Petersen, "American Efforts to Reduce the Fertility of Less Developed Countries," in Nick Eberstadt, ed., *Fertility Decline in Less Developed Countries* (New York: Praeger, 1981). R. T. Ravenholt, "The A.I.D. Population and Family-Planning Program—Goals, Scope, and Progress," *Demography*, 5 (1968), 561-573.

activity ordinarily refers to participation in the *labor force, but in the 1970 and 1980 enumerations the U.S. Bureau of the Census extended the range of the term's meaning. All persons aged 15 years and older were asked what their activity had been five years earlier. Responses were classified as working in a job or business (that is, in the civilian labor force), in the armed forces, or attending college. In 1980 those in the latter two categories were also asked what their *residence had been in 1975, so that military service and attendance at a college could be related to migration trends.

activity space, a term developed mainly by the French geographer Chombart de Lauwe, denotes the space where most of an individual's activities take place. It usually comprises a number of discontinuous areas, each related to family, neighborhood, work place, or another focus of social life.

REFERENCE: P. H. Chombart de Lauwe, *Paris et l'Agglomération Parisienne*, 2 vols. (Paris: Presses Universitaires de France, 1952).

actuary, one skilled in the calculation of insurance risks and premiums. Also, *actuarial*, pertaining to actuaries and their work; *actuaries' table*, an alternative designation of a *life table or, more specifically, a life table in which premium rates have been calculated from survival probabilities. Unlike demographers, who generally use life tables to analyze mortality as a mass phenomenon, actuaries are much more interested in the probability of an individual's survival or of the joint survival of husband and wife. One consequence is that actuaries have developed more precise methods of *interpolation and *graduation than are commonly used in demographic analysis. In what is called a "select table," the standard risks associated with age and sex are supplemented by others based on the state of health and sometimes other factors.

acute, of a disease, having a short and relatively severe course. Its opposite is *chronic. Alternatively, acute also characterizes an infectious or other curable disease, rather than a morbid condition marking the deterioration associated with *aging. In the United States during 1980, illnesses and injuries defined as acute resulted in 9.9 days of "restricted activities" per person. An estimated total of 68 million persons, or almost a third of the population, were injured or ill.

REFERENCE: U.S. National Center for Health Statistics, *Current Estimates from the National Health Interview Survey: United States, 1980* (Washington, D.C., 1981).

adaptation, a change by which an organism adjusts to its environment. Used originally in the context of biology or (human) ecology, the term is often used as a synonym for *accommodation or, more vaguely, the process by which an individual or social entity achieves a particular goal.

addiction signified in Roman law the formal transfer of a person by sentence of a court; hence, a surrender of anyone to a master. In English it came to mean an indulgence in habit-forming drugs, the self-surrender to an impersonal master. However, the relevant expert committees of the World Health Organization and the National Research Council proposed that the term "drug addiction" (as well as "drug habituation"), which had acquired various confusing connotations, be replaced by *drug dependence*. This latter term the committees defined as "an abnormal state arising from repeated medical or nonmedical use of a drug, either periodically or continuously." Their recommendation has not been widely followed as yet; even the two committees have retained names including the word "addiction." Note also *addict*, one who regularly uses opium, heroin, or another habit-forming drug.

As generally conceived, addiction consists in a psychic element, called habituation or psychic dependence, and a physical dependence usually associated with an acquired tolerance, or increased physiological resistance to a drug's initial effects. The relative importance of psychic and physical dependence is difficult to ascertain, and experts differ on how to link particular addictions to the two factors. In an interesting comparison with *alcoholism, Newman (1983) pointed out that the dividing line between alcoholics and run-of-the-mill drinkers is not whether they consume liquor (many alcoholics do not), but whether the consequences are pathological. In all cases of drug addiction detoxification can be accomplished easily and quickly, but the very high rate of recidivism has suggested that "once an addict, always an addict." It may be, however, that eventual failure has been due to the self-selection of those who seek help from clinics and, after their temporary "cure," continue to need help and find it in renewed use of drugs. The hypothesis got some support from the many veterans who, after using drugs in Vietnam, were treated without requesting detoxification and remained cured.

The U.S. National Institute on Drug Abuse (1981) projected young adults' use of marijuana, inhalants, hallucinogens, cocaine, heroin, and other opiates to the year 1995. The extrapolations were based on the estimated total number of users in the recent past, classified by sex, race, and residence in or out of metropolitan areas. The most striking feature of the study is not the projection itself but the built-in premise that the use of drugs by persons with the specified characteristics will not diminish over the next period. Addictions contribute to morbidity and mortality in various ways, and some statistics are startling. According to the usual estimate, more than half of fatal automobile *accidents in the United States, the principal cause of death of children and young adults, are linked to alcohol and drugs.

REFERENCES: Robert H. Newman, "The Need to Redefine 'Addiction,' " *New England Journal of Medicine*, 308 (May 5, 1983), 1097-1098. U.S. National Institute on Drug Abuse, *Demographic Trends and Drug Abuse, 1980-1995*, Research Monograph Series, no. 35 (Rockville, Md., 1981).

address register, the identification of addresses in and near large cities down to the level of a *block face, compiled in preparation for each of the recent censuses of the United States in order to facilitate coverage of all the households in the population. See also *residence.

ADMATCH (an acronym for Address Matching System), a computer program developed by the Census Use Study of the U.S. Bureau of the Census, is designed to help assign geographic codes to computerized records of data that include street addresses. Cf. *GBF/DIME; *UNIMATCH.

adnexa uteri, the medical term for appendages of the uterus, comprising the ovaries, oviducts, and ligaments. Removal of the adnexa is called *adnexectomy*. Their inflammation, called *adnexitis* or *pelvic inflammatory disease, may result from the use of *intra-uterine contraceptive devices.

adolescence, the process of growing up; the period that extends from the beginning of *puberty to full manhood or womanhood—from about 12 to about 20 years. Physical changes in both sexes are complex, but in females the transition is relatively clearly marked by the most important one, the onset and gradual development of regular *menstruation. Among males there is no such single index; pubic hair appears, the voice changes, the youth is able to ejaculate. Physiologically the organism of either sex is often in imbalance: the child may grow tall but not put on equivalent weight; endocrine malfunction may result in obesity or acne. Such biological factors sometimes help generate an emotional instability, the consequence also of a transitional cultural stage during which the person's role is more ambiguous than in childhood or adulthood. Apart from its physiological base, the concept of adolescence has varied connotations. Philippe Ariès (1962) has noted some of the patterns in the European past. A child of 5 to 7 years could move directly into the adult world, or a person of the lower classes could remain a "child" permanently unless he moved to a higher social status. The spread of schooling to the whole population blurred whatever distinctions there were between child, adolescent, and young adult—for all were engaged in learning and all were subject to discipline with the rod.

At the present time the age at which a person is permitted to vote, leaves school to enter the work force, or in other respects attains an adult role differs from one country to another; and one should not expect much consistency among the several indices used to define the supposedly common status. The biological process itself is marked by a period of adolescent subfecundity (sometimes mislabeled "adolescent sterility"); conception or giving birth, though possible, is less probable with the same exposure than at full maturity (Montagu, 1957; but see also *illegitimacy). The shift to adulthood is gradual also by cultural indicators; for example, many adolescents work intermittently or part-time before fully entering the work force, and the proportion of those of various ages who vote rises gradually from the electorate's minimum age. In any demographic context, therefore, there is a recurrent dilemma where to draw the line between childhood and adulthood. A fertility rate (the number of births per thousand fecund women), for example, differs greatly according to how many young adolescents are included in the base. In the censuses of some countries, as another instance, a question about economic activity is asked of all persons aged 10 and over, while in the United States, following the trend in the economically active population, the minimum age of respondents in most questionnaires was raised from 14 to 16 years.

REFERENCES: Philippe Ariès, *Centuries of Childhood: A Social History of Family Life* (New York: Knopf, 1962). Ashley Montagu, *The Reproductive Development of the Female, with Especial Reference to the Period of Adolescent Sterility* (New York: Julian, 1957).

adoption, the taking of an outsider into a kin group, investing him or her with the status of a congenital member. In Western societies the procedure is typically used either to legitimize a child born out of wedlock or to bring into the same family orphans and a couple (or, in some jurisdictions, a single person) that wants children. In the United States the Bureau of the Census used to survey children in institutions or foster homes (cf. Truesdell, 1935), but presently most of the analyses are by social workers. One of the more interesting is a longitudinal study of social-work agencies as they related to foster children (Shapiro, 1976). The widespread sentiment that whenever possible adoption should be substituted for foster care (for Britain, see Triseliotis, 1980) led in the United States to the Adoption Assistance and Child Welfare Act of 1980 (P.L. 96-272). Under its terms states that institute an adoption-assistance program receive federal funds to facilitate the placement of children with "special needs"—particularly, older, handicapped, or minority children (Calhoun, 1980).

In non-Western cultures adoption has a much wider range. A Latin American peasant, for example, might attain greater security or move up socially by being adopted into an upper-class family. Nineteenth-century Japan had no less than ten categories of adopted persons. One function of adoption was to regulate family size: the parents of too many children would pass one on to a childless friend. Since only-sons were exempt from military conscription, such a transfer was also used to evade the draft (Chamberlain, 1971). A detailed study of the records in several communities of Taiwan also shows a great variety and very large number of adoptions (Wolf and Huang, 1980). In demographic analyses adopted children can confuse the assumed relation between fertility and family size. Parents are sometimes asked to give the number of their *own children, but whether they always respond in a narrow biological sense is doubtful.

REFERENCES: John A. Calhoun, "The 1980 Child Welfare Act," *Children Today*, 9 (September-October, 1980), 2-4, 36. Basil Hall Chamberlain, *Things Japanese* (London: Routledge, 1939); reprinted as *Japanese Things* (Rutland, Vt.: Charles E. Tuttle Co., 1971). Deborah Shapiro, *Agencies and Foster Children* (New York: Columbia University Press, 1976). John Triseliotis, ed., *New Developments in Foster Care and Adoption* (London: Routledge & Kegan Paul, 1980). Leon E. Truesdell, *Children under Institutional Care and in Foster Homes, 1933* (Washington, D.C.: U.S. Bureau of the Census, 1935). Arthur P. Wolf and Huang Chieh-shan, *Marriage and Adoption in China, 1845-1945* (Stanford, Calif.: Stanford University Press, 1980).

adulthood, the state of being a fully mature person, varies according to the criterion used to define the end of *adolescence. The link between the two concepts is manifest from their common etymology: both derive from the Latin *adolescere*, "to grow up," with the past participle *adultus*, "grown up."

REFERENCES: Dolores Cabic Borland, "Research on Middle Age: An Assessment," *Gerontologist*, 18 (1978), 379-386. John Modell, Frank F. Furstenberg, Jr., and Theodore Hershberg, "Social Change and Transitions to Adulthood in Historical Perspective," *Journal of Family History*, 1 (1976), 7-32.

affinity, in anthropology, the relationship between persons or groups established by marriage, or descent and marriage; contrasted with *consanguinity. Also, *affinal*, reflecting a relationship of affinity, as in "affinal kin."

affirmative action, the composite of decisions by United States courts and rulings by federal agencies to render more effective the laws outlawing racial, ethnic, and sexual *discrimination and to set standards for admission to universities and for the hiring, training, and promotion of workers and employees. The meaning of the term changed during the years following passage of the key laws, and "affirmative action" can be understood only against a history of the legislation and its subsequent interpretation. Many state and municipal governments, business firms, and universities also have affirmative-action programs, which differ somewhat in scope and procedures. Partly because of the great complexity of the legal structure, there has been much debate over whether, or how much, members of ethnic minorities and women have benefited from the programs.

The equality guaranteed in the Declaration of Independence, which had been compromised by the acceptance of slavery in the Constitution, was given legal force in the Thirteenth, Fourteenth, and Fifteenth Amendments, which abolished slavery, guaranteed all citizens equal protection under the law, and secured the right to vote against racial discrimination. As can be seen from the debates in Congress on the three amendments, those who framed them wanted to outlaw all legal distinctions based on race; but the federal courts ignored this intent. The separate-but-equal doctrine, which the U.S. Supreme Court laid down in 1896, was not reversed until 1954, in *Brown* v. *Board of Education*. During the following decade, however, the Supreme Court consistently denounced racial distinctions in law as, in Chief Justice Stone's words, "by their very nature odious to a free people whose institutions are founded upon the doctrine of equality" (*Loving* v. *Virginia*, 1966). Over the same period Congress also repeatedly insisted that the society's main institutions be neutral with respect to race, enacting the Civil Rights Acts of 1957, 1960, 1964, and 1968 and the Voting Rights Act of 1965. That those laws were intended to establish standards under which race and ethnicity would make no legal difference (generally summarized as a "color-blind" norm) is clear from both their language and the debates in Congress. Opponents of the Civil Rights Act of 1964, for example, were worried about the possible effects of Title VII, which would prohibit discrimination in employment but might, they feared, lead to new racially determined preferences. The bill's sponsors adamantly rejected this interpretation, and finally Senator Hubert Humphrey became so exasperated with the continued skepticism that he declared, "If . . . in Title VII . . . any language [can be found] which provides that an employer will have to hire on the basis of percentage or quota related to color,. . . I will start eating the pages [of the bill] one after another."

However clear the mandate of Congress, it was ignored by federal agencies and federal courts, and the Supreme Court once again frustrated the will to establish color-blind institutions. As originally interpreted, the "equal opportunity" afforded under the new laws was taken literally: those in charge of dispensing various types of goods and services were to remove any biases built into their procedures. For instance, corporation recruiters visiting predominantly black colleges and universities, who numbered only 4 in 1960, grew to 50 in 1965 and to 297 in 1970 (Wilson, 1978, p. 107). Eventually, however, "equal opportunity" was interpreted to mean not the right to apply for all positions but the right to special dispensation in order to compensate for past discrimination. Because the discrimination had been not merely against individuals but against blacks, Hispanics, American Indians, and women as a class, all persons in these categories would be entitled to special remedial action. Obviously this list is not all-inclusive, and representatives of Italian-American and Slavic-American organizations have demanded similar quotas, based on the same kind of statistical evidence—for instance, that a far smaller proportion of these nationalities go to college, or that the top level of large corporations is markedly deficient in Poles, Greeks, and Yugoslavs (e.g., Illinois Department of Human Rights, 1982).

In short, the attempt to eliminate bias from access to certain important values in society went from equal opportunity as a goal, to using quotas to test the efficacy of programs instituted to realize that goal, to many instances of reverse discrimination. As implemented, the laws were not what their proponents had intended them to be; on the contrary, in many cases nothing mattered so much about a person applying for various types of preferment as his or her race or nationality or sex. How fast federal agencies and federal courts reversed the will of Congress is suggested by one fact: when institutions were forbidden to specify race or ethnicity (for example, on an employment application or in a student or faculty roster), this regulation often overlapped with the subsequent one setting de facto quotas for the hiring or promotion of workers or the admission of students. For a period, thus, business firms and universities were both prohibited from keeping records on race or nationality and required to maintain and report the stipulated balance among designated groups.

The effect of affirmative action on the composition of the work force is difficult to measure. Many who wrote on the subject have been faculty members and concentrated on whether labor standards in universities had changed appreciably. Criteria for hiring or promoting faculty, however, are usually much more specific than in the business world; generally an applicant for a position of professor must have a specific higher degree, preferably from an institution of standing, and must have published a minimum of so-and-so many papers, preferably in refereed journals. According to one careful study, the differences in status between male and female faculty have largely reflected differences in such objectively measured performance (Ferber et al., 1978).

Those applying for comparable positions in a commercial firm, however, can demonstrate their competence over a much wider range, and businesses often found it expedient to accommodate more fully to the law as it has been interpreted. Many more blacks and women acquired positions from which they usually would have been barred earlier. According to one analysis, however, demand factors (continuing discrimination and the segmentation of the labor market) combined with supply factors (lack of appropriate training or experience) to perpetuate patterns based on past discrimination (Lloyd and Niemi, 1979). However, the economic position of male and especially female blacks improved rapidly, because blacks were better educated than previously and, mainly for other reasons, all wages rose greatly in the South (Smith, 1978). Of the vast number of works on affirmative action, Nathan Glazer (1976, 1979) can be recommended as a detailed differentiation between the original law and the subsequent interpretation, which he terms "affirmative discrimination"; R. A. Rossum (1980) as a good analysis of "reverse discrimination"; and C. J. Livingston (1979) as a spirited defense of "affirmative action" against "equality of opportunity."

India has had a similar policy of providing preferential treatment to members of the so-called scheduled *castes and tribes and also to local ethnic groups in competition with migrants. As in the United States, the specific benefits include access to higher education and to particular types of employment (Weiner and Katzenstein, 1981).

REFERENCES: Marianne A. Ferber, Jane W. Loeb, and Helen M. Lowry, "The Economic Status of Women Faculty: A Reappraisal," *Journal of Human Resources*, 13 (1978), 385-401. Nathan Glazer, *Affirmative Discrimination: Ethnic Inequality and Public Policy* (New York: Basic Books, 1976); "Affirmative Discrimination: Where Is It Going?" *International Journal of Comparative Sociology*, 20 (1979), 14-30. Illinois Department of Human Rights, "Report of Public Hearing on the Department's Proposed Rules Governing Equal Employment Opportunity and Affirmative Action by State Executive Agencies" (Chicago: mimeographed, 1982). C. J. Livingston, *Fair Game? Inequality and Affirmative Action* (San Francisco: W. H. Freeman, 1979). Cynthia B. Lloyd and Beth

T. Niemi, *The Economics of Sex Differentials* (New York: Columbia University Press, 1979). R. A. Rossum, *Reverse Discrimination: The Constitutional Debate* (New York: Marcel Dekker, 1980). James P. Smith, *The Improving Economic Status of Black Americans* (Santa Monica, Calif.: Rand Corporation, 1978). Myron Weiner and Mary Fainsod Katzenstein, *India's Preferential Policies: Migrants, the Middle Classes and Ethnic Equality* (Chicago: University of Chicago Press, 1981). William Julius Wilson, *The Declining Significance of Race: Blacks and Changing American Institutions* (Chicago: University of Chicago Press, 1978).

Afghanistan: The Central Statistics Office publishes a *Statistical Year Book* in English and Dari editions, as well as a quarterly review of statistics in Dari with some sections in English. The country's first census was in 1979, and a summary of the results was published in English—''Preliminary Results of the First Afghan Population Census,'' *Demographic Statistics Publication*, no. 1 (1981). Address: Prime Ministry, P.O. Box 2002, Kabul.

African Demography Group (Groupe de Démographie Africaine), founded in 1964, is subsidized through France's Ministry of Cooperation. The group is administered by a permanent nucleus consisting of one delegate each from the ministry and the four French organizations mainly concerned with studying the population of francophone Africa: the National Institute of Demographic Studies (INED), the National Institute of Statistics and Economic Studies (INSEE), the Bureau of Scientific and Technical Overseas Research (ORSTOM), and the Demography Institute of Paris (IDP); see also *France: Demographic Institutions. Each year representatives of these five organizations meet and plan their joint efforts. It was through the group's initiative that ORSTOM undertook the first *multi-round surveys, and its subsequent work has also been concentrated on the methodology of demographic work in African countries. Beginning in 1979 the group has published the serial *Études et Documents*. The group itself has no office, but further information concerning it can be obtained from Groupe de Démographie Africaine, INSEE-Coopération, 18 boulevard Adolphe Pinard, 75675 Paris Cédex 14, France.

REFERENCE: Anon., ''Profile 6: The Groupe de Démographie Africaine,'' *Population Index*, 47 (1981), 13-19.

African society usually includes not the whole of the continent but either sub-Saharan Africa or what is called Tropical Africa, the area between the Sahara and the Limpopo River, the northern boundary of South Africa (see *Southern African society). How many societies exist in either region is both a difficult and a disputatious question—perhaps as many as a thousand if one counts the peoples, perhaps as few as forty if one counts the largest social units. The topography of Tropical Africa is simple—high mountains along the east and a long slope to the west dominated by the enormous Congo River basin. Temperatures differ by latitude and altitude, but the principal determinant of life's chances is typically rainfall, which varies greatly.

In "traditional Africa," which can be dated as recently as 1900, only a few peoples lived mainly from hunting and gathering. Most were farmers or herdsmen or both, often with hunting as a supplement. Agriculture was generally of the rudest sort; a woman put a seed or a tuber in a hole made by a digging stick and then covered the hole with a kick. Cattle were so valued as status symbols that the idea of thinning out a herd to prevent overgrazing would have been inconceivable (see also *sleeping sickness). In many respects the main social group was the clan, uniting a *kinship unit and directing various collective activities. Around the time of the European Middle Ages, there arose several large kingdoms. The usually alien rulers exacted tribute from as many subjects as they could control. The revenue of some kings depended on trade in raw materials and slaves, and the ends of caravan routes became large commercial centers (Kimble, 1962).

The vast area of Tropical Africa varies in many respects, but there is a uniform lack of truly adequate population data. A summary of earlier estimates by R. R. †Kuczynski (1948-53) dismissed censuses, counts, poll-tax estimates, and vital statistics with a verve that makes this work livelier reading than one would anticipate. A later survey (Brass, 1968) provides a basis for assessing the changes during the interim. In some instances there was a decline even from the generally poor vital statistics of the earlier period, and in spite of much activity the overall improvement in coverage and accuracy was not significant. Techniques used to develop estimates from partial data depend on conditions that often are not satisfied. The reasonably good report of distribution by age on which such calculations largely depend is lacking; many, perhaps most, Africans do not know how old they are. When reported ages merely reflect such markers as puberty, menopause, and the like, not only are the ranges excessively broad but the transfer to yearly ages can be precarious. For instance, several countries showed an apparent excess of women aged 20-40, since those both younger and older who had borne children were transferred to what the census officials arbitrarily defined as the childbearing period. In any case, a deduction from spotty statistics depends on an assumption that certain other factors remain constant, which hardly describes the postcolonial political and social chaos of much of the continent. Even by the narrow definition of *refugee that the United Nations uses, there were over a million in Tropical Africa in the mid-1970s, with a consequent all but incalculable disruption of social life, not to mention population counts (Gould, 1974).

These points can be made more effectively in the smaller context of a single country. When Nigeria became independent in 1960, it was the largest and wealthiest nation of the whole area, with a body of civil servants who had been trained by their white predecessors to take over their functions. The euphoria in the country was shared by many foreign observers, who minimized the problems to be faced. Within Nigeria an estimated 248 languages are spoken, some by no more than several hundred, others by as many as 5 million, and in important instances by millions also in adjoining countries. Once the factitious unity engendered by the struggle for independence was shattered, this diversity came to the surface. Since power was exercised largely through regional institutions, the relative size of the regions' populations became crucial. According to the census that the British had administered in 1952-53, the Northern Region (populated largely by Fulani and Hausa) had a population of 17.6 million out of a total of 31.8 million, thus getting an absolute majority in the Federal House. By 1962, when independent Nigeria held its first census, the East and West (where the most important people was the Ibo) supposedly had increased by 70 percent over the decade, contrasted with 30 percent in the North. The data were discarded, and according to another census the following year the North had increased in twelve months from 22.5 to 29.8 million, a result that was also rejected. The two censuses were symbolic of the tensions that soon escalated into a civil war in which so many Ibo (or Biafrans) were slaughtered that the charge of genocide was seemingly justified (see Adepoju, 1981; Nwankwo and Ifejika, 1970; Campbell, 1976). In the Brass book, the summary appraisal by Etienne van de Walle was realistic as late as 1968: "The very size of [Nigeria's] population is uncertain after the last censuses, its mortality is unknown, and its fertility can only be guessed.... No sophisticated procedure upon which we would base even a mere guess about what this population would be 10, 15, or 25 years ahead is justified. Unfortunately this is still true of a large part of Africa." Whether there has been a significant improvement since that was written depends partly on how much faith one places in subsequently developed techniques for the estimation of population data. Alternatively, it depends on whether the small populations that have been intensively studied are representative of Tropical Africa as a whole (cf. Cantrelle, 1974).

The evidence available indicates that a relatively low fertility prevailed over much of sub-Saharan Africa. This was the consequence not of an accepted limit to family size but of the large number of childless marriages. The high incidence of venereal and other diseases, whose effect is often aggravated by family and social disorganization, has been studied for some years by a French physician and ethnologist, who describes one region of the Central African Republic as "a country adrift" (Retel-Laurentin, 1979; cf. Frank, 1983). In many other places the level of health has been greatly improved over the past several decades, and if efforts to combat diseases elsewhere succeed, one should anticipate a considerable increase in fertility. How family size is viewed is suggested by a 1977-78 fertility survey in Kenya: the respondents were designated as "modern" if they had ever even once used an efficient contraceptive method and if they expressed a desire for fewer than six children (Dow and Werner, 1982, 1983). The beginning of a significant decline in family size would appear in fertility differentials, which are generally lacking or, when they do appear in the data, the contrary of what Western experience would lead one to anticipate. The effect of education is unexpected. According to one survey, women with primary schooling showed a rise in fertility, and those with secondary education an insignificant decline; only the tiny minority who completed secondary schooling had significantly smaller families (Caldwell, 1981). Of the fourteen countries in the world with apparent birth rates over 50 per 1,000 population, all are either in Africa or the adjacent Middle East; all have family systems set by either Islamic norms or the strong descent lineages of Tropical Africa.

In 1981 delegations from twenty-six African countries convened in Nairobi to consider the continent's population and development. In a preamble, the conference report noted that Africa's rate of population growth is the highest in the world: from 220 million in 1950 the population was said to have grown to 400 million in 1975 and was expected to reach 850 million in 2000 and 1,500 million in 2025. These rather startling figures were followed, however, by very cautious recommendations. National planners should take population into account, but "the diversity of national, cultural, and political contexts constitutes a richness from which the continent can derive great benefit when searching for a true African definition of population education." "Access to fertility regulation services should be assured," but only because family planning is needed to improve health. There was no mention of limits to family size or to the rate of population growth, and nothing was said about how feasible the recommendations are (Parliamentary Conference on Population and Development in Africa, 1981).

The one issue on which the Nairobi conferees spoke out forcefully was migration: "it is imperative that everything be done to reduce the high rate of urbanization in view of the intractable problems created by the influx of people into the larger cities." It was proposed to generate jobs and set up schools in rural areas, to create medium-sized towns that would deflect the present flow to large cities, and to establish "resettlement schemes." These rather drastic policies were not novel; they have been suggested or attempted in various countries of Tropical Africa (cf. Abumere, 1981). As in other places and times, when political prudence makes it difficult to face up to population growth directly, policymakers try rather to change the distribution of population.

REFERENCES: S. I. Abumere, "Population Distribution Policies and Measures in Africa South of the Sahara: A Review," *Population and Development Review*, 7 (1981), 421-433. Aderanti Adepoju, "Military Rule and Population Issues in Nigeria," *African Affairs*, 80 (1981), 29-47. William Brass et al., *The Demography of Tropical Africa* (Princeton, N.J.: Princeton University Press, 1968). John C. Caldwell, "Fertility in Africa," in Nick Eberstadt, ed., *Fertility Decline in Less Developed Countries* (New York: Praeger, 1981). Ian Campbell, "The Nigerian Census: An Essay in Civil-Military Relations," *Journal of Commonwealth and Comparative Politics*, 14 (1976), 242-254. Pierre A. Cantrelle, ed., *Population in African Development*, 2 vols. (Liège: IUSSP, 1974). Thomas E. Dow, Jr., and Linda H. Werner, "Modern, Transitional, and Traditional Demographic and Contraceptive Patterns among Kenyan Women," *Studies in Family Planning*, 13 (1982), 12-23; "Prospects for Fertility Decline in Rural Kenya," *Population and Development Review*, 9 (1983), 77-97. Odile Frank, "Infertility in Sub-Saharan Africa: Estimates and Implications," *Population and Development Review*, 9 (1983), 137-144. W.T.S. Gould, "Refugees in Tropical Africa," *International Migration Review*, 8 (1974), 413-430. George H. I. Kimble, *Tropical Africa*, 2 vols. (New York: Doubleday-Anchor, 1962). R. R. Kuczynski, *Demographic Survey of the British Colonial Empire*,

3 vols. (New York: Oxford University Press, 1948-53). Arthur Agwuncha Nwankwo and Samuel Udochukwu Ifejika, *Biafra: The Making of a Nation* (New York: Praeger, 1970). Parliamentary Conference on Population and Development in Africa, *Conclusions and Recommendations*, reprinted in *Population and Development Review*, 7 (1981), 719-725. Anne Retel-Laurentin, *Un Pays à la Dérive: Une Société en Régression Démographique, Les Nzakara de l'Est Centrafricain* (Paris: J. P. Delarge, 1979).

age, the time that a person has lived, is the most important variable in most demographic analyses. In population statistics the concept is ordinarily understood to be a person's age at his last birthday, in actuarial practice often that at his nearest birthday. In China a child, assigned the age of 1 year at birth, becomes a year older at the beginning of each successive lunar year; by the Chinese reckoning, thus, everyone is between 1 and 3 years older than by the Western convention. Ordinarily the most efficient way of obtaining this basic datum would be to ask for the date of birth, but this has seldom been done. In the United States census of 1980, respondents filled in the quarter-year during which they were born, as well as giving the month and year of their last birthday and their age in years as they interpreted it. In such population models as the *life table or a *cohort table of fertility, the convention is to use an exact age correct to the nearest day; the period designated as ''20-24,'' then, means the 5-year interval from the twentieth birthday to the day before the twenty-fifth birthday.

The difficulties in gathering data on ages in less developed countries can be illustrated by the experience in Bangladesh. Since there are virtually no vital statistics, all information must be gathered in censuses. If an enumerator were to ask the mother of a young boy, ''What was your son's age on his last birthday?'' the response would probably be, ''What is 'birthday'?''—for there is no such concept in the culture. The enumerator must resort to a common device—matching the person's age against a series of events prominent enough to remain in everyone's memory (see *time). ''Was he born when the village high school was set up?'' elicits the response, let us suppose, ''He was a suckling baby then.'' Infants are breastfed for about three years, which is thus the range of error possible from accepting such a response. With adults there may be other problems—a strong reluctance to tell one's age; a confusion among the Western, the Bengali, and the Muslim calendars, all of which are in use in Bangladesh. The erratic shapes of single-year *population pyramids suggest how many recorded ages are only approximate (Ahmad, 1975).

Even literate populations, however, include many who do not know their age, do not report it precisely, or refuse to state it at all. As estimated by Giorgio †Mortara, the last generation's top expert on Latin American populations, in 1950 half a million Brazilian women aged 30 to 69 declared their ages to be 15 to 29; and are the females of Brazil vainer than the women of other countries— or the men? There is typically a tendency toward what is called *age heaping* or age preference—that is, moving the reported age up or down several years to a digit ending in 5 or 0, avoiding an unlucky number like 13, marking the onset of maturity at age 18 or 21, exaggerating the longevity of the very old, and so on. Since there is generally a smooth progression from those of one actual age to the next, various techniques, such as the computation of an *age ratio, can be used to correct such misreporting (see Zelnik, 1964; National Academy of Sciences, 1981). Formerly those who responded inadequately to the question about their age were aggregated into a separate category labeled "unknown age"; presently they are usually distributed among the population with reported ages. Two methods have been used for this allocation—assignment according to the distribution of persons whose other characteristics in prior aggregate tabulations are similar (called the "cold-deck" method), or, during the processing of the current data, assigning the age of the last earlier person whose other characteristics were similar (called the "hot-deck" method).

*Errors in age data that are aggregated into 5-year or broader categories are generally smaller, since any misreporting within each year affects the total only slightly. Such an aggregate is termed an *age group—an unfortunate designation suggesting an internal coherence that, of course, does not typically exist—or age interval. In anthropology the several patterns of differentiation are distinguished as follows: age "grades," comprising the hierarchy from childhood to revered elderly status through which each person may advance; age "classes," those age grades set apart by enough common features to generate a loose sentiment of unity, such as among teenagers or "the young marrieds" in Western societies; and age "groups," formally organized sectors of the population that in parts of Africa, for instance, have institutionalized mutual obligations, distinctive symbols, and specific functions. In this narrower sense, industrial societies have no age groups. Age grades are universal: *infancy, *childhood, *adolescence, *adulthood, and *old age (which sometimes is associated with *senility). These are set in part by biological factors, but only in part; when each individual moves from one to the next depends also on how the particular culture defines each stage. The transition may be gradual or marked by a *rite of passage that sharply distinguishes successive stages.

In any society, irrespective of conventional definitions, every important role is concentrated in a particular age range. Many of the phenomena analyzed in social disciplines, therefore, depend in considerable part on the age structure (or "age composition"), the relative distribution by age. It is well known that a society's fertility depends on the proportion in the fecund ages, or that the size of the *work force is closely related to the number of persons of working age. One should also note, among less obvious examples of the pervasive influence of a population's age structure, that the overall crime rate varies with the relative number of young males, the sector from which most criminals are drawn, or that the markets for various types of commodities can change radically with shifts in the proportion of young or old (see Chaddock, 1936; Davis and van den Oever, 1981).

The simplest measure of a society's age structure is its median age, which divides the population into two equal parts, one older and the other younger.

For almost all purposes this is a better index than the commonly used mean (or average) age. When the median is over 30 years, the population is considered "old," contrasted with a "young" one with the median under 20 years. In the United States in 1980 it was exactly 30 years; half the population "can't be trusted" (Robey, 1981). When the median is rising, one says that the population is "aging"; when it is falling, the population is "younging." Such appellations are only suggestive, for the measure gives no hint of how the distribution around the median may be changing (see Coale, 1964). For example, the percentage aged 65 years and over, by a common convention designated as the "aged," could be increasing while the median age was going down, for fertility and the consequent proportion of children also affect the median. A full distribution by age can be represented graphically in the familiar *population pyramid. See also *age at marriage, *age-cost profiles, *age group, *age of childbearing, *age ratio, *age-specific rate.

REFERENCES: Bahauddin Ahmad, "Census Age Data of Bangladesh," *Asian and Pacific Census Newsletter*, 1 (May, 1975), 7-10. Robert E. Chaddock, "Age and Sex in Population Analysis," *Annals of the American Academy of Political and Social Science*, 188 (1936), 185-193. Ansley J. Coale, "How a Population Ages or Grows Younger," in Ronald Freedman, ed., *Population: The Vital Revolution* (Garden City, N.Y.: Doubleday-Anchor, 1964). Kingsley Davis and Pietronella van den Oever, "Age Relations and Public Policy in Advanced Industrial Countries," *Population and Development Review*, 7 (1981), 1-18. National Academy of Sciences, *Age Misreporting and Age-Selective Underenumeration: Sources, Patterns, and Consequences for Demographic Analysis* (Washington, D.C., 1981). Bryant Robey, "Age in America," *American Demographics*, 3 (July-August, 1981), 14-19. Melvin Zelnik, "Errors in the 1960 Census Enumeration of Native Whites," *Journal of the American Statistical Association*, 59 (1964), 437-459.

age at marriage means the age at first *marriage; it is thus differentiated from age at *remarriage. It can be calculated from the vital statistics or from the data of censuses or surveys—usually separately for the two sexes or, very often, only for females. The median age at marriage is usually calculated from *period data—that is, relating to all those who married during a given year. However, a *cohort measure, the mean age at marriage of all those who were born in a given year, can be estimated from responses to a question in a census or survey from which the marriage experience of each birth cohort can be reconstructed—omitting, however, those who had died before the date of the count. The *singulate mean age at first marriage*, a measure devised by John †Hajnal (1953), approximates the average age at first marriage from census figures independent of differences in age structure; it is especially useful for countries where marriage registration is inadequate. The idea was developed in a paper by Gudmund Hernes (1972), who calculated the resultant of two forces on members of a cohort: social pressure to get married rises as the proportion married of the cohort increases, but as they age members of the cohort have fewer chances to get married. See also *adolescence; *birth interval.

In each society the typical age at marriage fluctuates about a norm set by cultural institutions. These short-time variations often are responses to economic factors—a poor harvest, for instance, or a rise in unemployment. The norm itself, which can be a major determinant of fertility, has ranged widely from a tradition of *child marriage in India, through generally low ages in less developed countries, to a significant postponement of marriage in modern Europe (see *Ireland). An influential paper of Hajnal's (1965) described the "European marriage pattern," which was distinguished by a uniquely high age at marriage and a no less uniquely high proportion that never married at all. In a number of recent studies attempts have been made to fill in the sketchy outline that Hajnal had traced. As one would expect from a detailed analysis of the data available, the picture was mixed (Gaskin, 1978; cf. R. M. Smith, 1979; Watkins, 1980, 1981). The principal support for the theory is less early statistics than the institutions that impeded early marriage (cf. Laslett, 1977). Modernization seemingly includes a shift to the European pattern, which in Asia is competing with traditional norms (Peter C. Smith, 1980; cf. Blayo, 1978; Henry and Piotrow, 1982). If most in a society marry late, some are likely to postpone getting a spouse indefinitely, which is why a high proportion of the never married is a usual second element of the European pattern (cf. Dixon, 1978).

In the United States the median ages at first marriage fell sharply during the years following World War II and then rose again. For women it went from 22.0 years in 1890 to 20.8 years in 1970 and back to 22.1 years in 1980; and for men, in the same years, from 26.1 to 23.2 to 24.6. In 1980, among those aged 20-24, half the women and two-thirds of the men had not married for the first time (U.S. Bureau of the Census, 1981). The seeming reasons for the reversal are apparent. Young women are now more likely to weigh marriage against a career as alternative options (Cherlin, 1980). More generally, the loosening of restrictions on extramarital sex has reduced the impetus to seek a formal sexual partner (Modell, 1980). Whether the recent shift in marriage patterns contributed significantly to the concomitant decline in fertility is difficult to judge, for family size and the timing of births are so often controlled by contraception.

REFERENCES: Yves Blayo, "Les Premiers Mariages Féminins en Asie," *Population*, 33 (1978), 951-986. Andrew Cherlin, "Postponing Marriage: The Influence of Young Women's Work Expectations," *Journal of Marriage and the Family*, 42 (1980), 355-365. Ruth B. Dixon, "Late Marriage and Non-marriage as Demographic Responses: Are They Similar?" *Population Studies*, 32 (1978), 449-466. Katharine Gaskin, "Age at First Marriage in Europe before 1850: A Summary of Family Reconstitution Studies," *Journal of Family History*, 3 (1978), 23-36. John Hajnal, "Age at Marriage and Proportions Marrying," *Population Studies*, 7 (1953), 111-132; "European Marriage Patterns in Perspective," in Glass and Eversley, *Population in History* (1965). Alice Henry and Phyllis T. Piotrow, "Age at Marriage," *International Encyclopedia of Population*, 1, 22-30. Gudmund Hernes, "The Process of Entry into First Marriage," *American Sociological Review*, 37 (1972), 173-182. Peter Laslett, "Characteristics of the Western Family Considered over Time," *Journal of Family History*, 2 (1977), 89-115. John Modell, "Normative Aspects of American Marriage Timing since World War II," *Journal of Family History*, 5 (1980), 210-234. Peter C. Smith, "Asian Marriage Patterns in

Transition," *Journal of Family History*, 5 (1980), 58-96. Richard M. Smith, "Some Reflections on the Evidence for the Origins of the 'European Marriage Pattern' in England," in Christopher C. Harris and Michael Anderson, eds., *The Sociology of the Family: New Directions for Britain* (Keele, England: University of Keele, 1979). U.S. Bureau of the Census, "Marital Status and Living Arrangements: March, 1980," *Current Population Reports*, Ser. P-20, no. 365 (October, 1981). Susan C. Watkins, "Variation and Persistence in Nuptiality: Age Patterns of Marriage in Europe, 1870-1960," doctoral dissertation, Princeton University, Princeton, N.J., 1980; "Regional Patterns of Nuptiality in Europe, 1870-1960," *Population Studies*, 35 (1981), 199-215.

age-cost profiles, a mode of representing the needs and expenditures typical of each age bracket and, thus, the overall schedule of consumption associated with a particular age distribution.

REFERENCE: Josephus van den Boomen, "Age-Cost Profiles: A Common Denominator?" in IUSSP, International Population Conference, Manila, 1981, *Solicited Papers* (Liège, 1981).

age group, the standard term for persons of several contiguous ages considered as a unit. In an abridged *life table, for instance, those aged precisely from 20 to 24 years comprise one "age group." The connotation of a certain coherence rather than merely a patterning of parts, which is the usual meaning of the word *group* in other contexts, is thus lacking. Some demographers have therefore substituted "age category" or "age bracket," but their usage has not been generally adopted.

age of childbearing (also called the age of mothers or maternal age) can be designated for a female population by either a mean or a median, which typically differ very little. Both measures are usually calculated from the birth rates specific to 5-year age groups during one year. They can be interpreted, then, as relating to a synthetic *cohort of women—that is, a hypothetical category that has during its members' lifetime the fertility experience recorded in a single calendar year.

age ratio, the population of a given age divided by one-third of the sum of the populations of that age and the preceding and following ages, times 100. For any age, P_n , the formula for the age ratio is as follows:

$$\frac{P_n}{1/3(P_{n-1} + P_n + P_{n+1})} \times 100$$

Barring extreme fluctuations in past births, deaths, or migrations (of which an analyst would usually be aware), the three age groups in the formula should form a nearly linear series, and the age ratio should therefore approximate 100. If it differs very much from that anticipated value, the reported ages are probably in error, and the ratios can be used to suggest the needed corrections. With appropriate adjustments, the formula can be applied to age groups of a number of successive years, but the greatest utility is in evaluating reported single-age values, which generally deviate much more from a linear series.

age-specific rate is a very common refinement of simpler *rates of almost any demographic or social phenomenon; for there is hardly any human activity that does not vary considerably by age, whether because of physiology or of culture. Even when an event is possible at any age—death, for example—the likelihood of its taking place is far less at some ages than at others. An age-specific death rate, then, is the number of persons in a designated age range who died during a year per 1,000 persons of the midyear population in the same age range. More generally:

$$_nr_x = \frac{_nE_x}{_nP_x} \times 1,000$$

where n = the number of years in the age bracket (usually but not necessarily set at 5)
x = the initial age in the bracket
E = the number of events
P = the size of the subpopulation in the age bracket
The principal limitation of age-specific rates is that they are represented in a schedule, useful for analysis but difficult to interpret at a glance. For that reason an array of age-specific fertility rates, for example, can be summed into the single *total fertility rate.

aggiornamento (Italian for ''bringing up to date''), the movement in *Roman Catholicism to bring the religion, according to its proponents, in closer accord with the modern world; begun under the papacy of John XXIII (1958-63) and carried out in large measure by the Second Vatican Council (1962-64). Though the changes in theology and liturgy have been important, with a marked trend toward support of ecumenical efforts, doctrines related to *celibacy, *contraception, and other matters most closely related to population were not changed. See also *Humanae Vitae.

agglomeration, the process of concentration in space of people, economic activities, or other entities; also, the consequence of this process. The term is most commonly used in spatial economics. Cf. Alfred †Weber.

aggregation, the addition of figures concerning small units into summary data on larger ones; also *aggregative*, pertaining to aggregation; *disaggregation*, the breaking up of data on composite units into figures pertaining to either smaller units or individuals. See also *ecological correlation; *segregation. In the context of demography, aggregation typically refers to the combination of data about individuals into those about populations. As in other disciplines, the correspondence is often less simple than it might seem. When Alfred †Kinsey tried to estimate the amount of sexual activity at various ages, he took reports of 16-year-old adolescents, say, together with retrospective accounts of men of all subsequent ages on their behavior at age 16. Somewhat similarly, Raymond †Pearl's widely used measure of the efficacy of *contraception aggregates women by the number of months they use a particular method, though their reasons for discontinuing it may place them in quite different categories. The more careless and more fecund become pregnant, leaving a more and more homogeneous residue of satisfied and highly motivated users, including all the sterile and most of the subfecund.

aging is a continuous and universal process, but individuals differ considerably in what is termed their biologic age, or their functioning capacity as set by both genetic and environmental factors, including their chronologic age. Whether a life insurance company grants a policy to a particular applicant, for instance, depends not only on how many years he or she has lived but also on such rough indications of biologic age as the person's parents' longevity, medical history and present state of health, and occupation. In a demographic analysis one usually assumes that variations in the rates of aging balance out and that chronologic ages thus distinguish more or less homogeneous categories.

The power of self-renewal and the ability to reproduce the species, the main features that set living beings apart from inert matter, both decline with advancing age (cf. *Hayflick limit). Of other physiological functions that have been intensively studied—the amount of physical work one can do, the speed of nerve conduction, the amount of acid secreted by the stomach's mucous membranes, the maximum filtration rate of the kidney, the cardiac output, the maximum rate at which one can breathe—in each case a person aged around 30 will have lost only about 1 percent of the initial capacity. Thereafter the depletion is faster, and a loss of about 40 percent of initial capacity increases the probability of death almost a thousandfold. On the other hand, Fries and Crapo (1981, chap. 9) speak of "the plasticity of aging"; for the timing of many of the symptoms that herald the onset of irreversible *chronic diseases that eventually lead to disability or death is affected by *smoking, diet, and other elements of the person's life-style.

One also speaks of the aging of a population—that is, a rise in its median age (e.g., Clark and Spengler, 1980; Fry, 1980; Quadagno, 1980). Such a change in the age structure can take place by a shift in any of its determinants, but in fact the principal reason that Western populations have become older has not been an extension of the expectation of life but rather the decline in fertility. With a smaller proportion of children, a population lacks a counterbalance to the older age brackets (see also *dependency ratio). For the remainder of this century, if a probable projection proves to be correct, aging of the United States population will be at a slower rate than in the recent past (Uhlenberg, 1977). See also *age; *life span; *nutrition; *old age.

REFERENCES: Robert L. Clark and Joseph J. Spengler, *The Economics of Individual and Population Aging* (Cambridge, England: University Press, 1980). James F. Fries and Lawrence M. Crapo, *Vitality and Aging: Implications of the Rectangular Curve* (San Francisco: W. H. Freeman, 1981). Christine L. Fry, ed., *Aging in Culture and Society: Comparative Viewpoints and Strategies* (New York: Praeger, 1980). J. S. Quadagno, *Aging, the Individual and Society* (New York: Basic Books, 1980). Matilda White Riley, ed., *Aging from Birth to Death: Interdisciplinary Perspectives* (Washington, D.C.: American Association for the Advancement of Science, 1979). Bernard L. Strehler, "The Origins of Senescence," *Transactions of the Society of Actuaries*, vol. 19, Part II (1967), D429-D440. Peter R. Uhlenberg, "Changing Structure of the Older Population of the United States of America during the Twentieth Century," *Gerontologist*, 17 (1977), 197–202.

aid, a summary term in the context of international relations for a transfer of money or its equivalent from wealthy to poorer countries, was eminently successful in its first important manifestation, the Marshall Plan, through which the United States spent some $17 billion in order to help in the reconstruction of war-devastated Western Europe (see Price, 1955). It was relatively easy to rebuild the industrial plants of fully developed countries, where the population's skills and work habits facilitated the reestablishment of production. A second type of aid, the use of Western medicine, physicians, and other death-control facilities to reduce the *mortality of less developed countries, has also been remarkably effective. It is often forgotten that the reason for the rapid growth of population in those countries was not a rise in fertility but rather a sharp decline in the death rate, with a consequent shift in the age structure that encouraged a continuing high birth rate.

Aid presently refers also to far less successful types of programs. In spite of the tremendous sums allocated to stimulate the economies of less developed countries, the results have generally been disappointing even to proponents of the programs. By the mid-1970s about 70 percent of the government-financed aid for nonmilitary purposes was by Western democracies, about 30 percent by the Soviet Union and other Communist states, OPEC countries, and such poor countries as India, which has been both a major recipient and an important donor. Amounts have increased, even if discounted for inflation. From 1965-67 and 1975-77, in billions of current dollars per year, the aid from all Western countries rose from 6.1 to 14.0; from the United States from 3.4 to 4.2 (*Economist*, April 28, 1979). According to the sharpest critics, the aid has in fact been counterproductive, hampering the rise of private industry by fostering an inefficient state bureaucracy (e.g., Bauer, 1976).

In general the most destitute got little, the relatively well off got most. In 1973 the U.S. Congress passed a law setting "New Directions" in foreign aid, which subsequentially was to be targeted at the "poor majority," in paticular the rural poor, of less developed countries. Impatient with the slow pace with which this radical change was implemented, Congress further restricted the latitude that had been given to the U.S. Agency for International Development (AID; see the discussion of the agency under *United States: Federal Agencies). The difficulties are great, for the typical less developed country is governed by an urban elite often fearful of a possible revolt by the rest of the cities' population, while the rural poor are typically remote from power centers. When AID hired a consulting firm to recommend how to carry out the new directive, it proposed, perhaps not surprisingly, that AID should be given wider options again (Mickelwait et al., 1979).

With growing population becoming an ever more salient problem in many less developed countries, some Western analysts had proposed as early as the 1960s that the funding of economic projects should be limited to those nations that at least tried to curb their fertility; but at first this was generally considered to be too delicate a subject to broach formally. By the 1970s receiving nations often had both industrialization and family-planning programs funded from abroad. Much of the international funding of birth control has been through the *U.N. Fund for Population Activities and the *International Bank for Reconstruction and Development. The interpretation of the record during its first decade by Rafael M. †Salas (1979), the executive director of the UNFPA, is generally sanguine (see also Som, 1977; Crane and Finkle, 1981). The amounts allocated to the UNFPA for "population assistance" in less developed countries, mainly by the United States, rose from $6 million in 1961 to $345 million in 1977. Whether such outlays were effective has also been a polemical issue. With the data usually available, it is difficult to estimate the fertility trend in a less developed country and, even more so, to say how much *family-planning programs contributed to a decline, if at all.

In the United States the principal agency allocating funds for the control of population has been AID, whose record has been repeatedly criticized in Congress. In testimony before the House Select Committee on Population (February 9, 1978), Kingsley †Davis, perhaps the most distinguished American demographer not himself involved in family-planning programs, offered the following critique: "The inadequacy of these [family-planning] policies is suggested by the fact that population growth in the less developed countries as a whole has *not* slowed down, but has *increased* . . . . During each half decade from 1950 to 1975, the rate of population growth in the less developed countries increased. The rate was 9.95 percent in 1950–55, and 12.26 percent in 1970–75. According to projections, . . . the rise in rate is due to continue for another half decade, after which a slow decline will set in. However, . . . the absolute increase of population in the less developed countries is projected to go on increasing despite a slight decline in the rate. In 1995-2000, the 5-year increase will be 451.4 million, whereas in 1950-55 it was only 163.6 million. These figures do not indicate that the effort to limit population growth has been successful or will be successful. On the contrary, it looks to be probably the most tragic failure in the entire history of the human species."

REFERENCES: Peter T. Bauer, *Dissent on Development* (rev. ed.; Cambridge, Mass.: Harvard University Press, 1976). Barbara B. Crane and Jason L. Finkle, "Organizational Impediments to Development Assistance: The World Bank's Population Program," *World Politics*, 33 (1981), 516-553. Donald R. Mickelwait, Charles F. Sweet, and Elliott R.

Morss, *New Directions in Development: A Study of U.S. Aid* (Boulder, Colo.: Westview Press, 1979). H. S. Price, *The Marshall Plan and Its Meaning* (Ithaca, N.Y.: Cornell University Press, 1955). Rafael M. Salas, *International Population Assistance: The First Decade* (Oxford: Pergamon Press, 1979). Ranjan K. Som, "Assistance to Fertility Regulation within the United Nations System," *U.N. Population Bulletin*, no. 10 (1977), 36-62.

Alan Guttmacher Institute, founded in 1968, was until 1977 the research division of the Planned Parenthood Federation of America; it is now a special affiliate. It is one of the principal private agencies in the United States that sponsor family-planning programs and policies. Its Division of Research and Planning, with a staff of sixteen headed by Jacqueline Darroch Forrest, in 1980 spent about $250,000 on research, or a fifth of the institute's budget. Publications: *PPWP Washington Memo*, biweekly; *Family Planning Perspectives*, bimonthly; *International Family Planning Perspectives*, quarterly. Addresses: 360 Park Avenue South, New York, N.Y. 10010; 1220 Nineteenth Street, N.W., Washington, D.C. 20036.

Albania: The Bureau of Statistics publishes a biennial *Statistical report* in Albanian. Address: Drejtoria e Statistikës, Tirana.

alcoholism, a pathological dependence on alcohol, is difficult to define more precisely. A number of pioneers in the first half of the nineteenth century helped classify it as a disease (Bynum, 1968). But since it frequently begins as a self-indulgence, alcoholism is not entirely a physiological problem; and one reason for the success of Alcoholics Anonymous, a worldwide organization with some 17,000 local groups in the United States, is that its therapy focuses on the psychological factor. A narrowly medical diagnosis is complicated also by the great individual differences in tolerance and in the specific pathology associated with overdrinking. Alcohol may be a contributory cause of death from various diseases (especially but not exclusively cirrhosis of the liver) and behavior patterns (especially automobile accidents and suicides). The Honolulu Heart Study, for example, analyzed the effect of alcoholism on mortality from coronary heart disease, cancer, and stroke, as well as cirrhosis of the liver (Blackwelder et al., 1980). An English study analyzed deaths of alcoholics by age, sex, and various causes of death for the period 1953-74 (Adelstein and White, 1976).

   Among both primitive peoples and higher civilizations, the attitude toward drinking ranges from those that deem alcohol to be essential or blessed to those that ban it altogether (Pittman and Snyder, 1962; Mandelbaum, 1965). In the United States group differences in the incidence of alcoholism have been associated less with social class than with ethnicity; rates of "problem drinking" used to be highest among the Irish, lowest among the Jews and Italians (Room, 1968; Wechsler et al., 1970). This pattern, more or less consistent from the beginning of the twentieth century to the 1960s, seems to have changed; in 1977 the

ALGORITHM   31

Federation of Jewish Philanthropies of New York, acknowledging that the disease was a growing problem among Jews, set up a Task Force on Alcoholism (*New York Times*, January 23, 1977). During the 1970s deaths from both alcoholism and various associated causes were rising in the United States, especially among black males, as well as in most countries of Western Europe and, to the degree one can determine, the Soviet Union. American corporations and trade unions have initiated control programs based on therapy rather than discipline (DuPont and Basen, 1980). See also *addiction.

REFERENCES: A. M. Adelstein and Graham White, "Alcoholism and Mortality," *Population Trends*, no. 6 (1976), 7-13. William C. Blackwelder, Katsushiko Yano, George C. Rhoads, and Abraham Kagan, "Alcoholism and Mortality," *American Journal of Medicine*, 68 (1980), 164-169. William F. Bynum, "Chronic Alcoholism in the First Half of the 19th Century," *Bulletin of the History of Medicine*, 42 (1968), 160-185. R. L. DuPont and M. M. Basen, "Control of Alcohol and Drug Abuse in Industry—A Literature Review," *Public Health Reports*, 95 (1980), 137-148. David G. Mandelbaum, "Alcohol and Culture," *Current Anthropology*, 6 (1965), 281-293. David J. Pittman and Charles R. Snyder, eds., *Society, Culture, and Drinking Patterns* (New York: Wiley, 1962). Robin Room, "Cultural Contingencies of Alcoholism," *Journal of Health and Social Behavior*, 9 (1968), 99-113. Henry Wechsler, Harold W. Demone, Jr., Denise Thum, and Elizabeth H. Kasey, "Religious-Ethnic Differences in Alcohol Consumption," *Journal of Health and Social Behavior*, 11 (1970), 21-29.

aleatory, a term sometimes used in statistics, is a direct transliteration of the French *aléatoire* or the Italian *aleatorio*, which are usually (and preferably) translated as "random."

Algeria: Demographic Institutions

The Algerian Association for Demographic, Economic, and Social Research (AARDES), established in 1964, was in 1981 under the direction of Mohamed †Boukhobza. It has conducted studies of differential fertility, the family, and internal migration. Address: Association Algérienne pour la Recherche Démographique, Économique, et Sociale, 15 rue Hamani, Algiers.

The Office of Statistics and National Accounts publishes an *Annuaire Statistique* and a *Bulletin Trimestriel de Statistique*, both of which contain data on the population and its characteristics. The office includes a Division of Social and Demographic Statistics, which is responsible for publishing population data, and the National Office for Population Censuses, which conducts the country's censuses. Address: Direction des Statistiques et de la Comptabilité Nationale, Sous-Direction des Statistiques Sociales et Démographiques, and Commissariat National du Recensement de la Population, Boîte Postale 55, Alger-Bourse, Algiers.

algorithm had until recently (and still has in other languages) a rather general meaning more or less equivalent to that of "formula." A common example is Euclid's algorithm—that is, the rule for finding the greatest common divisor of two positive integers. With the increased use of the *computer for such exercises as the *simulation of population growth, the word has acquired a more restricted meaning—namely, the calculation of an assigned quantity by an iterative process that converges on the true value. Some analysts contrast an algorithmic process, one that guarantees a solution to a problem in a finite number of steps if at least one solution exists, with a heuristic process, which may help find a solution but does not guarantee it.

alien, a person who is the subject of one country and residing in another and is thus defined legally as a foreigner; also, pertaining to such a person or his condition. Though seemingly a straightforward concept, aliens in fact are delineated by the enormously complex laws of *nationality, which vary greatly from one country to another. Since most immigrants enter a population as young adults, generally their age structure is markedly different from that of natives (see also *arrivals). In the United States a question on citizenship was asked in the censuses of 1820, 1830, 1870, 1890 through 1950, and 1970—that is, whenever immigration was a political issue of some importance. In 1980, when the question was included only in the long form circulated to a 20-percent sample, the lack of full data was criticized by those concerned about illegal immigrants. A second set of data is available through the registration of aliens by the U.S. Immigration and Naturalization Service in 1940 and annually since 1951. The difference in the figures has been amazingly great—for example, in 1940 between a census count of about 3.5 million aliens and a registration of about 5 million.

alienation, in the sense of estrangement, became a subject of wide interest following the publication in the 1930s (in English translation, only in 1964) of Karl †Marx's so-called "Paris Manuscripts of 1844" (see Feuer, 1962). In this early work Marx held that the more wealth a worker acquires the poorer he becomes, for "the increasing value of the world of things proceeds in direct proportion [with] the devaluation of the world of men." The main drift of efforts to define the concept in a sociological context has been to break it down into three major components: powerlessness, normlessness, and social isolation (Lystad, 1972). The importance of alienation in demography relates principally to the fact that those who do not believe enough in any future to plan typically also do not practice family planning. Some in the depressed classes, in other words, have many children not because they lack contraceptives, but rather lack the will to use them. This thesis was first enunciated at length in some of Lee †Rainwater's books (e.g., 1965), and it has been the principal subject of a series of empirical studies by Theodore †Groat and Arthur †Neal (e.g., 1970, 1975, 1980). In the usual analysis of fertility, however, and particularly in formulations of antinatalist policies, the rationality of *Economic Man is generally taken as a postulate. In the debate whether it is in the interest of peasants to have large families, with most Western demographers on one side and many nationalist or neo-Marxist analysts on the other, neither addresses the problem posed by the concept of alienation—that for many in the less developed countries conditions of life are such that potential parents often do not weigh the advantages against the disadvantages of having another child.

REFERENCES: Lewis Feuer, "What Is Alienation? The Career of a Concept," *New Politics*, 1 (1962), 116-134. H. Theodore Groat and Arthur G. Neal, "Alienation Correlates of Catholic Fertility," *American Journal of Sociology*, 76 (1970), 460-473; "Alienation Antecedents of Unwanted Fertility: A Longitudinal Study," *Social Biology*, 22 (1975), 60-74; "Fertility Decision Making, Unintended Births, and the Social Drift Hypothesis: A Longitudinal Study," *Population and Environment*, 3 (1980), 221-236. Mary H. Lystad, "Social Alienation: A Review of Current Literature," *Sociological Quarterly*, 13 (1972), 90-113. Lee Rainwater, *Family Design: Marital Sexuality, Family Size, and Contraception* (Chicago: Aldine, 1965).

allometric function, one that is used to measure a difference, has the general equation $A = a^{b^p}$, with a and b set to fit a particular example. When used to convert land areas into estimates of urban populations, its validity depends not only on the *goodness of fit but on the stability of the function over time; the first generally holds, but the second does not. For example, in the United States urbanized areas of 100,000 or more population covered 66 square kilometers in 1950, but two-thirds more in 1970.

REFERENCE: Daniel R. Vining, Jr., and Stephanus J. H. Louw, "A Cautionary Note on the Use of the Allometric Function to Estimate Urban Populations," *Professional Geographer*, 30 (1978), 365-370.

altitude of very high mountains is associated with low fertility, and a debate about the reasons for this relation has flourished because of the difficulty in distinguishing cultural from physiological factors. Many of the small settlements at very high altitudes lose young adults by out-migration, with a consequent reduction in the birth rate of those places. On the other hand, the small amount of oxygen in the air can cause hypoxia, a deficiency of oxygen reaching body tissues, which affects fecundity adversely. Most of the studies pertain to the Andes (e.g., Abelson et al., 1974), occasional ones to the Himalayas (Gupta, 1980).

REFERENCES: Andrew E. Abelson, Thelma S. Baker, and Paul T. Baker, "Altitude, Migration, and Fertility in the Andes," *Social Biology*, 21 (1974), 12-27. Ranjan Gupta, "Altitude and Demography among the Sherpas," *Journal of Biosocial Science*, 12 (1980), 103-114.

amalgamation, the blending of physical types into a new one through successive generations of interbreeding. According to some analysts, this is the ultimate stage of *assimilation, the melting pot in a literal sense. In the United States, however, where a very high proportion of blacks have some white forebears, anyone known to have some Negro ancestry has generally been considered black. In other words, the social definition of *races is typically far more important than a person's physiological antecedents.

AMBUSH, a simulation program used by anthropologists for tracing the effects of fertility and mortality schedules, rules of marriage and descent, density-dependent infanticide, and other characteristics of closed breeding groups.

REFERENCE: Nancy Howell and Victor A. Lehotay, "AMBUSH: A Computer Program for Stochastic Microsimulation of Small Human Populations," *American Anthropologist*, 80 (1978), 905-922.

amenorrhea, absence of the menses, may indicate a pregnancy and its aftermath, the menopause, or some pathological blockage of menstruation. It persists following a childbirth, particularly if the woman breastfeeds the infant, and prolonged *lactation is thus a means of preventing conceptions, though not a particularly effective one. See also *birth interval.

REFERENCE: Robert G. Potter, Jr., and Frances E. Kobrin, "Distributions of Amenorrhoea and Anovulation," *Population Studies*, 35 (1981), 85-99.

American Anthropological Association (AAA), founded in 1902, is a professional society of anthropologists, educators, students, and others interested in the biological and cultural origin and development of mankind. It had a claimed membership of 10,000 and a paid staff of 25 in 1983. Its activities include conducting research and compiling statistics. Among its publications is the *American Anthropologist*, a quarterly. Address: 1703 New Hampshire Avenue, N.W., Washington, D.C. 20009. See also *anthropology.

American Association for the Advancement of Science (AAAS), the largest and broadest scientific organization in the United States, was founded in 1848 and in 1980 claimed as members 130,000 individuals and 285 scientific societies, including the *Population Association of America. AAAS has sponsored several international projects related to population, and its Office of International Science cooperates with the Committee on Population and Demography of the National Science Foundation in reviewing anthropological research on human fertility and periodically publishes the findings. "Cultural Factors in Population Programs," an AAAS program, resulted in several papers at the 1974 World Population Conference in Bucharest. Publications: *Science*, weekly; other journals and monographs. Address: 1515 Massachusetts Avenue, N.W., Washington, D.C. 20005.

American Economic Association (AEA), the country's principal professional association of economists, was founded in 1885. In 1983 it claimed a membership of almost 20,000. Its publications include the scholarly quarterly *American Economic Review* and the quarterly annotated bibliographical *Journal of Economic Literature*, both of which often include items related to population. Address: 1313 Twenty-first Avenue South, Nashville, Tenn. 37212.

American Fertility Society (AFS), an American organization founded in 1944 and until 1966 called the American Society for the Study of Sterility, had a claimed membership in 1980 of 7,400 medical and biological scientists interested in research on the determinants of fertility. Most of the papers in its monthly periodical, *Fertility and Sterility Journal*, pertain to domestic or laboratory animals, and those about humans are generally highly technical. It also publishes a quarterly *Newsletter*. Address: 1608 Thirteenth Avenue South, Suite 101, Birmingham, Ala. 35256.

American Indians, the aboriginal population of the Western Hemisphere, pose both scholarly and policy problems related to demography. Estimates of the pre-Columbian population of the Americas have risen prodigiously through the decades, from A. L. †Kroeber's 8.4 million (1939) through Ángel †Rosenblat's 13.4 million (1945) to Henry F. †Dobyns's 90-112 million (1966) (see also Denevan, 1976). Obviously the basic data are poor enough to allow much latitude for interpretation. All estimates start from some relatively recent date and work back through accounts of massacres, epidemics, and other causes of extraordinary mortality to a presumed pre-contact population. The violence and imposed hardships sometimes characterized as "genocide" were generally the least significant factors with respect to the number of persons affected. Far more important were smallpox, measles, and other infectious diseases, which were deadly among a population that had not acquired any degree of immunity.

A third component of population loss, the disappearance not through death but through race mixture and reclassification, was especially important south of the Rio Grande. The censuses of Latin America used to attempt with great precision to delineate the degrees of miscegenation among whites, Indians, and Negroes, with not only *mestizo*, *mulato*, and *lobo* as the first generation but *morisco*, *costizo*, *cambujo*, *sambahigo*, *calpamulato*, *jíbaro*, *coyote*, *albarazado*, and so on as indicators of various degrees and types of crossing (cf. *race). A significant influence in revising the self-perception of Brazilian intellectuals, for example, was Gilberto Freyre's *Masters and Slaves* (1946), which taught the many persons of mixed blood who were rising in the social structure that miscegenation represented not only no defect but the country's greatest asset (Skidmore, 1964; cf. Spalding, 1972). In Mexico, where mestizos have become dominant both culturally and politically, the census does not define Indians by racial criteria. A person who wears Indian clothes and speaks only an Indian language is "Indian"; one who wears European clothes and speaks only Spanish is not.

The estimated 1492 population north of Mexico has generally been set at about a tenth of the total in the New World, ranging from 849,000 (Mooney, 1928) to 1 million (Kroeber and Rosenblat) to 9.8-12.3 million (Dobyns), and then back to 1,845,000 (Thornton and Marsh-Thornton, 1981; see also Thornton, 1980, 1981). Contrasted with the Aztec, Mayan, or Incan civilizations, the inhabitants of the present territories of the United States and Canada were at a lower level of culture. The Indians of North America spoke a total of 221 mutually unintelligible languages, and such other basic cultural elements as means of subsistence, religion, and family organization also differed greatly. According to Harold E. Driver (1969), in some areas the extended family was the largest cultural unit, in some a band or village; by the eighteenth century, the League of the Iroquois (with a total population of 10,000 to 17,000) was the largest and best organized federation—which, however, split during the American Revolution to support both sides. In short, not only was the concept of "Indian" (as well as the name) a product of white contact, but many of the "tribes" with which treaties were signed also had a dubious existence.

The fact that colonies, states, and the federal government signed treaties with Indian tribes, however, gave them the status of foreign powers, and the entire ethnic minority thus acquired a unique place in American law. Policy has been not only inconsistent but cyclical, alternating between emphases on facilitating acculturation and encouraging Indians to maintain their own culture. Beginning in 1819 Congress appropriated money to missionary societies to teach Indian children how to read and write and to instruct their parents in "the mode of agriculture suited to their situation and the habits and arts of civilization." After the Louisiana Purchase opened up a vast expanse of fresh territory to land-hungry whites, the Indian Removal Act of 1830 set a pattern of exchanging Indian lands for other lands west of the Mississippi. Many of the Indians in the Southeast were moved, some of them several times, to eastern Oklahoma and other Indian Territories or reservations. Then a contrary policy led to the enactment of the Dawes Act of 1887, whose supporters saw it as the first step toward ending the reservation system and integrating Indians into the general population. The Indian Reorganization Act of 1934, a brainchild of John Collier, reversed the policy of trying to integrate individuals and revivified the tribes and strengthened the usually conservative chieftains (see Kelly, 1975). Though essentially a failure, the 1934 Act had an important negative influence, undermining the prior policy without establishing a viable new one.

The effects of these repeated reversals have been in some respects worse than those of either policy alone. Removal from their earlier land damaged the tribes' economies considerably, and in the recent period the more Indians are tied to their relatively unproductive economy, the more they require outside assistance. Federal support of various types and particularly the successful claims against the government for past wrongs have been inducements for many Indians to identify themselves with their tribe, countering both the pan-Indian movement and the inclination of many younger Indians to find a place in the general American culture.

The federal Bureau of Indian Affairs often used to define "Indian" as a person with at least one-quarter "Indian blood"; but this is in several respects less than adequate. In a volume on relevant federal law, the long section on "Definitions of 'Indians'" opens with a warning against any simple interpretations: "Legally speaking, an Indian is what the law legislatively defines, or juridically determines, him to be. General definitions do not apply'' (U.S. Department of the Interior, 1958, p. 4). Each legal definition—enrollment in a tribe, tribal membership, adoption (e.g., of a wholly white person)—has its own background of legislation and court decisions, which varies from tribe to tribe. Some of the legal disabilities of Indians have been onerous, but sometimes the benefits of government wardship or of membership in a particular wealthy tribe have been substantial. It is often not only convenient but possible for a single individual, depending on the context, both to be and not to be an Indian. The ambiguity, thus, pertains not only to whether marginal types should be included but also under what circumstances each such person will include himself. According to a report in the *New York Times* (March 21, 1976), a presumably authentic Mohawk commented that one consequence of federal programs had been a large-scale production of ''instant Indians.''

Indians not taxed—that is, living on reservations or in Indian Territories—were first counted in the 1890 census (cf. Johansson and Preston, 1978). Because of variation in how precisely the next several censuses defined ''Indian,'' the numbers enumerated went up and down, as though the population were suffering from recurrent disasters. Not only are these figures virtually useless, but one can hardly suggest how they might be improved. More recently, it seems from a detailed analysis that many who were registered as white at birth and who were counted as white in the 1960 census identified themselves as Indian in 1970, presumably because of the resurgence of ethnic sentiment during the decade (Passel, 1976). Poor as the counts have been, they are sufficiently close to reality to show that Indians have been increasing in population at a faster rate than any other identifiable group (see also *accidents).

In 1980 the Bureau of the Census collected fuller information on Indians. As was the rest of the population, Indians were asked to fill in either a ''short form'' giving only basic demographic data or, in a randomly selected 20 percent of the total, a ''long form'' with supplementary questions on employment, occupation, income, and housing. On all federal and state reservations and in the historically Indian areas of Oklahoma, every household with at least one American Indian, Aleut, or Eskimo was asked to supplement the short form with questions similar to those in the long form but adapted specially to these minorities. Additional items were included on tribal affiliation and enrollment, the year the respondent moved to the reservation and the place of residence one year earlier, what and where health services were received, how much time it took to travel to the health facility, and the methods of paying for the services. At the time of writing the results of the enumeration were not available.

REFERENCES: William M. Denevan, ed., *The Native Population of the Americas* (Madison: University of Wisconsin Press, 1976). Henry F. Dobyns, ''Estimating Aboriginal American Population: An Appraisal of Techniques with a New Hemispheric Estimate,'' *Current Anthropology*, 7 (1966), 395-416. Harold E. Driver, *Indians of North America* (2nd ed.; Chicago: University of Chicago Press, 1969). S. Ryan Johansson and Samuel H. Preston, ''Tribal Demography: The Hopi and Navaho Populations as Seen through

Manuscripts from the 1900 U.S. Census," *Social Science History*, 3 (1978), 1-33. Lawrence C. Kelly, "The Indian Reorganization Act: The Dream and the Reality," *Pacific Historical Review*, 44 (1975), 291-312. A. L. Kroeber, *Cultural and Natural Areas of Native North America* (Berkeley: University of California Press, 1939). James Mooney, *The Aboriginal Population of America North of Mexico* (Washington, D.C.: Smithsonian Institution, 1928). Jeffrey S. Passel, "Provisional Evaluation of the 1970 Census Count of American Indians," *Demography*, 13 (1976), 397-409. Ángel Rosenblat, *La Población Indígena de América desde 1492 hasta la Actualidad* (Buenos Aires: Institución Cultural Española, 1945). Thomas Skidmore, "Gilberto Freyre and the Early Brazilian Republic," *Comparative Studies in Society and History*, 6 (1964), 490-505. Karen Spalding, "The Colonial Indian: Past and Future Research Perspectives," *Latin American Research Review*, 7 (1972), 47-76. Russell Thornton, "Recent Estimates of the Prehistoric California Indian Population," *Current Anthropology*, 21 (1980), 702-704; "Demographic Antecedents of a Revitalization Movement: Population Change, Population Size, and the 1890 Ghost Dance," *American Sociological Review*, 46 (1981), 88-96. Thornton and Joan Marsh-Thornton, "Estimating Prehistoric American Indian Population Size for United States Area: Implications of the Nineteenth Century Population Decline and Nadir," *American Journal of Physical Anthropology*, 55 (1981), 47-53. U.S. Department of the Interior, *Federal Indian Law* (Washington, D.C., 1958).

American Medical Association (AMA), founded in 1847, is the country's largest and most prestigious professional society of physicians, with a claimed membership of over 220,000 and a paid staff of 945 in 1980. It provides information on research and advances in therapy, food and nutrition; on quackery and health legislation. It represents the profession before governmental bodies, helps set standards in medical schools and teaching hospitals, maintains a library, and in general acts as the intermediary between medicine and other professions. Vehemently opposed to socialized medicine, it has accepted Medicare and Medicaid as inevitable (see the discussion under *United States: Federal Agencies). Among its serial publications, the most general, the weekly *Journal of the American Medical Association* (*JAMA*), often has articles peripherally related to population studies. Address: 535 North Dearborn Street, Chicago, Ill. 60610.

American Protective Association (APA), a nativist organization founded in 1887, by the mid-1890s had a claimed membership of almost 2.5 million. These were the decades during which the main source of immigrants to the United States shifted to Southern and Eastern Europe, with many Catholic newcomers. The principal theme of APA propaganda was anti-Catholicism, mixed with such progressive stands as support of female suffrage and the separation of church and state. After the 1894 election some fifty-eight members of Congress, as well as legislators in ten or more states, were open members of the APA. Thereafter it declined as rapidly as it had risen and disbanded officially in 1911, when its last president died. Its anti-Catholicism survived in the various movements to set quota restrictions to immigration.

REFERENCE: Donald L. Kinzer, *An Episode in Anti-Catholicism: The American Protective Association* (Seattle: University of Washington Press, 1964).

American Psychological Association (APA), founded in 1892, is the principal professional society of psychologists in the United States, with a claimed membership of 50,000 in 1980. Its Population and Environmental Psychology Division includes those members interested in developing the relation between psychology and demography and in stimulating research on issues like the motives underlying decisions such as whether or not to have a child. It publishes *Population and Environment: Behavioral and Social Issues* (formerly *Journal of Population*), quarterly, as well as a newsletter. Address: 1200 Seventeenth Street, N.W., Washington, D.C. 20036.

American Public Health Association (APHA), a professional organization of persons concerned with community health founded in 1872, claimed a membership of over 30,000 in 1980. It maintains a Population Section for members interested in population issues and family planning. Its International Health Program conducts projects on family planning, maternal and child health, and nutrition in such less developed countries as Costa Rica, Ecuador, Thailand, and the Philippines, with funding from the U.S. Agency for International Development (AID). Publications: *American Journal of Public Health*, monthly; *The Nation's Health*, popular monthly; *Salubritas*, a quarterly newsletter in English, Spanish, and French; *Mother and Children*, a quarterly newsletter in English, French, and Spanish; *Washington Newsletter*, monthly. Address: 1015 Fifteenth Street, N.W., Washington, D.C. 20005.

American Social Health Association (ASHA), an American national voluntary health organization founded in 1912, was known until 1959 as the American Social Hygiene Association. It is dedicated to the prevention and control of venereal disease and in 1980 claimed a membership of 14,000. The association engages in biomedical research through its Venereal Diseases Research Fund and operates a national VD Hotline (800-227-8922). Publications: *Helper* and *Hotline*, quarterlies. Address: 260 Sheridan Avenue, Suite 307, Palo Alto, Calif. 94306.

American Sociological Association (ASA) was founded in 1905 as the American Sociological Society (the name was changed because of the unfortunate implication of the prior acronym). As the principal American association of professionals in sociology and related fields, it claimed 13,000 members in 1984. One of its twenty-one sections, made up of those interested in population studies, has included many of the country's demographers in academia. Main publications: *American Sociological Review*, bimonthly; *Contemporary Sociology: A Journal of Reviews*, bimonthly. Address: 1772 N Street, N.W., Washington, D.C. 20036.

American Statistical Association (ASA), founded in 1839, claimed a membership in 1980 of 14,000 persons interested in the theory, methodology, or application of statistics. At its annual meetings the Social Statistics Section often includes quantitative analyses related to demography. Its several publications include the *Journal of the American Statistical Association*, a professional quarterly; *American Statistician*, a quarterly for shorter commentaries and notes; and *Amstat News*, a newsletter. Address: 806 Fifteenth Street, N.W., Washington, D.C. 20005.

amniocentesis, the tapping and analysis of the amniotic fluid surrounding a fetus. Amniocentesis can give advance notice of complications that may occur during childbirth or of such genetic abnormalities as Down's syndrome (mongolism) and spina bifida. The sex of a child can also be determined, but the test is not recommended merely to satisfy parents' curiosity. If it is known relatively early in the gestation period that the child will suffer from an incurable defect, a woman may choose to undergo an *abortion rather than carry it to term.

ancestors, or lineal forebears, double in number in each generation, since each person has two parents, four grandparents, and so on. Indeed, the doubling is thrown off by such factors as remarriages and multiple births, but these cause relatively small deviations from the standard succession. If we ignore aberrational factors, in the roughly 64 generations since the beginning of the Christian era, the number of ancestors of each person is 2^{64}, or 18,446,744,073,709,551,616. The size of the figure strongly suggests how much overlap there must have been as a consequence—at least by the definitions of some religions and cultures— of "incestuous" relations.

In the 1980 enumeration the U.S. Bureau of the Census eliminated the question in prior schedules on the country of birth of the respondent's parents (cf. *foreign stock) and substituted for it, "What is this person's ancestry?" The open-ended item, asked of a sample of the entire population, was processed into figures using a code with over 400 categories, and those who identified themselves with two ancestries were assigned two code numbers. Except that ancestry was self-identified, it was essentially the same as the "national origin" used earlier to set immigration quotas; see *migration policies and controls.

ancient world, which for Western historians comprises mainly Greece, Rome, and the extensions of their civilizations by imperial conquest, has generated an enormous body of writings, including many on population. As generally with *historical demography, the extant quantitative data of this protostatistical era were typically collected for nondemographic purposes. So-called censuses omitted such sectors of the population as slaves and often women and children. Lists of grain shipments to Rome from the rest of the empire require a rather hazardous guess about the per capita consumption in order to be translated into the number of people who consumed it. The rolls drawn up as part of the administration of taxes, military conscription, and similar governmental functions covered only particular subpopulations and also stimulated even those persons to evade the count whenever possible. Data on mortality from *epitaphs are even worse. The primitive life tables drawn up by the famous Roman jurist Ulpian (A.D. 170?-228), which were used by the courts to settle property disputes, were presumably based on the death rates of the well-to-do.

Manipulating these unsatisfactory sources produces a range for the population of Rome at the time of Augustus (who reigned from 27 B.C. to A.D. 14), for instance, from a low of 250,000 to a high of 1.6 million (Maier, 1954). The estimated population of the empire at the same time was between 50 and 70 million; in the third century, between 50 and 100 million (Boak, 1955, pp. 5-6; cf. Crawford, 1977; Lassère, 1977). With the figures on the population so uncertain, those on the components of its growth are obviously no better.

One important determinant of family size is how long marriages endure. From estimates of the average ages at marriage and of life expectations at birth, Keith Hopkins (1965) judged the mean duration of first marriages in Rome to be only 10 to 14.6 years. Even so, some means of controlling fertility, even if illegal, were often used (cf. Wilkinson, 1978). Earlier the Greek city-states not only had permitted infanticide but under certain conditions prescribed it. In Rome it was limited by various legal restrictions and finally made a capital offense. Out of the twenty-two ancient medical writers whose works are extant and not on irrelevant topics, eleven discussed contraceptive methods and fifteen spoke of methods of abortion. Their recommendations combined superstition with effective practice. Even Soranus, the best of them, recommended that the woman hold her breath during the sexual act or drink something cold immediately after it and, on the other hand, prescribed spermicides that physicians were still advocating in the 1930s. That the family size in Rome declined is suggested by the *Leges Julia et Papia-Poppaea, decrees intended to encourage marriage and reproduction.

From tombstone inscriptions in Roman Italy, Julius †Beloch (1886, pp. 48-51) calculated the age-specific death rates *per 1,000 deaths*. The median life expectations of adults and children seemingly differed only slightly, ranging from 10-11 years at age 50 to only 17-18 at age 10. But these data included virtually no infant deaths. Age-specific mortality with life expectations at birth of 20 to 30 years (the probable range at that time) would describe a U-shaped curve, reflecting a very high infant and child mortality, a sharp decline in adolescence and early adulthood, and then a gradual rise. The curves drawn from Roman data, however, lack the left arm of this U, all rising from an initial low point (Hopkins, 1966). These not very satisfactory sources pertain mostly to what might be termed normal periods, but mortality was raised greatly by periodic wars, famines, and epidemics, and by the breakdown of social order. Those who have witnessed hundreds of their neighbors die of hunger or disease do not themselves continue their usual pursuits in accordance with established norms. Often they flee their homes, carrying the blight with them.

The lack of empirical data and conceptual clarity did not prevent the ancients from developing population policies. The pronatalist efforts of the Greek city-states, applied to populations ridiculously small by modern standards, were usually intended to maintain a static number rather than to stimulate an increase (see †Aristotle; †Plato). The arena for Roman policy was far larger, and it was more consistently pronatalist. As imperial hegemony spread from Italy to the far reaches of the Mediterranean and beyond, it would appear that the center suffered from moral decay, the dissolution of the family, and the slower growth of population (e.g., Landry, 1936). As the empire gradually disintegrated, no central authority took its place. Many believed that the end of the world was at hand, and various sects competed in offering dogmas appropriate to the apocalypse. Early Christian doctrine, which evolved in such a social environment, in some respects continued classical themes, transmitted by neo-Platonists and consolidated especially by †Augustine and, several centuries later, Thomas †Aquinas (Noonan, 1965).

REFERENCES: Julius Beloch, *Die Bevölkerung der Griechisch-römischen Welt* (Leipzig: Duncker & Humblot, 1886). Arthur E. R. Boak, *Manpower Shortage and the Fall of the Roman Empire in the West* (Ann Arbor: University of Michigan Press, 1955). Michael H. Crawford, "Rome and the Greek World: Economic Relationships," *Economic History Review*, 2nd Ser., 30 (1977), 42-52. Keith Hopkins, "Contraception in the Roman Empire," *Comparative Studies in Society and History*, 8 (1965), 124-151; "On the Probable Age Structure of the Roman Population," *Population Studies*, 20 (1966), 245-264. Adolphe Landry, "Quelques Aperçus Concernant la Dépopulation dans l'Antiquité Gréco-romaine," *Revue Historique*, 61 (1936), 1-33. Jean-Marie Lassère, *Ubique Populus: Peuplements et Mouvements de Populations dans l'Afrique Romaine de la Chute de Carthage à la Fin de la Dynastie des Sévères (146 av. J.C.-235)* (Paris: Centre National de la Recherche Scientifique, 1977). F. G. Maier, "Römische Bevölkerungsgeschichte und Inschriftenstatistik," *Historia*, 2 (1954), 318-351. Noonan, *Contraception*. L. P. Wilkinson, "Classical Approaches to Population and Family Planning," *Population and Development Review*, 4 (1978), 439-455.

Ancor, an anchor-shaped intra-uterine device developed by Michael S. Burnhill.

androgen, any substance in the body that tends to enhance the person's maleness, such as the hormones testosterone and androsterone, which when injected counteract the side effects of castration.

REFERENCE: R. I. Dorfman and R. A. Shipley, *Androgens* (New York: Wiley, 1964).

Anglo is used in areas of the United States with large proportions of *Hispanics to designate any white person who is not of Spanish background, irrespective of nationality. In other parts of the country the term *Anglo-American* is sometimes used in the same broad sense, and sometimes is limited to those with Northwestern European forebears. WASP, standing for White Anglo-Saxon Protestant, began as an opprobrious designation of snobbish patrician types, but it quickly spread to virtually all non-Catholic, non-Jewish whites and lost the intended bite of the original epithet.

Angola: The government's Bureau of Statistical Services publishes a statistical yearbook in Portuguese and a shorter pamphlet, *Statistical information*, with table titles in English and French. Address: Direção dos Serviços de Estatística, C.P. 1215, Luanda.

animal populations, a topic of considerable importance in itself, can be studied by demographers as a way of understanding the narrowly biological determinants of population size and growth (e.g., Andrewartha, 1961; Begon and Mortimer, 1981; Chauvin, 1973). More specifically, it may be that some of the advanced methods used routinely in the study of animal populations can be applied to human populations of past periods or of less developed countries, where often the principal problem is also a paucity of accurate data. For example, a recent text begins with a section on mathematical models and proceeds with discussions of such overlapping topics as spatial distribution and growth in numbers (Elseth and Baumgardner, 1981). Since it is seldom possible to count all the animals in a particular area, the usual counterpart of a census is to count those in one or more representative subareas called "quadrats" (the counterpart of a survey), or to mark, release, and recapture individuals, noting the relation between marked and unmarked categories. If one can assume a closed population in which marked individuals are distributed homogeneously, then

$$P = N \times \frac{M}{R}$$

where P is the estimated population; M is the number captured, marked and released; and N is the number captured on a subsequent occasion, including R marked ones. Two types of *life tables are constructed by analysts of animal populations, an "age-specific" or cohort table similar to that used by actuaries, and a "time-specific" or cross-sectional one when it is impossible to estimate the ages of individuals within acceptable limits (e.g., Dempster, 1975). The first aphid life table was approached through a series of simulations until the match with empirical observations was considered to be satisfactory (Gilbert, 1976, chap. 9). See also *crowding; *ecology; *environment; *mathematical demography.

REFERENCES: H. G. Andrewartha, *Introduction to the Study of Animal Populations* (Chicago: University of Chicago Press, 1961). Michael Begon and Martin Mortimer, *Population Ecology: A Unified Study of Animals and Plants* (Oxford: Blackwell Scientific Publications, 1981). Rémy Chauvin, "Vues de Démographie Animale," *Population*, 28 (1973), 231-260. J. P. Dempster, *Animal Population Ecology* (New York: Academic Press, 1975). Gerald D. Elseth and Kandy D. Baumgardner, *Population Biology* (New York: Van Nostrand, 1981). Neil E. Gilbert, *Ecological Relationships* (San Francisco: W. H. Freeman, 1976).

annexation, the incorporation of adjacent territory into a political unit. A major factor in the increased population of cities has been the annexation of the smaller units that had grown up around them. The extension of a nation-state's expanse is also often by annexation, which is both more effective and less obtrusive than imperialist ventures at a distance. During the Second World War, as a prime instance, the Soviet Union incorporated some 670,000 square kilometers inhabited by almost 24 million non-Russian people.

annulment, a legal decree invalidating a marriage because of a fault in the original contract. It is distinguished from a *divorce in that the parties revert to the status of ''single''; the contract is voided from the date of its inception rather than from the date of its dissolution. Where statistics on annulments are compiled, they strongly suggest that they function mainly as a substitute for divorce. In jurisdictions like Nevada, where divorces have been granted with little trouble, there are few annulments; in those like New York, which used to grant divorces only on the single ground of adultery, there were many. See also *Roman Catholicism. An *annulment rate* is computed as the number of annulments during a year per 1,000 in the base population, which may be designated as the total population, the married population, or the latter specified by age and sex.

anomie, normlessness, was resurrected from the Greek by Émile †Durkheim to denote the cause of one type of suicide. With the spelling *anomy*, it had already existed in English to designate the disregard of law, particularly divine law. In the sense of personal disorganization, anomie is often a factor in such social pathologies as *alcoholism or *addiction, as well as procreation not governed by rational choices (see *alienation).

anovulation, the absence of *ovulation in a woman, as during a pregnancy or after an abortion or a birth, when the interruption in the production of ova is normally indicated by an absence of *menstruation. There may also be anovular cycles, however—that is, menstrual cycles during which there is no ovulation.

anthropology, ''the study of man and his works,'' is in this review limited to the analysis of living primitives, thus omitting research based on written records (see *historical demography) or the remains of extinct peoples (see *paleodemography), or that concerned with *population genetics or *ecology. Supposedly the most expeditious way to start a study of a small people would be with a census, classifying the population by sex and approximate age (and therefore by role), placing each person in his geographical and social setting, and thus laying a base for a more detailed analysis of almost any other specific topic. As we know from some ethnologists' personal reminiscences, when such a house count used to be made, it was often seen as busy work; few of the classical ethnographies suggest an even marginal interest in demographic topics. We know more about kin structure than about family size, more about beliefs in the afterworld than about the expectation of life, more about the structure of roles than of age categories. When Ludwik †Krzywicki (1934) compiled the data available two generations ago, this was a collection of figures mostly too poor to be useful. The serious study of population developed in anthropology after that book was published (cf. Nag, 1978).

Much of the more recent work, comprising especially but not exclusively instructional materials, has been based on borrowings from other disciplines. Two papers in the *Annual Review of Anthropology*—by Paul T. †Baker and William T. Sanders (vol. 1, 1972), and Kenneth M. Weiss (vol. 5, 1976)—give a good idea of how population anthropology was then defined, the problems encountered by those working in it, and some of the results to date. The tendency still to link the subdiscipline with archeology and *animal populations, both put in an evolutionary schema, presumably reflects the paucity of narrower, more specific data and theory. The longer review in the volume edited by Brian Spooner (1972) defines the range of the discipline to include both prehistoric and literate populations.

Many demographers used to assume that fertility among primitives had to be close to the physiological maximum in order to match their high mortality. More recent evidence (as in the symposium in *Human Biology*, vol. 48, February, 1976) indicates that fertility has varied greatly and that births have virtually always been controlled to some degree. Similarly, there is no reason to expect an overall uniformity in the mortality of primitive peoples, independent of their habitat, standards of sanitation, nutritional norms, patterns of violence, and therapeutic skills. There is suggestive evidence that both the dominant causes of death and the expectations of life differ considerably (e.g., Acsádi and Nemeskéri, 1970). In other words, the discipline may be working its way to documenting what in cultural anthropology has become a commonplace—that, within the range set by the lack of civilization, there is a far wider variation in the population characteristics of primitive peoples than the merely negative definition would imply. See also *age, *diffusion.

Relative to earlier work in ethnology, the greatest innovation has been the use of computer simulation. At a conference in the United States sponsored by the Social Science Research Council, for instance, one of the four sessions was on Anthropology and Social Systems (Dyke and MacCluer, 1973). In a paper by Eugene A. Hammel and David W. Hutchinson, an initial population of 65 persons with fertility and mortality at presumed prehistoric levels was run for a century with no incest taboo and with four different types of taboo, thus offering a new insight on a much discussed topic. In a comment on the relation between empirical data and model, the Canadian demographer Nancy Howell remarked, ''I would use model life tables and scorn ad hoc mortality curves as a waste of time. When the mortality experience of hundreds of human populations is known in detail, it is wasteful to postulate patterns that have never been observed.''

REFERENCES: George Acsádi and János Nemeskéri, *History of Human Life Span and Mortality* (Budapest: Akadémiai Kiadó, 1970). Bennett Dyke and Jean Walters MacCluer, eds., *Computer Simulation in Human Population Studies* (New York: Academic Press, 1973). Ludwik Krzywicki, *Primitive Society and Its Vital Statistics* (London: Macmillan, 1934). Moni Nag, *Population Anthropology: An International Directory of*

Contributors and Their Works, for the Population Commission, International Union of Anthropological and Ethnological Sciences (New York: Population Council, 1978). Brian Spooner, *Population Growth: Anthropological Implications* (Cambridge, Mass.: M.I.T. Press, 1972).

antibacterial, a generic term to denote a substance that destroys *bacteria or suppresses their growth or reproduction; also, pertaining to such substances. The antibacterials can be classified into several types; antiseptics, which are antibacterial through a physical or chemical action; such substances as sulfanilamide, which interferes with the metabolism of the bacteria; *antibiotics; and such natural substances as certain enzymes.

antibiotic, coined in 1945, means a chemical substance produced by microorganisms that, in dilute solutions, can destroy bacteria or inhibit their growth; by extension, also close chemical derivatives of the natural product, even though they do not occur in nature. Antibiotics have been used widely in the treatment of infectious diseases since 1929, when Alexander Fleming noted that the fungus *Penicillium notatum* inhibited the growth of cultures of staphylococcus, one of the bacteria that cause pneumonia. Like the penicillins, other antibiotics also typically have a particular antibacterial effect—which can be reduced, however, by a growing resistance following continual use. Those antibiotics that attack a wide spectrum of bacteria, such as the tetracyclines, are particularly likely to cause allergic reactions.
    REFERENCE: F. C. Sciavolino, "Antibiotics," in D. M. Considine, ed., *Chemical and Process Technology Encyclopedia* (New York: McGraw-Hill, 1974).

antibody, a type of serum globulin developed in the body or artificially in the laboratory in response to an infection or an ingestion of an *antigen. The antibody responsible for immunity to an infectious agent is called "protective." Loosely, a sensitizing antibody is one attached to body cells that renders them susceptible to destruction by body defenses. Compare *immunity.

antigen, a protein or other compound of high molecular weight that, when foreign to the bloodstream of an animal, stimulates the formation of a specific, homologous *antibody with which it reacts. The portion of an antigenic molecule or complex that determines its immunological specificity is called its *haptene*.

Antigon, a closed, kite-shaped *intra-uterine device first developed in Denmark; also called a "polygon."

Antigua: The government's Statistics Division publishes a *Statistical Yearbook* that includes population data. Address: Ministry of Planning, Development and External Affairs, St. John's.

antinatal, opposed to births, as in "antinatal policy," an intention by the state or one of its units to reduce fertility. Traditional methods of contraception are sometimes called "antinatal practices."

anti-Semitism was apparently coined by Ernest Renan (1823-92), the French philologist and historian. Though the term dates only from the nineteeth century, the hatred of *Jews that it denotes is as old as history. Such classical writers as Tacitus, Plutarch, and especially Apion condemned Jewish "depravity" for some of the same reasons that recurred again and again, including even the suspicion that in their religious rites they drank the blood of Gentile children. The charge that Jews killed Christ was long the pivot of Christian attitudes. England expelled Jews in 1290, France in 1394, Spain in 1492; in the various principalities of Germany they were designated "servants of the state" and both restricted to petty trades and heavily taxed. In 1555 Pope Paul IV required them to wear a badge of identity that marked them as separate and inferior, to live apart in what were later called *ghettos, and to be barred from designated professions and occupations. Luther's "honest advice" was that their synagogues and their homes should be destroyed and that under pain of death rabbis should be prohibited from teaching (cf. Rogow, 1968). In his work on the destruction of European Jews, Raul Hilberg (1967) begins his account of the Nazi *Holocaust with tables in parallel columns, giving in the first a series of anti-Semitic regulations from canon law or pre-Nazi civil law, and in the second a list of the often remarkably similar measures in National Socialist Germany. Whatever the consistency in anti-Jewish attitudes and acts, the rationale changed with the historical setting. In Western Europe many Jews had lost their religious identity and either converted to Christianity or become agnostics. The ostensible basis of hostility shifted from religious or mercantile to social-class and, under the Nazis, racial. Current anti-Semitism in Communist and Islamic states is largely nationalist, based on a willful confusion of *Judaism with Zionism.

Their group history has influenced the demographic characteristics of Jews, and not only through the extraordinary mortality in *pogroms or the Nazi death camps. The mass movement of Europeans to the United States or other countries of immigration was usually of unattached young males, but very often among Jews it was a family migration, with a consequent wider distribution among age groups and a better balance between the sexes. The new intellectual forces of the eighteenth century, which were reflected in Jewish thought in a counterpart to the Enlightenment, have often been depicted as a new and paradoxical threat to Jewish survival, for the assimilation of a small minority could mean its disappearance. Whether or not they were religious, Jews migrated mainly to large cities, where they formed self-protective communities in which they continued the skills they had learned in the old country, sometimes as furriers, for instance, more often as merchants. The typically low *fertility of emancipated Jews has been plausibly explained as the effect of their upward mobility against a barrier of continuing anti-Semitic discrimination.

REFERENCES: Raul Hilberg, *The Destruction of the European Jews* (Chicago: Quadrangle Books, 1967). Arnold A. Rogow, "Anti-Semitism," in *International Encyclopedia of the Social Sciences*, 1, 345-349.

antiseptic, an agent that inhibits the growth of microorganisms without necessarily destroying them, contrasted with germicide or disinfectant, which destroys infectious organisms. The first antiseptic was carbolic acid, which Joseph Lister (1827-1912) used to sterilize surgical instruments and wounds in a process he termed "antiseptic surgery." Subsequently a wide variety of substances were found to be antiseptic, but for many purposes they have now been replaced by *antibiotics.

apportionment,   the distribution of legislative seats among the territorial units entitled to representation. Since the districting principle is often based on population, it implies a recurrent count so that the boundaries of the districts can be periodically adjusted to maintain the relatively equal (or other stipulated) number of voters in each. In the United States Constitution, thus, the decennial census is called for in order to adjust congressional districts to changes in the population. As early as 1883, apportionment was applied also to membership in the civil service; and in recent years more and more federal grants and other values have been distributed proportional to the population. Alleged underenumeration, therefore, is a recurrent complaint among local officials. See also *gerrymander.

REFERENCE: Leon Gilford, Beverly D. Causey, and Naomi D. Rothwell, "How Adjusting Census Counts Could Affect Congress," *American Demographics*, 4 (September, 1982), 30-33, 43-44.

area, the most general term for any portion of the earth's surface, specified more or less arbitrarily by any of a number of referents to suit the context or the convenience of the analyst. In contrast, a *region usually connotes a certain geographic, economic, or cultural homogeneity; a *territory typically is associated with biology or politics.

area sampling, a method of *sampling based on dividing the area being studied into small subareas roughly equivalent with respect to relevant characteristics. Of these subareas, a randomly chosen sample is fully investigated.

area studies, a class of multidisciplinary university programs in the United States devoted to the languages, life conditions, cultures, and social systems of a specified geographic area—for example, Latin America, the Soviet Union, Southeast Asia. The new emphasis developed after the Second World War as a means of training scholars in depth about places of political and economic interest. With respect to the analysis of population, such programs made it possible to place the determinants of fertility or the causes of infant mortality, say, in a full cultural-social-economic context.

REFERENCES: Joseph Axelrod and Donald N. Bigelow, *Resources for Language and Area Studies* (Washington, D.C.: American Council on Education, 1962). Robert H. Hall, *Area Studies, with Special Reference to Their Implications for Research in the Social Sciences* (New York: Social Science Research Council, 1947). Lucian W. Pye, ed., *Political Science and Area Studies: Rivals or Partners?* (Bloomington: Indiana University Press, 1975).

Argentina: Demographic Institutions

The Bariloche Foundation, a private agency, established a Population Studies Center (CENEP) in 1974. Under the direction of Alfredo E. †Lattes, it has conducted research on the population of Argentina. Since 1978 it has published a serial, *Cuadernos del CENEP*. Address: Centro de Estudios de Población, Fundación Bariloche, Casilla 4397, Correo Central, 1000 Buenos Aires.

The Center for Urban and Regional Studies (CEUR), a private agency, was established in 1962 as one unit of the Torcuato di Tella Institute; it conducts research on urbanization, housing, and regional development. In 1980 its director was Oscar Yujnovsky and the head of research was César A. †Vapñarsky. Address: Centro de Estudios Urbanos y Regionales, Instituto Torcuato di Tella, Bartolomé Mitre 2212, 1939 Buenos Aires.

The Center for Economic Research, founded in 1960 as another unit of the same institute, was directed in 1980 by H. L. Dieguez. Its analyses of development planning and economic history sometimes include population as one factor. Address: Centro de Investigaciones Económicas, Instituto Torcuato di Tella, Superi 1502, 1939 Buenos Aires.

GOVERNMENT STATISTICAL BUREAUS

The national Department of Health Statistics publishes regularly not only vital and health statistics but series on the evaluation of data and methods of investigation, health and mortality surveys, and analyses of data. Address: Departamento de Estadística de Salud, Alsina 301-6, Oficina 6052, Buenos Aires.

The National Bureau of Migrations publishes a quarterly report on immigration, titled simply *Inmigración*. Address: Dirección Nacional de Migraciones, Buenos Aires.

The National Institute of Statistics and Censuses publishes a quarterly statistical bulletin, a statistical yearbook, and an irregular series on particular demographic topics. The most recent census report was for 1980. Address: Instituto Nacional de Estadística y Censos, Hipólito Yrigoyen 250, 0032 Buenos Aires.

arid, dry, with deficient precipitation; hence, of land, bare or barren. The first step toward the amelioration of aridity has been an attempt to define it more precisely—at least into the three-way classification of extremely arid, arid, and semi-arid (White, 1956). The index of aridity is usually given by the formula

$$I = \frac{P}{T + 10}$$

where P is the precipitation in millimeters and T is the temperature in degrees Centigrade. However, this is only one of a dozen formulas that specialists use to define and classify the subject of their studies (cf. Nir, 1974, Appendix). In 1977 the United Nations sponsored a conference in Nairobi on desertification, by which is usually meant dessication of an area as a result not of natural forces but of human activities (cf. Walls, 1980).

REFERENCES: Dov Nir, *The Semi-arid World: Man on the Fringe of the Desert* (New York: Longman, 1974). James Walls, *Land, Man and Sand: Desertification and the Solution* (New York: Macmillan, 1980). Gilbert F. White, ed., *The Future of Arid Lands* (Washington, D.C.: American Association for the Advancement of Science, 1956).

arithmetic progression, a series of which each item differs from the preceding one by the addition of a constant; thus, x, $(a + x)$, $(2a + x)$, ... $(an + x)$. It is contrasted with a *geometric progression; see also †Malthus.

array, in statistical usage, means the arrangement of a set of empirical observations by some rule—for example, in order of magnitude. Setting an array is a usual first step toward the *classification of data into convenient and meaningful subunits.

arrivals, or total arrivals, include all categories of persons entering a country, comprising temporary and permanent immigrants, visitors, and natives returning from a residence abroad. Those going in the opposite direction make up *departures*. Most countries do not collect the comprehensive data that the United Nations has recommended on what are termed, however clumsily, "nonimmigrant arrivals" and "nonemigrant departures." See also *migration, international.

artificial insemination, the use of a syringe or other instrument to place semen in a female's genital tract in order to fertilize an ovum, has been used mainly in the breeding of horses and cattle. American laws concerning its application to humans have made a distinction according to whether the donor is the husband: insemination with a third party's semen constitutes adultery, and the child of such an impregnation is illegitimate. In a number of state legislatures bills were introduced to change the law. In California, for example, the Civil Code (Sec. 7005) was amended in 1975 to hold that, if artificial insemination is administered with the written consent of the husband and under the direction of a physician, the husband is treated in law as the natural father, while the identity of the donor is secreted in a file that may be opened only under exceptional circumstances. In the moral teaching of the Roman Catholic church, it was once held that artificial insemination with the husband acting as donor may be licit if the semen is not obtained by masturbation or another forbidden practice. In 1949, however,

Pius XII averred that all artificial insemination is to be absolutely rejected as a violation of natural law, and this ruling has remained in force (Liebard, 1978, pp. 96-100, 173-179; McKeever, 1967).

REFERENCES: Odile M. Liebard, ed., *Official Catholic Teachings: Love & Society* (Wilmington, N.C.: McGrath Publishing Co., 1978). P. E. McKeever, "Artificial Insemination (Moral Aspects)," in *New Catholic Encyclopedia*, 1, 922-924.

Aryan, Sanskrit for "noble" or "nobleman," had, like many of the locutions that people use to designate themselves, overtones of greatness or superiority. This connotation was taken over by nineteenth-century racists and particularly their Nazi successors to designate the ostensibly superior Northern Europeans. In modern usage the word refers to the Indo-European group of languages or to the language from which they all hypothetically derived.

ASCII (an acronym for American Standard Code for Information Interchange), a system of seven-bit codes that can be specified as one of the options on the nine-track tapes sold by the U.S. Bureau of the Census. Cf. *EBCDIC.

asepsis, the surgical procedure by which infection is inhibited by the use of sterile instruments and clothing—including, in what is termed integral asepsis, the freeing of the entire operating room and air of living germs. In contrast, antisepsis means inhibiting the growth of microorganisms already present.

Asia Foundation, a government-supported American organization founded in 1954, has had field offices in nineteen Asian countries. With a three-year grant from the U.S. Agency for International Development (AID), it expanded its work related to population, generally by helping to fund public or private family-planning programs already in existence. By 1981 this type of activity had been cut to a single antinatalist program in Bangladesh, plus whatever ancillary efforts were made in other countries as part of rural development. The foundation publishes *Asia Foundation News*, bimonthly. Address: P.O. Box 3223, San Francisco, Calif. 94119.

Asian and Pacific Development Center (Centre de Développement pour l'Asie et le Pacifique) was established in 1980 with funding from the U.N. Economic and Social Commission for Asia and the Pacific (ESCAP) by combining four prior regional centers for research and training. Its announced programs include the maintenance of a secure food supply, the mobilization of human resources, and securing an adequate place for women in economic development. One of the component organizations, the Social Welfare Development Center for Asia and the Pacific, had cooperated with the *U.N. Fund for Population Activities (UNFPA) in preparing a seven-volume work on migration in the area, *Migration and Resettlement: Rural-Urban Policies* (1980). Address: Pasiaran Dula, P.O. Box 2224, Kuala Lumpur 01 02, Malaysia.

Asians and Pacific Islanders, one of the aggregates used by the U.S. Bureau of the Census in classifying the population by *race. In *complete-count tabulations it included persons who identified themselves as Japanese, Chinese, Filipino, Korean, Asian Indian, Vietnamese, Hawaiian, Guamian, or Samoan. In such tabulations based on a complete count, comprising over fifty more nationalties, the residual category "Other Asians and Pacific Islanders" was transferred to "Other races"; but in tabulations based on a sample of the population, those in this residual category were included among Asians and Pacific Islanders.

assimilation, the most general term to denote the interpenetration of groups of two or more cultures. As developed by American analysts of immigrant or racial groups, the concept of assimilation has varied somewhat in its characteristics. Generally it is understood to include *acculturation and *integration, but it is distinguished from *accommodation, which implies a tolerance on one side and a giving way on the other. In the "race relations cycle" of Robert E. †Park and Ernest W. †Burgess, assimilation was supposedly the last phase of an inevitable and irreversible process, following contact, competition, conflict, and accommodation. In fact, assimilation is neither an inevitable nor a one-way process. Such peoples as, for instance, the *Jews have lived for millennia among strangers without necessarily entirely losing their distinguishing characteristics. Among immigrants to the United States, the relatively insecure first generation usually sought to disappear totally into the general population, but the third generation often tried to reverse the process and establish nativist associations of various types in order to maintain or revive the specific ethnic culture (Hansen, 1938). Currently analysts often contrast assimilation with the continuation of differences in a pattern of cultural pluralism (Abramson, 1980).

REFERENCES: Harold J. Abramson, "Assimilation and Pluralism," in *Harvard Encyclopedia of American Ethnic Groups* (Cambridge, Mass.: Harvard University Press, 1980). Milton M. Gordon, *Assimilation in American Life: The Role of Race, Religion, and National Origins* (New York: Oxford University Press, 1964). Marcus Lee Hansen, *The Problem of the Third Generation Immigrant* (Rock Island, Ill.: Augustana Historical Society, 1938; reprinted in *Commentary*, November, 1952, pp. 492-500).

Association for Jewish Demography and Statistics, an international organization founded in 1957, maintains a documentation center in Jerusalem. It claimed 75 members in its American branch in 1980. Publication: *Jewish Population Studies*. Address: 4320 Cedarhurst Circle, Los Angeles, Calif. 90027.

Association for Population/Family Planning Libraries and Information Centers—International (APLIC-Int.), an American nonprofit organization founded in 1968, develops documentation and similar services for demographers and professionals in family planning. It conducts an annual conference and publishes the proceedings. With a claimed membership of 159 in 1980, it has been funded mainly by the *U.N. Fund for Population Activities (UNFPA).

Among its publications is a quarterly information bulletin, *APLICommunicator*. Addresses: 105 Madison Avenue, New York, N.Y. 10016; 165 South Second Avenue, Clarion, Pa. 16214.

Association for Vital Records and Health Statistics (AVRHS) before 1980 was called the American Association of Registration Executives (1933-58) and the American Association for Vital Records and Public Health Statistics (1958-80). It claimed a membership in 1980 of 220 officials of state and local health agencies who meet annually and discuss their common problems in maintaining an effective statistical system. It maintains no permanent office, and its affairs are conducted by officers who are newly elected each year.

Association for Voluntary Sterilization (AVS), an American organization established in 1937, was known earlier as Birthright, Inc.; Human Betterment Association of America; and Human Betterment for Voluntary Sterilization. It acquired its present designation in 1949. AVS acts as a worldwide clearinghouse for scientific information on *sterilization and for propaganda in favor of its voluntary use. Males or females considering the operation are given advice and are referred to one of about 2,000 cooperating physicians in the United States. AVS also has an International Project, funded by the U.S. Agency for International Development (AID) with a sum that makes up about three-quarters of the association's total budget. AVS publishes three quarterlies, *Bio-Medical Bulletin*, *IPAVS Newsletter*, and *AVS News*. The best statement of the association's purposes and achievements is a book by H. Curtis Wood, Jr., who was its president for some fifteen years—*Sex without Babies: A Comprehensive Review of Voluntary Sterilization as a Method of Birth Control*. Address: 708 Third Avenue, New York, N.Y. 10017.

Association Internationale des Démographes de Langue Française (AIDELF; International Association of Francophone Demographers), founded in 1977, has a membership of about 150, most of them in Europe. Its purpose is to promote the study of population by fostering exchanges among francophone scholars, including those whose first language is not French. Address: c/o Institut National d'Études Démographiques, 27 rue du Commandeur, 75675 Paris Cédex 14, France.

Association of American Geographers (AAG), the professional society of geographers in the United States, was founded in 1904. It has sponsored research on topics related to population—for example, an Urban Project to assess how human needs are met in America's twenty largest metropolitan areas. "Specialty Groups" of the association include: Population, Urban, Environmental Studies, Cultural Ecology, and Medical. Publications: *Annals*, quarterly; *Professional Geographer*, with shorter articles. Address: 1710 Sixteenth Street, N.W., Washington, D.C. 20009.

REFERENCE: Preston E. James and Geoffrey J. Martin, *The Association of American Geographers: The First Seventy-Five Years, 1904-1979* (Washington, D. C.: Association of American Geographers, 1978).

Association of Planned Parenthood Physicians (APPP), until 1973 the American Association of Planned Parenthood Physicians, is an American organization founded in 1963 "to establish an ongoing interest in family planning in order to promote the stability and health of the family through responsible parenthood." It claimed a membership of 850 in 1980. Publication: *Advances in Planned Parenthood*, quarterly, which ceased publication in 1981. Address: 810 Seventh Avenue, New York, N.Y. 10019.

Association of Public Data Users (APDU), an American consortium founded in 1975, included in 1981 about seventy-five business firms, universities, research institutes, federal and state agencies, libraries, and other organizations with an interest in machine-readable statistical products. It publishes an annual *Directory of Members' Data File Holdings*. Address: P.O. Box 9287, Rosslyn Station, Arlington, Va. 22209.

astrology can affect the spacing of births in believers' families, for whether a person will prosper during his lifetime allegedly depends on whether he is born at an auspicious time. The effect on fertility, if any, is difficult to ascertain in Western countries, but it is quite apparent among Chinese populations and even in so modernist a country as Japan. "The year of the fiery horse," which recurs only once every sixty years, is grossly inauspicious for female babies. At the last such occasion, Japan's crude birth rate fluctuated sharply from 18.6 in 1965, to 13.7 in 1966, and then to 19.3 in 1967. Avoidance of the unlucky year was effected partly by shifting birth registration (fooling fate, as it were), but partly through a genuine temporary decline in fertility.

REFERENCES: Jean-Noël Biraben, "L'Année 'Cheval et Feu,' " and "Quelques Précisions sur l'Année 'Cheval et Feu,' " *Population*, 23 (1968), 154-159 and 24 (1969), 119-123. Allan Chapman, "Astrological Medicine," in Charles Webster, ed., *Health, Medicine and Mortality in the Sixteenth Century* (New York: Cambridge University Press, 1979).

asymptote, the limiting position of a tangent to a curve, which makes contact at an infinite distance from the origin. In demography the term has been used especially in discussions of the various *logistic curves used to project the population growth of particular areas. In that context the asymptote marks the maximum population feasible under the stipulated conditions.

attitude, a predisposition to act; thus, a psychological link between values and the behavior based on them. Demographic research was broadened greatly when questions on the number of children, for instance, were supplemented with ones on the size of family desired. See also *KAP.

attribute, a qualitative characteristic, like sex, as contrasted with a quantitative characteristic, or *variable, like age.

Australia: Demographic Institutions
The Academy of the Social Sciences in Australia, founded in 1952 as the Social Sciences Research Council of Australia, changed its name in 1971. It promotes research and teaching in all the social sciences, and in 1980 its director was W. D. †Borrie, one of the country's principal demographers. Address: National Library Building, Canberra A.C.T. 2600.

The Australian Development Assistance Agency was established in 1974 to administer aid to less developed countries, including the funding of antinatalist programs in Bangladesh, Pakistan, and Papua New Guinea, as well as contributions to multilateral organizations. Address: P.O. Box 887, Canberra A.C.T. 2601.

The Australian Population Association, founded in 1980 as a private professional society, has a central office in Canberra and the intention of establishing a branch in each state. As of mid-1981, it had about 200 members. Address: Secretary, A.P.A., c/o Department of Immigration and Ethnic Affairs, Canberra A.C.T. 2616.

UNIVERSITY AND OTHER RESEARCH INSTITUTES

The Australian Institute of Aboriginal Studies, of which the principal in 1980 was P. J. Ucko, has published monographs that in some cases include analyses of the population of native Australians. Address: P.O. Box 553, Canberra A.C.T. 2601.

The Australian Institute of Urban Studies, of which the president in 1980 was Burnet MacFarlane, deals in its research with urbanization and city planning. It published a *Bibliography of Urban Studies in Australia* (1977). Address: P.O. Box 809, Canberra A.C.T. 2601.

The Department of Demography of the Australian National University, headed since 1970 by John C. †Caldwell, has conducted research on all aspects of Australia's population; population problems in Southeast Asia, the Pacific Islands, and Africa; and settlers in Australia as related to its immigration policy. Address: P.O. Box 4, Canberra A.C.T. 2600.

The A.N.U. Survey Research Center, of which the director in 1980 was K.R.W. Brewer, has conducted various surveys pertaining to population or demographic methods. Address: Australian National University, P.O. Box 4, Canberra A.C.T. 2600.

The Center for Applied Social and Survey Research, Flinders University of South Australia, was directed in 1980 by Robert J. Stimson. Its wide range of research monographs has included some pertaining to demography and particularly population geography. Address: Bedford Park, South Australia 5042.

Macquarie University offers an undergraduate program in demography and a master's program in population and development. In 1981 both were headed by John H. †Pollard, professor of actuarial studies. Address: North Ryde, N.S.W. 2113.

The Planning Research Center of the University of Sydney was directed in 1980 by S. Domicelj. Its research has related to the populations of Australia, Southeast Asia, the Pacific area, and Africa, usually focusing on urban and regional planning. Address: Department of Town and Country Planning, Sydney, N.S.W. 2006.

GOVERNMENT STATISTICAL BUREAUS

The Australian Bureau of Statistics, headed in 1980 by Roy J. Cameron, conducts the country's censuses and provides regular estimates of the size and characteristics of the population. It publishes annual compilations of births, deaths, perinatal deaths, causes of death, marriages, divorces, and overseas arrivals and departures, as well as monthly and quarterly summaries, an overall *Year Book*, and a biennial compilation of social indicators. Address: P.O. Box 10, Canberra A.C.T. 2616.

The national Department of Immigration and Ethnic Affairs publishes a quarterly statistical survey of immigration and an annual compilation. Address: Canberra A.C.T. 2616.

Austria: Demographic Institutions

The Austrian Academy of Sciences, a private association, in 1976 established an Institute of Demography, of which the director in 1980 was Lothar †Bosse. Its research has been focused on the decline of fertility in Austria and in Western Europe generally and on the prospective changes in age structure and dependency ratio. Its publications include the semi-annual *Demografische Informationen*, begun in 1981. Address: Institut für Demographie, Österreichische Akademie der Wissenschaften, Hintere Zollamtstrasse 4, A-1033 Vienna.

The Interdisciplinary Institute for Urban and Regional Studies, University of Economics, was directed in 1980 by W. B. Stohr. Its program of research and training has been related to population geography and the work force, among other demographic subfields. Address: Interdisziplinäres Institut für Raumordnung, Hochschule für Raumordnung, Hasenauerstrasse 42/8, A-1190 Vienna 19.

The International Institute for Applied Systems Analysis (IIASA); see the entry under *International.

The Salzburg Institute for Regional Research, of which W. Haslauer was president in 1980, conducts studies on the Salzburg area, including population and labor-force projections. Address: Salzburger Institut für Raumforschung, P.O. Box 2, A-5033 Salzburg.

UNIVERSITY RESEARCH INSTITUTES

At the Vienna Technical University the Actuarial Institute under K. H. Wolff teaches its students the standard range of life-table construction and population projections. Address: Institut für Versicherungsmathematik, Technische Universität Wien, Gusshausstrasse 25-29, A-1040 Vienna.

At the same university the Institute for Econometrics and Operations Research, established in 1972, was directed in 1980 by Gustav †Feichtinger. Its research program has included such demographic elements as the family cycle, nuptiality and divorce, population-economic interrelations, and mathematical demography. Address: Institut für Unternehmungsforschung, Technische Universität Wien, Argentinierstrasse 8, A-1040 Vienna.

Also at the same university the Institute for Urban and Regional Research, of which the director in 1980 was Dieter Bökemann, has included relevant portions of demography in its instructional and research program. Address: Institut für Stadt- und Regionalforschung, Technische Universität Wien, Karlsgasse 13, A-1040 Vienna.

Several units of Vienna University include population in their programs. The Institute for Economic and Social History under Michael Mitterauer has studied historical demography and, in particular, changes in the Austrian family structure since the seventeenth century. Address: Institut für Wirtschafts- und Sozialgeschichte, Universität Wien, Dr. Karl-Lüger-Ring 1, A-1040 Vienna.

The Geographical Institute at the same university has population geography in its program. Address: Geographisches Institut, Universität Wien, Universitätsstrasse 7/V, A-1010 Vienna.

The Social Science Research Center at the same university, directed in 1980 by Leopold †Rosenmayr, conducts research related to population and social planning. Address: Sozialwissenschaftliche Forschungsstelle, Universität Wien, Dr. Karl-Lüger-Ring 1, A-1040 Vienna.

GOVERNMENT STATISTICAL BUREAUS

The Austrian Central Statistical Office includes a Division for Population Statistics, of which the director in 1980 was Heimold †Helczmanovszki. It conducts the country's censuses and issues regularly a *Demographisches Jahrbuch* and a *Statistisches Handbuch*, as well as a number of more specialized reports, including an annual compilation of traffic accidents. Its analysis of the state and movement of the country's population includes some notable contributions to demographic history. Address: Abteilung für Bevölkerung, Österreichisches Statistisches Zentralamt, Neue Hofburg, A-1014 Vienna.

The Ministry for Health and Environmental Protection issues jointly with the Central Statistical Office an annual report, *Bericht über das Gesundheitswesen in Österreich im Jahre—.*Address: Bundesministerium für Gesundheit und Umweltschutz, Stubenring 1, A-1010 Vienna.

automation, used loosely as a synonym of "mechanization," means more precisely a change in production techniques by which several steps are consolidated into a single process (so-called Detroit automation) or one using a feedback principle (Bolz, 1974; Froomkin, 1968). Like most dramatic improvements in technology, automation has resulted in shifts in the work force, though the occasional fearful predictions of increasing unemployment have not been well based (cf. Forslin et al., 1979). The development of robots continues the same advance along another path (Chin, 1981).

REFERENCES: Roger W. Bolz, *Understanding Automation* (Novelty, Ohio: Conquest Publications, 1974). Felix Chin, *Automation and Robots: A Selected Bibliography* (Monticello, Ill.: Vance Bibliographies, 1981). Jan Forslin, Adam Sarapata, and Arthur M. Whitehill, eds., *Automation and Industrial Workers: A Fifteen-Nation Survey* (New York: Pergamon, 1979). Joseph N. Froomkin, "Automation," in *International Encyclopedia of the Social Sciences*, 1, 480-489.

autopsy, the postmortem examination of a body, is legally required in most jurisdictions of the United States only when the person was not under the care of a physician, when his identity or the cause of death is unknown, or when violence was involved or suspected. The percentage of all deaths in the United States followed by an autopsy, 19.1 in 1958 and again in 1972, fell uninterruptedly from the latter date to 15.7 in 1978. The main reason is that autopsies are seldom performed following deaths from the three leading causes—heart diseases, cancers, and stroke. With deaths from homicide, suicide, and accidents, the percentages followed by autopsies increased (U.S. National Center for Health Statistics, 1980). According to some data, medical knowledge would advance much faster if autopsies were regularly performed following all deaths. Dr. John M. Prutting and the Foundation for the Advancement of Medical Knowledge (21 East Ninetieth Street, New York, N.Y. 10028), of which he is president, have argued this position in a number of publications. However, what is deemed to be the desecration of a dead body is opposed strongly by many individuals and in some ethical systems (e.g., Jakobovits, 1958).

REFERENCES: Immanuel Jakobovits, "The Dissection of the Dead in Jewish Law: A Comparative and Historical Study," *Tradition*, 1 (1958), 77-103. John M. Prutting, "Lack of Correlation between Antemortem and Postmortem Diagnoses," *New York State Journal of Medicine*, 67 (1967), 2081-2084. U.S. National Center for Health Statistics, "Final Mortality Statistics, 1978," *Monthly Vital Statistics Report*, vol. 29, no. 6, Supplement 2 (September 17, 1980).

average, any of several measures of central tendency of an array of values. Without specification, it is usually understood as the *mean, but sometimes, or alternatively, as the *median, the *mode, or even the harmonic mean or a weighted measure.

axiate pattern, an arrangement of city streets of which the main characteristic is that several thoroughfares radiate from a central point.

B

baby boom, the unanticipated rise in the fertility of most Western countries in the late 1940s and most of the 1950s, reversing the prior secular decline. In the United States fertility went up during the 1950s not only overall but especially among the social category that previously had led the long-term decline, the urban middle class with relatively high levels of education and income. At first it was thought that the rise represented no more than births postponed during World War II, but eventually it became evident that a genuine increase in family size was taking place (e.g., Grabill et al., 1958; Rindfuss and Sweet, 1977, chap. 3). In several respects this was for demographers one of the most significant phenomena of the postwar period. The assurance with which census bureaus had offered population projections was totally shattered, and there was a salutary reworking of the theories that had been used to explain fertility trends. Of these the most radical shift came with the thesis of Richard †Easterlin (1961, 1980) that there is a tendency for large cohorts to produce small families and for the resultant small cohorts to produce comparatively large families (see also Welch, 1979). It was more generally recognized that the control of reproduction affected not only the number but also the timing of births. The so-called boom babies represented a high fertility potential when these large cohorts reached the age of marriage and childbearing; but the "echo" of the baby boom, anticipated on the basis of age structure, was postponed year after year, and eventually came so weakly that some analysts continued to dispute its arrival. The large cohorts also affected the societies into which they were born. School populations grew prodigiously and then declined as the boom babies moved up into the work force, with sizable disruptions of one institution after another. The political revolts of the 1960s have been interpreted, somewhat more dubiously, as largely a consequence of the very high proportion of teenagers and young adults (see also Robey, 1982).

REFERENCES: Richard A. Easterlin, "The American Baby Boom in Historical Perspective," *American Economic Review*, 51 (1961), 869-911; *Birth and Fortune: The Impact of Numbers on Personal Welfare* (New York: Basic Books, 1980). Wilson H. Grabill, Clyde V. Kiser, and Pascal K. Whelpton, *The Fertility of American Women*

(New York: Wiley, 1958). Ronald R. Rindfuss and James A. Sweet, *Postwar Fertility Trends and Differentials in the United States* (New York: Academic Press, 1977). Bryant Robey, "A Guide to the Baby Boom," *American Demographics*, 4 (September, 1982), 16-21. Finis Welch, "Effect of Cohort Size on Earnings," *Journal of Political Economy*, 87, Part 2 (1979), S65-S97.

bachelor and **spinster** are defined in the IUSSP *Multilingual Demographic Dictionary* simply as a person (respectively, a male and a female) who has never married. In a demographic context, however, the relevance of the two categories is how they relate to family structure and natality, and this depends not only on his or her status but also on the person's age. Whether a country's fertility is cut by a custom of postponing marriage to beyond puberty, for instance, can be estimated only if civil status is specified by age. Usually the age data available in various countries' statistics do not lay a basis for cross-cultural studies and in any case generally have little to do with the typical age at marriage set in each culture. Moreover, *marriage itself is not a clearcut concept: the division between it and *consensual union is often not sharp, and the important distinction between first and subsequent marriages is often not made in national statistics.

bacteria (sing., bacterium), unicellular organisms considerably larger than viruses, are usually composed of both DNA and RNA (see *virus). They are classified by their shape, which may be spherical (cocci), straight and cylindrical (bacilli), or curved (vibrios). Some can survive with no host, but others only within a living body, in some cases that of a human being. Their relative pathogenicity—the extent to which they can damage their host—depends mainly on how fast they spread through the tissues (what is called their invasiveness) and the toxic substances that are released when a bacterium breaks down. Among the most important diseases caused by bacteria are tonsillitis, scarlet fever, pneumonia, and meningitis (all airborne); tuberculosis of the lung, bone, kidney, or other organs (borne by air or milk); cholera and typhoid (transmitted by water or food); osteomyelitis (transmitted by direct skin contact); gonorrhea (spread by sexual contact); and the plague (spread by the bite of a flea from an infected rat or other rodent).

Bahamas: The government's Department of Statistics conducts the country's censuses, the most recent of which was in 1980. It publishes an annual *Statistical Abstract* that includes population data and an annual *Vital Statistics Report*. *Social Statistics Report* (February, 1982) was the first of a regular series that will present demographic-social data. Address: P.O. Box N3904, Nassau.

Bahrain: The government's Directorate of Statistics publishes an annual *Statistical Abstract* in English and Arabic that includes population data. Address: Ministry of State for Cabinet Affairs, P.O. Box 235, Manama.

balancing equation, one designation of a schematic view of the most basic relations studied in demography:

$$P_t = P_0 + (B - D) + (I - O)$$

where P_t is the population at the end of the period under consideration and P_0 the population at the beginning, B and D are the births and deaths during the period, and I and O are the in-migrants and out-migrants during the period. Other terms used have included the "inflow-outflow relationship" and the "component equation."

Bangladesh is the poorest of the world's sizable countries, and rapid population growth will help to keep it so. In some respects similar to its larger neighbors, this Muslim country has fewer physical resources than India or Pakistan, and a smaller proportion of its people are literate or skilled.

The country consists largely of the combined deltas of the Ganges, Brahmaputra, and Meghna rivers. In most years the flooding of about a third of the land area lays down a highly fertile deposit of silt, but variation in the timing and amount of monsoon rains can cause severe crop damage. From the great famine of 1769-76, in which almost a third of Bengal's population died, to the Bengal famine of 1943, which caused between 2 and 2.5 million deaths, the area has been under continual threat of catastrophe. This precarious relation with the physical environment was aggravated by political control under the rule successively of the Moghul empire, the East India Company, British India, and independent India. The creation of Pakistan in 1947, brought about with much violence and enormous, partly forced migrations, merely shifted the center of power from Delhi in India to Karachi in West Pakistan. And the war of independence by which East Bengal or East Pakistan became Bangladesh cost an estimated half million lives. An independent country only since 1971, Bangladesh started its national existence with an extraordinarily heavy historical burden.

The population is overwhelmingly rural, 91 percent in 1974 and still 86 percent in 1981. Of the total area under cultivation in 1977, 80 percent was in rice, 4 to 5 percent in jute, and 2.5 percent in pulses, with the balance in various other crops. Though the level of living is low in the countryside, the control of mortality has been steadily improved. With some fluctuations the estimated crude death rate fell from 46 in 1901-11 to 19 in 1961-74. Mortality varies greatly, however, among the social classes, which are stratified by the amount of land that is owned or otherwise controlled. In the famine year of 1975, the crude death rates in one district ranged in order from 12.2 among those with more than 1.2 hectares up to 35.8 among the landless proletariat (Colin McCord, 1976; cited in Arthur and McNicoll, 1978). The principal causes of death overall are diarrheal diseases (including some cholera), tuberculosis and other respiratory diseases, tetanus, and chronic diseases of old age.

Virtually all families typically observe strict *purdah: women work at home, very seldom in the fields (see also *Islam). Most girls marry around age 15 or 16; by age 20 only 10 percent of the women are still unmarried, and fewer than 0.1 percent never marry. For males the average age at marriage is in the mid-20s, with a larger spread than among females. Families are large and have become in effect larger by the decline in mortality. In the 1930s only about half of the children born grew to be adults; in the 1970s about three-quarters did. Completed family size is about seven children, and it is kept to this figure mainly by the effect of extended breastfeeding. "Bangladesh is basically a society that does not use contraceptives" (Alamgir, 1982). If demand for contraceptives were completely satisfied, fertility might be cut by about 15 percent—to a birth rate of 40 per thousand! Children are regarded, correctly, as a good investment; according to one village study, the average boy becomes a net producer by age 12; by age 15 he has made up for his prior consumption; and by age 22 he has repaid the investment in both himself and one sister (Cain, 1977).

According to the census of 1981, the population of Bangladesh was almost 90 million. It is the densest rural population in the world, with 1,375 persons per square mile (531 per square kilometer). Government policy is nominally antinatalist, but not effectively so. For decades a law has been in existence setting the minimum age at marriage at 16 for females and 18 for males, but it has never been seriously enforced. Proposals in the early 1980s included raising the age still further and enforcing the limitation, liberalizing the law on abortion, and especially trying to create a favorable attitude toward smaller families. The projected population in the year 2000, according to various estimates in 1975, ranged between 128 and 159 million. In their very full and informed analysis, W. Brian Arthur and Geoffrey †McNicoll (1978) estimated that the population would grow by about two-thirds to the end of the century, with very little decline in fertility and, even so, an increase in per capita income. See also *Bangladesh: Demographic Institutions.

REFERENCES: Mohiuddin Alamgir, "Bangladesh," in *International Encyclopedia of Population*, 1, 53-58. W. Brian Arthur and Geoffrey McNicoll, "An Analytical Survey of Population and Development in Bangladesh," *Population and Development Review*, 4 (1978), 23-80. Mead Cain, "The Economic Activities of Children in a Bangladesh Village," *Population and Development Review*, 3 (1977), 201-227.

Bangladesh: Demographic Institutions

With its serious and widely noted population pressure, Bangladesh has received funds from the United Nations, the U.S. Agency for International Development (AID), and comparable British and Scandinavian government agencies, as well as private foundations and family-planning organizations. The money, used not to conduct research but mainly to reduce the excessive growth of the population, is dispensed principally through two agencies. Under the Ministry of Health and

Population Control, the Population Control and Family Planning Division administers the government's efforts to reduce fertility (address: Bangladesh Secretariat, Dacca-5). Among several private organizations, the Bangladesh Family Planning Association conducts a parallel effort (address: 2 Naya Paltan, Dacca-2).

The Statistics Division in the Ministry of Planning publishes a monthly statistical bulletin, an annual *Statistical Pocket Book*, and a more complete statistical yearbook, all giving estimates of the country's population and its characteristics. Address: Bangladesh Secretariat, Dacca-2.

The Bangladesh Institute of Development Studies, a training and research center established in 1957, was in 1982 under the direction of Monowar Hossain, acting head. Its publications include the quarterly *Bangladesh Development Studies* and such bibliographic guides as *POPINDEX Bangladesh: Bangladesh Literature on Population Control and Its Allied Subjects* (1978). Address: Adamjee Court, Motijheel Commercial Area, Dacca-2.

In 1964 the University of Dacca set up an Institute of Statistical Research and Training, which in 1982 was directed by M. †Obaidullah. It publishes two journals, *Rural Demography* and the *Journal of Statistical Research*. Its studies have been concentrated on contraception. Address: Science Annexe, Dacca-2.

The International Center for Diarrheal Disease Research, founded in 1960, was known until 1978 as the Cholera Research Laboratory. It is a nonprofit center for research and training, funded by a number of states and intergovernmental bodies. Under William B. Greenough III as director, it had a staff of 743 in 1981, and its research has developed far from the original focus on cholera to include many topics related to demography. Its series of *Scientific Reports*, instituted in 1977, numbered 44 by 1981. Address: G.P.O. Box 128, Dacca-2.

The government's Bureau of Statistics conducts the country's censuses, of which the last was in 1981. Address: Dacca.

baptism, a Christian rite of purification by water that frees the person from sin and makes him or her a member of a church. Most Christian churches require baptism, either by total immersion (as among Baptists) or by a symbolic sprinkling, either in infancy or at the age of consent or conversion. Before civil vital statistics were institutionalized in Europe, churches kept better records of baptisms than of births; in England and Wales, for instance, a significant underregistration of births continued until the 1860s or later (Glass, 1951). What to set as the ratio of births to baptisms has been a constant problem among historical demographers who use parish records as a source. For lack of a better rule, analysts have generally used a fixed ratio for areas or time periods known to be quite different in other characteristics (cf. Krause, 1958; 1965).

REFERENCES: D. V. Glass, "A Note on the Under-registration of Births in Britain in the Nineteenth Century," *Population Studies*, 5 (1951), 70-88. John T. Krause, "Changes in English Fertility and Mortality, 1781-1850," *Economic History Review*, 11 (1958), 52-70; "The Changing Adequacy of English Registration, 1690-1837," in Glass and Eversley, *Population in History*.

Barbados: The Barbados Statistical Service issues a *Monthly Digest of Statistics* that includes data on births, deaths, migration, and population by sex. Address: National Insurance Building, Fairchild Street, Bridgetown. There is also an annual report on vital statistics, issued by the Registration Office, Supreme Court of Barbados, Bridgetown.

barefoot doctors, rural workers trained to carry out rudimentary sanitary measures, preventive medicine, and therapy. The term, first used to designate a program in Communist China, has sometimes been extended to other less developed countries that use similar quasimedical personnel. See also *Chinese medicine.

barrier methods are types of contraception that block the entry of spermatazoa into the uterus, such as the *condom or the *diaphragm.

barrio, Spanish for a quarter or precinct of a city, is sometimes used to denote a shantytown. The usual designation of such slum neighborhoods is *barriada* or *pueblo joven* in Peru, *rancho* in Venezuela, *callampa* in Chile, *villa miseria* in Argentina, *tugurio* in Colombia, and *favela* in Brazil. See also *bidonville; *squatter.

basal body temperature is the temperature of the body at absolute rest. In the female it changes during the menstrual cycle, and it thus can be used to determine the days during which a woman is fecund. The *rhythm method of contraception that is based on measurement of body temperature is notably more efficient than earlier practices.
   REFERENCE: J. P. Royston and R. M. Abrams, "An Objective Method for Detecting the Shift in Basal Body Temperature in Women," *Biometrics*, 36 (1980), 217-224.

base, a magnitude used as a standard of reference, as in the denominator of a ratio or the figure used to calculate an *index number. In a time series, the *base period* may be of any duration but is preferably taken to be several years, in order to reduce the likelihood of choosing one with a short-term aberration from the general trend. The *base population* is the figure used in the calculation of demographic rates, either the number of people in a country or other area in a crude *rate, or the specified segment of that total in a refined rate.

baseline, an alternative for *base to designate the beginning of a progression from which subsequent change is measured, as a "baseline census," "baseline survey," "baseline observation." Another term with the same meaning is *benchmark*.

basic data (or raw data, primary data, sometimes crude data) are those that have not been adjusted, standardized, or otherwise changed to correct for an estimated miscount or in order to facilitate interpretation.

Battelle Memorial Institute (BMI), an American nonprofit public-purpose organization founded in 1929 and with a staff of 7,300 in 1981, conducts research on a contract basis for industrial firms or government agencies, mostly related to the physical sciences, supplementarily to education, urban problems, and other social issues. In 1977 BMI established a Population and Development Policy Program in its International Development Study Center in Washington, D.C. In the same year it established in its Seattle branch a Program for the Introduction and Adaptation of Contraceptive Technologies (PIACT), designed to increase the acceptance and use of contraception in less developed countries. With funds provided by American foundations, the U.N. Fund for Population Activities, and Britain's Overseas Development Administration, PIACT maintains regional offices in Manila and Mexico City. In 1979 it established a health division, Program for Appropriate Technology in Health (PATH), to develop and promote the technology for international health programs. Publications include *Product Information Memorandum*, a bimonthly abstract service on current technical information on contraception; *PIACT Product News*, a quarterly; *PIACT Papers*, bimonthly. Addresses: Main office, 505 King Avenue, Columbus, Ohio 43201; 4000 N.E. Forty-first Street, Seattle, Wash. 98105; 2030 M Street, N.W., Washington, D.C. 20036.

BEA, an areal unit of the United States, is named after the U.S. Bureau of Economic Analysis, which in the 1960s instituted the accounting system based on it (see the discussion under *United States: Federal Agencies). Each BEA is made up of a Metropolitan Statistical Area, plus the surrounding functionally related counties. All the BEAs together include the entire land area of the United States.

REFERENCES: Martha Farnsworth Riche, "The BEA," *American Demographics*, 5 (July, 1983), 34-35. Sam Bass Warner, Jr., and Sylvia Fleisch, *Measurements for Social History* (Beverly Hills, Calif.: Sage, 1977).

behavioral environment, that portion of a person's environment that elicits a behavioral response, resulting in a conscious utilization or transformation. The term is associated with geographers like William Kirk, who have used the concepts of Gestalt psychology to analyze the interrelation of action and space.

REFERENCES: William Kirk, "Problems of Geography," *Geography*, 48 (1963), 357-371. R. D. Sack, *Conceptions of Space in Social Thought: A Geographic Perspective* (Minneapolis: University of Minnesota Press, 1980).

behavioral sciences, sometimes defined as the scientific study of individual behavior and human relations, are distinguished from social sciences by the usual inclusion of a larger component of psychological or social psychological concerns. The term, which the *Ford Foundation coined in the 1950s in the label of a new program, spread quickly. With the passage of time, however, the supposed distinction between "behavioral" and "social" sciences has become blurred, and the two designations are now used more or less synonymously. See also *earth sciences; *life sciences.

Belgium: Demographic Institutions

There are two professional demographic societies, the Dutch-language Belgian Demographic Society with 100 members (address: Vereniging voor Demographie, Keierveld 5, B-3020 Herent), and the French-language Belgian Demographic Society with 75 members (address: Société Belge de Démographie, Centre de Démographie, Institut de Sociologie de l'Université Libre de Bruxelles, 44 avenue Jeanne, B-1050 Brussels).

The Administration Générale de la Coopération au Développement, the government agency to administer assistance to less developed countries, has funded family-planning programs in Tunisia and Zaire, among other countries. Address: 5 place du Champs de Mars, B-1050 Brussels.

UNIVERSITY AND OTHER RESEARCH INSTITUTES

The Ministry of Public Health and the Family includes a Population and Family Study Center, founded in 1962. In 1980 it was under the direction of Jean †Morsa (the French-speaking section) and R. L. †Cliquet (the Dutch-speaking section). Since 1966 it has conducted national surveys on fertility, the results of which are published in its journal, *Population et Famille/Bevolking en Gezin*, originally one bilingual journal and later divided into two, one in each of the two languages. Like all official bureaus in Belgium, it has a double name and address, one in Dutch and one in French: Centrum voor Bevolkings- en Gezinsstudiën, Manhattan Center, Toren H2, Kruisvaartenstraat 3, B-1000 Brussels; Centre d'Étude de la Population et de la Famille, Manhattan Center, Tour H2, 3 rue des Croisades, B-1000 Brussels.

The Center for Interdisciplinary Research on Economic Development, a private organization, was established in 1967. Under the direction in the early 1980s of Jacques Dorselaer, it has conducted research on urbanization, internal migration, and the work force in Latin American countries. Address: Centre pour la Recherche Interdisciplinaire sur le Développement, 152 rue Valduc, B-1170 Brussels.

The Institute for Research on Central Europe, of which the director in 1980 was S. Muselay, has published monographs on such characteristics of Eastern Europe as ethnicity, economic development, and the work force. Address: Institut de Recherches de l'Europe Centrale/Instituut voor Onderzoek van Midden-Europa, Blijde Inkomstraat 108, B-3000 Louvain.

The Interuniversity Program in Demography was established in 1970 as the Werkgroep voor Demographie. It fosters comparative research efforts especially on Belgium and Africa, focusing on marriage and the family, fertility, population trends, and similar studies, as well as postgraduate instruction leading to a master's or doctor's degree. Its activities are noted in an *IPD Newsletter*. Address: c/o Centrum Sociologie, Vrije Universiteit Brussel, Pleinlaan 2, B-1050 Brussels.

A Computer Bank of Social Documentation was established at the University of Liège in 1973. Under the direction of Étienne †Hélin, it has moved toward an ultimate goal of putting on computer tape demographic and social data about Belgium from 1800 to date. Address: Service du Traitement Automatique de la Documentation Sociale, Université de Liège, 3 Place Cockerill, B-4000 Liège.

At the Catholic University of Louvain (Dutch-language), one sector of the Sociological Research Institute is a Group for Sociology of the Family and Population, which in the early 1980s was under the direction of Wilfried †Dumon. It has concentrated on the sociology of the family, particularly as this relates to population trends. Address: Katholieke Universiteit Leuven, Van Evenstraat 2B, B-3000 Louvain.

The Catholic University of Louvain (French-language) has a Department of Demography that was until the mid-1970s under the direction of Guillaume †Wunsch, who was succeeded by Hubert †Gérard. Its research interests have included the populations of Belgium and Africa, and the use of models in demography. Address: Département de Démographie, Université Catholique de Louvain, 1 Place Montesquieu, B-1348 Louvain-la-Neuve.

The Free University of Brussels (French-language) has a Center for Demography in its Sociology Institute, which in 1980 was under the direction of Robert †André. Its research, concentrated on the population of Belgium, is typified by a three-volume *Analyse Démographique de la Mortalité en Belgique* (1978). Address: Centre de Démographie, Institut de Sociologie de l'Université Libre de Bruxelles, 44 avenue Jeanne, B-1050 Brussels.

The Free University of Brussels (Dutch-language) includes a Center for Population and Family Studies, which in 1980 was under the joint direction of Ron J. †Lesthaeghe and Jan Geluck. Its research has included all aspects of Belgium's population: demographic and macro-economic simulations, historical demography, population policy, and fertility surveys. Address: Vrije Universiteit Brussel, Pleinlaan 2, B-1050 Brussels.

GOVERNMENT STATISTICAL BUREAUS

The National Bureau of Statistics is responsible for conducting the country's censuses, the most recent of which was in 1981. It publishes annually a statistical yearbook and one of regional statistics, a pocket statistical yearbook, and a bulletin, *Bevolkingsstatistieken* or *Statistique de la Population*, comprising vital statistics and the causes of death. A monthly general statistical bulletin is supplemented by a more specific quarterly on demographic statistics. Address: Institut National de Statistique, 44 rue de Louvain, B-1000 Brussels; Nationaal Instituut voor de Statistiek, Leuvenseweg 44, B-1000 Brussels.

The Ministry of Public Health and the Family publishes in Dutch and French a *Statistical yearbook of public health* with the full range of vital data. Address: Ministère de la Santé Publique et de la Famille, Quartier Vésale, B-1010 Brussels; Ministerie van Volksgezondheid en Gezin, Rijksadministratief Centrum-Vesalius, B-1010 Brussels.

Belize: The government's Central Planning Unit publishes an annual *Abstract of Statistics* that includes population data. Address: Ministry of Finance and Economic Development, Belmopan.

Benin: Demographic Institutions

The National Bureau of Statistics and Economic Analysis is responsible for conducting the country's censuses, the last of which was in 1979. It includes an Office of Demographic and Social Statistics, in 1981 headed by Emmanuel Amoussou. Address: Institut National de la Statistique et de l'Analyse Éco-nomique, and Service des Statistiques Démographiques et Sociales, Boîte Postale 323, Cotonou.

The Ministry of Foreign Affairs publishes an *Annuaire Statistique* that includes population data. Address: Ministère des Affaires Étrangères, Cotonou.

beriberi, a food-deficiency disease prevalent in East Asian countries, derives from the Singhalese for "I cannot," indicating that the person is too weak to do anything. The condition is caused mainly by a deficiency in vitamin B_1 (thiamine) and is frequently associated with a diet consisting largely of polished rice, which has the nutritious shell removed.

Berlin wall was built in 1961 by the East German government to seal off East Berlin from the portion of the city governed by Bonn. The twentieth anniversary of its construction in 1981 was celebrated by proclaiming it "a victory for socialism"—no mere bombast but the truth. The number fleeing to the West was cut from more than 234,000 in the single year 1961 to an annual average of slightly more than 2,000 in the subsequent period. More generally, the Berlin wall is the most palpable example of how Communist totalitarianism mainly affects international migration—by preventing it.

REFERENCE: Frederick W. Hollmann, "The Demographic Effect of Migration on an Urban Population: Migration to and from West Berlin, 1952-1971," in Alan A. Brown and Egon Neuberger, eds., *Internal Migration: A Comparative Perspective* (New York: Academic Press, 1977).

Bermuda: Demographic Institutions

The Statistical Department is responsible for conducting the country's censuses, the last of which was in 1980. Address: Hamilton.

The Statistician's Office in the Finance Department publishes an annual *Digest of Statistics* that includes population data. Address: Hamilton.

betrothal, a mutual promise or contract for a future marriage, can be relatively binding or mainly symbolic depending on the culture's norms. Among that sector of the American population that anticipates a marriage with an "engagement" (the word *betrothal* would be archaic in such a context), it implies a tentative testing of the two partners, a quasicontract that usually can be broken with no formal consequences. What is termed *sponsalia* in the canon law of the Roman Catholic church, or formal promises to marry at a future date, do not constitute an absolute or diriment impediment to another marriage. Among pious Hindus, at the other pole, the betrothal (*shadi*) often takes place in early childhood or even infancy, and there is a second ceremony at puberty that corresponds to a Western wedding. The ban on the remarriage of widows, however, applies also to females who have been betrothed, very often to considerably older males, with the consequence that Indian censuses typically record some tens of thousands of child widows.

bias, in this context the characteristic of a statistical result derived from a systematic distortion, is contrasted with *random errors, which generally more or less balance out over the whole. Any element of an investigation may introduce a bias. A biased sample is one that incorporates a systematic (but often hidden) error; a method of coding that repeatedly shifts the record from the true value in the same direction is biased; if a survey includes questions on sex roles, using only male (or only female) questioners may bias the replies of the respondents. Perhaps the most insidious bias results from the tendency of most persons to shift *responses concerning their own attitudes toward what they take to be the norm of their society or social class. See also *errors.

bidonville, French for shantytown or *squatter settlement; literally, tin-can town, from the flattened gasoline cans of which hovels are often built.

bilateral aid, that from one country to another one, may pertain to the funding of family-planning programs as one important example. It is contrasted with *multilateral aid*, which is channeled through such intermediary agencies as the *U.N. Fund for Population Activities or the *International Planned Parenthood Federation.

bilingualism and **diglossia,** the ability to use two or more languages, are distinguished by analysts of languages: the first term refers to individuals, and the second to populations. The fact that diglossia and bilingualism can be disjunctive presents a problem in the interpretation of census or survey statistics, which are gathered from individuals who may or may not be members of speech communities. There are four possible combinations between the two (Fishman, 1972, chap. 5): (1) A monolingual population made up of monolingual individuals, the simplest case, is restricted to very small and isolated speech communities. (2) A country with both diglossia and bilingualism is approximated in Paraguay. The rural population there once spoke only Guarani; but a substantial portion particularly of those that moved to the towns learned Spanish, which also in the countryside is the language of education, the courts, and other government institutions. As a consequence, more than half the population uses both languages. (3) In a society with quite distinct social classes and little movement between them, it sometimes happens that each class has its own language. In pre-1914 Europe, for instance, the elites often spoke French and the mass of the common people another language. The small amount of low-level communication required between master and servant was likely to be in a sharply curtailed version of either language—that is, a pidgin. (4) Bilingualism without diglossia, finally, can be exemplified by the United States of roughly 1880-1920, the period of mass immigration. Newcomers to the country who spoke their native languages had a strong motivation to learn English, but their children were usually monolingual in English (see *assimilation).

REFERENCE: Joshua Fishman, *Language in Sociocultural Change: Essays* (Stanford, Calif.: Stanford University Press, 1972).

biobehavioral sciences, a term proposed in 1982 in a study sponsored by the Institute of Medicine of the National Academy of Sciences. This new composite discipline would combine biology and medicine with psychology, psychiatry, and other social disciplines and thus supposedly furnish a basis for understanding how human behavior affects health and disease. Approximately three out of four deaths in the United States result from cardiovascular ailments, cancers, or accidents and violence—which the study panel subsumed under life-style.

bioethics, the system of moral principles governing situations related to life processes, are discussed at length in Warren T. Reich, ed., *Encyclopedia of Bioethics*, 4 vols. (New York: Free Press, 1978). Each year the Center for Bioethics, Georgetown University, Washington, D.C., issues a *Bibliography of Bioethics*. Under the rubric are most of the demographic processes about which there are ethical differences, including particular types of contraception, abortion, and euthanasia.

biological control, the control of pests by such "natural means" as bringing in their predators and introducing sterilized males that will mate with females but produce no offspring.

biology, the systematic study of living organisms, includes in the most general sense their evolution, structure and function, physiology and anatomy, manner of life, reproduction and development. In fact, however, all border lines of biology are obscure. Such new disciplines as biochemistry and biophysics, which link living matter to the inanimate substances of which it is constituted, have revived the age-old dispute of whether the concepts and laws of biology can be reduced to those of physics and chemistry. At the other pole, the social disciplines, though manifestly dealing with living beings, are not ordinarily classified as part of biology. But what has been one main criterion distinguishing them, that human behavior is governed largely by cultures, has been challenged by practitioners of *sociobiology, who hold that in different degrees cultures can be found also among at least the higher animals and that, on the other hand, biological imperatives set the main patterns of human cultures.

Biology is important in the study of populations because it pertains to that part of fertility and mortality determined by the nature of the organism rather than by particular environments or norms. A convenient way of separating out this physiological element is to study *animal populations through such subdisciplines as, among others, population biology, *population genetics, and particularly *ecology; but links between these and standard demography are not well established. One important virtue of †Malthus's principle of population is that he tried to analyze man both as an animal, subject to the physiological drives of sex and hunger, and as a member of society, motivated and able somewhat to control these appetites. Malthus was attacked both by traditional Christians for including man as part of nature, living in accord with the same biological laws as other species, and by many liberal critics for his alleged overemphasis of animalic drives.

BIOMED, known alternatively as BMD, BIMD, or Biomedical Computer Programs, was developed in the early 1960s for many types of medical-demographic research.

REFERENCE: W. J. Dixon, *BMD Biomedical Computer Programs* (Berkeley: University of California Press, 1970).

biometeorology, the study of short-term influences of the weather on life processes, is sufficiently well established as a subdiscipline to have its own quarterly, the *International Journal of Biometeorology*, which in 1984 was in its twenty-eighth year. Papers are published on such topics as day-to-day and seasonal fluctuations in mortality in Houston, Texas, and Kyoto, Japan. Both of these studies were in volume 23 (1979). See also *climate.

biometry, or biometrics, denotes the exact measurement and mathematical analysis of vital phenomena. The term was coined in association with the journal founded by Karl †Pearson, *Biometrika*, and is often understood more narrowly as a tool of eugenics. "The primary object of biometry," Francis †Galton wrote, "is to afford material that shall be exact enough for the discovery of incipient changes in evolution which are too small to be otherwise apparent." The more general term has been *biostatistics*, and the usual designation for a practitioner is *biostatistician*.

birth, defined in a medical dictionary as "the act or process of being born," would seem to be unambiguous, but imprecision can arise from setting the boundary between "live birth" and "stillbirth." If a *fetus is expelled "alive" by one or another criterion but expires shortly after the trauma of birth, should one consider that a live birth or not? Practice has not been consistent among various jurisdictions, and the problem of setting an international standard will probably be aggravated by the dispute about when human life begins. Some opponents of *abortion hold that humans exist from the moment of conception and that, therefore, any mode of what they term feticide is a form of murder.

The World Health Organization (WHO) has tried to establish uniform records by a careful definition of *fetal death. The difference in the number of births would not ordinarily be great, but the distinction can affect much more the rate of infant mortality, which has often been taken as an important indicator of a country's general well-being (see *mortality, infant). In any case, birth statistics are collected locally, with each registration supposedly taking place shortly after the event. This means that, as with other vital statistics, the process is likely to lag well behind census counts in both accuracy and completeness. Many nations simply exclude certain areas and collect data only from the remainder; and partly for this reason most countries, including virtually all classified as less developed, have markedly incomplete natality statistics. In the United States, Texas, the last state, was brought into the birth-*registration area only in 1933. Even after that date, as subsequent *matching studies showed, registration (especially for nonwhite races) was sometimes below the 90 percent used as the criterion for admission. An estimation of births from census data is hampered by the fact that the most serious underenumeration is often that of infants and young children, especially but not exclusively those that died before the date of the census. Various techniques have been devised to estimate the children of various ages omitted from a census and thus to correct the registration of births over the preceding period.

When a rural or a suburban woman goes to an urban hospital to have her baby delivered, the birth may be registered as taking place in the city or in her place of residence; practice differs, and the discrepancy can be great. In most industrial nations registration follows so shortly after the birth that the use of the date of registration to mark the timing of the birth does not introduce a serious error. But in some less developed countries children may be registered, for example, only when they start school; and in Oriental countries an effort is often made to avoid a registration in a year designated as unlucky (cf. *astrology). Probably the most important lacuna in current American statistics pertains to whether the child was born out of wedlock. Some states do not require that legitimacy status be reported on birth certificates, and the U.S. National Center for Health Statistics produces national estimates of *illegitimacy on the assumption that race-specific illegitimacy ratios in nonreporting states are the same as for reporting states in the same geographic region (cf. Berkov and Sklar, 1975; Chamblee et al., 1979).

*Fertility measures obviously depend on the record of births as their base, but since this record is often so inadequate, much effort has gone into devising alternative measures that give useful estimates.

REFERENCES: Beth Berkov and June Sklar, "Methodological Options in Measuring Illegitimacy and the Difference They Make," *Social Biology*, 22 (1975), 356-371. Ronald F. Chamblee, William B. Clifford, and R. David Mustian, "Validation of an Inferential Approach for the Measurement of Illegitimacy," *Demography*, 16 (1979), 49-54. Shryock and Siegel, *Methods and Materials of Demography*, chap. 16.

birth certificate, the document attesting to the fact and conditions of each live birth, is in the United States signed by the physician or other professional in charge, or, in the case of an unattended birth, by either one of the parents. It must be filed with the local registrar within a designated period; and this local authority—for example, a city or county health department—verifies the completeness and accuracy of the information on the parents' and child's names, residence, and other details (see certificate on page 74). A copy of the certificate is filed for local use, and the original is passed on to the state registrar or bureau of vital statistics. Eventually a copy is transmitted to the U.S. National Center for Health Statistics (see the discussion under *United States: Federal Agencies), to become one element in the compilation of natality data. The system has worked imperfectly, especially in the past in the United States (see *registrations areas), as well as currently in most less developed countries.

birth history, a record provided by the mother of all her live births and their dates, often supplemented with information on fetal, infant, and child deaths, the date(s) and duration of marriage(s), and the use of contraceptives. The data are used for an intensive study of the fertility of a small population or of a sample of a large population. See also *birth roster.

birth interval, or interbirth interval, the period between successive births, depends on three factors: the length of the gestation period, which for a child of normal birth is commonly approximated at nine months; the length of the sterile period following each birth, which varies particularly according to whether the child is breastfed and, if so, at what age it is weaned; and the subsequent *fecundability, or probability of conception per unit of time. In large families it is typical that, except for the children born toward the end of the mother's fecund period, the interval between successive births is more or less independent of the birth order, which strongly suggests that for any particular couple each of the three factors is approximately constant. Couples that use contraceptives generally try to control both the number and the *spacing of their children, but usually the efficiency is greater if the intention is to restrict the size of the family than if it is only to set a longer birth interval (Srinivasan, 1966; Whelpton, 1964).

The fecund years of women can be divided conceptually into pregnancy, sterile periods associated with pregnancy, and intervals during which the woman is susceptible to conception; and one can construct a model based on those three sectors and such other variables as the use-effectiveness of contraceptives, fetal mortality, and the total length of the reproductive period (Sheps and Menken, 1973). Roland †Pressat (1972, pp. 245-256) introduced the terms *protogenetic interval*, that between marriage and the first birth, and *intergenetic interval*, that between successive births or successive confinements. The lengths of the two in a population not using contraceptives approximate, respectively, 14 months and (with females aged 20-25 years, when fecundity is at the highest point) 24 months; the difference of 10 months is made up of a postpartum sterile period

TYPE
OR PRINT
IN
PERMANENT
INK

SEE
INSTRUCTIONS
HANDBOOK

U.S. STANDARD
CERTIFICATE OF LIVE BIRTH

BIRTH NUMBER

CHILD

1. CHILD—NAME | LOCAL FILE NUMBER | FIRST | MIDDLE | LAST
2. SEX
3a. DATE OF BIRTH (Mo., Day, Yr.) | 3b. HOUR
4a. HOSPITAL—NAME (If not in hospital, give street and number) | 4b. CITY, TOWN OR LOCATION OF BIRTH | 4c. COUNTY OF BIRTH

CERTIFIER

I certify that the stated information concerning this child is true to the best of my knowledge and belief.
4d. NAME AND TITLE OF ATTENDANT AT BIRTH IF OTHER THAN CERTIFIER (Type or print)
5a. (Signature) ▲
5c. DATE SIGNED (Mo., Day, Yr.)
5d. CERTIFIER—NAME AND TITLE (Type or print)
5e. MAILING ADDRESS (Street or R.F.D. No., City or Town, State, Zip)

REGISTRAR

6a. (Signature) ▲
6b. DATE RECEIVED BY REGISTRAR (Month, Day, Year)

MOTHER

7a. MOTHER—MAIDEN NAME | FIRST | MIDDLE | LAST
7b. AGE (At time of this birth)
7c. STATE OF BIRTH (If not in U.S.A., name country)
8a. RESIDENCE—STATE | 8b. COUNTY | 8c. CITY, TOWN OR LOCATION | 8d. STREET AND NUMBER OF RESIDENCE
8e. INSIDE CITY LIMITS (Specify yes or no)
8f. MOTHER'S MAILING ADDRESS—If same as above, enter Zip Code only

FATHER

9. FATHER—NAME | FIRST | MIDDLE | LAST
10a.
10b. AGE (At time of this birth)
10c. STATE OF BIRTH (If not in U.S.A., name country)

I certify that the personal information provided on this certificate is correct to the best of my knowledge and belief.
11a. (Signature of Parent or other Informant) ▲
11b. RELATION TO CHILD

INFORMATION FOR MEDICAL AND HEALTH USE ONLY

12. RACE—MOTHER (e.g., White, Black, American Indian, etc.) (Specify)
13. RACE—FATHER (e.g., White, Black, American Indian, etc.) (Specify)
14. BIRTH WEIGHT
15a. THIS BIRTH—Single, twin, triplet, etc. (Specify)
15b. IF NOT SINGLE BIRTH—Born first, second, third, etc. (Specify)
16. IS MOTHER MARRIED? (Specify yes or no)

EDUCATION—MOTHER (Specify only highest grade completed)
Elementary or Secondary (0-12) | College (1-4 or 5+)

EDUCATION—FATHER (Specify only highest grade completed)
Elementary or Secondary (0-12) | College (1-4 or 5+)

PREGNANCY HISTORY (Complete each section)

LIVE BIRTHS (Do not include this child)
17a. Now living — Number ☐ None
17b. Now dead — Number ☐ None

OTHER TERMINATIONS (Spontaneous and Induced)
17c. Before 20 weeks — Number ☐ None
17d. After 20 weeks — Number ☐ None

17e. DATE OF LAST LIVE BIRTH (Month, Year)
17f. DATE OF LAST OTHER TERMINATION (as indicated in d or above) (Month, Year)

18. DATE LAST NORMAL MENSES BEGAN (Month, Day, Year)
19. MONTH OF PREGNANCY PRE-NATAL CARE BEGAN First, second, etc. (Specify)
20. PRENATAL VISITS Total number (If none, so state)
21a.
21b.
22a. APGAR SCORE 1 min.
22b. 5 min.

23. COMPLICATIONS OF PREGNANCY (Describe or write "none")
24. CONCURRENT ILLNESSES OR CONDITIONS AFFECTING THE PREGNANCY (Describe or write "none")
25. COMPLICATIONS OF LABOR AND/OR DELIVERY (Describe or write "none")
26. CONGENITAL MALFORMATIONS OR ANOMALIES OF CHILD (Describe or write "none")

DEATH UNDER ONE YEAR OF AGE Enter State File Number of death certificate for this child

MULTIPLE BIRTHS Enter State File Number for mate(s)
LIVE BIRTH(S)
FETAL DEATH(S)

plus a mean time to conception. Henri †Léridon (1977, pp. 85-95) separated the two factors by analyzing cases when the infant died. The physiological effects are confounded, however, by the fact that in some cultures sexual intercourse is taboo for a period after the birth of a child, sometimes for as long as the child is being nursed (cf. Gray, 1981). When a woman's reproductive period is interrupted by divorce or the breaking off of a consensual union, such an extension of the birth interval can reduce fertility significantly (e.g., Blake, 1961, pp. 246-250). See also *age at marriage; *amenorrhea; *lactation.

REFERENCES: Judith Blake, *Family Structure in Jamaica: The Social Context of Reproduction* (New York: Free Press of Glencoe, 1961). R. H. Gray, "Birth Intervals, Postpartum Sexual Abstinence, and Child Health," in Hilary J. Page and Ron J. Lesthaeghe, eds., *Child Spacing in Tropical Africa: Traditions and Change* (New York: Academic Press, 1981). Henri Léridon, *Human Fertility: The Basic Components* (Chicago: University of Chicago Press, 1977). Roland Pressat, *Demographic Analysis: Methods, Results, Applications* (Chicago: Aldine, 1972). Mindel C. Sheps and Jane Menken, *Mathematical Models of Conception and Birth* (Chicago: University of Chicago Press, 1973). S. K. Srinivasan, " 'The Open Birth Interval' as an Index of Fertility," *Journal of Family Welfare*, 13 (December, 1966), 40-44. P. K. Whelpton, "Trends and Differentials in the Spacing of Births," *Demography*, 1 (1964), 83-93.

birth-marriage ratio is ordinarily understood as the number of legitimate live births during a year divided by the number of marriages during the same year. Obviously the two populations are different, and the index is now little used. More meaningfully, the measure can be applied to a birth *cohort of women who have reached the end of their reproductive years, in which case it is equivalent to the mean number of children of ever married women in the cohort.

birth order, or **birth rank,** is the ordinal number of a live-born child as related to all the other live-born children of the same mother. In the case of multiple births, the preferable usage is to number each child separately. A birth-order rate relates the number of live births of order *n* to women of a specified age or duration of marriage or both. See also *parity.

birth probability is defined as the number of live births during a year per 1,000 women who at the beginning of the year are at risk of having a birth. The rate is usually specified for the woman's age or *parity or both.

birth process (or **death process),** types of *stochastic processes of a population in which at each point in time there is a stated probability that an individual will give birth (or die). The model may also include such other factors as migration into or out of the population. Applications to demography are obvious, but the terms are used also in such other fields as particle physics.

birth-residence index is, for a specified area, the proportion of those that had been born there relative to the number living there at the time of a census or other count. It is a measure, thus, of migration at any time from birth onward and therefore indicates only very roughly the total of internal and international migration over a period. The mortality of nonmigrants obviously affects the count, and not necessarily by a similar proportion in all areas.

birth roster, a list of the *children ever born to a woman, together with their dates of birth and such supplementary information as their sex, whether still alive, and whether living at home or elsewhere. A roster can be compiled from a *population register, a *survey, or a *census. See also *birth history.

birth weight, the weight of a fetus or newborn measured preferably within the first hour of life, before a significant postnatal weight loss has occurred. A birth weight of less than 2,500 grams (about 5.5 pounds) is used as an operational definition of immaturity, which is an important cause of infant deaths. In the 1950s and 1960s, when the infant mortality of the United States was relatively high compared with that of other advanced countries, the difference was often explained by the superiority of socialized medicine in European nations. In fact, however, a higher proportion of immature births were saved in the United States, with a subsequent far greater risk of death. Compared with Sweden or the Netherlands (the two countries with the best recorded control of infant mortality), the attempts of American obstetricians to save a higher proportion of infants with a dangerously low birth weight accounted for 85 to 90 percent of the difference in neonatal mortality.

REFERENCES: Helen C. Chase, *International Comparison of Perinatal and Infant Mortality: The United States and Six West European Countries* (Washington, D.C.: U.S. National Center for Health Statistics, 1967); "Infant Mortality and Its Concomitants, 1960-1972," *Medical Care*, 15 (1977), 662-674.

births averted, or **births prevented,** are terms used by those who evaluate the supposed effects of a birth-control program. It is given sometimes as a total figure since the program started, sometimes as the number of births averted per 1,000 acceptors (see *acceptance). The calculation, however, is based on a supposition concerning the fertility that would have been experienced compared with the one after the program started. For instance, if a woman had borne all the children the couple wanted and used the facilities provided by the program to prevent any more births, all the births so averted would be counted as part of the program's success, as though no other method were available to limit the size of the family.

Black Death, an attack of the *plague and specifically the one that devastated Europe in the mid-fourteenth century. Presumably the disease came from China, turning up first in Constantinople in 1347. In the fall of that year it was reported in Sicily, and during 1348 it spread throughout the Mediterranean basin to Italy, France, and Spain, reaching Paris in June, London in September. From London it went west to Dublin (1349), north to York (1349) and Scotland (1350). From Italy and France it traveled to various German cities, reaching East Prussia in 1350 and Russia in the spring of 1352. In each place it struck in epidemic form several times and continued endemically for some 80 years. The mortality figures from contemporary sources reflect a variation from one place to another and are often exaggerated, but even the more conservative estimates of present-day scholars indicate an almost unparalleled loss of life. J. C. †Russell (1948, pp. 214-232) estimated that most European nations sustained a depletion of 20 to 25 percent in the first attack of 1348-50, and of 40 percent by the end of the century. Urban death rates were probably higher than the average, because of the greater contagion in congested areas, and the depopulation of cities was aggravated by a mass exodus of their terror-stricken inhabitants. Since pregnant women seem to have been particularly susceptible, the stupendous loss could not be quickly repaired.

REFERENCE: J. C. Russell, *British Medieval Population* (Albuquerque: University of New Mexico Press, 1948).

blacks or **Negroes** were brought to the Americas as slaves, and that fact conditioned their status in all countries of the Western Hemisphere, though not always in the same way or to the same degree (cf. *Brazil). Importation of slaves into the United States was prohibited in 1807 under penalty of forfeiting both vessel and cargo. By a law passed in 1819 informers were offered a bounty of $50 for each imported slave apprehended, and the following year slave trading was made a capital offense. The forebears of most American blacks, thus, were brought from Africa before 1808, and after that date plantation owners found it increasingly expensive to replace slaves that died. It was therefore in their interest to maintain their property in good condition, and some scholars—though not all—now hold that the material conditions of slaves were based on adequate nutrition and living quarters and that most of their children were born in stable two-parent households (see *slavery). This does not mean, of course, that the psychic burden of human bondage was lessened. Most slaves were illiterate and brutalized, and the whole of the South had to bear such of the institution's costs as special police forces, mail censorship in order to intercept abolitionist writings, and the impairment of academic freedom at Southern universities.

Some slaves became freedmen before the Civil War. "Free persons of color," who constituted 14 percent of the Negro population in the 1830s, lived mostly not in the black belt of the large plantations but in Northern or Southern cities and small towns. In the District of Columbia half the Negroes were free in 1830, more than three-quarters by 1860. There and elsewhere they established their own schools and reduced illiteracy sometimes to nil and always to well below that of even the most favored urban slaves. The Dunbar High School that free blacks founded in the capital maintained a record of extraordinary excellence until well into this century (Sowell, 1974). It is true that from about 1830 to 1865, under the ever more stringent restrictions based on *race rather than civil status, free Negroes in various portions of the South did not have the right to vote, to bear arms, to assembly peaceably, to move freely, to educate themselves, to testify against whites, to engage in various occupations. Even so, property rights, which were not abrogated, enabled the free Negroes to accumulate an estimated $50 million in real and personal wealth by 1860. Those who escaped from slavery before the general emancipation, in short, had an enormous and enduring advantage; they and their descendants were the principal leaders of the black community up to about the time of World War I (Sowell, 1978).

The Emancipation Proclamation of January 1, 1863, became effective only after the Civil War ended and particularly after several laws and three amendments to the Constitution gave freedmen the same civil rights as whites (cf. *affirmative action). With the South under the control of an occupying Union army, blacks were able to attend schools, to vote and hold local office, to work in occupations that had been barred to them. In the presidential election of 1876, the Democratic candidate, Samuel J. Tilden, presumably won, but the Republicans refused to concede on the grounds that returns from several states were in dispute. Eventually Southern Democrats agreed to sanction the election of Rutherford B. Hayes, the Republican nominee, on condition that the federal troops be withdrawn from the South. The political and civil rights of blacks were quickly eroded once the troops were withdrawn, giving way to segregation and discrimination and, when deemed necessary to enforce Jim Crow, to lynch mobs (Woodward, 1974). Without the formal reinstitution of slavery, white domination was reimposed. One reaction was a large migration of Negroes to Northern cities, well under way during the last decades of the nineteenth century. By 1900 New York, Philadelphia, and Chicago were the homes of thousands of modest black workers and small businessmen, who were on generally good terms with their white neighbors. As late as 1910 more than two-thirds of Chicago's blacks lived in neighborhoods of which most residents were white.

The gradual improvement in Northern race relations was reversed, however, by the eventual size of the in-migration, particularly after the movement of workers from Europe was interrupted by World War I. The record-breaking northward migration during the century's first decade nearly tripled in 1911-20 and doubled again in 1921-30. Like newcomers from Europe, blacks from the South were generally ill prepared for their new environment, and every antagonism between them and whites, or between them and the previously settled blacks, was aggravated by the depression of the 1930s. E. Franklin Frazier, the foremost black social analyst of the past generation, studied the effects of "the disintegrating forces in the city" in the gloomiest terms. "Illegitimacy, which was a more or less harmless affair in the country, has become a serious economic and social problem. At times students of social problems have seen in these various aspects of family disorganization a portent of the Negro's destruction'' (Frazier, 1966, p. 363). What had been mainly Southern institutions—*segregation of housing; overt and general *discrimination in employment by businesses and by local, state, and federal governments; branches of the Ku Klux Klan—spread to the North. The disintegration of black communities was so great that their leadership was largely taken over by a tiny number of immigrants from the British West Indies.

The rise from this new nadir began during World War II, accelerated during the postwar economic boom, and received legal substance from the Supreme Court's decision in 1954 that segregated facilities are unconstitutional and from the civil rights laws of the 1960s (Long and DeAre, 1981; U.S. Bureau of the Census, 1979). These were major steps, it was believed, toward the full integration of Negroes into American society. According to the thesis most fully expounded in Gunnar †Myrdal's massive *An American Dilemma* (1944), the differences between the races were either of no importance (skin color) or the consequence of discriminatory institutions (lower intelligence scores resulting from poorer schools). Thus, once the self-reinforcing pattern was broken, remnants of racial antagonism would be dissipated following a ''principle of cumulation,'' and eventually the distinction between black and white would be of no greater social significance than that, say, between dark and blond hair. Paradoxically, the marked reduction in discrimination led not to such a lessening of perceived racial differences, but the opposite.

Population statistics on American Negroes, not surprisingly in view of their social history, have generally been incomplete and inaccurate (e.g., Farley, 1968). Attempts to rework the count have focused on the post-emancipation period, for data on slaves lack even the reliable figures on age needed for a reconstruction (but see Eblen, 1972, 1974). That the annual intercensal increase of the black population fell off from about 3 percent at the beginning of the record to well under 2 percent, as shown in the table, followed the trend of the rest of the population and therefore might have been expected—but not the erratic jumps in these figures. As the prime example, the rate of increase from 1860 to 1870, 0.9 percent, rose to 3.0 percent during the following decade. Enumeration in the South was especially poor in 1870, the first census after the Civil War, and as judged by Francis A. Walker, the superintendent of the census, the count of blacks in particular was ''inadequate, partial, and inaccurate, often in a shameful degree.'' The simplest way to adjust the census figures is to remove these jumps by smoothing the decline in the rate of increase. This was done by John Cummings (1918) and then, apparently independently, by Kelly Miller (1922), who carried the calculation one decade farther. However, the underlying premise, in Miller's words, that the growth of the black population ''behave[d] more or less normally,'' contradicts the decided abnormality of many factors affecting the fertility and mortality of blacks. The dilemma remains no matter what method of adjustment is used: should one assume that aberrations were

Black Population of the United States, 1790-1980, according to Census Enumerations and Several Subsequent Adjustments

	Census Counts					
	Population (thousands)	Average Annual Intercensal Increase (%)	Percent of Total	Cummings (1918) and Miller (1922)	Bogue et al. (1964)	Coale and Rives (1973)
1790	757	—	19			
1800	1,002	2.8	19			
1810	1,378	3.2	19			
1820	1,772	2.5	18			
1830	2,329	2.7	18			
1840	2,874	2.1	17			
1850	3,639	2.4	16			
1860	4,442	2.0	14	4,442		
1870	4,880	0.9	13	5,392		
1880	6,581	3.0	13	6,581		7,241
1890	7,389	1.3	12	7,760		8,535
1900	8,834	1.8	12	8,834		9,921
1910	9,828	1.1	11	9,828		11,182
1920	10,463	0.6	10	10,763		12,340
1930	11,891	1.3	10		12,226	13,546
1940	12,866	0.8	10		13,175	14,753
1950	15,042	1.6	10		15,226	16,749
1960	18,916	2.3	11		20,014	20,684
1970	22,580	1.9	11			24,388
1980	26,505	1.7	12			

entirely an artifact of poor enumeration, or partly also a result of the experiences of the counted population?

The reconstruction of Donald J. †Bogue et al. (1964) was based on the postulate that "the most reliable data available" for the black population were the total census count without reference to age and the death registration by age (but cf. Zelnik, 1965). In a more elaborate reconstruction of the black population from 1880 to 1970 (Coale and Rives, 1973), it was assumed that this was a closed population approaching stability up to 1880 and that subsequent deviations from that path could be used to calculate the population structure and fertility (see *population, closed; *population, stable). For cohorts born after 1935, vital statistics corrected for underregistration were also used. Reynolds †Farley (1965, 1970) followed essentially the same procedure. Reconstructions of the growth based on a stable-population model, however, depend on age data, which are also highly inaccurate (cf. Zelnik, 1969). Even in the 1960 census, when general reporting was improved by asking for the year of birth rather than the age, a high proportion of blacks said that they had been born, for example, in 1890, 1900, or 1910—thus continuing to round off their ages to the nearest multiple of 10 (cf. *age).

However unsatisfactory the census data are, vital statistics on blacks have typically been worse. When Texas was admitted to the two *registration areas in 1933, statistics on births and deaths became national for the first time. The last states to reach the modest standards set for admission were mostly in the South, and even after being admitted some still did not register the requisite 90 percent of births and deaths, particularly those of blacks. Whatever is said about the fertility or mortality of the past, thus, must be tempered by a general observation that the data are usually loose enough to permit of several interpretations (cf. Tolnay, 1981).

Even if enumeration and registration had been satisfactory, the continuity of the record would have been distorted by the fundamental change that took place in Negroes' self-identity (cf. Banks and Grambs, 1972). For many years after emancipation, when it was difficult to advance or, in the worst periods, even to maintain oneself, the occasional individual who succeeded usually modeled himself on the white middle class. Once the barriers had been significantly lowered and large sectors of the race could improve their status, this widespread upward mobility was accompanied by a new emphasis on ethnic values. As one indication of the change in identity, one can note the succession of official or quasi-official designations (cf. Low and Clift, 1981, pp. 656-657). For some decades after the Civil War the usual polite group name was "Colored," which avoided the connotation of both blackness and African origin. The designation "black" became taboo during the first decades of this century, but "negro" and eventually "Negro" (which is Spanish for "black") was coming into increasing use over the same period. During the 1960s usages began to diverge among group leaders. Roy Wilkins, long head of the National Association for the Advancement of Colored People (NAACP), wrote in his syndicated column that he would continue to call himself a "Negro," but younger or more radical spokesmen insisted on being called "blacks" (or "Blacks"), reflecting their "black consciousness" and their desire for "black power." During the same period the link to Africa, once regarded as especially offensive, began to be emphasized in such terms as "African American" or, more frequently, "Afro-American." Each of such changes in designation was insisted on with great emotional fervor, and in the 1980 census schedule the U.S. Bureau of the Census resolved the resulting dilemma by offering respondents a wide choice of designations.

The successive group names that the minority preferred exemplify a more general point that can be illustrated also with other indicators. For example, in the 1950s the ideal Negro girl or woman had a light skin, thin lips, and "good" hair. The slogan, "Black is beautiful," often repeated over the next decades, was intended to transform much more than this perception of feminine beauty. During the "Colored" period, some of those light enough to pass as white shifted their racial identity altogether. No estimate of the number who moved into the white population can be taken as more than a plausible guess, but apparently passing was once relatively common, more prevalent in the United States than in countries with a recognized intermediate sector of mixed ancestry (cf. Bontemps and Conroy, 1966). Supposedly fewer Negroes have attempted to move across the racial line more recently, both because of their easier access to many good jobs and because of the rise in "black pride." As one aberrant reflection of that pride, some black spokesmen have designated *illegitimacy and the *one-parent family as not a problem but a culture trait of blacks—or, if a problem, then the fault exclusively of whites (cf. Rainwater and Yancey, 1967; Shimkin et al., 1978). Such opinions echoed those in the West Indies and Africa, where the proponents of *négritude were proclaiming a frankly racist ideology (cf. Petersen, 1976).

In the decades from roughly the 1880s to the 1950s, differences among Negroes were overwhelmed by the humiliating discrimination to which everyone with a dark skin was subject. The subsequent period, with the substantial improvement in the income and well-being of *some* blacks, has made statistics broken down by race somewhat misleading, for along every dimension Negroes are divided into two distinct subgroups. Blacks who took full advantage of the improved opportunities during the 1960s contrast with those who, because of age, region, or family structure, found it difficult or impossible to do so. If we control for these three factors, blacks closed the income gap between themselves and whites as early as 1970. "There was no apparent difference between the income of white and Negro husband-wife families outside the South where the head was under 35 years" (U.S. Bureau of the Census, 1971; cf. U.S. Bureau of the Census, 1979). Many analysts have noted the slowing rate of upward movement, both in journal articles on "Illusions of Black Economic Progress" (Darity, 1980) and in more substantial works to show that hopes of advancement are "still a dream" (Levitan et al., 1975). For in contrast to those blacks moving into the middle class are the female heads of households who must play the roles of both parents and the unskilled black teenagers—who are unable to get a first job at the minimum wage set by law (cf. Glasgow, 1980). The argument of William Julius Wilson (1978) that the significance of race has declined in the United States is buttressed by several dozen such contrasts between middle-class and lower-class blacks.

Demographic phenomena, to the degree that adequate data exist, also often describe bimodal curves. Differences by race in mortality, particularly in infant mortality, have often been used to measure whether, and if so how much, the gap in living conditions has been reduced. But inconsistent inaccuracies in the population figures used as the denominator of death rates can have a significant effect (e.g., Tomasson, 1961). In Southern states the proportion of black births attended by physicians increased from between 22 and 68 percent in 1950 to between 70 and 96 percent in 1968, yet the gap in those states between white and black neonatal mortality remained amazingly constant—presumably in considerable part because more black deaths were reported at the later date (Shin, 1975). Some infants die because of the conditions under which they were born: irrespective of race, illegitimate babies and those born to young teenagers have a lesser chance of surviving. In order really to assess the "mortality and morbidity disadvantages of the black population of the United States" (Sutton, 1971), in other words, it would be necessary to correct the faulty data, to distinguish between lack of medical services and other causes, and to differentiate between middle-class and lower-class blacks with respect to their rates of illness and death. In the vast mass of data that are regularly collected and analyzed, this has not been done.

The same contrast is found in fertility patterns. More blacks than whites have had no children, on the one hand, and six or more children, on the other. Childlessness was once typically diagnosed as a symptom of poor health, due particularly to the prevalence of venereal diseases (McFalls, 1973). But the families that now have the fewest children are often those of middle-class blacks, the ones least likely to suffer from such concomitants of social and family disorganization. A sector of a population that is moving up the social scale generally has a lower *fertility, and this effect is typically exaggerated in a minority rising under especially difficult circumstances. Those who see no chance of improving their situation, on the contrary, are usually oriented to the immediate present; to plan anything, including the number of one's off-spring, implies a faith in the future, a faith that is lacking in many lower-class blacks, who often continue to produce the numerous progeny once usual in the rural South (cf. *alienation).

When a population is congregated at the two ends of a continuum, so that the pattern of many characteristics describes a ∪-shaped curve, analyzing a trend in terms of the average not only passes over this most significant feature but draws our attention to the bottom of the ∪, where the fewest individuals are to be found.

REFERENCES: James A. Banks and Jean Dresden Grambs, eds., *Black Self-Concepts: Implications for Education and Social Science* (New York: McGraw-Hill, 1972). Donald J. Bogue, Bhaskar D. Misra, and D. P. Dandekar, "A New Estimate of the Negro Population and Negro Vital Rates in the United States, 1930-60," *Demography*, 1 (1964), 339-358. Arna Bontemps and Jack Conroy, *Anyplace But Here* (New York: Hill and Wang, 1966). Ansley J. Coale and Norfleet W. Rives, Jr., "A Statistical Reconstruction of the Black Population of the United States, 1880-1970: Estimates of True Numbers by Age and Sex, Birth Rates, and Total Fertility," *Population Index*, 39 (1973), 3-36. John Cummings, *Negro Population, 1790-1915* (Washington, D.C.: U.S. Bureau of the Census, 1918; reprinted, New York: Arno Press, 1968). William A. Darity, Jr., "Illusions of Black Economic Progress," *Review of Black Political Economy*, 10 (1980), 153-168. Jack E. Eblen, "Growth of the Black Population in *ante bellum* America, 1820-1860," *Population Studies*, 26 (1972), 273-289; "New Estimates of the Vital Rates of the United States Black Population during the Nineteenth Century," *Demography*, 11 (1974), 301-319. Reynolds Farley, "The Demographic Rates and Social Institutions of the Nineteenth-Century Negro Population: A Stable Population Analysis," *Demography*, 2 (1965), 386-

398; "The Quality of Demographic Data for Nonwhites," *Demography*, 5 (1968), 1-10; *Growth of the Black Population: A Study of Demographic Trends* (Chicago: Markham Publishing Co., 1970). E. Franklin Frazier, *The Negro Family in the United States* (rev. ed.; Chicago: University of Chicago Press, 1966). Douglas G. Glasgow, *The Black Underclass: Poverty, Unemployment, and Entrapment of Ghetto Youth* (San Francisco: Jossey-Bass, 1980). Sar A. Levitan, William B. Johnston, and Robert Taggart, *Still a Dream: The Changing Status of Blacks since 1960* (Cambridge, Mass.: Harvard University Press, 1975). Larry Long and Diana DeAre, "The Suburbanization of Blacks," *American Demographics*, 3 (September, 1981), 16-21, 44. W. Augustus Low and Virgil A. Clift, *Encyclopedia of Black America* (New York: McGraw-Hill, 1981). Joseph A. McFalls, Jr., "Impact of VD on the Fertility of the U.S. Black Population, 1880-1950," *Social Biology*, 20 (1973), 2-19. Kelly Miller, "Enumeration Errors in the Negro Population," *Scientific Monthly*, 14 (1922), 168-177. Gunnar Myrdal, *An American Dilemma: The Negro Problem and Modern Democracy*, 2 vols. (New York: Harper, 1944). William Petersen, "A Comparison of a Racial and a Language Subnation: American Negroes and Flemish," *Ethnicity*, 3 (1976), 145-173. Lee Rainwater and William L. Yancey, *The Moynihan Report and the Politics of Controversy* (Cambridge, Mass.: M.I.T. Press, 1967). Demitri Boris Shimkin, Edith M. Shimkin, and Dennis A. Frate, eds., *The Extended Family in Black Societies* (The Hague: Mouton, 1978). Eui Hang Shin, "Black-White Differentials in Infant Mortality in the South, 1940-1970," *Demography*, 12 (1975), 1-19. Thomas Sowell, "Black Excellence: The Case of Dunbar High School," *Public Interest*, no. 35 (Spring, 1974), 3-21; "Three Black Histories," in Sowell, ed., *Essays and Data on American Ethnic Groups* (Washington, D.C.: Urban Institute, 1978). Gordon F. Sutton, "Assessing Mortality and Morbidity Disadvantages of the Black Population of the United States," *Social Biology*, 18 (1971), 369-383. Stewart E. Tolnay, "Trends in Total and Marital Fertility for Black Americans, 1886-1899," *Demography*, 18 (1981), 443-463. Richard F. Tomasson, "Bias in Estimates of the U.S. Nonwhite Population as Indicated by Trends in Death Rates," *Journal of the American Statistical Association*, 56 (1961), 44-51. U.S. Bureau of the Census, "Differences between Income of White and Negro Families by Work Experience of Wife and Region, 1970, 1969, and 1959," *Current Population Reports*, Ser. P-23, no. 39 (1971); "The Social and Economic Status of the Black Population in the United States: An Historical View, 1790-1978," *Current Population Reports*, Ser. P-23, no. 80 (1979). William Julius Wilson, *The Declining Significance of Race: Blacks and Changing American Institutions* (Chicago: University of Chicago Press, 1978). C. Vann Woodward, *The Strange Career of Jim Crow* (3rd rev. ed.; New York: Oxford University Press, 1974). Melvin Zelnik, "An Evaluation of New Estimates of the Negro Population," *Demography*, 2 (1965), 630-639; "Age Patterns of Mortality of American Negroes: 1900-02 to 1959-61," *Journal of the American Statistical Association*, 64 (1969), 433-451.

blindness ranges from "total blindness," the inability to perceive light, to "vocational blindness," the inability to continue in the same line of work because of what could be a relatively minor impairment of vision. The precise designation varies from country to country; in the United States blindness is generally defined as a central visual acuity, uncorrected, of 20/200 or less in the better eye. This means that the person being tested can see at 20 feet what one with normal vision could see at 200 feet. "Normal" is defined as 20/20 vision or better. Persons afflicted with some types of blindness can see clearly but only over a very limited area, as though they were looking through a gun barrel. The count of blind persons is adequate in a few nations (for example, Britain), relatively poor in others, and hardly more than indicative in less developed countries. From these quite incomplete data one can derive a rate the world over of about 0.2 or 0.4 percent of the population. The major factor in recent increases has been the growing proportion of the elderly; well over half of the legally blind in the United States, for instance, are aged 65 and over. See also *disability.

block, in common parlance the distance along a street between two cross-streets, is similar to what is termed by the U.S. Bureau of the Census a *block face*, or the street along one side of a city block. A block, alternatively, is defined as a usually rectangular space in a city bounded by streets and suitable for buildings. A *census block* is ordinarily the same but can be larger or smaller depending on how it is identified on the map prepared in advance of each census. The block is the smallest area for which census data are published, though each block face can be identified from the basic-record tapes. Blocks are combined into *block groups*, which in turn are subunits of each metropolitan *census tract. See also *chunk.

blood groups are classified according to whether the red blood cells of one person can be mixed with those of another without forming clumps. Karl Landsteiner (1868-1943), an Austrian-born American biologist, received the Nobel Prize in 1930 for demonstrating the incompatibility of the groups now designated A, B, AB, and O. Subsequently researchers identified almost two dozen types of blood groups in addition to this original ABO system. The discovery of the Rh groups in 1939-40 led to the knowledge of their role in causing what is called hemolytic disease of the newborn. That blood groups are inherited according to Mendelian laws has made them extremely useful in physical anthropology, perhaps the best indicator of past interbreeding and thus, inferentially, of prehistoric migrations. The classification is much more discriminate than that based on such gross somatic characteristics as skin color; for example, the so-called Lutheran blood groups are concentrated in only one portion of the Caucasoid race, and the antigen Lu^a can be present in blacks as well as whites, though apparently not in Asians, Eskimos, or Australian aborigines.

REFERENCES: A. G. Erskine and Wladyslaw W. Socha, *Principles and Practice of Blood Grouping* (2nd ed.; St. Louis: Mosby, 1978). E. A. Mourant, *The Distribution of Human Blood Groups* (Oxford: Blackwell, 1954). R. R. Race and Ruth Sanger, *Blood Groups in Man* (5th ed.; Philadelphia: F. A. Davis, 1968).

boarder, an unrelated person who takes his meals with others in a "boarding house," residing either there or elsewhere. Compare *lodger.

boat people, a journalists' term for *refugees from Vietnam after the consolidation of the country under the Communist regime. Included were past or potential political dissidents plus the whole of the ethnic Chinese minority. Stripped of all their belongings and sent off in leaky boats, about half perished en route to one of the adjacent countries, and the impoverished masses that did land often damaged the economies of Vietnam's non-Communist neighbors. According to the London *Economist* (June 25, 1979), at that date new arrivals were entering the remaining havens at the rate of 50,000 per month, and the total awaiting resettlement was about 300,000. At the same date there were some 235,000 Indochinese refugees in the United States, with about 5,000 more entering each month.

REFERENCE: Barry Wain, *The Refused: The Agony of the Indochina Refugees* (New York: Simon and Schuster, 1981).

Bolivia: Demographic Institutions

The Center for Social Research of the National Academy of Sciences, founded in 1972 as a private organization, in 1980 was under the direction of Antonio J. Cisneros Cabrera. Its research has focused on those areas of population that affect economic development: urbanization, human resources, female work outside the home, and the like. Findings are published in the center's monographs, of which nineteen had been published by 1979. Address: Centro de Investigaciones Sociales, Casilla 6931, Correo Central, La Paz.

The Center for Social and Economic Development, a private organization founded in 1966, organizes research and distributes information, mainly on the country's rural population. Addresses: Centro para el Desarrollo Social y Económico, Avenida Camacho 1333, Casilla 6124, La Paz; Calle Junín 6062, Casilla 1420, Cochabamba.

The National Institute of Statistics is responsible for conducting the country's censuses. It issues a yearbook of vital statistics, a monthly statistical bulletin, and an annual compendium of health statistics. Address: Instituto Nacional de Estadística, Ministerio de Planificación y Coordinación, Calle Bolívar 688, La Paz.

border, loosely, a *boundary between administrative units or geographical regions; more precisely, the region just inside such a boundary. See also *frontier. (With a capital B, ''the Border'' refers to that between England and Scotland, a wild country much celebrated in folklore and the so-called Border ballads.) Political problems related to the overlap of national cultures and economies are usually designated as ''border problems''; ''boundary problems'' relate to disputes over where the line should be drawn. The ''border problems'' of the United States and Canada, according to one symposium, range over all the two countries' economic, social, and cultural relations (see Wagner, 1977), but more attention has been centered on those between the United States and Mexico. About four million people live on either side of this 1,966-mile boundary. On the southern side are *ciudades trampolinas*, staging areas for those from the interior awaiting their chance to slip across (see *migration, illegal). Each day an estimated 40,000 Mexicans who have the much coveted "green card" cross the border to work, and perhaps an equal number go to shop, perhaps having to pay a bribe of 20 pesos in place of the usually larger tariff that they avoid (cf. Miller, 1981). There is a National Border Program or PRONAF (for Programa Nacional Fronterizo) to develop communities along Mexico's northern border, and American firms with labor-intensive industries are encouraged to establish plants there (Dillman, 1970; Hansen, 1981).

REFERENCES: C. Daniel Dillman, "Urban Growth along Mexico's Northern Border and the Mexican National Border Program," *Journal of Developing Areas*, 4 (1970), 487-508. Niles Hansen, *The Border Economy: Regional Development in the Southwest* (Austin: University of Texas Press, 1981). Tom Miller, *On the Border: Portraits of America's Southwestern Frontier* (New York: Harper & Row, 1981). J. Richard Wagner, ed., "Border Problems of the United States and Canada: Issues of the Seventies," *Social Science Journal*, 14 (1977), 1-69.

borough, one of the dozen terms derived from the word for "fort" or "fortified town," has acquired quite different meanings in the various English-speaking countries. In England it means a town or urban constituency represented in Parliament or one with a royal charter but lacking the more dignified status of a "city." In some states of the United States it is the name used for what is generally termed an incorporated *place. In New York City it is one of the five constituent political units.

Botswana: The Central Statistics Office conducts the country's censuses, the most recent of which was in 1981. It publishes an annual *Statistical Abstract* that includes population data. Address: Private Bag 0024, Gaborone.

boundary, a sharply defined line marking the division between administrative units or geographical regions. It is contrasted with *border, or that region just inside the boundary, and with *frontier, an often loosely demarcated zone.

REFERENCE: J.R.V. Prescott, *Boundaries and Frontiers* (London: Croom Helm, 1978).

bourgeois (-ie), originally the French words for the "burghers" who lived in the "new burg," or mercantile quarter of the cities of early modern Europe. This nucleus of the middle class gradually evolved the institutions of both economic and political liberty. Inside the walls of the cities, whatever their differences in wealth, all men eventually were of equal civil status. The bourgeoisie were not consciously missionaries, but by their independent existence they challenged and eroded the hierarchical structure of feudalism. Marx regarded it as the most revolutionary class in history; in the *Communist Manifesto* he and Engels wrote that "the bourgeoisie cannot exist without constantly revolutionizing the instruments of production ... and with them the whole relations of society.'' More recently, Marxists, including especially the more ideological of Soviet writers on population, have used "bourgeois" to designate both the presumably distinctive patterns of population growth in the West and the theories developed by Western demographers to explain them (see, for example, B. IA. †Smulevich; M. IA. †Sonin). As the principal Soviet delegate to the 1954 World Population Conference in Rome, T. V. †Riabushkin divided the world according to what he saw as the dominant issue, "the struggle between two trends in the underlying questions of theory and practice of population statistics—the reactionary one, connected with neo-Malthusian ideas, and the progressive one, led by the delegates of the Soviet Union and the People's Democracies.'' Remarkably, if one now applies this rationale to sectors of the Soviet population itself, it is the Muslim minorities that are progressive and the Russian and other Slavic nationalities that are "bourgeois."

Bow, an *intra-uterine device in the shape of a tied bow, first developed by Charles H. Bernberg.

Boyce-Clark shape index, used to classify the shapes of geographical areas, has the following formula:

$$\text{S.I.} = \sum_{i=1}^{n} \left(\frac{r_i}{\sum_{i=1}^{n} r_i} \times 100 - \frac{100}{n} \right)$$

where r represents radials from a central node, and n the number of radials used. The S.I. of a circle is zero, and all other geometric forms have positive values, increasing in size as they deviate more and more from an approximation of a circular one. The authors exemplified the formula with indices of a number of Standard Metropolitan Areas of the United States, and geographers have since applied it to other sets of data.

REFERENCE: R. R. Boyce and W.A.V. Clark, "The Concept of Shape in Geography," *Geographical Review*, 54 (1964), 561-572.

brain drain, the emigration of highly qualified professionals or technicians, especially from less developed to industrial countries. Such international migrants constitute a relatively new phenomenon. Less than one in a hundred of the enormous number of immigrants to the United States up to 1925 were professionals (Fortney, 1972), and the much higher proportion during subsequent decades was mainly refugees, politically rather than economically motivated to relocate in another country. Immediately following the Second World War, the term was coined (also in French, *exode des cerveaux*, and in German, *Auszug des Geistes*) to distinguish these professionals and technicians from previous migrants, who had been mainly young unmarried men of modest background. The considerable body of usually disputatious writings has a wide range of concepts, indicators, data, and interpretations, often reflecting sharp disagreement (cf. Beijer, 1972; Guha, 1977). There are essentially two points of view. One group of disputants defend the interest of less developed countries, which can ill afford to lose the services of highly skilled persons whose education the state has often subsidized. A somewhat similar complaint has been voiced concerning even the movement between developed countries, as of physicians, chemists, and physicists from Britain to the United States. On the other side are those who defend the right of individuals to seek the most suitable place to work and live, regardless of country. How complex the debate has become is suggested by the fact that those who used to demand that American barriers to international migration be lifted later condemned the consequences of a relaxation of controls. As the major receiving country, the United States has been the chief target of critics, and one of the principal issues has been the 1952 immigration statute, which eliminated the preference for West Europeans explicit in the earlier regulations and thus permitted the entry of far larger numbers from Asia and Africa. According to a detailed analysis, however, the new law provided no impetus to a brain drain from South America (Rockett, 1976) and may even have inhibited the movement (Bernard, 1970).

The debate has been muddled by a typical lack of complete and accurate statistics on emigration from less developed countries (e.g., Henderson, 1970). Some states have imitated the Communist norm and imposed legal barriers to emigration, which are evaded by many who never appear in the statistics (cf. Inhaber, 1975). To estimate effects of migration accurately, moreover, one would need data not only on return migration but also on the number and skills of those moving in both directions—statistics that are almost never available (Friborg and Annerstedt, 1972; Marr, 1977). The results of a comparison of losses through education abroad depend mainly on whether one used as a base the number of students from each country in, for example, the United States, the number studying both at home and abroad, or the country's demand for high-level manpower (Myers, 1972). Similarly, of Asian students in the United States, 77.8, 58.2, or 38.6 percent did not return home, depending on how one defined "non-return" (Oh, 1973a, 1973b).

REFERENCES: Gunther Beijer, *Brain Drain: A Selected Bibliography on Temporary and Permanent Migration of Skilled Workers and High-Level Manpower, 1967-1972* (The Hague: Nijhoff, 1972). T. L. Bernard, "United States Immigration Laws and the Brain Drain," *International Migration*, 8 (1970), 31-38. J. A. Fortney, "Immigrant Professional: A Brief Historical Survey," *International Migration Review*, 6 (1972), 50-62. Göran Friborg and Jan Annerstedt, *Brain Drain and Brain Gain of Sweden* (Stockholm: Swedish National Science Research Council, 1972). Amalendu Guha, "Brain Drain Issue and Indicators on Brain Drain," *International Migration*, 15 (1977), 3-20. Gregory Henderson, *The Emigration of Highly Skilled Manpower from the Developing Countries* (New York: U.N. Institute for Training and Research, 1970). Herbert Inhaber, "The Brain Drain from India," *Social Biology*, 22 (1975), 250-254. W. L. Marr, "The United Kingdom's International Migration in the Inter-war Period: Theoretical Considerations and Empirical

Testing," *Population Studies*, 31 (1977), 571-579. R. G. Myers, *Education and Emigration: Study Abroad and the Migration of Human Resources* (New York: McKay, 1972). T. K. Oh, "A New Estimate of the Student Brain Drain from Asia," *International Migration Review*, 7 (1973a), 449-456; "Estimating the Migration of U.S.-Educated Manpower from Asia to the United States," *Social and Economic Studies*, 22 (1973b), 335-357. I.R.H. Rockett, "Immigration Legislation and the Flow of Specialized Human Capital from South America to the United States," *International Migration Review*, 10 (1976), 47-61.

Brass's method, named after William †Brass, permits the estimation of a population's fertility from data that with conventional calculations would be insufficient. Common to the several variations are three premises: that the fertility reported for a single year has remained constant during the past 15 or 20 years, that the *parities reported by the younger women are accurate, and that any error in the reference period affects the level of current fertility but not the relation among parities. In what is termed the *P/F ratio method*, reported parities (P) are related to parity-equivalent estimates of fertility (F) to get a correction factor. Thus, the estimation depends essentially on comparing *cohort with *period fertility in order to adjust both into a consistent pattern. Sometimes the method is used with marriage cohorts rather than age cohorts, a possibly useful refinement when data are available and when the age at marriage is changing rapidly. Brass (1975) also revised the method to compare first births rather than all births— that is, the proportions of women who had at least one child and the number of first births during a given year.

REFERENCES: Carmen Arretx, "Fertility Estimates Derived from Information on Children Ever-Born Using Data from Successive Censuses," in IUSSP, International Population Conference, Liège, 1973, *Contributed Papers* (1973–74). William Brass, "The Derivation of Fertility and Reproduction Rates from Restricted Data on Reproductive Histories," *Population Studies*, 7 (1954), 74-87; "The Estimation of Total Fertility Rates from Data for Primitive Communities," in World Population Conference, Rome, 1954, *Proceedings* (1956-57); "The Graduation of Fertility Distribution by Polynomial Functions," *Population Studies*, 14 (1960), 148-162; "Notes on the Brass Method of Fertility Estimation," in Brass et al., eds., *The Demography of Tropical Africa* (Princeton, N.J.: Princeton University Press, 1968); *Methods for Estimating Fertility and Mortality from Limited and Defective Data* (Chapel Hill, N.C.: Laboratories for Population Statistics, University of North Carolina, 1975). Ansley Coale, Allan G. Hill, and T. James Trussell, "A New Method of Estimating Standard Fertility Measures from Incomplete Data," *Population Index*, 41 (1975), 182-210. G. E. Omyemaeke Ogum, "The Distribution of Births in Some African Populations: An Empirical Test of the Adequacy of the Negative Binomial Model," *Genus*, 34 (1978), 153-164.

Brazil, with an expanse of almost 3.3 million square miles (8.5 million square kilometers), is the fifth largest country in the world. It covers nearly half of South America and borders on all but two of the other ten republics. Writers have sought metaphors to dramatize its enormous size, as well as the enormous problems that have gone with it—"half a continent," the "infinite country," a "complex giant." In capsule form, the country's complicated history can be divided into a few fairly distinct periods (cf. James Rowe, 1967; Smith, 1972):

1822-89:	the Empire under a dynasty founded by a scion of the Portuguese royal house, which ruled with the support of the coffee plantation owners. This backing was lost when the large slave population was emancipated in 1888.
1889-1930:	the First Republic, with continued dominance by the rural upper class but also a gradual development of manufacturing in the growing cities, which absorbed a large immigration.
1930-45:	rule by Getúlio Vargas over a "New State." With the backing of the new industrialists and reform-minded army officers, he centralized state power and expanded its control over education, social welfare, and public health.
1945-64:	the Second Republic, an interim between two periods of rapid development.
1964-?:	under a group of army officers, Brazil as a prominent NIC (Newly Industrializing Country). During the first decade the Gross National Product more than trebled, approaching $200 billion by the end of the 1970s and becoming the tenth largest in the world. Gross differences widened between the wealthy and the underemployed. Beginning in 1979, the promised "decompression" or "redemocratization" was begun with a general amnesty to prisoners; following the rise in the world price of oil, there was a sharp downturn from the economic boom. In the most recent period, Brazil has been on the verge of defaulting on its enormous foreign debt (Macrae, 1979; Merrick and Graham, 1979; Sanders, 1980).

The growth of Brazil's population during the last several decades is well documented (see also *Brazil: Demographic Institutions). Beginning in 1940 the censuses were conducted under the supervision of Giorgio †Mortara or, after he returned to Italy, following the procedures he had set. By his estimate the underenumeration in 1940 was only 1.7 percent (compared with 1.4 percent in the United States count of the same date). The 1960 census was of lesser quality and was not fully tabulated until 1978, but the two subsequent ones were better. From a probable 3 million around 1800 and 10 million in the 1870s, the population grew to 52 million by 1950, 93 million in 1970 and an estimated 134.4 million in 1984. The census count of 119 million in 1980, though slightly smaller than some projections had indicated, was more than six times the 18 million in 1900 (Merrick and Graham, 1979; Patricia Rowe, 1981; Smith, 1974, chap. 3).

From the last decade of the nineteenth century, the rapid growth was due in significant part to the large immigration following the abolition of slavery in 1888. Up to 1957 a total of 4.8 million persons came from—in order of their number—Italy, Portugal, Spain, Japan, and various other countries. In 1934 the government set a quota equal to 2 percent of the influx from each country over 1884-1934 (both the regulation and its date are similar to laws enacted in the United States), and by the 1960s immigration had become negligible (Smith, 1972). The increase in the population from abroad was added to the rapid natural growth, the consequence of the typical decline in mortality combined with fertility long sustained at a high level. According to the estimates of Moreira et al. (1978), the average annual rates of natural increase were as follows:

$$
\begin{array}{ll}
1849\text{-}70 & 1.4\% \\
1950s & 2.9\% \\
1960s & 2.8\% \\
\end{array}
$$

In the 1970s, the annual growth of the population (including net migration) was still at an average of 2.8 percent. If this rate holds, the population will double in twenty-five years.

The crude death rate, estimated at around 32 in the middle of the nineteenth century, fell to 12 in the 1960s and 10 in the late 1970s. Over the same period, comparable estimates of the crude birth rate were 46.5, 40, and 39 (see also Carvalho, 1974; Mortara, 1954). According to a number of studies, the urban populations show the expected inverse relation between social class and family size (Hutchinson, 1961, 1964; Miró, 1964). It would seem, however, that the upper class is diverse, and that the spread of modernist ideas is less direct than in societies lacking so strong a patrician tradition (cf. Kahl, 1968).

Difficulties associated with this growth in numbers were aggravated by an extraordinarily rapid urbanization. The few small centers established in the co-lonial period had been intended as administrative outposts of royal power. And in the early nineteenth century the populations of Brazil's cities generally grew more slowly than those of their regions, or in some cases underwent absolute declines (Morse, 1975). Though from 1888 the largest centers (São Paulo, Rio de Janeiro, Salvador, Recife) received many freed slaves, immigrants, and coun-trymen displaced from the subsistence sector, politics was still largely controlled by the planter class. The gradual shift in power was accelerated with Vargas's centralization of government functions and his encouragement to urban industries (Kuznesof, 1982). Yet as late as 1940 the urban sector (including villages and hamlets with an administrative function) made up slightly less than a third of the population. During the 1950s the net rural-urban migration totaled 6.5 mil-lion, and during the 1960s, 10.3 million—as T. Lynn †Smith (1974, chap. 13) remarked, a mass exodus from country to city probably unparalleled in the entire history of mankind. The notorious *favelas*, shantytowns that ring every city, have represented a stage in the painful adaptation of poor in-migrants to urban life. By 1970, with more than 56 percent of the population classified as urban,

Brazil had passed the halfway mark, the criterion that some demographers once used to indicate the transition from less to more developed. Since most of the cities are close to the coast, the rural-urban migration reinforced the differences in population density, very high in the east, very low in the west. The new capital of Brasília was located in the interior in the hope of reversing this trend, but the road between it and the coast actually facilitated a still larger movement out of the interior.

Until the 1970s Brazil's population policy, to the extent that it had any, was pronatalist. According to Peter McDonough and Amaury DeSouza (1981), the public demand for contraceptives has been in contrast with an elite ambivalence over whether to furnish them; but this view is not in accord with that of such other sources as Moreira et al. (1978). The literal translation of "family planning," *planejamento familiar*, was widely understood to mean that the government would impose a "plan" for each family, and this interpretation generated a widespread fear rather than a demand. It was to allay this apprehension that in 1978 the president, after describing the heavy burdens that rapid population growth imposed, declared that in his opinion birth limitation should not be forced but rather based on the informed will of the parents. The Catholic church in Brazil, once strongly opposed to birth control, is now split on this and related issues, and so are members of most professions. The sale of contraceptives was until very recently illegal, and their distribution is still hampered by ignorance and cost. BEMFAM, a private family-planning organization founded in 1965 (the popular designation derives from the Portuguese words for family welfare), was granted tax-exempt status in 1971, and from 1973 it has undertaken a wider distribution of contraceptives in accordance with formal agreements it made with state governments.

Ethnically the population of Brazil is as mixed as any in the world, and race has been a significant determinant of social and economic relations. Estimates of the size of the aboriginal population in the present area of Brazil are even less well based than those of North America. There were no cultures at the level of the Incas, and the smaller peoples spoke many languages—those in the Ge family (of which about fifty languages still survive) along the coast, and Arawakan and Cariban farther west (Steward, 1949). As recently as the 1950s, whites first discovered a tribe in the vast inland, the Xetá—bands of twenty or thirty persons wandering over a fixed territory gathering food on the way and sleeping in temporary shelters built each evening (Loureiro Fernandes, 1959). Of the original number of Indians in the areas settled by Portuguese, many probably died from enslavement and disease, while others disappeared into the category of *mestiço*, or mixed Indian-white. During the colonial period and Empire, there were very few white women, and, in the graphic description of Gilberto Freyre (1946, pp. 91, 325), "Brazil would appear to have been syphilized before it was civilized. . . . [A] 'barbarous superstition' held that those suffering from gonorrhea would be cured if they contrived to have intercourse with a [slave] girl at the age of puberty." Partly because there were not enough

Indians to serve as slaves and they died off in too large proportions, they were soon replaced by blacks imported from Africa.

Of the approximately 11.3 million African slaves shipped to the New World up to the year 1870, some 4.2 million, or about 37 percent, were taken to Brazil (see *slavery). The outnumbered white males mated as freely with them as they had previously with the Indians, and already the several degrees of race crossing were acquiring new designations. After the emancipation a variety of European immigrants were added to the mixture, plus Chinese and especially Japanese from Asia. In the last decades of the nineteenth century, intellectuals trying to expound an ideology of Brazilian nationalism were impeded by the anthropological theories then prevailing. Arthur de †Gobineau, the French racist, found the Brazilians "a population totally mulatto, vitiated in its blood and spirit, and fearfully ugly"; Louis Agassiz, the American naturalist, discovered there a proof of "the deterioration consequent upon an amalgamation of races, more widespread here than in any other country in the world" (Skidmore, 1974, pp. 30-31). At first Brazilians were inclined to accept this judgment, but some found solace in the thesis that the Brazilian population was gradually getting whiter. This "bleaching" was ascribed to such hardly plausible factors as the greater potency of white genes, but according to T. Lynn Smith (1974, pp. 66-67), "there can be little doubt that the Brazilian population is steadily becoming whiter in color," most obviously by the mass immigration from Europe, but also by the differential mortality favoring upper (that is, whiter) classes and the readier access of lighter males to darker women. Racist dogma, adumbrated originally concerning the issue of abolition, became prominent again in the 1920s, when Brazil was debating its immigration policy. Those in favor of a larger influx were also agreed on the absolute necessity of recruiting even agricultural laborers from Europe (Skidmore, 1974, pp. 141, 196). Of the counter statements, the most influential was Gilberto Freyre's work (1933), later translated as *The Masters and the Slaves* (1946). Not only had generations of miscegenation, he maintained, not done the irreparable damage charged to it, but it was Brazil's immense asset. He told Brazilians that they could be proud of their uniquely mixed tropical civilization; and some, especially the many *mestiços* rising in social status, were happy to accept his advice.

Brazil has been widely cited by sociologists in the United States as a model of racial harmony and justice; and in 1951 Brazil's Ministry of Foreign Affairs published—in English—*An Essay on Race Amalgamation* (Gordon, 1951), with a foreword by Freyre in which he cited his country as "of greater importance day by day as an experiment and perhaps as an example to be followed." His suggestion was accepted by UNESCO, which sponsored a large-scale study of Brazilian race relations (cf. Bastide, 1957). The results were not quite what its sponsors anticipated. One of those engaged in the project was the Brazilian sociologist Florestan Fernandes, whose study on *The Negro in Brazilian Society* (1969) wrote finis to the image of racial equality. In the concluding chapter of his study, Thomas Skidmore (1974, p. 218) held that in the 1970s Brazilians were still living with the intellectual legacy of the earlier compromise with racism. "They are still implicit believers in a whiter Brazil, even though it may no longer be respectable to say so" (see also Sanders, 1981).

REFERENCES: Roger Bastide, "Race Relations in Brazil," *International Social Science Bulletin*, 9 (1957), 495-512. José Alberto Magno de Carvalho, "Regional Trends in Fertility and Mortality in Brazil," *Population Studies*, 28 (1974), 401-421. Florestan Fernandes, *The Negro in Brazilian Society* (New York: Columbia University Press, 1969). Gilberto Freyre, *The Masters and the Slaves: A Study in the Development of Brazilian Civilization* (4th ed.; New York: Knopf, 1946). Eugene Gordon, *An Essay on Race Amalgamation* (Rio de Janeiro: Cultural Division, Ministry of Foreign Relations, 1951). Bertram Hutchinson, "Fertility, Social Mobility, and Urban Migration in Brazil," *Population Studies*, 14 (1961), 182-189; "Colour, Social Status and Fertility in Brazil," *América Latina*, 8 (October-December, 1964), 3-25. Joseph A. Kahl, *The Measurement of Modernism—A Study of Values in Brazil and Mexico* (Austin: University of Texas Press, 1968). Elizabeth Anne Kuznesof, "Brazilian Urban History: An Evaluation," *Latin American Research Review*, 17 (1982), 263-275. José Loureiro Fernandes, "The Xetá—A Dying People in Brazil," *Bulletin of the International Committee on Urgent Anthropological and Ethnological Research*, no. 2 (1959), 22-26. Norman Macrae, "Oh, Brazil: A Survey," *Economist* (August 4, 1979). Peter McDonough and Amaury De-Souza, *The Politics of Population in Brazil: Elite Ambivalence and Public Demand* (Austin: University of Texas Press, 1981). Thomas W. Merrick and Douglas H. Graham, *Population and Economic Development in Brazil: 1800 to the Present* (Baltimore: Johns Hopkins University Press, 1979). Carmen A. Miró, "The Population of Latin America," *Demography*, 1 (1964), 15-41. Morvan de Mello Moreira, Léa Melo da Silva, and Robert McLaughlin, "Brazil," Population Council, *Country Profiles* (New York, 1978). Richard Morse, "The Development of Urban Systems in the Americas in the Nineteenth Century," *Journal of Interamerican Studies and World Affairs*, 17 (1975), 4-26. Giorgio Mortara, "The Development and Structure of Brazil's Population," *Population Studies*, 8 (1954), 121-139. James W. Rowe, "A Note on Brazil," American Universities Field Staff, *Reports*, East Coast South America Ser., vol. 13, no. 5 (1967). Patricia M. Rowe, "Brazil," U.S. Bureau of the Census, *Country Demographic Profiles*, ISP-DP-19 (Washington, D.C., 1981). Thomas G. Sanders, "Human Rights and Political Process in Brazil," American Universities Field Staff, *Reports*, South America, no. 11 (1980); "Racial Discrimination and Black Consciousness in Brazil," American Universities Field Staff, *Reports*, South America, no. 42 (1981). Thomas E. Skidmore, *Black into White: Race and Nationality in Brazilian Thought* (New York: Oxford University Press, 1974). T. Lynn Smith, *Brazil: People and Institutions* (4th ed.; Baton Rouge: Louisiana State University Press, 1972); *Brazilian Society* (Albuquerque: University of New Mexico Press, 1974). Julian H. Steward, "The Native Population of South America," in Steward, ed., *Handbook of South American Indians* (Washington, D.C.: U.S. Bureau of American Ethnology, 1949).

Brazil: Demographic Institutions

The Brazilian Association for Population Studies, established in 1977 with funding by the Ford and Rockefeller Foundations, has been directed by João †Lyra Madeira as president. Its main purpose is to encourage interdisciplinary contacts between demographers and other social scientists in Brazil. Address: Associação Brasileira de Estudos Populacionais, Caixa Postal 2245, ZC-100, 20,000 Rio de Janeiro, R.J.

The Society for Family Welfare in Brazil (BEMFAM), a private philanthropic organization established in 1965, has indicated its interest in doing research on many aspects of population and its effect on the society. Apparently its main activity relates to a training and information program on family planning. Address: Sociedade Civil Bem-Estar Familiar no Brasil, Rua das Laranejiras no. 308, Rio de Janeiro, R.J. See also *Brazil.

UNIVERSITY AND OTHER RESEARCH INSTITUTES

The Brazilian Center for Analysis and Planning (CEBRAP), a private agency established in 1969, was in 1980 under the direction of C. P. Ferreira de Camargo, president. Its population program covers both formal and social demography with a concentration on Brazil. Its papers are published in *Estudos de População,* of which five had appeared by 1980. Address: Centro Brasileiro de Analise e Planejamento, Alameda Campinas 463, 01404 São Paulo, S.P.

The Latin American Center of Social Science Research (CLAPCS), established in 1957, studies such social-cultural issues as social mobility, income distribution, ethnic composition, fertility, birth control, and sterilization. It has conducted studies in a number of South and Central American countries. Address: Centro Latino-Americano de Pesquisas em Ciências Sociais, Praia de Botafogo no. 184, B-205, Caixa Postal 9012, Rio de Janeiro, R.J.

The Bank of Northeast Brazil established in 1971 a Study Group in Demography and Urbanization (GEDUR) of which Hélio Augusto de Moura was director of research in 1980. Its main concern has been to analyze the relation between demographic and economic variables as a guide to planning and policy. Address: Grupo de Estudos de Demografia e Urbanização, Banco do Nordeste do Brasil S/A, Rua Larga do Rosario 245, 50,000 Recife, Pernambuco.

The federal Ministry of the Interior in 1974 established a Division of Demographic Studies (SUDENE), which in 1980 was under the direction of Edilberto Xavier de Albuquerque. Its purpose is to provide information on the population and labor market of northeast Brazil as a base for instituting social-economic policies. Address: Superintendencia do Desenvolvimento do Nordeste, Avenida Professor Moraes Rego, Sala 827, Cidade Universitaria, 50,000 Recife, Pernambuco.

The public University of Brasília has in its Department of Social Sciences a Central Institute of Human Sciences, which in 1980 was headed by G. A. Soares. Its teaching and research include population factors, particularly as these relate to economic development and government policy. Address: Departamento de Ciências Sociais, Universidade de Brasília, Campus Universitario-Asa Norte, 70,000 Brasília.

At the public University of São Paulo there was established in 1964 a Center of Rural and Urban Studies, of which Eva Alterman Blay was president in 1980. Its analyses of Brazil and especially the local region include population variables. Address: Centro de Estudos Rurais e Urbanos, Universidade de São Paulo, Rua Maria Antonia 294, São Paulo, S.P.

The private University of the Vale do Rio dos Sinos has had since 1970 a Center for Documentation and Research on Economic Development, Population, and the Family. Under the direction of Pedro Calderan †Beltrão, it has conducted research on such particular aspects of Brazil's population as spatial distribution and the growth of squatter settlements in the Rio Grande do Sul state. Address: Centro de Documentação e Pesquisas—Desenvolvimento, População e Familia, Universidade do Vale do Rio dos Sinos, Caixa Postal 275, 93,000 São Leopoldo, R.S.

The Federal University of Minas Gerais established in 1968 a Center for Regional Development and Planning (CEDEPLAR), which was under the direction of Clélio Campolina Diniz, later succeeded by José Alberto Magno de Carvalho. It offers a master's program in economics with concentrations in economic demography, urban and regional economics, or economic theory, as well as conducting research in these areas. Address: Centro de Desenvolvimento e Planejamento Regional, Universidade Federal de Minas Gerais, Rua Curitiba 832, 30,000 Belo Horizonte, M.G.

GOVERNMENT STATISTICAL BUREAUS

The Brazilian Institute of Geography and Statistics (IBGE) is the government agency responsible for conducting the country's censuses, the most recent of which was 1980. It issues the journal *Boletim Demográfico*, a statistical yearbook, a quarterly statistical bulletin, an annual national household survey, an irregular summary of civil registrations, and an annual *Statistical Summary*, the last in English as well as Portuguese. Address: Fundação Instituto Brasileiro de Geografia e Estatística, Avenida Franklin Roosevelt 166, 20,000 Rio de Janeiro, R.J.

In 1967 IBGE established a Department of Population Studies, subsequently called the Department of Population and Social Statistics. Under the direction of Nelson do Valle Silva, it has analyzed all aspects of Brazil's population, reporting some of the findings in its *Revista Brasileira de Estatística*. Address: Departamento de Estatística de População e Sociais, Fundação Instituto Brasileiro de Geografia e Estatística, Rua Visc. Niteroi 1246, Rio de Janeiro, R.J.

The government Secretariat of the Economy and Planning established in its Department of Statistics a unit to analyze national data and construct population projections as an adjunct to economic plans. Address: Coordinadoria de Análise de Dados, Departamento de Estatística, Secretaria de Economia e Planejamento, Avenida Cásper Líbero no. 464, 0100 São Paulo, S.P.

bride and **bridegroom,** the woman and the man, respectively, taking part in a wedding ceremony. Particularly with respect to the woman, the designation is used for some period before and after the marriage. In vital statistics the words are sometimes used to refer to those married during a particular year, as in "the brides of 1980."

Brown v. *Board of Education of Topeka*, 347 U.S. 483 (1954); 349 U.S. 294 (1955), cases before the U.S. Supreme Court, overruled the "separate but equal" doctrine stated in *Plessy* v. *Ferguson*. In 1955 the court ordered that desegregation proceed "with all deliberate speed," leaving it to federal district courts to implement this ruling. In those courts the interpretation was extended to include "de facto segregation"—that is, a preponderance of one race brought about not as a matter of policy but as a reflection of residential patterns. See also *desegregation; *segregation.

Brunei: The government's Statistics Section publishes a biennial *Statistical Yearbook* that includes population data. Address: Economic Planning Unit, State Secretariat, Bandar Seri Begawan.

Buddhism derives from "the Buddha," or "the Enlightened One," the designation given to the Indian sage Siddhartha Gautama (c. 563-483 B.C.). The religion he founded evolved into many sects roughly grouped into three main branches— Hinayana (Lesser Vehicle) or Theravada (Doctrine of the Elders) in Ceylon, Burma, and Southeast Asia; Mahayana (Great Vehicle) in China, Korea, and Japan; and in Tibet a combination of these with the indestructible essence, or Vajrayana (Diamond Vehicle). Excluding China, where the status of any religion is indeterminate, adherents number well over 150 million, though the numerous marginal sects whose members can be included or not make any total highly dependent on how the boundary is set.

   In Tibet Buddhism was fully established under Mongol protection in the thirteenth century; and for the six centuries until 1959, when Communist China annexed it, the country was the prototypical Buddhist society (see Michael, 1982). The many sects and subsects cooperated through an allocation of functions, with monk-bureaucrats controlling both religious and secular administration. Several hundred of them ran the country, while others managed the monasteries and their estates, taught classes, or performed religious services. For the recent past the proportion of monks has been estimated as high as 40 percent of the adult male population, but this figure probably reflected their greater visibility in Lhasa, where they were concentrated. Over the whole country perhaps one man in three became a monk, and of women a far smaller proportion became nuns. Though Buddha's ethical teaching is sometimes summed up in his advocacy of a "middle path" between ascetic self-castigation and sensual indulgence, in fact most of this extraordinarily high percentage were celibates. Tibet may have been the world's one culture in which religious *celibacy significantly reduced fertility—though the data are too poor to prove the case.

As a consequence of the quintessential importance of reincarnation, Buddhism has shown an indifference unique among the world's major religions to such basic worldly institutions as the family. No religious ritual marks a marriage or a birth; sex is a fact of nature, controlled by laws against "sexual misconduct," which has not included premarital relations, for instance. According to a survey by Bryce Ryan (1954), attitudes toward birth control in Ceylon (now Sri Lanka) were not based on doctrine but were associated rather with the level of education: none of the best educated monks or priests found in Buddhism any opposition to contraception, but nine-tenths of the least educated held that preventing a birth is tantamount to murder.

In the Mahayana school the originally austere ethical doctrine evolved into what could be termed a polytheistic religion with a complex metaphysical elaboration; and this version was carried north to China and then, together with other elements of Chinese culture, to Korea and Japan. Japanese civilization in particular is closely linked to Buddhism, which had a decisive effect on its painting, sculpture, architecture, music, and drama. But whether it significantly influenced behavioral patterns related to population is doubtful; the moral guidance that its adherents derived from the religion was thin, for the major concern of Buddhist seers was not the problem of good and evil but rather the nature of being. Moreover, in religion as in other matters, the Japanese have shown a genius for reconciling opposites into a paradoxical compendium that uniquely suits them.

REFERENCES: Franz Michael, *Rule by Incarnation: Tibetan Buddhism and Its Impact on Society and State* (Boulder, Colo.: Westview Press, 1982). Bryce Ryan, "Hinayana Buddhism and Family Planning in Ceylon," in Milbank Memorial Fund, *The Interrelations of Demographic, Economic and Social Problems in Selected Underdeveloped Areas* (New York, 1954). Ninian Smart, "Buddhism," in *Encyclopedia of Philosophy*, 1, 416-420.

buffer state, a small independent country situated between two larger and potentially hostile ones, which might reduce the friction between them. The classic instance is Belgium, which was created in the post-Napoleonic settlement in order to separate France and Germany. Other examples have been Afghanistan between British India and Tsarist Russia; Nepal between India and China; Thailand between the colonies of Britain and France.

Bulgaria: Demographic Institutions

The Institute of Sociology at the Bulgarian Academy of Sciences conducts research on all aspects of the country's society, including population, and publishes some of the results in its journal, *Sotsiologicheski Problemi*. Address: 39 Blvd. Vitosha, Sofia 21.

The government's Central Statistical Office conducts the country's censuses. It publishes a statistical yearbook, a shorter statistical reference book, an annual bulletin of principal demographic indices, an annual review of public health, and the serial *Statistika*. Address: Tsentralno Statistichesko Upravlenie, Ministerskiya Suvet, 10 September 6th Street, Sofia.

The government's Information Bureau publishes annually a summary of all population data, *Naselenie*, in Bulgarian with table titles also in Russian. Address: Komitet po Edinna Sistema za Sotsialna Informatsiya, Ministerskiya Suvet, 2 Pl. Volov Street, Sofia.

Burma: The government's Central Statistical Organization conducts the country's censuses. It publishes a *Statistical Yearbook* that includes population data. Address: New Secretariat, Strand Road, Rangoon.

Burundi: Demographic Institutions

The Central Census Bureau is responsible for conducting the country's censuses, the last of which was in 1979. Address: Bureau Central de Recensement, Ministère de l'Intérieur, Bujumbura.

The Department of Statistical Research publishes an *Annuaire Statistique* that includes population data. Address: Département des Études Statistiques, Ministère du Plan, Boîte Postale 1156, Bujumbura.

business cycle, in a modern society the periodic fluctuation in aggregate economic activity, marked by successive stages of expansion, downturn, contraction, and upturn. Generally each full cycle lasts from two to ten years. The intensity of the contraction is distinguished, not very precisely, by the alternative labels of "recession" and "depression." Manifestly there is an interaction between business cycles and population trends, but not one that can be exactly demarcated. According to a thesis developed by Brinley †Thomas (1973), migration from Britain to the United States was largely regulated by the periodic demand for labor. During the depression of the 1930s, marriage and fertility rates in Western countries declined, to rise again during the postwar recovery in the *baby boom. In a theory developed most fully by Richard †Easterlin (1961, 1966, 1968), periodic fluctuations in fertility and thus in the size of the labor force are linked to business activity. See also *economics.

REFERENCES: Richard A. Easterlin, "The American Baby Boom in Historical Perspective" and "Economic-Demographic Interactions and Long Swings in Economic Growth," *American Economic Review*, 51 (1961), 869-911 and 56 (1966), 1063–1104; *Birth and Fortune: The Impact of Numbers on Personal Welfare* (New York: Basic Books, 1980). Simon Kuznets, *Capital in the American Economy: Its Formation and Financing*, National Bureau of Economic Research, Studies in Capital Formation and Financing, no. 9 (Princeton, N.J.: Princeton University Press, 1961). Joseph A. Schumpeter, *Business Cycles: A Theoretical, Historical, and Statistical Analysis of the Capitalist Process*, 2 vols. (New York: McGraw-Hill, 1939). Brinley Thomas, *Migration and Economic Growth: A Study of Great Britain and the Atlantic Economy* (2nd ed.; London: Cambridge University Press, 1973). Dorothy Swaine Thomas, *Social Aspects of the Business Cycle* (New York: Dutton, 1925).

C

calendar method of contraception means a periodic abstinence from coitus following a calculation of the woman's days of fecundity based on the calendar. The *rhythm method is a considerably more effective control if it follows changes in the woman's *basal body temperature.

callback, in the jargon of the U.S. Bureau of the Census, an enumerator's second or subsequent visit to a residence where no one was found at home. The number of callbacks, which prolong the enumeration and increase the cost, rose as the proportion increased of two-person households with both working away from home during the day.

Calvinism, the branch of Protestantism derived from the French theologian John Calvin (1509-64), whose main doctrines are to be found in the several thoroughly revised editions of his *Institutes of the Christian Religion.* According to his teaching, knowledge of God can be sought only through knowledge of oneself, by nourishing one's subjective awareness of the divine will. However, because of the inborn human resistance to His commands, an attempt to know God can never be fully realized; and the refusal to obey His commands, rooted in man's pride and self-love, spreads corruption through the whole of life. Those destined to be saved will receive on this earth a mere foretaste of the fruits due them at the final resurrection, but this foretaste will "allure us to the desire of heavenly benefits" (Wallace, 1959).

   In the first important study in the sociology of religion, *The Protestant Ethic and the Spirit of Capitalism*, Max †Weber undertook to show how this conception of the supreme being affected the believers' secular behavior. Since God is defined as ultimately unknowable and transcendental, no elaborate ritual evolved in Calvinism as a way of seeking His intervention. The link drawn between earthly prosperity and the promise of heaven made the "foretaste" doubly attractive, both for itself and as a sign of later redemption. Thus, their hope of resurrection encouraged men to a self-denying pursuit of day-to-day economic activities. As one Calvinist commentator pointed out, Weber's main example of a "Calvinist," Benjamin Franklin, was the deist son of a Quaker; and, more generally, he defined the ideal type of Calvinists so broadly that there was only a slight overlap with those who called themselves followers of Calvin. The hypothesized psychological link between hope for salvation and worldly asceticism, supported by a macroscopic correlation, in fact suggested that the Reformation brought about not only a "spirit of capitalism" but the rationalization of life altogether (Graham, 1971).

How Calvinist teachings affect behavioral patterns more directly related to population is difficult to pin down. Except for Augustinian Catholicism (from which Calvinism partly derived), probably no other world religion has emphasized sin so much or related it so closely to sexuality. The disease of concupiscence, man's "natural viciousness," induces him to corrupt all the many good things with which God filled the world. Within every man there is a struggle between spirit and flesh, and the flesh must be mortified if man would obey God's command. According to the ordinance that Calvin drew up for Geneva, a marriage, made "in the name of God" even if by secular authority, should always be without compulsion, between persons who come together of their own free will. Calvin's abomination of adultery was so great that he condemned even the double standard; either husband or wife, if innocent, could petition for divorce from an adulterer, who was not permitted to remarry. That contraception had no place in the family was obvious; it was hardly necessary to voice its illicit status.

Of all the places in the modern West strongly influenced by Calvinism, perhaps the prototype is the Netherlands. A Reformed pastor, Abraham Kuyper, constructed a political party based on Calvinist principles, which in a Christian coalition with a Catholic party governed the country with only short interruptions from the 1880s to the Second World War. The noble defense of democratic principles associated with Protestantism was spelled out in a full extension of suffrage, the easier access of lower classes to education, and other measures. But for several decades the hostility to birth control and the great emphasis on the family as a breeding unit made Holland a demographic anomaly—the country in Northwest Europe with the highest population density, one of the lowest death rates, and the highest fertility.

REFERENCES: W. Fred Graham, *The Constructive Revolutionary: John Calvin and His Socio-economic Impact* (Richmond, Va.: John Knox Press, 1971). Ronald S. Wallace, *Calvin's Doctrine of the Christian Life* (Edinburgh: Oliver and Boyd, 1959). Nicholas Wolterstorff, "Calvin, John," in *Encyclopedia of Philosophy*, 2, 7-9.

Cameroon: Demographic Institutions

The Institute for Demographic Training and Research (Institut de Formation et de Recherche Démographiques, or IFORD), Yaoundé, is described under *United Nations.

The Bureau of Statistics and Public Accounting in the Ministry of Economic Affairs and Planning collects and publishes official statistics. It includes an Office of Research, Projections and Forecasts, and a Central Bureau of the Census (headed in 1980 by Rose-Alice Njeck), which is responsible for conducting the country's censuses, the most recent of which was in 1976. Address: Direction de la Statistique et de la Comptabilité Nationale, Service des Études, des Projections et des Perspectives, and Bureau Central du Recensement, Ministère de l'Économie et du Plan, Boîte Postale 660, Yaoundé.

The Office of Health and Demographic Statistics in the Ministry of Public Health conducts health surveys of the country and publishes national health statistics. In 1980 it was headed by Jean Joel Keuzeta. Address: Service des Statistiques Sanitaires et Démographiques, Ministère de la Santé, Yaoundé.

Canada had an estimated population in mid-1984 of just over 25 million. In the 112 years since 1871, the first census after Confederation, the population grew from about 3.7 million, increasing by annual rates of about 4 percent when both fertility and immigration rates were high, or as low as 1 percent when families were small and few entered the country. As in most Western countries, the *population pyramid, broadly based a century ago, now reflects the recent drop in fertility and the increasing proportion at advanced ages.

Canada's area of 3.8 million square miles is some 200,000 more than that of the United States, but most of this vast expanse is virtually uninhabited. Almost all Canadians live within a few hundred miles of the American border, and the vast distances separating thinly populated regions have encouraged the persistence of local patriotisms. Ontario wanted the Confederation arranged in 1867, but the other provinces were at best unenthusiastic. All four Maritime Provinces were reluctant to join: New Brunswick voted against federation and was induced to reverse its stand by skillful politicking and money; in Nova Scotia a vote was avoided; Prince Edward Island came in only in 1873, when its financial straits made union more attractive; and Newfoundland postponed its assent until 1949 and then joined also for the same reason. Of the francophone delegates, twenty-two voted against Confederation, and the twenty-seven who voted for it were motivated to give up some of their independence at least partly by their fear of being annexed to the United States. The history of the western provinces, finally, has been decisively shaped by their opposition to Ontario's economic and political domination. As the Canadian historian Arthur †Lower (1946, p. 348) put it, "The Dominion of Canada was to reach the Pacific without the inner concept *Canada* having been born."

The English and French components in particular have maintained their more or less distinct separate cultures. With almost no immigration, the francophone population grew from the approximately 65,000 persons settled in Quebec by 1765 to about 4.3 million in the early 1950s, when Alfred †Sauvy (1970) wrote his *Théorie Générale de la Population*. With a perceptible note of envy, he commented that "if the population of France had multiplied in the same proportion, it would today be much larger than that of the entire world" (vol. 1, pp. 41-42). French Canadians, most of whom were either farmers or low-level urban workers, were dominated by a Catholic church well known for its orthodoxy.

They pursued what their nationalist leaders called "la revanche des berceaux": by filling their cradles with numerous progeny, they would avenge the British victory and eventually become a majority of the Canadian electorate. But British Canada grew faster by immigration; virtually all the immigrants to the country not only went to anglophone regions but, at least until recently, assimilated almost wholly to the anglophone sector (Petersen, 1955; Hawkins, 1972; Beaujot, 1978; Beaujot and McQuillan, 1982).

Traditionally Canada's immigration policy was set according to short-term manpower requirements, with little consideration given to long-term demographic, social, and cultural consequences. Most immigrants came from Europe, especially from Britain. In 1973 the government appointed a task force to undertake a "Canadian Immigration and Population Study," and in 1975 it published a four-volume "Green Paper"—that is, a basis for public discussion rather than a "White Paper," or a statement of government policy (Hawkins, 1975; Richmond, 1975). The prior emphases on filling gaps in the work force and facilitating family reunions were continued, but under a new law immigrants were admitted from whatever country without discrimination. The change in policy was similar to that brought about in the United States by the Immigration and Nationality Act of 1952, and in both countries the most important effect was to increase substantially the proportion of newcomers from Asia and other less developed areas (cf. Boyd, 1976).

For two centuries the dominant concern of French Canadians had been group survival, and to the end of preserving their language and religion they sacrificed many of the advantages associated with modernization. From 1945 on, however, the years they spent in school increased notably, the church's influence on secular matters was cut, the anomalously high fertility fell, and intellectuals fashioned a cosmopolitan culture whose quality matched or sometimes surpassed that of anglophone Canada (cf. Keyfitz, 1963). As one element of this transformation, especially significant in this context, the University of Montreal established a department of demography that has produced studies of Canada's population and ethnic structure in greater quantity and often of higher quality than all the rest of the universities and research institutes together (see, e.g., Lebel-Péron and Péron, 1979). In spite of Quebec's cultural renaissance, the use of French seemingly continued to decline (e.g., Castonguay, 1982; Lachapelle and Henripin, 1982; Maheu, 1978), and English Canadians continued to dominate the upper levels of Quebec's commercial and industrial firms. The frustration generated by this contrast between rising ability and lagging opportunity was undoubtedly heightened by the extraordinarily wide attention given to John Porter's analysis of social class and power in Canada, *The Vertical Mosaic* (1965), which pictured a society whose class (and thus ethnic) relations were all but frozen (but see also Rich, 1976). French-English antagonisms were officially recognized in a two-volume *Report* of the Royal Commission on Bilingualism and Biculturalism (1967-68). Following the lead given in that government document, Canada set a policy requiring most upper civil servants throughout the country to be (or become) bilingual. In Quebec, on the contrary, a law was passed setting French as the province's dominant (and, so it seemed, eventually only) language of work and education. The ruling was applied in ways both ridiculous and damaging to the province's economy: the insistence that air traffic controllers use French almost closed down Quebec's airport; and some commercial firms, both small and large, moved out of the province, taking capital and jobs with them. The Parti Québécois, which had won the provincial election in 1976, lost the subsequent referendum to decide whether Quebec should become an independent country.

Like the concern over race in the United States, the heightened awareness of Canadian-*Canadien* differences stimulated other groups in the society to seek similar kinds of recognition. In both countries native Indians have been the subject of many analyses and government reports (e.g., Valentine, 1980). One of Canada's important ethnic groups is the sizable Ukrainian community, which started to demand some of the privileges being given to francophones (cf. Isajiw, 1976). Canada's ethnic statistics are far superior to those of the United States; the census has included a question on religious affiliation, and immigrants are classified by both nationality and religion (see also *Canada: Demographic Institutions). Thus, for example, one can separate the effects of Catholicism and francophone nationalism in an analysis of fertility trends (e.g., Krótki and Lapierre, 1968), and the insoluble puzzle of which "Russian" immigrants to the United States were Jews has no counterpart in Canada.

Like most Western countries, Canada has liberalized earlier restrictions related to population and also extended its welfare program to support the family (e.g., Kantner et al., 1974). Family allowances, initiated in 1946, were altered several times over the following decades; according to the schedule set in 1973, in most provinces parents have received C$20 per month for each child through age 17. The law prohibiting the provision of contraceptive information or services, in effect since 1882, was repealed in 1970. Two years later the Health and Welfare Department established a family-planning division, which has coordinated federal efforts to provide information and train family-planning and health staff. Implementation of the program is a responsibility of the provinces, which have varied considerably in their policy. In theory contraceptives are free to "persons in need" and to others through the federal government's medical insurance, but in fact their availability depends on whether family planning has been incorporated as part of public clinics and hospitals. Abortions were prohibited until 1969, when a new law permitted them only in hospitals and only if at least two of a three-physician committee certified that continuation of the pregnancy would probably endanger the woman's life or health. By 1980 only 30 percent of all public general hospitals had established such abortion committees, and of those 19 percent reported no abortions during that year. In apparent disregard of federal legislation, Quebec funded abortions performed in several nonhospital clinics (Tietze, 1983, p. 9).

Canada's population, in sum, is interesting for a number of reasons. The trends in fertility and mortality have been similar to those in other Western countries, and the ups and downs of immigration followed patterns noted in other major receiving countries; but these processes have been recorded in statistics often more detailed than elsewhere. The one major lack, and a very important one, is that emigrants from Canada are not accurately counted, and the effect of immigration on population growth and structure, therefore, cannot be adequately appraised until after each census. Canada also has a particularly rich fund of old parish records, and work there in historical demography is probably more significant than in any other country outside Europe. French-English hostility, finally, has been linked for several centuries to comparative rates of growth, and few areas of the world provide so rich a fund of material to analyze the country's demographic competition.

REFERENCES: Roderic P. Beaujot, "Canada's Population: Growth and Dualism," *Population Bulletin*, 33 (April, 1978), 1-47. Beaujot and Kevin McQuillan, *Growth and Dualism: The Demographic Development of Canadian Society* (Toronto: Gage Publishing, Ltd., 1982). Monica Boyd, "Immigration Policies and Trends: A Comparison of Canada and the United States," *Demography*, 13 (1976), 83-104. Charles Castonguay, "The Decline of French as Home Language in the Quebec and Acadian Diaspora of Canada and the United States," in Raymond Breton and Pierre Savard, eds., *The Quebec and Acadian Diaspora in North America* (Toronto: Multicultural History Society of Ontario, 1982). Freda Hawkins, *Canada and Immigration: Public Policy and Public Concern* (Montreal: McGill-Queen's University Press, 1972); "Canada's Green Paper on Immigration Policy," *International Migration Review*, 9 (1975), 237-249. Wsevolod W. Isajiw, ed., *Ukrainians in American and Canadian Society* (Jersey City, N.J.: M. P. Kots Publishing, 1976). Andrew Kantner, Wendy Dobson, and Hervé Gauthier, "Canada," Population Council, *Country Profiles* (New York, 1974). Nathan Keyfitz, "Canadians and Canadiens," *Queen's Quarterly*, 70 (1963), 163-182. Karol J. Krótki and Évelyne Lapierre, "La Fécondité au Canada selon la Religion, l'Origine Ethnique, et l'État Matrimonial," *Population*, 23 (1968), 815-834. Réjean Lachapelle and Jacques Henripin, *The Demolinguistic Situation in Canada: Past Trends and Future Prospects* (Montreal: Institute for Research on Public Policy, 1982). Suzanne Lebel-Péron and Yves Péron, "Bibliographie sur la Démographie Récente des Groupes Ethno-linguistiques au Canada," Département de Démographie, Université de Montréal, *Canadian Ethnic Studies* (1979). Arthur R. M. Lower, *Colony to Nation: A History of Canada* (Toronto: Longmans, Green, 1946). Robert Maheu, "Les Transferts Linguistiques au Québec entre 1975 et 1977," *Cahiers Québécois de Démographie*, vol. 7, Special no. 3 (1978). William Petersen, *Planned Migration: The Social Determinants of the Dutch-Canadian Movement* (Berkeley: University of California Press, 1955). John Porter, *The Vertical Mosaic: An Analysis of Social Class and Power in Canada* (Toronto: University of Toronto Press, 1965). Harvey Rich, "The Vertical Mosaic Revisited: Toward a Macrosociology of Canada," *Journal of Canadian Studies*, 11 (1976), 14-31. Anthony H. Richmond, "The Green Paper—Reflections on the Canadian Immigration and Population Study," *Canadian Ethnic Studies*, 7 (1975), 5-21. Alfred Sauvy, *General Theory of Population* (New York: Basic Books, 1970). Christopher Tietze, *Induced Abortion: A World Review, 1983* (New York: Population Council, 1983). Victor F. Valentine, "Native Peoples and Canadian Society," in Raymond Breton, Jeffrey G. Reitz, and Valentine, eds., *Cultural Boundaries and the Cohesion of Canada* (Montreal: Institute for Research on Public Policy, 1980).

Canada: Demographic Institutions

There are two professional societies of demographers. The English-speaking Federation of Canadian Demographers has about 120 members. The francophone Association des Démographes du Québec, with about 130 members, has published since 1971 its *Cahiers Québécois de Démographie*. In 1977 a joint organization was established to foster relations between the two, the Federation of Canadian Demographers/Fédération Canadienne de Démographie, which organizes a joint conference every three years. Some francophone Canadians are also active in the *Association Internationale des Démographes de Langue Française (AIDELF), which is briefly discussed in its own entry.

The Canadian International Development Agency (CIDA), the federal bureau through which aid is distributed to less developed countries, is similar in its functions to the U.S. Agency for International Development (AID). In 1970 CIDA began granting funds to population programs, with Charles Nobbe supervising the usually modest allocations mostly through international agencies. It has also funded population programs in Botswana, Gambia, Zambia, India, and Sri Lanka under the supervision of the Family Planning Federation of Canada. Of the CIDA budget, 5 percent is allocated to research, particularly on how the expenditure of the remaining 95 percent is related to the agency's goals. One of those formerly active in this research was Walter †Mertens. Address: 112 Bank Street, Ottawa K1A OG4.

UNIVERSITY AND OTHER RESEARCH INSTITUTES

The Canadian Council on Urban and Regional Research, a private organization established in 1962, was headed in 1980 by Meyer Brownstone, president. Its research is focused on urbanization and city and regional planning, and some of the results appear in its *Urban Forum/Colloque Urbain*. Address: 251 Laurier Avenue West, Ottawa K1P 5J6.

The Groupe de Recherche sur la Famille Québécoise, of which S. Monast was secretary-treasurer in 1980, does research and documentation on the family in Quebec. Address: Chartierville-Compte-Compton, Quebec.

The Institut National de la Recherche Scientifique—Urbanisation, a public organization founded in 1970, was directed in 1980 by J.-C. Thibodeau. Its studies of urbanization have included analyses of migration and the regional development around Montreal. Address: 3465 rue Duroder, Montreal H2X 2C6.

The Institute for Research on Public Policy, a private organization funded by the federal and provincial governments and by private donations, began its operations in 1975 with a large-scale study of Canada's population, in which the work of Leroy †Stone and Jacques †Henripin was supported. In 1980 its research program was focused on six main topics, one of which was ethnic and cultural diversity. It has several offices throughout Canada, with the main research office at 60 Queen Street, Ottawa K1P 5Y7.

The International Development Research Center/Centre de Recherches pour le Développement International (CRDI/IDRC) is a publicly supported institute headed in 1980 by W. D. Hopper, president. It has published monographs on less developed countries throughout the world, including bibliographic essays on rural development in Latin America, low-cost sanitation technology, Canadian development assistance, rural health care and the training of health manpower, and related topics. Address: 60 Queen Street, P.O. Box 8500, Ottawa K1G 3H9.

The Social Science Federation of Canada/Fédération Canadienne des Sciences Sociales, a private foundation established in 1940, was headed in 1980 by J. E. Trent, executive director. It promotes research in all the social disciplines, including demography and statistics. Address: 151 Slater Street, Ottawa K1P 5H3.

The University of Alberta established in 1966 a Population Research Laboratory in its sociology department. Parameswara Krishnan, its director in the mid-1970s, was succeeded by L. W. Kennedy. Its research has concentrated on demographic topics related to Alberta or Edmonton, and some of the findings have been published in its journal, *Canadian Studies in Population*. Address: Edmonton, Alberta T6G 2H4.

In the geography department of the same institution, the *International Geographical Union established in 1976 a Commission on Population Geography under the chairmanship of Leszek A. †Kosiński. In 1980 the chairmanship was shifted to John I. Clarke at the University of Durham, England.

The University of British Columbia established in 1972 a Data Library under the direction in 1980 of L. G. Ruus. It is a storage center of documentation, including especially computer tapes, pertaining to all the social disciplines. Address: 2075 Wesbrook Place, Vancouver, B.C. V6T 1W5.

Brock University has an Institute of Urban and Environmental Studies, of which W. A. Matheson was acting director in 1979. It has studied, for example, migration in relation to regional development in Canada and Ecuador. Address: St. Catherines, Ontario L2S 3A1.

Carleton University has set up a Social Science Data Archives, of which H. Barshtyn was director in 1980. It both collects documentation on surveys and public opinion polls and uses its data to conduct research. Address: Department of Sociology and Anthropology, Colonel By Drive, Ottawa K1S 5B6.

At Laval University there is a Centre International de Recherche sur le Bilinguisme/International Center for Research on Bilingualism, of which J. G. Savard was director in 1980. Its research on sociolinguistics in Canada necessarily overlaps with the demography of ethnicity. Address: Grand Séminaire 60 sud, Ste-Foy, Quebec G1K 7P4.

The University of Montreal has a Department of Demography, founded in 1964 by Jacques †Henripin. In 1980 it was under the direction of Jacques †Légaré and included such promising young scholars as Hubert †Charbonneau and Colette †Carisse. Its very active staff has published more than a hundred works, mainly on French Canada but also on demographic methods and, because of the particular interests of some members, on francophone Africa. Address: Département de

Démographie, Université de Montréal, C.P. 6128, Succursale "A," Montreal, Quebec H7E 1L4.

The University of Sherbrooke established in 1970 a Center for Research in Regional Management, which in 1980 was directed by Claude Greffard. Its work on urban and regional planning and on industrial development has overlapped with several types of demographic analysis. Address: Centre de Recherches en Aménagement Régional, Université de Sherbrooke, Sherbrooke, Quebec J1K 2Rl.

The University of Toronto has a Center for Urban and Community Studies, of which L. A. Bourne was director in 1980. Its research has been on Canada's urban system and on factors related to housing in cities. Address: 150 St. George Street, Toronto M5S 1A1.

The University of Western Ontario established in 1974 a Population Studies Center under the continuing direction of T. R. †Balakrishnan. Its research has related to most aspects of Canada's population, as well as to family planning in less developed countries and family demography. Address: London, Ontario N6A 5C2.

York University established in 1967 an Ethnic Research Program in its Institute for Behavioral Research. It was headed for some years by Anthony H. †Richmond, who has an established reputation in the analysis of ethnic relations; subsequently by David Gold as coordinator. The program concentrates on the study of such important issues in Canada as a comparison of immigrant groups, ethnic stratification, and French-English relations. Address: 4700 Keele Street, Downsview, Ontario M3J 1P3.

GOVERNMENT STATISTICAL BUREAUS

The Department of Manpower and Immigration collects and analyzes statistics on migration in Canada and thus helps set the number of persons admissible. It includes an Immigration and Demographic Policy Group, which publishes an annual compilation of immigration statistics. Address: Ottawa K1A 0J9.

The Department of National Health and Welfare includes a Family Planning Division through which the federal government exercises its responsibility to assure access to all Canadians who want such services. It disseminates information, helps train personnel involved in family planning, promotes research, and subsidizes programs. Address: Brooke Claxton Building, Ottawa K1A OK9.

Statistics Canada, formerly the Dominion Bureau of Statistics, compiles, analyzes, and publishes statistical data on population, commerce, and other matters, combining the functions in the United States of the Bureau of the Census, the Bureau of Labor Statistics, and the Bureau of Economic Analysis. It conducts the Canadian censuses, taken in years ending in 1 and 6, and prepares population projections and estimates of the labor force. The Demography Division, headed in 1980 by Anatole †Romaniuk, prepares postcensal and intercensal estimates, population projections, and various demographic simulations. Its research is consciously policy-oriented, and in addition to the *Canada Year Book, Vital Statistics*, and other basic statistical compilations, it has published, for example, an annual report on therapeutic abortions. Address: Ottawa K1A OT6.

cancer, a cellular tumor, is a principal cause of death in most countries. The word derives from the Greek for "crab," presumably because the sharp pain is reminiscent of its pinch. The disease was first specified when the English physician Percivall Pott (1713-85) noted the high incidence of scrotal cancer among chimney sweeps. In 1838 the German biologist Johannes Müller (1801-58) demonstrated that various types of tumors are composed of cells; and one of his students, Rudolf Virchow (1821-1902), generalized this finding into the hypothesis that all disease is ultimately a malfunctioning of cells. Early in the twentieth century several pathologists proved independently that, when cancer cells are implanted in a healthy host of the same species, it develops new cancer cells. Successively physical, chemical, and biological agents were used experimentally to produce cancers; the theory was propounded that x-rays induce cancers through mutational aberrations; according to other investigators certain enzymes linked to heredity are conducive to cancer (Braun, 1977).

Some tumors are benign—that is, localized, with a limited growth, and not dangerous to life; one common example is warts. Malignant tumors, which grow diffusely and destroy the normal tissue with which they come in contact, are classified into three categories, which make up about 95 percent of all cases occurring in adults. Carcinoma, or cancer of the epithelium (the lining of the body's internal or external surfaces, including the skin, mouth, stomach, kidney, liver, and so on), comprises about 85 percent of cancers of adults. Sarcoma, or cancer of connective tissue composed of closely packed cells embedded in a homogeneous mass (such as bone, cartilage, or muscle), comprises only about 2 percent of cancers, with the rate constant over the whole age range. Leukemia, a disease of the blood-forming organs, occurs mainly among the very young and the elderly; among adults it makes up about 8 percent of all cancers. Cancers are also classified according to their site; their presumed cause (e.g., aniline or dye-workers' cancer, smokers' cancer of the lips, throat or lungs); and their particular characteristics (e.g., soft or hard, tubular).

Research on the more than one hundred relatively common diseases associated with an anomalous cellular differentiation has suggested a wide range of etiologies: heredity, particular foods or food additives, *smoking or other life-styles, the occupational environment of certain industrial workers, and the pollution of air and water; according to the sum of such studies, living is dangerous. We are at a very early stage in the growing knowledge about what cancers are, how they act on the body, and how they can be controlled. It has been argued with some plausibility that the epidemiologic data on cancer (as well as heart diseases) are often interpreted with a political inference. If the main cause is the person's way of life, then he or she is responsible; if it is pollution or another general condition of the environment, then the blame can be shifted to society as a whole

Attribution of Cancer Deaths in the United States to Different Factors

Factor or Class of Factors	Best Estimate	Range of Acceptable Estimates
Diet	35%	10 - 70%
Tobacco	30	25 - 40
Infection	10?	1 - ?
Sex relations, pregnancy, childbirth	7	1 - 13
Occupation	4	2 - 8
Alcohol	3	2 - 4
Geophysical factors	3	2 - 4
Pollution	2	<1 - 5
Medicines and medical procedures	1	0.5 - 3
Industrial products	<1	<1 - 2
Food additives	<1	-5 - 2

Source: Doll and Peto (1981), Table 20.

(Tesh, 1981; cf. Whelan and Stare, 1976; Cullen et al., 1976; Handler et al., 1982).

A recent summary of epidemiological evidence strongly suggests that two factors, diet and tobacco, cause a minimum of one-third and more probably two-thirds of the deaths in the United States attributed to cancer (see table). Little is now known about the relation between specific foods and cancer. Of the dozen hypotheses presently regarded as most promising, one or two may turn out to be both true and important. The link to smoking, on the contrary, is well established, and in that case control of the disease is completely subject to each individual's decision. Several of the factors ascribable to society have received much attention, but pollution, industrial products, and occupational hazards impose rather small risks as carcinogens. Food additives are ranked with a token percentage of less than one, and the possibly protective effect of antioxidants and other preservatives is indicated in the range starting at -5 (Doll and Peto, 1981).

In another recent study, some of the same causes were considered not in isolation but in combination with a wide range of other factors. By analyzing the components of variation among factors related to population, income, climate, air contamination, radiation, consumption (including cigarettes, alcohol, water, milk), and ethnicity, a "best" explanatory set of four major factor pools was reduced to income, three environmental factors, four related to consumption, and four to ethnicity. Appropriately combined, these twelve accounted for between 30 and 90 percent of the observed variation, depending on the site of the cancer and the sex of the patient. Whether large-scale cross-sectional geographic analysis of mortality and its many correlates adds to our information has been challenged, but so full a study at least points to possibly useful paths for further research (Wellington et al., 1979).

One of the few surveys in a less developed country indicates that when corrected for differences in age structure the rate is more or less the same as in the United States (Edington and Maclean, 1965; cf. Mettlin and Murphy, 1981). Cancer, it would seem, is a disease of industrial society only in the sense that more people live longer in developed economies and thus reach the ages with higher incidences of cancers (cf. Campbell, 1980). In comparisons over time, changes in diagnostic practices may introduce sizable errors (Percy and Dolman, 1978; Percy et al., 1981).

Each year about a million persons in the United States are diagnosed as having cancer, and of these more than a third die from the disease. An advanced case often brings an enormous financial burden and prolonged emotional stress to the patient's family. It was estimated that in 1977 the direct and indirect costs of malignant neoplasms in the United States were $29-$35 billion, or about a tenth of the cost of all diseases (Rice and Hodgson, 1981). If the vast efforts to find a cure for cancer succeeded, these deaths would be avoided and apparently the death rate would be cut by nearly 18 percent. However, as masses of people moved into the higher ages, they would die in increasing proportion of heart diseases, for instance, and the long-term reduction in mortality would be, in all likelihood, far less than so simple a calculation would suggest (Keyfitz, 1977).

REFERENCES: Armin C. Braun, *The Study of Cancer* (Reading, Mass.: Addison-Wesley, 1977). H. Campbell, "Cancer Mortality in Europe: Site-Specific Patterns and Trends, 1955 to 1974," *World Health Statistics Quarterly*, 33 (1980), 241-280. Joseph W. Cullen, Bernard H. Fox, and R. N. Isom, eds., *Cancer: The Behavioral Dimensions* (New York: Raven Press for the National Cancer Institute, 1976). Richard Doll and Richard Peto, *The Causes of Cancer: Quantitative Estimates of Avoidable Risks of Cancer in the United States Today* (New York: Oxford University Press, 1981). G. M. Edington and C.M.U. Maclean, "A Cancer Rate Survey in Ibadan, Western Nigeria, 1960-63," *British Journal of Cancer*, 19 (1965), 471-481. Philip Handler et al., "On Some Major Human Diseases," in National Research Council, *Outlook for Science and Technology: The Next Five Years* (San Francisco: W. H. Freeman, 1982). Nathan Keyfitz, "What Difference Would It Make If Cancer Were Eradicated?" *Demography*, 14 (1977), 411-418. Curtis Mettlin and Gerald P. Murphy, eds., *Cancer among Black Populations* (New York: Alan R. Liss, 1981). Constance Percy and Alice Dolman, "Comparison of the Coding of Death Certificates Related to Cancer in Seven Countries," *Public Health Reports*, 93 (1978), 335-350; Percy, Edward Stanek, III, and Lynn Gloeckler, "Accuracy of Cancer Death Certificates and Its Effect on Cancer Mortality Statistics," *American Journal of Public Health*, 71 (1981), 242-250. Dorothy P. Rice and Thomas A. Hodgson, *Social and Economic Implications of Cancer in the United States*, U.S. National Center for Health Statistics, DHHS Publication no. (PHS) 81-1404 (Washington, D.C., 1981). Sylvia Tesh, "Disease Causality and Politics," *Journal of Health Politics, Policy and Law*, 6 (1981), 369-390. Dorothy Gaites Wellington, Eleanor J. Macdonald, and Patricia F. Wolf, *Cancer Mortality: Environmental and Ethnic Factors* (New York: Academic Press, 1979). Elizabeth M. Whelan and Fredrick J. Stare, *Panic in the Pantry: Food Facts, Fads and Fancies* (New York: Atheneum, 1976).

canvass derives from the French word meaning to sift through a canvas sheet, hence to examine thoroughly, hence to go through a district soliciting support for a particular commercial product or political candidate or, for example, health or family-planning program. A canvass thus can present the same problems concerning sampling as a *survey.

Cape Verde Islands: Demographic Institutions
The Office of Censuses and Research is responsible for conducting censuses, the last of which was in 1980. Address: Direção de Recenseamentos e Inquéritos, Praia.

The National Statistical Office publishes a quarterly bulletin of statistics, *Boletim Trimestal de Estatística*, that includes population data. Address: Serviço Nacional de Estatística, Praia.

capital, the inputs to an economic enterprise during the interval before the outputs can be available for sale, is usually classified into fixed capital, or buildings and equipment needed at the start of production; working capital, or materials used continuously through the process; and money capital, or the funds needed to pay for these inputs. What is now usually termed *economic development is conventionally defined as the accumulation of a capital stock; and however great the differences in human terms, the process is similar in free-enterprise and state-controlled economies. Less developed countries have often invested in grandiose but inappropriate projects like national airways or mammoth steel plants, and this tendency has helped popularize an alternative use of investment funds, to improve the education and health of the work force, or what is known as *human capital.

capital cities, literally the "heads" of the nations or other jurisdictions, sometimes combine commercial, economic, cultural, and administrative functions; sometimes lack all but the last. After the United States was founded, the two largest colonial cities, Philadelphia and New York, served alternately as the national capital. The rivalry between them, as well as between the North and the South, was resolved by building Washington at a central point. This avoidance of the largest population centers as capital sites was followed also by some of the states: the capital of Missouri is Jefferson City (not St. Louis); of Texas, Austin (not Houston or Dallas); of Illinois, Springfield (not Chicago); of New York, Albany (not New York City). Both types of capital are found elsewhere in the world. The dominance of Paris in France's economy, culture, and politics has been regarded as a major problem, and in various ways efforts have been made to decentralize control. In contrast, that West Germany established its capital in the small provincial town of Bonn some analysts have interpreted as an important influence on its political decisions. When many of the world's colonies achieved independence in the years following the Second World War, there was sometimes a sentiment to choose as their capitals cities that had a native tradition and were located near the countries' geographical centers. In fact, almost without exception they chose cities created by Western trade and imperial rule, typically the largest urban aggregate and in some cases the only real one—for example, in Southeast Asia, Karachi, Colombo, Rangoon, Bangkok, Kuala Lumpur, Jakarta, and Manila. In Africa there was the same tendency, with Algiers, Tunis, Dakar, Accra, and Lagos established as capitals in the western region, for example (though Morocco selected Rabat rather than Casablanca). In Latin America the overwhelming dominance of Mexico City, for instance, or Buenos Aires, has both reflected and aggravated the countries' social-economic-political centralization, and in less developed countries generally a principal goal of *urban policy has been to inhibit the growth of such metropolises. Only *Brazil has tried to set up a separate administrative center, building its capital of Brasília far from the coast, the site of all the large cities.

capture-recapture data, used to estimate the size of *animal populations, have been adapted to estimate the human populations of areas with deficient statistics.
    REFERENCE: A. E. El-Goul, *The Estimation of Human Population by the Capture-Recapture Method*, Monograph Series, no. 5 (Khartoum, Sudan: Development Studies and Research Center, University of Khartoum, 1977).

carcinogen, a *cancer-producing substance. Also, *carcinogenesis*, the production of cancer; *carcinogenic*, producing cancer; *carcinogenicity*, the tendency to produce cancer.

cardiovascular, pertaining to the heart and blood vessels—that is, the circulatory system as a whole. See *heart disease.

CARE was founded in 1945 as the Cooperative for American Remittances to Europe, a federation of organizations to aid victims of the war in Europe. With an expansion of its activities, it changed its name to Cooperative for American Relief Everywhere, an American federation of 28 religious, nationality, labor, and other associations, funded by individual contributions and government grants. With a staff of 473 in the United States and overseas in 1980, it contributes food, equipment, and self-help materials to needy people in thirty-seven less developed countries throughout the world. In 1962 the Medical International Cooperative Organization (MEDICO), which had been established in 1958, became associated with CARE; it provides medical personnel to hospitals and clinics in less developed countries. In 1966 CARE provided the equipment for family-planning clinics in Egypt, and since that first population project it has supported similar activities in various countries of Asia, the Middle East, and Africa. Address: 600 First Avenue, New York, N.Y. 10016.

carrier, an individual infected with a disease without showing its manifest symptoms, who thus helps diffuse the infection among others.

carrying capacity, the maximum number of people who can be supported indefinitely from a given environment. As a simple ratio, the concept implies that members of the aggregate are independent of one another, an assumption seldom true of a human population. Thus, the carrying capacity is usually a function of the society's organization rather than merely of the resources and life conditions in the biophysical environment.

REFERENCES: Michael A. Glassow, "The Concept of Carrying Capacity in the Study of Culture Process," in Michael B. Schiffer, ed., *Advances in Archaeological Method and Theory* (New York: Academic Press, 1978). P. W. Porter, "The Concept of Environmental Potential as Exemplified by Tropical African Research," in Wilbur Zelinsky, Leszek A. Kosiński, and R. Mansell Prothero, eds., *Geography and a Crowding World* (New York: Oxford University Press, 1970).

cartogram, a type of map in which topographic space is altered to reflect a particular statistical datum, such as population size or density. Though the relation among units is often grossly distorted, the shapes and contiguity are maintained, so that readers can still easily recognize the topography.

REFERENCE: B. D. Dent, "Communication Aspects of Value-by-Area Cartograms," *American Cartographer*, 2 (1975), 154-168.

case history, a detailed account of an individual and his characteristics during the course of an illness, for example. Compare *genealogy.

case rate, for a given year and with respect to a specific disease, is the number of reported cases per 100,000 population. Since the risk of contracting a disease often varies greatly by age and other characteristics, a case rate is perhaps even less satisfactory than most other crude *rates. The proportion of persons contracting a disease who die of that disease is called a *case fatality rate*.

caste, from *casta*, Portuguese for "race," is used to translate two Hindi words, *varna* and *jati*. A varna (literally, "color") is each one of four steps in a hierarchy of purity: Brahman, Kshatriya, Vaisya, and Sudra (priest, warrior or ruler, merchant, and peasant). Society is divided into three levels, the "twice-born" top three varnas, who undergo a rite of passage that makes them full members; the "once-born" Sudras; and the Untouchables, Scheduled Castes, or Avarnas, who are below the line of pollution. A jati (from *jan*, to give birth to) is one of the perhaps 3,000 breeding units of Hindu society, setting the limits of the hierarchically arranged endogamous groups. Castes exist in nearby societies affected by India, but the use of the word to characterize race relations in such a country as the United States is more confusing than helpful.

"The Hindu social order," in the words of a Western demographer, "is the most thoroughgoing attempt known in history to introduce absolute inequality as the guiding principle in social relations" (Davis, 1951, p. 170). Under traditional Hindu law, the punishment for identical offenses was ranked by varna, with the

Brahman getting least and the Untouchable most. The British introduced the principle of equality under the law but interfered as little as possible with the religion from which the gross inequity derived. Modernist Indians who oppose the caste system have often stressed those elements that generally have been disappearing with increasing education, urbanization, and westernization. In particular, the association between caste and occupation, which some analysts believe was fundamental in the system's origin, is now no more than vestigial. But the antithesis in Hinduism between purity and pollution, which underlies the present caste system as an "irruption of biological into social life" (Dumont, 1970, p. 49), pervades personal and group relations and shows little or no tendency to become less important. Caste associations have adapted successfully to India's secular institutions, subsidizing their members' higher education, for instance, or voting as a bloc to ensure that the caste's interests—and thus the caste system—will be protected (Srinivas, 1962; Kolenda, 1978).

Much attention has centered on those below the line of pollution. They were called "Untouchables" until the status, and in theory the designation, were outlawed by India's Constitution of 1950. †Gandhi called them "Harijans," Children of God (or persons whose father is unknown—that is, bastards), and this is still a common term among caste Hindus. Ex-Untouchables usually use the term "Scheduled Caste," which derives from the lists first compiled in British India of groups that were to receive special access to education and political office (cf. Isaacs, 1964, chap. 2). The number of persons in this status depends in part on how one classifies marginal groups; something like 80 million Indians, or 18 percent of the 1971 population, are outcasts (cf. Chandra Sekhar, 1972). Their disabilities are suggested by the Untouchability (Offences) Act of 1955, which outlawed such prevalent practices as denying persons so designated access to temples, shops, restaurants, water sources, and other public accommodations and conveyances, particular occupations and trades, and hospitals and schools. However, the law was hardly enforced; a fraction of 1 percent of the population was ever charged, and the infrequent convictions resulted in minuscule fines. Since the accused, prosecutor, and judge were all caste Hindus, the outcast gained little by the law. Legal and social disabilities are reinforced, morever, by class relations; most Untouchables are landless peasants, who are pressured to work for low wages by the caste-Indian landowners. India's two Communist parties have concentrated on organizing members of the Scheduled castes, and in certain parts of the rural South the Communist Party of India (Marxist) is widely known as the Harijan party.

REFERENCES: A. Chandra Sekhar, "Religion," *Census of India, 1971*, Series 1, Paper 2 (New Delhi, 1972). Kingsley Davis, *The Population of India and Pakistan* (Princeton, N.J.: Princeton University Press, 1951). Louis Dumont, *Homo Hierarchicus: An Essay on the Caste System* (Chicago: University of Chicago Press, 1970). Dilip Hiro, *The Untouchables of India* (London: Minority Rights Group, 1975). Harold R. Isaacs, *India's Ex-Untouchables* (New York: John Day, 1964). Pauline Kolenda, *Caste in Contemporary India: Beyond Organic Solidarity* (Menlo Park, Calif.: Benjamin/Cummings

Publishing Co., 1978). M. N. Srinivas, "Caste: A Trend Report and Bibliography," *Current Sociology*, 8 (1959), 135-183; *Caste in Modern India and Other Essays* (New York: Asia Publishing House, 1962).

Casti Connubii ("On Christian Marriage"), a papal encyclical of 1930, was interpreted against even some ecclesiastical opposition as sanctioning the *rhythm method of limiting the size of families, provided there is a "serious motive" for avoiding childbearing. It marked the first important break in modern times with the Roman Catholic emphasis on the moral worth of large families irrespective of any contrary considerations.

REFERENCE: Alvah W. Sulloway, *Birth Control and Catholic Doctrine* (Boston: Beacon, 1959).

category, a sector of a population distinguished by one or more characteristics common to all its members but, unlike a *group, with no internal coherence. Alternative designations include bracket, grouping, and subpopulation, as well as sector.

Catholic Action, defined in the encyclical *Ubi Arcano Dei* (1922) as "the participation of the laity in the hierarchic apostolate for the defense of religious and moral principles, for the development of a wholesome and beneficent social order under the guidance of the ecclesiastical hierarchy, outside and above political parties, with the intention of restoring Catholic life in society and in the family." In later years the term was used more generally to apply to all organized movements of the Catholic laity, of which the most important and numerous were in some of the countries of continental Europe. The specific aim of defending the family has been through measures designed to oppose contraception and other forbidden practices. See also *Roman Catholicism.

cause of death reflects, of course, both the medical concepts and the statistical organization of a particular culture, and one must stress that in most less developed countries the markedly incomplete registration of deaths is also deficient with respect to this crucial datum. According to the partial record of British India, whose mortality data were far better than those of most other colonies, 60 percent of the registered deaths were due to "fever" and over 25 percent to a catch-all "other causes." In Ceylon two frequently cited causes of death still in the 1950s were *rathe* (literally, "redness"), and *mandama* (literally, "wasting"); *Grahaniya*, once the name of a she-demon that killed young children and then a synonym for *mandama*, was coded as such (Davis, 1951, chap. 6; Padley, 1959).

Even within the context of modern medicine the cause of death is a more complex concept than one might suppose. When most deaths resulted from infectious diseases, whether a host invaded by a microorganism succumbed depended also on the person's hereditary resistance, age, sometimes sex, past medical history, and various other ancillary factors. At the present time, with *heart disease, *cancer, *strokes, and *accidents the principal factors in most of the mortality in advanced countries, stipulating a single "cause" is sometimes more or less arbitrary, as one can see from analyzing the basic data on *death certificates (cf. *excess mortality; *risk). As specified by a physician or coroner and later compiled into a nation's vital statistics, each single or multiple cause of death supposedly conforms with the *International Classification of Diseases, Injuries, and Causes of Death, in which various cross-cultural compromises have had to be made. Yet the most interesting and often the most important characteristic of mortality is the relative chance of dying either within a specified period or eventually from a given cause at each particular age—what is termed a cause-specific mortality rate (Preston et al., 1972). This rate differs considerably, however, depending on whether it is based on the "underlying cause," the usual base of reports, or "multiple causes," including all the medical conditions listed on the death certificate (Manton and Stallard, 1982).

In 1978, as the table below shows, the United States death rate per 1,000 population was 8.83 (or, adjusted for the age structure, 6.06). The two leading

Age-Adjusted Death Rates by Cause, United States, 1978

	Rate per 100,000 Population	Percent Change, 1968-1978	Ratio of	
Cause			Male to Female	Nonwhite to White
All causes	606.1	−18.5	1.80	1.37
1. Diseases of the heart	207.6	−22.7	2.04	1.15
2. Malignant neoplasms	133.8	3.6	1.50	1.22
3. Cerebrovascular diseases	45.3	−36.5	1.19	1.63
4. Accidents	44.3	−19.5	2.85	1.21
5. Influenza and pneumonia	15.4	−42.8	1.83	1.50
6. Diabetes mellitus	10.4	−28.8	1.02	2.02
7. Cirrhosis of the liver	12.5	−10.1	2.17	1.86
8. Arteriosclerosis	6.0	−37.5	1.28	0.93
9. Suicide	12.0	10.1	2.98	0.58
10. Mortality in early infancy[a]	(10.1)	—	(1.29)	(1.92)
11. Bronchitis, emphysema, and asthma	6.8	−46.9	2.92	0.73
12. Homicide	9.6	15.7	3.64	5.57
13. Congenital anomalies[a]	(5.9)	—	(1.10)	(0.95)
14. Nephritis and nephrosis	2.8	−28.2	1.59	3.59
15. Septicemia	2.6	116.7	1.48	2.55

[a]Since these causes of death affect infants, the rates are not adjusted to the age structure in 1940, and the ratios are based on the infant mortality rate in 1978.

Source: U.S. National Center for Health Statistics, "Final Mortality Statistics, 1978," *Monthly Vital Statistics Report*, vol. 29, no. 6, Supplement 2 (September 17, 1980).

causes of death, Diseases of the heart and Malignant neoplasms (cancers), accounted for 58.4 percent of the total, and the next two, Cerebrovascular diseases (stroke) and Accidents, for 9.1 and 5.5, respectively. Changes during the prior decade and the ratio of deaths by sex and color are also shown in the table. The decline in deaths from Bronchitis, emphysema, and asthma was factitious, based on changes in classification. More than half of the age-adjusted rate for Accidents was specified as motor-vehicle accidents, for which the rate declined less than for others during the prior decade.

REFERENCES: Kingsley Davis, *The Population of India and Pakistan* (Princeton, N.J.: Princeton University Press, 1951). Kenneth G. Manton and Eric Stallard, ''Temporal Trends in U.S. Multiple Cause of Death Mortality Data: 1968 to 1977,'' *Demography*, 19 (1982), 527-547. Richard Padley, ''Cause-of-Death Statements in Ceylon,'' *Bulletin of the World Health Organization*, 20 (1959), 677-695. Samuel H. Preston, Nathan Keyfitz, and Robert Schoen, *Causes of Death: Life Tables for National Populations* (New York: Seminar Press, 1972). U.S. National Center for Health Statistics, ''Final Mortality Statistics, 1978,'' *Monthly Vital Statistics Report*, vol. 29, no. 6, Supplement 2 (September 17, 1980).

Cayman Islands: The Department of Finance and Development conducts the censuses, the last of which was in 1980. Address: Georgetown.

celibacy, which derives from the Latin for ''single'' or ''unmarried,'' now usually means a single life bound by vows not to marry, as in a monastic order of *celibates*. In the Roman Catholic church, priestly celibacy was a recurrent issue of contention, tied by its supporters to the ideal of virginity, which some recommended even between marriage partners (Noonan, 1965, pp. 276-279). More mundanely, the formal institutionalization of clerical celibacy contributed to the Roman church's organizational independence: as the aristocracy became the dominant class of secular society, the church remained a relatively open upward route for able commoners, for not even bishops could have legitimate heirs. In recent years celibacy has been a disputatious issue in the church; it has been recognized as an important reason for the lagging enrollments in seminaries and for the decisions of thousands of priests and nuns to return to secular life. In 1967, the same year that Pope Paul VI reaffirmed the traditional position in the encyclical *Sacerdotalis Caelibatus*, a symposium at the University of Notre Dame questioned this position (Frein, 1968). According to a survey cited there, of more than 3,000 American priests, 62 percent favored optional celibacy and 92 percent thought that those already married should be reinstated as priests while remaining with their wives.

One might think that clerical celibacy would reduce the fertility of the population in which it prevails, but the proportion of priests and nuns is typically too small to have a discernible overall effect. In the United States, of the total of some 50 million Roman Catholics, only about 0.5 percent are celibates. In Ireland, where the proportion has been higher, it is likely that many of those who put off getting married—a prolonged reaction to the famine of the 1840s—became priests or nuns, rather than the other way round. The one country where celibacy may have cut the fertility was pre-Communist Tibet; see *Buddhism.

"Celibacy" and "celibate" are occasionally used to refer to nonclericals, though less often in English than in French. The usual term in a demographic context is the "never married" or, if sex is to be specified, *"bachelor" or "spinster." A "celibate" may be understood, not merely as one who has not yet married, but as "a confirmed bachelor"—that is, someone who for other reasons is no more likely to wed than someone bound by religious vows.

REFERENCES: George H. Frein, ed., *Celibacy: The Necessary Option* (New York: Herder and Herder, 1968). Henry C. Lea, *History of Sacerdotal Celibacy in the Christian Church* (1867; reprinted, New York: Scribner, 1952). Noonan, *Contraception*.

cellular city, a city composed of a number a weakly related and therefore relatively self-contained enclaves.

REFERENCE: Amos H. Hawley, *Urban Society: An Ecological Approach* (New York: Ronald Press, 1971), chap. 5.

CENSPAC, a computer program developed by the U.S. Bureau of the Census, is designed to retrieve, sort, rank, and print data from summary tape files, to combine two files into a new tape, and to do simple calculations. Since the program is written in COBOL (Common Ordinary Business Language), a computer language that generally is less familiar than some others, getting a computation under way can be time-consuming. However, once the software has been installed, calculations are remarkably cheap, and private companies have complained of what they regard as unfair competition from a tax-supported agency.

REFERENCE: Cheryl Russell, "In Richmond with CENSPAC," *American Demographics*, 3 (January, 1981), 38-41.

CENSTAT, a computer program developed by Westat, Inc., retrieves, processes, and displays census tables from summary tapes of the U.S. Bureau of the Census.

census, the counting of a population and the recording of whatever characteristics are included in the questionnaire, or *schedule*, concerning either individuals or households. Since sometimes the term applies to counts of other entities (for example, in the U.S. Census of Manufactures), it may be necessary in some contexts to specify an enumeration of people as a population census. This is defined by a United Nations agency as "the total process of collecting, compiling, evaluating, analyzing, and publishing or otherwise disseminating demographic, economic, and social data pertaining at a specific time to all persons in a country or in a well delimited part of a country" (United Nations, 1980, p. 2). Ideally, such a count is made by a government, whose representatives (called enumerators) try to make sure that *responses in the strictly defined territory are counted without omission or duplication. In principle, the *enumeration* of the entire population is simultaneous, completed during a single day; since ordinarily this is impossible, one day is set as the date of the census and demographic events occurring after it are excluded. Censuses are preferably repeated at regular intervals.

Where the first census took place, an honor that various countries have claimed, depends on how precisely one defines the term. Many ancient peoples—the Egyptians, Hebrews, Greeks, and Romans, among others—took counts of those portions of the population that paid taxes or could be conscripted for military service. In medieval Europe some cities had enumerations, but these typically counted only a portion of the inhabitants. The national bookkeeping of the mercantilist era included at least the intention of keeping track of the number of people, and the "political arithmetic" associated with such counts marked the beginning of modern demography. The first enumeration of a total population may have been in New France (present-day Quebec), and the earliest accurate counts that any country made of its own population were in Scandinavia. In the full sense, thus, censuses are a product of modern Western societies. Because of England's importance as the first industrial nation, the development of population statistics there is of especial interest (Glass, 1973). In the United States a census was stipulated in the Constitution in order to adjust the *apportionment of representatives in Congress to changes in population distribution. Though the American count was not the first in history, the regular series that began in 1790 was the earliest. See U.S. Bureau of the Census under *United States: Federal Agencies.

By modern practice there must be a considerable preparation before the actual enumeration starts. Geographers mark the census areas on large-scale *maps; others design the schedule and preferably test it in a trial survey. What is meant by *population must be specified, whether a *de facto* or a *de jure* count or some compromise between the two. In recent United States censuses direct interviews have gradually been replaced by self-enumeration through mailed questionnaires; and the use of samples has increasingly supplanted the canvass of the entire population. After the count is completed efforts are made routinely to discover underenumeration and other *errors, estimate their size, and if possible make appropriate adjustments before the data are published. See also *editing; *matching.

No census is limited to a count of people, and which of their characteristics are included has varied from one country or time to another. Several overall principles apply. The information gathered should be important enough to warrant the extra expenditure. The question should be capable of eliciting a definite answer; thus, the vague demands in opinion polls for what are termed open-end responses are ruled out. That sex and age are virtually universal items in all demographic instruments reflects the fact that they are relatively unambiguous and also essential components of social analyses of any kind. If possible, questions should not excite fear, hostility, or any other motive for providing false information; but the more important the data, very often the more reluctant people are to respond fully and truthfully. Even *age may not be as neutral an item as it seems to be. According to surveys by the U.S. Bureau of the Census, the question that Americans find most objectionable is the one asking their income; it has been retained because the information (even if sometimes distorted by this hostility) is deemed too important to omit. Validity of the data is affected also by the general attitude toward the government. In a democracy the political consequences of a truthful answer in a census schedule are typically nil, but under *totalitarianism it may be dangerous to respond either truthfully or falsely. In short, censuses are like any other social instrument in that they reflect both general human frailties and the particular flaws of the state administering the counts.

REFERENCES: Glass, *Numbering the People*. Shryock and Siegel, *Methods and Materials of Demography*, chap. 2. United Nations, Department of International Economic and Social Affairs, *Principles and Recommendations for Population and Housing Censuses*, Statistical Papers, Ser. M, no. 67 (New York, 1980).

census tract, as defined by the U.S. Bureau of the Census, a subdivision of a metropolitan area with a relatively homogeneous population of 4,000 to 8,000. Not only census data but also vital and health statistics, for instance, are often broken down by census tracts, which thus afford the possibility of a comparative analysis using a wide range of variables.

centenarian, a person aged 100 years. Paradoxically, there are relatively more centenarians reported in some primitive cultures than in advanced countries, and the decreasing percentage enumerated in the West also seems to suggest that the simpler life of the past was more healthful. As long ago as in a volume supplementary to the 1900 census of the United States, the real reason was given for the trend: when states were ranked by the proportion reportedly 100 years or over and by the proportion illiterate, there was a correlation of 0.714 between the two series (Young, 1906). In India, as an example of less developed countries, there is a strong tendency to exaggerate longevity (Raman, 1980). Among the populations that supposedly have the highest proportion of centenarians are some of those living in the Soviet Caucasus, and Zhores Medvedev (1974, 1975) has made a detailed analysis of the data. The most famously longevous person, a man named Vakutia who allegedly was 130 years old in 1959, actually was 78; he had deserted from the army during World War I and used forged documents to assume his father's name. More generally, the area of the Soviet Union where most of the alleged centenarians have lived had no civil birth registration, and nine-tenths of the churches were destroyed together with their records. Not one of the approximately 500 who claimed to be between 120 and 170 could produce any reliable document of birth, education, marriage, or military service, any one of which would have been at least a partial validation. In the Caucasus as elsewhere, the number of centenarians has fallen off with improved record keeping—in that case by about half in 50 years. If one revises the data to correct for the tendency of unsophisticated populations to exaggerate the proportion of the extremely old (e.g., Rosenwaike, 1979), the maximum *life span turns out to be 114 years.

REFERENCES: Z. A. Medvedev, "Caucasus and Altay Longevity—A Biological or Social Problem?" *Gerontologist*, 14 (1974), 381-387; "Aging and Longevity—New Approaches and New Perspectives," *Gerontologist*, 15 (1975), 196-201. M. V. Raman, "The Census Centenarians," *Journal of the Institute of Economic Research*, 15 (1980), 15-18. Ira Rosenwaike, "A New Evaluation of United States Census Data on the Extreme Aged," *Demography*, 16 (1979), 279-288. Allyn A. Young, "Age," in *Supplementary Analysis and Derivative Tables: Special Report on the Twelfth Census* (Washington, D.C.: U.S. Bureau of the Census, 1906).

Center for Migration Studies [of New York], an institute to facilitate education and research on migration and ethnicity. Its quarterly, *International Migration Review*, includes a regular updating of United States laws and regulations on immigration. Address: 209 Flagg Place, Staten Island, N.Y. 10304.

Center for Population Activities (CEFPA), an American organization founded in 1975, provides training for prospective managers of family-planning and health programs. It has conducted workshops in various countries of Latin America, Africa, the Middle East, and Asia, as well as in Washington, D.C. Most of its funding comes from contracts with the U.S. Agency for International Development (AID). Address: 1717 Massachusetts Avenue, N.W., Washington, D.C. 20036.

center of population, the point comparable to a center of gravity, assuming a uniform and uninterrupted areal surface on which each resident is equal in weight and exerts an influence proportionate to his distance from the point. In the United States (not including the two noncontiguous states of Alaska and Hawaii), the center of population has moved steadily westward along the 39th parallel at a rate of four or five miles a year, from northeastern Maryland in 1790 to a quarter-mile west of DeSoto in Jefferson County, Missouri, in 1980. See also *gravity model; *median location.

Central African Republic: Demographic Institutions

In 1975 there was established in the capital a Regional Center for Population Studies, directed in 1980 by Félicien †Diafouka. Its main purpose has been to improve the collection of vital statistics, including those on education and health. It publishes a *Bulletin Trimestriel de Liaison* to report on its activities. Address: Centre Régional d'Études de Population, Boîte Postale 1418, Bangui.

The Central Census Bureau conducts the country's censuses, the last of which was in 1975. Address: Bureau Central du Recensement, Bangui.

The National Statistical Office publishes irregularly a statistical yearbook giving estimates of population size and distribution and the main household characteristics.

Address: Direction de la Statistique Générale et des Études Économiques, Ministère de la Coopération, du Plan et de la Statistique Générale, Boîte Postale 954, Bangui.

central business district, an area in a city containing the principal concentration of retail stores, financial firms, and the central offices of corporations, usually located where the city's main routes of travel converge. In Ernest †Burgess's schema of urban patterns, this was the nucleus around which concentric zones evolved. In cooperation with local statistical committees, the U.S. Bureau of the Census identified the central business districts in the central cities of Standard *Metropolitan Statistical Areas and other cities of 50,000 or more people. However, in 1980 some eligible cities chose not to participate in the program, and the bureau did not plan to process the data it collected.

central city, an urban place constituting the focal point of a metropolitan area; alternatively, the "central place," or city regardless of size with the minimum aggregate travel from a surrounding tributary area. Central places may be scaled according to the sizes of their *hinterland. In the usage of the U.S. Bureau of the Census, the largest city, or the dominant one though it is not the largest, is called the central city of a *Metropolitan Statistical Area or of an *Urbanized Area. See also *metropolis.
    REFERENCE: R. D. McKenzie, *The Metropolitan Community* (New York: McGraw-Hill, 1933).

central place theory, the systematic study of how a region's principal place relates to the rest through the spatial distribution of people, agriculture and manufacturing, administration and services. The goods and services provided to consumers depend on the minimum sales needed to support production ("the threshold") and on the distance consumers are willing to travel for each type of purchase ("the outer range of goods"). In any area the number of establishments will be between a maximum, equal to the demand for the commodity divided by the threshold, and a minimum, equal to the same demand divided by the outer range of goods. The most efficient pattern is one that achieves the maximum distribution at the least cost. See also Walter †Christaller; *location theory; J. H. †Thünen; Alfred †Weber.
    REFERENCE: Brian J. L. Berry and Chauncy D. Harris, "Central Place," in *International Encyclopedia of the Social Sciences,* 2, 365-370.

central plaza, the main square in the center of a typical Spanish city around which social life revolved (Ricard, 1950). Following a carefully developed urban policy embodied in the sixteenth-century Laws of the Indies (Nuttall, 1921, 1922), Spanish American cities as far apart as Bogotá in Colombia and Concepción in Chile, as well as practically every one in between, were built according to the same plan. "A uniformity of city layout has been rubber-stamped all over

the face of the continent no matter what the site, hill or dale, valley or pampa"
(Violich, 1944, p. 28). The preference of the upper-middle class for the environs
of the plaza has affected the whole city, and still today it is generally difficult
to move schools or other public buildings from their traditional central location
to a presently more convenient and rational site. As a consequence, Latin American
city planners regard overcentralization as probably their most serious problem.

REFERENCES: Zelia Nuttall, "Royal Ordinances Concerning the Laying Out of New
Towns," *Hispanic American Historical Review*, 4 (1921), 743-753; 5 (1922), 249-254.
Robert Ricard, "La Plaza Mayor en España y en América Española," *Estudios Geográficos*,
11 (1950), 321-327. Francis Violich, *Cities of Latin America: Housing and Planning to
the South* (New York: Reinhold, 1944).

centrifugal and **centripetal forces,** terms used in urban geography, relate to
factors that impel homeowners or business firms away from the expensive and
congested *central business district or, on the contrary, toward the greater
accessibility at the center.

REFERENCE: C. C. Colby, "Centripetal and Centrifugal Forces in Urban Geography,"
Annals of the Association of American Geographers, 23 (1932), 1-20.

CENTS, an acronym for Census Tabulation System, is a computer program
designed by the U.S. Bureau of the Census for processing the censuses of other
countries. A supplementary program that makes it easier to use CENTS without
sacrificing its advantages, called CENTS-AID, was developed by Data Use and
Access Laboratories (DUALabs; see under *data processing).

REFERENCE: U.S. Bureau of the Census, *CENTS: Census Tabulation System*, Ser.
ISPC 4, no. 4 (rev.), November, 1973.

cephalic index is defined as the maximum width of a skull as a percentage of
the maximum length measured just above the eyebrow ridges. Peoples used to
be characterized as *dolichocephalic* (long-headed) if their typical cephalic index
was below 75, *mesaticephalic* (with heads in the middle range) if between 75
and 80, and as *brachycephalic* (short- or broad-headed) if it was above 80.
Presently the index is discredited as a means of classifying races, but paleontologists
still use it as one criterion for the classification of skeletal types.

cervix, or cervix uteri, the lower and narrow end of the uterus, between the
body and the mouth of the organ. A cervical cap or *diaphragm that fits over
the cervix to prevent the entrance of any sperm into the uterus is an effective
means of *contraception.

Chad: The government's Bureau of Statistics and of Economic and Demographic
Studies publishes an *Annuaire Statistique* that includes population data. In 1980
Guelengdoukssia Ouaidou Nassour headed the bureau's Demographic Office.
Address: Direction de la Statistique, des Études Économiques et Démographiques,
Ministère de l'Économie, du Plan et des Transports, Boîte Postale 453, N'Djaména.

Chandrasekar-Deming technique was named after C. †Chandrasekaran (sometimes spelled Chandrasekar or Chandra Sekar) and W. Edwards †Deming. It is a means of improving the quality of registration by collecting birth and death rates from two independent sources and using the four figures, together with the given registration, to compute a final estimate. The main difficulty is that an omission of a birth is generally not independent of an omission of a death in the same locality, and the procedure includes a means of estimating this correlation. In spite of some criticism, the technique has been used in less developed countries in Africa, the Middle East, and Asia.

REFERENCES: C. Chandra Sekar and W. Edwards Deming, "On a Method of Estimating Birth and Death Rates and the Extent of Registration," *Journal of the American Statistical Association*, 44 (1949), 101-115. John C. Rumford and Samuel Greene, "A Study of the Correlation Bias of Unrecorded Events by Two Independent Enumeration Systems," *Population Studies*, 33 (1979), 181-188.

chi square, a measure of the significance of difference between observed frequencies and those expected on the basis of some hypothesis.

$$\chi^2 = \sum \frac{(0_i - e_i)^2}{e_i}$$

χ is the Greek letter chi, and the measure is called the chi-square test. For an event i, 0_i is the observed frequency and e_i the expected frequency. Depending on the number of *degrees of freedom, the values of χ^2 at various *significant levels are as follows:

Degrees of Freedom	Level of Significance			
	.20	.10	.05	.01
1	1.6	2.7	3.8	6.6
2	3.2	4.6	6.0	9.2
3	4.6	6.3	7.8	11.3
4	6.0	7.8	9.5	13.3
5	7.3	9.2	11.1	15.1

and so on.

Chicago school of sociology was made up of persons in that and some related disciplines at the University of Chicago during the first three or four decades of this century. It was the site of the world's first graduate department in sociology, which was enormously influential in establishing several sometimes quite disparate trends in the discipline. Though in retrospect the main emphasis is said to have been on research, the very important developments in social psychology by G. H. Mead and W. I. †Thomas continued the so-called armchair philosophizing of the earlier period. The emphasis most closely related to demography was the rise of human *ecology under Robert E. †Park and Ernest W. †Burgess; from the study of "the city"—in the main, Chicago itself—theories were propounded that supposedly applied to urban populations anywhere. Park, Louis †Wirth, and Franklin Frazier did much to stimulate the study of ethnic relations. See also *New Home Economics.

REFERENCE: Ernest W. Burgess and Donald J. Bogue, eds., *Contributions to Urban Sociology* (Chicago: University of Chicago Press, 1964).

child abuse, or the battered-child syndrome, became a well known phenomenon in the United States very suddenly in the 1960s. Under both common and American statutory law, parents' rights to control the upbringing of their children could not be easily abridged, whether by physicians, social workers, or police. When it became known that parents or other adults often beat or otherwise maltreat infants and children enough to inflict serious physical damage, all fifty states passed laws making parents more accountable. Very quickly hundreds of cases of child abuse were recorded in one jurisdiction after another—a prime instance of a statistical series created not from given levels of incidence but out of a sharply increased awareness.

REFERENCES: Richard J. Gelles, *Family Violence* (Beverly Hills, Calif.: Sage Publications, 1979). David G. Gil, *Violence against Children: Physical Child Abuse in the United States* (Cambridge, Mass.: Harvard University Press, 1970). Saad Z. Nagi, *Child Maltreatment in the United States: A Challenge to Social Institutions* (New York: Columbia University Press, 1977).

child care is traditionally the role of the mother, and in most American families that pattern continues. Or, more broadly, it is the traditional responsibility of females in the household—the mother assisted by older daughters in a large family, or by a grandmother, other female relative, or servant acting in place of the mother if she works outside the home. According to sample surveys in the United States, most working mothers still used such arrangements in the early 1970s (Waite et al., 1977). That the verb "to baby-sit" and the noun "baby-sitter" had come into general usage during or shortly after World War II (Wentworth and Flexner, 1960, p. 12) suggests one of the main pressures for change: the shortage of male labor during the war stimulated a great acceleration in female employment. In the usual connotation of the word, a baby-sitter is responsible for the care of a young child only during an occasional absence of the parents; but sometimes a woman, often a mother herself, provides care for several other young children during the hours when working mothers are busy. Thus, as demand for care facilities increased, the ideological commitment to the home as the proper place for childrearing was lessened.

This change was evident also in public programs. The federally funded Aid to Families with Dependent Children (AFDC) (see *United States: Federal Agencies) was initially devised specifically to provide an income to indigent women in order to enable them to stay home and raise their own children.

Though the funding for AFDC continued to grow, it was supplemented by another federal program to finance day-care centers for working mothers (Rosenberg, 1972). According to 1974 data published by the U.S. Senate Finance Committee, publicly subsidized day-care centers cost about $1,000 per child-year, or, extrapolated to the whole of the eligible preschool population, a total of $7 billion. This was considerably under the potential eventual outlay: agencies were supposed to meet "federal interagency day-care requirements," which mandated one employee per child up to 6 weeks of age, one per four children aged 6 weeks to 3 years, and one per five children aged 4 to 5 years. If these standards had been met, the cost per child-year in the mid-1970s would have been, according to various estimates, between $1,600 and $4,000, or a national total between $11 billion and $28 billion. Both the number of personnel and the cost were considerably higher than in the private sector (Bruce-Briggs, 1976; cf. Lueck et al., 1982).

Private day-care centers, which had started as adjuncts to churches or other community establishments, proliferated during recent decades. Around 1970 the first private chain was set up, Mary Moppets Day-Care Schools, which a decade later had 83 units in some fifteen states, some franchised and some company-owned. Two chains had considerably larger revenue by the end of the 1970s: Mini-Skools, with a gross income of $16 million from 82 centers in eight states and Canada, and Kinder-Care Learning Centers, with $13 million from 250 units in 24 states. In 1979 the usual rates ranged from $35 to $50 for a five-day week. As a corporate venture, baby-sitting was still enough of a novelty to continue to develop new patterns; for example, Palo Alto Preschools, which operated 22 centers, leased space from churches during the week and paid them a percentage of their gross revenue. See also *Soviet society; *women in the work force.

REFERENCES: B. Bruce-Briggs, "Getting a Handle on Day Care," *Wall Street Journal* (September 27, 1976). Marjorie Lueck, Ann C. Orr, and Martin O'Connell, "Trends in Child Care Arrangements of Working Mothers," *Current Population Reports*, Ser. P-23, no. 117 (June, 1982). Beatrice Rosenberg, *Federal Funds for Day Care Projects*, Children's Bureau, Pamphlet no. 14 (Washington, D.C.: U.S. Government Printing Office, 1972). Ralph Shaffer, "Booming Babysitting Business Is Joining the Corporate World," *Christian Science Monitor Service* (December, 1979). Linda J. Waite, Larry E. Suter, and Richard L. Shortlidge, Jr., "Changes in Child Care Arrangements of Working Women from 1965 to 1971," *Social Science Quarterly*, 58 (1977), 302-311. Harold Wentworth and Stuart Berg Flexner, *Dictionary of American Slang* (New York: Crowell, 1960).

child custody is the legal norm by which one or another adult is given control of a child. Under English common law the father's right to custody was virtually always supported by courts and other public authorities, even with respect to nursing infants. In early cases in the United States a difference was made according to the child's age, with the father's superior right applying only to older children. In the twentieth century both parents have been given equal rights, with the best interests of the child as the deciding factor. In practice, however, this meant that the mother acquired custody, particularly of younger children, unless her behavior was shown to have been unsuitable. In particular, extramarital sexual relations used to be regarded as proof of unfitness, but the standard is changing. Since 1971 the U.S. Supreme Court has invalidated at least six state statutes concerning child custody on the ground that due process was not followed and the right to privacy was violated. One must conclude that the law is being revised, a fact of considerable importance in view of the large number of divorces.

REFERENCE: Nora Lauerman, "Nonmarital Sexual Conduct and Child Custody," *University of Cincinnati Law Review*, 46 (1977), 647-724.

child density, a term sometimes used in relation to family-planning programs, is the ratio of the number of a couple's children to the number of years they have been married.

child labor was routine in preindustrial societies. In Europe the practice was taken over from agriculture to *cottage industry and the early stages of factories. By a decree of 1668, for example, Jean-Baptiste †Colbert, controller general of France's finances, commanded every resident of Auxerre to send his children into workshops to learn lace-making at the age of 6 years or pay a fine of 30 sous per child. In England's dispute about child labor during the first decades of the nineteenth century, parents were often the most vehement defenders of the tradition by which the father was also the master of a work team comprising his wife and children (e.g., Smelser, 1959, pp. 188-199). Child labor during early industrialization, in other words, was not the innovation it is often assumed to have been, but rather a new target of reformers. Over the ensuing period fewer and fewer children were employed in industrial countries, partly because of specific prohibitions, partly because of the demand for greater skills. By present norms the new regulations were hardly excessively restrictive. A Russian law of 1884 prohibited factory labor for children under 12 (Griffin, 1977). In the United States a 1916 law prohibiting the sale in interstate commerce of goods made by children under 14, or by those under 16 who worked more than eight hours a day, was declared unconstitutional two years later (Berger and Johansson, 1980). Generally the most important factor in reducing child labor has been compulsory *education up to a specified age. The historic decline of American children and teenagers in the labor force, thus, was matched almost precisely by a rise of the same age groups in the school population. A statistical adjustment in the definition of the work force was needed, and the lower limit of the labor pool, or those in the population capable of gainful work, has been raised twice in the United States, from 10 to 14 years between the 1930 and 1940 censuses, and from 14 to 16 in 1967.

In today's less developed countries some tens of millions of children are in the work force (cf. International Labor Organization, 1979). In 1979 about fifty participants from a wide range of African countries met in Yaoundé, Cameroon, to exchange views on how to bring the practice under control (International

Institute of Labor Studies, 1981). In the phrase "child labor," however, both words are ambiguous; and a preliminary step to reform, or even to measuring the prevalence of the phenomenon, should be a clarification of the term. In an interesting paper, Gerry Rodgers and Guy Standing (1981) distinguished several types of children's activities that had been noted in various less developed countries. Very often girls of 10-12 years are engaged in work about the house, and children of both sexes work on family farms. This is quite different from the millions in bonded labor; in India, for instance, children are sometimes bonded at the age of 8 and, since they seldom get enough to pay off the debt, often work as grossly underpaid servants for their whole lives. Laws prohibiting the wage labor of children sometimes merely encourage misreporting; in a Nigerian survey virtually the entire work forces of some industries consisted of "apprentices." In such circumstances child labor is not merely a reflection of poverty but also of how the labor market is structured, and one can assume it is an important factor in the continuing high fertility; cf. *wealth-flow theory.

REFERENCES: Lawrence R. Berger and S. Ryan Johansson, "Child Health in the Workplace: The Supreme Court in *Hammer* v. *Dagenhart* (1918)," *Journal of Health Politics, Policy and Law*, 5 (1980), 81-97. Frederick C. Griffin, "Improving the Conditions of Child Labor in Russia: The Law of June 1884," *European Studies Review*, 7 (1977), 359-370. International Institute of Labor Studies, *The World of Work and the Protection of the Child* (Geneva, 1981). International Labor Organization, *Children at Work* (Geneva, 1979). Gerry B. Rodgers and Guy Standing, "Economic Roles of Children in Low-Income Countries," *International Labour Review*, 120 (1981), 31-47. Neil J. Smelser, *Social Change in the Industrial Revolution: An Application of Theory to the British Cotton Industry* (Chicago: University of Chicago Press, 1959).

child marriage as an institution is associated especially with India, where a long tradition has been gradually eroded over the past century or more. In 1860 sexual intercourse with a wife under 10 years of age was prohibited. In the 1880s reformers were led by Behramji Malabari (1853-1912), a Bombay journalist, who was able to picture the horror of a young girl forced into marriage in such harrowing detail that the issue was difficult to evade (see also *child abuse). The nationalist movement, however, did not face up to it directly. In order to appeal also to orthodox Hindus opposed to any change in tradition, the Indian National Congress, founded in 1885, excluded such issues as child marriage from its deliberations and allocated them to a separate organization, the National Social Conference, which was based on a secular ideology (see Jordens, 1975). It was not until 1929 that the Sarda Act raised the minimum ages at marriage to 18 for boys and 14 for girls, subsequently increased to 15 and, in 1978, to 18 (Sadashivaiah et al., 1981). According to the best estimate available, the average age at females' marriage over a longer period rose from 12.77 years in 1891-1901 to 15.38 in 1941-51 (Agarwala, 1962; cf. Malaker, 1979). A sample survey in 1956 showed a total fertility of 730 per 1,000 females married at 14 or under, and 680 for those married at 17 to 19 years; the difference is less than one might anticipate because the extra years of exposure were affected by the subfecundity during *adolescence (Rele, 1962).

In the most recent period, it would seem that both opinion and practice have been changing rapidly. According to a 1970 survey of a sample of Calcutta's population (many of whom had migrated to the city from rural areas), some 70 percent of husbands and 30 percent of wives had married at or above 21 and 18 years, respectively. Perhaps more significantly, well over half of the respondents held that ideally girls should marry at 18, and over three-quarters set 21 as the ideal age for men (Raman, 1979). The new law that in 1978 set these ages as the new minima partly reflected these trends. According to the debates over the law, however, its purpose was less to prevent child marriages than to inhibit population growth.

REFERENCES: S. N. Agarwala, *Age at Marriage in India* (Allahabad: Kitab Mahal, 1962). J.T.F. Jordens, "Hindu Religious and Social Reform in British India," in Arthur L. Basham, ed., *A Cultural History of India* (Oxford: Clarendon Press, 1975). Chitta R. Malaker, "A Note on the Estimation of Mean Age at Marriage in India," *Sankhyā*, Ser. B, 40 (1979), 236-243. M. V. Raman, "Opinion of Calcutta Couples on Ideal Age at Marriage for Boys and Girls," *Journal of the Institute of Economic Research*, 14 (1979), 17-27. J. R. Rele, "Some Aspects of Family and Fertility in India," *Population Studies*, 15 (1962), 267-278. K. Sadashivaiah, A. S. Ramesh, and J. S. Sinha, "Age at Marriage in India: The Implications of the New Legislation in the Light of 1971 Census Data," *Journal of Family Welfare*, 27 (March, 1981), 39-45.

child-woman ratio, or the number of young children per 1,000 women in the fecund ages, is used in place of a fertility rate when census data but not vital statistics are available for a population. One might suppose that children up to the first birthday would be the closest equivalent of births; but since often such infants are grossly underenumerated, the convention is to use children aged 0-4 years. As in fertility rates, the specification of the fecund years may differ. In symbolic form, then, the ratio is

$$\frac{P_{0-4}}{f_{15-44}} k \quad \text{or} \quad \frac{P_{0-4}}{f_{15-49}} k$$

or the population under 5 years per 1,000 females aged either 15 to 44 or 15 to 49 years. See also *fertility measures.

REFERENCES: Donald J. Bogue and James A. Palmore, "Some Empirical and Analytic Relations among Demographic Fertility Measures, with Regression Models for Fertility Estimation," *Demography*, 1 (1964), 316-338. B. S. Tuchfield, L. L. Guess, and W. D. Hastings, "The Bogue-Palmore Technique for Estimating Direct Fertility Measures from Indirect Indicators as Applied to Tennessee Counties, 1960-1970," *Demography*, 11 (1974), 195-205. G.S.L. Tucker, "A Note on the Reliability of Fertility Ratios," *Australian Economic History Review*, 2 (1974), 160-167.

childbearing period, better termed the *fecund period*, comprises the years from puberty to menopause during which a female is capable of conceiving. See *fecundity; *fertility measures.

childhood, the period of life between infancy ànd puberty. The word *child*, which derives from the Gothic for "womb," originally meant fetus or newborn infant, as still in "with child" or "childbirth." In current usage the limits of childhood depend on the context and are seldom precise; so-called childhood diseases, for example, are concentrated in a certain age range but also affect others. In demography the lower limit is set by the convention that *infancy ends after the first year. It is usual to divide the subsequent period between preschool children, aged 1 or 2 to 5 years, and school-aged children, from 6 to *puberty. The distinction is pertinent, for instance, in the fact that a mother is more likely to seek work outside the home once her children have reached the higher age class. Of course, the boundaries of childhood depend in part on how the particular society defines this status, a truism that was exemplified in Philippe †Ariès's thesis that in the Middle Ages children were seen as young adults. This work helped establish a new focus of social history (e.g., Hanawalt, 1977; Kroll, 1977), as well as a more specific interest in present populations. For example, Hervé †LeBras (1979) has analyzed census data of Western Europe from 1945, Magda McHale et al. (1979) the world population under 15 classified by region.

REFERENCES: Philippe Ariès, *Centuries of Childhood: A Social History of Family Life* (New York: Vintage, 1962). Barbara A. Hanawalt, "Childrearing among the Lower Classes of Late Medieval England," *Journal of Interdisciplinary History*, 8 (1977), 1-22. Jerome Kroll, "The Concept of Childhood in the Middle Ages," *Journal of the History of the Behavioral Sciences*, 13 (1977), 384-393. Hervé LeBras, *Child and the Family: Demographic Developments in OECD Countries* (Paris: Organization for Economic Cooperation and Development, 1979). Magda C. McHale, John McHale, and Guy F. Streatfield, "World of Children," *Population Bulletin*, 33:6 (1979).

childless, in the usual convention of demographers a characteristic principally of women, is defined as never having borne a live child, whether or not there were pregnancies ending in an abortion or a stillbirth. Thus, a woman who had borne children all of whom died would not be denoted childless. A couple may be childless because one or the other is sterile or because the couple decided against having children. However different the two causes, without a specific interview they are often difficult to distinguish empirically (cf. Grabill and Glick, 1959). In Western countries couples who chose not to have children have often been subject to such social pressures as inequities in taxes, insurance rates, and sometimes even wages. Childless couples are now sufficiently numerous to form meaningful interest groups, which small associations have tried to organize in the United States and Western Europe.

According to research in the United States, Britain, and Canada, the number of deliberately childless couples, once an anomaly, rose spectacularly during the 1970s (e.g., Poston and Gotard, 1977; Baum and Cope, 1980; Veevers, 1980). According to a Current Population Survey in June 1980, 36.7 percent of American women aged 18-44 had no children, and of those aged 18-34, 11 percent said they did not expect ever to start a family (cf. Pebley, 1982). The reasons given relate principally to the women's work outside the home. Between 1968 and 1978 the number of two-income families in the United States grew by 4.5 million, or to just over half of all married couples. With an average annual income about $4,000 higher than that of a traditional family in which only the husband worked, such couples could afford many conveniences and amenities, particularly if the high *cost of bearing and rearing children was not deducted (Hayghe, 1981). It should be recalled, however, that the same pattern led demographers earlier to predict—falsely—that the *fertility of Western nations would decline without such a major interruption as the *baby boom.

REFERENCES: Frances Baum and David R. Cope, "Some Characteristics of Intentionally Childless Wives in Britain," *Journal of Biosocial Science*, 12 (1980), 287-299. Wilson H. Grabill and Paul C. Glick, "Demographic and Social Aspects of Childlessness: Census Data," *Milbank Memorial Fund Quarterly*, 37 (1959), 60-86. Howard Hayghe, "Two-Income Families," *American Demographics*, 3 (September, 1981), 35-37. Anne R. Pebley, "Childless Americans," *American Demographics*, 4 (January, 1982), 18-21. Dudley L. Poston, Jr., and Erin Gotard, "Trends in Childlessness in the United States, 1910-1975," *Social Biology*, 24 (1977), 212-224. Jean E. Veevers, *Childless by Choice* (Toronto: Butterworths, 1980).

children ever born, whose number is asked of female respondents in many censuses, surveys, or population registers, comprise a less straightforward concept than might seem to be the case. The procedure recommended by the United Nations for the 1970 censuses suggests the alternative options: The question should be put to all women aged 15 years and over, whether married or not; and the number recorded should include all live-born children, legitimate or not, of the present or a prior marriage, living or dead, resident with the mother or not. Note that by this criterion adopted children, foster children, and stepchildren should not be included. Comparisons of national statistics are affected by differences in definition and scope and, perhaps more importantly, by relevant norms. In some cultures even to mention a deceased child brings bad luck to living ones. In the West an adoptive mother may be unwilling to tell anyone that the child was not born to her. Old women anywhere may forget past births followed shortly by infant deaths. In the United States the question has been asked in most censuses since 1890, but up to 1960 only of women who had ever been married. In 1970 and 1980 all females aged 15 years or over were queried regardless of their marital status, but most tabulations in 1970 were restricted to those who had ever been married. See also *birth roster.

REFERENCE: Shryock and Siegel, *Methods and Materials of Demography*, pp. 507-513.

Chile: Demographic Institutions

The Chilean Association for the Protection of the Family (APROFA), established in 1965, promotes family planning as one means of combating abortion. It provides training for physicians and other medical personnel, and gives instruction on responsible parenthood to teachers and parents. Address: Asociación Chilena de Protección a la Familia, Avenida Santa María 0494, Santiago.

Inter-American Statistical Training Center (CIENES), Centro Interamericano de Enseñanza de Estadística. See *Organization of American States.

UNIVERSITY AND OTHER RESEARCH INSTITUTES

Latin American Demographic Center (CELADE), Centro Latinoamericano de Demografía, is discussed in the entry on the *United Nations.

The Catholic University of Chile has an Institute for the Planning of Urban Development, which in 1980 was directed by Andres Necochea. Its studies of urbanization and regional planning include migration as a major component. Address: Instituto de Planificación del Desarrollo Urbano, Universidad Católica de Chile, Casilla 16002, Correo 9, Santiago.

The Institute of Sociology at the same university, directed in 1980 by José Alvarez Madrid, has concentrated on an analysis of work and the professions, thus of the labor force and population. Address: Instituto de Sociología, Casilla 114-D, Santiago.

The University of Chile's Department of Public Health and Social Medicine was established in 1970. It engages in teaching and research in demography and such related fields as biostatistics, epidemiology, public health, and hospital administration. Address: Departamento de Salud Pública y Medicina Social, Universidad de Chile, Avenida Independencia 939, Santiago.

GOVERNMENT STATISTICAL BUREAUS

Annual compilations of births and deaths, broken down into the usual classification, are published by the Ministry of Public Health. Address: Ministerio de Salud Pública, Santiago.

The National Statistical Office conducts the country's censuses. It also publishes an annual *Compendio Estadístico*, which overlaps largely with its *Anuario Estadístico* (last published in 1976) and its supposedly annual *Demografía* (last published in 1975). All three contain estimates of the population size, distribution, and characteristics. Address: Instituto Nacional de Estadísticas, Casilla 7597, Correo 3, Santiago.

China (People's Republic of China), associated with one of the oldest of the world's cultures, is its most populous nation. It was changed radically by the revolutions of 1911 and 1949, but some characteristics have remained fixed or only somewhat altered. For example, the idealization of authority instilled by *Confucianism survives in a state ruled by the Communist Party; and the archaic therapy of *Chinese medicine was artificially revivified by Communist nationalists. See also *Taiwan.

In Western sociological texts, classical China is usually cited as the prototype of a "familial society," one based on the joint *family in which three or more generations live under one roof as a social, religious, and economic unit. The decision when and whom to marry does not rest with the two participants but with their elders, and adolescents can undertake such roles as parenthood while they are still socially immature, for they will not bear the main responsibility for the care of their children. The property and the income from it, along with the earnings of all the family members, constitute a common fund out of which the needs of all are met. The larger the joint family, the greater the realm and the honor of the patriarch who rules it. Supposedly this system results in a very high fertility, for constraints are removed from young people, and the elderly are markedly pronatalist (cf. Lang, 1946). Whether the supposed ideal was often followed, however, is doubtful. Peasants could hardly afford many children; and the gentry, though considerably better off, had to consider the absence of primogeniture and the repeated division of the land. According to one of the best empirical reconstructions of gentry life, the average size of the family was under five persons—that is, two parents and just under three children (Chang, 1955, pp. 112-113).

The notion that veneration of the family was equivalent to virtually unlimited procreation, however widespread, is plainly wrong. Marital coitus was regarded as inauspicious or even dangerous on the first, seventh, fifteenth, twenty-first, twenty-eighth, and twenty-ninth days of each lunar month; on the sixteenth day of the fifth month; during solar or lunar eclipses, the days of equinoxes and solstices; when there was an earthquake, rain, thunder and lightning, great heat, or great cold; after washing the hair, a long trip, heavy drinking or eating; when the man was tired, very excited, too old; during the woman's menstruation, for one month following the birth of a child, and after the woman had reached age 40; during twenty-seven months following the death of a parent; permanently after the birth of a grandchild. In various texts only some of these rules are stressed, but books and astrological calendars denoting the auspicious and inauspicious days still circulate in Taiwan (and possibly also in Mainland China). If all the basic rules are observed, intercourse on only about a hundred days per year is permitted in order to bring forth a healthy and lucky son (Eberhard and Eberhard, 1967).

Even so, China's traditional precepts favored a large progeny sufficiently to push population growth to recurrent disaster (cf. Orleans, 1972, 1976). Only about a tenth of the country's enormous expanse is arable, and the centuries of exploitation by a vast farming population have resulted in excessive run-off and a soil that is relatively infertile. During the past two millennia there has been an average of almost one *famine per year. Most were over only a portion of the country; the worst were nationwide. But without exception every district has experienced a famine at least several times during each normal lifetime, the consequence of crop failure, droughts, floods, and locusts or other pests, all aggravated by the rapacity and incompetence of officials. In the province of Hupei, for example, of the 267 years from 1644 to 1911, only 27 were entirely free of disaster (including those for which the record is known to be incomplete). What may have been the worst famine of pre-Communist China struck four northern provinces in 1877-78. Cannibalism was reported, and local magistrates ignored the laws prohibiting the sale of children to enable parents to buy a few days' food. The dead, buried in mass graves by the tens of thousands, numbered some 9 to 13 million who in those two years perished from hunger, disease, or violence (Ho, 1959). Not surprisingly, many Chinese sought a better life by emigration, and their descendants, the *Overseas Chinese of Southeast Asia, make up sizable proportions of the populations of those countries.

Under such conditions a count of the population is not likely to be very accurate, and China's so-called censuses present scholars less with data than with puzzles. Since the territory was not fixed from one period to another, it is often uncertain how much of the outlying regions was included in population counts. Within whatever territory, the tax or conscription laws underlying each census, the stringency with which they were enforced, and the care with which records were kept all varied greatly from one time or locality to another. That the population supposedly increased by 78 million from 1911 to 1912 is only the most striking example of how little the figures mean (Ho, 1959, p. 79).

The Communist regime conducted a census in 1953 under the supervision of Soviet experts. The astounding 583 million then enumerated were about 100 million more than the population the government itself had previously estimated, and according to Western analyses the reported total may even have been a considerable undercount (Aird, 1960, 1967; U.S. Bureau of the Census, 1961). However, to this day the full results of the 1953 census have not been made public. An unannounced census was taken in 1964, and some of the data began to appear, with no reference date or source, only in 1972. The first published citation of the 1964 census was in a 1974 paper on esophageal cancer in a medical journal; it gave no figures but merely stated that the age-sex structure in 1964 had been used to standardize rates. Even the total count was first made public only in 1981 (Aird, 1982). In the meantime, a new census originally scheduled for 1980 and then for 1981 actually got under way in 1982 (cf. Pressat, 1982). The official total as of July 1, 1982, was 1,008,175,288 (or, including estimates for Taiwan, Hong Kong, and Macao, 1,032,000,000). In the same release, the Mainland total in 1964 was given as 694,581,759, which represented an average annual growth over the 18 years of 2.09 percent (cf. Li, 1983).

Since the establishment of a Communist state, its course has shifted periodically from relative moderation to violent liquidation of whatever social gains had been made. All demographic topics—measurement, number of people, population policy—followed these pendulum swings (Ashbrook, 1967; Orleans, 1981). During the establishment of power (1949-52), according to preliminary official figures, about 2 million "bandits" and about 2.5 million "landlords" were executed and some 15 million "counterrevolutionaries" were "liquidated" (Chandrasekhar, 1959). Subsequent studies helped substantiate these figures. A decree of February 21, 1951, had called for the death penalty for a long list of vaguely defined crimes—instigating the masses to opposition, damaging the solidarity between the government and the people, spreading rumors, and so on. The most detailed analysis of how this was carried out was made by the American Federation of Labor, which estimated a total of 14 million killed over a period of 5 years. Probably the figure was reasonably accurate, for the regime did not hide its mass murder; on the contrary, every effort was made to publicize the killings in order to quell any antigovernment sentiments in the rest of the population (Walker, 1955, chap. 9).

The most important step during the First Five-Year Plan (1953-57) was a massive and rapid *collectivization of agriculture. The enemy was still defined as the landlords and "rich" peasants, who were to be eliminated so that their lands could be distributed among the poor peasantry. In fact, as earlier in the Soviet Union, land was coalesced into collectives; and a succession of self-contradictory policies—reflecting partly differences in the Party leadership and partly a uniform ignorance of agriculture—was imposed on the rural population. Sweeping aside targets sketched out in a Second Five-Year Plan, the Party quickened the pace in a Great Leap Forward (1958-60) in which China's vast population was to be treated like an economic asset; "man," according to one Party leader, "should be viewed as a producer rather than a consumer." Agricultural collectives were supposed to be converted into "people's communes" comprising about 25,000 people each; all private plots were to be abolished, and each worker would be paid a wage of usually 100 yuan (or $40) *per year*, half in money and half in kind. As this official figure suggests, material incentives were to be dispensed with; the whole population was to be imbued with the same fervor that had inspired the Party during its struggle for power. The commune was intended also as a complete substitute for the home; each had great mess halls, nurseries and kindergartens, and tailor shops, so that women could be liberated and work side by side with men in the fields. Of this program, portions were carried out piecemeal and then abandoned when tens of thousands were transported off to start some other vast project (Chu, 1962; Michael, 1977, chaps. 5-6).

The Great Leap Forward culminated in the man-made famine of 1959-61. In 1959 the government officially ordered that the following be included in foodstuffs: rice husks, bean waste, potato leaves, pumpkin flowers, wild plants, and algae. Newspapers published novel recipes with such ingredients. Rice straw soaked in lime solution, dried, ground into powder, and mixed with flour was served in restaurants to those who had ration coupons. In 1960, when the state permitted the sending of food parcels from Hong Kong, more than a thousand firms were established there with a combined shipment of 200,000 parcels per day. Such figures suggest how many died of starvation and accompanying disease, but one can only state that the total was in the tens of millions (Chu, 1962).

During the Great Retreat of 1961-65 every effort was made to reconstitute China's agriculture. Vast numbers of urban dwellers were shipped off to the countryside, either for periodic disciplining or permanently. Even two of the most publicized industrial achievements, the Wuhan steel works and the Anshan industrial complex, were cut back; only the chemical industry, which manufactured fertilizers and insecticides needed for food production, was exempted. Peasants were once again encouraged to tend tiny private plots, and other private enterprise was permitted to reappear in the form of petty traders and craftsmen. After some—certainly not all—of the damage had been repaired, the Party shifted again to reckless activism in the Great Proletarian Cultural Revolution (1966-69). Schools were dismissed so that the country's children and youth could be organized into Red Guards, who attacked, verbally and physically, all who deviated from absolute adherence to orthodoxy. Some 30 percent of the country's transport was placed at the disposal of the Red Guards, who set up camps in the middle of overcrowded cities. Half a generation now lacks the minimum preparation to acquire technical or professional skills, of which the great shortage has become more acute (cf. Butterfield, 1983, passim). Any hope of a Soviet-Chinese rapprochement, and thus of a renewal of Soviet aid, was quashed. With an emphasis again on "spiritual" incentives, those who wanted to pay for efficient and conscientious work with good wages were denounced for their "economism." This self-destructive spasm, which most Westerners find puzzling, can be explained only as a desperate attempt by Mao Tse-tung, the Party chairman, to retain power against the rest of the Party leadership (cf. Michael, 1977, chap. 7).

Mao died in 1976, and there was another swing of the pendulum, expressed most significantly in foreign policy: new trade and diplomatic relations were established with Japan, the United States, and other Western powers. Of the myriad problems that faced Mao's successors, according to the usual testimony of Western observers, two were on the way to being solved—the provision of food for China's millions and the control of its population growth. In fact, the evidence for either success is less than certain.

Since the famine of 1959-61, China has imported vast amounts of grain. In view of the state's concern about "face," one could take this as an implicit indication of severe food shortages, which were reported also by many refugees in Hong Kong and elsewhere. More substantial evidence appeared in the Party's so-called self-criticism, always sharpened during a struggle for control (London and London, 1979). All production statistics are thrown into doubt by the charge of the State Statistical Bureau that the data were falsified as a "general condition." The manner of falsification varied, but not the fact that the statistics were altered or, in some instances, simply invented. During the Great Leap Forward the region of loess soil (*huang t'u*) extending some 200,000 square kilometers across six northwestern provinces had been "blindly reclaimed," expanding agricultural land by destroying forest and pasture, with a consequent serious erosion. The once grain-rich province of Szechwan was struck by a massive drought in 1977-78 just as it was recovering from the famine of 1976. In the province's Chengtu City beggars were everywhere visible, and the occasional sale of children and brides was revived. Moreover, so long as the struggle at the top was not fully resolved, local Party cadres dared not go Right or Left, and their indecisive control kept production disorganized. In 1978, according to a Communist periodical in Hong Kong cited by Butterfield (1983, p. 15), the grain ration of 200 million Chinese peasants was less than 330 pounds per year. "That is to say," the journal noted, "they are living in a state of semistarvation."

Until recently the claim that Communist China had effected a significant decline in mortality could not be tested with any meaningful data. In 1980, for the first time, the state released age-specific mortality statistics from a survey of the population in 1975. The claimed crude death rate was 7.3 per thousand population, and the expectation of life from birth was 66.2 years. The latter figure is high for a less developed country, but two American demographers concluded that it was probably based on 80-90 percent of the adult population. The level of infant and child mortality was not indicated, and no data were provided from which a guess could be made (Banister and Preston, 1981). Whether one judges these figures to be approximately correct depends at least in part on one's general appraisal of the regime. If indeed the mortality was cut as much as was claimed, then the pressure to reduce fertility was increased accordingly.

In 1978 Article 53 of China's Constitution was revised to read, "The State advocates and encourages birth control." At the Party congress that ratified this change, Mao's successor, Hua Kuo-feng, specified the goal to be sought— to reduce the annual growth of the population to less than 1 percent within 3 years. In 1980 a new marriage law was adopted (see *Population and Development Review*, 7, 1981, 369-372). Minimum ages were raised by 2 years, to 22 for males and 20 for females, with a later marriage to be encouraged, as before. "Husband and wife are in duty bound to practice family planning." The care of dependents remained squarely within the immediate family, though parents who would have to depend on their children for support in their old age were encouraged to have only one child. Rather intrusive controls were combined with the denigration, derived from classical Marxism, of the family institution: no difference was permitted between legitimate and illegitimate offspring, and divorce was to be granted on demand from the two partners. Urban couples with one child who pledged to use contraceptives to hold their family size to that figure could apply for a "one-child certificate," which entitled them to a monthly stipend until the child reached 14 years, preferential treatment in schooling for the child and in housing, jobs, and pensions for themselves. Rural one-child couples, similarly, were to receive additional monthly work points, the basis for reckoning the payments in cash and kind. If a worker or official had three or more children, 6 percent of the combined income of husband and wife would be deducted for "welfare expenses." By such measures it was intended to achieve zero population growth by the end of the century (Chen and Kols, 1982; Mosher, 1983; Orleans, 1979, Introduction).

According to the age data reported in the 1982 census, half of the population was under 21 years, and each year up to the end of the century more than 11 million couples will reach childbearing age. These statistics indicate how difficult it will be to realize the government's population program. In his report on the Sixth Five-Year Plan for Economic and Social Development (1981-85), Premier Zhao Ziyang set a target of 1.06 billion by 1985:

> The whole society must pay full attention to this problem. We must take effective measures and encourage late marriage, advocate one child for each couple, strictly control second births, and resolutely prevent additional births so as to control population growth.... Persuasive education must be conducted ... to change radically the feudal attitude of viewing sons as better than daughters.... The whole society should resolutely condemn the criminal activities of female infanticide and maltreatment of the mothers, and the judicial departments should resolutely punish the offenders according to law [translated in *Population and Development Review*, 9, 1983, 181-184].

That *infanticide should be condemned at so high a level suggests that it must be fairly prevalent. For centuries a strong preference for sons has been ingrained in China's normative and institutional systems, and many peasants amend the official slogan "One couple, one child" to read "This couple, one son" (cf. Goodstadt, 1982; Mosher, 1983).

Official estimates of the annual growth rate during the period 1949-74 average out at about 1.9 percent; Western estimates run somewhat higher to around 2.0-2.15 percent (Howe, 1978, chap. 1). Very roughly, then, the program called for a cut in the rate of growth by perhaps as much as half within 3 years. According to official reports, already in mid-1978 the rate had reached the target in six provinces, or over two-fifths of the total population. This is incredible, but what is to be believed? There is no evidence that even Chinese officials then knew what the population was, not to say what the birth rate might have been to the nearest hundredth.

In two papers Ansley †Coale (1981) analyzed whatever data were available and concluded that a remarkably low level of fertility had been achieved. In a very full review John †Aird (1981) noted various social-cultural factors that might result in smaller families or in a continuation of pronatalist attitudes. The Party cadres, competing to show the best records in fulfilling the new quotas, at least in some instances used coercion. It was charged in the Chinese press that overzealous provincial organizers had imposed fines, cut food rations, and otherwise used "cruel persecution" against those exceeding their birth quotas, in some cases driving them to suicide (Aird, 1981, pp. 186-193; cf. Mosher, 1983). Coale, Aird, and Leo †Orleans, three of the best American authorities, thus more or less agree that fertility remained high until the early 1970s and then declined markedly. Until better statistics become available, this is the most probable guess.

REFERENCES: John S. Aird, "The Present and Prospective Population of Mainland China," in Milbank Memorial Fund, *Population Trends in Eastern Europe, the USSR and Mainland China* (New York, 1960); "Estimating China's Population," *Annals of the American Academy of Political and Social Science*, 369 (1967), 61-72; "Fertility Decline in China," in Nick Eberstadt, ed., *Fertility Decline in the Less Developed Countries* (New York: Praeger, 1981); "Population Studies and Population Policy in China," *Population and Development Review*, 8 (1982), 267-297. Arthur G. Ashbrook, Jr., "Main Lines of Communist Economic Policy," in U.S. Congress, Joint Economic Committee, *An Economic Profile of Mainland China* (Washington, D.C., 1967). Judith Banister and Samuel H. Preston, "Mortality in China," *Population and Development Review*, 7 (1981), 98-110. Fox Butterfield, *China: Alive in the Bitter Sea* (New York: Bantam Books, 1983). Sripati Chandrasekhar, *China's Population: Census and Vital Statistics* (Hong Kong: Hong Kong University Press, 1959). Chung-li Chang, *The Chinese Gentry: Studies on Their Role in Nineteenth Century Chinese Society* (Seattle: University of Washington Press, 1955). Pi-chao Chen and Adrienne Kols, "Population and Birth Planning in the People's Republic of China," Johns Hopkins University, Population Information Program, *Population Reports*, Ser. J, no. 25 (January-February, 1982). Valentin Chu, "The Famine Makers," *New Leader* (June 11, 1962), pp. 13-21. Ansley J. Coale, "Population Trends, Population Policy, and Population Studies in China" and "A Further Note on Chinese Population Statistics," *Population and Development Review*, 7 (1981), 88-97, 512-518. Wolfram Eberhard and Alide Eberhard, "Family Planning in a Taiwanese Town," in Wolfram Eberhard, *Settlement and Social Change in Asia* (Hong Kong: Hong Kong University Press, 1967). Leo F. Goodstadt, "China's One-Child Family: Policy and Public Response," *Population and Development Review*, 8 (1982), 37-58. Ping-ti Ho, *Studies on the Population of China, 1368-1953* (Cambridge, Mass.: Harvard University Press, 1959). Christopher Howe, *China's Economy: A Basic Guide* (London: Paul Erek, 1978). Olga Lang, *Chinese Family and Society* (New Haven, Conn.: Yale University Press, 1946). Li Chengrui, "On the Results of the Chinese Census," *Population and Development Review*, 9 (1983), 326-344. Miriam London and Ivan D. London, "Hunger in China: The Failure of a System?" *Worldview*, 22 (1979), 44-49. Franz Michael, *Mao and the Perpetual Revolution* (Woodbury, N.Y.: Barron's, 1977). Steven W. Mosher, *Broken Earth: The Rural Chinese* (New York: Free Press, 1983). Leo A. Orleans, *Every Fifth Child: The Population of China* (Stanford, Calif.: Stanford University Press, 1972); "A Selective Bibliography of the Demography of China," *Population Index*, 42 (1976), 653-693; ed., *Chinese Approaches to Family Planning* (White Plains, N.Y.: M. E. Sharpe, 1979); "China's Population Policies and Population Data: Review and Update," in U.S. House of Representatives, Committee on Foreign Affairs, 97th Congress, 1st Session, *Committee Reprint* (Washington, D.C.: U.S. Government Printing Office, 1981). Roland Pressat, "La Population de la Chine: Bilan des Trente Dernières Années," *Population*, 37 (1982), 299-316. U.S. Bureau of the Census,

"The Size, Composition and Growth of the Population of Mainland China," *International Population Statistics Report*, Ser. P-90, no. 15 (Washington, D.C., 1961). Richard L. Walker, *China under Communism: The First Five Years* (New Haven, Conn.: Yale University Press, 1955).

China (People's Republic of China): Demographic Institutions

Like much else in the country, China's demographic and statistical operations have gone through violent changes (see *China). The statistical system, gradually built up during the mid-1950s to a modest functional level, was destroyed during the Great Leap Forward: statistics were declared to be "a weapon of the class struggle" and not "a mere display of objective facts." The subsequent slow rebuilding, which started in the early 1960s, was set back again by the Cultural Revolution. In effect, the responsibility for keeping records was transferred from professionals to "the masses" under local Party committees. The consequence was a flood of what later was designated as "boasting, exaggeration, and omission of facts." It is not known whether the State Statistical Bureau continued to exist in skeletal form. In retrospect, it was admitted that "many statistical agencies were abolished, many statistical workers persecuted, and many statistical data destroyed." The rebuilding with another turn of the wheel was slower than a decade earlier (Aird, 1982; Orleans, 1981).

It is difficult to grasp the immensity of the difficulties to be overcome. The Cultural Revolution, when many universities and schools were closed, left a half generation illiterate at worst or, at best, lacking any higher education. The Party's reassurance that its "leadership over statistical work is not meant to interfere with how statisticians make their reports" is not quite believed. Many who work with statistics, according to the *People's Daily* (December 7, 1979), "are fearful some problems may arise that will get them into trouble." The number of statistical workers is small, their level of competence is low, and they are not inclined to accept the current line that even unpleasant truths should be accurately reported. As the content of local registers makes its tortuous route from team to brigade to commune to county to province to the capital, the journey will not improve the quality of the data being transmitted.

A census following those of 1953 and 1964 was announced for 1980 and again for 1981; it took place in 1982 (cf. *China). One can hardly imagine that the count was of adequate quality. Various training programs had been established, but the necessary preparatory work was still in process while the enumeration was under way. Under †Liu Cheng (Liu Zheng), director of the Institute of Population Research at the Chinese People's University, Peking, a committee worked at compiling (or constructing, for many terms did not exist in Chinese) a demographic dictionary. Textbooks were put together, mostly by Liu and his colleagues. Two four-year programs were set up in 1982, at People's University with about thirty students and at Fudan University, Shanghai, with about twenty. The first two years were to cover only preparatory work in statistics, economics, and sociology, and in 1982 the content of the training in demography during the subsequent two years had not yet been finally set (cf. Mertens, 1981). The count was supervised by the Population Census Office, Peking; and a 64-page summary pamphlet, *The 1982 Population Census of China (Major Figures)* was issued by the Department of Population Statistics of the State Statistical Bureau, as well as by the Economic Information Agency, Hong Kong.

A one-month course was given by three foreign demographers, under the direction of Walter †Mertens—Jacques †Henripin of the University of Montreal, Warren †Robinson of Pennsylvania State University, and †Kuroda Toshio of Nihon University, Tokyo. The lectures had to be translated, and the instructors were warned that the interpreters would be unfamiliar with the subject matter and any special vocabulary, and that few of the students knew anything of developments in demography and social science "in the last thirty years." The students were to be the faculty in a number of other demography programs.

The U.N. Fund for Population Activities, with Walter Mertens as advisor, has given support for the establishment of ten population centers under the direction of Ms. Fan Zhong-ming in the Ministry of Education. The centers are as follows:

Population Research Group
Anhui University
Hofei (Hefei)

Institute of Population Research
Chinese People's University
Peking (Beijing)

Population Research Group
Chungshan (Zhongshan) University
Kwangchow (Guangzhou)

Population Research Group
Department of Economics
Fudan University
Shanghai

Population Research Group
Hopei (Hebei) University
Paoting (Baoding)

Population Research Group
Department of Economics
Kirin (Jilin) University
Changchun

Population Research Group
Department of Economics
Lanchow (Lanzhou) University
Lanchow

Institute of Population Economics
Peking (Beijing) College of Economics
Peking

Population Research Group
Department of Economics
Peking (Beijing) University
Peking

Institute of Population Research
Szechwan (Sichuan) University
Chengtu (Chengdu)

The Chinese Academy of Social Sciences has a population program in its Institute of Social Sciences, also supported by the U.N. Fund for Population Activities.

There are also additional centers under the Ministry of Education but not supported by UNFPA. Some of these have been partially developed; others are just beginning. These centers are:

Population Research Group
Amoy University
Amoy

Population Research Group
Chengchow (Zhengzhou) University
Chengchow

Population Research Office
Heilungkiang (Heilongjiang) University
Harbin

Population Research Group
Honan (Henan) Normal University
Kaifeng

Population Research Group
Hopei (Hebei) Teacher Training University
Shihkiachwang (Shijiazhuang)

Population Research Group
Department of Statistics
Liaoning College of Finance and Economics
Dairen (Dalian)

Population Research Group
Institute of Economic Research
Nankai University
Tientsin (Tianjin)

Population Research Group
Nanking (Nanjing) University
Nanking

Society for Demography
Sian Chiaotung (Xian Jiaotong) University
Sian (Xian)

Population Research Group
Szechwan (Sichuan) College of Finance and
    Economics
Chengtu (Chengdu)

Population Research Office
Department of Economics
Tsinan (Jinan) University
Kwangchow, Kwangtung (Guangzhou,
Guangdong)

Population Research Group
Department of Economics
Wuhan University
Wuhan

REFERENCES: John S. Aird, "Population Studies and Population Policy in China," *Population and Development Review*, 8 (1982), 267-297. Walter Mertens, "Demographic Research and Training Report on Activities, June 1981-November 1981," *Report to the U.N. Office of Technical Cooperation* (1981). Leo A. Orleans, "China's Population Policy and Population Data: Review and Update," in U.S. House of Representatives, Committee on Foreign Affairs, 97th Congress, 1st Session, *Committee Reprint* (Washington, D.C.: U.S. Government Printing Office, 1981). H. Yuan Tien, "Demography in China: From Zero to Now," *Population Index*, 47 (1981), 683-710.

Chinese Americans, a tiny minority, are noteworthy because of some special characteristics. Most of the early immigrants were indentured laborers, so-called coolies, whose status often verged on slavery. Partly for this reason, partly because of a frankly racist opposition, a series of impediments were imposed on Chinese, first in California and then nationally (cf. Hansen, 1970). In 1870 they were barred from citizenship. In 1882 Chinese immigration was suspended for ten years, and the bar was renewed each decade until 1924, when the Immigration Act permanently prohibited the immigration of aliens ineligible for naturalization. Of the total of some 36 million persons listed as entering the United States from 1820, when the inadequate record starts, to 1924, only about 1 percent were Chinese. There was an illegal inflow of indeterminate size, but any figures on gross immigration considerably overstate the number who remained, for Chinese were the prototypical *sojourners. Virtually all were young males; of the more than 100,000 Chinese enumerated in the censuses of 1880 and 1890, only about 4,000 were females (Lyman, 1974).

The response of the Chinese to discrimination was to retreat—by migration back home, by living in separate quarters more or less cut off from the general population, and by concentrating on occupations that did not compete with non-Chinese, such as serving the Chinese community itself with exotic foods and commodities or catering to tourists. The relative isolation was reinforced by community organizations, which helped assimilate newcomers into the China-towns (Petersen, 1978). Recent immigrants from Hong Kong (or, in many cases, via Hong Kong from northern China), who are admissible under new regulations set in 1952, are often unable to adjust either to established Chinese communities, most of whose inhabitants speak Cantonese, or to the general American society (cf. Sung, 1975; Tsai, 1980). In 1980 the number of Chinese Americans enumerated was 806,027.

In spite of all impediments, Chinese Americans have shown a number of marked successes. According to 1970 census figures, they had completed an average of 12.4 years of schooling, compared with 12.2 for the total population. Of employed males aged 16 years and over, 28.7 percent of the Chinese were in professional or technical occupations, just over double the proportion of the total population. The median 1969 income of the Chinese-American males, however, was $5,223, well under the $6,444 for all American males.

REFERENCES: Gladys C. Hansen, *The Chinese in California: A Brief Bibliographic History* (San Francisco: San Francisco Public Library, 1970), annotated references for the period 1850-1968. Stanford M. Lyman, *Chinese Americans* (New York: Random House, 1974). William Petersen, "Chinese Americans and Japanese Americans," in Thomas Sowell, ed., *Essays and Data on American Ethnic Groups* (Washington, D.C.: Urban Institute, 1978). Betty Lee Sung, *Statistical Profile of the Chinese in the United States, 1970 Census* (Washington, D.C.: Manpower Administration, U.S. Department of Labor, 1975). Frank Wen-hui Tsai, "Diversity and Conflict between Old and New Chinese Immigrants in the United States," in Roy S. Bryce-Laporte, ed., *Sourcebook on the New Immigration: Implications for the United States and the International Community* (New Brunswick, N.J.: Transaction Books, 1980).

Chinese medicine in its traditional state consisted not only of the well publicized acupuncture and the less known moxa (a mass of wormwood leaves burnt on the skin as a cautery) but—in the words of an early Western authority, William R. Morse (1934)—of "a far-reaching and interlocking relationship of the practices of medicine with superstition and religious practices, magic, divination, sorcery, astrology, alchemy, palmistry, geomancy, physiognomy, necromancy, spiritism, demonology, fortune telling, etc.'' In a word, it differed in no essential from the Western medicine of the Middle Ages and was as effective in preventing a mortality that probably fluctuated between high and disastrously high. The demonstrable superiority of scientific therapies developed in the West, however, has not broken the attachment of people to herbs and practices millennia old, as is evident from not only the Chinese quarters in Western cities but even from modern Japan. Most of the population of pre-Communist China had little chance to make any comparison, for the slight intrusion of Western medicine was concentrated in the coastal cities.

According to Chinese accounts, their medicine dates from the legendary culture heroes Shen Nung and Huang-ti of the third millennium B.C., reaching a kind of apex of codification during the Han dynasty (206 B.C.-A.D. 220). Underlying the practices was a homeostatic concept of health and disease; the crucial factor in maintaining health is harmony or equilibrium of the dual forces in the universe, *yin* and *yang*, and the five elements of which the universe is composed—wood, fire, earth, metal, and water. Medical practice was highly derivative from these theoretical concepts (Croizier, 1968).

That a revolutionary regime intent on modernization should have reinforced a system of medicine praised for its ancient origins is on the face of it remarkable. The move was partly a reflection of Chinese Communists' nationalism, partly an accommodation to the masses' preference, and partly an expedient by which **''barefoot doctors''* could be put in the field after only a half-year of formal training. A strange amalgam of traditional and Western medicine is reflected in a 1,200-page compendium entitled *Peasant Village Physician's Handbook* (see the review and summary in *Science*, 178 (1972), 394-395). Much of the material relates to sanitation or nutrition rather than medicine—''extinguish the four pests,'' namely, rats, flies, mosquitoes, and bedbugs; build secure latrines; eat proper food. Diseases are diagnosed and classified by methods familiar in the West, but then subclassified with the classical terminology in the section on treatment. This consolidation has been achieved and maintained by a new system of medical education that is intended to bring together the best of both types of practice (Orleans, 1969). Whatever success in therapy there might have been is impossible to judge, for the lack of adequate statistics is matched by a heavy ideological infiltration (Gibson, 1972). See also *Indian medicine.

REFERENCES: Ralph C. Croizier, *Traditional Medicine in Modern China: Science, Nationalism, and the Tension of Cultural Change* (Cambridge, Mass.: Harvard University Press, 1968). Geoffrey Gibson, ''Chinese Medical Practice and the Thoughts of Chairman Mao,'' *Social Science and Medicine*, 6 (1972), 67-93. William R. Morse, *Chinese Medicine* (New York: Hoeber, 1934). Leo A. Orleans, ''Medical Education and Manpower in Communist China,'' *Comparative Education Review*, 13 (1969), 20-42.

chiropractic, a school of therapy founded by D. D. Palmer in Davenport, Iowa, and successfully promoted by his son, B. J. Palmer, in the years following 1895. According to its main thesis, all illness results from an interference in the nervous system from "subluxations," or slight dislocations of the spinal column. Originally, thus, all treatment consisted of manipulation of the spinal column, which later practitioners supplemented with various other nostrums. More or less restricted to the United States and Canada, it has achieved a certain degree of respectability, with chiropractors licensed since 1974 in all states and chiropractic colleges authorized to teach and supervise the licensing of new practitioners.

REFERENCE: Walter I. Wardwell, "Orthodox and Unorthodox Practitioners," in Wallis and Morley, *Marginal Medicine.*

chlormadinone, a progesterone derivative used with an estrogen as an oral contraceptive.

cholera, an acute infectious disease, marked by severe diarrhea, vomiting, and dehydration. It is spread by a microorganism, *Vibrio cholerae,* discharged from patients' bowels and typically disseminated in drinking water. Asiatic cholera spread to Western Europe and America in the 1820s and 1830s, and for a period it became there one of the most dreaded diseases, killing in a most unpleasant manner about half of those infected (Rosenberg, 1962). As early as 1849, the London physician John Snow correctly guessed its cause and mode of transmission, and in 1883 the vibrio was isolated by Robert Koch, the German bacteriologist. The initial control was not through effective therapy but rather by the construction of sewage systems that effectively separated excreta from drinking water—and this has yet to be done in most less developed countries.

Today's air travel can spread diseases with alarming rapidity. In the 1960s a variant called cholera El Tor swept through the Far East from Korea to Pakistan and southward to Indonesia, and in 1970 it appeared in Italy, France, and Spain and stimulated a hysterical response there. This outbreak was followed by a good deal of new research (Felsenfeld, 1966). Presently the most important treatment is to restore the body fluid lost in evacuations, which number up to forty a day. In the treatment that prevailed until very recently, about twenty liters of saline fluid per patient had to be infused intravenously, while at the same time correcting the chemical imbalance—processes that require a medical staff and clinical facilities distributed over the whole of the affected area. In the current therapeutic technique the patient drinks a solution of glucose, sodium chloride, potassium chloride, and sodium bicarbonate, as well as receiving the antibiotic tetracycline, which kills the vibrio (Adams, 1973). Infection can be inhibited by vaccination, but the principal preventive measures still relate to sanitation rather than medicine. It used to be that countries did not report cholera cases, for the governments were fearful of its reputation as a killer and ashamed of the countries' inadequate hygiene (cf. Hanlon, 1981). According to the ac-

counting of the World Health Organization, the cases in 1979 numbered 54,179—
38,842 in Asia, 18,996 in Africa, and the rest in scattered reports from Europe
(*World Health*, August, 1980, p. 39).

REFERENCES: Mary M. Eichhorn Adams, "Cholera: New Aids in Treatment and
Prevention," *Science*, 179 (1973), 552-555. Oscar Felsenfeld, "A Review of Recent
Trends in Cholera Research and Control," *Bulletin of the WHO*, 34 (1966), 161-195.
Joseph Hanlon, "Cholera Can Be Controlled," *World Health* (April, 1981), pp. 8-11.
Charles E. Rosenberg, *The Cholera Years: The United States in 1832, 1849, and 1866*
(Chicago: University of Chicago Press, 1962).

cholesterol, a fatlike, pearly substance, $C_{27}H_{45}OH$, found in all animal fats and
oils, in bile, blood, brain tissue, milk, egg yolk, nerve fibers, the liver, kidneys,
and adrenal glands. It is present in the most frequent type of gallstones, hardened
arteries, various cysts, and some types of cancerous tissue. A learned dispute
developed in the 1970s whether a diet with smaller amounts of animal fat would
reduce the probability of developing a *heart disease. As one expert remarked,
"A generation of research on the diet-heart question ended in disarray. . . . One
of the originators of the diet-heart hypothesis, E. H. Ahrens, wrote in 1969 and
has restated in recent congressional testimony, 'It is not proven that dietary
modification can prevent arteriosclerotic heart disease in man'" (cf. Mann,
1977). This debate was not resolved by a highly publicized study conducted by
the U. S. National Heart, Lung, and Blood Institute, which issued a long-awaited
report in 1984. Some 3,806 men aged 35 to 59 with cholesterol levels in the
upper 5 percent of the national range were examined regularly over as long as
a decade. A test group were administered doses of cholestyramine, which reduced
their cholesterol level by an average of 8.5 percent, and a control group were
given a placebo. Those who took the drug had 19 percent fewer heart attacks
and 24 percent fewer deaths from heart disease than those in the control group.
Since all participants were restricted to a low-cholesterol diet, however, the study
left moot the most puzzling question, whether cholesterol in one's diet affects
the amount of cholesterol in the blood and thus the risk of heart disease (cf.
Kolata, 1984).

REFERENCES: Gina Kolata, "Lowered Cholesterol Decreases Heart Disease," *Science*, 223 (January 27, 1984), 381-382. George Mann, "Diet-Heart: End of an Era,"
New England Journal of Medicine, 279 (1977), 644-650.

Christian Science, a religious sect distinguished mainly by its theory of disease
and therapy, was founded by Mary Baker Eddy (1821-1910), who wrote: "That
which [God] creates is good, and He makes all that is made. Therefore the only
reality of sin, sickness, or death is the awful fact that unrealities seem real to
human, erring belief, until God strips off their disguise." In accordance with
this doctrine, members of the church do not accept medical treatment, and they
have opposed such public-health measures as compulsory vaccination. The
denomination has survived and prospered in part by adaptations through

interpretation, in part by ignoring such prohibitions as of contraception. Its membership is mainly American, with about 2,400 churches; the far smaller numbers in other countries are mainly in Western Europe. Most of the adherents are of the middle class and often well above the median age of the population. The number of members, about a quarter million a generation ago, has apparently been declining, principally because those dying off have not been replaced by new recruits.

REFERENCE: Arthur E. Nudelman, "The Maintenance of Christian Science in Scientific Society," in Wallis and Morley, *Marginal Medicine*.

Christianity, the religion based on the teaching of Jesus, whom his followers regarded as the "Anointed King" or "Savior" (Hebrew, *Messiah*; Greek, *Christos*) and hence were called Christians. Many of the doctrines associated with one or another denomination pertain to family life, fertility, contraception, and other matters relevant to demography; but they have varied so greatly that they can best be discussed under some branches of Christianity (*Calvinism, *Christian Science, *Eastern Orthodox Churches, *Lutheranism, and *Roman Catholicism), certain of the more influential individuals (Thomas †Aquinas, †Augustine, Ernst †Troeltsch) and various particular topics (*celibacy, *church, *denomination, *Fundamentalism, *Humanae Vitae, *Vatican Council II).

chronic, of a disease, long continued, nonreversible; not acute. Usually the condition is defined operationally simply in terms of the duration of the malady, such as a morbid condition lasting for three months or more (U.S. National Health Interview Statistics) or one that is permanent or needs a long period of care. Obviously such a criterion depends in part on the state of knowledge; once it is known what causes a morbid condition, it may not be chronic in this sense, whether the cause is genetic (such as hyperthyroidism) or environmental (such as pellagra). It is possible to estimate the prevalence of particular chronic diseases from mortality data (Manton and Stallard, 1982). In 1980, according to estimates by the U.S. National Center for Health Statistics (1981), "chronic conditions" in the United States resulted in a limited activity for 14.4 percent of the population, including 10.9 who were restricted in carrying out a "major" activity, defined as work, housekeeping, or school. These figures were essentially the same as in the immediately prior years.

In a proposed new definition, James Fries and Lawrence Crapo (1981, chap. 7) suggest that "chronic" should be applied to the nearly universal diseases that mark the loss of organ functions with *aging. The effects of a chronic disease in this sense can only be postponed. Some ailments that presently last for a long time (e.g., rheumatoid arthritis or ulcerative colitis) may be eventually curable; but truly chronic diseases (atherosclerosis, emphysema, some cancers, diabetes, osteoarthritis, cirrhosis) mark the fact that the human *life span is finite. They typically proceed from certain types of life-style through discernible but subclinical symptoms to eventually severe conditions and *disability or death. With the lesser importance of infectious diseases, chronic conditions have become the most important causes of death in all developed countries. One who has lived his full span and succumbs finally to old age has what Fries and Crapo term a "natural death," as contrasted with a "premature death," the consequence of a curable disease or a trauma.

REFERENCES: James F. Fries and Lawrence M. Crapo, *Vitality and Aging: Implications of the Rectangular Curve* (San Francisco: W. H. Freeman, 1981). Kenneth G. Manton and Eric Stallard, "The Use of Mortality Time Series Data to Produce Hypothetical Morbidity Distributions and Project Mortality Trends," *Demography*, 19 (1982), 223-240. U.S. National Center for Health Statistics, *Current Estimates from the National Health Interview Survey: United States, 1980* (Washington, D.C., 1981).

chunk, in the jargon of *PGE surveys, a small village, hamlet, or small precinct of a town. A chunk is made up of several "blocks," each comprising 50 to 100 dwellings or 200 to 500 residents. Several chunks make up a "PGE area," the sampling unit in such a survey, which may range up to a population of 5,000 to 10,000.

church, the generic term for a religious organization, refers also to the church-sect typology expounded by Ernst †Troeltsch. A sect is small, with a voluntary membership based on a literal interpretation of the gospel and an undeviating observance of the rules it sets down. A church, representing a compromise with secular society, is universal in membership, with an elaborate ritual, a sizable personnel structured into a hierarchy, and typically some accommodation to infractions of religious norms. The American sociologist Howard Becker expanded the typology into ecclesia (equivalent to church), sect, *denomination and cult. The principal relevance to demography is twofold: the difference in social controls set by the several types of organization (see *religion), and the usual gross underenumeration of members of sects or cults.

circle, in the terminology of Louis †Henry (1976, pp. 274-277), a permanent or transitory group in which relations lead to endogamous marriages. It is "complete" when all of the permitted marriages have taken place, and "transitory" when the young unmarried persons have to leave the circle to look for mates.

REFERENCE: Henry, *Population*.

circulation, an alternative designation for certain types of internal migration, is used to stress the fact that many movements are of short duration and recurrent. Other terms that indicate the same characteristics include repeat migration, circular migration, wage-labor migration, seasonal mobility, movement of *sojourners, *transhumance, and *commuting. Essentially a differentiation can be made between movements that involve a change in the permanent place of residence (*migration) and those that do not (circulation).

REFERENCES: Murray T. Chapman, "On the Cross-Cultural Study of Circulation," *International Migration Review*, 12 (1978), 559-569; "Circulation," in *International Encyclopedia of Population*, 1, 93-98.

citizen, one who owes allegiance to a state and is entitled to reciprocal protection from it, is contrasted with *alien. As suggested by its etymology, the word *citizen* meant originally a townsman, especially an inhabitant of a city who enjoyed its privileges as a free man or burgess. In present usage the concept applies to the larger nation-state, but there is still a suggestion of membership in a community by the contrast with *subject*, which implies allegiance to a sovereign. In its recommendations for the 1970 censuses, the United Nations classified citizenship only as one among "other useful topics." The practice of countries has varied depending in part on their laws concerning *nationality. According to the Fourteenth Amendment to the U.S. Constitution, "All persons born or naturalized in the United States, and subject to the jurisdiction thereof, are citizens of the United States and of the State wherein they reside." In the United States censuses, therefore, questions on citizenship have been asked only of foreign-born residents, and of them only intermittently. In 1970, for instance, only the foreign-born included in a 5-percent sample were asked whether they had been naturalized and the approximate year when they had immigrated. In 1980 the long form asked foreign-born respondents for the country of birth, citizenship, and date of immigration; it omitted the question on the countries of birth of the enumerated person's parents, asked in 1970, and on their mother tongues, last asked in 1920. The number in the "foreign stock," comprising the foreign-born plus the native-born of one or both foreign-born parents, thus can no longer be derived from current data.

city, an inhabited place granted certain powers and privileges by a higher government; loosely, a relatively large and important inhabited place. The word derives from *civitas*, which Romans used to designate the independent tribes of Gaul and later their seats of government. In England, as episcopal sees settled in the older towns, a "city" became identified with a "cathedral town," and there the designation has remained largely honorific: a "city," so designated by an ecclesiastic or royal authority, has the same powers as a county borough. In the United States a city is a self-governing entity to which the state government has delegated the right to provide municipal services. Elsewhere in the world a city is commonly an administrative appendage of the central government.

Both in common parlance and in the social sciences, however, "city" is typically used as a rough synonym of *town or large town—that is, a more or less dense aggregation of population that, because of its occupational and institutional organization and its location on the principal transportation and communication routes, serves as the region's focal point. It is the medium, for example, through which the region relates to the nation and the world at large. As recent developments in transportation and communication resulted in a greater differentiation and specialization, the functions of single cities prior to the twentieth century were often taken over by a system of cities arranged in an approximate hierarchy of administrative specialization. However, many urban functions have shifted to suburbs or smaller towns, partly because metropolitan life has often become troublesome or even dangerous. Among the twenty-five largest American cities in 1982, ten had lost population since the 1980 enumeration, from Detroit, by 5.3 percent, to Memphis, by 0.1 percent. Those cities that continued to grow over that period were in the Southwest—Houston, which in 1982 was the fourth largest city after New York, Los Angeles, and Chicago by 8.2 percent; as well as San Jose, San Diego, Phoenix, Dallas, and San Antonio, each of which grew by more than 4 percent (*American Demographics*, 6 [July, 1984], 16).

city-state, the designation that developed during the nineteenth century for the Greek *polis*, which in French is called a *cité*. It is a political unit, characteristic of ancient Greece or Renaissance Italy, concentrated in a single town. In fact, the city-state was more than a city, for it contained agricultural areas; and it was hardly a state as this term has been understood in modern times.

civil divisions, territorial units that the nation-state has set, typically determine the first criterion by which the country's population is classified. Civil divisions are ranked by size and importance into what are termed—not entirely consistently—primary, secondary, and tertiary. In various countries around the world, the commonest names for primary units are district, province, island, department, parish, state, and *region; for secondary ones, *county, district, and commune; and for tertiary, *township or its equivalent in other languages. Even within the United States terminology is far from consistent. There are fifty states (plus the District of Columbia), and the subdivisions of states are called counties except in Louisiana ("parishes") and Alaska ("election districts"). In addition to counties there are the "independent cities" of Baltimore, St. Louis, and thirty-two in Virginia. So-called minor civil divisions are named townships in most states, but *towns in New England, New York, and Wisconsin. There are also thousands of administrative units of various types—school districts, taxation districts, and so on; generally the U.S. Bureau of the Census does not publish figures for these.

A classification of population by civil divisions has obvious but very limited uses. Since American states, counties, and townships, for example, do not ordinarily constitute meaningful social-economic units, most analyses either accept the limitations of the classification (discussing trends in "the South" or "the Middle West," for instance) or use a totally different typology based on occupation, race, income, or some other index of social units that are not arbitrarily delineated.

civil liberties and **civil rights,** often used synonymously, can be usefully distinguished. "Civil liberties" are of individuals, who have the right to be protected against certain specific governmental acts or, by the government, against the harmful acts of private persons or groups. "Civil rights" has come to refer mainly to ethnic minorities, the right of a group to a specified type of equality (cf. *affirmative action). Both types of rights, though justified philosophically by natural law, derive in fact from the legal authority of a state. They differ fundamentally from the recently popular concept of *human rights, which supposedly exist apart from any institution to define and maintain them.

civil service, originally a composite of all but military and judicial public employees, was applied first to those in British India and subsequently to those in the home country. Both in Britain and in the United States, the term became associated with a reform of the spoils system of political appointments. In present usage in the United States, civil service means either a specific portion of public employees so designated in federal or state law or, more loosely, that portion of the nonmilitary labor force engaged in government rather than private employment. In most countries of the world, the proportion of the work force in government employment has risen greatly. Between 1950 and 1975 one out of every four new entrants to the nonfarm labor force in the United States worked for a government. The increase was most evident in state and local governments, as the table indicates (Tucker, 1981). These figures, however, understate the amount of tax dollars used to pay for government service, for tens of thousands of consultants of diverse types also get sometimes very sizable fees, though they are classified in nongovernment employment. The number of persons working for the federal government in research organizations, universities, and elsewhere outside federal agencies has been estimated as high as 8 million—more than 2 million for the Department of Defense, almost a million for the Department of Health and Human Services, and the balance for various other bureaus (Bennett, 1981).

Government Employees, United States, 1920-80

	Number of Employees (thousands)	Percent of Nonfarm Labor Force		
		Total	**Federal**	**State and Local**
1920	27,340	9.5	n.a.	n.a.
1930	29,409	10.7	1.8	8.9
1940	32,361	13.0	3.1	9.9
1950	45,197	13.3	4.3	9.1
1960	54,189	15.4	4.2	11.2
1970	70,880	17.7	3.9	13.9
1980	90,564	17.9	3.2	14.8

Source: John T. Tucker, "Government Employment: An Era of Slow Growth," *Monthly Labor Review*, 104 (October, 1981), 19-25.

At least in theory the efficiency of most workers or employees is maintained at a reasonable level by competition in the labor market. Estimating the efficiency of government employees, however, is difficult—some say impossible; for in virtually every activity there are multiple and often conflicting objectives. Some critics of the trend contend that as government takes over previously private functions, they are typically carried out less effectively (cf. Bahl et al., 1980).

REFERENCES: Roy Bahl, Jesse Burkhead, and Bernard Jump, Jr., eds., *Public Employment and State and Local Government Finance* (Cambridge, Mass.: Ballinger, 1980). James T. Bennett, "How Big Is the Federal Government?" Federal Reserve Bank of Atlanta, *Economic Review* (December, 1981), pp. 43-49. John T. Tucker, "Government Employment: An Era of Slow Growth," *Monthly Labor Review*, 104 (October, 1981), 19-25.

civilization derives from *civis*, Latin for "citizen," and its several ranges of meaning are suggested by this etymology. The social analysts of earlier centuries who traced an upward path from savagery to a future utopia sometimes labeled the highest stage "civilization," thus reinforcing the prior contrast between the ways of life of "urbane" city dwellers and those of rural "boors" (from *boer*, Dutch for peasant) or "clodhoppers." The differentiation was in some respects similar to that now made between developed and less developed countries: those in the first category live longer and more comfortably, with smaller families that are better cared for. According to some analysts, however, the movement away from the soil to the cities resulted in a loss of man's natural being, and this connotation of the term was strongly reinforced by the Romantic movement in literature. In England a number of nineteenth-century writers—among others, Samuel Taylor Coleridge, Thomas Carlyle, and Matthew Arnold—denounced civilization as "artificial" or "mechanical" and contrasted it with *"culture," which they held to be "natural" and therefore good. In other words, according to the world view of the person using the word, "civilization" can imply either the progress associated with urban-industrial societies or the excessive sacrifice made to attain that progress.

clan, which anthropologists used originally to denote a patrilineal kin group in Teutonic or Scottish society, was extended to mean any descent group, usually unilateral, as in Australia or Africa. The meaning varies with the analyst. See also *sib.

clandestine marriage, a marital pattern in medieval Europe, evolved from earlier customs. In the twelfth century, when Gratian compiled *The Harmonization of Conflicting Decrees* (known as the *Decretum*), he noted that from Roman times the common criterion of a valid marriage was consent. If a couple exchanged consent in secrecy, by late medieval law they had conferred the sacrament on themselves and established a valid marriage. Many recent commentators, therefore, have identified clandestine marriage with the *consensual union of today. Subsequently, however, the church set additional conditions, and partners in a clandestine marriage could be charged before an ecclesiastical court and fined.

REFERENCE: Beatrice Gottlieb, "The Meaning of Clandestine Marriage," in Robert Wheaton and Tamara K. Hareven, eds., *Family and Sexuality in French History* (Philadelphia: University of Pennsylvania Press, 1980).

classification is the systematic distribution of data into distinct categories as a first step in the analysis of their interrelation. Demographic statistics are basically the result of counting populations but also of counting subunits, and thus of distinguishing one class of population from another. The rationale for classifying rural-urban residence, types set off by *ethnicity or *race, *occupations or other sectors of the labor force, and so on is both troublesome and often inadequate. If only to maintain comparability from one census to the next, statisticians are reluctant to make too many or too fundamental revisions, as some theorists of classification might consider appropriate.

REFERENCES: Ingetraut Dahlberg, "Classification Theory, Yesterday and Today," *International Classification*, 3 (1976), 85-90. Irene Hess, V. K. Sethi, and T. R. Balakrishnan, "Stratification: A Practical Investigation," *Journal of the American Statistical Association*, 61 (1966), 74-90. Peter H. Raven, Brent Berlin, and Dennis E. Breedlove, "The Origins of Taxonomy," *Science*, 174 (1971), 1210-1213.

clearinghouse is used in the jargon of librarians as a loose synonym of library or documentation center. In a report evaluating five such agencies in Asia whose holdings were focused on population and family planning, the three terms were distinguished as follows: a *library* is a collection of books and similar materials, arranged and classified for easy retrieval by a user who has taken the initiative in seeking the information. A *documentation center* publishes and distributes bibliographies of its holdings, and responds to the requests thus stimulated by reproducing its holdings. A *clearinghouse* goes beyond such services by searching for any information that has been requested, in part through contacts with other similar agencies, and it processes the materials to suit the particular needs of diverse users. More generally, the report is of interest for its detailed discussion of such institutions' functions and how they can best be fulfilled.

REFERENCE: U.N. Fund for Population Activities, *Evaluation Report to UNFPA on Clearinghouses and Documentation Centres in the Field of Population and Family Planning in Asia* (New York, 1977).

climacteric, the combination of endocrine, somatic, and psychic changes in the female at the time of her *menopause. The term is sometimes applied to the male's normal diminution of sexual activity, but loosely, for it usually takes place over a considerably longer period.

climate, the weather typical of a region as indicated by the mean temperature, rainfall, wind velocity, and other measurements, is an obvious factor in determining the probability of human settlement, particularly of primitives who lack the means of countering unfavorable factors. A number of geographers, of whom Ellsworth †Huntington was the most prominent, have assigned an exaggerated importance to climatic differences and changes in determining the broad path of history. The human species, however, is enormously adaptable; and the irrigation systems of the past or the current desalination of sea water can expand agriculture and thus settlement even to deserts. *Climatology*, the study of weather elements over long periods (as contrasted with *meteorology*, which is concentrated on short-term changes) is still in its infancy, and greater knowledge may well lead to greater control.

clinic and **clinical** derive from the Greek for ''couch'' or ''bed''; and in medical terminology the primary meaning of ''clinical'' pertains to the bedside and thus to the actual observation and treatment of patients, as distinguished from ''theoretical'' or ''experimental.'' Thus, a ''clinic'' or ''clinical lecture'' is instruction at the bedside, an examination of patients before a class of students. Sometimes the reference is to patients irrespective of their location: a ''clinic'' can also mean a part of a hospital or medical school used for the treatment of out-patients; ''clinical psychology'' is a body of knowledge and skills useful in helping persons with behavioral disabilities or mental disorders. In popular usage, however, the word clinical has acquired the connotation of cold and sharp, dispassionate and laboratory-like—virtually the opposite of ''with a bedside manner.''

cliometrics, an originally derisive term for quantitative history, particularly works based on extensive calculations with the electronic computer; from Clio, the Muse of history. Two issues seem to be at stake: how wide an interpretation one can legitimately draw from existent statistics, and whether the quantification of certain kinds of qualitative information is permissible. See also *historical demography.
    REFERENCE: Robert P. Swierenga, ed., *Quantification in American History: Theory and Research* (New York: Atheneum, 1970).

clips, devices used to effect a reversible sterilization when snapped on the vas deferens or the fallopian tubes to prevent, temporarily, the passage of sperm or ova.

Club of Rome, an international study group of businessmen and other concerned persons, was established in 1968 to seek solutions to various global problems, including especially those related to the rapid growth of the world's population. In 1981 there were seventy-five members (out of the hundred to which membership is limited) in thirty-five countries. The very pessimistic conclusions in its well publicized first report, *The Limits of Growth* (1972), were considerably revised in its second report, *Mankind at the Turning Point* (1974), which received a good deal less attention. Address: Via Giorgione 163, I-00147 Rome, Italy. There is also an Association for the Club of Rome, which was founded in the

United States in 1976. In 1980 it had a staff of 2 and claimed 150 members out of the 500 to which membership is limited. Address: 1735 DeSales Street, N.W., Washington, D.C. 20036. See also *environmentalism; *Global 2000.

cluster sampling, a method of *sampling a population classified into "clusters," of which a sample is drawn. All the individuals in the sample clusters are included. For example, if all the residents in each small area are defined as one cluster, the sample of clusters can be designed so that one can determine the probability that each person in the whole population will be included. Depending on that probability, responses can be weighted so that the results will approximate those that would have been given by the total population. With an adeptly drawn sample, the interviewers' travel time can be cut considerably.

coding, an early step in the processing of raw empirical data, converts them into categories that can be transferred to punch cards or another type of processing equipment. If a question is asked on income, for instance, the responses are divided into ten (say) class intervals, which are then converted into the positions 0 to 9 in one column of the punch card. Because coding is both time-consuming and prone to error, many questionnaires are precoded; thus, a person would be asked not to give his income but to check a box that corresponds to a particular income range. Similarly, most of the questions in the 1980 United States census were answered by filling in a circle next to a designation of ethnicity, for example; and later a camera picked up this darkened spot, which was converted into information to be included in the various subtotals.

cohabitation, the living together of a man and woman, whether in a *consensual union or in a legal or marriage.

cohort, all persons who experience an event (such as birth or marriage) in the same year (or other time period) and who are analyzed thereafter as one category. Without specification, the word ordinarily means what is more accurately termed a birth cohort. Though the word in this sense is a recent neologism, the concept is familiar. In the United States college alumni organize themselves into "classes," and the class of any given year, which spent four years of undergraduate life building up common memories, has this experience for the rest of its members' lives. In France *classe* is more likely to refer to those called to military service at a particular time; *une classe creuse* ("a hollow class") means one that reflects in its small size a period of particularly low fertility. See also *generation.

By a *cohort analysis,* one brings into a single framework both physiological determinants associated with age and the cultural influences from a particular life experience. It is routine, for example, to control for age in fertility rates— but even with this control these have varied considerably from one period to another. As one instance, many of the American women who reached the best age for childbearing during the depression of the 1930s had no children, but then had their first child after 1945, when they were much older than the usual *primipara (cf. Whelpton, 1954). A cohort can be used in the study of social change (Ryder, 1965), of such a particular social change as urbanization (Taeuber, 1965), of such physiological-social processes as aging (Riley, 1973-74; Carlsson and Karlsson, 1970). As these examples suggest, though cohort analysis began in the study of fertility and has been concentrated there, it is useful over a much wider range.

When it is impossible to find data pertaining to a real cohort, it is sometimes possible to fashion what is called a *synthetic cohort* (or a hypothetical or fictitious cohort), which is constructed by treating cross-sectional data by age as if they represented the same persons aging over time. To take a very simple example, several sociologists have analyzed how college life changes attitudes by recording at one particular time those of freshmen, sophomores, juniors, and seniors. From responses on marital status in a census, as another example, one can construct a nuptiality table—though this will be incomplete if only because many of the married persons will have died before the date of the enumeration.

REFERENCES: Gösta Carlsson and Katarina Karlsson, "Age, Cohorts and the Generation of Generations," *American Sociological Review*, 35 (1970), 710-718. Matilda White Riley, "Aging and Cohort Succession: Interpretations and Misinterpretations," *Public Opinion Quarterly*, 37 (1973-74), 35-49. Norman B. Ryder, "The Cohort as a Concept in the Study of Social Change," *American Sociological Review*, 30 (1965), 843-861. Karl E. Taeuber, "Cohort Population Redistribution and the Urban Hierarchy," *Milbank Memorial Fund Quarterly*, 43 (1965), 450-462. P. K. Whelpton, *Cohort Fertility* (Princeton, N.J.: Princeton University Press, 1954).

cohort-survival, a method or model for the analysis of population change, is contrasted with what might be termed *components-of-change* models. The latter combines figures on births, deaths, and migration into the *balancing equation to arrive at a total population at a specified time after the date of the base figure. With a cohort-survival model, one begins with the age distribution at a given date and repeatedly applies age-specific rates of fertility, mortality, and migration to new age distributions that are successively generated. See also *population projections.

coil, one of several *intra-uterine devices, Margulies coil, Saf-T-Coil, Spring coil.

coitus interruptus, sexual intercourse in which the male withdraws the penis from the vagina before he ejaculates. It is a widely used method of contraception, effective enough to cut fertility in the mass but hardly dependable for individuals who desire a relative certainty of avoiding pregnancy. Those who have studied the decline of fertility in Western Europe during the third stage of the *demographic transition generally hold that withdrawal was one of the commonest methods of birth control.

coitus reservatus, or karezza, sexual intercourse in which the male deliberately suppresses or postpones ejaculation. Reportedly it was the principal means of contraception used in Oneida Community, the utopian establishment in New York State that John Humphrey Noyes founded in 1848 and led for several decades. Eventually social experimentation was discontinued, and the venture was converted into a joint-stock company. During the interim the community practiced "complex marriage," a combination of polygamy and polyandry. Understandably, practitioners did not often discuss their customs publicly, but apparently in this tightly knit group coitus reservatus was a reasonably effective means of controlling fertility.

REFERENCE: Lawrence Foster, *Religion and Sexuality: Three American Communal Experiments of the Nineteenth Century* (New York: Oxford University Press, 1981), chap. 3.

collective behavior denotes types of conduct in situations that lack an unambiguous norm, including especially such mass phenomena as panics and crazes. Typically such behavior is relatively spontaneous and of short duration. Few analysts have tried to apply the concepts and insights developed in this branch of sociology to the problems in demography where it might apply—for example, the imitative pattern of a migration stream (but see the discussion of "America fever" in Lindberg, 1930) or the fad of childless families (but see Veevers, 1972).

REFERENCES: John S. Lindberg, *The Background of Swedish Emigration to the United States* (Minneapolis: University of Minnesota Press, 1930). G. T. Marx and J. L. Wood, "Strands of Theory and Research in Collective Behavior," *Annual Review of Sociology*, 1 (1975), 363-428. Jean E. Veevers, "The Violation of Fertility Mores: Voluntary Childlessness as Deviant Behavior," in Carl F. Grindstaff and Paul C. Whitehead, eds., *Deviant Behavior and Societal Reaction* (New York: Holt, Rinehart and Winston, 1972).

collectivization, the consolidation, typically by force, of individually owned agricultural holdings into large state farms. The prototype is the collectivization of agriculture in the Soviet Union, which began in 1928 and continued through the early 1930s, a process in which some millions of peasants were killed or deported to labor camps. In Soviet law a distinction is made between a *kolkhoz*, or collective farm ostensibly owned by its members, and a *sovkhoz*, or state farm whose workers are state employees; but in many respects it is a distinction without a difference. The draconian methods needed to take over the peasants' land resulted in a massive *famine and a chronically weak agriculture, periodically bolstered by imports from capitalist countries and by reluctant and "temporary" permission to supplement production with that on small private plots (Jasny, 1949; Millar and Nove, 1976; Nove, 1977). See also *Soviet society.

The extension of collectivized agriculture to Eastern Europe was generally less brutal, and in Poland and Yugoslavia the process was halted and in part reversed. The large communes organized in *China during the Great Leap Forward (1958-61) proved to be an expensive failure and were greatly modified, with propaganda and political pressure supplemented by economic incentives.

REFERENCES: Naum Jasny, *The Socialized Agriculture of the USSR: Plans and Performance* (Stanford, Calif.: Stanford University Press, 1949). James R. Millar and Alec Nove, "A Debate on Collectivization: Was Stalin Really Necessary?" *Problems of Communism*, 25 (July-August 1976), 49-62. Nove, "Can Eastern Europe Feed Itself?" *World Development*, 5 (1977), 417-424.

college town, in the United States a relatively small urban place in which a high proportion of the population consists of the faculty, staff, and students of one or more institutions of higher education. Before 1950 unmarried students were enumerated as residents of their parents' homes, typically not in that town. Beginning with the census of that year, students were designated as residents of the college towns where they were studying, and the change in definition increased the recorded population of such towns considerably, as well as effecting marked changes in the reported median age, income, level of education, and so on through a whole list of other characteristics. For example, the number of inhabitants of Chapel Hill, the site of the University of North Carolina, increased from 3,654 in 1940 to 9,177 in 1950, mostly because of this reclassification (see also *residence). From 1970 to 1980 it grew by 24 percent compared with 16 percent for North Carolina; College Station, home of Texas A&M University, more than doubled in population while the state increased by 27 percent; Ithaca, the site of Cornell University, increased by almost a tenth though New York State lost nearly 4 percent in population. This growth from students will not continue at the same pace, but it is anticipated that college towns will continue to increase in population, since many persons retire there and the towns are often becoming the sites of high-technology industries. The politics of college towns is often skewed; Berkeley, California, as the prime example, has probably the most radical municipal government in the country. According to a national market survey, over a period of six months only 17 percent of the male students and 21 percent of the females purchased contraceptives (Walsh, 1984).

REFERENCE: Doris Walsh, "Consider Collegetowns," *American Demographics*, 6 (April, 1984), 17-21.

Colombia: Demographic Institutions

The Colombian Association for the Study of Population, a private organization established in 1964, was in 1980 under the direction of R. Salazar, executive director. Its action-research unit has produced studies of fertility, family planning, and the status of women, often published in its journal, *Estudios de Población*. Address: Asociación Colombiana para el Estudio de la Población, Carrera 23, no. 39-82, Bogotá.

The Colombian Association of Medical Faculties (ASCOFAME) set up in

1955 a Health Division, which in 1980 was under the direction of Ricardo Galan Morera. Its main purpose has been to work out policies on medical education and the delivery of health services, and to this end it has conducted research on differential fertility and its relation to the availability of contraception, internal migration, health, and the development of agriculture. Its Division of Education and Continuing Education began a basic training program in 1959, with instruction on maternal and child health, community health, and teaching aids. A Documentation Center, which distributes materials on population and other subjects to the public and prepares bibliographies, was established in 1970. Address: Asociación Colombiana de Facultades de Medicina, Calle 45A, no. 9-77, Bogotá.

UNIVERSITY AND OTHER RESEARCH INSTITUTES

The University Center for Research on Population (CUIP), a private organization founded in 1964, conducts research on population and family planning in Colombia and other countries of Latin America. It also offers postgraduate training in demography and health, and its documentation center distributes materials on population and birth control. Address: Centro Universitario de Investigaciones sobre Población, Apartado Aéreo 2188, Carrera 4 Sur no. 36-00, Bogotá.

The Regional Population Center, a private organization founded in 1973, was in 1980 under the direction of Guillermo †López Escobar. It conducted a national survey on the prevalence of contraception, and investigated the sexual knowledge and opinions imparted in schools. A study group on the effect of family planning on the demographic, economic, and social structure published a work on fertility decline from 1964 to 1975. The center also trains physicians and other medical personnel in family planning and undertakes community education in Colombia and elsewhere in Latin America. Address: Corporación Centro Regional de Población, Carrera 6a, no. 76-34, Apartado Aéreo 24846, Bogotá.

The Colombian Institute of Social Development, a private nonprofit organization, was founded in 1958. It conducts research and sponsors seminars on such public questions as family and population and social-economic development. Address: Instituto Colombiano de Desarrollo Social, Calle 16, no. 4-75/79, Apartado Aéreo 11966, Bogotá.

Nariño, one of the *departamentos* along the southern boundary, set up in 1968 its own Institute of Population Problems, which in 1980 was directed by Luciano Mora-Orejo. It has published an economic-demographic study of the Southern Highlands and a methodological monograph on internal migration. Address: Instituto de Problemas Demográficos de Nariño, Apartado Aéreo 25669, Bogotá.

The University of the Andes has a Center for the Study of Economic Development (CEDE), directed in the mid-1970s by Guillermo Perry, succeeded by Rafael Isaza Botero, who later became rector of the university. It has conducted research on fertility and internal migration in Colombia. Address: Centro de Estudios sobre Desarrollo Económico, Universidad de los Andes, Calle 18A, Carrera 1-E, Bogotá.

The University of Antioquia has a Center of Economic Research, of which F. Javier Gómez was director in 1980. Its studies of economics have included population as one factor. Address: Centro de Investigaciones Económicas, Universidad de Antioquia, Apartado Aéreo 1226, Medellín.

In the medical faculty of the National University of Colombia there is a Center of Demographic Studies, headed in 1980 by Italo Mirkow. Its research has been focused on fertility and family planning in Colombia. Address: Centro de Estudios Demográficos, Facultad de Medicina, Universidad Nacional de Colombia, Apartado Nacional 2509, Bogotá.

At the same university there is a Center of Research for Development, of which J. O. Melo was director in 1980. Its policy-oriented research includes population as it is related to rural-urban development, housing needs, and other factors. Address: Centro de Investigaciones para el Desarrollo, Ciudad Universitaria, Bogotá.

GOVERNMENT STATISTICAL BUREAU

The National Statistics Bureau (DANE), which in 1980 was directed by Humberto Gallego G., conducts the census and the annual family survey and collects statistics on education, health facilities, prices, and other social-economic indicators. It publishes the annuals *Economía y Estadística* and *Anuario Demográfico* and issues a monthly bulletin; it also maintains a data bank that is available to the public. Address: Departamento Administrativo Nacional de Estadística, Apartado Nacional 8798, Bogotá.

Colombo Declaration on Population and Development was adopted by an International Conference of Parliamentarians on Population and Development at Colombo, Sri Lanka, in 1979. Representatives of fifty-eight countries participated, and the propositions in the declaration were often phrased in ambiguous terms so as to permit a seeming agreement. Perhaps the most forthright recommendation was that aid to population programs be raised to one billion dollars by 1984, or more than tripled over five years. The text is reproduced in *Population and Development Review*, 5 (1979), 730-736.

colonia, Spanish for "colony" or, in Mexico, "neighborhood," is used in the Southwest of the United States to designate an unincorporated village or small town (hence, one with low or no taxes and therefore inadequate facilities) inhabited by Mexican Americans, very often recent immigrants.
    REFERENCE: John Huey, "Sagebrush Slums," *Wall Street Journal*, May 30, 1979.

colony derives from the Latin *colonia*, a "settlement" (whence Cologne), and the related word *colonus*, a "settler." In its primary meaning, thus, colonization denotes the planting in a new territory of offshoots from a parent state, community, or tribe with which continuing relations are maintained. Since this new territory is often already occupied, the new land must be taken and held forcibly, and the subjugated area is subsequently exploited for the benefit of the invaders—a system designated as *imperialism, colonialism, or neocolonialism.

color, or skin color, is one of the conventional characteristics setting off one *race from others. Especially when judged by enumerators or other interviewers, color is often an ambiguous criterion, since it varies considerably within racial categories as defined by physical anthropologists. As used by the U.S. Bureau of the Census, color means either white or "nonwhite," the latter comprising all non-Caucasian persons in the population. The reason for the two-part classification is that in many jurisdictions virtually all nonwhites are blacks, and it would be excessively expensive to print a full breakdown by race concerning every variable. Objections to the term came from analysts of such parts of the country as the Southwest, where significant proportions of nonwhites are Indians, Chinese, Japanese, and so on, with social and demographic characteristics quite different from those of Negroes. In 1969 the term nonwhite was dropped and supplanted by "Negro and other races"—which is to be interpreted as Negro and other *nonwhite* races. The change of designation, thus, did nothing to mitigate the confusion of official statistics.

COMECON is the acronym for the Council for Mutual Economic Assistance. It was established in 1949 by the governments of the U.S.S.R. and Eastern European countries in order to effect a "socialist division of labor," with the national economies coordinated according to plans largely set by Moscow. Later Mongolia and Cuba joined as members, and Vietnam and North Korea as observers. COMECON publishes in Russian a *Statistical yearbook of member states of the Council for Mutual Economic Assistance*; the 1979 edition was published in English by IPC International Press, London. Address: Soveta Ekonomicheskoi Vzaimopomoshchi, Prospekt Kalinina 56, Moscow G-205, U.S.S.R.

REFERENCES: William E. Butler, ed., *A Source Book on Socialist International Organizations* (Alphen–aan-den-Rijn: Sijthoff & Noordhoff, 1978). Ferenc Kozma, *Economic Integration and Economic Strategy* (The Hague: Martinus Nijhoff, 1982). Roy E. H. Mellor, *Eastern Europe: A Geography of the Comecon Countries* (London: Macmillan, 1975).

Comité International des Sciences Historiques (CISH; International Committee of Historical Sciences), founded in 1926, is made up of national historical associations in forty-eight countries plus twelve international organizations. Address: 28 rue Guyusmar, F-75006 Paris, France. Its activities are carried out in part by the Commission Internationale de Démographie Historique (International Commission of Historical Demography); address: c/o CISH, 270 boulevard Raspail, F-75014 Paris, France. See also *historical demography.

commensalism, from the Latin *com* and *mensa*, "eating at the same table," is used in ecology to denote the parallel activity of organisms that make similar demands on their joint environment. In human ecology the meaning has been extended to include an interdependence based on, for instance, common interests.

commercial distribution of contraceptives, the usual process in Western countries, is exceptional in less developed ones. In the abstract it would seem advantageous to distribute contraceptives through the network of small shops that sell basic consumer goods in even the most backward areas, rather than waiting for the establishment of special programs or, even longer, for medical clinics; but in fact family-planning facilities are generally administered by public bureaucracies. If the price of contraceptives proved to be too high for the typical potential user, it could be subsidized with far less money than the cost of whole *family-planning programs. To promote, distribute, and sell contraceptives at a low subsidized price through existing outlets has been termed *social marketing* (Altman and Piotrow, 1980; cf. Obaidullah, 1980). One of the first such projects was in India; from 25 million in the late 1960s, the total sale of condoms rose to 160 million in 1978-79, of which 118 million were Nirodhs, the subsidized brand. Some twenty-seven countries have had similar programs to distribute condoms, oral contraceptives, or spermicides—though, of course, two of the commonest methods, IUDs and sterilizations, can hardly be sold in shops. The estimated cost per couple-year of protection ranged from $1 in Colombia to $5 in Bangladesh; and there have been complaints of delays in deliveries and other bureaucratic complications. It is probable that a system that requires the couple, or one of the two, to pay part of the cost will result in a higher use-effectiveness than with contraceptives "accepted" partly in response to pressure. Yet many of the papers on the commercial distribution of contraceptives, such as those by Therel †Black (1973, 1976, 1979), seem to be arguing for an aberrant position as contrasted with the standard government program.

REFERENCES: Diana L. Altman and Phyllis T. Piotrow, "Social Marketing: Does It Work?" *Population Reports*, Ser. J, no. 21 (1980). T.R.L. Black, "Rationale for the Involvement of Private-Sector Marketing Institutions in Family Planning in Africa," *Studies in Family Planning*, 4 (1973), 25-32; "Community-Based Distribution: The Distributive Potential and Economics of a Social Marketing Approach to Family Planning," in R. V. Short and Dugald T. Baird, eds., *Contraceptives of the Future* (London: Royal Society, 1976). Black et al., "The Application of Market Research in Contraceptive Social Marketing in a Rural Area of Kenya," *Journal of the Market Research Society*, 21 (1979), 30-43. M. Obaidullah, *Household Distribution Evaluation Study: Free Initial Household Distribution/Commercial Resupply* [of contraceptives] (Dacca: Institute of Statistical Research and Training, University of Dacca, 1980).

Commission on Population Growth and the American Future, often referred to as the Rockefeller Commission after John D. Rockefeller III, its chairman, was established by the U.S. Congress in 1970. It included Senators and Congressmen, distinguished citizens, representatives of foundations, members of the black community, a Mexican American woman, a Puerto Rican, Catholics, physicians, youth (including a 19-year-old student)—and academic demographers headed by Charles †Westoff of Princeton University as executive director. Differences in points of view among the commission's members were too great to be resolved and were finally all noted in an introduction to its final report entitled "A Diversity of Views." A number of research reports were commissioned (see Westoff, 1973), and a *Report* was written with slight relation to them. In effect, President Nixon rejected the *Report*, and Congress took no action at all concerning it. This reaction might have been expected, for among the recommendations were several highly controversial policies: Federal funds should be provided to implement education on population and sex. Child-care services should be encouraged. Illegitimate children should be accorded equal status socially, morally, and legally, with more subsidies to those willing to adopt them. The Equal Rights Amendment to the U.S. Constitution should be approved. Minors should be given contraceptives. Sterilization and abortion should be available on demand. The nation should welcome and prepare for zero population growth, keeping immigration at its current level and imposing criminal sanctions against those who employ illegal aliens. The list of such recommendations was followed by particular members' statements of disagreement. More fundamentally, the commission was one symptom of the hectic environmentalism of the 1960s and early 1970s, a mood that was changing during its term in part because some of these proposals were adopted, in greater part because of the sharp and unexpected decline in the American birth rate.

REFERENCE: Charles F. Westoff, "The Commission on Population Growth and the American Future: Its Origins, Operations, and Aftermath," *Population Index*, 39 (1973), 491-507.

Committee for Comparative Behavioral Studies in Population was established in 1974 with funding from the Ford Foundation and the International Development Research Center of Canada. Address: C.P.O. Box 3528, Seoul, South Korea.

Committee for International Cooperation in National Research in Demography (CICRED; Comité International de Coopération dans les Recherches Nationales en Démographie) developed out of a 1971 meeting of demographers in Lyon, France; and CICRED was formally founded in 1972 as the Committee for International Coordination of National Research in Demography; the name was changed to the present one in the late 1970s. The U.N. Fund for Population Activities (UNFPA) agreed to assist in coordinating the work of demographic research institutes throughout the world, and the first task that CICRED undertook was to make a list of such centers. It acts as a clearinghouse for research projects conducted anywhere by national or international organizations, and it has sponsored seminars on population growth and on international migration. It has a membership of 171 research centers in 69 countries. Publications: *Liaison Bulletin*, in English, French, and Spanish; *Directory of Demographic Research Centers*, in English and French (2nd ed., 1980); *A Repertory of Research Projects in Priority Areas of Demographic Study* (2nd ed., 1975); *Socio-economic Differential Mortality in Industrialized Societies*, no. 1 (1981), no. 2 (1982). Address: 27, rue du Commandateur, F-75675 Paris Cédex 14, France.

REFERENCE: "Le Comité International de Coordination des Recherches Nationales en Démographie (CICRED): Organisation et Fonctionnement," *Population*, 28 (1973), 491-510.

commune, a form of social organization in which members own no property and share equally in the product of their labor, has been used to denote two quite different types of association. Under the influence of such utopian socialists as Charles †Fourier and Robert †Owen, small groups of zealots established communes in New England and the Middle West, for instance; and such minuscule independent societies have been organized by dissidents and *dropouts in California and elsewhere in the American West. Communes in Communist countries, though started by the state with the promise of some local independence, were consolidated into state farms organized to bring peasants under stricter control. See *China; *collectivization; *communism; *kibbutz.

REFERENCE: A. E. Bestor, *Backwoods Utopias* (Philadelphia: University of Pennsylvania Press, 1950).

communication, in the broadest sense of the transmission by language or another means of values, knowledge, or attitudes, is pertinent to the study of population even in the simplest case, the communication between two individuals. According to some organizers of *family-planning programs in Latin America, for instance, their efforts are impeded by the norm that husband and wife shall not discuss marital intimacies, and certainly not intercourse or birth control. Regarding mass communication, the dominant concern in research has been influence—what attitudes are or can be revised by reading or television, how such changes are facilitated or blocked by factors like the gaps associated with social class, ethnicity, or race; see also *diffusion. Much of what we think we know about non-Western peoples is based on the implicit assumption that, when questioned about private matters by an anthropologist or a *survey researcher, they respond more or less accurately, or at least with no more dissimulation than one would expect from Westerners. The rather few replications, such as those by Oscar †Lewis (1963) or Mahmood Mamdani (1972), suggest that there may have been more of researchers' credulity than of respondents' truthfulness as the foundation of many reports.

REFERENCES: Oscar Lewis, *Life in a Mexican Village: Tepoztlán Restudied* (Urbana: University of Illinois Press, 1963). Mahmood Mamdani, *The Myth of Population Control: Family, Caste, and Class in an Indian Village* (New York: Monthly Review Press, 1972).

communism was coined by obscure French secret societies in the 1830s. It was related to various words indicating some sort of commonality, in particular the French verb *communer*, to render available to all, to share; *Communion*, a sharing with God; *community*, which derived from a Latin word meaning "fellowship" and in the Middle Ages acquired the meaning of a "body of fellows." From this start the term *communism* took on meanings that are not only distinct but mutually contradictory. The word can denote (1) a small *utopian *commune; (2) the ideology of Karl †Marx and Friedrich †Engels as expounded in *The Communist Manifesto* (cf. Wolfe, 1965); (3) the future perfect commonwealth into which the present "socialist" *Soviet society is allegedly evolving (Semenev, 1981); (4) the present society of the U.S.S.R., mainland *China, and their satellites, particularly as contrasted with the "socialist" or "social democratic" parties of the West (cf. Medvedev, 1981); and (5) one of the variants of Soviet ideology and practice that developed in what has been termed Eurocommunism or polycentrism, meaning various Communist parties or countries that differ according to each national background (Westoby, 1981).

There are fundamental differences among these types (which can be indicated by using a capital C to denote a Communist state as contrasted, for example, with the communism practiced on a *kibbutz). Nevertheless some portions of the ideology are more or less common to the whole range. One typical theme is hostility to the family, for the strong bond between parent and child is the means by which are transmitted the allegedly false beliefs and practices of the general (or *bourgeois) society. Many utopian societies, therefore, instituted a communal rearing of the children, and in the first years after the revolution the Soviet Union attempted to set up a similar system. Another theme common to both classical *socialism and the first decades of the Soviet Union is the allegation that overpopulation is the consequence, not of too many people, but of an unjust and inefficient social order. Sometimes this position has been reinforced by hostility to birth control. Typically communists of all types have denounced the conventional differences between sex roles, but in usual practice the subordinate position of women has been maintained.

REFERENCES: Roy Medvedev, *Leninism and Western Socialism* (London: Verso, 1981). V. S. Semenev, "The Theory of Developed Socialism and Its Growth into Communism," *Soviet Studies in Philosophy*, 19 (1981), 3-32. Adam Westoby, *Communism since World War II* (New York: St. Martin's Press, 1981). Bertram D. Wolfe, *Marxism: One Hundred Years in the Life of a Doctrine* (New York: Dial Press, 1965).

community, a population characterized by one or another form of commonality; usually, a population with its own territory and a network of relationships through which it conducts its daily life; generally, a village or a small town. Sometimes the meaning is extended to include a city or a metropolitan area, thus discarding the implication of intimacy and mutual awareness in the smaller unit. By analogy, in ecology it means an association of different species of plants or of plants and animals occupying the same circumscribed area. Sometimes the word is used to designate any category of persons with a common interest, as a community of scholars, of property owners, of proponents of an ideology.

REFERENCES: George A. Hillery, Jr., "Definitions of Community: Areas of Agreement," *Rural Sociology*, 20 (1955), 111-123. Robert A. Nisbet, *The Sociological Tradition* (New York: Basic Books, 1966), chap. 3. Roland L. Warren, *The Community in America* (Chicago: Rand McNally, 1963).

community contact, in countries with deficient vital statistics, is a village head, religious leader, or other knowledgeable person from whom information is gathered about births, deaths, and marriages.

commuting, periodic travel between the home and the place of work or other destination (cf. O'Farrell, 1975). The radius of the maximum daily volume of commuting is one index of the approximate boundary of a trade area or of a *community. According to surveys of American workers in 1977 and 1979, only about 4 percent walked to work, 2 percent worked at home, and the remainder (apart from the 3 percent who did not respond to this question) commuted. Of those who used vehicles, almost three out of four went by private automobile or truck, and another 17 to 18 percent traveled in car pools. After decades of subsidies to public transportation, it is used by about 6 to 7 percent of those who travel to work by any type of vehicle (U.S. Bureau of the Census, 1981, 1983).

REFERENCES: P. N. O'Farrell, *The Journey to Work* (New York: Pergamon, 1975). Bryant Robey, "A Commuter's Friend," *American Demographics*, 2 (June, 1980), 44-47. U.S. Bureau of the Census, "Selected Characteristics of Travel to Work in 20 Metropolitan Areas: 1977," *Current Population Reports*, Ser. P-23, no. 105 (1980); "The Journey to Work in the United States: 1979," *Current Population Reports*, Ser. P-23, no. 122 (1983).

compage, a recent adaptation of the general term *compages*, which means a system of conjoined parts, a complex structure. As used by geographers in regional analysis, compage denotes a highly diversified but unitary complex.

REFERENCE: Derwent Whittlesey, "Southern Rhodesia: An African Compage," *Annals of the Association of American Geographers*, 46 (1956), 1-97.

comparative method refers ordinarily not merely to a procedure of clarifying the resemblances and differences among social phenomena in order to discern causal relations, but to what Auguste †Comte called the "comparative or historical method." Whole societies of the world today are classified and then ordered in a presumed temporal sequence, ranging from primitive to civilized (cf. Bock, 1956; Nisbet, 1969, chap. 6). The *demographic transition is a striking instance of the type of comparative method that has been most criticized. To trace the course of population of nineteenth-century Europe offers no valid clues to the future trend in presently less developed countries, contrary to the assumptions underlying one usual interpretation of the demographic transition.

REFERENCES: Kenneth E. Bock, *The Acceptance of Histories* (Berkeley: University of California Press, 1956). Robert A. Nisbet, *Social Change and History: Aspects of the Western Theory of Development* (New York : Oxford University Press, 1969).

competition, a relation in which two or more persons, firms, or other entities influence one another through making demands in excess of the available supply of a commodity or other value. Most familiar in the context of economics, competition is also a basic concept of ecology. Robert †Park and Ernest †Burgess (1924) called it "the elementary, universal, and fundamental" form of human interaction, typically without direct contact and not involving conflict. So defined, the concept of competition was part of their Darwinian orientation.

REFERENCE: Robert E. Park and Ernest W. Burgess, *Introduction to the Science of Sociology* (Chicago: University of Chicago Press, 1924).

complete-count, in the usage of the U.S. Bureau of the Census, a designation of questions in an enumeration that are asked of the entire population, or of data based on the responses to those questions. When complete-count responses are cross-classified against those from a sample of the population, the resultant figures are designated as sample data. For example, if the population is broken down by sex (complete-count) and, for males and females separately by years of schooling (in 1980 asked of only about 19 percent of the population), the table would include a notation that it is based on sample data.

completed family size, or **completed fertility,** the average number of *children ever born to women beyond the fecund age span, is one of the best *fertility measures for the analysis of long-term trends (see also *family size). Fluctuations that result, for instance, merely from changes in spacing patterns affect all annual measures, whether simple ones like the crude birth rate or more elaborate ones like the gross reproduction rate. In one application of completed family size, it was defined operationally as the number of children ever born to women aged 45-49 years, married once, whose husbands were still living with them at the time of the enumeration. From census data the authors of the study were able to compare American fertility by major occupational groups in 1910, 1940, and 1950 (Grabill et al., 1958, Table 54). If the age range is taken to be women 45 years and over, the number of children of successively older sectors gives an approximate indication of the decline in fertility over a considerable period. So used, the measure has particular flaws, for underreporting of children probably increases with the age of the mother, particularly for the higher ages, and longevity is related in a complex fashion with completed family size. Trends in marriage and in childlessness can be included by calculating the children ever born per woman, per wife, and per mother (Grabill et al., 1958, Tables 9 and 16).

A somewhat similar measure, based on reports of anticipated rather than completed fertility, is the *lifetime births expected*. In the United States in 1979, this averaged 2.2 per 1,000 wives aged 18-24 years, which had declined from 2.9 in 1967 to the lower figure by 1975. The more precise figure in 1979, 2.164 births, is barely more than is required to replace the two parents. The same downward trend is apparent from cross-sectional data by age bracket: in 1979 the lifetime births expected were 2.835 for women aged 35-39, 3.351 for those aged 30-34, 2.049 for those aged 25-29, and 2.052 for those aged 18-24 (U.S. Bureau of the Census, 1980).

REFERENCES: Wilson H. Grabill, Clyde V. Kiser, and Pascal K. Whelpton, *The Fertility of American Women* (New York: Wiley, 1958). U.S. Bureau of the Census, "Fertility of American Women: June, 1979," *Current Population Reports*, Ser. P-20, no. 358 (December, 1980).

component analysis, the approximation of the change in a particular area's population using the *balancing equation. Each ten years, for instance, everyone in a population becomes ten years older, taking on the demographic rates of the higher age. The age and sex structure changes, thus, both by differentiation of the characteristics of the original residents and by additions or depletions through births, deaths, and migrations.

compulsuation, a neologism to denote a combination of COMPULSion and persUATION in fertility-control programs.

REFERENCE: Kumudini V. Dandekar, "Compulsuation for Sterilization: An Unprecedented Revolution," *Journal of the Institute of Economic Research*, 11 (1977), 1-8.

computer, a device for processing information, has a long history. Its principles were fully worked out by Charles †Babbage (1792-1871), an English mathematician at the University of Cambridge. He designed an "analytical engine" that would change its operations following the results of its own calculations. Numbers would be fed in by patterns of holes on cards, a "store" would hold partial results, and the results of a calculation would be printed. Though he worked on the machine for years, Babbage was unable to solve the engineering problems in arranging the wheels and rods so that they would perform accurately and speedily (Morrison and Morrison, 1961). In other words, the development of the modern computer depended on electric power and particularly on the miniaturization of electronic circuits.

Electronic computers are of two basic types, analog and digital. With an analog computer, such physical quantities as distance or voltage are directly represented by an electric charge or current, and these representations are all related to one another in a manner analogous to that in the real world. Development was rapid during World War II, when techniques were devised for ballistics calculations, and the analog computer has been used for such problems in the physical sciences as the design of airplanes (Ivall, 1960, chaps. 3-6).

Virtually all computers used in demography or related disciplines are of the second type, electronic digital computers or, briefly, digital computers. Input through a keyboard, punched card, or other route is fed into the system by way of a binary language, written as 1 or 0 and translated for the computer as the presence or absence of an electric charge. Each element of this digital message,

0 or 1, is called a "bit," a contraction of "binary digit." In the computer's storage or "memory" is held information subject to recall in the form of "words," made up typically of sixteen, thirty-two, or sixty bits. Each word represents data to be manipulated or instructions to be executed, or in some instances either one or the other under different specified conditions. An arithmetic unit in the computer performs the usual arithmetical and essentially similar logical operations; and a control unit interprets the memory's instructions, some of which are affected by the results of these operations. As a computation progresses, its result is emitted in an output of, for instance, magnetic tape or printed paper. The distinctive feature of a computer, then, is its ability to store, interpret, and, when appropriate, modify its operation in the processing of quantitative data.

For relatively simple mathematical problems one can begin with an "algorithm," a precisely described step-by-step procedure for arriving at a solution. More generally, the series of actions that a computer is called on to perform is called its "program," which is described in a special "language." Programs and other specially prepared routines are called "software," in contrast to the mechanical and electronic components, the computer's "hardware." Of computer languages, one of the first and possibly most important is FORTRAN, a contraction of "FORmula TRANslator" (Davidson and Koenig, 1967, chaps. 1-2). Other languages include ALGOL, PL/I, and APL. Any of these languages has to be translated through a "compiler" into a "machine code," the electrical language of the computer. More recently programs have been developed that use an approximation of Standard English.

The most obvious application of computer technology to population analysis is in the processing of *censuses. The preliminary step of *coding written entries on census forms, or their conversion into symbols that can be used as input to the computer, is both an expensive process and one likely to introduce errors. In recent United States censuses most of the basic information has been "precoded"; that is, alternative answers to each question were printed on the schedule itself, and the respondent was instructed to fill in appropriate circles so that a "scanner" could "read" the data directly. By 1960 a new piece of equipment called FOSDIC (Film Optical Sensing Device for Input to Computers) was producing as much in one minute as a 1950 punch operator had turned out in a day. By 1970 the production of printed reports and microfilms was also controlled by computer operations; with a Linotron photocomposer each page of statistics was reproduced on a sheet of photographic film or photosensitive paper, and the device processed 6-point characters at a rate of 1,000 per second.

In 1980 the computer was used more intensively. After the data were transferred to computer tape, various totals and subtotals were compared with the appropriate field counts. For small areas this check was called a *diary review*; more elaborate programs were devised to check the tapes on states, metropolitan areas, and minor civil divisions. For the average enumeration district—800 persons living in 300 housing units—the tolerance of error was 16 persons and 6 housing units; and if any of the tabulated data varied by more than that small proportion, an analyst rechecked the original questionnaires and corrected the tape. If he thought it necessary, he could even have the local enumeration repeated. *Editing was more elaborate than in 1970. Many details omitted from the printed volumes were made available, as also with the 1970 count but on a larger scale, in a series of computer tapes (*American Demographics*, 1981). In short, the use of the computer in the processing and printing of census volumes has made it possible to attain a speed of production unimaginable a generation ago and, at the same time, to reduce appreciably the number of errors.

More generally, population data from any source can be assembled, processed, and tabulated most expeditiously with the use of an electronic computer. Errors of many types can be both uncovered and either corrected or, more frequently, adjusted so as to conform to the range of true responses in the most probable fashion. For example, by the current practice in the United States, unreported ages are neither so recorded nor distributed proportionately among the reported ages, but rather denoted to be the same as those of persons with about the same years of schooling, marital status, age of spouse, and employment status; and with a program the rather elaborate computation can be performed automatically (see *editing). The number of detailed cross-tabulations that the Bureau of the Census printed was more than doubled from 1960 to 1970, because improvements in computation made it easier and cheaper to derive them. The entire array of data on individuals can be converted into family (or household) statistics with a program including only three additional pieces of information: the number of persons in the family; the type of unit (subfamily, secondary family, primary individual, or secondary individual); and the relation to the head (if not the head, then spouse, child, or other). "Canned" routines derive specified figures automatically—subtotals, percent distributions, measures of central tendencies or dispersion, standardized or seasonally adjusted rates, and so on.

The whole discipline of cartography has been revolutionized by the possibility of reproducing maps on a computer screen and calculating with a built-in program such standard measures of each area as its center of population (cf. Chu, 1978). Computer *simulation is used not only to construct *population projections but as a means of analyzing the effect of sometimes small changes over long periods of time (Dyke and MacCluer, 1973).

REFERENCES: *American Demographics, A Researcher's Guide to the 1980 Census* (Ithaca, N.Y., 1981). Gregory Chu, "EWPI Workshop Explores Census Mapping," *Asian and Pacific Census Forum*, 5 (August, 1978), 4ff. Charles H. Davidson and Eldo C. Koenig, *Computers: Introduction to Computers and Applied Computing Concepts* (New York: Wiley, 1967). Bennett Dyke and Jean Walters MacCluer, eds., *Computer Simulation in Human Population Studies* (New York: Academic Press, 1973). T. E. Ivall, *Electronic Computers: Principles and Applications* (London: Iliffe, 1960). Philip Morrison and Emily Morrison, eds., *Charles Babbage and His Calculating Engines: Selected Writings by Charles Babbage and Others* (New York: Dover, 1961). Nancy D. Ruggles, ed., *The Role of the Computer in Economic and Social Research in Latin America* (National Bureau of Economic Research; New York: Columbia University Press, 1974).

concentration, like many verbal nouns, has a double meaning, either the process of increasing unevenness in the distribution of population or an end point in that process, the degree of unevenness at a given time. The usual measures are the *Lorenz curve and Corrado †Gini's "concentration ratio." Otis Dudley †Duncan (1957) recommended a new "index of concentration," for which he used the symbol Δ. If k is the number of areal units, and X_i and Y_i are the cumulated percentages of population and area, respectively, the index of concentration is the maximum of the set of k values of $(X_i - Y_i)$. Since the value of the index varies considerably according to the size of the areal unit chosen, there can be no single answer to the question of how concentrated a population is. See also *segregation.

REFERENCE: Otis Dudley Duncan, "The Measurement of Population Distribution," *Population Studies*, 11 (1957), 27-45.

concentration camps, internment centers used especially by the Nazi and Soviet states to incarcerate and punish sectors of their own populations. There were some 2,000 camps in Nazi Germany and Nazi-occupied Europe, including the death camps in which about eight million persons, among them five to six million Jews, were systematically slaughtered (see *holocaust). The number of Soviet camps and the number killed in them are more difficult to specify, but the latter figure is at least twenty million (Buber, 1949; Hilberg, 1967; Solzhenitsyn, 1973-77). The places in the United States where Japanese Americans were incarcerated during the Second World War, though identified with various euphemisms, were also concentration camps (Petersen, 1971, chap. 4).

REFERENCES: Margarete Buber, *Under Two Dictators* (London: Gollancz, 1949). Raul Hilberg, *The Destruction of the European Jews* (Chicago: Quadrangle, 1967). William Petersen, *Japanese Americans: Oppression and Success* (New York: Random House, 1971; Washington, D.C.: University Press of America, 1984). Aleksandr I. Solzhenitsyn, *The Gulag Archipelago, 1918-1956*, 3 vols. (New York: Harper & Row, 1974-77).

concept, the meaning given to a term, constitutes the first step from raw empiricism to the formation of theories. The term "homosexual," for instance, has been successively conceived as a sin, a disease, and an alternative life-style. The definition of "disease," thus, depends in part on the concept of homosexuality. The mental process by which concepts are formed out of a combined cognition and perception is called *conception*; social groups, whether nations or families or anything in between, are defined in part by the fact that they share many conceptions. Some demographers, who see their data as unambiguous, tend to pass over the distinction between term and concept. But even a variable that can be measured exactly and unambiguously—a person's age, for example—acquires part of its significance from the meaning the person and the society give to being so and so many years old.

REFERENCE: Abraham Kaplan, *The Conduct of Inquiry: Methodology for Behavioral Science* (San Francisco: Chandler, 1964).

conception, the fecundation of the ovum. Also, *conceptive*, able to conceive; *conceptus*, the product of conception throughout the period of gestation. The average number of menstrual cycles from the beginning or the resumption of sexual intercourse without the use of birth control to a conception is called the *conception delay* (cf. Henry, 1976, chap. 16). It varies, of course, with the woman's age and other factors determining her level of fecundity.

REFERENCE: Henry, *Population.*

CONCOR, a computer program developed by Julio Ortúzar of the Latin American Demographic Center (CELADE), Santiago, Chile, for the editing of census and survey data for CONsistency and CORrection. The system permits the conversion of non-numerical data to a numerical form, with which various checks can be made for consistency, conformity with the norms set, and other criteria.

REFERENCE: Michael J. Levin, "Census Editing and Imputating Work Group," *Asian and Pacific Census Forum,* 5 (November, 1978), 7ff.

concubinage, the regular cohabiting of a man and a woman who are not married, is defined by the lack of such formal ceremonies as a wedding, and it typically connotes also an inferior status for the woman and fewer legal rights for her and her children. It is a common term in social anthropology; sociologists and demographers are more likely to use *consensual union for an essentially similar institution, though a concubine can be a supplement to a regular marital relationship rather than a substitute for it.

condom, a sheath to cover the penis during coitus in order to prevent impregnation or infection. Gabriele †Fallopio (1523-62), the famous Italian anatomist, recommended a moistened linen sheath as a protection against syphilis and claimed that not one of the 1,100 men for whom he prescribed it became infected. In the eighteenth century condoms made of the dried gut of a sheep were widely used in Western Europe; Giacomo Casanova called them "English overcoats," and James Boswell complained that they reduced the pleasure of the sexual act. Currently in the United States condoms made from the cecum (the pouch with which the large intestine begins) of young lambs are much prized by those who use them, who comprise 2-4 percent of the American market. Most condoms today are made of latex, or vulcanized rubber; and the standards set by manufacturers as reinforced by federal inspection have resulted in products with virtually no flaws, though varying from brand to brand.

As a means of fertility control, condoms have had a curious history. In France they were prohibited for decades as contraceptives while sold everywhere as prophylactics. Traditionally, the birth-control movement has focused its efforts on the female, and this policy has resulted in its refusal to dispense the best known male contraceptive. This bias, moreover, was transferred to overseas efforts to reduce the fertility of less developed countries. Many of the writings on the condom from the late 1960s on, thus, have advocated that the well subsidized state efforts recognize a safe and relatively effective means long since widely used simply by individual initiative (see also *commercial distribution of contraceptives). The main fault of the condom as a contraceptive is not in the product but in the user; "among those people using condoms for family planning, the modal response across eight countries was that they were used 'not very often' " (Westinghouse Population Center, 1972).

REFERENCES: Consumers Union of United States, Inc., "Condoms: A Report Based on Laboratory Tests and on Detailed Questionnaires Filled out by Nearly 19,000 Readers," *Consumer Reports*, 44 (1979), 583-589. George Washington University Medical Center, "The Modern Condom: A Quality Product for Effective Contraception," *Population Report*, Ser. H, no. 2 (1974). Myron H. Redford et al., eds., *The Condom: Increasing Utilization in the United States* (San Francisco: San Francisco Press, 1974). Westinghouse Population Center, *Survey of Global Patterns for Contraceptive Distribution in the Private Sector in Selected Developing Countries* (Columbia, Md., 1972).

confidence, in the language of statistics, pertains to the facts that for large samples (arbitrarily, of thirty or more) the distribution around the mean approximates that of a normal curve and that therefore one can find any actual mean with a certain probable accuracy from a table of the areas under standard normal curves. The chosen percentage is the *confidence level*, which falls between two confidence limits in what is called a *confidence interval*.

REFERENCES: Thomas J. Espenshade and Jeffrey M. Tayman, "Confidence Intervals for Postcensal State Population Estimates," *Demography*, 19 (1982), 191-210. Johann Pfanzagl, "Estimation: Confidence Intervals and Regions," in *International Encyclopedia of the Social Sciences*, 5, 150-156.

confidentiality of records concerning individuals has long been a concern of the census officials of democratic countries (e.g., Bulmer, 1979). In the United States, the personal information gathered in a census has been carefully guarded even from other government agencies, and care is taken not to publish data in a form that would make possible the identification, say, of the only wealthy resident of a small community (cf. *suppression). According to a 1929 decision in one of the few legal challenges to the U.S. Bureau of the Census's policy, protection against the use of census data to any respondent's detriment is "akin to the protection afforded by the prohibitions against the evidential use of communication between attorney and client, priest and penitent, and physician and patient" (cf. Petersen, 1970, pp. 226-267). So adamantine a statement has not, however, settled this complex issue, which has been greatly aggravated by the wider use of the electronic *computer with its stupendous powers to store and retrieve all the data it has received.

On February 24, 1981, the U.S. Supreme Court handed down a unanimous decision denying access to the list of addresses of persons counted in the 1980 census. Two local jurisdictions, Essex County, N.J., and Denver, were among the more than fifty that had challenged the results of the census, and these two claimed the right to examine the files in order to substantiate their allegation that large proportions, particularly of blacks, had been passed over. According to the Court's decision, "There is no indication in the Census Act that the hundreds of municipal governments in the fifty states were intended by Congress to be 'monitors' of the Census Bureau. . . . One purpose [of the confidentiality promised to respondents] was to encourage public participation and maintain public confidence that information given to the Census Bureau would not be disclosed." The Court also refused to hear two other cases challenging the results of the census, letting stand decisions by federal appeals courts in favor of the bureau.

Even in the abstract it is difficult to draw a line between appropriate and improper use of personal records. Exploiting computerized files to aid in the apprehension and conviction of criminals has been particularly controversial. The use of Social Security files to weed out double or triple recipients has been criticized by the media as an attack on the poor. Under the law the U.S. Social Security Administration must pass on information that the U.S. Immigration and Naturalization Service requests on the location of persons suspected of being illegally in the country; and the many such requests have been both denounced and applauded (Westin and Baker, 1972, pp. 36-39). As part of a special effort to include illegal aliens in the 1980 count, the Bureau of the Census conducted pretests in several areas of the Southwest; and according to statements in the press, the enumerators were sometimes followed by officers who arrested those so designated. A San Francisco newspaper, in another instance, reported on how the city's mayor had filled out her census form. Virtually nothing in American society is long secret, and the remarkable success of the Census Bureau in maintaining the privacy of individual records is ever threatened.

Two supranational agreements indicate the reactions to the problem in other democratic states. In 1980 the Organization for Economic Cooperation and Development (OECD) and the Council of Europe both adopted guidelines on the protection of privacy and the restriction of transborder flows of information about individuals. The agreements, not ratified at the time of writing by all the member countries, forbid the collection of personal data on religion, race, or politics and stipulate that information garnered for one purpose can be used only for that purpose. Those who oppose such regulations argue that they are both unnecessary and unenforceable (*Economist*, October 25, 1980).

REFERENCES: Martin Bulmer, ed., *Censuses, Surveys and Privacy* (London: Holmes and Meier, 1979). William Petersen, *The Politics of Population* (Gloucester, Mass.: Peter Smith, 1970). Alan F. Westin and Michael A. Baker, *Databanks in a Free Society: Computers, Record-Keeping and Privacy* (New York: Quadrangle Books, 1972).

confinement, the delivery of one or more viable fetuses. When there are multiple births, thus, the number of confinements during a particular period will be less than the number of births. A *confinement order* differs from a *birth order in the same manner; it is the ordinal number of a confinement as related to all other confinements of the same woman.

Confucianism, the doctrine associated with Confucius (551-479 B.C.), the most revered figure of Chinese civilization. Living in troubled times, he emphasized the value of tradition, order, and authority, establishing a comprehensive humanist philosophy focused on prescribing how individuals' behavior should contribute to social and political well-being. *Jen*, usually translated as "benevolence," was a central concept of his ethics and even more of that of Mencius (c.372-c.289 B.C.), who emphasized the personal element; and the ideal of *chün-tzu*, literally "son of a ruler" but connoting a superior man irrespective of background, was instilled in several dozen generations by the education system that was established following Confucian principles.

In the Confucian classics marriage was defined as "a union betwen two persons of different families, the dual object of which is to serve the ancestors in the temple and to propagate the coming generation." The crucial importance given to maintaining the lineage meant that the system was at least implicitly pronatalist. When China's familistic culture was transferred to the Japanese islands, however, the mode of continuing the family from generation to generation was adapted to the more straitened circumstances: in China the male line was guaranteed through a numerous progeny, but in Japan by sacrificing numbers to quality (but cf. *China). In neither setting was there an effective prohibition of fertility control. Indeed, Confucian scholars condemned both abortion and infanticide, but these remained the means of population control used routinely by, respectively, the urban gentry and the peasantry.

REFERENCES: Wing-tsit Chan, "Chinese Philosophy," in *Encyclopedia of Philosophy*, 2, 87-96. Sylvie Gay Sterboul, "Confucius, Ses Disciples et la Population," *Population*, 29 (1974), 771-794.

congestion, from the Latin for "heaped together," is used by traffic engineers and urban sociologists to denote an overcrowded condition, the coming together of too many people or vehicles. The term is used in medicine to mean an excessive or abnormal accumulation of blood in a particular part of the body; local hyperemia.

Congo: The National Center of Statistics and Economic Studies, a government agency, includes an Office of Demographic and Social Statistics, established in 1977 under the direction of Raphael Mfoulou. Its purpose is to collect, analyze, and publish demographic and social statistics, and it has tried to improve the registration of vital events. Its four volumes on the 1974 census were to include a full statement on methodology as well as detailed tables and analyses. The *Statistical Yearbook*, published irregularly by the National Center, includes estimates of population by region and principal characteristics, and its *Monthly Bulletin of Statistics* is sometimes devoted to a presentation of particular demographic data. Address: Direction des Statistiques Démographiques et Sociales, Centre National de la Statistique et des Études Économiques, Boîte Postale 2031, Brazzaville.

Congressional District, one of the areas in the United States that elects each of the 435 members of the House of Representatives. After each enumeration there may be a redistricting to reflect changes in the size and location of the population. The U.S. Bureau of the Census publishes data classified by Congressional Districts, generally with maps showing their boundaries in relation to those of counties. See also *apportionment.

Congressional Information Service, a private firm, abstracts and indexes public documents and sells its products for annual subscription fees. The *CIS/Index* is a guide to the working papers of the U.S. Congress, including everything but the readily available *Congressional Record* and bills, resolutions, and laws. *American Statistics Index* is a similar service pertaining to federal statistical publications, and *Statistical Reference Service* to statistical publications from state and local governments, trade and professional associations, academic research centers, corporations, and commercial publishers. The *Index to Current Urban Documents* covers the country's 268 largest cities and counties. *IIS: Index to International Statistics*, of which the first issue was published in 1983, is a monthly guide to English-language publications of all the important international organizations. Address: 7101 Wisconsin Avenue, Washington, D.C. 20014.

consanguinity, a social relationship based on descent from a putative common ancestor, either lineal or collateral (that is, linked to the same ancestor but not by a direct line of descent). Consanguinity is contrasted with *affinity. The blood ties suggested by the word's etymology are usual but not necessary, for in some cultures *adoption is very common, and descent is typically reckoned not through the "genitor," or biological father, but, when there is a distinction to be made, through the "pater," or sociological father.

consensual union, a relatively stable family-like unit with no religious or legal sanction. It is contrasted on the one hand with *family, on the other hand with what are euphemistically termed "visiting unions," which last for only a short time (see also *concubinage). Common-law or de facto unions exist in all societies, but they are especially common in Latin America (cf. Baade, 1975). Around 1950, the estimated proportion of the "married" population in fact living in consensual unions ranged from under a tenth in Chile to over half in Panama and almost three-quarters in Haiti; and probably neither the order of countries nor the approximate figures have changed appreciably in the interim. These examples suggest that with modernization there is a tendency toward a higher proportion of legitimate marriages. However, the proportion of unmarried couples living together has been high, and recently often rising, also in Western Europe and the United States.

Since the late 1960s the legal status of children in the United States born outside wedlock has changed dramatically (see *illegitimacy), and American courts have also been called on to decide what rights and obligations continue after a consensual union ends. The traditional law denied any implication of an economic return for providing "sexual services" but recognized the claim, for example, to property that had been accumulated through a joint effort. In the much publicized case of *Marvin* v. *Marvin*, 135 Cal. Rptr. 815 (1976), the California Supreme Court all but removed the prior difference between a divorced wife and a woman whose consensual partner left her. Indeed, under that ruling, "meretricious sexual services" do not establish a right to what has become known as "palimony," but "even if sexual services are part of the contractual consideration, any severable portion of the contract supported by independent consideration will still be enforced." In short, "a nonmarital partner may recover ... the reasonable value of support received if he can show that he rendered services with the expectation of monetary reward." To date courts in other states have been reluctant to follow the lead of California, especially the finding that merely implied contracts are enforceable.

The 1980 census of the United States introduced a new category, "partner or roommate," to indicate an unmarried adult sharing living quarters with a nonrelative of the opposite sex. Conceivably such households might comprise an elderly woman who rented a room to a male college student, for example, or an old man with a live-in female nurse, but a comparison of the ages suggests that most are consensual unions. According to census statistics, the number of unmarried couples living together increased from 523,000 in 1970 to 1,560,000 in 1980. At the latter date, in almost two-thirds of the cases both partners were under 35 years of age; in a fifth both were under 25. Well over a quarter of the unmarried couples had children present. This trend has received a good deal of attention (cf. *POSSLQ), but one should keep in mind that compared with the 1.56 million unmarried couples in 1980 there were 48.2 million married ones (U.S. Bureau of the Census, 1981). Consensual unions, still anomalous in the United States, are seemingly often equivalent to trial marriages, a first step toward a more formal union.

REFERENCES: Hans W. Baade, "The Form of Marriage in Spanish North America," *Cornell Law Review*, 61 (1975), 1-89. Paul C. Glick and Arthur J. Norton, "New Lifestyles Change Family Statistics," *American Demographics*, 2 (May, 1980), 20-23. Glick and G. B. Spanier, "Married and Unmarried Cohabitation in the United States," *Journal of Marriage and the Family*, 42 (1980), 19-30. U.S. Bureau of the Census, "Marital Status and Living Arrangements, March, 1980," *Current Population Reports*, Ser. P-20, no. 365 (October, 1981).

conservation was popularized in the United States, both as a term and as a movement, by Gifford Pinchot (1865-1946), the country's first professional forester and chief of the U.S. Forest Service after President Theodore Roosevelt established it. As Pinchot used the word, it referred to federal programs to regulate the use of forests and other public lands so that their products would be available also to future generations. He was opposed not only by business interests but also by such wilderness enthusiasts as John Muir, who prized forests as repositories of spiritual beauty and not as sources of timber (cf. Hays, 1959). Many persons associated with the movement presently dislike the word and prefer *environmentalism. As an editor of *Field & Stream* noted, Pinchot was a hunter, and "people who believe that no creature should be killed, that no forests should be cut, . . . should be called ultra-preservationists, radical environmentalists, unrealistic extremists, or residents of the twilight zone, but please, please, don't call them conservationists. They are not" (Reiger, 1978). Others have broadened the meaning of "conservation" from its initially narrow range of public control. According to one biologist, early conservationist measures included, for example, the penalties imposed by the first Norman kings of England to prevent the further encroachment of agriculture on their hunting preserves (Alison, 1981). And the International Union for the Conservation of Nature and Natural Resources (1980), with the "advice, cooperation, and financial assistance" of several United Nations agencies, prepared a quite elaborate "World Conservation Strategy." The three main objectives of the program were "to maintain essential ecological processes and life-support systems, to preserve genetic diversity, and to ensure the sustainable utilization of species and ecosystems." Every country in the world was urged to review its current conservation measures and to expand them to include especially those requirements designated as priority.

REFERENCES: Robert M. Alison, "The Earliest Traces of a Conservation Conscience," *Natural History*, 90 (May, 1981), 72-77. Samuel P. Hays, *Conservation and the Gospel of Efficiency* (Cambridge, Mass.: Harvard University Press, 1959). International Union for the Conservation of Nature and Natural Resources, *World Conservation Strategy: Living Resource Conservation for Sustainable Development* (New York, 1980). George Reiger, Letter to the *New York Times* (January 10, 1978).

Consolidated Metropolitan Statistical Area (CMSA), a megalopolitan unit used by the U.S. Bureau of the Census to designate several contiguous *Metropolitan Statistical Areas. This designation of CMSA was adopted in 1983; previously the name had been Standard Metropolitan Consolidated Area (SMCA) and, before that, Standard Consolidated Area (SCA). In 1970, when the unit was established under the first of these designations, only two were noted—the New York-Northeastern New Jersey SCA, comprising four SMSAs plus two New Jersey counties, and the Chicago-Northwestern Indiana SCA, comprising two adjacent SMSAs. In 1981 the criteria as well as the name were changed. An SMCA consisted of two or more contiguous SMSAs, each at least 60 percent urban, with a combined population of at least one million. On the basis of the 1980 census, the U.S. Office of Management and Budget designated four new SMCAs, bringing the total to seventeen, including one in Puerto Rico.

REFERENCE: U.S. Bureau of the Census, *Data User News* (July, 1981), pp. 3-4.

constant activity rates, used in projecting the work force, are based on the assumption that the age-sex-specific rates observed in a recent census or survey do not change over the period of the projection. Any change in the work force, thus, is ascribed either to growth of the population or to shifts in its age-sex structure. Manifestly the premise is often invalid, and sometimes more accurate projections can be made by including some shifts in employment as one factor.

consumer price index (CPI), a measure of the changing value of money in the purchase of certain typical consumer goods; an indication, thus, of the rate of inflation or, theoretically, of deflation. In the abstract the construction of such an index is simple, but the calculation can be complicated by, among other factors, the choice among several alternative formulas, the selection of a suitable base period, and the decision whether to weight particular components. Though discussions of the *population optimum have generally neglected this factor, it is manifestly pertinent to consider changes in the consumer market resulting from inflation.

REFERENCE: Ethel D. Hoover, "Index Numbers: Practical Applications," in *International Encyclopedia of the Social Sciences*, 7, 159-165.

consummation of a marriage takes place with the first sexual intercourse after the wedding ceremony. In many legal systems a marriage is not completed until it has been thus consummated, and the lack of any sexual relations between the couple is a valid ground for an *annulment.

consumption, the ultimate use of goods and services, differs greatly among social classes and nations. According to Ernst †Engel's law, the higher a person's income, the smaller the proportion he spends on food; and the same relation holds for countries. Among the world's nations with adequate statistics, there is a high correlation between the *food rate*, or the percentage of money used to buy food, and such measures of general well-being as the infant mortality rate (cf. Stigler, 1954). The pattern of expenditure varies with many factors—income, family size, locale and thus the relative availability of various goods, and a more or less unanalyzable residual labeled "taste" (cf. Nicosia and Mayer, 1976). In the usual analysis of economists, the overall choice of consumers includes three major discretionary components—the purchase of durable goods, short-term borrowing, and voluntary savings (cf. Schipper, 1964). That is, in such a view demand and saving/borrowing are taken to be parts of a single integrated framework. The different allocation of expenditures in high- and low-income countries can be estimated; if one currency unit is added to the expenditure per capita, it is distributed as follows (Lluch et al., 1977):

Category of Consumption	Low-income Countries	High-income Countries
Food	39%	17%
Housing	12	21
Transportation	9	21
Clothing	7	8
Other	33	33

Especially among the increasingly cosmopolitan inhabitants of advanced economies but also in most less developed countries, the tempo of change in consumption has been rapid during the twentieth century. But even in populations suffering from severe lacks, many have refused to eat imported foods defined as unsuitable in their cultures. African peoples, for instance, remain conservative in their food habits, clinging tenaciously to diets that are inadequate and to taboos that aggravate their lacks.

REFERENCES: Constantino Lluch, Alan A. Powell, and Ross A. Williams, *Patterns in Household Demand and Saving* (New York: Oxford University Press, 1977). Francesco M. Nicosia and Robert N. Mayer, "Toward a Sociology of Consumption," *Journal of Consumer Research*, 3 (1976), 65-75. Lewis Schipper, *Consumer Discretionary Behavior: A Comparative Study in Alternative Methods of Empirical Research* (Amsterdam: North-Holland Publishing Co., 1964). George J. Stigler, "The Early History of Empirical Studies of Consumer Behavior," *Journal of Political Economy*, 62 (1954), 95-113.

contagious, of diseases, means capable of being transmitted from one person to another. Also, *contagion*, the communication of such a disease or the disease itself. Contagious is loosely used as a synonym of *infectious*, which describes diseases caused by such parasites as bacteria, viruses, protozoa, or fungi. All infectious diseases are contagious but some (e.g., leprosy) are barely so. Some neuroses, on the other hand, are so contagious that they can develop into a crowd mania. Infection, the invasion of the body by pathogenic micro-organisms, is distinguished from *infestation*, the invasion of the body by such arthropods as insects, mites, or ticks. *Communicable*, a more general term meaning capable of being transmitted from person to person, is sometimes used as a loose equivalent of either contagious or infectious.

conterminous, in the phrase "conterminous United States," comprising the forty-eight adjoining states and thus omitting Hawaii and Alaska. Particularly concerning any measure of centrality, the usual practice is to omit the distant parts of the country.

contingency table is one consisting of two or more rows and two or more columns, in which the values in each of the cells are cross-classified by two criteria. The simplest form is a fourfold table, in which each of the variables is dichotomized. If the frequencies in the four cells are as follows,

a	*b*
c	*d*

then the *coefficient of association* is calculated by the equation

$$Q = \frac{ad - bc}{ad + bc}$$

Like a coefficient of *correlation, this varies between 1.00 and -1.00, with zero indicating a total lack of association.

continuation ratio (often called a continuation rate) is used in the analysis of birth-control programs. It is the proportion of acceptors who continue to use the services offered for a specified period. The complement is called the *termination ratio* (or rate). See also *acceptance.

continuous, noted of a *parameter or a *variable, taking values without jumps from one to the next, as opposed to *discrete*, which describes an array of values that includes gaps or intervals from one set to another. The distinction is less observed in empirical studies than one might suppose. Age, for instance, is clearly a continuous variable; no unit of time, no matter how minute, can represent the process of aging without imposing on it a series of artificial jumps. And in most demographic studies the unit is a year or 5-year bracket, rather large periods relative to the person's lifetime.

contraception, the preventing or impeding of conception. Also, *contraceptive*, pertaining to contraception; anything used to prevent or impede conception. The terms are the most precise and least ideological of a group of near synonyms. *Neo-Malthusianism* (or sometimes simply Malthusianism) refers to the movement that developed during the latter decades of the nineteenth century in several Western countries. Its demand for the public dissemination of knowledge about simple contraceptives was embedded in a truncated version of †Malthus's theory, a simplified utilitarianism derived from Jeremy †Bentham, atheism or at least vigorous secularism, a quasi-anarchist opposition to socialism, and several other minor or local strains all irrelevant to its ostensible central purpose. Marie †Stopes in England and Margaret †Sanger in the United States, two pioneers in disseminating contraceptives, wanted to distinguish themselves from this tradition, and both adopted the term *birth control* to designate their use of clinics to offer medical services with a minimum of economic or social theorizing. From the beginning this "control" of births connoted the reduction of fertility, which was hardly an urgent issue during the interwar decades, when many Western demographers were concerned about a seemingly imminent depopulation. Birth-control clinics started to treat subfecundity, and in their propaganda they stressed that their contraceptive services were intended not to prevent births but to regulate their number and spacing—what eventually came to be called *planned parenthood*.

Birth control is sometimes used loosely to denote any means whatever to reduce the number of one's offspring, but contraception clearly does not include *abortion or *infanticide, which take place after conception has occurred. Whether permanent or periodic abstinence or prolonged *lactation should be regarded as contraceptive depends on the motive of the persons involved. Priestly *celibacy is practiced for religious reasons. The interruption in sexual relations by the death of a spouse or a divorce, which can very significantly reduce a population's fertility, is manifestly not purposeful. And many cultures impose periods of abstinence within marriage—while the woman is menstruating, during the gestation period, and for some time after the birth of a child; whenever solemnity or mourning is appropriate; when magical signs indicate that a conception would be unlucky. In industrial societies, however, one of the commonest types of periodic abstinence is the *rhythm method of contraception. Two other controls that require no drugs or devices are *coitus interruptus (or "withdrawal") and *coitus reservatus, but these are not defined as "natural" by those who make this distinction.

What is termed a *contraceptive prevalence survey* has been used particularly in less developed countries to gather data on family planning. A standardized interview is administered to a representative sample of women in their fecund ages. In addition to the standard questions on knowledge, attitudes, and use, respondents are asked about the source of contraceptive services, their cost, and other relevant questions. Up to 1980, surveys had been conducted in sixteen countries or parts of countries in Asia, Latin America, and the Middle East (cf. Morris et al., 1981).

The range of contraceptives that has been used is wider than many people suspect. In nineteenth-century America, the circulation of books, pamphlets, and newspapers recommending this or that method of preventing a birth was sometimes enormous. Frederick Hollick's *The Marriage Guide*, first published in 1850, went through over 300 printings, with a total sale of almost a million copies. The more or less accurately described methods, whether advocated or condemned, included abstinence or infrequent intercourse, a rhythm method based on an inaccurate timing of ovulation, intercourse without ejaculation, coitus interruptus, *condoms, "womb veils" (that is, *diaphragms), a *sponge or *douche, and abortion. In 1864 a New Hampshire physician complained that the 123 types of diaphragm he knew of were converting the vagina into "a Chinese toy shop." Also recommended were such chemicals and extracts as ergot, cotton root, aloes, savin, tansy, opium, iodine, lemon juice, vinegar, prussic or sulfuric acid, and Lysol! Electric devices were said to render the semen sterile. The more startling items in this listing, it is true, were in the inventory of quacks, but one should keep in mind that even in the best medical circles knowledge of the physiology of reproduction was slight and often faulty (Wells, 1978). Nor have the means used to avoid childbearing necessarily improved among the lower classes of Western societies. According to a recent survey of mothers of six or more children in the English city of Leeds, one reasonably effective method still was what was variously termed "pulling out," "being careful," "being sensible," or "getting off at Hillgate," the bus stop before the one for home. Folk methods of inducing a menstrual flow included a drink consisting of milk stout boiled with two or three teaspoons of nutmeg, a solution of Tide detergent or Epsom salts, quinine, or various "female pills" obtainable from a druggist or herbalist. Not surprisingly in view of such alternatives, almost half of the sample interviewed preferred female *sterilization to any other type of contraception or abortion (Chamberlain, 1976).

The contraceptive means used by better informed persons, many chosen with a physician's or a clinician's advice, also vary in effectiveness, relative safety, and price. Some of the simplest methods persist from the past: coitus interruptus, rhythm, an astringent douche, the condom. The standard contraceptive of middle-class Americans was once the diaphragm, combined typically with a spermicidal foam, cream, or jelly. Male and female sterilization has become far more significant both in Western countries and worldwide. But the two most prominent means are *oral contraceptives and *intra-uterine devices.

A perfect contraceptive, one might say, is one that never permits an accidental pregnancy, but this result would depend also on the couple's fecundity, their intelligence and care in using it, and the period over which it is used. As the term is ordinarily understood, the effectiveness of contraceptives means not their theoretical efficacy but how they work when used by a sample of fallible humans. Motivation can be measured to some degree through survey questions; a couple that wants only to space their children, for example, may be more careless than one that wants to restrict their family to the present number of children. The period over which contraceptives are used has been measured with a formula devised by Raymond †Pearl to give the number of pregnancies per 100 woman-years of use:

$$R = \frac{\text{Number of pregnancies} \times 1{,}200}{\text{Total months of use}}$$

This became a standard measure, recommended in specialist texts (e.g., Pincus, 1965, pp. 297-299; Henry, 1976, pp. 101-104). With the formula, however, one gets a rather inexact approximation of the actual proportion of failures; for among any sample of women that start to control births, those that discontinue over the following months are not representative of the whole. Any who find the particular method objectionable shift to another; any who have an accidental pregnancy are presumably less conscientious or more fecund. Month by month, the original heterogeneous population is reduced to a more and more homogeneous residue of satisfied, highly motivated users, including all the sterile and most of the subfecund. If the observed rates are corrected by using a *multiple-decrement table, the values of R calculated at intervals of several months start higher than the adjusted rates and gradually decline to a figure below the corrected one (Potter, 1963).

Taking this factor into account, Christopher Tietze (1970; see also Trussell, 1974; Schirm et al., 1982) has ranked the commonest contraceptives as follows:

Probably the most effective: female sterilization, with male sterilization a bit less so; oral contraceptives of the combined type, with sequential medication a bit less so; the rhythm method based on measurement of the basal body temperature; and *injectable progestational agents.
Highly effective: intra-uterine devices; the diaphragm with spermicidal cream or jelly; the condom; the so-called minipill, which provides a continuous ingestion of small doses of progestogen only, without estrogen.

Less effective: such chemical contraceptives as vaginal foams, jellies, and creams, foaming tablets, and suppositories; the rhythm method based on the calendar; coitus interruptus. Least effective: post-coital douche; prolonged lactation.

The efficiency of any means of contraception cannot be equated with effectiveness in reducing the fertility of the population that uses it. A single failure may result in conception, but a contraceptive success must be repeated at each new ovulation. Thus, a method with an 80 percent efficacy reduces fertility only by about half (Ryder, 1965).

REFERENCES: Audrey Chamberlain, "Gin and Hot Baths," *New Society* (July 15, 1976), pp. 112-114. Henry, *Population*. Leo Morris et al., "Contraceptive Prevalence Surveys: A New Source of Family Planning Data," *Population Reports*, Ser. M, no. 5 (1981). Gregory G. Pincus, *The Control of Fertility* (New York: Academic Press, 1965). Robert G. Potter, Jr., "Additional Measures of Use-Effectiveness of Contraception," *Milbank Memorial Fund Quarterly*, 41 (1963), 400-418. Norman B. Ryder, "The Measurement of Fertility Patterns," in Mindel C. Sheps and Jeanne C. Ridley, eds., *Public Health and Population Change* (Pittsburgh: University of Pittsburgh Press, 1965). Allen L. Schirm, T. James Trussell, Jane Menken, and William R. Grady, "Contraceptive Failure in the United States: The Impact of Social, Economic and Demographic Factors," *Family Planning Perspectives,* 14 (1982), 68-75. Christopher Tietze, "Ranking of Contraceptive Methods by Levels of Effectiveness," *Excerpta Medica*, International Congress Series, no. 224 (1970). Trussell, "Cost versus Effectiveness of Different Birth Control Methods," *Population Studies*, 28 (1974), 85-106. Robert V. Wells, "Fertility Control in Nineteenth-Century America: A Study of Diffusion, Technique, and Motive," in American Academy of Arts and Sciences, "Historical Perspectives on the Scientific Study of Fertility in the United States" (Boston: mimeographed, 1978).

control, in an experimental situation, the population or other entity used as a standard. Ideally it should be as nearly identical to the test population as possible in every respect except in the characteristic being tested, where the contrast should be as great as possible.

The phrases "birth control" and "population control," routine in demographic contexts and seemingly self-explanatory, in fact are often confused. Growth of a population depends not only on the decisions of potential parents on whether to have children but also on the relative number of such persons—that is, on the age structure.

conurbation, in Britain an urban aggregate comprising two or more contiguous but politically independent municipalities. Somewhat loosely used after the term was coined by Patrick †Geddes early in this century, conurbations were officially defined in the 1951 census as "continuously urbanized areas surrounding large population centers, which are to a greater or lesser extent focal points of economic and social activity." All the areas so designated in 1951 had populations of a million or more. In most recent analyses the term has been replaced by either metropolitan area or metropolitan labor area.

REFERENCES: D. E. C. Eversley and Lucy Bonnerjea, *Changes in the Size and Structure of the Resident Population of Inner Areas* (London: Social Science Research Council, 1980). L. M. Feery, "Conurbations in England and Wales," in World Population Conference, Rome, 1954, *Proceedings*, 4 (1956-57), 615-626. J. Douglas McCallum, "Statistical Trends of the British Conurbations," in Gordon E. Cameron, ed., *The Future of British Conurbations: Policies and Prescriptions for Change* (London: Longman, 1980).

convergence hypothesis, the proposition that in the modern era—because of the functional requirements of modern technology and the standardization resulting from frequent interaction—the division of labor and related structural characteristics of all societies, including those of less developed countries, are becoming increasingly similar. In an important variant of the theory, the point of view is advanced that the political-cultural differences between democratic and totalitarian states are diminishing.

REFERENCES: John W. Meyer, John Boli-Bennett, and Christopher Chase-Dunn, "Convergence and Divergence in Development," *Annual Review of Sociology*, 1 (1975), 223-246. Ian Weinberg, "The Problem of the Convergence of Industrial Societies: A Critical Look at the State of a Theory," *Comparative Studies in Society and History*, 11 (1969), 1-15. Bertram D. Wolfe, "Some Reflections on the Convergence Theory," *Western Politica*, 1 (Autumn, 1966), 3-14.

CONVERSE, a computer program used to estimate the effectiveness of family-planning programs. An annual stream of acceptors, classified by type of method used and age bracket, is fed in, and the number of births averted over each time period is calculated. The program also yields birth rates as an output variable. See also *TABRAP.

REFERENCE: Dorothy L. Nortman et al., *Birth Rates and Birth Control Practice: Relations Based on the Computer Models TABRAP and CONVERSE* (New York: Population Council, 1978).

Cook Islands: The Statistics Office conducts the country's censuses, of which the last was in 1981. It publishes a *Quarterly Statistical Bulletin* that includes population data and a quarterly *Overseas Migration Statistics*. Address: Central Planning Bureau, P.O. Box 125, Rarotonga.

correlation, a specific relation between two or more quantitative variables or ranks, measured by a coefficient of correlation that conventionally ranges between -1 and $+1$. A perfect negative correlation means that with each increase in one variable there is a comparable decrease in the other; a perfect positive correlation means that with each increase in one there is a comparable increase in the other. The intermediate value, zero, means an absence of any correlation, but not necessarily that the variables are independent. For example, from his general thesis that the suicide rate depends on the degree of social integration, Émile †Durkheim held that suicides should be relatively more frequent among city dwellers and relatively less so among Jews. However, most Jews live in cities, and an observed zero correlation between the proportion of Jews in a population and its suicide rate might mean that the positive correlation has been hidden by a negative one. More generally, any correlation should be interpreted as a causal relation only after alternative interpretations have been tested and eliminated.

corruption in political terminology implies a contrary standard, a moral norm of integrity that is violated; but in many less developed countries one finds what Stanislav Andreski (1968) called "kleptocracy," or corruption as a system of government (cf. Kotecha and Adams, 1981). Where virtually the only road up is by public office, it is seen by almost all as a means of personal enrichment. Though venality is hardly unknown in Communist countries (in Poland a bribe is called "a socialist handshake"), Western Europe, and the United States, it is commonest in Africa, the Middle East, and Latin America. In developed economies corruption is an aberration; in less developed ones it is very often the rule (Wraith and Simpkins, 1964).

The pervasive effects of venality on political, economic, and social life are seldom documented, of course, and generally are passed over altogether in tomes on economic development or compilations of data by international agencies. Appointments to any sort of office are made on the basis of family or kin ties, even if the candidate is notoriously unsuitable. A test of competence, if it is used, may be irrelevant, for passage into and through a university is also governed in large part by favoritism and bribery. The vast sums expended by Western countries on military or economic aid have helped enrich the sector of the population in charge of dispensing it.

Where almost everything else in a social environment is corrupt, so also is the subject matter of demography. Andreski noted that there were hospitals in West Africa where patients had to pay a nurse to bring them a chamber pot; where a physician treated only those who bribed him, in order of the size of the bribe; where those in charge of the dispensary stole the medicaments and sold them either to the patients or to traders. When food is scarce, those assigned to distribute relief supplies see them as another means of self-enrichment.

When population counts set the distribution of political power, one can hardly assume anywhere that they are made without regard to this key function (see *African society). Many of the items in public statistics, moreover, are indices of personal or national prestige—industrial production, food crops, literacy, expectation of life, and so on; and while it is obvious that such figures often cannot be accepted as given, it is impossible to know what correction would be reasonable in each case.

REFERENCES: Stanislav Andreski, *The African Predicament: A Study in the Pathology of Modernisation* (London: Michael Joseph, 1968.) Ken C. Kotecha and Robert W. Adams, *African Politics: The Corruption of Power* (Lanham, Md.: University Press of

America, 1981). Steven W. Mosher, *Broken Earth: The Rural Chinese* (New York: Free Press, 1983), chap. 4. Ronald Wraith and Edgar Simpkins, *Corruption in Developing Countries* (New York: Norton, 1964).

cost, when defined in a dictionary as the amount paid for something purchased, is equivalent to what economists term an *outlay*. As they use the word, cost includes what is called *opportunity cost*, or the value of alternatives that have to be forgone in order to make a particular purchase or follow a particular course of action. Thus, one of the main costs of having a child may be that, at least for a period, the wife stops working outside the home. Indeed, since opportunities exist in an only partly predictable future, the opportunity cost may be incurred not by quitting a job but by failing to seek one or even by neglecting to train adequately for one. Since such potential sacrifices cannot be calculated precisely, a decision not to have a child that is in fact based on nonmonetary factors is often rationalized in economic terms. To the degree, however, that potential parents' decisions are based on calculated choices, the direct and opportunity costs of each child at the level of each social class are important data.

This rationale has been exemplified with United States data in a number of interesting studies by Thomas J. †Espenshade. In general, for various income levels, the first child costs more than twice as much as the second. In 1960-61 the combined cost of bearing and raising three children up to their 18th birthdays amounted to 59.1 percent of the income earned by a lower-income family, 47.4 percent for the middle income, and 38.8 percent for the upper income (Espenshade, 1973). Inflation affected few activities more than childrearing: over only the three years 1977-80 the cost rose by a third, to a possible $85,000 per child (Espenshade, 1977, 1980; see also Callan, 1980; Edwards, 1981; Olson, 1983). Estimating the cost of rearing children indicates that, while this is generally one factor in a rational decision whether to have children, it is nonmonetary incentives that induce potential parents in Western societies to have any at all; for none of them can reasonably expect to profit financially from them (but see also *New Home Economics; *wealth-flow theory).

In the evaluation of *family-planning programs, several calculations of costs have been used. The cost per acceptor is the total expenditure for the program divided by the number of persons who have indicated a willingness to use its services. For the cost per birth averted, the denominator is the estimated number of births that did not take place because of the program's existence; see *births averted. For the cost per *couple-year of protection, the denominator is the estimated number of years that couples effectively used the contraceptives furnished.

Fertility and its control are not the only elements of demography that can be related to costs and benefits. Indeed, any act of an individual that takes place following an actual or hypothesized rational decision can be analyzed in the context of *Economic Man's behavior. The rationale is more persuasive when applied to aggregate data, with the implication that acts more or less determined by rational decisions are balanced out (see also *economics; *migration).

REFERENCES: Victor J. Callan, "The Value and Cost of Children: Australian, Greek, and Italian Couples in Sydney, Australia," *Journal of Cross-Cultural Psychology*, 11 (1980), 482-497. Carolyn S. Edwards, "The Cost of Raising a Child," *American Demographics*, 3 (July-August, 1981), 25-29. Thomas J. Espenshade, *Estimation of the Cost of Children and Some Results from Urban United States* (Berkeley: International Population and Urban Research, University of California, 1973); "The Value and Cost of Children," *Population Bulletin*, 32 (1977); "33 Percent Rise in Three Years: Raising a Child Can Now Cost $85,000," *Intercom*, 8 (September, 1980), 10-12. Lawrence Olson, *Costs of Children* (Lexington, Mass.: Lexington Books, 1983).

cost-benefit analysis, a mode of setting out the factors to be taken into account when making an economic choice, has been applied loosely to situations in which neither the costs nor the benefits can easily be reduced to monetary terms. For example, the American economist Stephen †Enke tried to show that in India and other less developed countries the cost of preventing a birth would be considerably less than that of the goods and services required for another person added to the population. He proposed that the government share this saving with the nonparents responsible through a subsidy for not having a (or another) child. Another economist, Gary †Becker, offered the thesis that prospective parents generally choose a certain number of children of a particular "quality" by contrasting the pleasure from parenthood against alternative ways of spending their money, time, and effort. Such concepts were applied in various types of analysis to estimate the cost effectiveness of family-planning programs in less developed countries (Yinger et al., 1983). According to an employee of the U.S. Agency for International Development, however, to increase the proportion of married women aged 15-49 in less developed countries from the 20 percent who were using contraceptives in the early 1980s to the 80 percent that would be required to stabilize the population would entail an investment of $4 billion a year—about four times the then current expenditure (Speidel, 1982).

REFERENCES: J. Joseph Speidel, "Cost Implications of Population Stabilization," in Ismail A. Sirageldin, David Salkever, and Richard Osborn, eds., *Evaluating Population Programs: International Experience with CEA/CBA* [cost-effectiveness analysis, cost-benefit analysis] (Baltimore: Population Center, School of Hygiene and Public Health, Johns Hopkins University, 1982). Nancy Yinger, Osborn, Salkever, and Sirageldin, "Third World Family Planning Programs: Measuring the Costs," *Population Bulletin*, 38 (February 1983), 1-35.

Costa Rica: Demographic Institutions
The Costa Rica Demographic Association (ADC) was founded in 1966; in 1980 its president was E. B. Cravarria. Its activities have related mostly to family planning, as has also its serial publication, *Planifamilia*. In 1974 it started a training program on contraception and related matters for physicians and nurses, and two years later it began research on population, family planning, health, and communication. Address: Asociación Demográfica Costarricense, Paseo Colón, Apartado 10.203, San José.

UNIVERSITY AND OTHER RESEARCH INSTITUTES

The Latin American Demographic Center (CELADE), with its main office in Santiago, Chile, has a branch in Costa Rica. Its activities are described in the entry on the *United Nations.

In 1975 the University of Costa Rica, a public institution, established an Institute of Social Research. Its work, concentrated on the economy of Costa Rica, pertains to demography only with respect to such topics as labor mobility or, more broadly, the interrelation of the economy and population. Address: Instituto de Investigaciones Sociales, Universidad de Costa Rica, Apartado Postal 49, Ciudad Universitaria, Rodrigo Facio, San José.

The School of Social Work at the same university has included population and family planning in various of its programs. Its documentation center, established in 1967, provides information on these and other topics. Since 1973 its staff has conducted research related to employment, migration, birth control, and similar matters; and in the same period it offered training in demography and family planning, first to its employees and then to the general public. Address: Escuela de Trabajo Social, Universidad de Costa Rica, Ciudad Universitaria, San José.

Also at the same university there is a Central American University Council (CSUCA), of which Eugenio Rodríguez Vega was president in 1980. It carries out research on migration, rural development, and the social structure of rural areas and publishes a journal, *Estudios Sociales Centroamericanos*. Address: Consejo Superior Universitario Centroamericano, Apartado 37, Ciudad Universitaria, San José.

At the National University of Costa Rica there is an Institute of Social and Population Studies (IDESPO), which conducts research on population and family planning, as well as a training program for university students and government officials. Address: Instituto de Estudios Sociales y de Población, Universidad Nacional Autónoma de Costa Rica, Heredia.

GOVERNMENT STATISTICAL BUREAU

The Central Office of Statistics and Censuses, which in 1980 was under the direction of René †Sánchez Bolaños, administers the census and vital statistics and publishes annual compilations. It also prepares life tables and population projections, and it has published the first results of its national survey of fertility. Address: Dirección General de Estadística y Censos, Apartado Postal 10163, San José.

cottage industry (sometimes termed "domestic industry" or the "domestic system") represented in Europe a continuation of late medieval institutions to the beginning of the nineteenth century. In England, for instance, a master spinner or weaver bought wool from a dealer and, with the assistance of his wife and children (as well as often three to six journeymen), processed it in his home.

As production became larger than a local market could absorb, merchants often advanced from simple marketing to a control of the whole process. The centralization into factories, partly because of the greater use of mechanical power, meant a decline of domestic industry and the rise of a new class of entrepreneurs. The pitiless exploitation of women and children that supposedly characterized early capitalism, paradoxically, was in fact a carry-over of the family organization of cottage industry to a new setting (Ashton, 1964, chap. 4; Mantoux, 1961, chap. 1).

Cottage industry conducted by a single family (or a near equivalent, with a very small number of hired workers) is common today in many less developed countries. Some analysts see it as a temporary residue from the inefficient traditionalist sector of a *dual economy, but this is not at all the universal view. Particularly in India, nationalists have argued that the British had destroyed the native economy in order to eliminate competition with Lancashire mills; and as one of its first acts, independent India established a Cottage Industries Board charged with revivifying rural small-scale enterprises. Indeed, in deference to †Gandhi and his followers, India's new constitution holds that "the State shall endeavor to promote cottage industries on an individual or cooperative basis in rural areas" (Article 43). The rationale behind this policy is not merely nationalistic. In an economy with limited investments and industrial skills—that is, a less developed country—the surplus labor can be absorbed usefully into enterprises that require little capital or technical ability (Rao, 1967; see also Child, 1977; Herman, 1956).

The relation of cottage industry to population variables, though seldom studied as such, is implicit in a number of general theories. Whatever decline in family size is associated with women's participation in the work force does not apply to work at home, where mothers can simultaneously perform quasi-industrial tasks and watch over their offspring. Indeed, since children are typically set to work from an early age, the system may encourage rather than depress a high natality (cf. *wealth-flow theory). The move to cities is probably reduced if economic opportunities arise outside them, and most less developed countries would regard this as a benefit. In the longer run, however, industrialization— and thus possibly modernization—may become more difficult to develop; cottage industry can be efficient only on a small scale, not to provide the economic basis for the rise in living standards that such countries are seeking.

REFERENCES: T. S. Ashton, *An Economic History of England: The 18th Century* (London: Methuen, 1964). Frank C. Child, *Small-Scale Industry in Kenya* (Los Angeles: African Studies Center, University of California, 1977). Theodore Herman, "The Role of Cottage and Small-Scale Industries in Asian Economic Development," *Economic Development and Cultural Change*, 4 (1956), 356-370. Paul Mantoux, *The Industrial Revolution in the Eighteenth Century* (New York: Harper & Row, 1961). R. V. Rao, *Cottage & Small Scale Industries & Planned Economy* (Delhi: Sterling Publishers, 1967).

Council for the Development of Economic and Social Research in Africa (CODESRIA) was founded in 1973 with research institutes in twenty-nine countries as members. Several years later it was established in Dakar under Abdalla S. Bujra as executive secretary. One area of research was the general field of population, including policy and family-planning programs. Publications: *Africa Development*, quarterly; *Africana*, bimonthly newsletter; *Africa Development Research*, annual. Address: Boîte Postale 3304, Dakar, Senegal.

Council of Europe (Conseil de l'Europe) was established in 1949 by twenty-one governments of Western Europe in order to safeguard their common heritage and to promote social and economic progress. Beginning in 1976 it has published a series, *Population Studies,* in English and French editions. It also publishes an annual compilation *Recent Demographic Developments in the Member States of the Council of Europe*, of which the fifth edition was issued in 1982. Address: Avenue de l'Europe, F-67006 Strasbourg Cédex, France.

Council of Professional Associations on Federal Statistics (COPAFS) consists of two representatives from each of twelve American professional associations, including the Population Association of America, the American Statistical Association, and the Society of Actuaries. It developed out of a Joint Ad Hoc Committee on Government Statistics, which had been set up in 1975 in order to review the federal statistical system and its products. Following the recommendation that its work be continued in a permanent liaison body, COPAFS was established in 1980. In 1982 its director was William H. Shaw, a former assistant secretary of commerce for economic affairs and a past president of the American Statistical Association. Address: 806 Fifteenth Street, N.W., Washington, D.C. 20005.

counseling, professional guidance and assistance to individuals, relates in many cases to demographic topics. Most counselors have had training in psychology, others in sociology, economics, theology, or another discipline—or in none. Counseling psychology, so designated from the early 1950s, developed out of vocational guidance, in existence since early in the century. Some fifty American universities offer doctoral programs in counseling psychology, and the relevant division of the American Psychological Association has recommended that appropriate standards be set. In contrast to clinical psychology, the primary focus is on normal people facing choices and plans that are or can be elements of everyone's life. Perhaps the dominant subcategory is marriage counseling, which generally consists of advice on whether to get married or assistance in coping with family problems. Related to this is counseling on sexual behavior or disorders of adults and adolescents, on contraceptives and abortions, on pregnancy and genetics. The professional background required varies from training in a field of learning (genetics) through some knowledge of the legal, institutional, and personal ramifications of various courses of action. Some counseling is based mainly on ethical choices—for example, whether interreligious marriages are suitable, whether one should ever undergo an abortion and if so under what conditions. In a society less secularized than modern industrial countries, such counseling is typically given by religious leaders following generally accepted moral principles, and the transfer to a pseudoscientific framework has not been wholly successful.

counterurbanization, the deconcentration of population from metropolitan areas by a net migration from the centers to rings or to nonmetropolitan sites.

REFERENCE: Brian J. L. Berry, ed., *Urbanization and Counterurbanization* (Beverly Hills, Calif.: Sage Publications, 1976).

country derives from the Late Latin *contrata regio* or *contrata terra*, a region or land set over against (*contra*) another and hence distinct from it. Three sets of meanings developed from this origin: a particular type of area, as in such a phrase as "hunting country"; a rural district as distinct from cities, or the "countryside" as a whole; and a more colloquial synonym for *nation or state. There is the same curious combination of meanings in the quite unrelated French *pays* (but note also *campagne*) and German *Land*.

county, an administrative subdivision of a nation. In Britain it is the principal local unit, with responsibility for police, education, health services, services to children, town and country planning, and maintenance of roads. In the United States the county is the primary subdivision of a state. It is governed by an elected board with legislative and administrative powers, including the right to tax and sometimes to borrow for local purposes; it is generally responsible for welfare, licensing, the registration of deeds, the compilation of vital statistics, and some planning and zoning. Counties in the United States have ranged in size from about 20 to about 20,000 square miles, and they have been far less stable than one might suppose. Depending on the topography, the survey techniques, the policy of the public-land office, the date of statehood, and the size and population of the state, a county may have changed several times, in some cases disappearing altogether. A county's population has also been influenced by its function, which was minimal in New England, strongly governmental in the South, and coordinated with minor civil units in the North and West. In 1980 there were 3,215 counties or equivalent areas in the United States, including 78 in Puerto Rico.

county group, in the usage of the U.S. Bureau of the Census, one or more counties (or another aggregation of contiguous places, whether or not they are counties) with a total population of 100,000 or more. Usually county groups have been defined so as to correspond with areas that are regarded as distinctive in that particular state.

couple is a common designation of a linked pair, either a man and wife, two intending to marry, or those living together in a stable union. It used to be applied less often to short-term liaisons, but recent publications have referred to "husband-wife couples" as a necessary specification. See also *one-parent family.

couple-years of protection is a concept used in calculating the efficacy of *family-planning programs. The estimated time during which each contraceptive is effective is multiplied by the number of such contraceptives supplied, giving an index of the maximum avoidance afforded. On the assumption that the risk of a pregnancy leading to a live birth is one per three years of unprotected sexual intercourse, the couple years of protection can be converted into the number of *births averted. As in other measures of success that administrators of such programs use, the *acceptance of a contraceptive is usually taken to be equivalent to its full and intelligent use.

courbe des populations, an index of metropolitanization, is given by the equation

$$\log y = A - a \log x$$
$$\text{or}$$
$$yx^a = 10^A$$

where x is a specified number of inhabitants
y is the number of places with more than x inhabitants
A and a are constants.

This is similar to Vilfredo †Pareto's law of income distribution.
    REFERENCE: H. W. Singer, "'The 'Courbe des Populations': A Parallel to Pareto's Law," *Economic Journal*, 46 (1936), 254-263.

couvade, a husband's simulation of childbirth during his wife's period of labor. As recently as the middle of the nineteenth century, it was usual to "faire la couvade" in southern France and the Basque country. According to the interpretation of some anthropologists, the function of the couvade was to involve the husband more fully in the process of reproduction and thus to tie him emotionally to the child (cf. *legitimacy). What could be deemed a functional equivalent has begun to develop among the American middle class; the husband is involved in a delivery at home or at the hospital, and he is encouraged to help care for the infant from birth onward.

crime, the sum of serious violations of a society's laws, is a subject of great complexity with an enormous body of writings. It overlaps with demography in several ways. Since particular crimes are typically committed by persons in a certain age range, and since crime in general is characteristic especially of young males, a population's age-sex structure is important in setting the incidence of crime. Less obviously and perhaps more dubiously, in-migrants to the cities during the early rise of industry may have become criminal in larger proportion than those who remained in the countryside. Any such contrast, however, is blurred by the differential development of reliable crime statistics (cf. Maltz, 1977). Similarly, the immigrants to the United States from roughly 1880 to 1920 were often typed as a potentially criminal element, but some evidence suggests rather that it was the next generation, with higher aspirations but a vestigial alien background, that more frequently broke the law.

That statistics on crime are inherently poor is a routine element of any discussion of the phenomenon. Some portion of the crimes committed are not discovered; many of those so identified are not "cleared" by arrests; of those arrested, many evade a trial or conviction. Each of these gaps in the record, moreover, reflects a differential incidence; as one obvious example, inexperienced criminals (who are generally younger) are more likely to be arrested, tried, and convicted than those who have gone through these processes before. Variation is usual also in the wording of parallel statutes, their interpretation by local courts, and the zeal and honesty with which police enforce them.

In the United States the basic set of criminal statistics is the Uniform Crime Reports that the Federal Bureau of Investigation compiles from records sent in by local administrations. Reporting rules are not followed consistently, with an allegedly systematic underreporting as a consequence in both the United States and Canada, which adopted a similar system (e.g., Silverman, 1980). In the early 1970s a second set of data on crime was instituted, the National Crime Surveys. The U.S. Bureau of the Census, acting for the Law Enforcement Assistance Administration of the U.S. Department of Justice, conducts periodic surveys of the victims of crime, of public opinion on law enforcement and related issues, and on particular subjects of topical importance. Individuals who have suffered from any of the more serious crimes (except, of course, homicide) are interviewed, and officials of commercial establishments that were victims of burglaries or robberies are also questioned. The two series generally give the same overall picture (cf. U.S. Law Enforcement Assistance Administration, 1980), partly because some lacks are common to the two sets of data and therefore do not show up in a comparison. According to statistics derived from victims, from 1973 to 1977-78 the rates of personal crimes of violence were unchanged except for a rise in those of theft and simple (that is, not aggravated) assault (U.S. Bureau of Justice Statistics, 1980). In 1982, however, the number of victims fell by 4.1 percent, or by the largest annual decrease ever reported (cf. Riche, 1984).

From the data of the National Crime Survey, paralleled by those of the Uniform Crime Reports, one gets a consistent demographic pattern of the perpetrators of serious crimes. For those aged 18-20 and those aged 21 or over, the highest proportions of criminals fall into color-sex categories as follows: (1) black males, (2) white males, (3) black females, and (4) white females (Hindelang, 1981). Overriding all the differences among local administrations and the lacunae in the statistics, this ranking indicates the importance of age-sex structure and race composition; see also *homicide. As the large cohorts born in the late 1940s and early 1950s grew to adolescence and early maturity, the crime rate increased irrespective of other factors; and as the median age of the population rises in the coming years, one can anticipate that the rate will tend to go down, or at least rise more slowly.

REFERENCES: Michael J. Hindelang, "Variations in Sex-Race-Age-Specific Incidence Rates of Offending," *American Sociological Review*, 46 (1981), 461-474. Michael D. Maltz, "Crime Statistics: A Historical Perspective," *Crime and Delinquency*, 23 (1977), 32-40. Martha Farnsworth Riche, "The Bureau of Justice Statistics," *American Demographics*, 6 (April, 1984), 40–42. Robert A. Silverman, "Measuring Crime: More Problems," *Journal of Police Science and Administration*, 8 (1980), 265-274. U.S. Bureau of Justice Statistics, *Criminal Victimization in the United States, 1978* (Washington, D.C., 1980). U.S. Law Enforcement Assistance Administration, *Sourcebook of Criminal Justice Statistics, 1979* (Washington, D.C., 1980).

cross-cousin is a first cousin (that is, an offspring of either parent's sibling) who is a child of a father's sister or a mother's brother. When the parental siblings are of the same sex, their children are called *parallel cousins*. In cultures that prohibit the marriage of parallel cousins, one between cross-cousins is often permitted or even preferred or prescribed.

cross-pressure, the inner conflict arising from contradictory motives on which a person's decision is based, as when his group loyalty pulls in one direction and the attitudes he has learned in another. In the United States, for instance, most Catholics and Jews were until recently Democrats, and a member of those religions personally inclined to vote Republican would sometimes "lose interest" in politics and abstain from voting. Or, in an example related to demography, even when Catholic norms still favored large families, most American Catholics who moved up the social ladder adopted the smaller family typical of the middle class, though possibly with some misgivings and feelings of guilt until the church's norms began to be challenged openly and more generally. All social change, one might say, results in a certain degree of cross-pressure among the individuals affected, some of whom find it difficult to adjust traditional to modernist norms. In the context of demography, whether in Western countries of the past or in currently less developed ones, this difficult transition is evident in the gradual institution of a small-family system.

cross-section analysis is based on observations of variables at one point in time; such data are contrasted with a time series or longitudinal data. The effect of four years of college on students' attitudes, to take a very simple example, can be analyzed by comparing members of the four classes, from freshmen to seniors. Or, in a broader instance of the same principle, the number of children born to women of successive ages can be used to predict the trend in fertility if one assumes that the age pattern of childbearing remains more or less fixed (cf. *Brass's method). From the frequent failure of such projections to forecast correctly, however, one should conclude that a cross-section analysis of contemporaneous events can do no more than suggest a cause-effect relation, which necessarily implies a lapse of time.

REFERENCES: Yair Mundlak, "Cross-Section Analysis," in *International Encyclopedia of the Social Sciences*, 3, 522-527. Robert V. Wells, "On the Dangers of Constructing Artificial Cohorts in Times of Rapid Social Change," *Journal of Interdisciplinary History*, 9 (1978), 103-110.

cross-tabulation, by which a population is broken up according to one variable along the horizontal dimension and, at the same time, according to another variable along the vertical dimension, is often a convenient method of presenting sets of data. It can also be the first step to their analysis, since procedures have been worked out to test for independence between the two variables, or their degree and type of association; see *contingency table.

REFERENCE: Graham J. G. Upton, *The Analysis of Cross-Tabulated Data* (New York: Wiley, 1978).

crowding, as used to designate the residential density of population, is both a contentious and an ambiguous term. Though sometimes used pejoratively as equivalent to "overcrowding," in other contexts crowding designates no more than a neutral measure. According to some American authorities, if more than one person per room live together, their condition is called "overcrowding" (cf. Baldassare, 1979, chap. 1). But the standard for such a judgment is largely cultural; most of the inhabitants of Singapore, to cite an extreme instance, would be delighted with what in the United States is defined as overcrowding. Even within the American middle class, the "livability" of a home (as some architectural analysts term it) depends largely on the number, age, and sex of the family's children, apart from the amount of space for each of them. Much of the recent concern about the effects of crowding, whether physiological or social, evolved from studies on *animal populations (for convenient summaries, see Choldin, 1978; Galle and Gove, 1978; Hawley, 1972). Whatever the results of such experiments, they leave unanswered the most fundamental question—how pertinent are they to an understanding of human behavior?

Crowding should not be confused with neighborhood density, or the number of persons per residential area. In modern American cities crowding and density are more or less independent of each other, with typical correlations below 0.3 (Carey, 1972). The relation between the two in typical areas can be represented in tabular form:

Persons per Areal Unit	Persons per Room	
	Below average	Above average
Below average	Stereotype of suburbia (e.g., Westchester County)	Slum in Western U.S. cities (e.g., Oakland, Watts)
Above average	High-rise luxury apartments or public housing	Stereotype of an urban tenement district

So long as infectious diseases were important causes of death, either overcrowding or a high neighborhood density endangered public health. In all Western countries, thus, urban death rates were higher than rural until some time in the nineteenth century, when sanitation systems became effective enough to counteract the effects of congestion. Shortly thereafter, there was typically a reversal in the healthfulness of the two sectors, for effective medical facilities developed first in cities and spread only gradually (and often incompletely) to the countryside. See also *population density.

REFERENCES: Mark Baldassare, *Residential Crowding in Urban America* (Berkeley: University of California Press, 1979.) George W. Carey, "Density, Crowding, Stress, and the Ghetto," *American Behavioral Scientist*, 15 (1972), 495-509. Harvey M. Choldin, "Urban Density and Pathology," *Annual Review of Sociology*, 4 (1978), 91-113. Omer R. Galle and Walter R. Gove, "Overcrowding, Isolation, and Human Behavior," in Karl E. Taeuber et al., eds., *Social Demography* (New York: Academic Press, 1978). Amos H. Hawley, "Population Density and the City," *Demography*, 9 (1972), 521-529.

crude rate is the simplest and the commonest measure of either demographic or social phenomena. It denotes the number of events during a year per 1,000 persons in the midyear population. Since the denominator typically includes persons not in the "population at risk"—that is, who do not contribute to the phenomenon being measured, or who contribute in a disproportionate degree— the crude *rate can be misleading when it is used to compare populations with markedly different age structures. The limitations of crude rates, however, have sometimes been exaggerated; they are easily calculated from data often readily available, and far more complex measures are not necessarily better indicators.

Cuba: Demographic Institutions

The Center of Demographic Studies of the University of Havana included among its members in the late 1970s Fernando González Quiñonez. Address: Centro de Estudios Demográficos, Universidad de la Habana, Calle 41 no. 2003, Marianao 13, Havana.

The Central Planning Board (JUCEPLAN) includes the Directorate for Statistics, which publishes the general *Anuario Estadístico de Cuba*, with volumes on *Matrimonios* and *Divorcios*, and a *Statistical Yearbook*, which contains population data. It also has a National Statistical Information System (SIEN), of which the head in 1982 was Efraín Fuentes. Address: Junta Central de Planificación, Gaveta Postal 6016, Havana.

The State Committee for Statistics (CEE) includes the Census and Surveys Office (ONCE), of which the director in 1978 was Máximo Gancedo Cabrera. A Demography Directorate had at its head in 1979 Oscar Ramos Piñol. Address: Comité Estatal de Estadísticas, Havana.

cultural relativism, an ethical position common among philosophers and especially anthropologists, can influence greatly any discussion of population phenomena. It has several facets (cf. Bidney, 1968): (1) At the most trivial level, a cultural relativist points out that every society determines what is right and good for its members. (2) If, however, those studying an alien society perceive it in terms of their own values, they may not be able to understand fully how it works. As A. L. †Kroeber (1950) wrote in a half-century review of his discipline's developments, "Anthropologists now agree that each culture must be examined in terms of its own structure and values, instead of being rated by the standards of some other civilization exalted as absolute—which in practice of course is always our own civilization." In theory, this principle of research could mean no more than trying, for the duration of one's contact with a band of cannibals or head-hunters, for instance, to act "as if" their customs were merely different, not in any way of lesser moral value. (3) The German philosopher Hans Vaihinger (1852-1933), best known for his book on *The Philosophy of "As If"* (1935), was a disciple of Immanuel Kant and cofounder of the journal *Kant-Studien*. Melville J. †Herskovits, of all American anthropologists the most articulate exponent of cultural relativism, also found support in Kant's philosophy and especially in the "spiritual anthropology" of the neo-Kantian Ernst Cassirer (cf. Herskovits, 1948, 1955). This link to the complexities of Kantian ethics gave the concept of cultural relativism a greater depth than could be derived from ethnographic studies alone. (4) Cultural relativism has sometimes been equivalent to moral relativism, or the doctrine that any culture's values and institutions can be judged (rather than merely examined) only by that culture's own standards. In 1947, the executive board of the American Anthropological Association expounded such a view in a "Statement on Human Rights" (Kluckhohn et al., 1947), which it submitted to the U.N. Commission on Human Rights. If the principle of individual rights were to apply to all of mankind, they declared, it would have to include a respect for the cultures in which the individuals were embedded. In order to assist in expanding the concept of human rights in this way, the executive board outlined "some of the findings of the sciences that deal with the study of human culture," as follows:

1.   The individual realizes his personality through his culture, hence respect for individual differences entails a respect for cultural differences.
2.   Respect for differences between cultures is validated by the scientific fact that no technique of qualitatively evaluating cultures has been discovered.
3.   Standards of values are relative to the culture from which they derive so that any attempt to formulate postulates that grow out of the belief of moral codes of one culture must to that extent detract from the applicability of any Declaration of Human Rights to mankind as a whole.

As some critics pointed out, one of the most remarkable features of this statement was its date, 1947, when the seemingly innumerable horrors of Nazi Germany were still being brought to light. Others have attacked the doctrine as intrinsically illogical (Dixon, 1977).

Among British anthropologists one of the most prominent proponents of cultural relativism was Bronislaw Malinowski. Although the Trobriand Islanders, the subject of his main works, were among the most primitive peoples in the ethnographic record, he insistently repeated that they should never be judged by the standards of European civilization. A diary that Malinowski (1967) kept in the Trobriands, published after his death by his widow, demonstrated how alien this public stance was to his actual thinking. While in his published works Malinowski always put the hateful word "savage" in quotation marks, in his journal he was jotting down his "general aversion for niggers," his wish that he could beat up informants "without starting a row," his feeling that he would like to "exterminate the brutes." Malinowski's example suggests that a product of a high civilization, however much he may profess cultural equality with primitives, may find it impossible to convince himself.

The anthropologists of Malinowski's generation were reacting—in the view of many today, overreacting—to the *ethnocentrism of the theory of progress as it was expounded in the eighteenth and nineteenth centuries (cf. *comparative method). To reject the notion that one's own society's values constitute a universal criterion, however, does not mean that all value systems are on a par. In many instances, moreover, the posture of neutrality has barely masked a hostility to modern Western civilization, particularly as exemplified in American society.

Paradoxically, the rise of cultural relativism to its prominent position in anthropology took place during the same years that the subdiscipline of applied *anthropology was developing. In Britain this started after the Boer War of 1899-1902; anthropologists were enrolled in the administrations of Britain's new African colonies in order to furnish those in charge with a more informed view of the peoples they controlled. In the United States a Society for Applied Anthropology was founded in 1941; some anthropologists were hired to facilitate the incarceration of Japanese Americans in concentration camps for the duration of the Second World War and, after the Allied victory, to describe the countries that would be occupied by American troops. In the postcolonial world much of the work of applied anthropologists has shifted to helping new governments or international agencies in carrying out health or family-planning programs—both of which generally attempt to change the values of the people involved (cf. Mair, 1968).

REFERENCES: David Bidney, "Cultural Relativism," in *International Encyclopedia of the Social Sciences*, 3, 543-547. Keith Dixon, "Is Cultural Relativism Self-Refuting?" *British Journal of Sociology*, 28 (1977), 75-88. Melville J. Herskovits, *Man and His Works: The Science of Cultural Anthropology* (New York: Knopf, 1948); *Cultural Anthropology* (New York: Knopf, 1955). Clyde Kluckhohn, Herskovits, Charles F. Voegelin, Cora DuBois, William W. Howells, Ralph L. Beals, and W. W. Hill, "Statement on Human Rights," *American Anthropologist*, 49 (1947), 539-543. A. L. Kroeber, "Anthropology," *Scientific American*, 183 (September, 1950), 87-94. Lucy Mair, "Applied Anthropology," in *International Encyclopedia of the Social Sciences*, 1, 325-330. Bronislaw Malinowski, *A Diary in the Strict Sense of the Term* (New York: Harcourt, Brace, 1967). Hans Vaihinger, *The Philosophy of "As If": A System of the Theoretical, Practical, and Religious Fictions of Mankind* (2nd ed.; London; Routledge & Kegan Paul, 1935).

culture derives from the Latin *cultus*, past participle of the word for "to till" or "to cultivate." Its original range of meanings was generated by a metaphorical extension from the culture (or cultivation) of wheat, to the culture of souls (note also "cult"), to the culture of minds. In the more abstract sense common today, it was introduced from the German by Edward B. Tylor (1871), who defined culture as "that complex whole which includes knowledge, belief, art, law, morals, custom, and any other capabilities and habits acquired by man as a member of society." As is clear from A. L. †Kroeber and Clyde Kluckhohn's exhaustive survey (1963), not even the theorists of anthropology and sociology use the term at all consistently. Though demographers often explain trends in one or another variable by cultural factors, many of them try to avoid any determinant that is difficult to quantify. As a prime instance, the thesis that the succession traced in the *demographic transition of the West will be followed some generations later by the same stages in less developed countries implies that in the long run the vast cultural differences between, say, nineteenth-century England and twentieth-century India are not decisive. See also *civilization.

REFERENCES: A. L. Kroeber and Clyde Kluckhohn, *Culture: A Critical Review of Concepts and Definitions* (New York: Vintage, 1963). Edward B. Tylor, *Primitive Culture* (1871; 6th ed., London: Murray, 1920).

culture area, an area distinguished by its uniform culture, contrasted with *natural area. The uniformity may be relative, varying on a gradient from an inner zone of maximum homogeneity to an outer one of relative heterogeneity.

REFERENCES: Robert W. Ehrich and Gerald M. Henderson, "Culture Area," in *International Encyclopedia of the Social Sciences*, 3, 563-568. A. L. Kroeber, *Cultural and Natural Areas of Native North America* (Berkeley: University of California Press, 1939). Clark Wissler, *Man and Culture* (New York: Crowell, 1923).

cumulative inertia, axiom of, states that the longer a person resides in a given locality, the less likely he will be to leave it, for the attachment to a place grows with a longer association with it.

REFERENCES: George C. Myers, Robert McGinnis, and George S. Masnick, "The Duration of Residence Approach to a Dynamic Stochastic Model of Internal Migration: A Test of the Axiom of Cumulative Inertia," *Eugenics Quarterly*, 14 (1967), 121-126. Karl E. Taeuber, "Duration-of-Residence Analysis of Internal Migration in the United States," *Milbank Memorial Fund Quarterly*, 39 (1961), 116-131.

CURB Project (an acronym for the Cost of Urban Growth), a study undertaken by the European Coordination Center for Research and Documentation in Social Sciences, with headquarters in Vienna. It is a comparison of Functional Urban Regions (FURs) in Europe, with rather inconclusive results.

REFERENCE: Roy Drewett, "Changing Urban Structures in Europe," *Annals of the American Academy of Political and Social Science*, 451 (1980), 52-75.

curbstoning, in the slang of survey research, a form of cheating by interviewers, who instead of calling on respondents fill in fictitious interviews, supposedly at the curb in front of their houses.

Current Population Survey (CPS), a serial publication of the U.S. Bureau of the Census, was started during the mid-1930s in order to collect data on the work force. Those original series are now published by the Bureau of Labor Statistics as the *Monthly Labor Review* and the *Monthly Report on the Labor Force*. Currently information is collected on a number of demographic topics from a national sample, used to provide estimates for the whole country and some of the larger states and *Metropolitan Statistical Areas (MSAs). An additional sample is collected in the District of Columbia and some of the smaller states. The national sample is made up of households and persons in *group quarters in 461 Primary Sampling Units (PSUs) comprising 923 counties and independent cities. From these PSUs a number of Ultimate Sampling Units (USUs) is selected. In 1975 the average number of households in the total sample was about 58,000, of which 3,000 were no longer used as living quarters; and of the remaining 55,000, interviews were conducted at about 45,000. Samples are rotated within each PSU following an elaborate design, which makes it possible to use the same procedures, personnel, and facilities for several of the surveys that the bureau conducts. The results of each survey are adjusted for sampling error and corrected for such biases as noncoverage and nonresponse. False *responses, even if seemingly trivial, can result in pronounced differences when the samples' data are expanded to national estimates. Questions on income are the most sensitive, with the highest proportion of *refusals (nonresponse, forbidden by law in a census, is permitted in a survey).

The resulting *Current Population Reports* (CPRs) are published in a number of series, which are illustrated by some of the typical reports issued during 1979, a normal year.

Series P-20, *Population Characteristics*
    no. 333, "School Enrollment—Social and Economic Characteristics of Students"
    no. 334, "Demographic, Social and Economic Profile of States"
    no. 338, "Marital Status and Living Arrangements"
    no. 339, "Persons of Spanish Origin in the United States"
    no. 341, "Fertility of American Women"
    no. 344, "Voting and Registration in the Election of November 1978"
Series P-23, *Special Studies*
    no. 78, "The Future of the American Family"
    no. 79, "Illustrative Projections of the World Population to the 21st Century"
    no. 80, "The Social and Economic Status of the Black Population of the United States: An Historical View, 1790-1978"
    no. 84, "Divorce, Child Custody, and Child Support"
Series P-25, *Population Estimates and Projections*. Calculated annually for each state and for the United States.

Series P-26, *Federal-State Cooperative Program for Population Estimates*. Estimates of
   county and MSA populations, prepared jointly by the bureau and agencies of those
   states participating in the program.
Series P-27, *Farm Population*. Prepared jointly with the Department of Agriculture.
Series P-28, *Special Censuses*. Particular places in the United States by arrangement with
   local authorities, plus an annual summary.
Series P-60, *Consumer Income*.

   A parallel series prepared by the International Demographic Data Center of
the Bureau of the Census is the *Country Demographic Profiles* (Series ISP-DP)
and the annual compilation, *World Population: Demographic Estimates for
Countries and Regions of the World* (Series ISP-WP). Through 1980, reports
were issued on the following countries: in 1977, Costa Rica, Ghana, Guatemala,
Honduras, Jamaica, Panama, Sri Lanka; in 1978, Chile, China (Republic of),
India, Kenya, Korea, Thailand; in 1979, Colombia, Indonesia, Malaysia, Mex-
ico, Nepal; in 1980, Morocco, Pakistan.
   REFERENCES: Daniel B. Levine and Charles B. Nam, "The Current Population
Survey: Methods, Content, and Sociological Uses," *American Sociological Review*, 27
(1962), 585-590. Lisa Sher, ed., *Subject Index to the U.S. Bureau of the Census' Current
Population Survey Reports* (2nd ed.; New York: Information Clearing House, 1981).
U.S. Bureau of the Census, *The Current Population Survey: Design and Methodology*,
Technical Paper 40 (Washington, D.C., 1978); "Subject Index to Current Population
Reports: December, 1980," *Current Population Reports*, Ser. P-23, no. 109 (September,
1981).

customs comprise neither mere habitual modes of behavior nor, at the other
extreme, those that are explicitly stipulated by a legal code or other institutional
guide. A custom is based on a precept whose claim to validity is tradition: since
it has always been done in this way, this is the way to do it. From the premise
that humans typically behave rationally, present-day analysts often prefer to
avoid the concept of custom and thus to interpret traditional patterns of behavior
in terms of their supposed function. The large families common in less developed
countries, for instance, may be a continuation of the past pattern of childbearing;
but Western demographers are likely to seek such rational motives as that in a
society without social security parents will need children to care for them in
their old age, that high fertility is the consequence not of desire but, for example,
of lack of access to contraceptives. See also *folkways.

Cyprus: The government's Department of Statistics and Research publishes an
annual *Demographic Report* in English and Greek and an annual *Statistical
Abstract* that includes population data. Address: Ministry of Finance, Nicosia.

Czechoslovakia: Demographic Institutions

The Government Population Commission, reorganized in 1971 from the earlier State Population Commission, issues *Population reports* (in Czech) several times a year, mainly on policy issues and its pronatalist programs. Following its recommendations, by 1977 local authorities reportedly had set up about half of a planned hundred marriage-counseling offices throughout the country. It has organized programs designed to help single persons find spouses—"Rendezvous" (1968-71), in which some 10,000 persons took part, and "Contact," in which 20,000 participated during 1972, its first year. Address: Palackeho Nam. 4, Prague 2.

At Charles University, Prague, a department in the natural sciences faculty teaches demography. In 1967-68 it cooperated with the Research Institute for Building and Architecture in a fertility survey of rural Bohemian women.

Several units of the Czechoslovak Academy of Sciences have done research on population. The Institute of Landscape Ecology has concentrated on surveys of small areas. A Commission for Historical Demography was established in 1967. Two units, the Czech Society for Demography, established in 1963, and the Slovak Demographic and Statistical Society, in 1968, have organized several international population conferences of demographers from socialist countries.

The Federal Statistical Office issues (in Czech) an annual, *Population change in the Czechoslovak Socialist Republic in the year—*, as well as a more general *Statistical yearbook* and a monthly *Statistical survey*. It also publishes two population quarterlies: *Demografie*, in Czech with Russian and English tables of contents and often summaries, has analytical papers; and *Demosta*, in Russian, French, English, and Spanish editions, comprises short and usually descriptive pieces. Address: Federální Statistický Úřad, Sokolovská 142, 18613 Prague 8-Karlin.

REFERENCES: *Bibliografie Československé Statistiky a Demografie* (Bibliography of Czechoslovak statistics and demography), issued periodically by Výzkumný Ústav Sociálně Ekonomických Informací (VÚSEI), Prague. Olga Vidláková, "Bevölkerungsforschung in der CSSR," *Zeitschrift für Bevölkerungswissenschaft* (1977), 55-74.

D

Dalkon shield, a type of *intra-uterine device developed by Irwin Lerner. It is shield-shaped, with five small appendages on either side and a partially closed interior. Approved by the U.S. Food and Drug Administration in 1974, the device was withdrawn from the market a year later after a series of court cases. A judgment was granted to one woman who became pregnant while wearing the shield and then had to have a hysterectomy; the penalty was $600,000 in compensatory damages and $6.2 million in punitive damages against A. H. Robins Company, the manufacturer. The judgment was appealed, but at the beginning of 1980 the company faced about a thousand other suits, apart from 800 that had been settled out of court or dismissed. In all likelihood the record with this particular device has affected the reputation of all IUDs.

data processing, the classifying and summarizing of empirical observations, depends greatly on the size of the population studied and the techniques available. The use of a *computer has not only increased enormously the speed of processing but has made it possible to produce as many cross-classifications as may be useful. In all types of data processing, a fundamental issue is how to define the unit—in census counts, for example, whether the person or the household, or in studies of morbidity whether the patient or the case (see also *record linkage). Though strictly speaking the processing adds nothing more than order to the mass of raw data, in fact it often overlaps with their subsequent analysis, at least by pointing to lines of further manipulation of the figures.

The use of computer techniques to process population data has resulted in a very active and competitive business among a large number of rapidly changing corporations and organizations (Riche, 1981, 1983; Russell, 1984). The American commercial firms active in the early 1980s include those listed here.

Allstate Research and Planning Center has used 1970 and 1980 census data to trace the potential labor market at the firm's location, depending on how far those in each occupation might be willing to commute. Address: 321 Middlefield Road, Menlo Park, Calif. 94025.

AUI Data Graphics has specialized in computer-generated maps to facilitate sales management, using census or other data. Address: 1701 K Street, N.W., Washington, D.C. 20006.

Biddle and Associates, Inc., has used census data to develop affirmative-action programs and help firms fulfill the legal requirements for equal employment opportunities. Address: 903 Enterprise Drive, Suite 1, Sacramento, Calif. 95825.

C.A.C.I. has evaluated sites and trading areas, as well as developing proprietary software and other products from census data. Address: 1815 North Fort Myer Drive, Arlington, Va. 22209.

California Survey Research has provided demographic data and analyses to firms interested in the California market. Address: 15250 Ventura Boulevard, Sherman Oaks, Calif. 91403.

CENEX was established in 1981 by four former senior officials of the U.S. Bureau of the Census, who have acted as expert witnesses in legal or regulatory cases. The firm has offered consulting services related to demographic or economic data. Address: 300 North Washington Street, Alexandria, Va. 22314.

Chase Econometrics, a consumer market service, has made quarterly forecasts of such demographic characteristics as household composition and income distribution. Address: 150 Monument Road, Bala-Cynwyd, Pa. 19004.

Claritas has provided population data for zip-code areas, school districts, congressional districts, and other small areas, all useful in pinpointing consumption patterns. Address: 1911 North Fort Myer Drive, Arlington, Va. 22209.

Compucon has provided computer-generated maps of census tracts, cities, or Metropolitan Statistical Areas. Address: P.O. Box 401229, Dallas, Texas 75240.

Compusearch has used census data and updated estimates from both the United States and Canada to offer its customers computerized market research. Address: 347 Bay Street, Suite 703, Toronto, Ontario M5H 2R7, Canada.

Criterion has provided census data and current estimates on population and income either in reports or on computer-generated maps, incorporating such additional information as travel-time contours in order to give the maximum data needed for sales promotion or the management of human resources. Address: 11100 Roselle Street, San Diego, Calif. 92121.

Data Resources, Inc. (DRI), a subsidiary of McGraw-Hill, has used computer models derived from economic-demographic trends to forecast consumer behavior. Address: 29 Hartwell Avenue, Lexington, Mass. 02173.

Datamap has produced computer-generated maps to facilitate the analysis of trade areas. Address: 9749 Hamilton Road, Eden Prairie, Minn. 55344.

David Bradwell and Associates has provided demographic data and analysis for clients interested in the western states, particularly California. Address: 880 Las Gallinas Avenue, San Rafael, Calif. 94903.

Demographic Laboratory (DEM/LAB) has been headed by Donald B. Pittenger, the author of a standard book on the techniques of population forecasting. It has produced estimates, projections, and analyses according to the particular needs of a customer. Address: 2065 Lakemoor Drive, S.W., Olympia, Wash. 98502.

Demographic Research Company, through its Rapidata system, has sold site and market information to both market researchers and city and state planners. Address: 233 Wilshire Boulevard, Santa Monica, Calif. 90401.

DISCUS (Demographic Information Services and Census Utilization Systems) has offered various services based mainly on census data. Address: 1776 South Jackson Street, Suite 702, Denver, Colo. 80210.

Distribution Sciences has sold computerized information on transportation— for example, by matching its data base of place names to geographic codes and coordinates. Address: 1350 East Touhy Avenue, Des Plaines, Ill. 60018.

Donnelley Marketing Information Services, a subsidiary of Dun and Bradstreet, has sold products based on both its own direct-mail business and census and other public sources. Its ZIProfiles have offered up-to-date population data for each of the more than 37,000 zip-code areas. Main address: 1351 Washington Boulevard, Stamford, Conn. 06902.

DUALabs (Data Use and Access Laboratories, Inc.), a nonprofit organization, has provided computer programs for the analysis of such statistics as census files and fertility survey records. Illustrative of its special programs is the preparation of two reference manuals, *Ethnic Statistics: Using National Data Resources for Ethnic Studies* and *Ethnic Statistics: A Compendium of Reference Sources*. Together with Elsevier North Holland, it publishes the journal *Review of Public Data Use*. Its clients have included various sectors of the United Nations and government agencies of both the United States and less developed countries. Address: 1515 Wilson Boulevard, Arlington, Va. 22209.

Financial Marketing Groups, Inc., has created information systems for retailers by merging data from the census with those from sales accounts. Address: 1290 Avenue of the Americas, New York, N.Y. 10104.

Futures Group has included among its consulting services forecasts of consumer trends based on demographic and other characteristics. Address: 76 Eastern Boulevard, Glastonbury, Conn. 06033.

Geographic Data Technology, Inc., has specialized in selling highly detailed computer maps. Address: 13 Dartmouth College Highway, Lyme, N.H. 03768.

Geographic Systems has analyzed demographic data for the evaluation of sites and market analysis. Address: 100 Main Street, Reading, Mass. 01867.

Infomap has created computer maps with a combination of client and census data. Its *Atlas of Demographics: U.S. by County* contains a series of maps with sixteen color-coded demographic and socio-economic characteristics. Address: 3300 Arapahoe No. 207, Boulder, Colo. 80303.

International Data and Development (IDD) has offered up-to-date population, income, and other demographic estimates for census tracts and minor civil divisions. Address: P.O. Box 2157, Arlington, Va. 22202.

Kellex Data Corp. has produced reports and tapes showing the characteristics of those in particular occupations in any geographic area, useful for firms in complying with regulations concerning affirmative action. Address: 20B Village Square, Glen Cove, N.Y. 11542.

LAM Consulting, Inc. has produced, on a custom basis, longitudinal data particularly related to education, medicine, and communications. Address: 220 Albert, Suite 211, East Lansing, Mich. 48823.

Market Statistics has served marketing and advertising analysts with demographic data, in part through a system it calls CENTAB, which offers fast delivery of prepackaged census data. Address: 633 Third Avenue, New York, N.Y. 10017.

Metromail has sold small-area demographic statistics based on its own mailing lists. Address: 901 West Bond Street, Lincoln, Neb. 68521.

Modeling Systems has applied mathematical models to transportation problems, using the *DIME file of the U.S. Bureau of the Census as one data base. Address: 10 Emerson Place, Suite 3E, Boston, Mass. 02114.

National Decision Systems, Inc., has specialized in computer-produced reports linking demographic and geographic information. Address: 9968 Hibert Street, Suite 100, San Diego, Calif. 92131.

National Planning Association, an independent nonprofit organization, has offered subscriptions to two series of population projections. Address: 1606 New Hampshire Avenue, N.W., Washington, D.C. 20009.

National Planning Data Corporation (NPDC) has sold census-based computer services in both standard and custom forms. Address: P.O. Box 610, Ithaca, N.Y. 14850.

Orrington Economics, Inc., established in 1982 by Jack Goodman, who was formerly with the *Urban Institute, has offered market-research products based on census data that can be used with a microcomputer. Address: P.O. Box 3756, Arlington, Va. 22203.

Personnel Research, Inc. (PRI), has provided statistical analysis and other data useful to firms in complying with affirmative-action regulations. Address: 1901 Chapel Hill Road, Durham, N.C. 27707.

Planning Economics Group, Boston, was formed in 1979 by seven former executives of Data Resources, Inc.—a striking indication of how competitive the market is. This firm has also combined demographic and economic data for various types of business use. Address: 300 Unicorn Park, Woburn, Mass. 01801.

Public Demographics, Inc., was established in 1981 to apply demographic analysis to the solution of community problems. Address: 1 Walbrooke Circle, Scarsdale, N.Y. 10583.

Robinson Associates has combined census data with other types of statistics to develop marketing strategies. Address: 15 Morris Avenue, Bryn Mawr, Pa. 19010.

Sammamish Data Systems, started in 1982 by a long-time employee of the U.S. Bureau of the Census, has made 1980 census data available for use on microcomputers. Address: 1413 177th Avenue, N.E., Bellevue, Wash. 98008.

Sophisticated Data Research (SDR) has served market researchers with various types of data analysis. Address: 4360 Georgetown Square, Suite 810, Atlanta, Ga. 30338.

Tri-S Associates, Inc., has used census data to provide market research in

Texas, Arkansas, Louisiana, and Mississippi. Address: P.O. Box 130, Ruston, La. 71270.

Urban Data Processing has specialized in matching addresses with census tracts, so that owners of lists can identify each address by demographic characteristics. Address: 209 Middlesex Turnpike, Burlington, Mass. 01803.

Urban Decision Systems, Inc. (UDS), has offered customers a variety of computer services based on census data. Addresses: P.O. Box 25953, Los Angeles, Calif. 90025; P.O. Box 551, Westport, Conn. 06881.

Urban Science Applications, Inc., has combined census data with those from clients to develop computer graphics and maps with which to select optimal locations for various types of business. Address: 200 Renaissance Center, Suite 230, Detroit, Mich. 48243.

Vistar, Inc., has developed a software package called OCTAGON, similar to the *CENSPAC of the U.S. Bureau of the Census. Address: 659 West 61st Terrace, Kansas City, Mo. 64113.

Warren Glimpse and Co. has specialized in providing tapes from census summaries and instructing those who want to learn how to use census files. Address: 105A Oronoco Street, Alexandria, Va. 22314.

Wharton EFA, Inc., has developed economic and demographic forecasts for countries, Metropolitan Statistical Areas (MSAs), and states, using census data or updated estimates. Address: 3624 Market Street, Science Center, Philadelphia, Pa. 19104.

See also: *Association of Public Data Users; *Federal Statistics Users' Conference.

REFERENCES: Martha Farnsworth Riche, "Demographic Supermarkets of the Eighties," *American Demographics*, 4 (February, 1981), 15-21; "Data Companies 1983," *American Demographics*, 6 (February, 1983), 28-39. Cheryl Russell, "The Business of Demographics," *Population Business*, 39 (June, 1984), 1–40.

data sources related to population statistics are of several types, with different purposes, strengths, and weaknesses (cf. taxation). The *census is the comprehensive instrument, with the most detail about geographic areas, social groups, and the populations at risk for calculating various rates (see also U.S. Bureau of the Census under *United States: Federal Agencies). It is the primary means by which nations record the number and condition of their populations, and less developed countries are far better able to organize a periodic count from the capital than to establish a permanent registration office in every locality. The census is used also to supplement information from other sources about natality, mortality, and migration. By the time the mass of statistics has been processed and the volumes or tapes have become available, however, the information is no longer timely for many purposes.

In all countries *registration is generally by local authorities, with often a considerable variation in the completeness or the quality of the count. The function of the central bureau is not to collect data on births, deaths, marriages, divorces, and so on, but to set standards and compile the local statistics (see also U.S. National Center for Health Statistics, under *United States: Federal Agencies).

Sample *surveys have some obvious advantages: the questions can be focused precisely on the issues of immediate interest, and answers can be obtained promptly. But sampling errors preclude their use in apportionment or for the analysis of small subpopulations.

All countries gather statistics on international migrants, but these data are never entirely satisfactory. The measure of immigration is far better than that of emigration, and many persons manage to evade both counts (see *migration, international; *migration, illegal). In a nation that lacks internal passports as well as the full will to keep track of its inhabitants, it is very difficult to trace movements within the country. The congeries of estimates used in the United States, for instance, hardly warrants the designation "source" (see *migration, internal).

In many respects a *population register would afford the best record, for it combines much of the information available from all the other systems together with great timeliness. Except under optimum social and political circumstances, however, it is virtually impossible to establish and maintain a register, and at best it is rather expensive.

The *United Nations, like individual countries with respect to vital statistics, is not generally a data-collection agency. It recommends definitions of concepts and tries to establish uniform procedures, encouraging particularly less developed countries to enumerate their populations. The data compiled in the *Demographic Yearbook* and other publications are derived from the national statistical offices, either directly through an annual questionnaire sent to each of them or from the offices' own publications. The lacunas and inaccuracies in these data are not lessened by bringing them together into a single large and impressive volume. Statistics in the *Demographic Yearbook*, it is true, are rated as relatively reliable or not, with the latter printed in italics as a warning to the careful user. However, the distinction is based principally on the methods of estimation that had been used, as reported by the countries themselves. There is no way for an international technical agency to transgress the limitations imposed by untrained personnel, inadequate facilities, and the frequent desire to hide these faults. Such other units of the United Nations system as the *International Labor Organization, the *Food and Agriculture Organization, the United Nations Educational, Scientific, and Cultural Organization, the *World Health Organization, and particularly the regional commissions for Europe, Asia and the Pacific, Latin America, and Western Africa, all publish specialized data often related to population.

date in the sense of an appointment with someone of the opposite sex has been American slang since about 1905. The extensions to the verb "to date" and the phrases "my date," "blind date," and "heavy date" are all recorded from the 1920s. The spread of these phrases seemingly coincided with the decreasing importance of formal engagements, and that they all now sound dated may herald another shift in marital institutions.

dating as used in archeology means the timing of artifacts and thus also of prehistoric populations. In order of increasing precision, sequence dating means a classification from the oldest to the most recent; cross-dating, the linking of two such ordinal series; and absolute dating, the placing of a settlement on the calendar. The comparison of culture traits or geologic strata have been supplemented by dendrochronology (or counting the annual growth rings of trees) and especially radiocarbon dating. Each radioactive element (such as carbon-14) is transformed into a stable counterpart at a more or less fixed rate, and one can thus estimate the time elapsed since a fossil or artifact was deposited by measuring the ratio of the radioactive component to its inert product (cf. Protsch and Berger, 1973; Michels, 1973). However, when compared with other methods, radiocarbon dating has been found to be in serious error (e.g., Lee, 1981; Pearson et al., 1970), and sometimes other radioactive elements, such as potassium or argon, have been substituted for carbon (e.g., Aronson et al., 1977). More significantly, various more elaborate techniques have been devised (e.g., Haddy and Hanson, 1982; Ikeya, 1978).

REFERENCES: J. L. Aronson et al., "New Geochronologic and Palaeomagnetic Data for the Hominid-Bearing Hadar Formation of Ethiopia," *Nature*, 267 (1977), 323-327. A. Haddy and A. Hanson, "Nitrogen and Fluorine Dating of Moundsville Skeletal Samples," *Archaeometry*, 24 (1982), 37-44. M. Ikeya, "Electron Spin Resonance as a Method of Dating," *Archaeometry*, 20 (1978), 147-158. Robert E. Lee, "Radiocarbon: Ages in Error," *Anthropological Journal of Canada*, 19 (1981), 9-29. Joseph W. Michels, *Dating Methods in Archeology* (New York: Seminar Press, 1973). G. W. Pearson, J. R. Pilcher, M.G.L. Baillie, and J. Hillam, "Absolute Radiocarbon Dating Using a Low Altitude European Tree-ring Calibration," *Nature*, 270 (1970), 25-28. Reiner Protsch and Rainer Berger, "Earliest Radiocarbon Dates for Domesticated Animals," *Science*, 179 (January 19, 1973), 235-239.

DDT, or dichloro-diphenyl-trichloroethane, a powerful insecticide first used during the Second World War. It was a major factor in cutting dramatically the number of deaths from *malaria, but it has become the target of environmentalists who deplore its effect on the ecological balance. So far as we know, DDT is harmless to man, but with sufficient concentrations it has had demonstrably harmful effects on birds and other animals.

death, which once could be designated simply as the end of life, has become more complicated with the development of medical techniques through which, while some attributes of life are permanently lost, others can be maintained for a long time. The traditional definition given in *Black's Law Dictionary* (4th ed., 1968) was frequently cited in a series of American court cases: death is "the cessation of life, ... a total stoppage of the circulation of the blood and a cessation of the animal and vital functions consequent thereon, such as respiration, pulsation, etc." For example, in a 1952 case in Kentucky, the issue was which of two claimants died earlier. Based on this "whole-body" concept, the judgment was that a person who had been decapitated in an automobile accident was held to be alive as long as blood was being pumped out of the severed body. In 1968, an ad hoc committee of the Harvard Medical School proposed a new criterion, irreversible coma as indicated by a flat electroencephalogram; and this suggestion stimulated an extensive debate (e.g., Devins and Diamond, 1976-77; Black, 1977; Walton, 1979, chap. 3). One important legal dilemma is whether a person beyond resuscitation should be kept "alive" (e.g., Hirsh and Donovan, 1977). When a person is dead under one definition but alive under another, doctors become understandably reluctant to apply such life-saving techniques as the transplant of organs from a body recently "deceased." In 1969-70 Kansas passed the country's first statutory definition of death—or, in fact, two alternative definitions, whole-body and brain-oriented. As a commentator remarked, in Kansas there were two ways of dying. Similar acts were passed in a number of other states; and in New Mexico's law the term "human being" was substituted for the usual "person," suggesting that *human* life is not merely biological (Engelhardt, 1978). The question has not been fully resolved in the United States or anywhere else, though the debate has helped stimulate a great surge of interest in such topics as dying, its physiology, and the norms of grief and bereavement (e.g., Fulton, 1976). See also *cause of death; *euthanasia; *mortality.

REFERENCES: Ad Hoc Committee, "A Definition of Irreversible Coma," *Journal of the American Medical Association*, 205 (1968), 85-88. Peter McL. Black, "Three Definitions of Death," *Monist*, 60 (1977), 136-146. Gerald M. Devins and Robert T. Diamond, "The Determination of Death," *Omega*, 7 (1976-77), 277-296. H. Tristram Engelhardt, Jr., "Definitions of Death: Where to Draw the Line and Why," in Ernan McMullin, ed., *Death and Decision* (Boulder, Colo.: Westview Press, 1978). Robert Fulton, ed., *Death, Grief and Bereavement: A Bibliography, 1845-1975* (New York: Arno Press, 1976). Harold L. Hirsh and Richard E. Donovan, "The Right to Die: Medicolegal Implications of In re Quinlan," *Rutgers Law Review*, 30 (1977), 267-303. Douglas N. Walton, *On Defining Death: An Analytic Study of the Concept of Death in Philosophy and Medical Ethics* (Montreal: McGill-Queens University Press, 1979).

death certificate, the attestation to the fact and circumstances of a person's having died, is a routine legal requirement in advanced countries, where it lays the empirical base for all measures of mortality, from the crude death rate to the most refined life-table functions. In the United States the form (see the Certificate of Death on page 215) must be filled in and signed by the attending physician or, under specified conditions, by a medical examiner or coroner. To the extent that they can be determined, the certificate gives details concerning the deceased—his or her date of birth, place of last residence, where the remains are buried, cremated, or removed to, and so on. In a demographic context, the most significant datum, the *cause of death, is also the most difficult to interpret. The standard form lists under cause an "immediate cause" and two "conditions, if any, which gave rise to immediate cause," as well as "other significant conditions contributing to but not related to cause." A surprisingly high proportion of death certificates are filled out carelessly. From 1911 to about 1945, the U.S. Bureau of the Census queried physicians who had filed apparently inadequate certificates, with a consequent reduction in the percentage listing ill defined or

CERTIFICATE OF DEATH

LOCAL FILE NUMBER   STATE FILE NUMBER

TYPE OR PRINT IN PERMANENT INK — FOR INSTRUCTIONS SEE HANDBOOK

DECEDENT

1. DECEDENT—NAME   FIRST   MIDDLE   LAST
2. SEX
3. DATE OF DEATH (Mo., Day, Yr.)
4. RACE—(e.g., White, Black, American Indian, etc.) (Specify)
5a. AGE—Last Birthday (Yrs.)
5b. UNDER 1 YEAR — MOS.   DAYS
5c. UNDER 1 DAY — HOURS   MINS.
6. DATE OF BIRTH (Mo., Day, Yr.)
7a. CITY, TOWN OR LOCATION OF DEATH
7b. COUNTY OF DEATH
7c. HOSPITAL OR OTHER INSTITUTION—Name (If not in either, give street and number)
7d. IF HOSP. OR INST. Indicate DOA, OP/Emer. Rm., Inpatient (Specify)

IF DEATH OCCURRED IN INSTITUTION SEE HANDBOOK REGARDING COMPLETION OF RESIDENCE ITEMS

8. STATE OF BIRTH (If not in U.S.A., name country)
9. CITIZEN OF WHAT COUNTRY
10. MARRIED, NEVER MARRIED, WIDOWED, DIVORCED (Specify)
11. SURVIVING SPOUSE (If wife, give maiden name)
12. WAS DECEDENT EVER IN U.S. ARMED FORCES? (Specify Yes or No)
13. SOCIAL SECURITY NUMBER
14a. USUAL OCCUPATION (Give kind of work done during most of working life, even if retired)
14b. KIND OF BUSINESS OR INDUSTRY
15a. RESIDENCE—STATE
15b. COUNTY
15c. CITY, TOWN OR LOCATION
15d. STREET AND NUMBER
15e. INSIDE CITY LIMITS (Specify Yes or No)

PARENTS

16. FATHER—NAME   FIRST   MIDDLE   LAST
17. MOTHER—MAIDEN NAME   FIRST   MIDDLE   LAST

INFORMANT

18a. INFORMANT—NAME (Type or Print)
18b. MAILING ADDRESS   STREET OR R.F.D. NO.   CITY OR TOWN   STATE   ZIP

DISPOSITION

19a. BURIAL, CREMATION, REMOVAL, OTHER (Specify)
19b. CEMETERY OR CREMATORY—NAME
19c. LOCATION   CITY OR TOWN   STATE
20a. FUNERAL SERVICE LICENSEE Or Person Acting As Such (Signature)
20b. NAME OF FACILITY
20c. ADDRESS OF FACILITY

CERTIFIER

To be completed by CERTIFYING PHYSICIAN Only

21a. To the best of my knowledge, death occurred at the time, date and place and due to the cause(s) stated. (Signature and Title)
21b. DATE SIGNED (Mo., Day, Yr.)
21c. HOUR OF DEATH   M
21d. NAME OF ATTENDING PHYSICIAN IF OTHER THAN CERTIFIER (Type or Print)

To be completed by MEDICAL EXAMINER or CORONER Only

22a. On the basis of examination and/or investigation, in my opinion death occurred at the time, date and place and due to the cause(s) stated. (Signature and Title)
22b. DATE SIGNED (Mo., Day, Yr.)
22c. HOUR OF DEATH   M
22d. PRONOUNCED DEAD (Mo., Day, Yr.)   PRONOUNCED DEAD (Hour)
22d. ON   22e. AT   M

23. NAME AND ADDRESS OF CERTIFIER (PHYSICIAN, MEDICAL EXAMINER OR CORONER) (Type or Print)

REGISTRAR

24a. REGISTRAR (Signature)
24b. DATE RECEIVED BY REGISTRAR (Mo., Day, Yr.)

CAUSE OF DEATH

25. CONDITIONS IF ANY WHICH GAVE RISE TO IMMEDIATE CAUSE STATING THE UNDERLYING CAUSE LAST

PART I   *(ENTER ONLY ONE CAUSE PER LINE FOR (a), (b), AND (c).)*   Interval between onset and death

(a) IMMEDIATE CAUSE
DUE TO, OR AS A CONSEQUENCE OF:
(b)
DUE TO, OR AS A CONSEQUENCE OF:
(c)

PART II   OTHER SIGNIFICANT CONDITIONS—Conditions contributing to death but not related to cause given in PART I (a)
26. AUTOPSY (Specify Yes or No)
27. WAS CASE REFERRED TO MEDICAL EXAMINER OR CORONER (Specify Yes or No)

28a. ACC., SUICIDE, HOM., UNDET. OR PENDING INVEST. (Specify)
28b. DATE OF INJURY (Mo., Day, Yr.)
28c. HOUR OF INJURY   M
28d. DESCRIBE HOW INJURY OCCURRED
28e. INJURY AT WORK (Specify Yes or No)
28f. PLACE OF INJURY—At home, farm, street, factory, office building, etc. (Specify)
28g. LOCATION   STREET OR R.F.D. No.   CITY OR TOWN   STATE

DEPARTMENT OF HEALTH, EDUCATION, AND WELFARE—PUBLIC HEALTH SERVICE—NATIONAL CENTER FOR HEALTH STATISTICS
1978 REVISION
HRA-152-1
Rev. 1/78

unknown causes of death. Some state vital statistics offices continued this practice, but with apparently less effect on the overall quality of the data. Like *birth certificates, death certificates move up through several levels, to be compiled eventually by the U.S. National Center for Health Statistics (discussed under *United States: Federal Agencies) into national mortality data. See also *autopsy; *registration areas.

decision-making, jargon for "manner of deciding" or simply "deciding," has become a prolific field in psychology, economics, and political science. It occurs in works on population, particularly in analyses of whether and how couples decide to have a child.
    REFERENCES: Linda J. Beckman, "Couples' Decision-Making Processes regarding Fertility," in Karl E. Taeuber et al., eds., *Social Demography* (New York: Academic Press, 1978). Thomas K. Burch, ed., *Demographic Behavior: Interdisciplinary Perspectives on Decision-Making* (Boulder, Colo.: Westview Press, 1981).

deficit fertility, as calculated from responses in a fertility survey, is the average number of children desired minus the number of children the parents have. See also *excess fertility.

degrees of freedom, a statistical term meaning the number of alternative values that can be assigned in a specified system while maintaining its definition. For example, if a sample is grouped into k intervals, there are $k - 1$ degrees of freedom; for if $k - 1$ frequencies are specified, the remaining one is determined.

del, written ∇, is the geometric mean of age-specific death rates, which can be used in place of a schedule of such rates as a summary index. It can be easily calculated, is unbiased, needs no standard population, and is directly comparable to the same index of another population.
    REFERENCES: Robert Schoen, "The Geometric Mean of the Age-Specific Death Rates as a Summary Index of Mortality," *Demography*, 7 (1970), 317-324; "Measuring Mortality Trends and Differentials," *Social Biology*, 23 (1976), 235-243.

demand for a commodity means, in economic analysis, the amount that potential purchasers would like to buy of it. In a competitive market, demand and supply together determine the prices of goods. The demand for any particular commodity depends on its price, the prices of other goods, the preferences of prospective consumers, and their income; the relation between the quantity of a good a consumer wants to buy and all the quantitative factors that determine this demand is called the *demand function*. A *demand curve* relates price per unit of a product to the quantity of the product a consumer would like to buy. *Effective demand*— that is, a desire for goods backed up by the ability to pay for them—was a crucial concept in the economic theories of †Malthus and John Maynard †Keynes, and both related the concept also to their population theories.

demographic accounts, one type of social accounting system, were so named by Richard †Stone (1971). In order to describe quantitatively how a social pattern changes over time and thus to provide a basis for research, policy analysis, and planning, he developed a manner of integrating information on human stocks and flows similar to that used for income or products. By "stocks" he meant the distribution into the conventional categories of population structure and composition, and by "flows" the transition from one category to another. By rephrasing standard demographic terms, he made it possible to apply an adaptation of double-entry bookkeeping to any changes in a population, extending the principle of the *balancing equation to shifts, for example, in occupation or marital status. In later works he applied the concepts of matrix algebra as used by economists in input-output studies.

REFERENCES: Kenneth C. Land and Marilyn M. McMillen, "Demographic Accounts and the Study of Social Change, with Applications to the Post-World War II United States," in F. Thomas Juster and Land, eds., *Social Accounting Systems: Essays on the State of the Art* (New York: Academic Press, 1981). Richard Stone, *Demographic Accounting and Model Building* (Paris: Organization for Economic Cooperation and Development, 1971); "The Relationships of Demographic Accounts to National Income and Product Accounts," in Juster and Land (1981).

demographic gap, an alternative designation for *natural increase, used especially when referring to the dramatically rapid fall in mortality contrasted with the more or less fixed fertility of less developed countries.

demographic transition, in its simplest meaning, designates the shift accompanying the *modernization of the West from Stage I, a relatively static population with high fertility and mortality, to Stage II, a rapid population growth based on a continuing high fertility and falling mortality, and then to Stage III, a relatively static population based on a new balance between low fertility and low mortality. This empirical generalization is one of the most sweeping and best documented trends of modern history. Among its first statements by American demographers were a 1929 paper by Warren S. †Thompson and a subsequent one by Frank W. †Notestein (1945). Essentially similar theses were presented in other countries, in Britain by A. M. †Carr-Saunders (1936) and in France by Adolphe †Landry (1934).

Even in these first works, and increasingly in the polemics that ensued from them, the demographic transition was more than a summary of population trends in the West. Causal links were hypothesized between the several stages and were taken as a reliable guide to predicting population growth in less developed countries; policy recommendations were offered that derived from this elaboration. The theory is both less unitary and more debatable than the empirical generalization identified by the same two words. Indeed, none of the theory's elements have escaped fundamental criticism.

The societies grouped together under the rubric "Stage I" comprise all that have not begun industrialization, from bands of hunters to great civilizations; and the points made concerning them, lacking any evidence from anthropology or historical demography, were thin and overgeneral. Because in such societies the control of mortality is typically precarious, many writers at least implied that, unless fertility is close to the physiological maximum, the population will die out. In fact, all societies virtually without exception use one or another means of population control; and the *family type that arose in preindustrial Europe, with large proportions that never married and the *age at marriage of the remainder well above puberty, restricted the growth of numbers almost as effectively as any means of contraception. The main importance of the point is that when beginning modernization undercuts such institutional checks, fertility is likely to rise—or at least to fall much less rapidly than the theory led one to suppose.

The secular fall in fertility was projected to what Notestein termed an "incipient decline" of Western populations. Since potential parents were typically weighing the cost of children against alternative ways of spending their money, time, and effort, and since the first child costs the most, particularly if the wife must stop working, the trend was presumed to be to one-child or even childless families. Those sectors of Western populations still breeding at or above a replacement level were seen as vestigial—social groups that for a short period only would lack a full physical, financial, and moral access to effective contraception. The so-called *baby boom—the significant increase in family size among just those social classes that had led the trend to a lower fertility—undercut not only the repeated predictions of population decline but the social theories on which they were based (Dorn, 1950).

The most significant conclusion drawn from the theory has been that the presumed history of the West could be used to predict the future of less developed countries. Note some of the more important differences between the two. Europe was relatively empty at the beginning of the long-term rise in numbers; India, Java, and Egypt started from very high population densities. The overflow from Europe went in the tens of millions to overseas destinations; today migration is everywhere restricted to, at most, a small fraction of the population increase. The West's decline of mortality resulted from successive improvements in agriculture, sanitation, and medicine; in the less developed countries, with the most advanced methods brought from the outside to societies often lacking any but primitive control of mortality, the fall in death rates has been many times faster. Since most of this decline has been in the mortality of infants and children, its effect on age structure has been to aggravate the high fertility: because of the broad-based *population pyramids, apart from other factors, the rate of increase will be relatively high for several generations (cf. Petersen, 1982).

It is true that population increase in the modern period has been faster than ever before in history and that this has been due mainly to the imbalance between a declining mortality and a temporarily fixed fertility. But the theories to explain this generalization were at first too broad and simplistic and have since become numerous and partly contradictory. We know more or less what has happened, but our theories about the causes of this broad transition are still fragmentary (but see Wrigley and Schofield, 1981; Knodel and van de Walle, 1982). An important effort to round out our knowledge has been a series of monographs at Princeton University on the shift in Europe's fertility (cf. Coale, 1973-74). One of the more interesting efforts to specify more precisely explanatory factors is the *wealth-flow theory of John C. †Caldwell (1977). But the net result of both empirical and theoretical work is to suggest that there is a far greater diversity than posited by the three-stage model.

REFERENCES: John C. Caldwell, "Towards a Restatement of Demographic Transition Theory," in Caldwell, ed., *The Persistence of High Fertility* (Canberra: Department of Demography, Australian National University, 1977). A. M. Carr-Saunders, *World Population: Past Growth and Present Trends* (Oxford: Clarendon, 1936). Ansley J. Coale, "The Demographic Transition Reconsidered," in IUSSP, International Population Conference, Liège, 1973, *Contributed Papers* (1973-74). Harold F. Dorn, "Pitfalls in Population Forecasts and Projections," *Journal of the American Statistical Association*, 45 (1950), 311-334. John Knodel and Etienne van de Walle, "Fertility Decline: European Transition," *International Encyclopedia of Population*, 1, 268-275. Adolphe Landry, *La Révolution Démographique: Études et Essais sur les Problèmes de la Population* (Paris: Sirey, 1934). Frank W. Notestein, "Population—The Long View," in Theodore W. Schultz, ed., *Food for the World* (Chicago: University of Chicago Press, 1945). William Petersen, "The Social Roots of Hunger and Overpopulation," *Public Interest*, no. 68 (1982), 35–52. Warren S. Thompson, "Population," *American Journal of Sociology*, 34 (1929), 959-975. E. A. Wrigley and Roger S. Schofield, *The Population History of England, 1541-1871: A Reconstruction* (Cambridge, Mass.: Harvard University Press, 1981).

demography, derived from two Greek words meaning "description of" and "people," was coined by the French political economist Achille †Guillard in his *Éléments de Statistique Humaine, ou Démographie Comparée* (1855). Men have been concerned about the components of population growth since ancient times; but the development of a separate discipline, with its own professional practitioners, associations, and journals, is a phenomenon of the recent past. Earlier writings about births and deaths, the growth in numbers, and the relation to other processes went by different names—political arithmetic (used to denote the pioneer efforts of such mercantilist essayists as John †Graunt, William †Petty, and Gregory †King) political economy (the term current at the time of †Malthus to designate the study of population, among other topics); and human statistics, or simply *statistics. Note also *demographer*, one versed in demography; *demographic*, of or pertaining to demography (or, in a loose usage perhaps better avoided, of or pertaining to population); *demographics*, population data related, for example, to a market for a particular commodity.

Demography can be defined narrowly or broadly. *Formal demography* consists of the gathering, collating, statistical analysis, and technical presentation of population data per se; it is based on the fact that within limits population growth is a self-contained process, with a more or less fixed interrelation among fertility, mortality, and age structure. *Social demography* or *population studies*, on the other hand, comprise analyses of how population interacts with social, economic, political, geographic, and biological factors, all part of what has been termed the determinants and consequences of population trends. From the 1950s on, there has been a shift from description or analysis to the recommendation of policy, with important consequences on how demographic data and techniques were viewed (cf. Hodgson, 1983).

In various settings around the world, demography developed from a base in biology or genetics, geography or ecology, public health or statistics, economics or sociology. Those who today identify themselves as demographers or who work on problems related to population continue to be associated with quite diverse fields and institutions. In the United States one demographer who noted this diversity remarked that his discipline is "appropriately" regarded as a "subfield of sociology" and as closely linked to human ecology (Hauser, 1965). Other demographers have defined the field as an entity in itself, made up of specific elements from sociology, economics, geography, statistics, and biology. Judith †Blake, who holds this view (see Blake, 1964), established such a department of demography at the University of California, Berkeley, but some years later it was dissolved. Other efforts in the United States to consolidate pertinent portions from existent disciplines have also not achieved their full goal. Demography remains in a somewhat anomalous position, with its own national and international professional societies, with dozens of journals, with an importance that is recognized by statesmen and funding agencies, but with still no firm identity (but see Nam, 1979). Students who acquire advanced degrees leading to a competence in demographic analysis typically must learn much that is irrelevant to that task and miss some of the learning that others regard as crucial (see also Caldwell, 1973-74; Glass, 1957).

During the past several decades there has been a stupendous increase in the number of persons and institutions engaged in work related to demography. In this work the principal research institutes are discussed under the countries in which they are located, but these brief notations can barely suggest how rapidly the field has grown. The expansion has not been entirely without problems. Much of the instruction in American institutions of higher learning, for instance, is less demography than what is ordinarily termed *population education, which is typically antinatalist propaganda sometimes combined with the training of field operatives. Partly because of the discipline's imprecise boundaries and identity, partly because the various elements of "the population problem" are often associated with fervently held political-moral positions, demography has proved to be highly vulnerable to popularized or even vulgarized intrusions.

In a survey of undergraduate offerings related to population, the faculty were classified into three types: Purists, with graduate training in demography and a commitment to the field, strongly inclined to stress the complexity of social issues. Propagandists, with little or no training in demography; their publications, if any, are on such subjects as birth control or sexuality, and they transmit to their students mainly their deep concern about "the population problem." And Popularizers, who include some materials on population in a wide range of courses, sometimes with a limited knowledge and occasionally with a modesty related to their lack of competence, but generally with a tendency to strengthen the influence of the Propagandists. The lack of consensus on what population education for undergraduates should include, the report concluded, results in a low level of some instruction, with a general overemphasis on population growth as the factor to be discussed and a frequent attempt to inculcate in students the importance of their having small families (Rogers, 1974; see also Toney et al., 1981).

REFERENCES: Judith Blake, "Issues in the Training and Recruitment of Demographers," *Demography*, 1 (1964), 258-263. John C. Caldwell, "The Teaching of Demography in the Social Sciences," in IUSSP, International Population Conference, Liège, 1973, *Contributed Papers* (1973-74). D. V. Glass, ed., *The University Teaching of the Social Sciences: Demography* (Deventer, Netherlands: IJsel Press, 1957). Philip M. Hauser, "Demography and Ecology," *Annals of the American Academy of Political and Social Science*, 362 (1965), 129-138. Dennis Hodgson, "Demography as Social Science and Policy Science," *Population and Development Review*, 9 (1983), 1-34. Charles B. Nam, "The Progress of Demography as a Scientific Discipline," *Demography*, 16 (1979), 485-492. Theresa F. Rogers, *Attention to Population on the Campus* (New York: Bureau of Applied Social Research, Columbia University, 1974). Michael B. Toney, William F. Stinner, and Yun Kim, "The Population Debate: A Survey of Opinions of a Professional Organization Membership [Population Association of America]," *Population and Environment*, 41 (1981), 156-173.

demometrics, a term parallel to "econometrics," is used to designate the more quantitative elements of *demography or, especially, *mathematical demography. It is infrequent in English but *démométrie*, its French equivalent, seems to be coming into general use.

Denmark: Demographic Institutions

Danish demographers are generally members of the *Scandinavian Demographic Society.

Copenhagen University includes a Demographic Section in its Statistical Institute. Demographic research and teaching were initiated there during the 1960s by Poul C. †Matthiessen, who has continued as its director. It has used the early statistics of Denmark to develop some very interesting projects in historical demography. Recent publications include an analysis of remarriage and period life tables for 1780-1939. Address: Københavns Universitet, Studiestræde 6, DK-1455 Copenhagen K.

Denmark Statistics was formerly known as the State Statistical Bureau (Statens Statistiske Bureau, 1850-1913) and then as the Statistical Department (Det Statistiske Departement, 1913-66). The current bureau includes a section that deals with population data, administering census statistics, and more specific population analyses. It publishes annually, in Danish and English, *Vital Statistics* and a *Statistical Yearbook*. When the Central Population Register was established in 1968, this effected a radical change in Danish population statistics. With data from the register it is possible to tabulate the distribution of the population by sex, age, civil status, and geographic area far more rapidly than was the case earlier. It also published *The population of Greenland* (in Danish; 1981). Address: Danmarks Statistik, Sejrøgade 11, DK-2100 Copenhagen.

The Ministry for Greenland issues regularly, in Danish and English editions, *Greenland in Figures* (vol. 6, 1981), which includes population data. Address: Ministeriet for Grønland, Copenhagen.

The Public Health Administration publishes an *Annual causes of death* and *Statistics on contraception and abortion* (annual), both in Danish with English summaries and table headings, as well as the serial *Vitalstatistik*. Address: Sundhedsstyrelsen, St. Korgensgade 1, Copenhagen.

REFERENCE: Poul C. Matthiessen, *Some Aspects of the Demographic Transition in Denmark* (Copenhagen: Københavns Universitets Fond til Tilvejebringelse af Læremidler, 1970).

denomination, a type of religious institution intermediate between *church and sect, such as, in the United States, the Episcopalian, Methodist, Baptist, Lutheran, and other major Protestant churches; in effect, the Roman Catholic Church, in spite of its history as an ecclesia; and, by extension, Reform, Conservative, and Orthodox Judaism and similar branches of other major religions. Like the sect, the denomination depends in principle on voluntary membership rather than on the universal allegiance due such an ecclesia as the medieval church. A denomination's demands on its members, as well as its claims to truth, are more modest than in either of the other types. Denominationalism, it has been argued, is the religious organization toward which a modern pluralist society tends (Niebuhr, 1957). At least according to some analysts, the ''mainline denominations'' (that is, the principal large Protestant churches omitting the Baptists and fundamentalist sects) are heading toward ''disestablishment.'' Clergy trained in modernist seminaries often come into conflict with traditionalist congregations; and, among teenagers and young adults, the well-to-do are less involved in church affairs than those in the lower classes (Nelsen and Maguire, 1980; Nelsen and Potvin, 1980). It is less true than several decades ago, thus, that a count of denominations' memberships would indicate the trend of social or political opinion; see also *religion.

REFERENCES: Hart M. Nelsen and Mary Ann Maguire, ''The Two Worlds of Clergy and Congregation: Dilemma for Mainline Denominations,'' *Sociological Analysis*, 41 (1980), 74-80. Nelsen and Raymond H. Potvin, ''Toward Disestablishment: New Patterns of Social Class, Denomination, and Religiosity among Youth?'' *Review of Religious Research*, 22 (1980), 137-154. H. Richard Niebuhr, *The Social Sources of Denominationalism* (New York: World, 1957).

dependency ratio measures the relation of the dependents in a population to those on whom they depend for their sustenance. In the abstract, it is both a simple and an important relation: young children and the aged can survive only if those who are working provide for them. In fact, the ratio can be no more than an approximate indicator of dependency, for the elements that are compared cannot be precisely defined. Many persons cannot be unambiguously designated as in or out of the *work force, and their statistical status thus depends in part on the classificatory rules used in a particular jurisdiction. The international trend toward early *retirement can increase the rate of upward mobility (Cantrell and Clark, 1982), but, on the other hand, it cuts down the productive sector of the population (cf. Stearns, 1976). To some extent, the population's age structure determines the range of occupations that can be filled: the young are stronger, the middle-aged more experienced (cf. Kaufman and Spilerman, 1982). Not only production but also consumption varies with age. The *cost of children to parents varies with, among other factors, the level of living of the country and the social class; the number, sex, and age of the children; the portion of childrearing costs paid by the state; and the age at which young people start to work and to help support their parents (cf. *wealth-flow theory). The proportion of each age-sex category that participates in the work force varies with current incidence of unemployment and of underemployment; the typical ages at which participation in the work force begins and ends; the custom regarding women's work outside the home. Adjusting for some of these factors can change the measure of dependency greatly (e.g., Kleiman, 1967).

Since it is difficult to define gainful work precisely, the dependency ratio is generally calculated from age groups of the population, as follows:

$$\text{Dependency ratio} = \frac{P_{0\text{-}14} + P_{65+}}{P_{15\text{-}64}} \times 100$$

Such an equation can give only a still looser impression of the ratio of working to nonworking sectors, for the overlap between age groups and sectors of the work force is no more than partial (cf. Leridon, 1962). For example, most of the housewives excluded by definition from the work force are in the active category delineated by age. Moreover, the boundaries of the age categories may have to be adjusted to changing circumstances; in most Western countries social childhood extends well beyond age 14, and in some, as we have noted, retirement often begins before age 65. With a declining fertility and a growing proportion of aged, the sum in the numerator of the formula may remain almost the same over the years; but its changing composition has important implications. Children are cared for mostly by their parents, old people very often by the state, and the shift in age structure tends to reinforce the neomercantilist trend of the twentieth century.

REFERENCES: R. Stephen Cantrell and Robert L. Clark, "Individual Mobility, Population Growth, and Labor Force Participation," *Demography*, 19 (1982), 147-159. Robert L. Kaufman and Seymour Spilerman, "The Age Structures of Occupations and Jobs," *American Journal of Sociology*, 87 (1982), 827-851. E. Kleiman, "A Standardized Dependency Ratio," *Demography*, 4 (1967), 876-893. Françoise Leridon, "Prévisions de Population Active: Trois Publications Internationales," *Population*, 17 (1962), 97-120. Peter N. Stearns, *Old Age in European Society: The Case of France* (New York: Holmes and Meier, 1976).

depopulation, a significant and permanent decline in the number of persons in a particular population unit, is a relative rarity in human history. In each of the several contexts where analysts have applied the term, it has often been a hyperbole: (1) Primitive peoples who depend for their subsistence on hunting and gathering may, like other species of predators, suffer from an acute shortage of food during a bad year; but typically the following season or two bring a recovery, in part by the very fact that there are fewer persons to be fed. (2) Much of the depopulation of *American Indians, as a different kind of example, seemingly was not physical but rather ethnic, a disappearance into the populations of mestizos that now dominate much of Latin America. In the United States census officials estimated as early as 1910 that only 56.5 percent of the Indians enumerated were full-bloods. The erratic shifts up and down in the counts of Indians have been due mainly to the different proportions of those of mixed ancestry that were so classified (for an extreme case, see Trosper, 1976; cf. also Pool, 1961). On the other hand, Indians did suffer from the increased deadliness of new weapons and from the hardships of mass removals to new territories. New diseases introduced by the first contacts with advanced peoples were generally more deadly among those that had not built up any immunity; and epidemics of measles or the common cold, for example, sometimes caused deaths in numbers that could really be termed a depopulation. (3) Another common use of the appellation "depopulation" pertains to *Landflucht* or "flight from the land." When the young go off to the cities, the aged left behind die off, and—in parts of Italy, for instance—"villages [were] all but abandoned, the houses uninhabited and in decay, grass growing in the streets, and in the gardens weeds choking whatever vegetables come up" (Foerster, 1924, p. 449). In many other places with high rates of out-migration, however, the abandoned land has generally been marginal in one sense or another—because of particularly oppressive landlords (as in much of Italy), because of the land's low fertility (as in Southern France, for example), because of the decline of industry (as in parts of New England). (4) A small island population is especially susceptible to loss because of its isolation. When men from Ithaca in Greece took advantage of the new opportunities opening up in the United States, the island's population declined by almost half from 1896 to 1951 (Lowenthal and Comitas, 1962). (5) The pronatalist propaganda during the first two decades of this century rose to a crescendo during the economic depression of the 1930s, when terms like "race suicide" or *The Menace of Under-population* (Charles, 1936) were used as titles of presumably sober analyses of the depopulation of Britain, France, Germany, or another Western country. (6) Depopulation in the form of *genocide is a phenomenon mainly of the twentieth century. It has been estimated that perhaps half of the world's Jews were killed in the *Holocaust, and some ethnic minorities of the Soviet Union have suffered comparable losses (e.g., Conquest, 1960; Dyadkin, 1983).

REFERENCES: Enid Charles, *The Menace of Under-population: A Biological Study of the Decline of Population Growth* (London: Watts, 1936). Robert Conquest, *The Soviet Deportation of Nationalities* (London: Macmillan, 1960). Iosif G. Dyadkin, *Unnatural*

Deaths in the USSR, 1928–1954 (New Brunswick, N.J.: Transaction Books, 1983). R. F. Foerster, *The Italian Emigration of Our Times* (Cambridge, Mass.: Harvard University Press, 1924). David Lowenthal and Lambros Comitas, ''Emigration and Depopulation: Some Neglected Aspects of Population Geography,'' *Geographical Review*, 52 (1962), 83–94. D. I. Pool, ''When Is a Maori a 'Maori'?'' *Journal of the Polynesian Society*, 73 (1961), 206–210. Ronald L. Trosper, ''Native American Boundary Maintenance: The Flathead Indian Reservation, Montana, 1860–1970,'' *Ethnicity*, 3 (1976), 275–303.

descendant, one linked through common descent from the same progenitors or *ancestors. In a formal analysis descent is generally reckoned from a single marriage through several generations.

desegregation, the process of reversing an ongoing *segregation or the resultant state, can be applied theoretically to the concentration of any type of population sector—age groups, occupational categories, and so on. In the United States, it has been used almost exclusively to designate a social movement to do away with compulsory (or, later, de facto) segregation by race in schools, housing, and other public or private institutions. See also *affirmative action.

design of a study or experiment includes the specification of the population and what sectors are to be analyzed (e.g., experimental versus control groups); the attributes that are to be studied (e.g., broad characteristics like sex and race, as well as those reflecting the narrower subject of the study); the rules denoting how stimuli or ''treatments'' are to be distributed (e.g., one or another method of *sampling); how the effect of the treatments is to be measured. A proper design facilitates the ascription of a probable cause-effect relation; a poor one can suggest a false conclusion from a spurious correlation.

detribalization, used particularly with reference to Africa, means the process by which persons are removed physically and culturally from their tribal life. Many of the in-migrants to cities may return to their native villages; probably most refugees also hope to do so. At what point their separation becomes definitive is generally impossible to determine, yet the issue can be important. When land or other values are divided among tribes, sometimes a portion is set aside for the detribalized—who must then be stipulated. More generally, the new nations of Africa have little natural coherence, and often their future is tied to a presumed lessening importance of tribes. See also *African society.

Development Associates, Inc., an American management and consulting firm, has specialized in training related to fertility control. By 1982 some 63,000 persons in Latin America and the Caribbean area had been trained in family planning and related activities, with funding from the U.S. Agency for International Development (AID). Under contracts with the U.S. Department of Health and Human Services, the firm has also trained contraceptive personnel in the United

226   DIABETES

States, organized conferences on natural family planning, and appraised the
effectiveness of education programs on nutrition. Address: 2924 Columbia Pike,
Arlington, Va. 22204.

diabetes, with no further specification, means the habitual discharge of an excessive
amount of urine, a symptom of various disorders. More narrowly defined, the
term refers to one of two diseases. In the normal functioning of the body, a
hormone produced by the hypothalamus and stored in the pituitary, vasopressin,
slows down the rate of urine formation. A patient with *diabetes insipidus*, a
chronic metabolic disorder marked by a great thirst and the passage of a large
amount of urine with no excess of sugar, can be relieved by the administration
of vasopressin or another antidiuretic. The more important disease commonly
called diabetes is properly known as *diabetes mellitus*, a metabolic disorder by
which a person becomes more or less unable to oxidize carbohydrates because
of a malfunctioning pancreas and the consequent lack of insulin, which is normally
produced by that gland. There are two major classes of patients with diabetes
mellitus. In one, including all younger patients, the so-called beta-islets of the
pancreas have been damaged by the action of the body's immune system in
combating another disease. Most of a second class of diabetics, who begin to
show the symptoms later in life, are chronically obese. For both classes the most
important element in the management of the disease dates only from the 1920s,
when two Canadian physicians isolated from the pancreas of stockyard animals
a pure extract of insulin, which is injected to compensate diabetics for its lack.
With obese patients this treatment can be usefully supplemented by prescribing
a special diet and exercise, and drugs have been developed to supplement the
action of the insulin.

The administration of insulin has saved many lives but also dramatically
increased the number of diabetics. Over the past four decades the reported
prevalence of diabetes mellitus in the United States has grown by more than six
times. The number of diabetics exceeds 5.5 million, plus an additional 4 to 5
million with similar abnormalities. Among disease-related deaths in this country,
the rank of diabetes moved from twenty-seventh at the turn of the century to
fifth in 1978 (see *cause of death). Secondary complications adversely affect
the blood vessels, the heart, the kidneys, the eyes, and the nervous system; and
diabetics are substantially more susceptible than nondiabetics to dying from a
number of other causes.

REFERENCES: Philip Handler et al., "On Some Major Human Diseases," in National
Research Council, *Outlook for Science and Technology: The Next Five Years* (San Francisco:
W. H. Freeman, 1982). Ira J. Laufer and Herbert Kadison, *Diabetes Explained: A
Layman's Guide* (New York: Dutton, 1976).

diagnosis, the art of recognizing a disease through its symptoms, is obviously
a crucial element of effective therapy, as well as of the compilation of accurate
data on the *cause of death. The trend in diagnosis over the past several decades
has combined two contradictory influences. On the one hand, the shift from

infectious diseases to less specific, less well understood causes of death—as, in particular, heart diseases, cancers, and strokes—has rendered diagnosis much more difficult. On the other hand, it has become possible with some new devices to make diagnostic tests that were impossible only a decade or two ago. A CAT (Computerized Axial Tomograph) scanner, for example, gives an immediate and comprehensive view of the condition of the vital organs, including the brain. More generally, the use of computers to relate statistically the incidence of various types of malfunction has begun to provide a better understanding of how the parts of the body interact.

dialect, a local or provincial variant of a *language. Whether a particular form of speech is regarded as one or the other sometimes depends on a historical accident. Martin Luther translated the Bible into the German that he spoke, which thus eventually became standard throughout the country. Very often the distinction is made on the basis of political power. In Belgium, for instance, the subordinate sector of the population used to speak a dialect called "Flemish"; now, with the rise of Flemings to equal power, their language is called "Southern Dutch."

REFERENCE: Einar Haugen, "Dialect, Language, Nation," *The Ecology of Language* (Stanford, Calif.: Stanford University Press, 1972).

diaphragm as a method of *contraception has a long history. For centuries past women inserted leaves and other substances into their vagina in order to block the entrance to the uterus. The Venetian adventurer Giacomo Casanova (1725–98) recommended that women squeeze half a lemon and then insert it over the cervix, thus getting both an obstructive cup and an astringent spermicide. In the nineteenth century there were dozens of "womb veils" available in the United States. The history of the modern cervical cap dates from 1882, when a German physician, Wilhelm P. J. Mensinga (writing under the pseudonym of C. Hasse) described the diaphragm that he had developed—a soft rubber cervical cup with a metal spring reinforcing the rim. It was introduced into Holland by that country's first female physician, Aletta †Jacobs, and from there spread to other West European countries as the "Dutch cap." Before the wide distribution of *oral contraceptives and *intra-uterine devices, the diaphragm with a spermicidal cream or jelly was the most effective contraceptive available, the standard method of middle-class women in industrial countries. The proportion using it declined sharply but from the mid-1970s apparently started to rise again, following negative reports on the pill and IUDs. Even with long-continued use, the diaphragm is completely safe, with no unpleasant side effects. Its use-effectiveness, however, is often below the risk-free protection that it theoretically provides, for it must be fitted to get the proper size and each time it is used it must be inserted with adequate care. Renewing the supply of spermicide, moreover, makes it more expensive than alternative methods. Because of such factors, no one has ever tried to introduce the diaphragm to less developed countries, but it may again become a standard contraceptive in the West.

REFERENCE: Judith Wortman, "The Diaphragm and Other Intravaginal Barriers: A Review," *Population Reports*, Ser. H, no. 4 (1976).

dichotomy, a technical term in several disciplines, has become a quasi-learned synonym for any type of cleavage or division. Derived from the Greek words for "two" and "cut," dichotomy applies most appropriately to a splitting of a unit into two subunits for the convenience of analysis or interpretation. Sometimes such a division exists in nature or fact (e.g., male, female; voted, did not vote) and need only be applied. These seemingly natural divisions, however, are often artifacts of arbitrary definitions (e.g., rural, urban; employed, unemployed); and the thoughtless use of such classifications may lead to false conclusions. No simple rule prescribes whether to dichotomize. In some instances, dichotomization has been used merely to separate out the few aberrant cases from a skewed distribution or otherwise to manipulate a set of data that seem to be intractable to routine analysis. In contrast, if a population is manifestly divided into two parts by a characteristic relevant to the study (e.g., in an analysis of political attitudes, those under and not under the minimum age of suffrage), or if a frequency distribution is clearly bimodal (as with many characteristics of American *blacks once the all-encompassing factor of discrimination was attenuated), a separate analysis of the two parts of a bimodal variable can be enlightening.

diffusion, the spread of ideas and artifacts from the place of origin to other peoples. Anthropological theory of the nineteenth and early twentieth centuries developed in large part through an intermittent debate on whether culture change can be explained as parallel inventions stimulated by analogous circumstances or, alternatively, as a diffusion from a few sources of cultural innovation (cf. Lowie, 1937). More recently studies by geographers, sociologists, market researchers, and others have concentrated on circumstances that encourage or impede the spread of new products (e.g., hybrid corn), new processes (e.g., contour plowing), or new ideas (e.g., birth control). In geography one of the important pioneers was Torsten †Hägerstrand (1968), a Swedish economist who developed simulation models to show how the range of information correlated with that of innovations. See also *Galton's problem.

REFERENCES: Lawrence A. Brown, *Innovation Diffusion: A New Perspective* (New York: Methuen, 1981). Torsten Hägerstrand, *Innovation Diffusion as a Spatial Process* (Chicago: University of Chicago Press, 1968). Robert H. Lowie, *The History of Ethnological Theory* (New York: Farrar and Rinehart, 1937). Everett M. Rogers, *Diffusion of Innovations* (New York: Free Press, 1962).

dilatation and curettage (D&C) is a surgical procedure sometimes used to perform an *abortion. Dilatation means the condition of an organ that has been stretched beyond its normal dimensions; curettage means the use of a curette, a kind of scraper or spoon, to remove growths or other matter from the interior walls of body cavities. The combination is a routine operation, for example, to remove abnormal cells from the uterus. In a D&C abortion, the cervical canal is stretched by the insertion of a series of metal dilators, each slightly thicker than the preceding one. When the canal has been sufficiently enlarged to permit the passage of instruments into the uterine cavity, the contents of the uterus are removed with a small ovum forceps, and then any remaining tissue is scraped out with a metal curette. In early pregnancy the use of a forceps may not be necessary. This used to be the standard procedure for first-trimester abortions, but it has been largely replaced by *suction curettage.

dilatation and evacuation (D&E), a surgical procedure used to perform an *abortion, usually between the thirteenth and sixteenth weeks of gestation, occasionally up to the twenty-first or even twenty-fourth week. The cervical canal is dilated with either a metal rod or laminaria, a dry seaweed that expands as it gradually absorbs moisture from the cervix. Once the canal has been opened, to the needed size, the physician uses whatever instruments may be needed to remove the fetus—forceps, suction cannula, or a sharp curette. The later in the pregnancy the operation is performed, the more difficult it becomes; and in any case, D&E requires greater technical skill than first-trimester abortions because the fetus is larger and fully formed.

DIME (an acronym for Dual Independent Map Encoding), a technique used by the U.S. Bureau of the Census to edit a geographic base file for completeness, or, in colloquial usage, that file itself. See also *GBF/DIME.

diminishing returns, a so-called law of classical economics, was an extension of †Malthus's principle of population. According to the usual formulation, the application of additional units of any one input (land, labor, or capital) to fixed amounts of the other(s) yields successively smaller increments of output. As later rephrased, the ''law'' became similar to the concept of the *population optimum: from the point of maximum, the economic return diminishes in both directions, with either more or less input of labor.

disability, once used as a synonym of *inability*, a general incapacity, was narrowed to designate specific instances of such a lack, particularly one associated with medical-legal jurisdiction. The concept developed especially after the proliferation of workmen's (now workers') compensation laws, starting in Germany in the 1880s and Britain a decade later and spreading to various states of the United States in the first two decades of this century. In order to provide a basis for any of the compensations provided under such laws (cash, medical care, and rehabilitation), it was necessary to define types of disabilities more precisely and to provide administrative means for applying these criteria in practice. The framework of compensation for occupational injuries was adopted in defining the welfare payments appropriate, for instance, to a ''blind'' person, with the renewed necessity of stipulating how this condition could be tested (cf. *blindness). In practice, then, a disability is a lack of physical or intellectual competence that is recognized as such by appropriate physicians and administrative boards (Nagi, 1969, 1975). The difficulties that such professionals encounter in setting an appropriate definition are similar to those in measuring the *health of a population; existent records pertain to that portion of the population with full access to medical facilities, and such efforts to transgress these limits as the National Health Survey or its counterparts in other countries are faced with virtually insurmountable blocks to adequate knowledge.

The likelihood of a person being disabled in the United States varies with— among other factors—age, sex, race, marital status, occupation, industry, urban or rural residence, income, family size, and region of the country. Some of these factors (such as age) are at least partly causal; others (such as occupation) are indicators of the different risks associated with the person's life-style; others (such as region of the country) are composites that would be difficult to interpret no matter how high a correlation was found. Some psychological factors may be more important than most of those in the list. The range of attitudes toward work—from a person who uses any excuse to have some time off to one who tries to keep going in spite of pain or serious handicap—is possibly related to marital status and family size, but certainly not very precisely. In recent years a greater effort has been made in the United States to absorb those with disabilities into the general economy. Under the Rehabilitation Act of 1973, as amended, and the Vietnam Era Veterans Readjustment Assistance Act of 1974, as amended, the principle of *affirmative action was extended to the handicapped. Since there proved to be a shortage of qualified persons suffering from one or another disability, employers were encouraged to make a special effort to locate and recruit them (Rabby, 1981).

In the 1970 census of the United States, persons were asked whether a disability limited the kind of work he or she could do, whether he or she was not able to work a full week (defined as 35 hours or more), or whether a disability kept the respondent out of the labor force altogether. These questions were repeated in 1980 and supplemented by another on whether a health condition made it difficult or impossible to use buses or other means of public transportation. The last item was included in spite of the fact that earlier replies in a sample survey that had been tested with reinterviews were too inconsistent to be useful.

REFERENCES: Saad Z. Nagi, *Disability and Rehabilitation: Legal, Clinical, and Self-Concepts and Measurement* (Columbus: Ohio State University Press, 1969); *An Epidemiology of Adulthood Disability in the United States* (Columbus: Ohio State University, Mershon Center, 1975). Rami Rabby, *Locating, Recruiting, and Hiring the Disabled* (New York: Pilot Books, 1981). Richard T. Smith and Abraham M. Lilienfeld, *The Social Security Disability Program: An Evaluation Study*, DHEW Publication No. (SSA) 72-11801 (Washington, D.C.: U.S. Government Printing Office, 1971). U.S. National Center for Health Statistics, *Synthetic State Estimates of Disability Derived from the National Health Survey*, Public Health Service Publication 1759 (Washington, D.C.: U.S. Government Printing Office, n.d.).

disaster derives from *astrus*, Latin for ''star,'' and thus meant originally an ill-starred event—what in legal terminology is termed an ''act of God,'' one that could not have been prevented by the exercise of reasonable foresight and care and which, therefore, incurs no human responsibility for damage. Research on such natural disasters as hurricanes, earthquakes, and tornadoes has been of two broad types: by physical scientists in an effort to improve prediction enough to provide adequate warning to potential victims and by sociologists concerning how people typically behave in a disaster and how public authorities can cope with its effects (e.g., Rossi et al., 1982). What is called ''disaster behavior'' has not differed greatly with the type of catastrophe. Some natural disasters, such as famines or floods, are subject to at least partial control but typically over a long period and with a considerable expenditure of money and personnel. And a third category, sometimes labeled man-made, is at least in theory altogether preventable—fires and explosions, rail and automobile *accidents, *wars, and so on. According to the compilation in a popular review (Cornell, 1979), the cost of natural disasters to the American economy in the mid-1970s was about $4 billion per year. By a very conservative estimate, the direct loss of life worldwide during the period 1947–67 was 388,775, with the causes ranked in order as floods; typhoons, hurricanes, and cyclones; earthquakes; gales and thunderstorms; volcanic eruptions; and other violent shifts in the weather or the earth's crust. In industrial countries there has been a long-term decline in lives lost but with a considerable rise in property damage. One analyst has proposed that disasters be ranked also by the amount of emotional stress they caused and on that basis has given ten historical events the following magnitudes (Foster, 1976):

World War II	11.1
Black Death	10.9
World War I	10.5
The 1936–38 purge in the Soviet Union	10.2
The atomic bombing of Hiroshima	8.2
The 1970 glacier avalanche in Yungay, Peru	8.1
The 1972 earthquake in Managua, Nicaragua	7.9
Mass poisoning from fungicide-treated grain, Iraq, 1971	7.4
Eruption of Mt. Pelée, Martinique, 1902	7.3
The attack of the Spanish Armada against Britain, 1588	7.2

The first three are classified as ''major catastrophes,'' the next three as ''catastrophes,'' and the others as ''disasters.'' One historian has reacted to the ''Foster scale'' by analyzing the Black Death in this new framework, with much richer detail on how the people reacted to mortality on so massive a scale (Lerner, 1981).

REFERENCES: James Cornell, *The Great International Disaster Book* (New York: Pocket Books, 1979). Harold D. Foster, ''Assessing Disaster Magnitude: A Social Science Approach,'' *Professional Geographer*, 28 (1976), 241–247. Charles E. Fritz, ''Disasters," in *International Encyclopedia of the Social Sciences*, 4, 202-207. Robert E. Lerner, "The Black Death and Western European Eschatological Mentalities," *American Historical Review*, 86 (1981), 533-552. Peter H. Rossi, James D. Wright, and Eleanor Weber-Burdin, *Natural Hazards and Public Choice: The State and Local Politics of Hazard Mitigation* (New York: Academic Press, 1982).

discrimination once reflected its Latin root in a meaning becoming rare in English, the act of noting or making a distinction. From this neutral connotation, it acquired the sense of making a careful or accurate distinction, as between fact and fancy. Then, in social analysis related to ethnic groups, the two sexes, age classes, and various other categories, it came to denote the treatment of one group differently from others for inappropriate reasons. Finally, as with the analogous term *prejudice, the relative merits of the categories being compared were implicitly ignored, and discrimination came to be widely defined as "practices and actions of dominant race-ethnic groups that have a differential and negative impact on subordinate race-ethnic groups" (Feagin and Eckberg, 1980); see also *affirmative action. In 1982 the U.S. Bureau of the Census issued a computer tape designed to assist employers in avoiding genuine discrimination. For each county, metropolitan area, and city of 50,000 or more, the tape breaks down those holding any of 504 occupations by race, sex, and Hispanic origin; and for the same geographical units, it gives the years of schooling completed by age and the other three classifications. Whenever a skill is determined by education rather than only by work experience, the combination of the two sets of data can furnish employment planners with pertinent information concerning the local situation (Riche, 1982). See also *data processing.

REFERENCES: Joe R. Feagin and Douglas Lee Eckberg, "Discrimination: Motivation, Action, Effects, and Context," *Annual Review of Sociology*, 6 (1980), 1-20. Martha Farnsworth Riche, "Measuring the Human Factor," *American Demographics*, 4 (September, 1982), 38-40.

disease, as suggested by its derivation from "ease," once meant unease or discomfort; hence, a cause of the discomfort. In the narrower sense common today, the word still retains a negative connotation: that is, what any culture regards as a "disease" depends on how it defines the norm that is broken, its concept of *health. Until the twentieth century the typical index of a population's level of health was its death rate, but some diseases with little or no effect on mortality considerably reduce efficiency, comfort, or well-being. The common cold, for instance, is a leading reason for absenteeism; those afflicted with trachoma, an eye infection prevalent in the Near East, eventually become blind if it is not treated, but they do not die appreciably earlier than their uninfected neighbors.

Presently *disease* is applied very broadly to any type of morbid process, whether or not its etiology, pathology, and prognosis are known and whether it affects the whole body or any part of it. It can also designate an individual case of such a morbid condition—an illness or ailment. The preference of physicians and epidemiologists is to classify diseases by their causes—as infectious, nutritional, genetic, and so on. But as we can see from the *International Classification of Diseases, Injuries, and Causes of Death, when the etiology is complex or unknown, the disease is likely to be grouped according to its site (e.g., diseases of the circulatory system) or process (e.g., mental disorders; complications of pregnancy, childbirth, and the puerperium).

Since a disease connotes a condition that can be prevented or cured—or, if not, results in death—the number of diseases has paradoxically increased with the advance of medical knowledge. Among the Bantu, for example, coughs and colds, fever and rheumatism, used to need no explanation; they were nuisances comparable to being in debt and just as unavoidable. Among primitives it is only the mysterious and dangerous process that requires the intervention of a medicine man. His diagnosis may be the malevolence of another person or a god; and his therapy is likely to include both incantations and specific medicaments: there is no sharp distinction between medicine on the one hand and magic or religion on the other (Sigerist, 1951, chap. II: 2). Such concepts of disease are likely to persist in developed societies, especially among the less educated classes or particular ethnic groups. As one respondent in "Regionville" remarked: "I'd look silly, wouldn't I, going to see a doctor for a backache. My mother *always* had a backache, as long as I can remember, and didn't do anything about it. It didn't kill her, either" (Koos, 1967, p. 36).

Belief systems that compete with modern medicine occur also among the middle classes. Most Christian Scientists, who hold that all disease is "error," are moderately well educated, as are many of the patients of chiropractors and naturopaths. Since not even the most efficient medicine eliminates pain and death, such competing faiths will never lack clients. Moreover, since bodily functions respond in some degree to mental states, a *placebo can be relatively effective under some circumstances (cf. Frank, 1971). See also *Christian Science; *chiropractic; *folk medicine.

REFERENCES: Jerome D. Frank, *Persuasion and Healing: A Comparative Study of Psychotherapy* (New York: Schocken, 1971). Earl Lomon Koos, *The Health of Regionville: What the People Thought and Did about It* (New York: Hafner, 1967; facsimile of the 1954 edition). Henry E. Sigerist, *Primitive and Archaic Medicine* (New York: Oxford University Press, 1951).

disengagement, in gerontology the process by which an old person breaks off or significantly alters his relations with other members of society.

REFERENCES: Elaine Cumming and William E. Henry, *Growing Old: The Process of Disengagement* (New York: Basic Books, 1961). Cumming, "Further Thoughts on the Theory of Disengagement," *International Social Science Journal*, 15 (1963), 377-393.

dispersed settlement, a rural patterning of dwelling places with farmhouses situated some distance from one another; contrasted with a *nucleated settlement*, with the homes concentrated in a hamlet or village.

dispersion, in statistical terminology, the degree of scatter of observations, usually measured by the average deviation from some central value; see *mean deviation, *standard deviation. In spatial analysis, deconcentration.

Displaced Persons (or DPs) were originally those *refugees who had survived a stay in Nazi concentration or forced-labor camps and were released after the Allied victory in the Second World War. Of the approximately 12 million, about 11 million were repatriated to their home countries; under the auspices of the U.N. Relief and Rehabilitation Administration (UNRRA), thousands were forced to return to the Soviet Union or Soviet-occupied territory, many of them ending up in new labor camps. Jews in particular were often unwilling to return to their home countries, and probably most of them wanted to be evacuated to Palestine. After a formal protest from the United States, the deplorable conditions of the refugee camps in Germany improved, and there was a backflow from Eastern Europe to camps in the American Zone. Against considerable opposition, a special immigration law was passed in the United States to admit a specified number of DPs (Bernard, 1975). Eventually about two-thirds of the Jewish DPs settled in Israel and about one-quarter, as well as most of the non-Jewish DPs, in the United States, Canada, and other countries. From this specific denotation, the meaning of "displaced persons" (spelled usually with lower-case letters) was expanded, and presently the term is often a loose synonym for refugees of any type. See also Eugene M. †Kulischer.

REFERENCE: William S. Bernard, "Refugee Asylum in the United States: How the Law Was Changed to Admit Displaced Persons," *International Migration*, 13 (1975), 3-20.

displacement has been used in demography in two related but different senses. In the theory of migration associated particularly with Francis A. †Walker and W. Burton †Hurd, it signifies the process by which immigrants take the place of natives in the labor force, or by which their unfair competition induces the natives to emigrate. Some analysts have used displacement, alternatively, as a loosely defined generalization from the *Displaced Persons officially specified in American laws concerning the admission of refugees.

dissolution of a marriage can be by *divorce, *annulment, or the death of one of the spouses. A dissolved marriage differs from a broken one in that the latter is understood usually to include also a legal separation.

distribution, the frequency of occurrence of persons or other entities or attributes over space or time. In economics, it means the relative amounts of goods and services that each investor, producer, or consumer receives; thus, it is distinguished from the marketing and circulation of goods, which refer to the physical spread of commodities over space. In statistics, it refers to the way that a set of individuals is classified with respect to one or more variables; for example, the population of a city might be classified by occupation (a univariate distribution) or cross-classified by occupation and income (a bivariate distribution).

division, or geographic division, is used by the U.S. Bureau of the Census to designate a subunit of the country's four *regions. The Northeast region is broken down into the New England and the Middle Atlantic divisions; the North Central region into an eastern and western division; the South into the South Atlantic, the East South Central, and the West South Central divisions; and the West into Mountain and Pacific divisions. See the map.

Regions and Geographic Divisions of the United States, 1980, as Defined by the U.S. Bureau of the Census

division of labor, a distribution of related tasks among members of a population, who thereby form a coherent system of symbiotic relationships. The economic consequence of a division of labor has been to increase production greatly, the social one, to distance workers much more from the final product. See also Émile †Durkheim; *occupation; Herbert †Spencer; *specialization.

234

REFERENCES: Émile Durkheim, *The Division of Labor in Society* (New York: Macmillan, 1933). Adam Smith, *The Wealth of Nations* (New York: Modern Library, 1937).

divorce, according to the recommended definition of the U.N. Statistical Commission, is "the final legal dissolution of a marriage . . . which confers on the parties the right to civil and/or religious remarriage, according to the laws of each country." Statistics on divorce are seldom satisfactory, for its incidence generally varies with the difficulty of getting one (cf. Crosby, 1980). In such countries as Ireland, the Philippines, and formerly Italy, where Roman Catholic norms have been reflected in a legal code that permits no divorces, a common substitute is *annulment. Early in the nineteenth century, when the laws of most American states had little or no provision for the formal ending of marriages, husbands sometimes broke them by moving west. Samuel H. †Preston and John McDonald (1979) have used both vital statistics and census data to estimate American cohort divorce rates from 1867 to 1970; though also related to business cycles and wars, they rose steadily with far less variability than period rates. The differential rate of divorce by social class in more recent times, similarly, is largely factitious: what the middle class achieves by divorce, the lower class often gets by separation or desertion. As long as the grounds differed greatly from one jurisdiction to another, such states as Nevada granted decrees to "residents" temporarily living there for the express purpose of getting a divorce; it has not been possible, therefore, to compare meaningfully the long-term rates of states. Those states in the divorce-*registration area, which has lagged well behind that for marriage, record divorces on a form similar to the one reproduced on page 237. The records are then compiled by the U.S. National Center for Health Statistics.

A *divorce rate* is the number of divorces during a year per 1,000 in the base population, which is designated as the whole population (yielding a crude divorce rate), the married population, or the latter specified by age and sex. The *divorce ratio* of any population used to be defined as the number of divorces during a year related to the number of marriages during the same period, but this virtually meaningless measure is now seldom used. As presently defined in a publication of the U.S. Bureau of the Census (1981), it is the number of divorced persons per 1,000 married persons living with their spouse; it is thus essentially the same as a refined divorce rate except that the data are derived from a census or survey. In the United States recent divorce ratios were as follows:

| Year | Total | Males | | Females | |
		White	Black	White	Black
1960	35	27	45	38	78
1970	47	32	62	56	104
1980	100	74	151	110	257

Form Approved
OMB No. 68R 1904

U.S. STANDARD
CERTIFICATE OF DIVORCE,
DISSOLUTION OF MARRIAGE OR ANNULMENT

TYPE OR PRINT IN PERMANENT INK FOR INSTRUCTIONS SEE HANDBOOK

COURT IDENTIFICATION (Court file number)

STATE FILE NUMBER

HUSBAND

1. HUSBAND—NAME
   FIRST | MIDDLE | LAST

2a. USUAL RESIDENCE—STREET ADDRESS

2b. CITY, TOWN OR LOCATION

2c. COUNTY

2d. STATE

3. BIRTHPLACE (State or foreign country)

4. DATE OF BIRTH (Mo., Day, Yr.)

WIFE

5a. WIFE—NAME
   FIRST | MIDDLE | LAST

5b. MAIDEN NAME

6a. USUAL RESIDENCE—STREET ADDRESS

6b. CITY, TOWN OR LOCATION

6c. COUNTY

6d. STATE

7. BIRTHPLACE (State or foreign country)

8. DATE OF BIRTH (Mo., Day, Yr.)

9a. PLACE OF THIS MARRIAGE—CITY

9b. COUNTY

9c. STATE (If not in U.S.A., name country)

9d. DATE OF THIS MARRIAGE (Mo., Day, Yr.)

10. DATE COUPLE SEPARATED (Mo., Day, Yr.)

11a. NUMBER OF CHILDREN EVER BORN ALIVE OF THIS MARRIAGE (Specify)

11b. CHILDREN UNDER 18 IN THIS FAMILY (Specify)

12. PETITIONER—HUSBAND, WIFE, BOTH, OTHER (Specify)

13a. ATTORNEY FOR PETITIONER—NAME (Type or print)

13b. ADDRESS
   STREET OR R.F.D. NO. | CITY OR TOWN | STATE | ZIP

DECREE

14a. I certify that the marriage of the above named persons was dissolved on:
   Month | Day | Year

14b. TYPE OF DECREE—DIVORCE, DISSOLUTION OR ANNULMENT (Specify)

14c. DATE OF ENTRY (Mo., Day, Yr.)

14d. COUNTY OF DECREE

14e. TITLE OF COURT

14f. SIGNATURE OF CERTIFYING OFFICIAL ▲

14g. TITLE OF OFFICIAL

HUSBAND

15. RACE—HUSBAND
Specify (e.g., White, Black, American Indian, etc.)

16. NUMBER OF THIS MARRIAGE
Specify (First, second, etc.)

17a. IF PREVIOUSLY MARRIED HOW MANY ENDED BY
DEATH?

17b. DIVORCE, DISSOLUTION OR ANNULMENT?

18. EDUCATION (Specify only highest grade completed.)
Elementary or Secondary (0-12) | College (1-4 or 5+)

WIFE

19. RACE—WIFE
Specify (e.g., White, Black, American Indian, etc.)

20. NUMBER OF THIS MARRIAGE
Specify (First, second, etc.)

21a. IF PREVIOUSLY MARRIED HOW MANY ENDED BY
DEATH?

21b. DIVORCE, DISSOLUTION OR ANNULMENT?

22. EDUCATION (Specify only highest grade completed.)
Elementary or Secondary (0-12) | College (1-4 or 5+)

1978 REVISION

In 1980 for every ten persons living in intact marriages there was one divorced person who had not remarried. As with *illegitimacy and other symptoms of family disorganization, the rates for blacks were extraordinarily high (see also Glick, 1979; Spanier and Glick, 1981). According to 1984 data from the Current Population Survey, between two-fifths and a half of the offspring of divorced parents spend about 5 years as children in a single-parent household, and about half of those whose parent remarries experience a breakup of the new family (Bumpass, 1984). See also *Fundamentalism, *Islam, *one-parent family, *remarriage, *Roman Catholicism.

REFERENCES: Larry L. Bumpass, "Children and Marital Disruption: A Replication and Update," *Demography*, 21 (1984), 1–82. John F. Crosby, "A Critique of Divorce Statistics and Their Interpretation," *Family Relations*, 29 (1980), 51-58. Paul C. Glick, "Children of Divorced Parents in Demographic Perspective," *Journal of Social Issues*, 35 (1979), 170-182. Samuel H. Preston and John McDonald, "The Incidence of Divorce within Cohorts of American Marriages Contracted since the Civil War," *Demography*, 16 (1979), 1-26. Graham B. Spanier and Glick, "Marital Instability in the United States: Some Correlates and Recent Changes," *Family Relations*, 30 (1981), 329-338. U.S. Bureau of the Census, "Marital Status and Living Arrangements: March 1980," *Current Population Reports*, Ser. P-20, no. 365 (October, 1981).

Djibouti: The government's Bureau of Statistics and Public Information publishes a quarterly *Bulletin de Statistique et de Documentation*, of which the annual special issue includes population data. Address: Service de Statistique et de Documentation, Ministère du Commerce, de l'Industrie, des Transports et du Tourisme, Boîte Postale 1846, Djibouti.

Domesday Book, the record of the survey that William the Conqueror had made of his new British territory in 1086. According to the man historians know as the Saxon Chronicler, "there was not one single hide nor rood of land, nor— it is shameful to tell but he thought it no shame to do—was there an ox, cow, or swine that was not set down in the writ." Domesday was primarily a "geld book," an account made for the purpose of levying the tax called the Danegeld. But it was also a compendium, unique for its period, of the population, its distribution into shires, and many of the inhabitants' characteristics.

REFERENCE: J. C. Russell, *British Medieval Population* (Albuquerque: University of New Mexico Press, 1948).

dominance, the control of an *ecological community by members of a particular species; in human ecology, the coordinating influence over a region's activities by the institutions concentrated in a city or metropolitan center.

REFERENCES: R. D. McKenzie, "The Concept of Dominance and World Organization," *American Journal of Sociology*, 33 (1927), 28-42. Eugene P. Odum, *Fundamentals of Ecology* (3rd ed.; Philadelphia: Saunders, 1971).

Dominican Republic: Demographic Institutions
The National Council on Population and the Family, established in 1968, was directed in 1980 by Luis González Fabra. It conducts training, research, and documentation, particularly as related to policy issues; and it has been responsible for the local component of the World Fertility Survey. Address: Consejo Nacional de Población y Familia, Apartado Postal 1803, Santo Domingo.

The National University Pedro Henríquez Ureña established in 1970 a Research Center, which in 1980 was under the direction of Ezequiel García. It has focused on migration and family planning in its research, and in 1975 it set up a documentation center on demography and family planning. Address: Centro de Investigaciones de la Universidad Nacional Pedro Henríquez Ureña, Avenida John F. Kennedy K.M. 5½, Santo Domingo.

The Secretariat of Health and Public Assistance publishes an annual volume, *Cuadros Estadísticos*. Address: Sección de Estadística, Secretaría de Sanidad y Asistencia Pública, Santo Domingo.

The National Statistical Bureau conducts the country's censuses, of which the last was in 1981. It issues irregularly a compilation including population data, *República Dominicana en Cifras*, and a more specific and detailed *Estadística Demográfica*. Address: Oficina Nacional de Estadística, Apartado de Correos no. 1342, Santo Domingo.

dormitory town, a *suburb primarily residential in its function, with minimum opportunities for employment within its boundaries. The term originated in Britain and is still used more commonly there; the American counterpart is "suburb," loosely defined, "residential suburb," or "bedroom community."

double effect, as used by Roman Catholic moralists, defines a situation when an action with a good and therefore acceptable effect runs the incidental risk of an unavoidable harm. For example, an abortion is licit if an ectopic pregnancy threatens the life of both mother and child; drugs are licit to control the pain of a terminal patient even if they may hasten his death.
REFERENCE: G. R. Dunstan, *The Artifice of Ethics* (London: SCM Press, 1978).

doubling time, the number of years it takes a population to double its size, given the annual rate of increase. A population growing at a constant rate can be calculated with the formula

$$P_1 = P_0 e^{ax}$$

where P_0 is the initial population and P_1 that at the end of a designated number of years, x; e is the base of natural logarithms; and a is the rate of growth per designated unit of time. By setting P_1 as equal to $2P_0$, one can determine the doubling time for each annual rate of growth. The following table shows the doubling times for particular countries, given their annual growth rates in 1978.

Country	Percent Annual Growth in Population	Doubling Time (years)
New Zealand	0.5	139
Spain	1.0	69
Sri Lanka	1.5	46
The world	2.0	35
Malaysia	2.5	28
Morocco	3.0	23
Honduras	3.5	20
Bahamas	4.0	17

If one adds to the growth of the population of the United States between 1970 and 1980 an approximate estimate of illegal immigration, the probable growth rate would be 1.0 percent, resulting in a doubling in 69 years.

douche, which in medicine is used to designate a stream of water, gas, or vapor directed against a part of the body or into one of its cavities, means specifically in the context of demography the rinsing of the uterus immediately after coitus as a means of controlling fertility. It is certainly one of the oldest means of *contraception, and it was given new prominence in the early days of the neo-Malthusian movement. In Charles †Knowlton's *Fruits of Philosophy* (1832), the subject of the notorious trial of Charles †Bradlaugh and Annie †Besant, the author recommended that before using the douche the woman should "add something to the water that should not hurt the woman but yet kill the tender animalcules or, in other words, destroy the fecundating property of the semen" (cf. Fryer, 1965, chap. 10). The recommended means in George R. Drysdale's *The Elements of Social Science* (1854), for decades the bible of the English birth-control movement, included "the injection of tepid water into the vagina immediately after intercourse"—which by its omission of the spermicide represented a retrogression from a work published several decades earlier (Ledbetter, 1976, chap. 1); see †Drysdale family.

REFERENCES: Peter Fryer, *The Birth Controllers* (London: Secker and Warburg, 1965). Rosanna Ledbetter, *A History of the Malthusian League, 1877–1927* (Columbus: Ohio State University Press, 1976).

dropout, originally a colloquial term for a person who has left school, the labor force, or another institutional setting of conventional life, has been incorporated into the jargon of social sciences. Though often a transient phenomenon, dropping out can be a serious social problem, associated with the sale and consumption of drugs and with an increased burden of dependency on the community. The number of dropouts depends on how this somewhat ambiguous term is specified, and any count is hampered by the fact that those in the category often try to avoid being included. In analyses of the school population, the dropout rate is calculated as a proportion of the pupils in a particular grade or of those in a specified age group. In a *panel study—that is, a survey in which the same respondents are questioned several times—the dropouts who cannot be located are typically concentrated in the less educated lower classes, and their omission therefore biases the sample more than their typically small proportion would suggest. See also *continuation ratio.

REFERENCES: Shryock and Siegel, *The Methods and Materials of Demography*, p. 323. Marion G. Sobol, "Panel Mortality and Panel Bias," *Journal of the American Statistical Association*, 54 (1959), 52-68.

dual citizenship can occur under several circumstances. For example, a child born of American parents abroad is counted as an American citizen (*jus sanguinis*), but the country in which he is born may also rate him as a citizen (*jus soli*). The principal difficulty for the individual usually arises from competing claims for military service, but the number of persons involved is usually too small to make a significant difference in population figures.

dual economy, the relation in a "dual society" between a native subsistence economy and a modernist one based on international trade. The term was coined by the Dutch economist J. H. Boeke and exemplified in his study of the Netherlands East Indies (present Indonesia). The units of exchange used in the two sectors there were both called the guilder but had values so different that hardly any transactions could take place across the chasm separating the sectors. Villagers in Java spent market days buying and selling their wares for as little as half a guilder-cent ($0.0012). Moreover, the premises on which Western economic theory is based do not apply, or apply only in part, to the native sector. There is typically what economists term a backward-sloping supply curve: higher wages or profits result not in a greater effort but in a smaller one, for the peasant's aim is only to meet his family responsibilities with the minimum work necessary. Policymakers, thus, cannot attain their ends using economic incentives, for these are likely to work in reverse. As early as the beginning of the nineteenth century, Java had a higher density of rural population than any European country had ever experienced, and all attempts to reduce the consequent pressure failed. Improvements in agriculture or extensions of arable land through irrigation generally resulted in more people. The resettlement of Javans to the outer islands (which the Indonesian government continued) transplanted Java's family-building norms there without solving the problem at home; see *transmigration. In Boeke's opinion, the population pressure could not be mitigated on a mass scale, but only by gradually bringing a larger and larger portion of the native economy into the world of Western production and thus introducing a dynamism that it lacked.

Boeke regarded his analysis as generally applicable to less developed countries, which typically have a marked asymmetry between traditional and modern production and distribution. The model has been analyzed by a number of other economists (e.g., Lewis, 1954, 1958; Fei and Ranis, 1964; Jorgenson, 1961,

1967), who usually have focused on factors linking the two sectors. For example, there is so large a pool of potential workers in the traditional economy that growth (measured principally or solely in the modernist sector) may be accompanied by rising unemployment (e.g., Sabolo, 1971). Modernization also often stimulates an explosive urbanization, and cities in less developed countries are viewed negatively because they represent in a concentrated form all the problems that a dual economy reflects or generates. Some analysts have argued that one way of bridging the gap between the two parts of the economy is to encourage an intermediate one, comprising *cottage industry or other small-scale enterprises, especially in rural areas (e.g., Child, 1977).

REFERENCES: J. H. Boeke, *Economics and Economic Policy of Dual Societies* (New York: Institute of Pacific Relations, 1953). Frank C. Child, *Single-Scale Rural Industry in Kenya* (Los Angeles: African Studies Center, University of California, 1977). J.C.H. Fei and Gustav Ranis, *Development of the Labor Surplus Economy* (Homewood, Ill.: Richard Irwin, 1964). Dale W. Jorgenson, "The Development of the Dual Economy," *Economic Journal*, 71 (1961), 309-334; "Surplus Agricultural Labor and the Dual Economy," *Oxford Economic Papers*, N.S., 19 (1967), 288-312. W. Arthur Lewis, "Economic Development with Unlimited Supplies of Labor" and "Unlimited Labor: Further Notes," *Manchester School*, 22 (1954), 139-191, and 26 (1958), 1-32. Yves Sabolo, "Sectoral Employment Growth: The Outlook for 1980," in Walter Galenson, ed., *Essays on Employment* (Geneva: International Labor Office, 1971).

dual record system, a means of collecting information on births and deaths (and occasionally other vital events) in places with a deficient registration. Two denotations of each event are sought, one by a continuous recording similar to, but independent of, the civil registration system, and the other by retrospective questions in a periodic household interview. When two reports refer to the same event, this overlap is called a "match"; the proportion of events in one collection duplicated in the other is its "match rate." The common terms "probable match" and "probable nonmatch"; "mismatch," "erroneous match," and "erroneous nonmatch"; "one-way match" and "two-way match" are self-explanatory. See also *matching; *PGE/ERAD/ECP.

DUAList, a series of five computer programs developed by the U.S. Bureau of the Census and designed to read and display tabulations from the summary tapes of the 1970 census. DUAList 4 (Population) permits the aggregation of data from different geographic areas, such as census blocks or census tracts.

dummy variable, in statistics a constant that, for the convenience of the analysis, is included in a mathematical expression in the form of a variable. In an experimental situation the *control that receives none of the test factor is given what is termed a "dummy treatment."

dust bowl, a region of low rainfall converted into a desert by wind erosion following excessive grazing or plowing. In the United States, the term was first applied in the 1930s to Oklahoma and adjoining states and then generalized to other man-made deserts. The designation of those migrants forced from their homes, "Okies," also became part of the language.

dwelling unit, either a whole house or a portion of it; the place of residence of a family, a comparable group living together, or a single person living alone. It is the usual statistical term, rather than "dwelling house," used in law.

dysgenics, the study of detrimental hereditary traits and, by their accumulation, the deterioration of a human stock. Eugenicists have often emphasized dysgenic factors, which are frequently both more clearly identifiable and indisputably hereditary, unlike such positive characteristics as, for instance, intelligence.

E

earth sciences, a regrouping of disciplines in American academia to include all sciences concerned with the study of the earth. To the traditional *geography and geology were added an increased emphasis on meteorology and oceanography, a bit of geophysics, and portions of paleontology and astronomy. See also *behavioral sciences; *life sciences.

Eastern Orthodox churches, as diverse in some respects as Protestantism, are also no less unitary. The differentiation from Roman Catholicism, which began as early as the Nicene Council (A.D. 325), was completed over the next millennium. With no disciplining papacy at the center, Orthodoxy proliferated into national churches throughout Eastern Europe and the Levant and schismatic churches of various types, some using a Slavonic liturgy, some a Greek, and others one in the vernacular. Monks were not ordained and thus did not constitute, as with the Western orders, auxiliary troops of the church; though distanced from the churches, the lay monks of the East yet influenced enormously the development of Orthodoxy. As contrasted with Western Christianity, Orthodox churches have been less rational and more mystical, more inclined to stress the brotherhood of believers rather than discipline in an ecclesiastical structure. One can do no more than guess at the number of adherents in Communist countries, but Nicolas Zernov (1961) estimated a world total in around 1960 of 150 million followers of the Byzantine rite, plus 21 million other Orthodox Christians.

Orthodox norms affecting the family and fertility generally do not differ significantly from those of Roman Catholicism. The adoration of the Virgin Mary, the Mother of God, was stressed more in the East, perhaps reflecting the greater penetration of neo-Platonist asceticism (cf. †Plato). Yet the sacrament of Orthodox marriage can be broken by a licit divorce and even followed by a second wedding with a lesser rite than the original "crowning." Priests may marry, but only once; the insistence on clerical *celibacy that is disrupting Roman Catholicism is not an issue. The very high fertility of pre-1914 Russia was in no sense the consequence of religious dictates. In sum, whatever effect Orthodoxy has had on population trends has been mostly indirect and probably less in sum than the effect in other countries of Roman Catholicism or of the major Protestant denominations at their high points.

REFERENCES: Ernst Benz, *The Eastern Orthodox Church: Its Thought and Life* (Chicago: Aldine, 1963). Nicolas Zernov, *Eastern Christendom: A Study of the Origin and Development of the Eastern Orthodox Church* (New York: Putnam, 1961).

EBCDIC (an acronym for Extended Binary-Code Decimal Interchange Code), a system of eight-bit codes that can be specified as one of the options of the nine-track tapes sold by the U.S. Bureau of the Census. Cf. *ASCII.

echo, with respect to a particular change in the age structure, the consequent reflection a generation later in higher or lower rates of vital events. The term is used particularly with reference to the *baby boom, the exceptionally high fertility in the late 1940s and early 1950s, and the anticipated high fertility when these large cohorts reached the ages of marrying and reproduction.

ecological community, the interacting individuals of various species in an *ecosystem.

ecological correlation, a designated relation between group characteristics based on the proportions recorded in territorial units, as contrasted with the usual sense of *correlation, in which the variables are characteristic of individuals. For example, since in the United States the votes of individuals are secret, conclusions concerning political preferences are often drawn from the percentages of blacks, Catholics, or whatever in various precincts, on the one hand, and the percentages in the precincts who voted Republican or Democratic, on the other hand. The frequent implicit purpose of such calculations, to infer the voting behavior of such subpopulations, involves a logical error: generally one may not conclude anything concerning individuals from aggregated data. This applies, of course, to any type of *aggregation—by social class, for instance; analysts have criticized "ecological correlation" specifically because territory affects the attributes of individuals less than other types of aggregates. In the United States the key paper drawing attention to this fallacy was by W. S. Robinson (1950). It was followed by expositions on some alternatives to ecological correlation (Duncan and Davis, 1953; Goodman, 1959). Somewhat later a number of analysts tried to show more precisely the reasons for the false conclusions and, thus, the conditions under which an ecological correlation can be accepted as valid (Firebaugh, 1978; Gove and Hughes, 1980; Hammond, 1973). It was concluded that discrepancies between micro- and macrolevel studies of voting result from the fact that individual welfare comprises two components, one government-induced and politically relevant and the other related to the life cycle and other politically irrelevant factors. If estimates of how changes in welfare affect voting are based on cross-sectional analyses of individual data, the calculation omits part of the effect of voters' interests on their behavior (Kramer, 1983).

REFERENCES: Otis Dudley Duncan and Beverly Davis, "An Alternative to Ecological Correlation," *American Sociological Review*, 18 (1953), 665-666. Glenn Firebaugh, "A Rule for Inferring Individual-Level Relationships from Aggregate Data," *American Sociological Review*, 43 (1978), 557-572. Leo A. Goodman, "Some Alternatives to Ecological Correlation," *American Journal of Sociology*, 64 (1959), 610-625. Walter R. Gove and Michael Hughes, "Reexamining the Ecological Fallacy: A Study in Which Aggregate Data Are Critical to Investigating the Pathological Effects of Living Alone," *Social Forces*, 58 (1980), 1157-1177. John L. Hammond, "Two Sources of Error in Ecological Correlations," *American Sociological Review*, 38 (1973), 764-777. Gerald H. Kramer, "The Ecological Fallacy Revisited: Aggregate- versus Individual-Level Findings on Economics and Elections, and Sociotropic Voting," *American Political Science Review*, 77 (1983), 92-111. W. S. Robinson, "Ecological Correlations and the Behavior of Individuals," *American Sociological Review*, 15 (1950), 351-357.

ecology, derived from the Greek for "the study of the house," has been extended to include the habitat in the broadest sense; the study, thus, of the interrelation between living beings and their *environment. Once the theory of evolution was accepted, with natural selection as the means by which new species developed, scholars' interest was bound to focus on how particular characteristics of plants or animals were encouraged or inhibited by the features of their "house." In the analysis of plant and animal life in what may be termed *bio-ecology*, to contrast it with *human ecology*, concepts and propositions were generated that were later applied to the collective life of humans in order to guide research initially on the forms and development of cities, and subsequently on a much wider array of settlements or communities broadly conceived. Epidemiologists, however, have used "human ecology" to denote their studies of environmental factors in the origin and spread of diseases. Anthropologists began by using the term to refer to environmental influences on particular culture traits, then extended the range to any interactions between environment and culture, especially in primitive societies. A specialization known as *population ecology* is the study of members of composite units—whether people or organizations—and of how their number and interrelation are regulated by the competition for the limited space in the common environment. Most recently, the word *ecology* has come into general use in connection with the management of the environment and programs to preserve wild life.

REFERENCES: Donald L. Hardesty, *Ecological Anthropology* (New York: Wiley, 1977). Hawley, *Human Ecology*. Eugene P. Odum, *Fundamentals of Ecology* (3rd ed.; Philadelphia: Saunders, 1971).

economic base, a concept used in the analysis of urban economies, is founded on a difficult and disputed distinction between activities essential to the city's well-being and those that support these "basic" or city-forming activities. It is the processing or trading of goods and the provision of services or capital, the equivalent of the export sector in a national economy, that supposedly underlie growth of a city's employment, income, and population.

REFERENCE: Ralph W. Pfouts, ed., *The Techniques of Urban Economic Analysis* (West Trenton, N.J.: Chandler-Davis, 1960).

economic development and **economic growth** are usually distinguished at least implicitly both from each other and from *modernization. When "economic growth" refers to a historic record of sustained and substantial rise in *Gross National Product or, more specifically, in product per capita, it is an empirical datum in the analysis of the modern era (Kuznets, 1959). Some, however, define "economic development" more or less synonymously, as "only such changes in economic life as are not forced upon it from without but arise by its own initiative, from within" (Schumpeter, 1961), or "the process whereby the real per capita income of a country increases over a long period of time" (Meier, 1970). In many contexts "development" has the additional connotation of an automatic progression according to a fixed schema, what used to be termed "evolution" in the nineteenth century and is still so designated in French. Thus, when a "traditional society" achieves what is called a take-off, "growth becomes its normal condition; compound interest becomes built, as it were, into habits and institutional structure" (Rostow, 1962). As used by many, "development" has come to mean also "change in the direction that the speaker thinks desirable" (Mair, 1975).

If the presently occasional usage becomes general, the distinction would be useful between economic growth, a historical or analytical process studied apart from political influences, and economic development, the consequences of policies proposed or adopted in order to initiate or accelerate economic growth. The branch of learning called "development economics" encompasses both, using theoretical constructs from Adam Smith on, sometimes combining these with theories from sociology, history, and other disciplines into the study of modernization, and applying all of this to the enunciation of either narrowly economic or broad social policy (cf. Powelson, 1979).

In the West the economic growth of the modern period was associated with a phenomenal increase of population, Stage II of the familiar *demographic transition. As the life-saving techniques of Western science were transferred to less developed countries, the consequent population explosion often impeded efforts to develop their economies. How high a proportion of demographic works relates in one way or another to changes or proposed changes in the economy is suggested in the useful classification developed by Nancy Birdsall (1977; cf. International Labor Office, 1979). Population can be viewed as the independent or the dependent variable, and its relation to development can be analyzed as a factor in the whole economy or in such key microsocial factors as family size. Many of the variables that correlate with either macro or micro factors, however, cannot be designated unambiguously as causes or consequences. For instance, if a woman works outside the home, she is likely to want fewer children; but if she has many children, she may be induced to augment the family income by working outside the home. Or, it has been shown in a number of countries that the larger the size of the family, the poorer the health of the children, but it is typical also that families of the lower classes are generally larger. Compared with the complexity of empirical reality, most research has been somewhat simplistic; in a review by William P. McGreevy and Nancy Birdsall (1974), only one study was considered to be "good," and all the rest of the seventeen examined were rated as "fair" or "poor." There is no consensus on any of the basic questions pertaining to economic-population relations—whether industrialization of the whole world is possible or, if so, desirable; whether *aid by developed to less developed countries is useful in the diffusion of modernist culture; and whether population growth should be, or can be, impeded as a precondition to significant economic development. One of the sharpest criticisms of the publications during a "profoundly unsatisfactory era—the Aristotelian era"—was in a review by John †Caldwell (1981) of an allegedly typical work of that period, *Population and Economic Change in Developing Countries*, edited by Richard †Easterlin. Hardly any of the authors in this symposium and very few of the discussants had ever lived or done research in a less developed country. Their generalizations, based mainly on Western experiences, were, according to this critique, sometimes dubious and sometimes flat wrong—such as the statement that the lower wages of women and children reflect their lower productivity rather than norms to maintain the social fabric. Both in this work and more generally, each less developed country is treated as an autonomous unit, though the influence of the West on social change—even if not necessarily on economic development—has been pervasive. Even so, in Caldwell's view, hardly anyone in such a setting has the wide range of options open to a middle-class American woman, which practitioners of the *New Home Economics postulate when they transfer their mode of analysis to less developed countries.

REFERENCES: Nancy Birdsall, "Analytical Approaches to the Relationship of Population Growth and Development," *Population and Development Review*, 3 (1977), 62-102. John C. Caldwell, Review of Richard Easterlin, ed., *Population and Economic Change in Developing Countries, Journal of Political Economy*, 89 (1981), 830-834. International Labor Office, *Population and Development: A Progress Report on ILO Research, with Special Reference to Labour, Employment, and Income Distribution* (2nd ed.; Geneva, 1979). Simon Kuznets, *Six Lectures on Economic Growth* (Glencoe, Ill.: Free Press, 1959). Lucy Mair, "Development," *Man*, 10 (1975), 607-612. William P. McGreevy and Birdsall, *The Policy Relevance of Recent Research on Fertility* (Washington, D.C.: Smithsonian Institution, 1974). Gerald M. Meier, *Leading Issues in Economic Development* (New York: Oxford University Press, 1970). John P. Powelson, *A Select Bibliography on Economic Development with Annotations* (Boulder, Colo.: Westview Press, 1979). W. W. Rostow, *The Stages of Economic Growth* (Cambridge, England: University Press, 1962). Joseph A. Schumpeter, *The Theory of Economic Development* (New York: Oxford University Press, 1961).

Economic Man, or *Homo œconomicus*, the personification of rational behavior. It was an axiom of Jeremy †Bentham's utilitarianism that every person seeks the maximum "pleasure" and tries to avoid as much "pain" as possible. Something of this view was incorporated into the classical economics that was evolving during Bentham's lifetime; but †Malthus's program to avoid the disasters of the positive checks, for example, consisted essentially in attempts to enhance the rationality of the overfertile. In the latter decades of the nineteenth century, when the thesis that all mankind behaves rationally was challenged, most economists avoided the issue by changing the axiom to a postulate: let us assume that in the marketplace at least rationality describes the modal behavior of most persons and proceed to develop theory from that base. That the issue is still with us is suggested by a recent work of Harvey †Leibenstein (1976). In his view, for Economic Man one should substitute "S.R. Man," with the initials standing for "selective rationality": people behave rationally in some contexts, less so in others, and not at all so in others. On the contrary, however, a fashion has developed to analyze *fertility as though virtually every potential parent carefully weighs the pros and cons of having another child and behaves accordingly; see *New Home Economics.

REFERENCES: Élie Halévy, *The Growth of Philosophic Radicalism* (Boston: Beacon Press, 1966; French original, 1928). Harvey Leibenstein, *Beyond Economic Man: A New Foundation for Microeconomics* (Cambridge, Mass.: Harvard University Press, 1976).

economics, conventionally defined as the study of how scarce resources are allocated among competing uses, ought logically to include population trends in its purview. For if the population increases, to take one example of the usual interrelation, until the children mature, demand will generally rise faster than supply, and consumption faster than production. Political economy, the composite discipline out of which modern economics arose, did include a simplified version of †Malthus's principle of population. By the end of the nineteenth century, however, it was possible to write a general treatise on economics with hardly any reference to population, and many economists today still work in the latter tradition.

Those in the discipline who in recent decades have written on demography have typically concentrated on one of several subspecialties (but see Schultz, 1981). The wealth of nations, the problem that classical economists dealt with concerning their own countries, has been broadened to include less developed countries, and the range of variables in the study of *economic development has brought the new subdiscipline of "development economics" closer to the original political economy (e.g., Goldberg, 1975; Robinson, 1975; Stamper, 1977). Partly reflecting this renewed emphasis and partly stimulating it, such population economists as Joseph †Spengler have reviewed the works of some of the most important analysts of the past two centuries, noting how each fitted population trends into his economic framework. The momentous expansion of *historical demography has stimulated a new interest in economic history, with a revised examination of how the level of living changed during the early modern period.

The factor in contemporary Western societies on which many economists have focused their analysis is fertility (but see also *migration; *mortality; *work force). By the 1950s not only were most American couples using contraceptives, but they generally preferred a small or a relatively small number of children; thus, the earlier differences in family size by social class, urban-rural residence, religion, or whatever were becoming too slight to distinguish by the gross comparisons of conventional social analysis. Demographers tried to refine their studies by using survey data on the use of contraceptives, the preferred family size, and other relevant attitudes; and to this effort economists brought their concept of *utility. Potential parents, it has been argued, weigh the *costs of childbearing against the benefits they derive from it and decide whether to have a (or another) child essentially in the same way as whether to purchase a major consumer product (Becker, 1960). This mode of micro-economic analysis has generated a substantial body of writings (e.g., Espenshade, 1972; Hoffman et al., 1978; Cramer, 1979; Thornton, 1979), as well as a good deal of criticism (e.g., Blake, 1968; Leibenstein, 1974); cf. Gary †Becker; *New Home Economics; *wealth-flow theory.

The middle-class American couple that decides to have a child must expect to pay out over some two decades something like $85,000 against a return only in such psychic values as family pride or the reproduction of oneself. If individuals in fact do rationally balance one against the other, they do so by applying nonmonetary values, which in the typical micro-economic presentation are subsumed under "taste." How a cohort's values develop has been the central theme of another economist, Richard †Easterlin. Simply put, his thesis is that change in the average size of American families is cyclical: large cohorts who enter the labor market are restricted in their job opportunities by their numbers, and they react by having fewer children; a generation later, when the consequent small cohorts seek employment, they get good positions and rapid promotions, and spend some of their income on larger families. The theory, a generalization from the *baby boom and the absence of the anticipated *echo, includes both sociological and economic elements. In some respects, thus, it also returns to the broader political economy of the early nineteenth century.

REFERENCES: Gary Becker, "An Economic Analysis of Fertility," in National Bureau of Economic Research, *Demographic and Economic Change in Developed Countries* (Princeton, N.J.: Princeton University Press, 1960). Judith Blake, "Are Babies Consumer Durables? A Critique of the Economic Theory of Reproductive Motivation," *Population Studies*, 22 (1968), 5-25. James C. Cramer, "Employment Trends of Young Mothers and the Opportunity Cost of Babies in the United States," *Demography*, 16 (1979), 177-197. Thomas J. Espenshade, "The Price of Children and Socio-economic Theories of Fertility," *Population Studies*, 26 (1972), 207-221. David Goldberg, "Socioeconomic Theory and Differential Fertility: The Case of the LDCs," *Social Forces*, 54 (1975), 84-106. Lois Wladys Hoffman, Arland Thornton, and Jean Denby Manis, "The Value of Children to Parents in the United States," *Journal of Population*, 1 (1978), 91-131. Harvey Leibenstein, "An Interpretation of the Economic Theory of Fertility: Promising Path or Blind Alley?" *Journal of Economic Literature*, 12 (1974), 457-479. Warren C. Robinson, ed., *Population and Development Planning* (New York: Population Council, 1975). T. Paul Schultz, *Economics of Population* (Reading, Mass.: Addison-Wesley,

1981). B. Maxwell Stamper, *Population and Planning in Developing Nations: A Review of Sixty Development Plans for the 1970s* (New York: Population Council, 1977). Thornton, "Fertility and Income, Consumption Aspirations, and Child Quality Standards," *Demography*, 16 (1979), 157-175.

ecosystem, an *ecological community and its physical environment viewed as a closed system within which a cycling of nutrients and a flow of energy take place. The special study of this interaction of living beings and nonliving matter (in technical terms, biotic and abiotic factors) is called "ecosystem ecology." In human ecology the term denotes a system of inputs and outputs among organized populations by which foodstuffs are cycled.

REFERENCES: Lee R. Dice, *Natural Communities* (Ann Arbor: University of Michigan Press, 1952). Eugene P. Odum, "The Strategy of Ecosystem Development," *Science*, 164 (1969), 262-270.

Ecuador: Demographic Institutions

The Ecuadorian Association for Family Welfare (APROFE), a private organization, started in 1969 to train medical and paraprofessional personnel in demography and in the techniques of contraception. In 1976 it expanded its activities to the dissemination of such information to the general public. Address: Asociación Pro-Bienestar de la Familia Ecuatoriana, Seis de Marzo no. 610 y Velez, Guayaquil.

The Ministry of Public Health directs a National Family Planning Program, of which the evaluation unit issued a report authored by Mario †Jaramillo Gómez, *Estudios de Evaluación* (Guayaquil, 1972). Address: Ministerio de Salud Pública, Programa Nacional de Planificación Familiar del Ecuador and Unidad de Evaluación de Programas de Planificación, Guayaquil.

The National Bureau of Statistics and Censuses, a unit of the National Planning Board, conducts the country's censuses, the most recent of which was in 1974 (one was announced for 1983). It publishes an annual compendium of vital statistics and an irregular statistical series that includes data on the population. The Center for Demographic Analysis, one unit of the bureau, constructs population projections, analyzes the relation between demographic and social-economic variables, and issues reports on employment, internal migration, mortality, and other factors related to the population. Another unit of the bureau, the Department of Censuses and Research, analyzes the results of enumerations. Address: Junta Nacional de Planificación y Coordinación Económica, Instituto Nacional de Estadística y Censos, Centro de Análisis Demográfico and Departamento de Censos y Encuestas, Avenida 10 de Agosto 229, Quito.

editing and **imputation** are used by census and other statisticians to denote various corrections of *errors and other changes made in the processing of data between their initial collection and the printing of the final version. Some such revisions are generally accepted as useful, but others are the subject of considerable controversy among professional demographers (cf. Cohen, 1982). In the United States the issues involved were given a thorough public airing when some of the results of the 1980 count were challenged in the courts because they were based on imputation.

When portions of a census form have been left blank or filled in with manifestly inaccurate or contradictory responses, if these lapses are discovered by a field supervisor, the best procedure is to return to the respondent and have the information corrected. This so-called "field editing," a valuable way to increase accuracy and completeness, is constrained only by the time and money available for the census. Subsequently, when data are fed into a computer, it can perform what is called a "validation check," detecting such keypunch errors as coding "3" for sex when only either "1" or "2" is permissible. The computer can also work out what is called a "redundant imputation," filling in a bit of information omitted on the form but unambiguously implied in other responses. For example, if a respondent has left blank the space specified in the form for sex, but if it is indicated by the given name, the marital status as the wife of a male, and so on, to denote the person "female" in the processed data adds to completeness with no sacrifice of accuracy. The computer can also correct such presumably impossible combinations in the reported data as a male "housewife," a "widow" aged 10 years, a native-born "alien," and the like. Sometimes, however, it may not be obvious which half of the contradiction is in error.

Other types of revisions are more questionable. In what Judith †Banister (1980) terms a "semi-informed" imputation, the computer uses bits of evidence from the rest of the questionnaire or from other sources to make a plausible, but not necessarily correct, emendation in the reported responses. In what she terms a "blind" imputation, a person's or household's existence and characteristics are assumed from data on presumably similar components of the population. In the 1960 census of the United States, for example, some "occupied" housing units had no one reported as living in them; and a total of 776,665 persons, or 0.4 percent of the official count, were imputed by replicating households in the same neighborhood on which there were data. In 1970, the census form asked a sample of households to give the 1969 wage or salary income for each person in the household who worked, but for 11 percent of the households some part of the total income was imputed. The difference between 0.4 percent and 11 percent, in some critics' view, is one between reasonable editing, to which they do not object, and so great a revision that the user of the resultant tables cannot always be sure what they mean.

The alternative to imputation is to revert to the procedure used in United States census reports before computer techniques were fully developed—that is, to list in each table a residual proportion labeled "Not stated" or "Unknown." This information is sometimes useful in itself, as an indication of how intrusive respondents find particular questions. Thus, those who opposed adding a question on religious affiliation to the 1960 census schedule, for instance, were seldom aware that in sample surveys a far higher proportion of respondents refused to give their income than their religion. Information that is typically used to compare subgroups in a population may be based on imputation rates that differ significantly from one group to another. From a question in the 1970 census on the number of children ever born, for example, the Bureau of the Census arrived at figures by imputing answers for 4.6 percent of all ever married women in the country, for 10.7 of ever married women aged 15-19, and for 20.0 percent of ever married black women aged 15-19 in the Northeast. Yet many using such statistics would be interested precisely in the contrast between the very young and older mothers or between black and white mothers—that is, in the parts of the data most suspect because of the way in which they were processed.

Imputation of data requires a computer. One program developed in Canada was never used even for the Canadian census, presumably because it was too complex (cf. Fellegi and Holt, 1976). Dubious practices of census bureaus become much worse when they are transferred to places lacking equipment or personnel of comparable quality. Most statisticians of less developed countries receive some training from their counterparts in the West, either in universities or directly through programs initiated by census administrators; and it may be no service to instruct them in procedures that depend on computers and software that are unavailable and that may encourage a sloppy enumeration in the belief that all errors in the count will eventually be corrected.

REFERENCES: Judith Banister, "Use and Abuse of Census Editing and Imputation," *Asian and Pacific Census Forum*, 6 (February, 1980), 1-2, 16-20. Steven B. Cohen, "An Analysis of Alternative Imputation Strategies for Individuals with Partial Data in the National Medical Care Expenditure Survey," *Review of Public Data Use*, 10 (1982), 153-165. Ivan P. Fellegi and D. Holt, "A Systematic Approach to Automatic Edit and Imputation," *Journal of the American Statistical Association*, 17 (1976), 17-35.

education is related to demography most directly in that, within the framework of any country's school system, the age structure largely determines the numbers that attend various grades. In all Western countries the large cohorts of the *baby boom, for instance, found the facilities at primary, secondary, and college levels to be successively overcrowded; and as much smaller cohorts followed them, in some instances the contrary adjustment entailed disruptive cuts in budgets and staffs. Education is often used to analyze demographic variables, especially fertility (Graff, 1979). Those who advocate improving the work force particularly of less developed countries through investment in so-called *human capital sometimes argue that this would also tend to reduce the country's average family size.

In the United States a question on schooling has been asked in every census since 1840, and these decennial data are supplemented regularly through sample surveys (cf. Folger and Nam, 1967). In 1970 about three-quarters of young people graduated from high school, contrasted with about one-third in the early 1930s. And in 1974 more than 60 percent of high school graduates entered college, contrasted with 39 percent in 1932. The sizable shift can be indicated also by other measures. Of persons 25 to 29, the percent of whites who had completed only 5 years or less of schooling fell from 3.4 in 1940 to 0.8 in 1978;

of nonwhites, from 26.7 to 1.3. Or, the median years of schooling completed rose for whites from 8.5 in 1920 to 12.9 in 1978; for nonwhites, from 5.4 to 12.7 (Grant and Lind, 1979). By various indices, in other words, the notorious difference between the educations of whites and blacks has been almost eliminated during the past several decades.

That years of schooling are used to measure education, however, assumes that each period spent in whatever school yields essentially equivalent results (cf. Mare, 1981). Another quantitative index—dollars spent per pupil enrolled— has been used repeatedly to demonstrate that throughout the United States facilities are not equivalent. The federal summary of statistics includes an index of quality called the National Assessment of Educational Progress. From 1969-70 to 1972-73, this showed a decline in all regions of the country, for both sexes and colors, at almost all levels of schooling and in places of almost every size, virtually irrespective of the education of the pupils' parents. From 1970-71 to 1974-75, there was a slight improvement in children aged 9, no change at age 13, and a continued decline at age 17 (Grant and Lind, 1979, Table 26). Between 1977–78 and 1981–82, the test scores of 9-year olds rose by only 1.0 percent and those of 13-year olds by 3.9 percent, but those of 17-year olds fell slightly. At age 17 the scores of blacks were 15 to 16 percentage points under the national average in reading, mathematics, and science; and those of Hispanics were 8 to almost 11 points under that modest norm (Grant and Snyder, 1983, chap. 1).

These data suggest that enrollment figures rose so dramatically partly because of the ever more prevalent practice of keeping children in school and promoting them from grade to grade, whether or not they had learned anything. In an extreme instance a young man who was graduated from a New York high school, having received H (for Honor) in English throughout his senior year, could not read traffic signs and therefore could not qualify for a driver's license (Lowe, 1961).

Secondary and college education has been linked to the work force by particular qualifications set for various occupations, either a high school or college diploma or a more specific certification or degree (Bowen, 1981). The consequence, particularly in less developed countries, has been what Ronald †Dore (1976) called the diploma disease, the adaptation of student, instructor, and institution to an overriding demand that formal qualification be attained even at the sacrifice of genuine learning. In the United States, as it became obvious that certification barriers often did not distinguish the better from the less qualified, a common response has been to denounce all such requirements as unfair, undemocratic, or racist.

REFERENCES: William G. Bowen, "Market Prospects for Ph.D.s in the United States," *Population and Development Review*, 7 (1981), 475-488. Ronald Dore, *The Diploma Disease: Education, Qualification, and Development* (Berkeley: University of California Press, 1976). John K. Folger and Charles B. Nam, *Education of the American Population* (Washington, D.C.: U.S. Government Printing Office, 1967). Harvey J. Graff, "Literacy, Education, and Fertility, Past and Present: A Critical Review," *Population and Development Review*, 5 (1979), 105-140. W. Vance Grant and C. George Lind, *Digest of Education Statistics, 1979* (Washington, D.C.: National Center for Education Statistics, 1979). Grant and Thomas D. Snyder, *Digest of Education Statistics, 1983–84* (Washington, D.C.: National Center for Education Statistics, 1983). Helen R. Lowe, ''The Whole-Word and Word-Guessing Game,'' in Charles C. Walcutt, ed., *Tomorrow's Illiterates: The State of Reading Instruction Today* (New York: Little, Brown, 1961). R. D. Mare, ''Trends in Schooling: Demography, Performance, and Organization,'' *Annals of the American Academy of Political and Social Science*, 453 (1981), 96-122.

Egypt, the most populous country of the Middle East, is typical of that diverse region. Like every other country except Lebanon (and, of course, Israel), Egypt is overwhelmingly Muslim. It has moved some distance toward modernism; less than Turkey, for example, but farther than most of the other countries in the Levant. Unlike Saudi Arabia, Egypt has not been transformed by its oil, which is nevertheless an important element of its economy. Egypt was briefly associated with Syria in the United Arab Republic, a short-lived attempt to work out pan-Arabism in state relations.

Only a decade after Mohammed's death in A.D. 632, his followers conquered Egypt and brought it both its Islamic religion and its Arabic language. From the beginning of the sixteenth century, Egypt was a province of the Ottoman Empire until Mohammed Ali (1769-1849), an army officer, succeeded in detaching it from Turkey and became the founder of a hereditary house in de facto control. His grandson Ismail, khedive (or viceroy) from 1863 to 1879, had traveled widely in Europe; he set about to complete his country's modernization, using profits from the sale of cotton for a vast expansion of primary education and massive public works. The major project was the Suez Canal, which, shortly after it opened in 1869, was taken over by Britain (cf. Abu-Lughod, 1965a). Its security, however, was under constant threat, and after several years of inter-mittent fighting, British forces occupied Cairo. With no formal annexation, Britain assumed control of Egypt's affairs. Evelyn Baring, Lord Cromer, the British consul-general from 1883 to 1907, put the country's finances in order with a revised tax system and freed the peasant from the corvée; his successors encouraged the growth of education and supervised the introduction of a liberal constitution. After Turkey's defeat in World War I, Egypt became a nominally independent kingdom, but an Anglo-Egyptian treaty restricting British forces to the Canal Zone was not signed until 1936. The nationalist sentiment building up through the decades finally, in 1952, culminated in the establishment of the Arab Socialist Republic under the head of a Free Officers Movement, Gamal Abdal Nasser (Vatikiotis, 1980).

The British role in Egypt was anomalous, and the irregularity of its presence undoubtedly aggravated Egyptian opposition. Britain was interested in Egypt and the Sudan only because of the canal, and in the canal only because of India; yet its influence on Egypt's economy and institutions was important, in some respects decisive. Reformers like Muhammad Abduh (1849-1905) had been seeking a way to accommodate Islam to modern life-styles (cf. Adams, 1968), but then and later one significant reinforcement of traditionalism was that for many Egyptians "modernist" was identified as "English."

Egypt is a large country of over 363,000 square miles (just under 200,000 square kilometers), but most of it is desert. About 98 percent of the population—that is, all but the few Bedouins—live on less than 5 percent of the land, the Nile valley and delta. "Egypt enjoys the dubious distinction," as John Waterbury (1978, pp. 85-111) remarked, "of demonstrating the basic resource ratios in stark simplicity." The perhaps 2.5 million inhabitants of the country when Napoleon invaded it in 1798-99 were no more than the present population of just the northern sector of Cairo. From that base to the estimated 47 million in 1984, the population increased not quite nineteen times, while the amount of cultivated land about doubled. The population density in 1980 was almost 3,000 per habitable square mile, close to the highest in the world (Gallagher, 1981). As typically when there are too many people to work small plots, the productivity of agricultural labor fell. In the mid-1950s Charles †Issawi (1954, p. 252) estimated that as much as half of the agrarian population was economically surplus in the sense that if those workers left the land the amount of food produced would not be cut. This "hidden unemployment" is not corrected in a family enterprise, for no peasant will fire a kinsman who is not needed; thus, the gross disparity between land and people understates the ratio between food produced and consumed. When Kingsley †Davis and Hilda Hertz †Golden (1954) devised the concept of *overurbanization, they cited Egypt as the prime instance of an "overurbanized" country—that is, one in which "the densely settled and impoverished countryside is pushing people into the cities because they have no other alternative." The urban sector, defined as those living in centers of substantial size, amounted to a quarter of the total in the 1930s, a third by 1950, two-fifths by 1965, and almost half around 1980. Most who moved to cities did so in spite of the lack of openings in urban occupations for which they were qualified.

In 1952, when Nasser took power, the country was overwhelmingly agricultural, and according to a 1980 estimate about 45 percent of the work force was still tilling the land. Yet in that year Egypt had to bring in from abroad $2.3 billion in food products, with cereals making up some 55 to 60 percent of its total imports. On a free market, staples would therefore be very expensive, but the government spent about $3 billion a year, or 11 percent of the Gross Domestic Product, in subsidizing food prices. The economy has not broken down only because of the sizable grants and loans fed into it. In 1977, when the International Monetary Fund (IMF) pressured Egypt to abandon price supports for household commodities, the response to the first moves in that direction was mass food riots (Carim and Mahiouz, 1981).

One way of reducing the pressure has been to extend the area under cultivation. The Aswan High Dam, built with Soviet assistance at a cost of approximately $1 billion, was the centerpiece of Nasser's economic program. When it was completed in 1971, the expectation was that it would double the acreage that could be cultivated. Only a fraction of the new irrigation, and only a third of the anticipated electric power, were realized; and drastic changes in the Nile valley ecology created many new problems. Even so, the greater emphasis given to agriculture in the 1980-84 government investment program was concentrated in a large-scale land reclamation project, with 200,000 to 250,000 hectares of desert to be brought under cultivation over the 5 years (Carim and Mahiouz, 1981).

A second way of mitigating population pressure has been to foster emigration. Until the mid-1960s few Egyptians left the country, either temporarily or permanently, for the necessary permission was seldom granted. In November 1964, for instance, of the 282 applications to emigrate, the Ministry of Labor approved only 27, as well as issuing 125 permits to work abroad. A government committee was established in 1969 to formulate new policy, and for several years outward movement was both encouraged and impeded with continuing restrictions. After Nasser's death in 1970, the partial shift to a market economy was reflected also in a freer movement abroad. Article 52 of the 1971 Constitution stipulated the right to emigrate either temporarily or permanently, but applications were still supervised by a large number of committees with vague jurisdictions and overlapping functions. Over two decades, with hesitations and some lapses, government policy changed successively from a reluctance to lose anyone from the population, to a quota system for professionals and skilled workers in short supply, to a relatively free movement, to an enthusiastic promotion of exporting surplus labor (Dessouki, 1982). Especially for those in the public sector, who earn far less than in equivalent private jobs, a contract to work in other Arab countries can be a bonanza. A professor, as one example, can increase his income tenfold by teaching at a Saudi university. In 1980, remittances from abroad amounted to $2.9 billion, which combined with oil sales, Suez Canal fees, and tourism have resulted in a quite sizable influx of income (Horton, 1981).

The most direct mode of controlling population growth, by a limitation of births, must be judged on the basis of grossly inadequate data (see also *Egypt: Demographic Institutions). As in less developed countries generally, the rapid increase in numbers followed a sharp reduction in mortality. The crude death rate, stable at about 27 from the 1920s through World War II, fell to 19 in the early 1950s, then to 15 in the 1970s and 11 in 1984. In most of the Arab world the birth rate in the 1920s and 1930s was close to 50 per thousand, and some analysts have put Egypt's fertility in the same category (e.g., el-Badry, 1965). In Pat Caldwell's view (1977), however, the very high population density and severe shortage of land had brought about a lower birth rate in Egypt, perhaps something under 44. Mohamed A. †el-Badry (1956) and Janet †Abu-Lughod (1965b) tried to use the data from the 1947 and 1960 censuses, respectively, to ferret out any patterns of differential fertility, but with no very satisfactory results. Completed family size in 1947 was estimated at 6.2 to 6.4 children; and from the analysis of the 1960 census, the indication was that fertility was rising.

Apparently the more or less stable birth rate began to fall during the 1960s, moving from the mid-40s to the mid-30s. Presumably this decline was due to the wider availability of contraceptives, both commercially and through private clinics, and then, after the government program was started in 1966, through its not very efficient services. From 1972 on, however, there was a steady rise in the estimated crude birth rates, from 34.4 in that year to 39.3 in 1979 (Gallagher, 1981) and 38 in 1984. Although these figures are not precise, the trend they show undoubtedly reflects the actual situation. That this rise in fertility indicated a failure of the national family-planning program has been pointed out by virtually every commentator—including President Anwar Sadat's wife, Jihan, who asserted in 1981 that all efforts up to that date had been futile. But why, apart from ineffective antinatalist efforts, should the birth rate have gone up? One study suggests that no single policy would work, because of the sizable differences between urban and rural populations, as well as between various regions of the country, and that therefore a differentiated program is advisable (Kelley et al., 1982).

According to the *wealth-flow theory, as long as it is in the economic interest of parents to bring more children into the world, they will be rather impervious to the antinatalist message of *KAP programs (John Caldwell, 1982). In an interesting application of this thesis to the Egyptian case, Pat Caldwell (1977) speculated that, for most of the population, children pay their own way and, indeed, that prosperity often rises with family size. Whenever the alternative would be to hire a worker, it is far cheaper to rear a child. In rural areas children do much work before and after school, the hours that in the hot climate are best for physical labor. The petty vendors in the cities bring their children into their ventures at a very young age, and with the subsidized food prices, they are cheap to feed. In short, if this argument is valid, the mere availability of contraceptives combined with propaganda favoring their use will not suffice to bring down fertility to acceptable levels.

How do those responsible for the carrying out of population planning react to such an argument? In 1972, John Waterbury (1978, pp. 49-65) interviewed twenty-three Egyptians involved either in the government's family–planning program or in related fields. His purpose was to find out how these administrators estimated the importance of the population problem, its causes and consequences, and the best way to cope with it. Most of the respondents were reluctant even to think of family planning as the acquisition of individual responsibility for that portion of one's life that is subject to control. The major exception to this pragmatic norm was Aziz †Bindary, in whose opinion "the real solution is the liberation of rural women and their entry into the work force. This *alone* is what will lead to a lowering of the birth rate and to the solution of population growth in Egypt." A somewhat similar view was expressed by the Governor of Fayyum Province: "No one practices planning other than those who understand the necessity of planning. And people who don't read or write don't understand. In my view family planning begins with the eradication of illiteracy, [and] for that reason I have decided to transfer a large part of the [provincial] family-planning budget to literacy programs'' (quoted in Waterbury, 1978, p. 68).

To the degree that the control of family size is more than a technical problem, the trend in Egypt in the early 1980s has not been encouraging. Anwar Sadat, who succeeded Nasser as president in 1970, set a new political and social-economic course, which in many respects aggravated the hostility of fundamentalist Muslims. He offered asylum to the Shah of Iran, a refugee from the Islamic regime; he signed a treaty with Israel, which all other Arab states regard as their main enemy; he shifted Egypt's general orientation toward the United States, Israel's ally. Opposition developed in several organizations said to be financed by the Libyan government and Saudi private sources: Gamaat Islameya (Islamic Societies), informal groups of fundamentalists particularly strong in the universities; the Jihad Group (the name means "Holy War"); and the Muslim Brothers, less strong than they once were but reputedly still influential. The strengthened religious sentiment was reflected in higher attendance at mosques, the spread of traditional dress to perhaps a third of the female students at universities, the larger number of protests that were more or less freely permitted if organized around a religious theme, the accommodation of the government to this trend. The president, as one instance, started to stress his first name, identifying himself as Mohammed Anwar al-Sadat (Horton, 1981). In 1980 a draft of a Law for the Protection of Ethics was published; it provided, among other things, for a special court to try any who advocated antireligious ideologies. Understandably it was opposed by all modernists, but at least some informed observers believed the government was succeeding in its effort to placate the extremists. An authoritative review of events in 1979-80 opened with the judgment that "Egypt could justify its claims to being 'an island of stability' " (Legum, 1981).

On October 6, 1981, Sadat was assassinated, to be succeeded by Vice-President Hosni Mubarak. Within a week of Mubarak's swearing in, an estimated four thousand suspects were arrested. According to the government's statement, there had been a plot to kill the entire secular leadership of the country and replace it with a fundamentalist regime. There would be little place in such a society, should it come into being, for women's work outside the home or an expansion of female education, which the two officials cited earlier deemed to be the surest routes to a control of Egypt's population (cf. *Islam; *purdah).

REFERENCES: Janet Abu-Lughod, "Tale of Two Cities: The Origins of Modern Cairo," *Comparative Studies in Society and History*, 7 (1965a), 430-460; "The Emergence of Differential Fertility in Urban Egypt," *Milbank Memorial Fund Quarterly*, 43 (1965b), 235-253. Charles C. Adams, *Islam and Modernism in Egypt* (New York: Russell and Russell, 1968). Mohamed A. el-Badry, "Some Aspects of Fertility in Egypt," *Milbank Memorial Fund Quarterly*, 34 (1956), 22-43; "Trends in the Components of Population Growth in the Arab Countries of the Middle East," *Demography*, 2 (1965), 140-186. John C. Caldwell, *Theory of Fertility Decline* (New York: Academic Press, 1982). Pat Caldwell, "Egypt and the Arabic and Islamic Worlds," in John C. Caldwell, ed., *The Persistence of High Fertility* (Canberra: Australian National University, Department of Demography, 1977). Enver Carim and Mohand Mahiouz, "Egypt," *Middle East Review, 1982* (Saffron Waldon, England, 1981). Kingsley Davis and Hilda Hertz Golden, "Urbanization and the Development of Preindustrial Areas," *Economic Development and Cultural Change*, 3 (1954), 6-24. Ali E. Hillal Dessouki, "The Shift in Egypt's Migration Policy, 1952-1978," *Middle Eastern Studies*, 18 (1982), 53-68. Charles F. Gallagher, "Population and Development in Egypt," 2 parts, American Universities Field Staff, *Reports*, nos. 31-32, Africa (1981). Alan W. Horton, "Egypt Revisited," American Universities Field Staff, *Reports*, no. 23, Africa (1981). Charles P. Issawi, *Egypt at Mid-Century: An Economic Survey* (London: Oxford University Press, 1954). Allen C. Kelley, Atef M. Khalifa and M. Nabil el-Khorazaty, *Population and Development in Rural Egypt* (Durham, N.C.: Duke University Press, 1982). Colin Legum, ed., *Middle East Contemporary Survey*, vol. 4: *1979-80* (New York: Holmes and Meier, 1981). P. J. Vatikiotis, *The History of Egypt* (2nd ed.; Baltimore: Johns Hopkins University Press, 1980). John Waterbury, *Egypt: Burdens of the Past, Options for the Future* (Bloomington: Indiana University Press, 1978).

Egypt: Demographic Institutions

For the Cairo Demographic Center, see the discussion under *United Nations.

The University of Alexandria includes teaching and research in population geography in its Faculty of Arts. Fathy M. †Abou-Aianah was a member in 1981. Address: University of Alexandria, 3 Al-Gueish Avenue, Shatby, Alexandria.

The Social Research Center at the American University in Cairo, founded in 1953, was in 1981 under the direction of Saad M. †Gadalla. Its program includes training and research related to social-economic development, family planning, rural and urban problems, and other facets of population studies. Address: 113 Sharia Kasr, El-Aini, Cairo.

At the University of Cairo, there is an Institute of Research and Statistical Studies, headed until his death in 1971 by Hassan †Hussein. The director in 1982 was Saad el-Din el-Shayal. Its research and training, as well as its *Egyptian Statistical Journal*, often relate to demography. Address: 5 El-Goheiny Street, Dokki, Cairo.

A Department of Population and Biostatistics was established in the Institute in 1963; in 1981 its chairman was Atef M. †Khalifa. Its research has been concentrated on fertility and family planning, particularly in rural areas, and some of the findings have been published in its *Egyptian Population and Family Planning Review*. Address: 5 Tharwat Street, Orman, Ghiza, Cairo.

The government's Population and Family Planning Board in 1980 was chaired by Aziz †Bindary. It publishes a journal, *Dirasat-Sukkaniyah/Population Studies*. It has undertaken a sample survey of contraceptive practices among the rural population and published the preliminary findings in Arabic. Address: P.O. Box 1036, Cairo.

The Central Agency for Public Mobilization and Statistics conducts the country's censuses, of which the last was in 1976. It publishes in Arabic annual summaries of vital statistics. Its more general *Statistical Yearbook*, which appears also in an English edition, has estimates on the size and main characteristics of the population. One unit of the agency, the Population Research and Studies Center, was established in 1971 and in 1980 was under the direction of Reda Kandil. It conducted a fertility survey in 1980 and published a four-volume report in 1983. Address: P.O. Box 2086, Nasr City, Cairo.

elasticity, in economics the relative responsiveness in one variable to changes in another; in the commonest usage, the percentage changes in supply and demand with a 1 percent difference in price are called the elasticity (or price elasticity) of supply and demand, respectively. Though the term is not common in demography, either the independent or the dependent variable can be population change.

elite, which was incorporated from the French so recently that it is still sometimes spelled with an accent, means the choice part of any class of people; specifically, the category of a society distinguished by its excellence, whether actual or claimed, and by the prestige and power associated with that quality. In the writings of Vilfredo †Pareto, who helped popularize the term, *elite* is value-free, denoting only those who score highest on a scale measuring some social value. According to what he called "the circulation of elites," there is a cyclical process of history by which new members are coopted into elites and, more fundamentally, one type of elite replaces another. Recently egalitarians have used *elite* (or such derivatives as "power elite" or "elitism") as a general pejorative, challenging not the superiority of any particular elite but rather the proposition that any sector of society can be superior.

REFERENCE: Vilfredo Pareto, *The Rise and Fall of the Elites*, with an introduction by Hans L. Zetterberg (New York: Bedminster Press, 1968).

ELL, or equivalent length of life, a demographic measure of economic development. One computes the length of life that, if it were identical for all persons in the population, would reflect the same social welfare as the actual distribution of deaths by age. Jacques Silber (1983), who proposed the new measure, compared it at length with a number of other indices of development.

REFERENCE: Jacques Silber, "ELL (The Equivalent Length of Life) or Another Attempt at Measuring Development," *World Development*, 11 (1983), 21-29.

El Salvador: Demographic Institutions

The Salvadoran Population Association began in 1969 as an informal group to collect and distribute demographic materials. The following year it started a program of research on various aspects of population and family planning, and the formal institution took place in 1977. The association trains physicians and others in the biology of reproduction and family planning, methods of contraception and especially sterilization. See *Políticas de Población y Desarrollo en El Salvador: Primera Reunión de Intercambio sobre Requerimientos de Investigación, San Salvador, 15 y 16 Diciembre, 1977* (San Salvador, 1978). Address:

Asociación Demográfica Salvadoreña, la Calle Pte. 1214, Apartado (06) 1338, San Salvador.

The Center of Population and the Family (CEPOFA) was established in 1975 to support the family as "a basic unit of society." It provides interested persons with a free informational bulletin and trains them in family planning by natural means. Address: Centro de Población y Familia, Avenida San José y Avenida Las Américas, Apartado Postal 1112, San Salvador.

The government's Bureau of Statistics and Censuses publishes an *Anuario Estadístico* and a biennial *El Salvador en Cifras*, both of which include population data. Address: Dirección General de Estadística y Censos, Calle Arce y 17 Avenida Sur no. 953, San Salvador.

The Ministry of Planning and Social-Economic Development issues twice each year a volume on *Indicadores Económicos y Sociales*, which includes estimates of all the basic demographic indicators. Address: Ministerio de Planificación y Coordinación del Desarrollo Económico y Social, Final Calle México y Avenida Los Diplomáticos, Barrio San Jacinto, San Salvador.

embryo, the early stage of development of a fertilized *ovum, in humans from about one week after fertilization to the end of the second (or, by some types of reckoning, the third) month.

embryology, the branch of zoology dealing with the development of the *embryo. Its importance in relation to demography is that a better understanding of the process of reproduction is likely to lead to new means of controlling it. See also *fetus, *ovum.

employment and **unemployment** are correlative terms, and the size of each thus depends in part on how the other is defined. Both together make up the *labor force, and how one delimits that entity also affects our conception of the two components. Partly because "unemployment" is a political issue of periodically great significance, its meaning and boundaries have remained rather imprecise.

So long as most workers were agriculturists, the concept of "employment" hardly arose. In good times and bad, with no sharp divisions by age, sex, or status, farmers, their families, and hired help worked the land, setting their hours by the natural rhythm of the seasons rather than by the *workweek. Something like this situation still obtains in much of the world, but in economically advanced countries the proportion of the *work force engaged in agriculture fell over several decades from more than half (a rough index of a "less developed country") to about a tenth or less. Comparative studies of agricultural labor are still difficult because, though women do much or even most of the work on a family farm, they are not treated consistently in the statistics of different countries— included or half-included as "unpaid family workers" in some cases, and in others omitted altogether since their work is equated with housework and is thus not a "gainful occupation."

Employment statistics developed along several routes. Unemployment insurance was made compulsory for some portions of the work force in Britain (1911), Austria (1920), and Germany (1927), and the records initiated with this reform eventually provided much information about *manpower more generally. The demobilization of armies after World War I, followed by the great depression of the 1930s, led in all developed countries to far wider measures to cope with unemployment and thus to efforts to measure it more accurately. As with such other paired concepts as *legitimacy-*illegitimacy, statistical attention has been focused less on the basic norm than on the social problem.

Data today are gathered from periodic surveys, registration at government unemployment offices, records on unemployment insurance or other types of relief, and trade-union rolls. According to the recommendations of the United Nations for the 1970 censuses, employed persons comprise all, including family workers, who had a job during a designated period or who had one from which they were temporarily absent because of illness or injury, vacation, or another temporary disorganization such as a strike or inclement weather. Unemployed persons comprise all who during the designated period were not working but were seeking work for pay or profit or, when employment opportunities were very limited, were not looking for a job because they believed that none was available for them. Persons who never worked are to be listed as unemployed if they were looking for a job, but to be classified separately. Those neither employed nor unemployed comprise the sector of the population that is not economically active: homemakers of either sex; students; persons who receive income from investments, pensions, and the like; those living on private or public relief. The minimum age is to be set in accordance with the national conditions, but in no case higher than 15 years (United Nations, 1967; see also International Labor Office, 1976).

The procedure in the United States, which evolved gradually over several decades, currently more or less follows the United Nations recommendations. Each month a sample of the civilian noninstitutional population aged 14 years and over are asked whether they worked for pay or profit during a specified week. Those who worked or were absent from their job for one of the reasons listed above are employed; those with no job who had been actively seeking work during the prior four weeks are unemployed. Full-time work is defined as thirty-five hours or more per week; the reasons for working fewer hours are classified as economic (no full-time jobs available) or individual (for example, poor health or personal preference). These data, published regularly by the U.S. Bureau of Labor Statistics, can be supplemented with information collected from "establishments" (that is, business firms) rather than households, and from totals of the Old Age, Survivors' and Disability Insurance (OASDI) records.

Even when the type of measure is similar, the concept of "unemployment" can differ considerably. Is someone to be counted who is marginal because of young or advanced age, marital status, or physical impairment? Is a "discouraged" person—that is, one not looking for work who might not accept any job for which he is suited—to be classified as unemployed; and how does one decide whether such an attitude exists? Is a part-time worker also partly unemployed? When official unemployment figures of other countries are compared with what they would be by American criteria, there are sometimes quite substantial differences (Myers, 1964). In the early 1960s, thus, the British rate of 1.9 percent would rise to 2.8 percent; the Italian rate of 6.3 percent would fall to 3.2 percent. In Japan unpaid family workers are included in the labor force if they worked one hour in the survey week, in the United States only if they worked fifteen hours or more. In Japan those temporarily laid off are classified as employed, in the United States as unemployed. Anyone who worked even one hour during the reference week is considered employed in the United States, but in Germany and Great Britain the reference period is a day. The "self-employed" are excluded from the employed category in many countries, but included in the United States and also in the denominator from which the rate of unemployment is calculated. As these examples suggest, the numerical figures even of industrial countries are not comparable without a good deal of adjustment (Gordon, 1968).

Various dissatisfactions with United States statistical procedures led to the establishment of a National Commission on Employment and Unemployment (Public Law 94-444, October 1, 1976), consisting of nine members appointed by the president with the consent of the Senate, seven broadly representative experts and two from the general public. The commission's charge was to assess the current concepts and methods of collection and analysis and to report its findings and recommendations within eighteen months. It began by issuing a series of narrow background papers by particular members or hired consultants, then published a preliminary report for public comment at the beginning of 1979 and, on Labor Day of that year, a final report, *Counting the Labor Force*, which was supplemented by three large appendix volumes, *Concepts and Data Needs*; *Data Collection, Processing, and Presentation: National and Local*; and *Readings on Labor Force Statistics*. According to the law by which it was established, the commission terminated its existence 180 days after the submission of its final report (see also Clogg, 1979; OECD, 1979).

The commission's recommendations related to definitions of concepts, methods of collecting and processing data, alignment of federal statistics with those collected by state and local agencies, and estimated costs of the changes it proposed. It judged the distinction between paid and unpaid work to be a sound basis for defining the labor force; thus, housework and similar activities around the home would continue to be omitted. Because the armed forces were made up of volunteers, the commission suggested that those stationed in the United States should be included in national employment figures. "Discouraged workers" should be left out of unemployment figures, but the commission recommended that those "marginally attached" to the labor force be redefined as follows: persons currently available for work and willing to accept a job who have actively sought one during the past six months. The lower limit of the age range included in the labor force should be 16 years, as in current practice, but young persons should be classified according to whether or not they are attending school. Volunteer work, omitted from the statistics as gathered, should be included in a special category since it contributes to the national output. More information should be gathered on the sources of income of unemployed persons, as well as whether those who are employed work full or part time. Up to the time of writing, none of these recommended changes had been implemented.

"Full employment," a goal of virtually every national policy, does not mean that everyone in the country has a job, but rather, in one of several possible definitions, that "unemployment does not exceed the minimum allowances that must be made for the effects of frictional and seasonal factors" (United Nations, 1949, p. 13). Frictional unemployment results from the time lag in the redeployment of labor: the shift of workers from one job to another or from one locality to another is not instantaneous; but the loss of income either to the individual or, in sum, to the nation is neither serious nor avoidable. Seasonal unemployment, on the contrary, can be a significant factor in the building trades, for instance, or in business enterprises dependent on agriculture or summer (or winter) sports. "Full employment" is defined by various nations' criteria as a labor market with no more than 1.5 to 4 percent of the work force out of jobs. Unemployment exceeding these proportions is in effect what is called "structural," the consequence of some basic long-term change in demand or technology. If the use of the private car declines as some economists have predicted, the automobile workers—heavily concentrated in a few midwestern states and with skills often not readily transferable to other jobs—would constitute a prime instance of structural unemployment.

For less developed countries and especially the rural sectors of their populations, "employment" and "unemployment" hardly apply even conceptually, not to say statistically. The term "underemployed," however, is ordinarily used with particular reference to such economies, though not very precisely. According to one recommended definition, a person of given training and work experience is underemployed if his hours of work are "inadequate in relation to specified norms or alternative employment." This underemployment may be "visible," directly measurable from survey data, or "invisible," reflecting a fundamental imbalance between labor and other factors in production and resulting in low productivity and income (International Labor Office, 1976, pp. 33-34). In India, as a typical example, an agriculturist is occupied on the average only about three months a year, and many landless laborers even less than that; and a substantial portion of the urban work force is no more fully occupied. In development plans for such countries, therefore, efficiency and speed are often sacrificed to the prior goal of absorbing people into labor-intensive projects (Coale and Hoover, 1958).

REFERENCES: Clifford C. Clogg, *Measuring Unemployment: Demographic Indicators for the United States* (New York: Academic Press, 1979). Ansley J. Coale and Edgar M. Hoover, *Population Growth and Economic Development in Low-Income Countries: A Case Study of India's Prospects* (Princeton, N.J.: Princeton University Press,

1958). Robert A. Gordon, "Employment and Unemployment," *International Encyclopedia of the Social Sciences*, 5, 49-60. International Labor Office, *International Recommendations on Labour Statistics* (Geneva, 1976). Robert J. Myers, "Unemployment in Western Europe and the United States," in Arthur M. Ross, ed., *Unemployment and the American Economy* (New York: Wiley, 1964). Organization for Economic Cooperation and Development, *Working Paper on Employment and Unemployment Statistics: Measuring Employment and Unemployment* (Paris, 1979). United Nations, *National and International Measures for Full Employment* (New York, 1949); *Principles and Recommendations for the 1970 Population Censuses*, Statistical Papers, Ser. M, no. 44 (New York, 1967).

enclave, an area completely surrounded by a territory with different characteristics, is contrasted with *exclave*, a disconnected section of territory situated in a foreign environment. For example, West Berlin is an enclave in East Germany, an exclave of West Germany. In the United States the term enclave is often used to refer to an urban ethnic neighborhood. See also *ghetto, *natural area, *neighborhood, *segregation.

endogamy and **exogamy** were coined by the Scottish theorist of social evolution, J. F. McLennan (1827-81), in his construct of the supposed history of family types. Today the terms are used particularly in the comparative analysis of family systems to denote the boundaries of permissible marriages. Rules of exogamy prescribe marriages outside a stipulated group—as a minimum (in the *incest taboo) the immediate family, and among primitive peoples also various lineages or territorial units. Rules of endogamy limit permitted spouses to members of specified groups, such as the *castes of Hindu India. In modern industrial societies the typical marriage system permits a person to marry whomever he or she chooses; generally the only absolute rule is the prohibition of incest. Selection of spouses, however, usually follows endogamous and exogamous customs; see also *intermarriage.

REFERENCES: Kingsley Davis, "Intermarriage in Caste Societies," *American Anthropologist*, 43 (1941), 376-395. Bronislaw Malinowski, *Sex, Culture, and Myth* (New York: Harcourt, Brace & World, 1962). Robert K. Merton, "Intermarriage and the Social Structure: Fact and Theory," *Psychiatry*, 4 (1941), 361-374.

energy, the capacity to do work, has been the key to man's rise to civilization. Primitive peoples depend on their own muscle power, supplemented in some instances by that of domestic animals; the cities of the ancient world could be built only by using whole armies of slaves. Wind power and nonelectric water power raised the potential substantially, but the first transformation to modern life came with the use of coal to produce steam. Today's sources of energy also include petroleum, natural gas, hydro-electricity, nuclear reactors, and solar radiation (e.g., Svalastoga, 1976; Stobaugh and Yergin, 1979; Longwell, 1982).

No kind of energy is without its problems. Some sources increase *pollution of the environment; others build up patterns of production that may falter when the supply of oil or natural gas or coal is depleted. Balancing the social gains against costs is difficult, for the equation involves such highly technical operations as the projection of demand and the estimate of future supplies of each source of energy. Unfortunately most of the argumentation has been highly emotional; see *conservation; *entropy; *environmentalism. William Blake's contrast between "dark Satanic mills" and "England's green and pleasant land" led without a break to the current worldwide opposition to nuclear power (e.g., Surrey and Huggett, 1976; McCracken, 1977). During the 1970s American environmentalists tried, usually with some success, to block the building of an Alaskan pipeline; to prevent the construction of oil refineries on the East Coast and of nuclear power plants anywhere; to limit offshore drilling and to oppose oil imports; to halt strip mining; and to discourage the construction of port facilities for the importation of liquefied gas. The subsequent "energy crisis" was in large part a political phenomenon, and no element of the continuing debate can be understood merely in technical terms. A good contrast is to be found between *A Time to Choose*, a report by the Energy Policy Project of the Ford Foundation (1974) and *No Time to Confuse*, a critique of that report by the Institute for Contemporary Studies (Adelman, 1975).

Population growth and well-being depend heavily on available energy, which in many respects can be substituted for food in the familiar axiom that people must have food in order to live. Agriculture has been revolutionized in part through artificial fertilizers manufactured in industrial plants. The process of removing salt from sea water, which is technically feasible, is impeded mainly by a lack of cheap energy; with it, deserts could become as productive as those in central and southern California. More generally, any progress in providing for a better and less expensive source of energy will mitigate the problems associated with the rapid growth of the world's population. According to the International Bank for Reconstruction and Development (1981), the greatest change in world development from the 1960s to the 1970s was the cost of energy. Over 40 percent of the substantial increase in exports from oil-importing countries was required to pay for the higher price of the imported oil. From one decade to the next the average annual growth in Gross National Product per capita changed as follows:

	Percent Annual Growth in GNP	
	1960-69	**1970-79**
All low-income oil importers	1.8	0.8
In Sub-Sahara Africa	1.7	−0.4
In Asia	1.8	1.1
All developed countries	3.5	2.7

In other words, the actions of the Organization of Petroleum-Exporting Countries (OPEC) were bothersome to industrial countries, but for many less developed countries, particularly in Africa, the very great rise in the price of oil was a disaster.

REFERENCES: Morris A. Adelman, ed., *No Time to Confuse: A Critique of the Final Report of the Energy Policy Project of the Ford Foundation* (San Francisco: Institute for Contemporary Studies, 1975). Ford Foundation, Energy Policy Project, *A Time to Choose* (Cambridge, Mass.: Ballinger, 1974). International Bank for Reconstruction and Development, *World Development Report, 1981* (New York: Oxford University Press, 1981). John P. Longwell, "Fuel Science and Technology," in National Research Council, *Outlook for Science and Technology: The Next Five Years* (San Francisco: W. H. Freeman, 1982). Samuel McCracken, "The War against the Atom," *Commentary* (September, 1977), pp. 33-47. Robert Stobaugh and Daniel Yergin, eds., *Energy Future: Report of the Energy Project at the Harvard Business School* (New York: Random House, 1979). John Surrey and Charlotte Huggett, "Opposition to Nuclear Power: A Review of International Experience," *Energy Policy*, 4 (1976), 286-307. Kaare Svalastoga, "Space, Population, Energy, and Information in Seven Nations, 1820-1970," *International Journal of Comparative Sociology*, 17 (1976), 30-47.

Enlightenment is used by cultural historians of the eighteenth century to designate the radically new philosophical and political ideas that spread throughout the Western world. Because in France these precepts culminated in a revolution, the word is sometimes more or less restricted to the "philosophes" who wrote a new summation of knowledge and wisdom in their *Encyclopédie*, together with their successors who overthrew the Bourbon monarchy. In many respects such men represented a new conception of humanity, but their postulates of population policy changed little from those of *mercantilism. †Montesquieu, Voltaire, Saint-Just, Rousseau—men who differed in most other respects—were all markedly pronatalist. Like †Colbert in an earlier century, France's revolutionary assembly used differential taxation as a spur to births; the new constitution itself proclaimed marriage and procreation to be essential parts of good citizenship. According to Voltaire, a nation was fortunate if its population increased by so much as 5 percent a century. Saint-Just, later one of the instigators of the Jacobin terror, held that misery could never follow from overpopulation but only from social institutions: one can usually depend on nature "never to have more children than teats," but to keep the balance in the other direction nature needs the state's assistance. The revolutionary utopianism expounded by †Condorcet, the proposition that with adequate political and economic institutions all population problems disappear, has reverberated ever since in Marxist writings.

REFERENCE: Anita Fage, "La Révolution Française et la Population," *Population*, 8 (1953), 311-338.

entropy was coined from *en*-ergy plus *trope*, "a turning," originally as a technical term in thermodynamics. In that context it means a quantity that partly specifies the thermal state of a system, such as, for example, the steam in a boiler. According to the second law of thermodynamics, an initially ordered state of any thermal system is virtually certain to randomize over a sufficient period of time; in its more familiar usage, then, entropy is the measure of disorder among the atoms making up the system. The term was taken over in cybernetics with a similar meaning, referring there to information rather than energy. Most recently entropy has been adopted by some of the more radical environmentalists in two discrete senses. The contrast between numbers of people and the amount of food they must consume has been adapted to the allegedly limited amount of what is termed ''free energy''—that is, energy that man can transform into useful work. Second, as society becomes larger and more complex, communication among its parts falters; ultimate dissolution can be averted only by reverting to a simple preindustrial state. The attraction of the concept of entropy, in short, is that it sums up in a seemingly scientific way the faith that everything in the modern world is becoming worse.

REFERENCES: Nicholas Georgescu-Roegen, *The Entropy Law and the Economic Process* (Cambridge, Mass.: Harvard University Press, 1971). Jeremy Rifkin and Ted Howard, *Entropy: A New World View* (New York: Viking Press, 1980).

enumeration, the counting of a population in a *census and the recording of whatever characteristics are included in the census schedule concerning either individuals or households. Also, *enumerator*, a person who conducts such a count.

enumeration district, according to the usage of the U.S. Bureau of the Census, a small area within a single political unit with clearly marked boundaries and a population of no more than 1,000 to 1,600, judged to be a reasonable work load of one enumerator. The so-called EDs are often changed from one census to the next in accord with shifts in the distribution of population. They serve mainly as the administrative field areas used in making assignments to enumerators. In recent censuses the first tabulations were by EDs, but no data were printed by these units.

environment, in bio-ecology the combination of physical and biological characteristics that for each organism make up its *ecosystem. The social environment of an individual, a population, a community, or a nation comprises all the populations or social systems to which the given unit is exposed. In general, then, with reference to any entity the term denotes everything external to it that influences it.

Environmental Fund, a private American association founded in 1973, has as its stated purpose to stop the growth of the world's population and then to reduce its size. It conducts various programs designed to acquaint Americans with the population problem, and it publishes an annual *World Population Estimate Sheet*, as well as *The Other Side*, a quarterly, and an annual *Special Report*. In 1982 the chairman of its board was Garrett †Hardin, an active propagandist for anti-natalist causes. Address: 1302 Eighteenth Street, N.W., Washington, D.C. 20036.

Environmental Impact Assessment (EIA), in the United States a formal judgment of how a proposed development would adversely affect the environment. Under the National Environmental Policy Act of 1969, an EIA was required prior to any federally sponsored major development, and laws in a number of states and in such other countries as New Zealand have set similar restrictions.

REFERENCE: Luna Bergere Leopold et al., *A Procedure for Evaluating Environmental Impact* (Washington, D.C.: U.S. Geological Survey, Circular 645, 1971).

environmentalism, the view that the environment largely determines the range of social variation, was dominant among geographers of the nineteenth century. A challenge to geographic determinism came in what was termed "human geography," as expounded especially by Paul †Vidal de La Blache, who was influential enough to change the typical professional position in France. In Britain and the United States, however, adoption of a new orientation was slower, since it was impeded by Ellen Semple's important exegesis (1911) of Friedrich †Ratzel's theories and by Ellsworth †Huntington's persistent assertion that climate is a dominant factor in human affairs. As late as the 1950s, the English geographer A. F. Martin published a paper entitled "The Necessity for Determinism" (Martin, 1952). With the increasingly sophisticated analysis of quantitative data, moreover, it has been possible to retain much of environmentalism in a new version, sometimes termed "social physics," which fails to be fully determinist or even mechanical only because of the probabilistic framework (Spate, 1968). See also *geography.

In a second sense now more common in the United States, environmentalism refers to a popular concern to preserve the setting of human life. Two of the more important stimuli to this social movement were Rachel Carson's *Silent Spring* (1962), first published in the *New Yorker* magazine and eventually in a widely sold paperback (cf. Graham, 1970), and *The Limits of Growth* (Meadows et al., 1972); see *Club of Rome. As propagated by such organizations as the Sierra Club, the Wilderness Society, and the National Audubon Society, environmentalism has often included a kind of pop demography, with far more fervor than competence in their widely distributed writings. According to a membership survey of several such environmental organizations, 81 percent agreed that any species denoted as endangered should be protected even at the expense of commercial activity; 65 percent that if the price of a beautiful and healthful environment is the cessation of further economic growth, it is a price worth paying (cf. the April 1980 issue of the *Natural Resource Journal*, vol. 20, pp. 217-358, which has a symposium by environmentalists). In short, environmentalism is much more than a development from *conservation; in greater part it is a reaction against such federal agencies as the Federal Power Commission, the

Bureau of Reclamation, and the Soil Conservation Service, which have carried out earlier mandates in a way the new advocates have found inadequate.

Notable among the many critiques of environmentalism in this sense are *The Doomsday Syndrome* (Maddox, 1972) and *Eco-Hysterics and the Technophobes* (Beckmann, 1972). The debate has not been on preserving the environment, on which there is essential agreement, but rather about what opponents regard as the extremist positions of environmentalist groups that aim to conserve natural resources irrespective of other desiderata. Critics stress that because a good environment, however defined, is one of several competing social objectives, measures to achieve it must be weighed against other goals. The argument is well presented in a small book with an eye-catching title—*People or Penguins: The Case for Optimal Pollution* (Baxter, 1974). Several economists have argued that the way to set environmental policy is by a cost-benefit analysis—that is, by a comparison of how much expenditure is required for how much improvement in well-being (e.g., Baumol and Oates, 1975; Mills, 1978; Swartzman et al., 1982). Such an analysis is not easily made, for some of the benefits sought are nonmonetary, and converting them into dollar values involves procedures that are themselves controversial. Even if the estimates in such a balance sheet cannot be made precisely, proponents argue that one should reckon the effect of a policy before adopting it. An early example of this approach was given in a volume prepared jointly by the U.S. Council on Environmental Quality and the U.S. Environmental Protection Agency (1972). According to this estimate, the minimum cost of an adequate environmental program would be, in constant 1958 dollars, 872.2 billion over 1972-76; the annual average of about $175 billion would amount to 22 percent of the 1970 national income. Ancillary costs, moreover, would be disastrous for some of the fifteen industry groups surveyed. In the canning industry, as a striking example, it was anticipated that the added cost of reducing pollution would squeeze small and even medium-sized plants out of the market. Of the 1,200 canning plants included in the survey, it was expected that one-third would have to close down, resulting in a loss of approximately 28,000 jobs, 90 percent of which were held by relatively unskilled workers.

Most environmentalists hold that population growth is a threat to a healthy environment (cf., e.g., *Global 2000). Whether this is so on a world scale has been challenged by Julian †Simon, among others, but the data are typically so poor that many of the points made by either side are difficult to judge. On a smaller scale, however, it is clear that growth of numbers has little or nothing to do with pollution. If the automobile uses up oil and iron and emits unpleasant and potentially dangerous fumes, the broader background to this phenomenon includes, apart from engineering factors, the affluence of the United States, which has made it possible for many or even most families to acquire a personal means of locomotion; the degeneration of the rail system and the failure to construct alternative means of mass transport comparable in efficiency to the railroads of Western Europe; the sheer size of the country, which meant that the commitment to automobiles and highways, once it was made, constituted an expenditure of billions in capital investment. In itself, population has hardly been significant even as an aggravating factor. As another example, cities as different as London and Pittsburgh cleaned their notoriously bad air not by expelling some of their inhabitants but by fiscal measures that enabled administrators to adopt technical improvements that had long been available.

REFERENCES: William J. Baumol and Wallace E. Oates, *The Theory of Environmental Policy: Externalities, Public Outlays, and the Quality of Life* (Englewood Cliffs, N.J.: Prentice-Hall, 1975). William F. Baxter, *People or Penguins: The Case for Optimal Pollution* (New York: Columbia University Press, 1974). Petr Beckmann, *Eco-Hysterics and the Technophobes* (Boulder, Colo.: Golem Press, 1972). Rachel Carson, *Silent Spring* (Greenwich, Conn.: Fawcett, 1962). Frank Graham, Jr., *Since Silent Spring* (Greenwich, Conn.: Fawcett, 1970). John Maddox, *The Doomsday Syndrome* (New York: McGraw-Hill, 1972). A. F. Martin, "The Necessity for Determinism," Institute of British Geographers, *Publications*, 17 (1952), 1-11. Donella H. Meadows, Dennis L. Meadows, Jørgen Randers, and William W. Behrens III, *The Limits of Growth: A Report for the Club of Rome's Project on the Predicament of Mankind* (New York: New American Library, 1972). Edwin S. Mills, *The Economics of Environmental Quality* (New York: Norton, 1978). Ellen C. Semple, *Influences of Geographic Environment, on the Basis of Ratzel's System of Anthropo-geography* (New York: Holt, 1911). O.H.K. Spate, "Environmentalism," *International Encyclopedia of the Social Sciences*, 5, 93-97. Daniel Swartzman, Richard A. Liroff, and Kevin G. Croke, eds., *Cost-Benefit Analysis and Environmental Regulations: Politics, Ethics, and Methods* (Washington, D.C.: Conservation Foundation, 1982). U.S. Council on Environmental Quality and U.S. Environmental Protection Agency, *The Economic Impact of Pollution Control: A Summary of Recent Studies* (Washington, D.C.: U.S. Government Printing Office, 1972).

epidemic, of a disease, widely diffused and spreading rapidly; attacking many people at the same time; recurrent or cyclical, with a high but occasional morbidity. As a noun, such a disease or such a concentrated attack of the disease. Epidemic is contrasted with *endemic*, with a low incidence but constantly present in a particular population. Note also *pandemic*, widely epidemic, affecting most of a population; *pandemia*, a nearly universal epidemic.

REFERENCES: John D. Post, "Famine, Mortality, and Epidemic Disease," and Andrew B. Appleby, "A Comment," *Economic History Review*, 2nd Ser., 29 (1976), 14-37, and 30 (1977), 508-512.

epidemiologic transition, a term coined by the epidemiologist Abdel †Omran (1971, 1977), emphasized the importance of disease in the *demographic transition. Mortality, he held, is a fundamental factor in population dynamics, and with its decline disease patterns shift from pandemics of infection to degenerative and man-made ailments. This shift particularly benefits children and young women. Three models of the epidemiologic-social-economic transition are identified: the classical Western (England), the accelerated (Japan), and the contemporary or delayed (less developed countries). This new jargon is based essentially on facts well known to every demographer and combined with such dubious implications as terming the momentously rapid decline of mortality in less developed countries part of a ''delayed'' transition.

REFERENCES: Abdel R. Omran, "The Epidemiologic Transition: A Theory of the Epidemiology of Population Change," *Milbank Memorial Fund Quarterly*, 49 (1971), 509-538; "Epidemiologic Transition in the U.S.: The Health Factor in Population Change," *Population Bulletin*, 32 (May, 1977), 1-42.

epidemiology, the systematic study of the differential distribution of diseases; also *epidemiologist*, a practitioner of epidemiology. Originally the subject was limited to the study of *epidemics, outbreaks of such infectious diseases as *cholera. In a broadened perspective it has become a major branch of public health, covering both the full range of diseases, noninfectious as well as infectious, and any cultural patterns that may explain their prevalence. The three elements of classical epidemiological analyses were the host, or human being with an individual degree of susceptibility or immunity to various infections; the agent, or carrier of the disease; and the environment, or the surrounding medium in which these two are most or least likely to interact. With the dramatic conquest of infectious diseases as causes of death, the emphasis has shifted from microorganisms to food deficiencies, such addictions as smoking, and various types and concentrations of pollutants. The methods of research in epidemiology and demography overlap greatly. In the typical start of an analysis in either discipline, the population affected by the variable being tested is classified by sex, age, occupation, race, and other social groupings in order to uncover clues that would explain whatever correlations are found. In both disciplines such data are often no more than indicative; for instance, some of the best epidemiologists refused to accept the statistical evidence that smoking cigarettes caused lung cancer until the data were confirmed by establishing direct physiological links.

REFERENCES: Charles F. Chapman, ed., *Biocultural Aspects of Disease* (New York: Academic Press, 1981). Brian MacMahon and Thomas F. Pugh, *Epidemiology: Principles and Methods* (Boston: Little, Brown, 1970). David Schottenberg and Joseph F. Fraumeni, eds., *Cancer Epidemiology and Prevention* (Philadelphia: Saunders, 1982). Hans Zinsser, *Rats, Lice and History: . . . The History of Typhus Fever* (New York: Bantam, 1960).

epitaphs, the inscriptions on tombstones, are a widely used source to estimate the mortality of the *ancient world. They have, however, several built-in errors. Tombstones were seldom erected for infants, a very important sector in any study of death rates. In Rome stones with data on the age at death were an institution mainly of the middle and lower-middle classes, with the top and the bottom of the social hierarchy lacking. Perhaps the most convincing demonstration of how inadequate epitaphs are as demographic data is Louis †Henry's comparison (1959) of nineteenth-century tombstones in a Lyon cemetery with vital statistics of the same period.

REFERENCES: Louis Henry, "L'Âge au Décès d'après les Inscriptions Funéraires," *Population*, 14 (1959), 327-329. T. H. Hollingsworth, *Historical Demography* (London: Hodder and Stoughton, 1969), pp. 272-274.

equilibrium is a term used with similar but not identical meanings in economics, psychology, sociology, ecology, and systems analysis, among other disciplines. Essentially it denotes a stable relation among specific elements of an interacting whole, either partial or general, either dynamic (or moving) or fixed. See also *homeostasis. In demography a common term is "equilibrium trap," the situation of less developed countries when small increases in capital result only in comparable increases of the population. A massive capital formation, according to the theory, is needed to produce a rise in per-capita income.

REFERENCES: Richard R. Nelson, "A Theory of the Low-Level Equilibrium Trap in Underdeveloped Countries," *American Economic Review*, 46 (1956), 894-908. Julian L. Simon, "There Is No Low-Level Fertility and Development Trap," *Population Studies*, 34 (1980), 476-486.

equity-fertility hypothesis, a refinement of the proposition that economic development leads to a decline in fertility, states that this is likely to be so only if the distribution of assets and income is equitable. Indicative findings were substantiated in an analysis of sixty-eight countries, where the correlations of fertility with income inequality were greater than those with female literacy, infant mortality, or per-capita income (Repetto, 1981). As with most data from less developed countries, however, these were subject to various types of criticism. A comparison between two Indian states helps clarify the thesis; Kerala's fertility has been lower than West Bengal's since the 1950s, though the distribution of income, consumption expenditures, and household assets has been less egalitarian in the former state. What Kerala did have was greater equity in education and health facilities (Nag, 1983).

REFERENCES: Moni Nag, "The Equity-Fertility Hypothesis as an Explanation of the Fertility Differential between Kerala and West Bengal," Population Council, Center for Policy Studies, Working Paper no. 96 (New York, 1983). Robert Repetto, *Economic Equality and Fertility in Developing Countries* (Baltimore: Johns Hopkins University Press, 1981).

errors occur in every type of demographic data, as in all other products of human endeavor, and a good deal of professional demographers' expertise is concentrated on pinpointing the deviations from accuracy, estimating their probable size, and making suitable adjustments (e.g., Bailar et al., 1982). There may be an overcount or an undercount—called with respect to a census an overenumeration or an underenumeration; with respect to vital statistics, an overregistration or an underregistration. Sometimes it is possible to gauge only the difference between the two, the net undercount, which may be considerably smaller than the gross miscounts in both directions. Even relatively small errors may result in a serious misinterpretation, for since they are never randomly distributed, the mistakes can be quite significant concerning the subpopulations where they are concentrated. The misreporting of a population characteristic, an error of a different type, can have a similar effect on the record. For instance, if some foreign-born are reported in a census as natives or if there is an underenumeration of the foreign-born, the consequence can be about the same.

In all *errors of coverage*, an undercount is generally more frequent and larger than an overcount. As long ago as in a volume supplementing the 1900 United States census, Walter F. †Willcox (1906, p. 88) defined the class most likely to be passed over, and the reason: "Census returns are obtained by enumerators who inquire from dwelling house to dwelling house, [but] a small minority have no dwelling house even in the loose sense in which that term is defined by the Census Office, namely, the place where a person regularly sleeps." More generally, sectors at a society's periphery—not only the homeless but casual laborers, criminals and near-criminals, and (in a different setting) those who live in the shantytowns that ring cities of less developed countries—are always the most difficult to count. Many such persons want no contact of any kind with officialdom, and they fit but poorly into the normal categories of occupation, regular income, or family life by which the majority are classified. The rising concern about "America's uncounted people" (Parsons, 1972; cf. Heer, 1968) is not due to a lesser efficiency in enumeration or to a proportionate increase in the types that are not included. Political power and many other values have come to be distributed according to the number of inhabitants in each area.

The problem cannot be fully solved, as was explicitly recognized in an appraisal by the National Academy of Sciences (1978) of plans for 1980. The committee's recommendations begin with the observation that "the 1980 census will be more costly than ever and probably more difficult than any in a century"—that is, since the notoriously incomplete counts in the South following the Civil War. The Bureau of the Census might use more Spanish-language schedules; it ought to consider testing various procedures that might improve efficiency or save money; it should emphasize more the recruitment and training of a competent staff (in fact, the local supervisors and enumerators were to be chosen by local Democratic Party bosses); it should use paid advertising to try to enlist public support; and so on. None of this was novel. The bureau had long conducted research on the causes of error (Hansen and Waksberg, 1970), especially on such possibly crucial issues as the effect of the interviewer on accuracy (Hanson and Marks, 1958).

In countries where enumerators are paid per person counted, there is sometimes a serious overcount. When political power depends on the regional distribution of the population, a census is hardly a neutral instrument (note the example of Nigeria, discussed under *African society). And in such a totalitarian state as the U.S.S.R. (see *Soviet society), the accuracy of any official datum must always be judged in context. Throughout the world marginal sectors of the population are often excluded, such as the "Indian jungle population" in parts of South America and the nomads in some countries of northern Africa. In the United States *American Indians living in tribal territories were included in the census for the first time in 1890, and the count since then has been markedly deficient.

Errors of classification can be exemplified by the misreporting of *age, which has been more discussed than any other type of error. Sometimes the question is poorly phrased: in a French census a person is asked for his date of birth, which is both unambiguous and probably less subject to falsification than the last or the nearest birthday, the way that "age" is defined in most other jurisdictions. Many respondents misstate their age—because they do not know it, because they answer carelessly and give it only approximately, or because out of vanity or other motives they deliberately falsify it.

In demographic data of all types there is often an attempt to find a reasonable quantitative index of a qualitative characteristic. In United States censuses, for example, *education is measured by the years of schooling completed—but over the decades the index has risen while more meaningful measures strongly suggest that the amount of learning has declined.

During the mass immigration from roughly 1880 to 1914, American port officials were supposed to classify newcomers by nationality, but they were harried, processing as many as 4,000 to 5,000 a day, and typically ignorant of the complex ethnic structure of the Russian, Austro-Hungarian, and German empires. Ukrainian immigrants, for instance, were sometimes so listed, and sometimes as Russians, Austrians, Galicians, or Ruthenians; and eventually each of these several categories was solemnly totaled. Studies of immigrant stocks invariably indicate an extraordinary upward mobility among "Russians"—who are, of course, very often Jews, an ethnic category not so designated because it is defined only as a religion. In the current period, there is a fundamental difference between asking a respondent where he and his parents were born (the basis for the "foreign stock" in census compilations) and asking him to define himself in any of a number of vague and shifting ethnic categories. People may lie in their replies to the first type of question, but there is a definite correct answer. Whether someone is an "American" *tout court*, a "Mexican American," a "Spanish-speaking" person, someone with a "Spanish surname," one of a group called *Hispanics," a "Chicano," or whatever—this depends sometimes on mere mood, sometimes on an identification of a paid worker for an ethnic or racial organization (cf. Siegel, 1974).

Enumerators in countries as different as Malaysia and the United States have made the same *error in recording*. When a woman who was asked how many children had been born to her answered "None," the reply was noted in such a way as to be coded "No answer." The number of childless couples, a most important datum for any analysis of fertility, was thus seriously misstated (el-Badry, 1961; cf. Palloni, 1981).

Generally speaking, the greatest improvements in demographic data have come with the reduction of *errors in processing* (but see also *editing). If the data collected are accurate and complete, the rate at which they appear in bound volumes or computer tapes has quickened amazingly in all industrial nations and, by the standards of the recent past, also in many less developed countries.

The *correction of errors* can be effected by various means, but only partly.

With some demographic data, such as the progression of ages in a *population pyramid or the near-balance between the numbers of males and females, one can assume a certain regularity and smooth out deviations. Data on ages, thus, can be adjusted by the use of *age ratios, or by computing age-specific *sex ratios (Henry, 1976, pp. 10-11). But in such extreme cases as widely practiced female *infanticide or a *war that has killed many males, a deviation from the presumed norm reflects not an error but the true situation. Whether smaller deviations are one or the other is often impossible to decide. The same is true of mathematical *models spelling out the interdependence of fertility, mortality, and age structure. Used to estimate the rates of countries with grossly deficient statistics, model life tables, for instance, are better than any available alternative, but still far short of what elsewhere would be deemed reasonable accuracy.

Any set of data can be checked for its internal consistency. In the processing of the 1970 United States census, the computer itself was programmed to.do the preliminary editing. A woman listed both as a wife and as single, for instance, the computer designated as "now married." Or, in another example, cited from a bureau release, "assume that a person reported as a 20-year-old son of the household head failed to indicate his marital status. Upon detecting this omission, the computer assigned him the same marital status as that of the last son that was processed in the same age group." This procedure, called "allocation of data," generally results in a greater validity than would distributing persons with missing characteristics proportionately over the whole of the population, which once had been the procedure followed.

Apart from such instances, the typical method of correcting errors is by *matching—that is, using one fallible source to check the accuracy and completeness of another. In any statistical series, there should be temporal consistency. Such characteristics as literacy or legal majority can be presumed to be permanent, and age changes at a regular rate. When data are collected in several ways—for example, in birth and death registrations and also in censuses—one set can be compared against the other. But even when in theory there should be a perfect match, as between the number of emigrants from Country A to Country B and the number of immigrants to Country B from Country A, the discrepancy may be surprisingly large (see *migration, international). Sometimes the matching is between an existent count and one specially made as a check, either a re-enumeration or more often a *post-enumeration survey. In the same report on the 1900 census that was quoted earlier, Willcox remarked, "A careful census is like a decision by a court of last resort—there is no higher or equal authority to which to appeal. Hence there is no trustworthy means of determining the degree of error to which a census count of population is exposed, or the accuracy with which any particular census is taken." The best way to reduce the number and importance of errors in other words, is not by finding suitable means of correcting them but by avoiding them in the first place.

REFERENCES: Mohamed A. el-Badry, "Failure of Enumerators to Make Entries of Zero: Errors in Recording Childless Cases in Population Censuses," *Journal of the*

American Statistical Association, 56 (1961), 909-924. Barbara A. Bailar, Roger A. Herriot, and Jeffrey S. Passel, "The Quality of Federal Censuses and Survey Data," *Review of Public Data Use*, 10 (1982), 203-218. Morris H. Hansen and Joseph Waksberg, "Research on Non-sampling Errors in Censuses and Surveys," *Review of the International Statistical Institute*, 38 (1970), 317-332. Robert H. Hanson and Eli S. Marks, "Influence of the Interviewer on the Accuracy of Survey Results," *Journal of the American Statistical Association*, 53 (1958), 635-655. David M. Heer, ed., *Social Statistics and the City* (Cambridge, Mass.: Harvard University Press, 1968). Henry, *Population*. Ian I. Mitroff, Richard O. Mason, and Vincent P. Barabba, *The 1980 Census: Policymaking amid Turbulence* (Lexington, Mass.: Lexington Books, 1983). National Academy of Sciences, *Counting the People in 1980: An Appraisal of Census Plans* (Washington, D.C., 1978). Alberto Palloni, "Adjusting Data on Children-Ever-Born for Nonresponse," *Social Biology*, 28 (1981), 308-314. Carole W. Parsons, ed., *America's Uncounted People* (Washington, D.C.: National Academy of Sciences, 1972). Jacob S. Siegel, "Estimates of Coverage of the Population by Sex, Race, and Age in the 1970 Census," *Demography*, 11 (1974), 1-23. Walter F. Willcox, "Special Reports, Supplementary Analyses and Derivative Tables," *Twelfth Census of the United States, 1900* (Washington, D.C.: U.S. Bureau of the Census, 1906).

estimation, in demography the stipulation of an *estimate*, or the approximate size or other characteristic of a population as inferred from a sample or other type of incomplete data, or from complete but only symptomatic data.

estrogen, one of several types of female *hormone produced principally in the ovaries. These hormones play an important part in both the menstrual and the reproductive cycles, and they bring about the female's secondary sex characteristics. Estrogen is also a generic term for any of several estrus-producing compounds, whether natural or synthetic, that affect the menstrual cycle and thus fecundity in a manner similar to one of the naturally produced female hormones. Several types of estrogen are typical components of *oral contraceptives. See also *estrus; *progestogen.

estrus and **anestrus** (alternatively, estrum and anestrum or diestrum) are the elements of the sexual cycle in most species of mammals. The same *hormone that controls ovulation also regulates the female's sexual desire. When a female animal is in heat, she seeks the male's advances; at all other times, she rejects them. Sexual union is thus narrowly physiological: its timing is determined by the animal's glandular flow, and the union has the single function of physical reproduction. In most primate species the female exhibits the estrous cycle in a vestigial form; but according to the slight evidence available, human females feel the strongest desire just before and just after menstruation, when fertile copulation is normally impossible, and the weakest desire just at the time of ovulation. In a dated but very ingenious study, the researcher interviewed wives of seamen, traveling salesmen, and other men who had to be away from home for considerable periods; the wives recorded the times of high sexual desire and related them to their menstrual cycle (Davis, 1929, chaps. 8-9; cf. Pearl, 1939, pp. 32-34). See also *sexual behavior.

REFERENCES: Katharine Bement Davis, *Factors in the Sex Life of Twenty-two Hundred Women* (New York: Harper, 1929). Raymond Pearl, *The Natural History of Population* (New York: Oxford University Press, 1939).

Ethiopia: Demographic Institutions

The U.N. Economic Commission for Africa (ECA) maintains a Population Division in Addis Ababa. See *United Nations for details.

The government's Central Statistical Office is the agency responsible for population censuses. It also issues a quarterly report on international migration statistics, an annual *Statistical Abstract*, and a *Statistical Bulletin*. Its Population and Social Statistics Department was headed in 1981 by Abdulahi Hasen. Address: P.O. Box 1143, Addis Ababa.

ethnicity derives via Latin from the Greek *ethnikos*, the adjectival form of *ethnos*, "nation" or "race"; and in many contexts *race and ethnic group have been used synonymously. In recent decades, however, a useful distinction has developed between a category distinguished by genetic heritage, a "race," and one set apart by such cultural characteristics as *language or *religion, an "ethnic group." In the United States, thus, *blacks, *Chinese Americans, *Japanese Americans, and other "nonwhites" are classified under one rubric, European nationalities under another (see also *color). The differentiation is hindered by the facts that in real life physiological and cultural features often overlap, and that neither criterion sharply delimits a sector of the population. See also Bureau of the Census under *United States: Federal Agencies.

That the English language never adopted a noun from the Greek *ethnos* has resulted in a number of makeshift alternatives. Such a phrase as "white ethnics" must still be considered slang; and if ever it becomes fully accepted into the language, it would have to be generalized from Poles or Italians, presently the typical referent, to Scots and Norwegians as well. In French there is a neologism, *ethnie*, which means all who adhere, for example, to French culture irrespective of national boundaries, thus including francophones in Belgium, Switzerland, Italy, and other countries. It is thus similar in meaning and political connotation to one use of the German *Volk*. At present the commonest substantive in English is "ethnic group," which is unfortunate in that it glosses over the crucial contrast between a group, which by definition has some degree of internal coherence and solidarity, and a subpopulation, category, grouping, aggregate, bracket, or sector, any of which suggest a patterned differentiation but not more. Residents of the United States who were born in Canada are so designated in American censuses; but in studies of ethnicity the information is of slight interest, for "Canadian Americans" have little or no sense of commonality, and seem barely aware of one another's existence. Yet the implication underlying the term "ethnic group" is that a population sector so called is either presently or at least poten-

ETHNICITY 281

tially bound by a sense of oneness, is more than an aggregate that happens to share a characteristic (like red hair, for instance, or left-handedness) with no relation to social, economic, or political configuration (Petersen, 1980).

Since no satisfactory system for classifying even one multi-ethnic population has ever been devised, it is not surprising that comparative studies based on such data are likely to falter. According to two early international surveys by the United Nations, thirty-nine countries divided their populations by a geographical-ethnic criterion, ten by race, eight by culture, twenty-two by a combination of race and culture, eleven by a combination of culture and geography, a few by origin as indicated by the language of the respondent's father, and several by "mode of life." But "even where the concept employed in several countries or census operations is apparently the same, . . . the meaning or definition of the concept may have changed and the amount of detail shown in the final tabulations may differ considerably. . . . There is always a considerable chance of deliberate falsification in connection with matters affecting social prestige" (United Nations, 1957, pp. 32-33). In short, since characteristics used to define a race or any of its approximate synonyms are "not uniform in concept or terminology, . . . it is impossible to define these concepts precisely" (United Nations, 1964, p. 38). No improvement was made over the interim, and in its recommendations for the 1970 censuses the United Nations denoted race and ethnic group a "useful" rather than a "recommended" topic.

Sometimes even the utility may seem doubtful. The U.N. Economic Commission for Africa, for instance, proposed that the populations of that continent be classified by race (African, European, Asian, and others)—thus evading the often more important, but also more sensitive, issue of ethnicity, the relative strength of tribal units within each African population. In Mexican censuses (following that country's usual perception of its ethnic pattern), an "Indian" is one who speaks an Indian language and wears Indian clothing; if he learns to speak Spanish and shifts from huaraches to shoes, he becomes a "mestizo." But if one gathers statistics on occupation, and if occupation in fact helps determine "ethnicity," is it appropriate to gather a second set of data on the largely derivative characteristics? (see also Shryock and Siegel, chap. 9). The frequent intermingling or confusion of physiological and cultural criteria makes it useful to coin such a term as "subnation" with which to denote either a race or an ethnic group or both.

If neither ethnicity nor race defines sharply bounded sectors of a population that can be as reliably classified as sex, for instance, or even urban-rural residence, then what is it, apart from the characteristics of the groupings, that determines whether and how a population is divided? The axiom underlying all other statements is that any society's subnations are classified only partly by their objective characteristics, partly by other criteria. The latter are chosen according to the view that the politically dominant group has of the whole society, and it is this group that is typically given the most statistical attention. In any taxonomy one main dimension is to divide "insiders," variously defined, from "outsiders." When the relative power of a subnation declines, however, it may retain its earlier place in a statistical classification. Designations of subnations are often changed from one synonymous term to another because of shifts in their emotional or political connotations, and an ethnic or racial group that deems its designation to be derogatory may demand not merely a new name but a reclassification. A decision not to include a particular subnation, although it is often justified by a statement that this ethnic differentiation is unimportant, is often based, on the contrary, on a reluctance to publicize ethnic-class or ethnic-political correlations. An important influence on any classification, finally, is the convenience and the budget of the administrative agency that does the work (Petersen, 1969).

How these principles work out in practice can be illustrated by the questions on race and ethnicity in the successive censuses of the United States (cf. Lowry, 1980). Issues deemed to be politically important as interpreted by social analysts or jurists were represented in queries to the population; and once posed, questions were sometimes retained in close to their original wording if only in order to maintain continuity in the record. The purpose of the census as stipulated in the Constitution is to provide an empirical base for periodic reapportionment, and the first censuses (1790-1820) therefore distinguished between those eligible and ineligible to vote—that is, between white citizens and unnaturalized aliens, slaves, tribal Indians, and, in some early schedules, "all other free persons, except Indians not taxed." The schedules during the next several decades merely elaborated this central theme. The first important shift came in 1870-80, reflecting the momentous increase in the number of immigrants, the shift of their dominant origin from Northwestern to Southern and Eastern Europe, and widespread concern about whether and how fully the newcomers were being assimilated. The principal criterion of ethnicity became birthplace, which divided the population into three broad categories: *foreign-born, native-born of foreign or mixed parentage (who together with the foreign-born make up the *"foreign stock"), and native-born of native parentage. In other words, only the first and second generations of European immigrants were to be classified by ethnicity; from the third generation on, no distinction has generally been made in the census classification. (And in 1980, the schedule did not ask for the country of birth of the enumerated persons' parents.) This fitted in with the social doctrine that America was a melting pot, a thesis that immigrants propounded most enthusiastically and that only a nativist minority challenged.

Races, however, continued to be distinguished irrespective of how many generations have lived in the United States, and this principle was permitted to prevail over the following decades. A special census of *American Indians was conducted in 1880 by John Wesley Powell; from 1890 on they were included in the regular count as a separate category and, most recently, divided according to tribe. A problem arose concerning sectors of the population that lie on the border between ethnic and racial. Before 1930 those born in Mexico and those of Mexican or mixed parentage were classified as part of the foreign stock, treated in the census like nationalities originating in Europe. In 1930 Mexican Americans were placed in the category "other races"—a defensible designation anthropologically, since a high proportion were mestizos. The change, however, became the occasion for protests from the Mexican government and the U.S. Department of State, and it resulted in a gross undercount of upper-class persons of Mexican descent, many of whom were of lighter complexion. In 1940 the Bureau of the Census shifted again and classified Mexican Americans by "mother tongue," the language spoken in early childhood; but a high proportion of those who by other criteria were "Mexican" reported this to be English. In 1950 the classification became "white persons of Spanish surname," and in 1980 the census schedule offered a choice among "Mexican," "Mexican American," "Chicano," and several other terms denoting *Hispanics or "Latinos."

The next major development had started in the 1960s, when a combination of laws, executive orders, judgments by federal courts, and interpretations by executive-branch agencies instituted a complex policy that can be subsumed under the label *affirmative action. *Discrimination based on race, color, religion, national origin, or sex was prohibited in public and private institutions and facilities, and preferential treatment was given not merely, as in earlier American law, to individuals suffering from various types of disability but to "disadvantaged minorities." Beneficiaries of a wide range of grants have been selected through some four hundred programs administered by over twenty-five federal agencies. Ethnic groupings were in effect defined as competitors for federal largesse, and the policy certainly stimulated the enormous increase in ethnic-oriented associations, which ostensibly reflected only a search for "roots." The jockeying for the official recognition that inclusion in the schedule affords resulted in the following list in 1980: "Is this person white; Black or Negro; Japanese; Chinese; Filipino; Korean; Vietnamese; Indian, American (print tribe); Asian Indian; Hawaiian; Guamanian; Samoan; Eskimo; Aleut; Other (specify)?" That a statistical agency under considerable financial pressure should try to determine the number of Aleuts in Massachusetts, or of Samoans in the several counties of Iowa, suggests how much the Census Bureau has been coerced. The Office of Management and Budget issued a directive in 1978 that set a minimum of five basic racial-ethnic categories for all federal statistics and reports on programs (*Federal Register*, vol. 43, no. 87, pp. 19269-70), and this was only the most authoritative of the many constraints under which the bureau has operated.

Moreover, beginning with the 1960 census and increasingly in the next two counts, the bureau instituted a system of self-enumeration. A marginal person's ethnic identity thus became whatever he said it was; in effect, he was asked whether he would like to be included in a vaguely defined category that would bring its members various preferments. If a potential member of nascent groupings did not know how to respond, most of them soon acquired quasi-official spokesmen to advise them. As a committee of the National Academy of Sciences (1978, pp. 71-72) noted, "It is by no means clear that persons in similar situations and with similar characteristics will answer in the same way. . . . [The] possibly wide variations in respondent behavior ... [may lead] to serious doubts about what the question measures and what its objective referent is.''

Criticism of the indicator used to define ethnic groupings and to measure their size is not intended to deny their reality and importance. Not only in the United States but throughout the world, ethnicity has become a much more significant principle of social stratification than anyone anticipated a generation ago (cf. Petersen, 1979; Said and Simmons, 1976). However ethnic groups and races are defined, they may differ significantly in their demographic behavior (cf. Bean and Frisbie, 1978). *Alcoholism in the United States was found to vary much more with ethnicity than with social class, and it may be that better data could furnish clues to other types of behavioral disorders and diseases. In some cases the higher mortality of those low on the economic scale can be plausibly ascribed at least in part to their ethnic characteristics, though obviously it is usually difficult to separate one causal factor from the other. Discrimination against a group whose members are motivated to rise may result in a smaller family size (see *fertility). Migration, both internal and international, is often shaped according to the ethnic composition of the sending population, and in the movement of refugees especially, economic or social determinants are often far less significant than ethnicity. In short, ethnicity is a salient factor not only in general social analysis but specifically in demography; and its importance is not reduced by the inadequate data generally available.

REFERENCES: Frank D. Bean and W. Parker Frisbie, eds., *The Demography of Racial and Ethnic Groups* (New York: Academic Press, 1978). Ira S. Lowry, *The Science and Politics of Ethnic Enumeration* (Santa Monica, Calif.: Rand Corporation, 1980). National Academy of Sciences, *Counting the People in 1980: An Appraisal of Census Plans* (Washington, D.C., 1978). William Petersen, ''The Classification of Subnations in Hawaii: An Essay in the Sociology of Knowledge,'' *American Sociological Review*, 34 (1969), 863-877; ed., *The Background to Ethnic Conflict* (Leiden: Brill, 1979); ''Concepts of Ethnicity,'' *Harvard Encyclopedia of American Ethnic Groups* (Cambridge, Mass., 1980). Abdul Said and Luiz R. Simmons, eds., *Ethnicity in an International Context* (New Brunswick, N.J.: Transaction Books, 1976). Shryock and Siegel, *Methods and Materials of Demography*. United Nations, *Demographic Yearbook, 1956* and *1963* (New York, 1957 and 1964).

ethnocentrism was coined by William Graham Sumner in his *Folkways* (1907). He defined it as a ''view of things in which one's own group is the center of everything, and all others are scaled and rated with reference to it.'' It leads all peoples ''to exaggerate and intensify everything in their own *folkways which is peculiar and which differentiates them from others. It therefore strengthens the folkways.'' See also *cultural relativism.

REFERENCE: William Graham Sumner, *Folkways: A Study of the Sociological Importance of Usages, Manners, Customs, Mores, and Morals* (Boston: Ginn, 1907).

ethnography and **ethnology**, used with various meanings by particular analysts, have become differentiated in their usual present definitions. Ethnography pertains to particular studies in depth of one well defined community or society or, more generally, to the branch of *anthropology concerned with producing such empirical studies. Ethnology is the theoretical counterpart, the subdivision of cultural anthropology that draws generalizations and constructs propositions from the data of ethnography.

ethology, the study of animal behavior; the counterpart in zoology of social psychology.

eugenics, coined by Francis †Galton in 1883, means the discipline related to efforts to improve the quality of mankind either by inhibiting the reproduction of the genetically inferior or by fostering the procreation of those with transmissible qualities deemed to be desirable—policies identified, respectively, as negative and positive eugenics. The eugenics movement is often associated with the extremists sometimes prominent in it or, more damagingly still, with policies that in totalitarian countries developed into *genocide. More broadly, the movement has been one phase of the modernist effort to better man's lot on earth; and the official societies in the United States, Britain, and elsewhere have included thoroughly responsible scientists, among them some important demographers. The interpenetration of demography and genetics has been great in Italy and Japan, for example; in the latter country the law under which abortion clinics were established had as its ostensible purpose the control not of population size but of its quality.

REFERENCES: Loren R. Graham, "Science and Values: The Eugenics Movement in Germany and Russia in the 1920s," *American Historical Review*, 82 (1977), 1133-1164. Frederick Osborn, "History of the American Eugenics Society," *Social Biology*, 21 (1974), 115-126.

Euiryong, a *gun* (or typically rural district) in South Korea, was the site of an experimental project in the distribution of contraceptives. In Area I a well paid canvasser visited every household that included one or more eligible women and offered them contraceptives or, if they preferred, the opportunity of having an IUD inserted or a sterilization performed. In Area II the procedure was the same except that it was preceded by a meeting at which contraception and this program were explained. In Area III a woman was selected at random from each group of ten eligible households and paid a small fee for explaining the project and distributing contraceptives to the other nine households. With all three procedures the reported use of contraceptives increased, and by very nearly the same proportions.

REFERENCE: Chai Bin Park, Lee-Jay Cho, and James A. Palmore, "The Euiryong Experiment," *Studies in Family Planning*, 8 (1977), 67-76.

Europe, a peninsula of the Eurasian land mass, has been understood differently in various epochs (cf. Rougemont, 1966). Except that the U.S.S.R. is excluded from it (see *Soviet society), this discussion pertains to the usual current definition, from Iceland southeast to Greece, from Finland southwest to Spain. On a global scale this is a relatively small expanse, but it is of far greater importance in world history than any other continent. In particular, much that is related to demography originated there—accurate censuses and vital statistics, and thus much of the methodology associated with them, including the recent developments in *historical demography; effective sanitation, medicine, and other death-control institutions (cf. Kunitz, 1983); the small-family system and birth-control ideology, together with relatively effective and safe contraceptive methods; industry, transportation, and communication of unique efficacy and all-pervasive in their impact on society; the democratic state and judicial system. To the extent that non-European countries share these characteristics, it is usually because of a large past immigration of Europeans, the indirect influence of colonization and trade, or the direct effect of Western-supported programs established, for example, to reduce mortality or fertility.

TRADITIONAL CONTROL OF FAMILY SIZE

In the seventeenth century or before, what John †Hajnal (1965) called the "European marriage pattern" developed in Scandinavia (excluding Finland), the British Isles, the German-speaking area, the Low Countries, and northern France (cf. Mitterauer and Sieder, 1982). In that region the ages at which young men and women married were well above puberty, and as many as one woman in five never married at all. In such preindustrial civilizations as *India or *China, in contrast, marriage was virtually universal and, for girls, at or very shortly after puberty. The contrast arose essentially from the different rules governing the formation of households (Hajnal, 1982; Laslett and Wall, 1972). Outside Northwest Europe it was the two families that arranged a marriage of adolescents; in Europe two mature adults came together following a period of courtship (see *romantic love). In the usual pattern outside Europe, females had no role except as wives and mothers, and a young couple could begin to procreate immediately since the burden of caring for infants was shared by the whole of a joint *family. In Europe, on the contrary, couples set up separate households that typically included servants who circulated from one family to another, eventually often settling down as an unmarried relative/servant in the home of a sibling. In China and India many children were needed to care for their parents in their old age. In Europe, when property was transferred to an heir he sometimes assumed a formal obligation to maintain the retired head; such "retirement contracts" were gradually supplemented with poor relief out of public funds. In other words, late marriage and nonmarriage could become so prevalent because the system provided reasonable alternatives. This removal of a large proportion of the population from the breeding pool, either for about a decade after puberty or permanently, cut Europe's fertility enough to set a good balance between population and the environment. In Asian civilizations, famines recurred with terrible regularity; but in modern Europe, except for the one disaster of the 1840s in Ireland, the frequent food shortages never grew to devastating proportions.

THE MODERN INCREASE IN POPULATION

According to a well reasoned estimate by Jean-Noël †Biraben (1979), the population of Europe without Russia increased by 7 percent in the seventeenth century and by 17 and 35 percent in the first and second halves of the eighteenth century. During the nineteenth century it doubled. This remarkable upsurge has been, of course, one of the major topics of modern demography; but it has yet to be fully explained. Migration apart, a population can grow only by a rise in fertility or a decline in mortality. The undoubted rise in *illegitimacy, however significant as a social trend, affected overall fertility only marginally; and for most countries of Europe we do not know what happened to marital fertility before some time in the nineteenth century. In *France certainly, and in Scandinavia probably, it fell during the eighteenth century; in other countries it may have remained more or less static (cf. Flinn, 1981, chap. 6). In any case, if one subtracts from the estimated growth in numbers the probably small rise in the birth rate, one must conclude that a substantial decline in mortality took place. This was once ascribed to improvements in medicine and public health, but two medical historians argued that there were hardly any such innovations before about 1850; in their view, the fall in the death rate was due to a better supply of food (McKeown and Brown, 1965; McKeown, 1976, 1978). On the other side, P. E. Razzell (1965, 1977) held that inoculation against smallpox was much more effective than most other analysts had thought and that the control of this one important disease largely explained the fall in the death rate. In short, the debate on this point has continued, with no resolution in sight.

By the beginning of the nineteenth century, the social institutions that had held Northwest Europe's fertility in check were becoming less effective. The guilds that forbade a man to marry until he had acquired a master's skill were obsolescent, and the migration to towns undercut the parallel controls in the rural population. When †Malthus advocated that men forgo marriage until they were able to care for their wives and children, his proposal was in fact that a pattern that had worked for more than a century not be allowed to disintegrate altogether. The way to inculcate a sense of responsible parenthood in the lower classes, Malthus averred, was to raise them to the level of the middle classes, so that they would adopt a new life-style that included a small-family norm (cf. Petersen, 1979, chap. 9). This policy of embourgeoisement is often called "social capillarity," the name given it by Arsène †Dumont (1890)—who, however, denounced the practice as the prime cause of France's empty cradles. The best study of the process is "a study of family planning among the Victorian middle classes" (Banks, 1954): those trying to rise to the positions that England's industrialization was opening up had many competitors, and to move up faster they cut the only major expenditures they could without losing face, the number of their children. Among the clergymen, doctors, lawyers, members of the aristocracy, merchants, bankers, manufacturers, and other males of the gentleman class who married between 1840 and 1870, the average age was a shade under 30 years.

THE TREND IN FERTILITY

To limit procreation by a long postponement of marriage required a strong self-discipline, and it was much easier to realize the same goal after contraceptives became more widely available. Within each country the small-family pattern gradually spread from the urban, secular middle class to the rest of the population. Certain categories maintained a larger family size for a generation or two— agricultural workers and pious Catholics, for instance; but by the 1930s and again, after the interruption of the *baby boom, in the most recent period, low fertility became more and more the general norm. The same diffusion took place internationally. Some countries lagged well behind France—the Netherlands in Northwest Europe, Italy in the South, and most of those in the East; but these differences in average family size have disappeared or in some instances have even been reversed. One factor was that most legal blocks to family limitation have been removed; contraceptives are legal now even in *Ireland, and in Italy one may also have a legal abortion.

One reinforcement of the downward trend in fertility was the increasing number of *women in the work force. Once females in sizable numbers started work outside agriculture, the usual pattern was that girls were employed until they married and then became housewives and mothers for the rest of their lives. In the first important modification, married women in their early 20s continued working outside the home, usually until they had their first child (and in the 1970s this was the norm in Sweden, the Netherlands, Belgium, and Italy). Another shift was that married women worked in their early 20s, left for a period of childbearing and rearing, and then returned to the work force around age 40 (this was the usual arrangement in England and France—and the United States). In Poland, Bulgaria, and Romania, however, between 60 and 70 percent of women aged 20-55 years, a vast majority of whom were married, were in the work force. One reason that fertility fell so precipitously in Eastern Europe was undoubtedly that women wanted to reduce the triple burden that combined family, reproductive, and economic functions (Szabady, 1973).

In the 1930s pronatalist measures were introduced by many European states, ranging in political orientation from Fascist Italy to democratic Sweden (cf. Kälvemark, 1980). From a review of several of the programs in Western Europe, D. V. †Glass (1940) concluded that they probably had no effect on fertility except possibly in Nazi Germany; and few analysts would disagree with this thesis. With the renewed fall in natality in the late 1960s and 1970s, there was a renewed effort to stimulate large families (cf. Simon, 1983). Countries like France and Sweden, which had pronatalist laws on the books, strengthened them. In West Germany some wanted to do the same, but in view of the record of

National Socialist policies, the government did not try to implement a comprehensive pronatalist policy (McIntosh, 1981; Wingen, 1980). Britain and the Netherlands took steps to facilitate childrearing for working women (Heeren, 1982). In Eastern Europe economic incentives were combined with restrictions on abortions, which together with coitus interruptus generally take the place of contraceptives in those socialist countries. In the view of Henry P. †David (1982), *family assistance has been effective there only for a very short time unless the value was continually increased (see also Andorka, 1978; Besemeres, 1980; Siampos, 1980).

Though there have been some surprising new developments in the control of mortality, the great unknown in projecting Europe's natural increase is future fertility. One can either project the secular decline in the birth rate to a stationary population or even a depopulation, or one can stress the variation in this long-term shift in family size and anticipate another rise from current levels. Several new life-styles may be seen as beginnings of new institutions or as temporary aberrations. Especially but not exclusively in Scandinavia, consensual unions have evolved into a widespread alternative form of mating, but what this indicates concerning fertility in the future is not clear (cf. Finnäs and Hoem, 1980). In Western Europe some women with remunerative and interesting jobs have forgone parenthood altogether (e.g., Baum and Cope, 1980), but the effect of this phenomenon on overall fertility will be slight unless a considerably higher proportion of Europe's couples remain childless. Social innovations of this type suggest how irrelevant such pronatalist measures as family assistance can be; subsidies pay for so small a proportion of the cost of rearing a child that probably decisions are affected only at the margin.

INTERNATIONAL MIGRATION

Europe's natural increase was sufficient to furnish a vast surplus that helped populate other continents. The usual estimate is that between 1800 and 1950 some 67 million persons migrated across an ocean and that of these some 60 million were Europeans (see *migration, international). Two out of three of the Europeans went to the United States, the others to Latin America, countries of the British Commonwealth, and other places around the globe. Analysis of this movement has never stopped, and in some recent studies statistics regarded as intractably poor have yielded more information than had been thought possible. The original passenger manifests from immigrant ships to United States ports have been analyzed (Erickson, 1981); names of Dutch emigrants were matched against those of passenger manifests (Swierenga, 1981); and the archival sources on emigration from the Germanies have undergone a new review (Adams, 1980). In the Great Migration up to 1914, the largest number left from Italy (cf. Albonico, 1981), the largest numbers relative to the sending populations from Ireland and Norway.

World War I not only interrupted the flow but changed its character permanently. The average number of persons departing each year from Europe in 1930-

35 was only 131,000, in 1936-39 only 147,000—the lowest figures in a century. One reason was restrictive quotas imposed by the United States and other countries of immigration, but a more important factor was the worldwide economic depression (Kirk, 1946, chap. 5; Kosiński, 1970, chap. 4). International migration within Europe, which partly took the place of overseas movements, had been sizable for many decades. Such an international center as Vienna attracted in-migrants not only from all over the Austro-Hungarian Empire but also from beyond its borders. There was a general drift westward, particularly to Germany and France, the only two countries that before 1914 had more than a million alien residents. Since many language and cultural communities overlapped international boundaries, there was often a movement to border regions, as of Italians to southeastern France. The many refugees set in motion by World War I and the Russian Revolution were a mere prelude to the flood following new totalitarian incursions and World War II. Migrations in Eastern and Central Europe from 1939 to 1955 totaled some 13 million Germans, mostly Volksdeutsche, or ethnic Germans, expelled from Eastern Europe after Germany's defeat in 1945 (cf. Arnold, 1980); 7.4 million Poles, repatriated from the Soviet Union or other countries, or transferred after a shift of boundaries; 2 million Czechs and Slovaks, repatriated or moved to areas vacated by Germans; half a million Yugoslavs, more than a third of a million Hungarians, and some hundreds of thousands of Romanians, Bulgarians, and others from the Balkans (Kosiński, 1970, Table 11; cf. Kirk, 1946, chap. 6).

In many of the countries of Western Europe, the economies expanded so rapidly after 1945 that they found it necessary to import foreign laborers, many of them the *Gastarbeiter or "guest workers," who ostensibly received work permits for a limited period and then would return home. They came mostly from countries along the Mediterranean and went mostly to Northwest and Central Europe, where they formed sizable alien blocs in certain areas. Opposition to "*Überfremdung*" was an important political issue in Switzerland; and after a downturn in Europe's economy, hostility became marked also in other countries. In West Germany, for example, fifteen prominent scholars and university professors, the so-called Heidelberg Circle, issued a manifesto denouncing the effects of Gastarbeiter on German society (*Die Zeit*, February 5, 1982; reprinted in translation in *Population and Development Review*, 8, 1982, 636-637); the government responded with a statement promising to take more effective measures both to end the illegal flow and to foster the acculturation of those in the country permanently (see *migration, illegal). Meanwhile the return migration of workers to their homelands was causing problems in Yugoslavia, for instance (cf. Chepulis, 1981; Künne, 1979; Mughini, 1981).

INTERNAL MIGRATION AND URBANIZATION

Some migration in Europe, though the people did cross international borders, has had the general characteristics of movements within a single nation—the ingathering of Volksdeutsche in Germany, for example, or the sojourns of Irish housemaids in middle-class English homes. One of the papers in an issue of the *Yearbook of Population Research in Finland*, on the contrary, concerned movement across the border between the Finnish and Swedish language communities within Finland (DeGeer, 1981). In Western Europe urbanization has been a major topic of analysis for decades; a recent annotated bibliography on the rural exodus in France has 582 pages (Pitié, 1980). The mass movement to East European towns is much more recent. In Bulgaria, as one instance, between 1947 and 1973 there was a net migration to urban places of 1.7 million people, and by the latter date 60 percent of the population was urban (Taaffe, 1977). Official opposition to the growth of cities is widespread (see also *urban policy). Several countries of Western Europe have tried to foster a dispersion from cities to small towns and villages, and at least one American analyst thought these efforts worth imitating (Sundquist, 1975). The more or less consistent counter-urbanization that a number of economists and geographers have documented in the United States may indeed be in process also in Europe, but according to an international survey, there was as yet no "clean break" with the past trend (Hall and Hay, 1980, chap. 7 and passim). Apparently the housing market had more to do with "flight from the city" than official policy (cf. Hammerschmidt and Stiens, 1980).

Some sixty scholars from the countries of Western Europe came together in the mid-1960s and drew up a "Plan Europe 2000" to mark the path to the end of the century (Hall, 1977). Four main areas were considered—education, industry, urbanization, and agriculture and the environment. Their major concerns related to demography were the growth of large cities and the destruction of the natural environment; though the decline in fertility was mentioned in passing, it got far less attention than in many subsequent analyses of Europe's problems. "The female dilemma" and "revolt of the old" are noted as "group problems," but, again, with far less urgency than others have given to the effect of women's work on the birth rate, or of the age structure on productivity. What Europe will be like in the year 2000 is difficult to discern, but we can state with some certainty that neither city planners nor demographers nor any other social scientists are likely to predict its contours very accurately.

REFERENCES: W. P. Adams, ed., *Die Deutschsprachige Auswanderung in die Vereinigten Staaten: Berichte über Forschungsstand und Quellenbestände* (Berlin: Free University of Berlin, Kennedy Institut für Nordamerikastudien Materialen, 1980). Aldo Albonico, "Un Decennio di Studi Italiani sull'Emigrazione in America Latina," *Studi Emigrazione*, 18 (1981), 49-78. Andorka, *Determinants of Fertility in Advanced Societies*. Wilhelm Arnold, ed., *Die Aussiedler in der Bundesrepublik Deutschland* (Vienna: Wilhelm Braumüller for the Forschungsgesellschaft für das Weltflüchtlingsproblem, 1980). J. A. Banks, *Prosperity and Parenthood: A Study of Family Planning among the Victorian Middle Classes* (London: Routledge and Kegan Paul, 1954). Frances Baum and David R. Cope, "Some Characteristics of Intentionally Childless Wives in Britain," *Journal of Biosocial Science*, 12 (1980), 287-299. John F. Besemeres, *Socialist Population Politics: The Political Implications of Demographic Trends in the USSR and Eastern Europe* (White Plains, N.Y.: M. E. Sharpe, 1980). Jean-Noël Biraben, "Essai sur l'Évolution du Nombre des Hommes," *Population*, 34 (1979), 13-25. R. L. Chepulis, "Migration Policies and Return Migration with Particular Reference to Yugoslavia," *Studi Emigrazione*, 18 (1981), 319-336. Henry P. David, "Eastern Europe: Pronatalist Policies and Private Behavior," *Population Bulletin*, 36 (February, 1982), 1-48. Eric DeGeer, "Migration and the Language Border," *Yearbook of Population Research in Finland*, no. 19 (1981), 62-86. Arsène Dumont, *Dépopulation et Civilisation: Études Démographiques* (Paris: Lecrosnier et Babé, 1890). Charlotte Erickson, "Emigration from the British Isles to the U.S.A. in 1831," *Population Studies*, 35 (1981), 175-197. Fjalar Finnäs and Jan M. Hoem, "Starting Age and Subsequent Birth Intervals in Cohabitational Unions in Current Danish Cohorts, 1975," *Demography*, 17 (1980), 275-295. M. W. Flinn, *The European Demographic System, 1500-1820* (Baltimore: Johns Hopkins University Press, 1981). D. V. Glass, *Population Policies and Movements in Europe* (Oxford: Clarendon, 1940). John Hajnal, "European Marriage Patterns in Perspective," in Glass and Eversley, *Population in History* (1965); "Two Kinds of Preindustrial Household Formation System," *Population and Development Review*, 8 (1982), 449-494. Peter Hall, ed., *Europe 2000* (London: Duckworth, 1977). Hall and Dennis Hay, *Growth Centres in the European Urban System* (Berkeley: University of California Press, 1980). A. Hammerschmidt and G. Stiens, " 'Stadtflucht' in Hochverdichteten Regionen—Gefahr oder Erfordernis?" *Informationen zur Raumentwicklung*, no. 11 (1980), 585-598. Hendrik J. Heeren, "Pronatalist Population Policies in Some Western European Countries," *Population Research and Policy Review* (Amsterdam), 1 (1982), 137-152. Catherine Jones, *Immigration and Social Policy in Britain* (London: Tavistock Publications, 1977). Ann-Sofie Kälvemark, *More Children of Better Quality? Aspects on Swedish Population Policy in the 1930s* (Uppsala: Studia Historica Upsaliensia, Uppsala University, 1980). Dudley Kirk, *Europe's Population in the Interwar Years* (Princeton, N.J.: Princeton University Press, 1946). Leszek A. Kosiński, *The Population of Europe: A Geographical Perspective* (London: Longman, 1970). Stephen J. Kunitz, "Speculations on the European Mortality Decline," *Economic History Review*, 2nd Ser., 36 (1983), 349-364. Wilfried Künne, *Die Aussenwanderung Jugoslawischer Arbeitskräfte: Ein Beitrag zur Analyse Internationaler Arbeitskräftewanderungen* (Königstein, West Germany: Hanstein, 1979). Peter Laslett and Richard Wall, eds., *Household and Family in Past Time* (Cambridge, England: University Press, 1972). C. Alison McIntosh, "Low Fertility and Liberal Democracy in Western Europe," *Population and Development Review*, 7 (1981), 181-207. Thomas McKeown, *The Modern Rise of Population* (London: Edward Arnold, 1976); "Fertility, Mortality and Causes of Death," *Population Studies*, 32 (1978), 535–542. McKeown and R. G. Brown, "Medical Evidence Related to English Population Changes in the Eighteenth Century," in Glass and Eversley, *Population in History* (1965). Michael Mitterauer and Reinhard Sieder, *The European Family* (Oxford: Basil Blackwell, 1982). Clara Mughini, "L'Emigrazione di Ritorno: Problemi e Prospettive per un Reinserimento Produttivo degli Emigrati in Jugoslavia," *Studi Emigrazione*, 18 (1981), 207-241. Petersen, *Malthus*. Jean Pitié, *L'Exode Rural: Bibliographie Annotée, France: Généralités, Régions, Départements d'Outre-Mer* (Poitiers: Centre de Géographie Humaine et Sociale, Université de Poitiers, 1980). P. E. Razzell, "Population Change in Eighteenth-Century England: A Reinterpretation," *Economic History Review*, 2nd Ser., 18 (1965), 312-333; *The Conquest of Smallpox* (Firle, Sussex: Caliban Books, 1977). Denis de Rougemont, *The Idea of Europe* (New York: Macmillan, 1966). George S. Siampos, ed., *Recent Population Change Calling for Policy Action with Special Reference to Fertility and Migration* (Athens: National Statistical Service and European Center for Population Studies, 1980). Julian L. Simon, "The Present Value of Population Growth in the Western World," *Population Studies*, 37 (1983), 5-21. James L. Sundquist, *Dispersing Population: What America Can Learn from Europe* (Washington, D.C.: Brookings Institution, 1975). Robert P. Swierenga, "Dutch International Migration Statistics, 1820-1880: An Analysis of Linked Multinational Nominal Files," *International Migration Review*, 15 (1981), 445-470. Egon Szabady, "The Social and Demographic Changes of Hungarian Society during the Last 25 Years," in B. W. Frijling, ed., *Social Change in Europe: Some Demographic Consequences* (Leiden: Brill, 1973). Robert N. Taaffe, "The Impact of Rural-Urban Migration on the Development of Communist Bulgaria," in Huey Louis Kostanick, ed., *Population and Migration Trends in Eastern Europe* (Boulder, Colo.: Westview Press, 1977). Klaus Unger, *Ausländerpolitik in der Bundesrepublik Deutschland* (Saarbrücken: Breitenbach, 1980). Max Wingen, *Bevölkerungsentwicklung als Politisches Problem* (Paderborn, West Germany: Ferdinand Schöningh, 1980).

European Center for Population Studies (ECPS), founded in 1953, comprises some 250 individuals professionally interested in demography as an interdisciplinary science. Its founder and director until his death in 1983 was Gunther †Beijer. Publications: *European Demographic Information Bulletin*, quarterly; irregular monographs. Address: 17 Pauwenlaan, 2566-TA The Hague, Netherlands.

European Economic Community, often called the Common Market, was established in 1958 in order to foster the integration of Western European economies. The member states abolished tariffs and other restrictions on trade in manufactured goods among themselves and established a uniform tariff against the rest of the world. It proved to be much more difficult to reach an agreement concerning agricultural goods, but one was gradually worked out. EEC, the usual acronym for the Common Market, can also refer to the European Economic Commission, the permanent organ of both the Community and two associated bodies, European Coal and Steel Community (ECSC) and the European Atomic Energy Community (EURATOM). Collectively all three are called the "European Communities." With respect to population, the most direct effect of EEC was its ruling, introduced at the end of the Community's "transition period" on December 31, 1969, that workers in any of the member countries were free to work in any of the others (see also *migration, international); the large number of Italian migrants, particularly to West Germany, thus acquired a status legally different from the *Gastarbeiter from other Mediterranean countries. Other Western European countries joined the founding nations, and certain less developed countries became associate members. The Statistical Office of the EEC publishes a number of serials with data on population: *Demographic Statistics*, with the standard population measures for member countries; *Population and Employment*; *Regional Statistics*; *Statistical Information*, quarterly; *Statistical Studies and Surveys*, annual; *Statistical Yearbook of the Associated African, Malagasy, and Mauritian States*. Address: 200 rue de la Loi, B-1049 Brussels, Belgium.

euthanasia, from the Greek words for "good" and "death," means the practice of painlessly killing persons suffering from an incurable and distressing disease, or, more often, allowing them to die by withdrawing life-sustaining medication or procedures. These two alternatives are sometimes designated, respectively, "positive" and "negative" euthanasia. Dispute over the moral and legal implications has a long history (cf. Triche and Triche, 1975), and it has sharpened during the past several decades. The Euthanasia Society of America, founded in 1938, has tried to achieve formal recognition of the "right to die"; and those opposed to this view have also become more active. The gap between the two points of view on ethical, medical, and legal aspects of euthanasia are seemingly unbridgeable, as is evident from a fairly well balanced volume representing both sides (Horan and Mall, 1977). Arguments, pro and con, are partly religious and partly pragmatic, both usually set in individual terms related to personal rights or obligations. With respect to medical institutions, similarly, one can argue that personnel and facilities can be far better used than in maintaining alive a sick person who wants to die, or that giving up on those afflicted with presently incurable diseases is likely to impede the advance of medical knowledge. Some physicians have half-evaded the moral arguments by redefining *death.

REFERENCES: Denis J. Horan and David Mall, eds., *Death, Dying, and Euthanasia* (Washington, D.C.: University Publications of America, 1977). Charles W. Triche III and Diane Samson Triche, *The Euthanasia Controversy, 1812-1974: A Bibliography with Selected Annotations* (Troy, N.Y.: Whitston Publishing Co., 1975).

ever married persons include not only the married (or, if the distinction is important, the currently married) but also those presently divorced or widowed. Sometimes the phrase *ever mated* is used in order to emphasize the same time reference.

evolution, which derives from the Latin for "unrolling" a scroll, signifies many types of gradual realization of a potential course of events. In modern times its primary meaning is the theory that varieties of plants and animals have come into being through a progressive diversification of their forebears, a thesis often adumbrated earlier but first convincingly expounded in Charles †Darwin's *On the Origin of Species* (1859). This theme not only permeated every corner of the biological sciences but affected, often crucially, both the social disciplines and moral philosophy. The extension of Darwinism to the widest conceivable range was initiated by Herbert †Spencer, who substituted "evolution" for "progress," which he had used earlier with the same meaning, in order to emphasize that the process had no ethical connotation. He defined evolution as "a change from a less coherent to a more coherent state, ... from the uniform to the multiform. ... While the more or less distinct parts into which the aggregate divides and subdivides are also severally concentrating, these parts are simultaneously becoming unlike—unlike in size, or in form, or in texture, or in composition, or in several or all of these. ... [In short,] evolution is definable as a change from an incoherent homogeneity to a coherent heterogeneity'' (cf. Peel, 1972). As ordinarily used, social evolution implies that change is natural, directional, immanent, continuous, and necessary. See also Franz †Boas, L. T. †Hobhouse.

REFERENCES: Robert A. Nisbet, *Social Change and History* (New York: Oxford University Press, 1969). J.D.Y. Peel, ed., *Herbert Spencer on Social Evolution* (Chicago: University of Chicago Press, 1972).

excess fertility, as calculated from responses in a fertility survey, is the number of children that parents have on the average minus the mean number they say they desire. See also *deficit fertility.

excess mortality, the proportion of deaths that could be avoided with certain specified improvements, has been used in two ways. In his work on the population of Europe, Dudley †Kirk (1946, pp. 180-182) contrasted each country's deaths with the number there would have been if Holland's age-specific rates in 1939 had obtained. For Europe as a whole, the ''excess deaths,'' so defined, amounted to 35 percent of the total number, and for Northwestern and Central Europe they were 23 percent. This was a dramatic way of stressing the effectiveness of the Dutch health system, much of which was closely associated with its specific culture and therefore not readily transferable to other nations. But Kirk took the whole of mortality as a unit, rather than deaths from each particular cause.

In recent years it has become almost routine to assert that the number of deaths from one or another cause could be avoided if a particular reform was effected. But with respect to the *risk of dying, populations are heterogeneous, and the several causes are not independent. It is not true that improved mobile units for coronary patients, or airbags in automobiles, or any other medical or social advance will save as many lives as are lost through the lack of each one. Death is merely deferred, and how long depends largely on age. Using the 1964 rates in the United States as a base, one would anticipate that the total elimination of cancers among males would add only 2.26 years to the expected life span, and the total elimination of deaths by motor vehicle accidents, only 0.87 year. Even these low figures may still exaggerate the benefit from an improvement in health or social controls, for the assumed homogeneity of the population is not typical. Those who travel by airplane are not subject to an automobile accident, and there are other relevant differences besides age that may be less obvious (Keyfitz, 1977, pp. 75-76).

REFERENCES: Nathan Keyfitz, *Applied Mathematical Demography* (New York: Wiley, 1977). Dudley Kirk, *Europe's Population in the Interwar Years* (Princeton, N.J.: Princeton University Press, 1946).

exile, one who is banished, compelled to live outside his native land; also, the alien place where such a person lives. An exile has no choice, in contrast with an *expatriate*, who chooses to live abroad. The differentiation between exile and *refugee is looser but at least implicit in most contexts. A person is exiled by some legal act directed against him as an individual; refugees flee in large numbers from a more general persecution or the fear of it.

exponential growth, though perhaps less familiar than the *arithmetic progression and *geometric progression underlying †Malthus's principle of population, is closer to the typical actuality. Growth (whether positive or negative) does not generally take place by an addition or a doubling during each year or other arbitrary period, but rather continuously. The formula for the rate of growth includes the symbol e, which is approximately equal to 2.71828 and is the base of natural or Napierian logarithms. For a period of n years during which the population grew from P_0 to P_n, the exponential rate of growth, r, can be derived from the formula

$$P_n = P_0 e^{rn}$$

as follows:

$$r = \frac{\log (P_n/P_0)}{n \log e}$$

A simpler formula gives approximately the same results, as follows:

$$r = \frac{2 (P_n - P_0)}{n(P_n + P_0)}$$

REFERENCE: Shryock and Siegel, *Methods and Materials of Demography*, pp. 379-380.

exposure residence, a mode of classifying the moves of migrants by the size of place of their successive residences. It is assumed that a resident is ''exposed'' to a particular range of specific social-cultural characteristics in each type of social setting, and the relative importance of moves, whether to the migrant or to society as a whole, can thus be estimated by adding up such exposures. If a farmer moves to another farm, or if a resident of a city moves to another urban place of about the same size, each of these migrants has been exposed to only one milieu; but if the farmer moves to the city, where he will have to change his occupation and otherwise adapt to urban ways, this would count as two exposures. In the cited paper, six sizes of place were used in the classification: rural farm, rural nonfarm, and urban places with populations of 2,500 to 9,999, 10,000 to 49,999, 50,000 to 499,999, and 500,000 and over.

REFERENCE: Karl E. Taeuber, William M. Haenszel, and Monroe G. Sirken, ''Residence Histories and Exposure Residences for the United States Population,'' *Journal of the American Statistical Association*, 56 (1961), 824-834.

extended city, in the 1970 and 1980 censuses of the United States, an incorporated place within an *Urbanized Area of which one or more portions were classified as rural. Criteria were set by the size of the rural area, its population density, and the percentage of the Urbanized Area included in it. Extended cities, so defined, were treated as rural and excluded from the Urbanized Areas.

external economies and **diseconomies,** together sometimes called "externalities," are the benefits and costs that affect economic decisions but are not controlled by a single firm or other entity. For example, the infrastructure of transportation and communication services might make an area more attractive to both industry and workers. The expulsion of smoke into the atmosphere and of other waste materials into streams, on the other hand, transfers certain costs from the manufacturer to the general community.

REFERENCES: Marcus Fleming, "External Economies and the Doctrine of Balanced Growth," *Economic Journal*, 65 (1955), 241-256. Tibor Scitovsky, "Two Concepts of External Economies," *Journal of Political Economy*, 62 (1954), 143-151.

extinct generation, a designation of a method of estimating the ages of the extreme aged, who very often do not report their own ages accurately (cf. *centenarian). Death statistics of a series of cohorts permit one to reconstitute the portion of the cohorts no longer surviving and thus to calculate death rates of the "extinct generations."

REFERENCE: Ira Rosenwaike, "A Note on New Estimates of the Mortality of the Extreme Aged," *Demography*, 18 (1981), 257-266.

exurbia, the residential area lying farther from the city than the suburban zone. According to the usual stereotype, the characteristics typical of suburbia are exaggerated in exurbia—greater wealth, longer commuting time, and more disorganized family life.

REFERENCE: A. C. Spectorsky, *Exurbanites* (Philadelphia: Lippincott, 1955).

F

family, without further specification, refers to what is more precisely termed the *nuclear family*, or a married couple and their minor children, all living apart from other kin. In his very influential *Social Structure* (1949), George P. Murdock called the nuclear family a universal institution, present in every known society either as the dominant form or as the basic unit within larger forms. Though this generalization has since been challenged, it remains true that, at least for demographers, the nuclear family is generally the norm by which other types are classified as aberrations or extensions. Variations may result from different patterns of *marriage and remarriage, from the *adoption of children, or from the *residence of other kin, boarders, or servants in a common *household. Where data are insufficient to control these complexities, the size of a "family" may be no more than a rough indicator of *fertility.

One of the complex types is the joint family, supposedly the form to which everyone aspired in classical India and China. As defined by the Indian sociologist Irawati †Karve (1968, p. 8), a *joint family* comprises "a group of people who generally live under one roof, who eat food cooked in one kitchen, who hold property in common, and who participate in common family worship and are related to one another as some particular type of kindred." In theory, the institution should have resulted in a higher fertility than in isolated nuclear families. Adolescents could marry and reproduce while still socially immature, since they would not bear the entire responsibility for the care of their children. The patriarch ruling the family complex, moreover, would generally encourage a growth in the number of persons under his control. Most fundamentally, many wants could be satisfied only through the kin group, so that all in it would cooperate to make it larger and more powerful. According to the several studies comparing fertility in joint and nuclear families, however, the difference is not so clear-cut, if only because with the statistics available the two types are not easily distinguished. At most one can assume that, in spite of the lack of empirical validation, the theory may hold for historic India, before modernizing disturbances became significant (cf. Bebarta, 1977; Burch, 1967).

Another important variation is the *stem family* (in French, *famille souche*), one of the forms that Frédéric †LePlay (1907) included in his typology. Supposedly the institution was developed in order to prevent the partition and repartition of family plots; the entire property went to a single heir, and his siblings either moved away or remained as unmarried members of the household. The typical unit, thus, consisted of a peasant, his wife and minor children, his unmarried brothers and sisters, and perhaps his aged father and mother, plus a number of farmhands or other relatives. More recent analysts have challenged LePlay's statement that this type, in any of the alternative meanings given the term "stem family," was the dominant one in early modern Europe (cf. Verdon, 1979). However, research has confirmed the main effect on fertility that LePlay postulated: a considerable proportion of the population remained single, and the normal age at marriage was many years beyond puberty. These two characteristics defined what John †Hajnal (1965) called the "European marriage pattern," which kept fertility (and thus probably also mortality) well under that in other preindustrial civilizations; see also *Europe.

When the theory of the *demographic transition is used to forecast trends in less developed countries from the historical pattern of nineteenth-century Europe, is this thesis supported by what we know of families in various cultures? A special issue of the *Journal of African History* on the family in Africa offered a wide variety of papers, of which two are relevant in this context. David Sabean (1983) compared the history of the family in Europe and Africa—beginning, however, with the difficulty that "in many African societies there is no equivalent term to the English (and European) word 'family' at all." In a second paper Gavin Kitching (1983) examined the possible relation between "proto-industrialization" (that is, traditionally organized rural handicrafts) and population change, an association that Peter †Laslett (1984) explored in his book on preindustrial England. Some parallels can be found, but also important differences.

The U.S. Bureau of the Census defines the family as any two or more members of a household who are related by blood, marriage, or adoption. This designation, which derives from the fact that the count is of *households rather than of families, is hardly the most suitable for an analysis of fertility. And in its recommendations for the 1970 censuses, the United Nations removed the family yet farther from the reproducing unit, defining it as "those members of a household ... who are related, to a specified degree, through blood, adoption, or marriage. The degree of relationship used in determining the limits of the family is dependent upon the uses to which the data are to be put and so cannot be precisely set for worldwide use." In other words, the common-sense notion of a unit comprising two parents and their children does not fit the usual statistics or those that would be collected if recommended procedures were adopted.

The U.S. Bureau of the Census also uses various other categories to designate usually minor aberrations from the norm defined by "household" or "family." A married couple with or without children, or one person with a child under 18, living as members of a household of which the *head or his/her spouse is a relative is termed a *subfamily*. The commonest example is a young couple living with the parents of the husband or wife. Since members of subfamilies are counted as part of the main household, the number of families in the statistics does not include subfamilies. A "married couple," defined for the census as a husband and wife enumerated as members of the same household, may be either a nuclear family or a subfamily. Similarly, a "parent-child group," consisting of a parent with no spouse present living with one or more children under 18 years, can form a household by itself or be one unit in a larger household. Before 1980 families were divided into "primary" and "secondary" depending on whether they did or did not include among their members the head of the household. Persons not living in family groups or in institutions are called *unrelated individuals. The coding of information or the programming of a computer according to these various definitions spells out what is termed the family composition of a population.

For several decades Paul †Glick was in charge of family statistics at the U.S. Bureau of the Census. In addition to dozens of anonymous reports based on the censuses from 1940 through 1970, he has written analytical studies related to such concepts as the *family cycle*, a now familiar term that he coined in 1947. In an academic field like family sociology, where the novel or the aberrational are often given more attention than the statistical or moral norm (cf. Macklin, 1980; Sweet, 1977), it is especially useful to base conjectures on solid data. Divorce and illegitimacy have risen, as well as such formerly anomalous patterns as one-person households, homosexual "marriages," and mothers of young children who work outside the home. It is a common practice to extrapolate recent trends and conclude that the family is a dying institution, not that it is "here to stay" (Bane, 1976; cf. Masnick and Bane, 1980). But "most Americans still experience some variation of the 'typical' family life cycle of the past; two out of three first marriages taking place today are expected to last 'until death do them part' " (Glick and Norton, 1977; cf. Thornton and Freedman, 1983). Particularly if one accepts the view that family size and the ills that may accompany it are to some degree cyclical, the recent social pathologies do not accurately forecast a long-term trend (cf. Easterlin, 1980, chap. 5).

REFERENCES: Mary Jo Bane, *Here to Stay: American Families in the Twentieth Century* (New York: Basic Books, 1976). Prafulla C. Bebarta, *Family Type and Fertility in India* (North Quincy, Mass.: Christopher Publishing House, 1977). Thomas K. Burch, "The Size and Structure of Families: A Comparative Analysis of Census Data," *American Sociological Review*, 32 (1967), 347-363. Richard A. Easterlin, *Birth and Fortune: The Impact of Numbers on Personal Welfare* (New York: Basic Books, 1980). Paul C. Glick and Arthur J. Norton, "Marrying, Divorcing, and Living Together in the U.S. Today," *Population Bulletin*, 32 (1977). John Hajnal, "European Marriage Patterns in Perspective," in Glass and Eversley, *Population in History* (1965). Irawati Karve, *Kinship Organization in India* (3rd ed.; New York: Asia Publishing House, 1968). Gavin Kitching, "Protoindustrialization and Demographic Change: A Thesis and Some Possible African Implications," *Journal of African History*, 24 (1983), 221–240. Peter Laslett, *The World We Have Lost Further Explored* (3rd ed.; New York: Scribner, 1984). Frédéric LePlay, *L'Organisation de la Famille, selon le Vrai Modèle Signalé par l'Histoire de Toutes les*

Races et de Tous les Temps (5th ed.; Tours: Mame, 1907). Eleanor D. Macklin, "Non-traditional Family Norms: A Decade of Research," *Journal of Marriage and the Family*, 42 (1980), 905–922. George S. Masnick and Mary Jo Bane, *The Nation's Families, 1960–1990* (Boston: Auburn House, 1980). George P. Murdock, *Social Structure* (New York: Macmillan, 1949). David Warren Sabean, "The History of the Family in Africa and Europe: Some Comparative Perspectives," *Journal of African History*, 24 (1983), 163–171. James A. Sweet, "Demography and the Family," *Annual Review of Sociology*, 3 (1977), 363-405. Arland Thornton and Deborah S. Freedman, "The Changing American Family," *Population Bulletin*, 38 (October, 1983), 1-43. Michael Verdon, "The Stem Family: Toward a General Theory," *Journal of Interdisciplinary History*, 10 (1979), 87-105.

family assistance does not ordinarily refer to the typical means by which the general community assumes a portion of the cost of rearing children—such as, to cite two important American examples, public schools and a reduction in the income tax for each dependent. Rather, it means an enhanced support given to actual or potential parents. Precisely what measures are deemed to be "family assistance," thus, depends on how the particular country defines the normal sustenance of a crucial social institution. Motives for establishing a system of family allowances have differed considerably. According to Roman Catholic teaching, the family is the natural unit of society and therefore should be protected more than it usually is in modern Western societies. Secularists have often advocated family assistance as a way to redistribute income and provide social welfare to the poor, who often are those with the largest families. And both Catholics and secularists have tried to use family subsidies in order to raise the country's fertility.

Apart from an abortive experiment with the *Speenhamland system, family assistance started in France in the 1870s, a period of economic depression throughout Europe. In order to relieve their workers' hardships, a number of employers paid those with children a supplementary wage based on the number of dependents they had to support. In order to avoid excessive burdens on a few employers, eventually all of those participating in the scheme contributed to one general fund from which allowances were dispersed to all eligible employees. The French government started a similar schedule of "family allocations" paid to civil servants and railroad workers. Undoubtedly everyone thought that the system would be discontinued when prosperity returned; but in France all three supportive ideologies—Catholic, meliorist, and pronatalist—were strong. Advocates succeeded in maintaining some family support and, after World War I, extending it considerably (Vadakin, 1958, chap. 2).

During the 1930s countries ranging in political orientation from Sweden or Britain to Nazi Germany or the Soviet Union initiated pronatalist measures that usually included one or more types of family assistance. Such laws or decrees can be exemplified by those in Italy, which used almost every device to maintain its high birth rate. Successively from 1926 to 1938, the Fascist government imposed a special tax on bachelors and married couples with few or no children; made the dissemination of information on contraceptives or abortion punishable by imprisonment; gave tax reductions to state employees with seven or more children, and to other workers with ten or more; granted birth premiums and family allowances; gave job preference to married men and women with relatively large families; gave priority to married men and women with families in the allocation of cheap houses and apartments; and required bachelors in the public service to marry before they could advance beyond a given level (Loffredo, 1950; Pendleton, 1978). Like Italy, most other countries used both coercion and encouragement, but whether either type of pronatalist device worked is not certain. In the most extensive analysis at the time, D. V. †Glass (1940) held that the only successful effort was possibly that of Nazi Germany, where he thought the stringent prohibition of abortion had the greatest influence. It may be, however, that family subsidies are ineffective as a cure of low fertility but, if introduced in order to preserve traditional mores rather than to restore them, can help maintain a relatively high natality (Petersen, 1955; cf. Cigno, 1983).

The family policies presently being implemented in various countries are based on the premise that family allowances of more or less the same amount and type both do and do not stimulate the parents to produce more children. Many governments of Eastern and Western *Europe have responded to the fall in fertility by reinstituting subsidies similar to those in effect during the 1930s. Obviously the sponsors of such measures hope that their policies will indeed raise the country's fertility, and they have on occasion argued that they have done so. The proposal that cash bonuses be used to reduce fertility, not only in less developed countries but also in the United States (e.g., Barnett, 1969; Enke, 1960), also implies a link between income and family size. On the other hand, most American advocates of family assistance argue for their position only as a means of achieving a more equitable distribution of income. They generally emphasize that such subsidies do *not* raise fertility—for otherwise the laws they support would not improve the status of the poor so much as increase their number (e.g., Hohm, 1975, 1976; Kelly et al., 1976; Presser and Salsberg, 1975; Wynn, 1970). The controversy goes back at least as far as the early nineteenth century, when †Malthus and others opposed the Poor Laws because, in their opinion, such supposed remedies did less to mitigate poverty than to foster it (Petersen, 1979, chap. 6). The dispute has continued so long in part because the issue is of great importance, but mainly because neither side can prove its case. Whether the birth rate of families given financial help rises or falls or remains constant is not the point, for the effectiveness of such pronatalist measures—if that is what the purpose is—must be measured against a hypothetical continuation of the fertility curve as it would have been lacking such a supposed stimulus (cf. *family-planning programs).

Once instituted, family subsidies often rise and also spread to other sectors of the population, and their cost thus tends ever upward. In a detailed study of this process in Germany of the 1950s and 1960s, Fritz Bünger (1970) argued against what he termed the "sprinkling-can principle" and urged that assistance be given only to those families in the direst need.

REFERENCES: Larry D. Barnett, "Population Policy: Payments for Fertility Limitation in the United States?" *Social Biology*, 16 (1969), 239-248. Fritz Emil Bünger, *Familienpolitik in Deutschland: Neue Erkenntnisse über den Einfluss des Sogenannten "Giesskannenprinzips" auf die Wirksamkeit Sozialpolitischer Massnahmen* (Berlin: Duncker und Humblot, 1970). Alessandro Cigno, "On Optimal Family Allowances," *Oxford Economic Papers*, 35 (1983), 13-22, 329. Stephen Enke, "Government Bonuses for Smaller Families," *Population Review*, 4 (1960), 47-50. D. V. Glass, *Population Policies and Movements in Europe* (Oxford: Clarendon, 1940). Charles F. Hohm, "Social Security and Fertility: An International Perspective," *Demography*, 12 (1975), 629-644; "Reply to Kelly, Cutright, and Hittle," *Demography*, 13 (1976), 587-589. William R. Kelly, Phillips Cutright, and David Hittle, "Comment on Charles F. Hohm's 'Social Security and Fertility: An International Perspective,' " *Demography*, 13 (1976), 581-586. Ferdinando Enrico Loffredo, "Demografica, Politica," *Enciclopedia Italiana*, Appendix I (1938), pp. 507-508; reprinted as part of the 1949 edition (1950). Brian F. Pendleton, "An Historical Description and Analysis of Pronatalist Policies in Italy, Germany and Sweden," *Policy Sciences*, 9 (1978), 45-70. William Petersen, "Family Subsidies in the Netherlands," *Marriage and Family Living*, 17 (1955), 260-266; *Malthus* (1979). Harriet B. Presser and Linda S. Salsberg, "Public Assistance and Early Family Formation: Is There a Pronatalist Effect?" *Social Problems*, 23 (1975), 226-241. James C. Vadakin, *Family Allowances: An Analysis of Their Development and Implications* (Miami: University of Miami Press, 1958). Margaret Wynn, *Family Policy* (London: Michael Joseph, 1970).

Family Growth in Metropolitan America, a series of three longitudinal interviews on the determinants of family size, is sometimes called the Princeton Study. The sample consisted of about one thousand urban, native, white American couples whose marriages were not disturbed by death, divorce, separation, or extensive pregnancy wastage. The first interview (1957) was conducted after the birth of their second child, the second (1960) to test the hypotheses concerning whether there would be a third child, and the third (1969-71) to round out the study after most of the women's childbearing period had passed. One major finding was that religious preference "is the strongest of all major social characteristics in its influence on fertility" (Westoff et al., 1963, p. 238). This datum, however, was a factitious consequence of the choice of the sample, which included Catholics with relatively large families but not rural Protestants or blacks with just as many children. Contrary to most earlier studies, Charles †Westoff and Raymond †Potvin (1967) found that among Catholic women the years of schooling are positively related with family size; in other words, the effect of education depends on what is taught. The study also analyzed "social capillarity": those rising in social status had fewer children on the average (cf. Westoff, 1956). Like the earlier *Indianapolis Study, this one uncovered no significant correlations between indices of psychological characteristics and fertility. See also *Growth of American Families.

REFERENCES: Charles F. Westoff, "The Changing Focus of Differential Fertility Research: The Social Mobility Hypothesis," in Joseph J. Spengler and Otis Dudley Duncan, eds., *Population Theory and Policy* (Glencoe, Ill.: Free Press, 1956). Westoff, Robert G. Potter, Jr., and Philip C. Sagi, *The Third Child: A Study of Prediction in Fertility* (Princeton, N.J.: Princeton University Press, 1963); "Some Selected Findings of the Princeton Fertility Study," *Demography*, 1 (1964), 130-135. Westoff and Raymond H. Potvin, *College Women and Fertility Values* (Princeton, N.J.: Princeton University Press, 1967).

family-planning programs, as the term is ordinarily understood, are government-administered efforts to provide birth-control information and means, and to induce members of a *target population to use them (see also *commercial distribution of contraceptives). According to the usual account, the first such program was set up by *India in 1951 (United Nations, 1972), though in fact that government was then and for two decades thereafter ambivalent about antinatalism of any kind. During the 1960s and 1970s several dozen countries adopted policies to cut their population growth and took some steps toward implementing them. From the first these policies were highly controversial, at first mainly with respect to whether population control was necessary and, if so, whether contraception, abortion, or sterilization is a licit and appropriate means of achieving it. Among Western demographers, virtually all of whom accept the necessity of reducing the fertility of some less developed countries, the debate has continued on the narrower issue of whether the programs generally work (cf. Nortman and Fisher, 1982; Yinger et al., 1983).

Demographers began their involvement in various programs with high expectations, based on the premise that large proportions of the rapidly increasing populations wanted to reduce the number of their children and lacked only the knowledge and means to do so (see also *KAP). A "demographic breakthrough" was imminent—"the end of the population explosion" (Bogue, 1964, 1967). This euphoria was undercut initially by experience in the field, later by trenchant criticism (e.g., Davis, 1967; Hernandez, 1981; Mamdani, 1972). A particularly instructive discussion came in an exchange between Paul †Demeny and Donald †Bogue (1979) on how the latter's predictions had worked out in the interim. In another representative analysis the authors argued that in four countries—Colombia, Thailand, Java-Bali, and South Korea—the decline in fertility over the period 1965-75 would not have occurred without the family-planning programs (Teachman et al., 1979). Why were state-sponsored projects effective in these instances, they ask, and not in other countries? (See also *island populations.) The will of a country's leaders to cut its natality is one important factor, but it can also lead, as it did in India, to a self-defeating coercion (Gwatkin, 1979).

Seemingly most proponents of family-planning programs have shifted to the more modest claim that, where other stimuli to a lower fertility existed, the programs were likely to accelerate the reduction and thus cut the time needed to realize a near-balance between fertility and mortality. A work by K. S. †Srikantan (1977), for instance, is a detailed study of "socio-economic thresholds for fertility decline"—that is, conditions in the society and economy that predispose a population to the *acceptance of proffered contraceptives. "Decline in natality," he wrote (p. 6), "is triggered initially when one or more of the associated variables reach certain threshold values"; but, if so, is the provision of birth-control facilities needed?

No end to the debate on the evaluation of family-planning programs is likely, for definitive judgments cannot be offered by either side (e.g., Chandrasekaran and Hermalin, 1975; Forrest and Ross, 1978). The purpose is to increase the number of *births averted, but this is defined in one analysis not as a decline in family size but as "a measure of the quantitative change in the expectations, assessed in terms of probabilities, of future births to a cohort of women resulting from the adoption or modification of birth-control practice by them or their husbands" (David Wolfers, in Chandrasekaran and Hermalin, 1975). A direct measure of fertility would be much more difficult, for in the less developed countries, where most of these antinatalist efforts are made, data on births are sometimes nonexistent and, where they exist, usually inadequate. The problem, moreover, is not to measure merely the change in natality, but rather the program's net effect on the hypothetical trend that there would have been without it. If the fertility rises, the program may have been successful in keeping it from rising more. If the target population was selected, as is very often done, for its probably readier acceptance of birth control, then the family size of that select group might well have declined apart from any intervention. By what is termed a "substitution effect," a couple controlling its conceptions independently may become involved in a program in order to get gratis the contraceptives that earlier it had had to pay for. Even if "acceptors" are all new contraceptors and all actually use the means they are given, extrapolating from that segment to the whole of a population—as is often done—is statistically highly dubious; for by definition acceptors are atypical with respect to the pertinent attitudes and behavior patterns. And if, finally, by a conscientious evaluation one concludes both that the fertility of the target population has fallen and that this decline was the direct consequence of the family-planning program, this still tells us very little about the long term—that is, about the number of children the couples will have over the whole of their fecund period. Even with the enormous number of studies based on far better data, the erratic ups and downs in the family size of Western countries remain essentially a puzzle.

REFERENCES: Donald J. Bogue, "The Demographic Breakthrough: From Projection to Control," *Population Index*, 30 (1964), 449-454; "The End of the Population Explosion," *Public Interest*, no. 7 (1967), 11-20. C. Chandrasekaran and Albert I. Hermalin, eds., *Measuring the Effect of Family-Planning Programs on Fertility* (Dolhain, Belgium: Ordina Editions for the IUSSP, 1975). Kingsley Davis, "Population Policy: Will Current Programs Succeed?" *Science*, 158 (1967), 730-739. Paul Demeny, "On the End of the Population Explosion," *Population and Development Review*, 5 (1979), 141-162; Bogue and Amy O. Tsui, "Reply," and Demeny, "Rejoinder," 479-504. Jacqueline D. Forrest and John A. Ross, "Fertility Effects of Family Planning Programs: A Methodological Review," *Social Biology*, 25 (1978), 145-163; "The Demographic Assessment of Family Planning Programs: A Bibliographic Essay," *Population Index*, 44 (1978), 8-27. Davidson R. Gwatkin, "Political Will and Family Planning: The Implications of India's Emergency Experience," *Population and Development Review*, 5 (1979), 29-59. Donald J. Hernandez, "The Impact of Family Planning Programs on Fertility in Developing Countries: A Critical Evaluation," *Social Science Research*, 10 (1981), 32-66. Mahmood Mamdani, *The Myth of Population Control: Family, Caste, and Class in an Indian Village* (New York: Monthly Review Press, 1972). Dorothy L. Nortman and Joanne Fisher, *Population and Family Planning Programs: A Compendium of Data through 1981* (New York: Population Council, 1982). K. S. Srikantan, *The Family Planning Program in the Socioeconomic Context* (New York: Population Council, 1977). Jay Teachman, Donald J. Bogue, Juan London, and Dennis P. Hogan, *The Impact of Family Planning Programs on Fertility Rates: A Case Study of Four Nations* (Chicago: University of Chicago, Community and Family Study Center, 1979). United Nations, *Measures, Policies and Programs Affecting Fertility, with Particular Reference to National Family Planning Programs* (New York, 1972). Nancy Yinger, Richard Osborn, David Salkever, and Ismail Sirageldin, "Third World Family Planning Programs: Measuring the Costs," *Population Bulletin*, 38 (February, 1983), 1-35.

family policy is generally so broadly interpreted that it can refer to almost any type of state intervention that, directly or indirectly, is intended to affect family life—including *family assistance and *family-planning programs; reflections of the shift in public attitudes toward *illegitimacy and the so-called *one-parent family (cf. Macklin, 1980); and the distribution of the burden of *taxation. Good reviews of some of these topics are given by Joan Aldous and Wilfried †Dumon (1980). The several types of policy, however, are often mutually contradictory (cf. Steiner, 1981).

REFERENCES: Joan Aldous and Wilfried A. Dumon, *The Politics and Programs of Family Policy: United States and European Perspectives* (Notre Dame, Ind.: University of Notre Dame, Center for the Study of Man, 1980). Eleanor D. Macklin, "Nontraditional Family Forms: A Decade of Research," *Journal of Marriage and the Family*, 42 (1980), 905-922. Gilbert Y. Steiner, *The Futility of Family Policy* (Washington, D.C.: Brookings Institution, 1981).

family reconstitution, a method of using *parish records to reconstruct the main demographic processes of the past, is associated with two French demographers, Michel †Fleury and Louis †Henry (1956, 1965). Some elements of their method were anticipated by, among others, Louis †Chevalier with data from France, Otto †Roller from Germany, and Hannes †Hyrenius from Estonia; but these were isolated efforts. One of the main advantages of the Fleury-Henry system is that identical forms have been used in research in various countries, facilitating greatly the comparison of the results. Jacques †Dupâquier (1979) has presented a synthesis of reconstruction surveys based on forty French parishes in the seventeenth and eighteenth centuries. The analysis goes well beyond the earlier genealogical studies, for the purpose is not merely to trace particular lineages but to search a whole parish register systematically and derive from it, using probability theory to fill in the gaps, as complete a record as possible of births, marriages, and deaths. The main deficiency in extant records is often that migrants disappeared from the registers, and those who remained over several generations in the same parish were probably atypical also in other respects. See also *genealogy; *inverse projection.

REFERENCES: Jacques Dupâquier, *La Population Française aux XVIIe et XVIIIe Siècles* (Paris: Presses Universitaires de France, 1979). Michel Fleury and Louis Henry, *Des Registres Paroissiaux à l'Histoire de la Population: Manuel de Dépouillement et d'Exploitation de l'État Civil Ancien* (Paris: INED, 1956); *Nouveau Manuel de Dépouillement et d'Exploitation de l'État Civil Ancien* (Paris: INED, 1965). T. H. Hollingsworth, *Historical Demography* (London: Hodder and Stoughton, 1969), chap. 5.

family size, as used by demographers, denotes several quite different quantities. The United Nations recommends one definition: the number of persons in a nuclear family, consisting generally of man, wife, and their children. In the usage of the U.S. Bureau of the Census, however, the term includes also any others in a household who are related to the head by blood, marriage, or adoption. What may be the commonest meaning today, the number of children that a family head and the spouse have, originated among European demographers. It is also the meaning given in one measure of fertility, the *completed family size, or the number of children who have been born to a woman who has passed her fecund period.

Predictive data on family size have been collected in a large number of polls. One reason is that the prior analysis of fertility—comparisons between urban and rural, or middle and working class, or Catholic and non-Catholic—became increasingly difficult as the earlier wide differences became smaller and smaller. Asking the individuals who would have the children what their plans were, it was thought, would help in forecasting the nation's fertility, the most erratic element of population projections. There is a considerable body of writings on whether best predictions are obtained by asking for the ideal, the expected, the intended, or the desired number of children; but the differences are not very great (cf. Girard and Roussel, 1982; *Growth of American Families). However the question is posed, results have been mixed. Sometimes statements of potential parents concerning their future families—and particularly concerning the "ideal family size"—merely reflect the level of fertility at the time of the poll, and thus have little or no predictive value (Trent, 1980; cf. Morgan, 1982). One test of reproductive goals against later natality showed, for example, a correlation of only 0.3 between the stated preference and the actual number of children twenty years later (Westoff et al., 1957; cf. Masnick, 1981). In another study, when Detroit women were re-interviewed after an interval of fifteen years, there was a generally good fit of their stated intentions with their completed fertility (Coombs, 1979; cf. O'Connell and Rogers, 1983). Most of the polling has been of women, but one cannot assume, especially but not exclusively in less developed countries, that the attitudes of husband and wife are identical, or that the wife will prevail in case of disagreement (Coombs and Fernandez, 1978). According to several studies, couples really have no genuine preference for a certain number of children; rather, after each child they decide anew in the context of the changed circumstances (Hout, 1978; Udry, 1983). Perhaps the best discussions of all the complications in using polling data to predict fertility are by Judith †Blake (1974) and Charles †Westoff and Norman †Ryder (1977).

REFERENCES: Judith Blake, "Can We Believe Recent Data on Birth Expectations in the United States?" *Demography*, 11 (1974), 25–44. Lolagene C. Coombs, "Reproductive Goals and Achieved Fertility: A Fifteen-Year Perspective," *Demography*, 16 (1979), 523–534. Coombs and Dorothy Fernandez, "Husband-Wife Agreement about Reproductive Goals," *Demography*, 15 (1978), 57–73. Alain Girard and Louis M. Roussel, "Ideal Family Size, Fertility, and Population Policy in Western Europe," *Population and Development Review*, 8 (1982), 323–345. Michael Hout, "The Determinants of Marital Fertility in the United States, 1968–1970: Inferences from a Dynamic Model," *Demography*, 15 (1978), 139–159. George S. Masnick, "The Continuity of Birth-Expectations Data with Historical Trends in Cohort Parity Distributions: Implications for Fertility in the 1980s," in Gerry E. Hendershot and Paul J. Placek, eds., *Predicting Fertility: Demographic Studies of Birth Expectations* (Lexington, Mass.: Lexington Books, 1981). S. Philip Morgan, "Parity-Specific Fertility Intentions and Uncertainty: The United States, 1970 to 1976," *Demography*, 19 (1982), 315–334. Martin O'Connell and Carolyn C. Rogers, "Assessing Cohort Birth Expectations Data from the Current Population Survey, 1971–1981," *Demography*, 20 (1983), 369–384. Roger B. Trent, "Evidence Bearing on the Construct Validity of 'Ideal Family Size,' " *Population and Environment*, 3 (1980), 309–327. J. Richard Udry, "Do Couples Make Fertility Plans One Birth at a Time?" *Demography*, 20 (1983), 117–128. Charles F. Westoff, E. G. Mishler, and E. Lowell Kelly, "Preferences in Size of Family and Eventual Fertility Twenty Years Later," *American Journal of Sociology*, 62 (1957), 491–497. Westoff and Norman B. Ryder, "The Predictive Value of Reproductive Intentions," *Demography*, 14 (1977), 431–453.

famine, an extreme and protracted shortage of food resulting in widespread deaths from starvation and from diseases aggravated by malnutrition (see *nutrition), cannot be sharply distinguished from somewhat less severe food shortages. There is often a tendency to label as famines shortages lasting a few weeks only, or a lack of particular nutrients resulting in food-deficiency diseases, or a more severe shortage in very small communities; but the term is better reserved for more general and more serious disasters.

Probably the worst famine in history was in four northern provinces of China in 1877–78. According to †Ho (1959, pp. 231–232), cannibalism was common, and local magistrates were ordered to overlook the prohibited sale of children so that their parents might buy a few days' food. During those two years, according to the estimate of a Foreign Relief Committee, from 9 to 13 million perished from hunger, disease, or violence. More generally, China is the land of famine, followed closely by India. In both traditional civilizations the family system encouraged a progeny that pushed population growth close to the number that regularly would consume all the food available, and both countries have suffered from periodic droughts and floods, as well as locusts and other pests, crop failures of other types, and inefficient government. The only modern famine in the Western world was that in Ireland in the 1840s (see Edwards and Williams, 1957). There had been a sharp decline in the age at marriage and a new dependence on the potato as the Irishman's staple. Following a potato blight that devastated the crop, between 0.5 and 1.0 million persons died out of a population of 8.2 million.

It is not possible to measure directly the mortality from a typical famine (but see Bongaarts and Cain, 1982). The registration of deaths, generally not very accurate in such areas, breaks down completely. But one can arrive at rough estimates, as exemplified from the Indian famine of the 1890s. India's population grew by 9.4 percent in the 1880s and by 6.1 percent in the first decade of the new century. If the growth had been by the average of these two figures, 7.8 percent, during the intervening decade, it would have been by some 19 million more persons, which Kingsley †Davis (1951, p. 39) estimated as the number lost by the famine.

Generally famines are intermediate between such natural *disasters as earthquakes or hurricanes and such social phenomena as *wars; as spelled out in †Malthus's principle of population, the growth of numbers beyond the means of subsistence is usually the consequence of both biological and cultural factors. Some recent famines, however, can be denoted as man-made—that in the Soviet Union in 1932–34, where the forced *collectivization of agriculture resulted in the death of about 5 million, or in Biafra, where the Nigerian civil war of 1967–69 culminated in a policy of genocide or, most recently, Cambodia, where the competition between two Communist regimes resulted in the death of perhaps a quarter to a third of the population from starvation and mass brutality (cf. Barron and Paul, 1977).

REFERENCES: John Barron and Anthony Paul, *Murder of a Gentle Land: The Untold Story of a Communist Genocide in Cambodia* (New York: Reader's Digest Press, 1977). M. K. Bennett, "Famine," in *International Encyclopedia of the Social Sciences*, 5, 322–326. John P. Bongaarts and Mead T. Cain, "Demographic Responses to Famine," in Kevin M. Cahill, ed., *Famine* (Maryknoll, N.Y.: Orbis Press, 1982). Kingsley Davis, *The Population of India and Pakistan* (Princeton, N.J.: Princeton University Press, 1951). R. Dudley Edwards and T. Desmond Williams, eds., *The Great Famine: Studies in Irish History, 1845–52* (New York: New York University Press, 1957). Ping-ti Ho, *Studies on the Population of China, 1368–1953* (Cambridge, Mass.: Harvard University Press, 1959).

farm would seem to be a fairly straightforward concept—a piece of land used for the cultivation of domestic plants or the raising of animals. In fact, however, the delineation of the *farm population* has varied so much from one country to another that international comparisons of such statistics as exist have a dubious value. Especially in less developed countries, a large proportion of the *food grown is on small family plots, of which the produce never enters either the commercial market or the statistics derived from market transactions (see also

*Gross National Product). The calculation of agricultural production, thus, may be understated, and the same is likely to be true of the population sector that grows the family's food. The work done by women and children is seen as an extension of housework and is not generally included in a compilation of the labor force. Males engaged in agriculture, on the other hand, often have other off-season or part-time jobs; and in some cases they are classified in these other sectors of the economy. With the enormous rise of agricultural productivity in advanced countries, the proportions of the population engaged in farming have declined dramatically; and if many of the young people are in the process of moving out of agriculture to other kinds of work, how should dependents be classified while they are still living at home?

The distinction between farm and nonfarm developed gradually in the United States censuses (Truesdell, 1960). Essentially the farm population has been defined by residence rather than occupation; it includes persons who live on a "farm," an entity whose definition has changed slightly over the years. The farm population has included some of the poorest and the best off: laborers, tenants, owners, and managers; illiterates and highly trained agronomists. The heterogeneity means that any generalizations that are not based on detailed statistics are likely to be misleading. Certainly it is inadequate to equate the farm population with the *rural one, in spite of the obvious overlap between the classification of households or families and that of geographic areas.

REFERENCES: Shryock and Siegel, *Methods and Materials of Demography*, pp. 168–174. Leon E. Truesdell, *Farm Population: 1880 to 1950*, U.S. Bureau of the Census, Technical Paper no. 3 (Washington, D.C., 1960).

fascism derives from *fasces*, a bundle of rods used as a symbol of authority in ancient Rome and also by the modern Italian movement. The term has been used narrowly to designate the party and government of Italy from 1922 to 1945 and, by some analysts, also as a generic designation (cf. Laqueur, 1976). Fascist Italy initiated some practices later adapted by Nazi Germany—the one-party state, with a dual set of institutions, one responsible to the state and the other to the Party; control of the press and terrorist elimination of key opponents; a "corporate" society in which all social classes would cooperate in the interest of the nation, with a consequent prohibition of strikes and lockouts (e.g., Salvemini, 1936). In spite of certain overlaps, as Gilbert Allardyce (1979) pointed out, the differences between Italian Fascism and German Nazism are as great and as important as their similarities. For the analysis of population in particular, the broader concept of *totalitarianism is more appropriate, since the Soviet-Nazi overlap is more significant. The pronatalist policy of the Fascist regime differed from similar efforts in other Western countries mainly in that it encompassed a full range, from the discouragement of celibacy and the encouragement of marriage to the subsidizing of large families and the inhibition of emigration (cf. Cannistraro, 1982; Loffredo, 1950). Like most other such policies, the one in

Italy failed to block the fall in fertility (Glass, 1940, chap. 5). See also *family assistance; Corrado †Gini.

REFERENCES: Gilbert Allardyce, "What Fascism Is Not: Thoughts on the Deflation of a Concept," with comments by Stanley G. Payne and Ernst Nolte, *American Historical Review*, 84 (1979), 367–398. Philip V. Cannistraro, "Demographic Policy," in Cannistraro, ed., *Historical Dictionary of Fascist Italy* (Westport, Conn.: Greenwood Press, 1982). D. V. Glass, *Population Policies and Movements in Europe* (Oxford:. Clarendon, 1940). Walter Laqueur, ed., *Fascism: A Reader's Guide* (Berkeley: University of California Press, 1976). Ferdinando Enrico Loffredo, "Demografica, Politica," *Enciclopedia Italiana*, Appendix I (1938), pp. 507–508; reprinted in the 1949 edition (Rome, 1950). Gaetano Salvemini, *Under the Axe of Fascism* (New York: Viking, 1936).

fecundability, the probability that a woman having regular sexual intercourse will conceive during one menstrual cycle in the absence of any attempt to prevent conception. As specified by Corrado †Gini, who seemingly coined the term, it means the probability of conception during any one month (rather than menstrual cycle) in the absence of contraception and outside the periods of gestation and of sterility following a childbirth. It is thus the usual way of summing up all the factors that affect fertility—physiological, cultural, and other—omitting only birth control and the bearing of a child. For women aged 20 to 29, the mean value is about 0.3; that is, women during their most fecund years will conceive in one menstrual cycle out of three during which they have regular sexual intercourse (Henry, 1976, pp. 98, 256). See also *natural fertility.

REFERENCES: Henry, *Population*. William H. James, "The Fecundability of U.S. Women," *Population Studies*, 27 (1973), 493–500.

fecundable, said of a woman, means capable of conceiving. An *infecundable* woman may be outside the reproductive age range, pregnant, in a state of postpartum sterility, or permanently sterile. See also *fecundability.

fecundity, the physiological ability to reproduce, is distinguished from *fertility, the realization of this potential, the actual birth performance as measured by the number of offspring. The two terms were long used synonymously, and it was only in 1934 that the *Population Association of America officially endorsed the differentiation that had been developing. The lay public and often physicians still use the two terms indifferently to mean the same thing. The cognates in Romance languages are also used synonymously in lay publications, but in demography the standardization of the etymological equivalents was not the same as in English. Thus, "fecundity" is translated into French as *fertilité*, into Spanish as *fertilidad*; and "fertility" is translated, respectively, as *fécondité* and *fecundidad* (IUSSP, Comisión del Diccionario Demográfico, 1959, chap. 6; Henry, 1981, chap. 6). In Italian the preferred usage in demography is the same as in these other two Romance languages, but some in the discipline do not follow it (Colombo, 1959, chap. 6).

The determinants of fecundity are difficult to specify precisely, for usually the only sure indication that a couple are able to have a child is that they have had one—in which case the conceptual differentiation between fecundity and fertility has no empirical equivalent. The most obvious factor is age; procreation is a function primarily of young adults. The capacity to reproduce, entirely lacking in childhood, begins to appear at puberty, develops gradually during *adolescence, reaches a high point at maturity, and then declines in middle age, relatively rapidly and completely in females, more slowly and apparently only partially in some males.

Fecundity is of course a characteristic of couples, but it is often regarded as one only of females. Sometimes the reduced ability of an elderly male to reproduce can be compensated by the high fecundity of a young wife. The precise timing of the decline in a female's fecundity, vice versa, is complicated by the fact that her childbearing is affected by the male's fecundity. Presumably it is possible to separate the physiological ability of the two sexes if the women are artificially inseminated, and such a study was made of French women by the Federation of Centers for the Study and Preservation of Human Sperm (CECOS). Among a population of 2,193 nulliparous women who had been artificially inseminated in one of the eleven centers that CECOS operates, the mean success rate per ovulation cycle fell with increasing age. The percentage conceiving within twelve cycles, 73 for those aged 25 years or under and 74 for those aged 26–30, fell to 61 at ages 31–35 and 56 at ages 36–40. The critical cutoff indicated by the study is 30 years (Fédération et al., 1982; DeCherney and Berkowitz, 1982). However, this conclusion has been challenged because, among other reasons, the rates of impregnation with artificial insemination are lower, age for age, than with natural sex relations (Bongaarts, 1982). The implications are important: women who want to postpone childbearing until they have completed their education and established themselves in a career either will or will not be able generally to combine the two roles successfully.

During the period when it is possible for a couple to have children, this ability is impaired by venereal disease or certain other ailments, including a nutritional deficiency (Bongaarts, 1979). It would seem that a high fecundity is hereditary (see *multiple births), but the evidence is muddied by the fact that when children remain in the same social-economic situation as their parents, their family size is likely to be more or less the same also for cultural reasons. The human ovum can be fertilized during only a day or two of each ovulation cycle, and during the rest of the month the woman is normally sterile (James, 1978; Potter, 1961). It has been established in the past several decades that prolonged breastfeeding reduces fecundity, and in some cultures the practice is used as a means of controlling family size (Bleek, 1976; Singarimbun and Manning, 1976); see also *lactation.

Though the word is seldom used in that sense, one might speak of the fecundity of populations—the ability to reproduce apart from either †Malthus's preventive checks or contraception. Perhaps the best estimate of the potential fertility of the human species is that derived from the *Hutterites, a religious sect that eschews birth control but enjoys the benefits of modern medicine. According to Christopher †Tietze's calculation (1957), if a woman married at age 15 and, throughout her fecund period, had the same number of children that Hutterites do in each age interval, she would bear an average of 12.6 children during her lifetime. We can take this to be the maximum physiological potential for a population (individual families have of course been larger). See also *altitude; *fecundability.

REFERENCES: Wolf Bleek, "Spacing of Children, Sexual Abstinence, and Breast-feeding in Rural Thana," *Social Science and Medicine*, 10 (1976), 225–230. John Bongaarts, "Malnutrition and Fecundity: A Summary of Evidence," in Center for Population Studies, *Working Papers*, no. 51 (New York: Population Council, 1979); "Infertility after Age 30: A False Alarm," *Family Planning Perspectives*, 14 (1982), 75–78. Bernardo Colombo, *Dizionario Demografico Multilingue: Volume Italiano* (Milan: A. Giuffrè, 1959). A. H. DeCherney and G. S. Berkowitz, "Female Fecundity and Age," *New England Journal of Medicine*, 306 (1982), 424–426. Fédération des Centres d'Étude et de Conservation du Sperme Humain, D. Schwartz, and M. J. Mayaux, "Female Fecundity as a Function of Age," *New England Journal of Medicine*, 306 (1982), 404–406. Louis Henry, *Dictionnaire Démographique Multilingue: Volume Français* (2nd ed.; Liège: Ordina Éditions, 1981). IUSSP, Comisión del Diccionario Demográfico, *Diccionario Demográfico Plurilingüe: Volumen Español* (New York: United Nations, 1959). William H. James, "The Length of the Human Fertile Period," *Population Studies*, 32 (1978), 187–194. Robert G. Potter, Jr., "Length of the Fertile Period," *Milbank Memorial Fund Quarterly*, 39 (1961), 1–31. Masri Singarimbun and Chris Manning, "Breastfeeding, Amenorrhea, and Abstinence in a Javanese Village," *Studies in Family Planning*, 7 (1976), 175–179. Christopher Tietze, "Reproductive Span and Rate of Reproduction among Hutterite Women," *Fertility and Sterility*, 8 (1957), 89–97.

Federal Statistics Users' Conference (FSUC), founded in 1956, was made up in 1980 of about 200 American business firms, labor unions, trade associations, research institutes, and state and local governments. Representatives of the member organizations met annually in Washington to review new developments in federal statistics on population trends, health and education, natural resources and economic growth, and other matters of interest. The Conference's thirteen committees included one on demography and another on manpower. The organization endeavored to get a prompter publication of federal data, the elimination of duplication in reporting, and a fuller regional and local analysis in existing statistical programs. It closed its office in 1984 when John Aiken, the executive director, retired. See also *Association of Public Data Users.

Federation for American Immigration Reform (FAIR), founded in 1979, advocates an overall revision of the relevant laws and procedures, particularly in order to curb illegal immigration. It publishes a monthly newsletter, *Immigration Report*, and a series of occasional *Immigration Papers*, of which the first was by the organization's chairman: John Tanton, "Rethinking Immigration Policy" (1979). Address: 2028 P Street, N.W., Washington, D.C. 20036.

feminism as a social movement is not a unitary phenomenon, for the goals have differed greatly from one historical era and one civilization to another (cf. Charvet, 1982). In most (perhaps even all) traditionalist cultures, women are subordinate to men. This lower status is quite explicit, for example, in both books of the Bible. Eve, who was created out of Adam's rib, tempted him and thus lost for all mankind the blessings of Eden; and the Church Fathers often recalled her deceitful behavior (cf. Daly, 1973). That wives should be submissive was given the force of religious faith.

I suffer not a woman to teach, nor to usurp authority over the man, but to be in silence. For Adam was first formed, then Eve. And Adam was not deceived, but the woman being deceived was in the transgression [I Timothy 2:11-14].

Women were to regard men as equivalent to God.

Wives, submit yourselves unto your own husbands, as unto the Lord. For the husband is the head of the wife, even as Christ is the head of the church. Therefore as the church is subject unto Christ, so let the wives be to their own husbands in everything [Ephesians 5:22-24].

The first meaning given to "equality," to put an end to this personal subordination of woman to man, was developed in the West as a corollary of the equal rights of men. In her enthusiasm for the French Revolution, Mary Wollstonecraft (1759-97), a notable pioneer of England's feminist movement, wrote *A Vindication of the Rights of Man* (1790) and then, two years later, *A Vindication of the Rights of Woman* (1792). A Women's Rights Convention that met in Seneca Falls, N.Y., in 1848 issued a declaration that even more pointedly derived from civil rights already won:

We hold these truths to be self-evident: that all men and women are created equal; that they are endowed by their Creator with certain inalienable rights; that among these are life, liberty and the pursuit of happiness; that to secure these rights governments are instituted, deriving their just powers from the consent of the governed [Rossi, 1973, pp. 416-417].

To begin with a premise expressed in phrases familiar to every American, and then to list all the ways that women were denied individual equality, made a powerful argument. The thesis that women are persons spread rapidly during the Victorian period, how rapidly is suggested by the extraordinary international popularity of Henrik Ibsen's play, *A Doll's House* (1879). The formal recognition of females as rational human beings, equivalent in a civil context to males, was achieved through women's suffrage, instituted in the West (except for such anomalies as Liechtenstein, which gave women the vote only in 1984) in the first decades of this century. Wherever else differences by sex had been written into law, these were often challenged and, if the differentiation was deemed to be irrelevant, overturned. In 1971, as one important example, courts voided an Idaho law stipulating that when a man and a woman had comparable claims to administer an estate, the former should be designated. "By providing dissimilar treatment for men and women who are similarly situated," the U.S. Supreme Court held, "the challenged [law] violate[d] the Equal Protection Clause [of the Constitution]" (*Reed* v. *Reed*, 404 U.S. 71 [1971]; cf. Wolgast, 1980, chap. 4).

Transferred to the economic sphere, the principle that men and women similarly situated should be treated the same evolved into a demand that those who did equal work should receive equal pay. Though this reform constituted an important gain for some *women in the work force, many continued to get smaller wages or salaries because they had jobs defined as low-paying women's work. Two more difficult reforms have been proposed: equivalent representation of males and females in every corner of the work force (a goal that will hardly be achieved in any country with a free labor market) and equal pay for equivalent work (which requires a decision, not readily accepted by the losing side, on what constitutes "equivalent").

As with most social movements, goals that had been accepted by most of the electorate were intertwined with others that both liberals and conservatives have found questionable or unacceptable. Women's political organizations generally include a highly vocal minority of lesbians, who have an agenda of their own (cf. Carden, 1974, pp. 81-83). Radical feminists like Germaine Greer and Kate Millett have revived the theme of Friedrich †Engels that a class struggle exists within the nuclear family, which must therefore be destroyed if women are to be truly liberated (cf. Charvet, 1982, chap. 3). An English group has labeled itself SCUM, or Society for Cutting Up Men. Not only such marginal types but a far more influential segment of Western populations has tried to eliminate the moral and legal differentiation between legitimate and illegitimate conceptions and births. In England it is the official policy of the National Council for One-Parent Families never to use the word "illegitimate" in its publications; and both there and in the United States, those who hold such opinions have succeeded in gaining general currency for the oxymoron "one-parent family." One reason that conservatives have often opposed feminist demands has been in order to defend the traditional family. Though a marriage of equals is a far nobler concept than one between a dominant male and his subordinate housewife, the egalitarian family is also more difficult to achieve and maintain. For when a wife had virtually no alternative to remaining with her husband, she generally made do with much that in a different setting would lead to a marital dissolution. However excellent in itself, the greater legal, economic, and social independence of women has also been an important factor in the rise in divorce.

The redefinition of women's domestic role seemingly implies that on the average wives will bear fewer children, but the relation between feminism and population is complex (cf. Birdsall, 1976). Women employed outside the home sometimes shift from family duties but sometimes they find ways to play the two roles simultaneously. Such a combination is seldom easy to achieve, but it has been facilitated by several new trends in Western institutions and folkways. Keeping house is far less burdensome with modern equipment, one-stop shopping, foods processed for quick preparation, and similar aids to middle-class American life. *Child-care centers, long established in some European and Communist societies, have become more important also in the United States. To the degree that household tasks are shared by the husband, the wife is freed from that portion of her traditional burden. Even with such aids, it is not a simple matter to adapt so central an institution as the family to new demands and strains, and students of the subject disagree sharply on whether the effort is succeeding. Neither Communist states nor most less developed countries have incorporated into their social and legal systems the principle of equal rights of men, a base from which the rights of women could be derived. Though the status of females in many of those countries is lamentable (see, for example, *Islam; *purdah), it has proved to be much more difficult than in the West to initiate reforms.

REFERENCES: Nancy Birdsall, "Women and Population Studies," *Signs*, 1 (1976), 699-712. Maren Lockwood Carden, *The New Feminist Movement* (New York: Russell Sage Foundation, 1974). John Charvet, *Feminism* (London: Dent, 1982). Mary Daly, "Social Attitudes towards Women," in *Dictionary of the History of Ideas* (New York: Scribners, 1973), 4, 523-530. Alice S. Rossi, ed., *The Feminist Papers* (New York: Columbia University Press, 1973). Elizabeth H. Wolgast, *Equality and the Rights of Women* (Ithaca, N.Y.: Cornell University Press, 1980).

FERMOD (presumably an acronym of FERtility MODel), a simulation model of reproduction that includes probabilities of pregnancy loss, expected length of pregnancy and of postpartum amenorrhea, and a varying fecundability.

REFERENCE: Robert G. Potter, Jr., and James M. Sakoda, "A Computer Model of Family Building Based on Expected Values," *Demography*, 3 (1966), 450-461.

fertility, the birth performance of a population, is contrasted with *fecundity, the physiological capacity to reproduce, and less sharply with *natality or the birth *rate, which are sometimes used more or less synonymously. See also *natural fertility.

The reasons for the great differences in the number of children per family, or in the fertility per unit of population, have become a topic of very active research in several disciplines, with no boundaries set on the range of variables to be included (cf. Andorka, 1978). Sizable bibliographies have annotated studies of fertility (e.g., Freedman, 1975; cf. Hawthorn, 1970) or of population policies (e.g., Driver, 1971). In fact, so much material has become available that it is difficult to organize. In a well known paper, Kingsley †Davis and Judith †Blake (1956) divided the determinants of family size by stages in the physiology of reproduction: continence, contraception, fetal mortality, and infant mortality (see *intervening variable). A second useful framework derives from significant developments during the past several decades in *anthropology and in *historical demography, which afford a far better guide to the past than the facile suppositions incorporated in the *demographic transition (cf. Knodel and van de Walle,

1979). Overlapping such a temporal sequence is the common contrast between industrial and less developed countries, a convenient though rough dichotomy that ignores so many variations in each of the two broad categories that it can be seriously misleading.

This discussion of fertility in general terms concentrates on analyses of Western and especially American fertility, if only because it would require a full book to do justice to the worldwide body of writings. American studies, moreover, are important beyond their locale, for whatever slight understanding was derived from them has been applied in developing a *population policy in less developed countries. This entry is followed by one on fertility measures, in which are expounded the many rates used with different types of data. The sequence here largely follows the development of demographic analysis, which after a rather narrow start has ramified into several social disciplines.

The study of differential fertility was the first and most obvious means of trying to make sense of observed variations. Differences among regions or other political subdivisions of nations are usually difficult to interpret, for the units are almost never homogeneous. Irrespective of other variations, urban fertility in the West has almost always been lower than rural; and this contrast was sometimes explained in ecological terms: city apartments or crowded neighbor-hoods permit expansion less comfortably than the one-family houses typical of villages or farms. A more plausible reason is that Western cities constituted the main driving wedge of a new social order. In less developed countries, where many in-migrants to cities are not upwardly mobile but are rather refugees from rural overpopulation, rural and urban fertilities are often close to equal, with urban sometimes higher (Robinson, 1963). See also *wealth-flow theory.

This fact suggests that differences by size of place are generally a special case of the inverse correlation between social class and fertility that has been observed in all modern Western countries. On the face of it, it is puzzling that those financially better able to care for children usually have had fewer of them, and analysts repeatedly hypothesized that the food of the middle classes, or some other elements of their way of life, was reducing the fecundity particularly of women. The actual reason was what Arsène †Dumont called "social capillarity": those seeking to rise to a higher status could move faster and farther if they had smaller family burdens. In Victorian England, where attractive positions were available in the developing industrial society, young men competing for them postponed marriage to an average age of 30 years, thus cutting their family size to well below that of those who remained at the bottom of the social-class hierarchy (Banks, 1954). In other words, it is not a high position that induces a low fertility, but rather the greater demands incurred in trying to move up (cf. Zimmer and Westoff, 1981). For those at the top, the lack of such pressures, combined with a typical concern about family continuity, has often resulted in a large progeny. Differentials by an index of social class—education, occupation, income, or some combination of such factors—are therefore ambivalent in many cases. In a review of more than 200 studies in less developed countries, few showed the expected negative correlation between education and fertility; most showed no relation or a positive one (Cochrane, 1979). Especially in less developed countries, the correlation between social class and family size is often positive in the traditionalist sector but negative in the modernist one, and the difficulty in distinguishing the two is compounded by the fact that many individuals are not so much in either sector as partially in both.

Differences in fertility by religion, ethnicity, race, or other cultural distinctions can sometimes be reasonably interpreted as variations on the same theme of social capillarity. Modern Western *Jews, for instance, have typically had the smallest families in their societies, for their remarkable success in climbing the social ladder was impeded by frequent anti-Semitism (Goldscheider and Uhlenberg, 1969). The same is true of such other minorities as *Japanese Americans, who had to reduce their family size more than others because for them social advancement was especially difficult. American *blacks show two patterns: those in the rural South, who generally lacked any hope of moving up, have had close to the highest fertility in the whole United States, but blacks advancing into the middle class have had many more childless families than whites (Farley, 1970; cf. Tolnay, 1981). In the usual view, the large families of earlier generations of Irish Catholics in the United States were simply a consequence of their religion. However, as young Irish Americans moved up—faster by some indices than any other subnation but Jews—it became routine to ignore the church's teaching on contraception in order to reduce the burden of dependents (cf. Greeley, 1972). Or, along another dimension of analysis, the movement of unprecedented numbers of married women into the labor force was indeed based on many aspirations, of which the first, however, was often the couple's hope of rising faster by combining two incomes with a smaller number of offspring.

The analysis of familial events by such broad categories as social class is based on the premise that by and large persons in the same place in the social structure, subject to the same pressures, will usually make more or less the same decisions—if they make any—concerning the spacing of children and the size of family. But overall determinants of fertility transgress the boundaries of such groupings. A consistent patterning by education shows the highest fertility among Americans with five to eight years of schooling and the lowest with sixteen or more years, and, among ethnic groups, the Mexican Americans with the highest fertility and Japanese Americans with the lowest. But all categories, whether social or cultural, generally adhere also to the national trend—a marked rise from 1945 to the 1960s and then a sharp fall. During both the postwar *baby boom and the subsequent decline in fertility, moreover, the trend has usually been toward convergence among subpopulations defined by any index (Rindfuss and Sweet, 1978).

One response of analysts to the diminishing returns from differential analysis was to start with data on birth or marriage *cohorts, for with them they could combine the effects on fertility of education or ethnicity, for instance, with the effects of each cohort's past history (Ryder, 1970). For example, women aged

40-44 generally have few children so close to the end of their fecund period; but the American cohorts born in 1911-15, many of whom postponed getting married—or, if married, having children—during the depression of the 1930s, had a high fertility late in their reproductive life.

A second new tack was survey research concerning how many children the respondent would like, the legitimacy of birth control or abortion, and other pertinent attitudes (cf. Swicegood et al., 1984). The results were usually not illuminating. In thirteen American polls between 1936 and 1966, male respondents gave a mean ideal *family size between 2.9 and 3.5 children, female between 2.7 and 3.6. In other words, over three decades encompassing the depression of the 1930s, World War II, and the years of postwar prosperity, reported shifts were within a range of less than one child (Blake, 1966; cf. Blake, 1974). The frequent attempt to get a greater precision by distinguishing among "ideal," "expected," "intended," and "desired" number of children helped not at all (cf. Hendershot and Placek, 1981). Changes in actual fertility were greater than the shift in reported attitudes, suggesting that many conceptions were not subject to rational control, or that those who were asked about future intentions were citing as their norm the current fertility level, or both. Even when the desired and the actual *family sizes coincide, it may be difficult to say which influences which; for instance, Catholics who would not use effective contraceptives and therefore expected larger families might also have said that this is what they wanted.

The inclusion of attitudes within its framework facilitated the extension of demographic research to other social disciplines. "Attitude" is, after all, a concept of social psychology, but such a typical work as *Psychological Perspectives on Population* (Fawcett, 1973) shows how difficult it is for those in another discipline to contribute significantly to demography. Does a decline in mortality, resulting in a higher rate of *natural increase, lead to a desire for fewer children as the most probable response (Davis, 1963; cf. Burch, 1975)? Applied to less developed countries, the presumed link between mortality and fertility seems to be contingent on various circumstances (e.g., Taylor et al., 1976). If we cannot be sure that the usual wish in "traditional" cultures is to maintain the "traditional" size of family, then what data or methodologies are available for the analysis of subtler attitudes?

In the subdiscipline called the *New Home Economics, an effort has been made to analyze how parents decide on the number of their children in the context of micro-economics (cf. Leibenstein, 1974). If one assumes that the rationality of *Economic Man extends to falling in love, getting married, pride of family, and other sentiments related to fertility, then one can postulate that the "demand" for children is analogous to the demand for such consumer durables as refrigerators or automobiles, relegating that portion of the data that does not fit to unanalyzed "tastes." Certainly some births follow from rational decisions to have children, but even within that portion—however large or small it may be—the effects of income on fertility, for instance, are not easy to specify (cf.

Rosenzweig and Wolpin, 1980; Simon, 1974). Since even after the fact the costs of having children are difficult to calculate, and since the benefits are largely nonmonetary and therefore calculable only by a dubious transfer to a quantitative scale, a model based exclusively on cost-benefit analysis is not likely to yield new insights on motivation (cf. *utility).

One way of studying the origins of attitudes toward family size is to study children's norms (Gustavus, 1975). People change as they mature, of course, but there may be more continuity than one expects. Female students who moved from Catholic to nonsectarian colleges, as well as those who moved in the other direction, adhered more to earlier preferences regarding family size than students who remained in the same setting, presumably because they felt impelled to defend their attitude (Potvin and Lee, 1974). The finding that attitudes learned in childhood often persist in a radically changed environment is slightly based, but its implications for population policy could be profound.

In some cases it is questionable whether *any* decision-making model is appropriate to the understanding of how conceptions take place. Many in the lower classes of industrial societies and especially of less developed countries—the population sectors, that is, with typically the most children, who constitute the greatest social problem—do not plan much of their lives. Even crude measures of such feelings as "meaninglessness," "powerlessness," "normlessness," "social isolation," or "alienation" can be significantly correlated with fertility (e.g., Groat and Neal, 1967, 1975, 1980). Lee †Rainwater (1965, p. 201) found some of the people he interviewed to be "quite passive and fatalistic about family planning; they do nothing because they do not think anything will help, or they go through the motions of using a method in which they have little confidence (and therefore do not use it very consistently)." In his American sample, the proportions that responded in this passive, fatalistic manner comprised 14 percent of middle-class Catholics, 24 percent of unskilled workers, but 63 percent of both white and black casual workers and unemployed. Among the so-called lower-lower class, in short, almost two out of every three did not believe enough in the future to plan anything, including their families. Such studies suggest that for persons like this sample motivation is lacking, not knowledge about birth control or access to contraceptives.

One of the best studies of attitude and motivation developed out of an attempt to explain the high fertility following World War II. During the 1930s, when the cohorts who produced the *baby boom were growing up, the straitened economy inculcated modest expectations in most young people. But when they entered the job market in the late 1940s and early 1950s, their competitive position was excellent. Because of their small cohorts, there was a shortage of young workers, relatively many of whom used veterans' benefits to attend college, thus becoming able to compete successfully even against older, more experienced employees. Thus, the income and prospects of potential parents were exceptionally favorable when measured against the comparatively difficult circumstances of their childhood homes. Many not only could afford all the material possessions they wanted but were able also to marry young and have a middle-sized family (Easterlin, 1961).

By the 1960s each of these conditions was repeated in reverse. The boom babies, growing up in homes where rising prosperity seemed to be the rule, extrapolated this upward trend in their own aspirations. Since a much larger proportion went to college than in earlier generations, a degree brought less of an advantage. Because of their very large numbers, they were a glut on the job market, very often for occupations demanding graduate degrees as well as for those lower on the social scale. Expecting more from life than their fathers and able to get less, these young people took steps to reduce their family responsibilities. The periods of both high and low fertility, thus, were the consequence not merely of economic conditions but of these combined with the relative size of the cohorts entering the work force and the social aspirations that they had acquired during their childhood and adolescence (cf. Easterlin, 1980; see also Smith, 1981).

REFERENCES: Andorka, *Determinants of Fertility in Advanced Societies*. J. A. Banks, *Prosperity and Parenthood: A Study of Family Planning among the Victorian Middle Classes* (London: Routledge and Kegan Paul, 1954). Judith Blake, "Ideal Family Size among White Americans: A Quarter Century's Evidence," *Demography*, 1 (1966), 154-173; "Can We Believe Recent Data on Birth Expectations in the United States?" *Demography*, 11 (1974), 25-44. Thomas K. Burch, "Theories of Fertility as Guides to Population Policy," *Social Forces*, 54 (1975), 126-138. Susan Hill Cochrane, *Fertility and Education: What Do We Really Know?* (Baltimore: Johns Hopkins Press, 1979). Kingsley Davis, "The Theory of Change and Response in Modern Demographic History," *Population Index*, 29 (1963), 345-366. Davis and Blake, "Social Structure and Fertility: An Analytical Framework," *Economic Development and Cultural Change*, 4 (1956), 211-235. Edwin D. Driver, *World Population Policy: An Annotated Bibliography* (Lexington, Mass.: Heath, 1971). Richard A. Easterlin, "The American Baby Boom in Historical Perspective," *American Economic Review*, 51 (1961), 869-911; *Births and Fortune: The Impact of Numbers on Personal Welfare* (New York: Basic Books, 1980). Reynolds Farley, *Growth of the Black Population: A Study of Demographic Trends* (Chicago: Markham, 1970). James T. Fawcett, ed., *Psychological Perspectives on Population* (New York: Basic Books, 1973). Ronald Freedman, *The Sociology of Human Fertility: An Annotated Bibliography* (New York: Wiley, 1975). Calvin Goldscheider and Peter R. Uhlenberg, "Minority Group Status and Fertility," *American Journal of Sociology*, 74 (1969), 361-372. Andrew M. Greeley, *That Most Distressful Nation: The Taming of the American Irish* (Chicago: Quadrangle Books, 1972). H. Theodore Groat and Arthur G. Neal, "Social Psychological Correlates of Urban Fertility," *American Sociological Review*, 32 (1967), 945-959; "Alienation Antecedents of Unwanted Fertility: A Longitudinal Study," *Social Biology*, 22 (1975), 60-74; "Fertility Decision Making, Unintended Births, and the Social Drift Hypothesis: A Longitudinal Study," *Population and Environment*, 3 (1980), 221-236. Susan O. Gustavus, "Fertility Socialization Research in the United States: A Progress Report," *Papers of the East-West Population Institute*, no. 35 (Honolulu, 1975). Geoffrey Hawthorn, *The Sociology of Fertility* (London: Collier-Macmillan, 1970). Gerry E. Hendershot and Paul J. Placek, eds., *Predicting Fertility: Demographic Studies of Birth Expectations* (Lexington, Mass.: Lexington Books,

1981). John Knodel and Etienne van de Walle, "Lessons from the Past: Policy Implications of Historical Fertility Studies," *Population and Development Review*, 5 (1979), 217-245. Harvey Leibenstein, "An Interpretation of the Economic Theory of Fertility: Promising Path or Blind Alley?" *Journal of Economic Literature*, 12 (1974), 457-479. Raymond H. Potvin and Che-fu Lee, "Catholic College Women and Family-Size Preferences: A Reanalysis," *Sociological Analysis*, 35 (1974), 24-34. Lee Rainwater, *Family Design: Marital Sexuality, Family Size, and Contraception* (Chicago: Aldine, 1965). Ronald R. Rindfuss and James A. Sweet, "The Pervasiveness of Postwar Fertility Trends in the United States," in Karl E. Taeuber et al., eds., *Social Demography* (New York: Academic Press, 1978). Warren C. Robinson, "Urbanization and Fertility: The Non-Western Experience," *Milbank Memorial Fund Quarterly*, 41 (1963), 291-308. M. R. Rosenzweig and K. I. Wolpin, "Testing the Quantity-Quality Fertility Model: The Use of Twins as a Natural Experiment," *Econometrica*, 48 (1980), 227-240. Norman B. Ryder, "The Emergence of a Modern Fertility Pattern: United States, 1917-66," in S. J. Behrman et al., eds., *Fertility and Family Planning* (Ann Arbor: University of Michigan Press, 1970). Julian L. Simon, *The Effects of Income on Fertility* (Chapel Hill: University of North Carolina, Carolina Population Center, 1974). David P. Smith, "A Reconsideration of Easterlin Cycles," *Population Studies*, 35 (1981), 247-264. C. Gray Swicegood, S. Philip Morgan, and Ronald R. Rindfuss, "Measurement and Replication: Evaluating the Consistency of Eight U.S. Fertility Surveys," *Demography*, 21 (1984), 19–33. Carl E. Taylor, Jeanne S. Newman, and Narindar U. Kelly, "The Child Survival Hypothesis," *Population Studies*, 30 (1976), 263-278. Stewart E. Tolnay, "Trends in Total and Marital Fertility for Black Americans, 1886-1899," *Demography*, 18 (1981), 443-463. Basil G. Zimmer, "The Impact of Social Mobility on Fertility: A Reconsideration"; Charles F. Westoff, "Another Look at Fertility and Social Mobility"; and Zimmer, "A Rejoinder," *Population Studies*, 35 (1981), 120-136.

fertility gods (or, more often, goddesses), an element of many religions or mythologies, are a striking indication of the strong pronatalist bent in most traditional cultures. A partial list includes: Amen (ancient Thebes), often identified with the sun god Ra and therefore called Amen-Ra. Astarte (Canaan), goddess of both fertility and the evening star. Cabiroi (Greece and Asia Minor), four gods of an obscure fertility cult. Demeter (Greece), goddess of fertility and the harvest. Dusares (ancient Jordan), god of fertility and the vine; he was born on December 25 of a virgin mother. Frey and Freyja (Norse), god and goddess of fertility or, respectively, of peace and plenty and of love. Gefion (Norse), goddess of fertility. Hathor (Egypt), goddess of love and fertility, sometimes represented as a cow. Inanna (Sumer), goddess of fertility, sister of the sun god Uttu and wife of Tammuz, lord of vegetation. Ishtar (Babylonia), variant of Inanna. Min (Egypt), fertility god whose festivals were celebrated with a pole-climbing contest. Nehalennia (Germanic), goddess of fertility and navigation. Osiris (Egypt), fertility god who gradually replaced the sun gods; also god of the dead. Pomona (Rome), goddess of fruit and fruitfulness. Priapus (Greece), god of fertility and gardens, represented as a misshapen dwarf. Vertumnus (Rome), fertility god, husband of Pomona. Xipe Totec (Aztec), god of spring, when he shed his diseased skin and started a new season of splendor.

REFERENCE: Richard Barber, *A Companion to World Mythology* (New York: Delacorte, 1979).

fertility measures vary in the data used to compute them, their relative complexity, their specific purpose, and their elegance (Henry, 1972; Le Bras, 1979). The commonest and least pretentious is the crude birth rate (or simply the birth rate), the number of births during a year per 1,000 in the midyear population. For countries with relatively complete *birth statistics, it ranges from under 10 to nearly 50, or in less developed countries with deficient registrations perhaps as high as 60. The birth rate has the same advantages and disadvantages as any other crude *rate: it is easy to compute from data often available, but the denominator includes a sizable proportion who do not contribute to the events measured in the numerator (in this case, children and the elderly, who cannot become parents).

It is usual in demography to measure fertility against the number of potential mothers rather than parents (see *fertility; *paternal fertility). In accordance with that convention, the first correction of the crude rate is the *general fertility rate*, or the number of births per 1,000 fecund women, usually specified as females aged 15 to 44 (or sometimes 15 to 49). Though women in this age range are usually physiologically capable of bearing a child, the probability that one will do so varies greatly because of both biological and cultural factors. It is possible to relate the birth performance more precisely to the potential, therefore, by calculating *age-specific fertility rates* (sometimes called age-specific birth rates), usually denoted by 5-year age groups. For any year, then, an age-specific fertility rate is the number of births to women of specified ages per 1,000 women of those ages in the midyear population. The calculation, of course, yields not a single figure but a schedule listing the numbers of births per 1,000 females aged 15 to 19, 20 to 24, and so on. One way of summarizing such a table or graph is to derive the median (or, less satisfactorily, the mean) age of all mothers at the time of the births during a year, in order to suggest any shifts in the typical ages at childbearing or whatever contrasts exist among various nations or subnations. Another summary figure is the *total fertility rate*, or the sum of the *age-specific rates, which, as noted above, are usually given by 5-year age brackets. This means that in order to get an annual measure, the sum has to be multiplied by 5, giving a figure that tells us how many children on the average each 1,000 women have while passing through their fecund years, assuming that the birth record of that single year is representative of the entire period. Since each woman typically has more than one child, the figure for a thousand women is several thousand—indeed a cumbersome measure.

The British demographer R. R. †Kuczynski devised two variations of the total fertility rate, the *reproduction rates. He took as the reproductive unit one woman rather than 1,000 women, and as the unit of reproduction a daughter who would take the place of her mother in the next generation rather than a child of either sex. The *gross reproduction rate*, then, is the ratio of female births in two successive generations, assuming no change in the age-specific birth rates and no deaths before the end of the childbearing period. If the age-specific female mortality is applied from a current life table to the mothers, the result is called the *net reproduction rate*, the ratio of female births in two successive generations, assuming no change in the age-specific fertility or mortality. That is, the gross rate measures fertility only, the net rate the difference between fertility and mortality. In fact, however, the gross and the net reproduction rates are population projections, half-disguised as measures of, respectively, fertility and natural increase.

Ansley †Coale (1970) devised a new measure of fertility, based on comparing the total fertility rate of any population with the highest one ever recorded. If a woman married at age 15 and, throughout her fecund period, had the same number of children that *Hutterites do in each age interval, she would bear an average of 12.6 children during her lifetime. If we take this to be the maximum physiological potential for a population (individual families have of course been larger), the reproduction of less prolific peoples can be related to this norm by what he termed the *index of overall fertility*.

These several rates can be adjusted in various ways for one purpose or another (cf. Romaniuk and Piché, 1972; Guest, 1974). Crude birth rates may be calculated from births corrected for underregistration or from a population corrected for underenumeration, or with both corrections. Any of the fertility rates may be calculated as the ratio of legitimate births to married women, or of illegitimate births to unmarried women. If parity is of special interest, one may calculate the rates of order-specific births either to all women or to women by age categories. For example, one can calculate the probability of births specific by age and parity of mothers—that is, the probability that a woman of a given parity and exact age x will bear a child before reaching exact age $x + 1$ (cf. U.S. National Committee on Vital and Health Statistics, 1965, Table C; Park, 1976). Age-specific fertility rates can be standardized by the age distribution of females in a standard population, yielding the so-called United Nations sex-age-adjusted rates (United Nations, 1956, pp. 42-44).

For a period or country lacking adequate registration but with usable censuses, one can substitute for fertility rates the *child-woman ratio* (sometimes called the fertility ratio), or the number of children aged 0-4 years per 1,000 women in the fecund period. For example, Walter †Willcox (1911) showed in a classic paper based on child-woman ratios that except for the single decade 1850-60 fertility in the United States had fallen continuously from 1810 on, rather than increasing or remaining stationary up to the time of the Civil War, as earlier investigators had thought. The ratio, however, can be a defective index for temporal or cross-cultural comparisons. The typically poor data on which the ratios are based may be improving much faster in some countries, or in some sectors of a population, than in others. The undercount of infants and children is usually large (thus, the ratio is based on children aged 0-4 years rather than 1 year, which would seem to be the logical counterpart of a fertility rate), but the magnitude of the underenumeration is not necessarily the same from one time or place to another. If infant mortality used to be high but has recently fallen, the relative level of the child-woman ratio can rise dramatically, suggesting an increase in fertility that would be spurious. For such reasons the trend in Mexican fertility for so recent a period as 1960-70 became an issue between two analysts who had studied that country intensively (Seiver, 1975, 1977; Hicks, 1974, 1977).

More elaborate methods have also been used to estimate fertility from two or more censuses or surveys but with no registration data. It is relatively easy to calculate r, the rate of growth between two counts, and fertility can be derived by using model life tables (see *models) to estimate the mortality. The principal fault of this method may be the often unrealistic assumption that there is no migration in either direction. If the age reporting in the censuses or surveys is trusted, one can use a reverse-survival technique, which involves the construction of an appropriate life table that specifies survivors back through time.

The common characteristic of the measures discussed so far is that they are so-called *period rates, based on cross-sectional data. The time subjected to direct analysis is short, usually a single year, though the process of family building can take place over decades. At least in Western societies, moreover, the occurrence and spacing of childbearing are typically controlled to some degree, so that no single year out of a variable schedule of births is likely to be representative of the whole. In fertility surveys, attempts have been made to convert events into processes by posing questions about both past and future "fertility behavior," but the response to neither kind of question has generally been valid enough to be very useful (Ryder, 1973, 1975). Contrasted with period rates are those that measure not the reproduction of this or that year but rather the total birth performance over the whole of a woman's fecund period. Generation reproduction rates, for instance, give the number of daughters that according to current age-specific mortality would survive to the exact ages of mothers at the time when their daughters were born (Woofter, 1947). Another such measure is the *completed family size, or the number of *children ever born to women who have reached the end of their childbearing period. This is one type of *cohort analysis (Hajnal, 1947; Whelpton, 1954). When women who have passed their fecund period are divided into successively older categories, the number of children they report indicates the decline in family size over a considerable time. Indeed, underreporting probably increases with age, particularly with the oldest women, and longevity is related to completed family size, so that such a record can only be approximate. The most serious limitations, however, of completed family size or any other such cohort rate is that it pertains mainly to the past, and the childbearing pattern of women who have survived their menopause offers no dependable clue to how the current process of family building will proceed. In order to get a complete picture of fertility, one needs both period and cohort data, which come from different kinds of sources.

During the past several decades attention with respect to fertility has been

focused largely on less developed countries. Since these lack, almost by definition, adequate statistics, various techniques have been devised to fill in the
gaps and repair the inaccuracies. Techniques of estimation have grown in number
particularly since *computers became available, and included here are only some
of the more important (Allen, 1980).

If two or more estimates are available, other values can be derived through
*interpolation and extrapolation by techniques that range from elementary to
advanced mathematics. Some of the methods (marginal fitting, osculatory interpolation) require a computer and, of course, persons able to operate it. The
principal drawback, however, is that many less developed countries lack the
accurate data base from which a series of further estimates could be generated.
If cross-sectional data exist for only a single date, they can be manipulated to
construct a synthetic cohort, which combines period data to show a hypothetical
experience over a number of years or a lifetime (see also *own children). If
there are several census counts or other types of period data, moreover, an
analysis based on such cohorts can be combined with a historical reconstruction
of fertility to afford a more complete view of its past trend.

From only one source of incomplete data, one can derive aggregate period
rates by postulating the stable population toward which current rates will converge
(cf. United Nations, 1968). However, the model assumes that current rates of
fertility and mortality will remain constant, which is often unlikely (cf. *population, quasi-stable), and that it is a closed population, though migration (typically skewed in its age-sex structure) is generally an important factor in population
change. It is often important, also, to use model life tables to estimate the effect
of infant and child mortality on fertility.

Which of these methods to estimate fertility is most appropriate depends first
of all on the kind, amount, and relative accuracy of the data available. A second
criterion is the mathematical complexity and particularly whether the estimation
requires the use of a computer. Some types of estimation lead to period rates,
others to cohort rates; some are suitable only for aggregate estimates, others for
those at a micro level. Whatever their inadequacies, estimates based on various
techniques of this type will certainly be developed during the years to come, for
the statistics needed for traditional measures will not become available in most
less developed countries during the foreseeable future.

REFERENCES: I. Elaine Allen, "Fertility Estimation: An Evaluation of Techniques
for Incomplete or Inaccurate Data," *Estadística*, 34 (1980), 173-195. Ansley J. Coale,
"The Decline of Fertility in Europe from the French Revolution to World War II," in
S. J. Behrman et al., eds., *Fertility and Family Planning* (Ann Arbor: University of
Michigan Press, 1970). Avery M. Guest, "The Relationship of the Crude Birth Rate and
Its Components to Social and Economic Development," *Demography*, 11 (1974), 457-
472. John Hajnal, "The Analysis of Birth Statistics in the Light of the Recent International
Recovery of the Birth Rate," *Population Studies*, 1 (1947), 138-164. Louis Henry, *On
the Measurement of Human Fertility* (New York: Elsevier, 1972). W. Whitney Hicks,
"Economic Development and Fertility Change in Mexico, 1950-1970," *Demography*,

11 (1974), 407-422; "Comments on Daniel A. Seiver's 'Recent Fertility in Mexico: Measurement and Interpretation,' " *Population Studies*, 31 (1977), 175-176. Hervé LeBras, "La Vraie Nature du Taux de Natalité," *Population*, 34 (1979), 91-107. Chai-bin Park, "Lifetime Probability of Additional Births by Age and Parity for American Women, 1935-1968: A New Measurement of Period Fertility," *Demography*, 13 (1976), 1-17. Anatole Romaniuk and Victor L. Piché, "Natality Estimates for the Canadian Indians by Stable Population Models, 1900-1969," *Canadian Review of Sociology and Anthropology*, 9 (1972), 1-20. Norman B. Ryder, "A Critique of the National Fertility Study," *Demography*, 10 (1973), 495-506; "Fertility Measurement through Cross-Sectional Surveys," *Social Forces*, 54 (1975), 7-35. Daniel A. Seiver, "Recent Fertility in Mexico: Measurement and Interpretation" and "A Reply to W. Hicks's 'Comments,' " *Population Studies*, 29 (1975), 341-354, and 31 (1977), 176-177. United Nations, *Methods for Population Projections by Sex and Age*, Population Studies, Ser. A, no. 25 (New York, 1956); *The Concept of a Stable Population: Application to Countries with Incomplete Demographic Statistics* (New York, 1968). U.S. National Committee on Vital and Health Statistics, *Fertility Measurement* (Washington, D.C.: National Center for Health Statistics, 1965). Pascal K. Whelpton, *Cohort Fertility* (Princeton, N.J.: Princeton University Press, 1954). Walter F. Willcox, "The Change in the Proportion of Children in the United States and in the Birth Rate in France during the Nineteenth Century," American Statistical Association, *Publications*, no. 93 (1911). T. J. Woofter, "Completed Generation Reproduction Rates," *Human Biology*, 19 (1947), 133-153.

fertility transition, that portion of the *demographic transition pertaining to the decline in the birth rate. Since many factors in this decline, whether in the past or possibly in the future, are not well established, the meaning of the fertility transition is generally not precise. With respect to broad social groups, it can suggest, for example, that families generally became smaller first among the urban middle class, then among the urban and rural lower classes. And with respect to individual motives, the term is a means of referring to the *wealth-flow theory, the thesis linking upward mobility with a restraint on producing progeny, and other social psychological explanations.

fetal death, according to the definition recommended by the World Health Organization (WHO), is one "prior to the complete expulsion or extraction from its mother of a product of conception, irrespective of the duration of pregnancy." After the separation the fetus does not breathe, its heart does not beat, the umbilical cord does not pulsate, the voluntary muscles do not move. The WHO also recommended that fetal mortality be classified into four categories according to the duration of the gestation period, as follows: early, twenty weeks or less; intermediate, twenty to twenty-eight weeks; late, twenty-eight weeks or over; and indeterminate. The term *stillbirth* would be abandoned according to this recommendation; what were termed stillbirths would be classified either as late fetal deaths or as neonatal deaths, according to whether any sign of life was evident after the complete expulsion of the fetus; see also *mortality, infant. Shortly after 1950, when the WHO recommended this definition, it was adopted by the United States, which revised the registration form to the one shown here

OMB No. 68R 1901

U.S. STANDARD

REPORT OF FETAL DEATH

STATE FILE NUMBER

TYPE OR PRINT IN PERMANENT INK
SEE HANDBOOK FOR INSTRUCTIONS

MOTHER

HOSPITAL—NAME (If not in hospital, give street and number)
1a.

CITY, TOWN OR LOCATION OF DELIVERY
1b.

COUNTY OF DELIVERY
1c.

DATE OF DELIVERY (Month, Day, Year)
2a.

HOUR OF DELIVERY
2b.

SEX OF FETUS
3   M

WEIGHT OF FETUS
4

MOTHER—MAIDEN NAME   FIRST   MIDDLE   LAST
5a.

AGE (At time of this delivery)
5b.

RESIDENCE—STATE
6a.

COUNTY
6b.

CITY, TOWN OR LOCATION   STREET AND NUMBER
5a.

INSIDE CITY LIMITS (Specify yes or no)
6c.

PREGNANCY HISTORY
(Complete each section)

IS MOTHER MARRIED? (Specify yes or no)
10.

DATE LAST NORMAL MENSES BEGAN (Month, Day, Year)
9.

LIVE BIRTHS

11a. Now living   Number   None ☐
11b. Now dead   Number   None ☐

OTHER TERMINATIONS (Spontaneous and Induced)
11d. Before 20 weeks   Number   None ☐
11e. After 20 weeks   Number (Do not include this fetus)   None ☐

RACE—(e.g., White, Black, American Indian, etc.) (Specify)
6c.

EDUCATION (Specify only highest grade completed)
Elementary or Secondary (0-12)   College (1-4 or 5+)
6d.

DATE OF LAST LIVE BIRTH (Month, Year)
11c.

DATE OF LAST OTHER TERMINATION (as indicated in d or e above) (Month, Year)
11f.

MONTH OF PREGNANCY PRENATAL CARE BEGAN First, second, etc. (Specify)
7.

PRENATAL VISITS—Total number (If none, so state)
8.

THIS BIRTH—Single, twin, triplet, etc. (Specify)
12b.

IF NOT SINGLE BIRTH—Born first, second, third, etc. (Specify)
10.

EDUCATION (Specify only highest grade completed)
Elementary or Secondary (0-12)   College (1-4 or 5+)
14d.

FATHER

FATHER—NAME   FIRST   MIDDLE   LAST
14a.

AGE (At time of this delivery)
14b.

RACE—(e.g., White, Black, American Indian, etc.) (Specify)
14c.

CAUSE OF FETAL DEATH

15.

PART I

IMMEDIATE CAUSE
(a)

Fetal or maternal condition directly causing fetal death.

DUE TO, OR AS A CONSEQUENCE OF:
(b)

Fetal and/or maternal conditions, if any giving rise to the immediate cause (a), stating the underlying cause last.

DUE TO, OR AS A CONSEQUENCE OF:
(c)

PART II

OTHER SIGNIFICANT CONDITIONS OF FETUS OR MOTHER: Conditions contributing to fetal death but not related to cause given in (a)

[ENTER ONLY ONE CAUSE PER LINE FOR (a), (b), AND (c).]

Specify Fetal or Maternal

Specify Fetal or Maternal

Specify Fetal or Maternal

FETUS DIED BEFORE LABOR, DURING LABOR OR DELIVERY, UNKNOWN (Specify)
16.

PHYSICIAN'S ESTIMATE OF GESTATION
17.   Weeks

AUTOPSY (Specify yes or no)
18.

MULTIPLE BIRTHS
Enter State File Number for mate(s)
LIVE BIRTH(S)

COMPLICATIONS OF PREGNANCY   (Describe or write "none")
19.

COMPLICATIONS OF LABOR AND/OR DELIVERY   (Describe or write "none")
20.

FETAL DEATH(S)

CONCURRENT ILLNESSES OR CONDITIONS AFFECTING THE PREGNANCY (Describe or write "none")
21.

CONGENITAL MALFORMATIONS OR ANOMALIES OF FETUS   (Describe or write "none")
22.

NAME OF PHYSICIAN OR ATTENDANT (Type or print)
23.

NAME OF PERSON COMPLETING REPORT (Type or print)
24.

TITLE

DEPARTMENT OF HEALTH, EDUCATION, AND WELFARE—PUBLIC HEALTH SERVICE—NATIONAL CENTER FOR HEALTH STATISTICS
1978 REVISION

for reporting a fetal death. However, only about half of the states changed the legal definition, and it is well known that registration is far from complete, especially for deaths after only a relatively short gestation period. Many of the data published, therefore, pertain only to deaths at twenty weeks or more, which in some states are the only ones that are supposed to be registered under the law. See also *abortion.

REFERENCE: U.S. National Center for Health Statistics, *Vital Statistics of the United States, 1975*, vol. II, "Mortality," Part A (Washington, D.C.: U.S. Government Printing Office, 1979), Sections 3 and 6.

fetus, an offspring developing in the uterus, called a zygote immediately after fertilization, a blastocyst during the first six or seven days, then an *embryo up to eight weeks after fertilization, and finally an infant after it is completely outside the mother's body, even before the cord is cut. Also *fetal*, pertaining to a fetus; *feticide*, the destruction of a fetus, a term often used by opponents of *abortion.

feudalism, the political-social system that prevailed in medieval Europe, varied considerably from one area or period to another; and scholars have debated which characteristics were essential and thus whether the somewhat similar institutions of Tokugawa Japan, for instance, should also be designated "feudal." In Europe land was held "in feud"—that is, in exchange for service, and their relation to land tenure defined the two main social classes, lords and vassals, or, when the latter were not permitted to leave the manor, serfs. Among the duties owed by tenants were military service and the corvée, such as work on local roads. Marc Bloch (1962) speaks of two ages of feudalism. During the first, Europe was on the defensive, under repeated attacks from Norse marauders, Muslim invasions, and the threat of further incursions from the east. The scant data suggest that the disintegration of the Roman Empire was accompanied by a depopulation, beginning in the third century, reaching a nadir around the year A.D. 600 and with a more or less static low level for several centuries thereafter. From the middle of the eleventh century to just before the *Black Death of the mid-fourteenth century, the population of England increased from 1.1 to 3.7 million, that of France (territory of 1328) from 4.0 to 13.5 million. Throughout Europe the decline that started with the outbreak of the plague in 1347-48 continued for about eighty years; and from 1430 to modern times the continent's population grew without interruption; see also *Domesday Book. Of the Holy Roman Empire's approximately 3,000 "cities" (that is, walled enclosures with charters) at the end of the Middle Ages, 2,800 had populations ranging between 100 and 1,000. Places whose names we know were hardly more than villages: London with 18,000 inhabitants in 1086, only 35,000 in 1377; Paris with 59,000 in 1292; and Venice with 78,000 in 1371.

REFERENCES: Marc Bloch, *Feudal Society* (London: Routledge and Kegan Paul, 1962). J. C. Russell, "Late Ancient and Medieval Population," *Transactions of the American Philosophical Society*, vol. 48, part 3 (1958).

field, used in physics to denote the range of electromagnetic forces, has been adapted to social disciplines in various ways. In psychology the term is associated especially with the German-American psychologist Kurt Lewin (1890–1947), who defined "field theory" so broadly that it is hardly differentiated from other broad generalizations: a method of analyzing causal relations and of building scientific constructs based on the thesis that events are determined only by forces in an immediate "field" (cf. Lewin, 1963; de Rivera, 1976). In anthropology and increasingly in other social disciplines, "field work" denotes a study of people and communities in their natural habitat, as contrasted with the use of library holdings and similar secondary sources; the differentiation is reflected in the distinction between *ethnography and ethnology. Similarly in demography, the field work associated with a census is the actual enumeration, as contrasted with the compilation, processing, and publication directed in a central office. *Field checking* was introduced in the 1960 census of the United States; before the raw data were forwarded, they were checked on the spot for internal consistency, incompleteness, and other manifest errors.

REFERENCES: Joseph de Rivera, ed., *Field Theory as Human-Science: Contributions of Lewin's Berlin Group* (New York: Gardner Press, 1976). Kurt Lewin, *Field Theory in Social Science: Selected Theoretical Papers*, edited by Dorwin Cartwright (London: Tavistock, 1963).

Fiji: The Bureau of Statistics publishes the annual *Vital Statistics in Fiji*, as well as the quarterly *Current Economic Statistics* and *Social Indicators for Fiji* (irregular), all of which include data on population. See also Martinus †Bakker. Address: P.O. Box 2221, Government Buildings, Suva.

filiation, relationship of kin, especially that of a son to his father. Also, the legal designation of the relationship between a parent and an illegitimate child.

REFERENCE: Alfred Nizard, "Droit et Statistique de Filiation en France: Le Droit de la Filiation depuis 1804," *Population*, 32 (1977), 91–122.

Finland: Demographic Institutions

The Finnish Demographic Society, originally a section of the *Scandinavian Demographic Society, became an independent association while retaining a link with its parent. It organizes annual meetings, of which the proceedings, mostly in Finnish, are published in the series *Suomen Väestötieteen Yhdistyksen Julkaisuja*. Address: Tilastokeskus, Annankatu 44, 00100 Helsinki 10.

The Statistical Society of Finland, founded in 1920, often includes demographic topics at its meetings, as well as at the triennial meetings of the Scandinavian statistical societies. In 1962 the society published the Finnish edition of the *Multilingual Demographic Dictionary*. Address: Tilastokeskus, Annankatu 44, 00100 Helsinki 10.

The Department for International Development Cooperation began in 1969 to support family-planning programs in other countries with contributions to the

U.N. Fund for Population Activities (UNFPA), the International Planned Parenthood Federation (IPPF), and the Development Center Population Program of the Organization for Economic Cooperation and Development (OECD). Address: Ministry for Foreign Affairs, Hallituskatu 17, 00100 Helsinki 10.

UNIVERSITY AND OTHER RESEARCH INSTITUTES

The Finnish Population and Family Welfare Federation includes a Population Research Institute, of which the director in 1980 was Aimo A. E. †Pulkkinen. In analyzes especially the fertility, mortality, and migration patterns in Finland. Many of the results are published in *Yearbook of Population Research in Finland* (since 1969 published in English), which also includes bibliographies of Finnish demographic research. Address: Kalevankatu 16, 00100 Helsinki 10.

The Institute of Development Studies at the University of Helsinki was in 1980 under the direction of Göran von Bonsdorff. Its work has been concentrated on less developed countries, including the effect of population growth there. Address: Unionkatu 40B, 00170 Helsinki 17.

Also at the University of Helsinki there is a Research Group for Comparative Sociology, of which Erik A. †Allardt was director in 1980. It analyzes survey techniques and conducts surveys on a wide range of attitudes and characteristics, including those pertinent to demographic analysis. Address: Mariankatu 10 A 13, 00170 Helsinki 17.

At the University of Turku, there is an Institute for Migration, which has fostered analyses of emigration from Finland or from Sweden and of the assimilation of Finnish immigrants in the United States. Address: Kasarmialue, rak. 46, 20500 Turku 50.

GOVERNMENT STATISTICAL BUREAU

The Central Statistical Office, founded in 1865, has continued the compilation and publication of population statistics that had started in 1749. In 1980 the director was Olavi Niitamo. The country's official population statistics are published in three series: vital statistics, causes of death, and population, including censuses in 1950, 1960, 1970, and 1975. Population statistics are also included in *Bulletin of Statistics* (in Finnish, Swedish, and English editions, published regularly since 1971), *Statistical Surveys* (in Finnish, Swedish, and English editions), *Report Series, Statistical Yearbook of Finland* (annual since 1879; currently also in an English edition), and *Finland in Figures* (1975, in English). Address: Tilastokeskus, Annankatu 44, 00100 Helsinki 10.

FIPS PUBS (an acronym for Federal Information Processing Standards Publications), a series issued by the U.S. National Bureau of Standards that, among other things, set the criteria by which states, *counties, *Metropolitan Statistical Areas, and other *places are defined in official United States documents and statistics.

flexitime, a recent translation of the German *Gleitzeit*, meaning the adjustment of office or factory schedules in order to alleviate rush-hour congestion or to accommodate women who combine work away from the home with housework and childrearing.

flow matrix, a model used to analyze patterns of migration and the future distribution of the population if the current movements continue unchanged.
    REFERENCE: Andrei Rogers, "A Markovian Policy of Interregional Migration," *Regional Science Association, Papers*, 17 (1966), 205–244.

focus-group research, a method of investigation developed in market research to test the effects of advertising and help introduce new products, has been adapted to *action-research on family planning and other demographic issues. Small groups (usually six to twelve persons) representative of the potential market for contraceptive services, for instance, are guided through an intensive review of their attitudes. Women unknown to one another, meeting away from relatives and neighbors and questioned sympathetically, would be willing, it is believed, to give fuller and more honest responses to queries on delicate topics. In this respect, focus-group research is viewed as a substitute for the more extensive, simpler *KAP surveys. Comments in the group are not in response to standardized stimuli, and the group's leader uses his or her own judgment to rate them as significant or not. On such a topic as how *machismo affects fertility in Latin America, however, that judgment may reflect the biases of professionals rather than the actual attitudes of the groups' participants (Stycos, 1981). The December 1981 issue of *Studies in Family Planning* is devoted entirely to focus-group research, including two general papers and two discussions of how the method was used in Mexico and Indonesia, respectively.
    REFERENCE: J. Mayone Stycos, "A Critique of Focus Groups and Survey Research: The Machismo Case," *Studies in Family Planning*, 12 (1981), 450–456.

folk medicine, although the subject of many papers, has seldom been rigorously defined; it is as ambiguous as "folk" itself. The term is clearly distinguished from Western medicine, but whether the traditional practices of various peoples should be arranged in a hierarchy from sorcery to such native systems as *Indian medicine and *Chinese medicine depends on the particular analyst's orientation.
    The theory and practice of health care among primitives, sometimes called "ethnomedicine," differ from one people to another but have several typical characteristics. The cause of an illness is magical—a curse, the breach of a taboo, the loss of soul, or the like. Appropriate therapy, thus, combines medical with religious or moral elements. How effective any supposed cure may be is generally impossible to determine; generalizations about the mortality of primitives are likely to be specious, for contact with higher cultures has influenced their death rates so much, both negatively and positively, that one can hardly reconstruct the life chances of isolated hunter-gatherer bands. Some of the var-

iation found is undoubtedly due to the different methods used in the surveys, but there is also no reason to anticipate an overall uniformity among primitive peoples independent of their habitat, standards of sanitation, nutritional norms, patterns of violence, and therapeutic skills (cf. Polunin, 1967); see also *paleodemography.

As former colonies attained their independence, one of the cultural heritages they often denounced has been the Western mode of therapy, substituting for it in whole or part something called "traditional medicine." According to a report of the World Health Organization (WHO) (1976), "African traditional medicine is one of the pillars of the cultural heritage of the Region. . . . An integration of the two systems (traditional and Western), without compromise of principle yet with full understanding on both sides, should enable the sorely underprivileged population to benefit from one of the fundamental human rights: the right to health." Whether supporting a system of therapy actually promotes good health depends, of course, on its efficacy; and on this there is a marked lack of consensus among interested parties. Those who attended a WHO-sponsored conference in Kampala, Uganda, were unable even to agree on the terms with which to discuss the issues. Some regarded the designation "healer" as a pejorative carry-over from colonial times; others refused to use the title "doctor" for a traditional practitioner. Those with Western training were inclined to include "witch doctors," "diviners," "seers," and "spiritualists" among the "healers." Tanzania has set up a Traditional Medicine Research Unit, which has proposed to collect the most commonly used herbs and other substances, test them for efficacy and side effects, standardize the recommended dosages, and establish a fee structure for their prescription. The press would be required to distinguish clearly between *mganga* and *mchawi* (Swahili for "traditional healers" and "supernatural practitioners"), though in most actual cases the two are intertwined (Miller, 1980).

It has been estimated that 90 percent of the rural populations of less developed countries depend on folk medicines (Ayenso, 1978). The one-time criterion of progress in health care, the supplanting of traditional concepts and therapies with scientifically based Western medicine, is now often regarded as ethnocentric. A bibliography on folk medicine is entitled *Resources for Third World Health Planners* (Singer and Titus, 1980). How do people react who are given a choice between the two systems? According to a detailed study of Tarascan Indians in west central Mexico, the villagers use the cheaper traditional healers for what they regard as relatively simple disorders but the more expensive *practicantes*, or nonphysician practitioners of Western medicine, for more serious illnesses (Young, 1981). The program that Tanzania has announced would break new paths, for until now subjective judgments have usually been the only basis for testing whether any of the specific medicines in folk pharmacopoeias are effective therapies. Cures are brought about, it would seem, mainly of ailments with a strong psychosomatic component; and the sick person's belief in the efficacy of the dose is an important factor in his recovery. A number of plants used by the

Hausa in West Africa to treat malaria, however, were tested in a laboratory to determine whether they generated in vitro a significant amount of an oxidizing agent, which would suggest that they might be of therapeutic value. Some did and some did not; by this criterion the range was from useless to potentially quite efficacious (Etkin, 1979).

Ethnic minorities in advanced societies sometimes carry over medical beliefs and practices from a folk past. According to a survey in a Texas town by Arthur Rubel (1960), for example, five illnesses were confined to Mexican Americans: *caída de la mollera* (fallen fontanel, or the displacement of the top of an infant's cranium), *empacho* (blockage of food in the intestinal tract), *mal ojo* (evil eye), *susto* (shock, which may be treated by drinking blessed water with floating herbs and palm leaves), and *mal puesto* (sorcery). Such beliefs (sometimes related to actual maladies) may persist perhaps because of the amazingly large gap in understanding between physician and lower-class patient (Samora et al., 1961). In 1981 a team of psychologists and psychiatrists found in Newark, N.J., eighty-six folk practitioners of "spiritual" or "occult" healing. The city's population is largely black (cf. *Science News*, vol. 119, 1981, p. 118). But members of the educated middle class are not immune to their own set of superstitions, some of which diverge no less from scientific knowledge. The remarkable revival of astrology, witchcraft, and other manifestations of the occult seems to flourish independently of social class or level of education (Truzzi, 1972). And Wilhelm Reich's variant of psychotherapy, a cult virtually exclusively of well-to-do intellectuals, was so patently fraudulent that the U.S. Food and Drug Administration successfully sued to block the sale of his "orgone accumulator." For those who use the term "folk medicine," one seeming function has been to disparage the superstitions of the lower classes while passing over those of the college graduates or others in the middle class.

REFERENCES: Edward S. Ayenso, *Medicinal Plants of West Africa* (Algonac, Mich.: Reference Publications, 1978). Nina L. Etkin, "Indigenous Medicine among the Hausa of Northern Nigeria: Laboratory Evaluation for Potential Therapeutic Efficacy of Anti-malarial Plant Medicinals," *Medical Anthropology*, 3 (1979), 401–429. Norman N. Miller, "Traditional Medicine in East Africa: The Search for a Synthesis," American Universities Field Staff, *Reports*, no. 22 (1980); Ivan V. Polunin, "Health and Disease in Contemporary Primitive Societies," in Don Brothwell and A. T. Sandison, eds., *Diseases in Antiquity: A Survey of the Diseases, Injuries, and Surgery of Early Populations* (Springfield, Mass.: Thomas, 1967). Arthur J. Rubel, "Concepts of Disease in Mexican-American Culture," *American Anthropologist*, 62 (1960), 795–814. Julian Samora, Lyle Saunders, and Richard F. Larson, "Medical Vocabulary Knowledge among Hospital Patients," *Journal of Health and Human Behavior*, 2 (1961), 83–92. Philip Singer and Elizabeth A. Titus, *Resources for Third World Health Planners: A Selected Subject Bibliography* (New York: Trado-Medic Books, 1980). Marcello Truzzi, "The Occult Revival as Popular Culture," *Sociological Quarterly*, 13 (1972), 16–36. World Health Organization, *Traditional Medicine and Its Role in the Development of Health Services in Africa* (Geneva, 1976). James Clay Young, *Medical Choice in a Mexican Village* (New Brunswick, N.J.: Rutgers University Press, 1981).

folk society, a small, isolated, nonliterate, and homogeneous community with a strong sense of group solidarity. The members' behavior is traditional and spontaneous, expressed through the family and the broader kin group as the main societal units. The term is identified especially with the American anthropologist Robert Redfield, whose life works represent a continual effort to define Ferdinand †Tönnies's concept of *Gemeinschaft with empirical referents. The conclusions of the first such application, a study of a small Mexican town, Tepoztlán, were challenged in a replication by Oscar †Lewis (1951).

REFERENCES: Oscar Lewis, *Life in a Mexican Village: Tepoztlán Restudied* (Urbana: University of Illinois Press, 1951). Robert Redfield, *Tepoztlán, a Mexican Village: A Study of Folk Life* (Chicago: University of Chicago Press, 1930); "The Folk Society," *American Journal of Sociology*, 52 (1947), 293–308; *The Little Community: Viewpoints for the Study of a Human Whole* (Chicago: University of Chicago Press, 1955).

folkways, coined by William Graham Sumner in his *Folkways*, he defined as "the habits of the individual and the customs of society which arise from efforts to satisfy needs . . . and so win traditional authority. . . . They can be modified, but only to a limited extent, by the purposeful efforts of men. In time they lose power, decline, and die, or are transformed." When the concepts of right and truth are brought in to justify them, folkways are raised to a higher plane, which Sumner called *mores*, "faiths, notions, codes, and standards of well-being . . . [that] pervade and control the ways of thinking in all the exigencies of life." See also *customs.

REFERENCES: James G. Leyburn, "Sumner, William Graham," in *International Encyclopedia of the Social Sciences*, 15, 406–409. William Graham Sumner, *Folkways: A Study of the Sociological Importance of Usages, Manners, Customs, Mores, and Morals* (Boston: Ginn and Company, 1907).

followback surveys, a term used by the U.S. National Center for Health Statistics, are conducted to check on the completeness and accuracy of the data the agency compiles on births, deaths, and infant deaths. In the National Natality Survey of 1980, as a typical example, questionnaires were sent to mothers, physicians, and hospitals concerning a sample of one out of each 350 births, with an anticipated response rate of 75–80 percent.

REFERENCE: U.S. National Center for Health Statistics, *Data Systems of the National Center for Health Statistics*, DHHS Publication no. (PHS) 82–1318 (Washington, D.C., December, 1981).

food is the complement of population, obviously in the sense that to survive people must eat, and hypothetically in the sense that under some conditions populations grow up to the level of the subsistence available. The latter thesis, a preliminary and crude version of †Malthus's principle of population that David †Ricardo and others incorporated into classical economics, is the so-called Malthusian theory that has dominated most discussions of how people relate to the food supply.

The production of food depends first of all on natural factors. More cultivable *land is still available for use than is under any type of crop, but it is located far from the dense populations of either industrial or less developed countries. Temperature and rainfall are sometimes the dominant determinants of agricultural production; but for centuries *irrigation has mitigated the dependence on rain, and some artifically produced varieties prosper in climates too harsh for the original plant. The subdiscipline of economic anthropology deals largely with the means of gathering or raising foodstuffs or, on a comparative basis, of how changes in such techniques affect the rest of a people's culture (e.g., Arnott, 1975; Oswalt, 1976).

The transition to modern population growth in England, the first of the industrial nations, was due largely to the prior revolutionary transformation of agriculture, which cut mortality drastically long before there was any significant advance in medicine or sanitation (McKeown et al., 1972). The development of large-scale mechanized agriculture on the plains of the United States and Canada, combined with improvements in transportation and in such subsidiary processes as canning, refrigerating, dehydrating, and freezing, made it possible to increase the world's production of food and to distribute it widely. Most recently, the propagation of new varieties of food grains, the "green revolution," overwhelmed the most optimistic expectations in those areas where the superplants flourish.

Little is known about how much food the world produces. For sizable portions—including the most populous nation, Communist China—no records are available, and some of the data that exist must be taken as very rough estimates (Diwan, 1977). In most less developed countries, much of the food is grown on small family plots, whose produce seldom finds its way into statistics. This means that the figures compiled, mainly from market transactions, are often considerably lower than what is grown and consumed. Each year the *Food and Agriculture Organization of the U.N. (FAO) compiles the national statistics, such as they are; and every decade or so it has supplemented these annual reviews with summary appraisals. According to these sources, during the first post-1945 decade agricultural production rose sufficiently both to repair the war damage and to make up for the increment to population. During the second postwar decade, food production continued to improve, more than keeping up with the growth of the population (FAO, 1955, 1965). Since the figures pertain to food production per capita, agricultural produce not used for human food and international shipments of food were excluded, and the increase of population was included. Most significantly, the earlier search for new land, according to FAO's recommendation, should be supplanted by a more efficient use of land that is already in use: the agency proposed that land permanently under crops in all less developed countries should be raised from 210 million hectares in 1962 to only 223 million in 1985 (FAO, 1970).

In the following period productivity declined in certain less developed countries, particularly in Africa. The tone of FAO reports changed, and the key chapter of *The State of Food and Agriculture, 1974* was reprinted to give it wider circulation (FAO, 1975). In November 1979 the message at the twentieth FAO conference in Rome was mostly gloom. "Even if we make the most enormous efforts to increase food and agricultural production," the director general asserted, some 250 million people still would be starving at the end of the century. In an agency of the United Nations, dominated as it is by representatives of the Third World, the real reason for this shift was left ambiguous. On a world scale, food production per capita has continued to exceed the growth of population. Specifically in Africa, according to a 1977 report by an FAO team, the plagues of locusts have been permanently eradicated. In short, the renewed threat of mass starvation has been the consequence not of faltering technology, nor even of more mouths than the economies of less developed countries can absorb, but of drought aggravated by social-political turmoil (Petersen, 1976; Poleman, 1977, 1981). Food production fell off in Africa mainly because during the postcolonial period hundreds of thousands have become refugees. In order that food be grown, there must be a settled population living in relative security from planting to harvesting, and the deterioration of this minimum security was the main new factor in the world's food production. See also *famine; *nutrition.

REFERENCES: Margaret L. Arnott, ed., *Gastronomy: The Anthropology of Food and Food Habits* (The Hague: Mouton, 1975). Romesh Diwan, "Projections of World Demand for and Supply of Foodgrains: An Attempt at Methodological Evaluation," *World Development*, 5 (1977), 497–506. Food and Agriculture Organization, *The State of Food and Agriculture*, 1955; 1965; *Provisional Indicative World Plan for Agricultural Development*, 2 vols., 1970; *Population, Food Supply and Agricultural Development*, 1975 (Rome: FAO). Bruce F. Johnston, "Food, Health and Population in Development," *Journal of Economic Literature*, 15 (1977), 879–907. Thomas McKeown, R. G. Brown, and R. G. Record, "An Interpretation of the Modern Rise of Population in Europe," *Population Studies*, 17 (1972), 345–382. Wendell H. Oswalt, *An Anthropological Analysis of Food-Getting Technology* (New York: Wiley, 1976). William Petersen, "An 'Optimist's' Pessimistic View of the Food Situation," *Social Science Quarterly*, 57 (1976), 365–374. Thomas T. Poleman, "World Food: Myth and Reality," *World Development*, 5 (1977), 383–394; "Quantifying the Nutrition Situation in Developing Countries," *Food Research Institute Studies*, 18 (1981), 1–58.

Food and Agriculture Organization of the United Nations (FAO), a Specialized Agency, was the end product of a series of conferences held during World War II to plan how damage from that conflict could be repaired; and eventually this initial goal was accomplished (cf. Jones, 1965). The permanent agency that ensued has as its stated goal to raise nutritional and living levels, particularly in less developed countries, and to improve the efficiency of producing and distributing food. FAO collects and interprets data related to these purposes and promotes national and international policies designed to mitigate what it sees as serious problems. In 1963 FAO's activities were significantly broadened with the start of the World Food Program, originally a three-year experiment but then

extended indefinitely. Under this program workers in such labor-intensive projects as road building, irrigation, and community development are paid with food
rather than money. In 1974 the United Nations set up the World Food Council,
which reports to the General Assembly through the Economic and Social Council
(ECOSOC); its headquarters, as is that of FAO, is in Rome, and the link probably
ties the FAO more closely to its parent body. There is also a Committee on Food
Aid Policies and Programs, which reports to both FAO and ECOSOC, with
special reports also to the World Food Council.

In 1973 FAO was authorized to include population policies and programs as
an integral part of its education and training in rural communities. It established
a Planning for Better Family Living Program (PBFL), which has combined an
antinatalist message with any aid given. Together with the *United Nations Fund
for Population Activities, FAO has undertaken various programs to emphasize
the relation between food production and population growth (FAO, 1981). In
its programs in agricultural colleges, rural extension, and home economics, FAO
has also brought in materials relating population growth to the resources available. In 1976 its Human Resources, Institutions, and Agrarian Reform Division
established a Population Documentation Center.

World data on the production and consumption of *food are published in
FAO's *Monthly Bulletin of Agricultural Economics and Statistics*, and in such
annual reviews as *The State of Food and Agriculture* and the *Production Yearbook*. Each decade since 1950 FAO has sponsored worldwide agricultural censuses, which are reported in special summaries. For lack of any comparably
authoritative statements on the current state of the food-population balance, most
discussants use these publications, often with little regard to either the difficulty
of compiling such figures or especially the strong and more or less consistent
alarmist bias in FAO reports.

Addresses: Via delle Terme di Caracalla, I-00100 Rome, Italy; liaison for
North America: 1776 F Street, N.W., Washington, D.C. 20437.

REFERENCES: Nick Eberstadt, "Hunger and Ideology," *Commentary* (July, 1981),
pp. 40-49. Food and Agriculture Organization, *FAO-UNFPA Projects: Bibliography*, 2
vols., also in French and Spanish editions (Rome, 1981). Joseph M. Jones, *The United
Nations at Work: Developing Land, Forests, Oceans, and People* (New York: Pergamon
Press, 1965).

Ford Foundation, the largest of the American private foundations. During the
year ended September 30, 1981, with assets of $2.6 billion, it dispensed a total
of $84.7 million in 1,921 grants, plus $4.4 million for programs. The foundation
has been engaged in activities related to population since 1952, with Oscar
†Harkavy as the program officer in charge, and in 1959 it began to fund research
also on reproductive biology and assistance to family-planning programs in less
developed countries. Together with the *Rockefeller Brothers Fund, it has furnished the major support to the *Population Council, which has been an important
source of funding for academic research and training programs in demography.

The total that the Ford Foundation expended in this area has ranged in recent years between $12 and $17 million annually, but population is not specifically mentioned among the foundation's current six major fields of interest, listed in 1982 as urban poverty; rural poverty, particularly in less developed countries; child care; human rights and social justice; education; and international politics and economics. Address: 320 East 43 Street, New York, N.Y. 10017.

foreign-born, by the usage of the U.S. Bureau of the Census, comprise all persons who are not classified as *native. Most immigrants have been young adults; they were born into American society, so to speak, at about the age of 20 and their ages ranged upward from that figure. This age structure (as well as old-country family norms) resulted in a very high fertility. After the laws restricting immigration were passed in the 1920s, the proportion of foreign-born in the population fell off—from about 15 percent in 1920 to about 5 percent in 1970. The number of immigrants rose slightly in the 1970s, but the high ages of many who came from 1880 to 1914 resulted in a higher mortality than among natives. The United States has asked the country of birth in every census since 1850, but the totals do not agree with those counted by the immigration service. For example, during the 1901-10 decade some 8.8 million immigrants were counted on their arrival, but the number of persons who declared themselves to be foreign-born in the 1910 census was only 3.8 million. Presumably many who have become acculturated and naturalized report themselves as native; this would seem to be especially true of those nationalities (such as Canadians) that have few if any differentiating characteristics and little sense of group solidarity. See also *alien.

The allocation of immigrants by nationality was particularly chancy during the several decades before 1914, when their number was sometimes more than a million a year. At the New York port of entry, officials who had no common language with those arriving had to register some 4,000 or 5,000 immigrants a day. Apparently they were often listed as natives of the country from which they had sailed, though many others than English left from Liverpool, or Germans from Hamburg. And what the officers did with the complex ethnic structures of Austria-Hungary and Russia, no one knows. Nor is the record for the more recent past without major flaws. The 1940 census schedule instructed the enumerator to distinguish between the Irish Free State and Northern Ireland, and the number from the latter was given as 106,000. When this instruction was shifted to the enumerator's manual in 1950, the number fell to 15,000, rising again to 68,000 in 1960, when the stipulation again was given on the schedule itself. For the countries of Central Europe, the allocation in 1950 was based on the person's surname, in 1960 on mother tongue; but neither index is an accurate measure of those who were born, say, in Czechoslovakia.

REFERENCE: Shryock and Siegel, *Methods and Materials of Demography*, chaps. 9, 20.

foreign stock, in the usage of the U.S. Bureau of the Census, first- and second-generation immigrants—that is, the *foreign-born plus their native-born children. See also *citizen.

frailty is defined in a demographic context as an individual susceptibility to dying independent of the three or four variables usually taken into account in analyses of mortality—age, sex, population group, and year. Including frailty in the construction of life tables makes a significant difference in life expectations.

REFERENCE: James W. Vaupel, "The Impact of Heterogeneity in Individual Frailty on the Dynamics of Mortality," *Demography*, 16 (1979), 439–454.

frame, a list, map, or other type of specification of the population from which a sample is to be drawn. If the frame of a sample survey is incomplete, out of date, or otherwise inaccurate, any conclusions based on the sample would be of doubtful value.

Framingham Study, an attempt to identify risks of heart disease associated with various physical and behavioral characteristics, took place in Framingham, Mass., a town some twenty-seven miles west of Boston. Included in the population were both workers in local factories and middle-class commuters to Boston offices. The study began in 1948 with a cohort of 2,336 men and 2,873 women aged 30 to 62 years. Every two years the surviving participants were given a physical examination that included an updated medical history, blood chemistries, body measurement, appraisal of vital capacity, chest X-ray, and electrocardiogram. Details of illness or death were collected from medical records and reports from family members. The results of these periodic examinations were reported in a series of thirty-two volumes, with an index in a separate volume (Kannel et al., 1967-78). The study confirmed the recommendations being developed elsewhere over the same decades—that the risk of heart disease can be reduced significantly by smoking fewer cigarettes, exercising regularly, keeping one's weight normal with a low-fat diet, and maintaining a normal blood pressure (cf. McQuade, 1980).

REFERENCES: William B. Kannel, Tavia Gordon et al., *The Framingham Study: An Epidemiological Investigation of Cardiovascular Disease*, 33 vols. (Washington, D.C.: U.S. Government Printing Office, 1967-78). Walter McQuade, "Good News from the House on Lincoln Street," *Fortune* (January 14, 1980), pp. 86-92.

France predated all other Western countries in the decline of its fertility. Its birth rate probably began to fall before the Revolution of 1789, and by 1800 fertility was an estimated 10 percent below its traditional level. In the middle of the following century, when the marital fertility rates of Sweden, Denmark, and England and Wales were close to 0.7 of the maximum ever recorded—that of the *Hutterites in the 1920s—the French index was around 0.5 and falling rather fast (cf. Knodel and van de Walle, 1979). Especially after France was defeated by Prussia in the war of 1870-71, French statesmen and scholars devoted much time and effort to understanding why families were getting smaller and how the trend could be reversed. It is noteworthy that †Malthus and Arsène †Dumont both explained the decline in the same way: as those in the lower classes endeavored to advance themselves, they found that with a smaller number of dependents they could move up faster and farther. For Malthus this embourgeoisement represented a most fortunate escape from the principle of population, but for Dumont it marked the unpatriotic selfishness of the rising classes. Fear of depopulation started in France and was long strongest there, but it spread to the rest of the West as well. Such eminent demographers as the American Joseph †Spengler (1938) and the German Hans †Harmsen (1927) also wrote major works on the decline of French fertility. By the 1930s, when the secular downward trend in the birth rate was reinforced by the temporary effects of the worldwide depression, demographic analysis throughout the West was concentrated on how to avoid what has since become known as *zero population growth.

The typical weaknesses of the neo-Malthusian movement were often aggravated in France by the country's special circumstances. The several rival leagues were associated closely with the extreme Left. Paul †Robin, founder of the League for the Regeneration of Humanity and of its publication, *Régénération*, was a genuine revolutionary, a one-time friend of Karl Marx. Eugène and Jeanne †Humbert, who put out a series of birth-control magazines (among others, *La Grande Réforme*, founded in 1931; and, after Eugène died in prison, *La Nouvelle Réforme*, established after World War II and published only until May, 1949), found some of their main supporters among anarchists. However, the two main parties of the Left, the Socialists and Communists, were either indifferent or hostile; and the movement also had little support in the middle class, where many were more likely to respond to nationalist or Catholic arguments for pronatalism (cf. Jean †Delteil; Paul †Haury).

In the nineteenth century the successive Republics had no overt population policy, but then the government took a series of both positive and negative pronatalist steps. Family allowances were given to mailmen and telegraph operators (1900), the army (1913), all civil servants (1916), and private employees with dependents (1932). In 1920 a law was passed forbidding abortion and the dissemination of contraceptives (see Henri †Fabre; Marie Andrée †Lagroua Weill-Hallé). These measures culminated in a Family Code, enacted in mid-1939 and put into effect under the Nazi occupation. It increased family subsidies and provided other types of family assistance, strengthened the prohibition of abortion, introduced measures designed to reduce infant and maternal mortality, and provided for *population education (see Bourgeois-Pichat, 1972; Watson, 1952, 1954). Within a few months of the end of World War II in 1945, the government established the National Institute of Demographic Studies (INED) and charged it with providing an accurate factual base for population policy. INED became one of the world's principal centers of demographic research and much of its work, as reported in its main journal, *Population*, has continued to relate to this original function. Periodic revisions in the schedule of family subsidies are analyzed by members of the INED staff. It was argued, for instance, that since the combined family assistance and tax deductions are still based on the premise that married women do not work outside the home, opportunity costs are high. Middle-income couples with three or more children in particular have to pay what was deemed to be a disproportionate share of the *cost of raising their families (Calot, 1980). Another feature has been a periodic survey of public opinion on family policy and French natality (e.g., Girard et al., 1975). See also *France: Demographic Institutions.

It is impossible to say how much the pronatalist measures affected the country's fertility, which went through the same general cycles as that in other Western countries: a postwar *baby boom, decline during the 1950s, a new high around 1962, and then a new decline. The entire December 1979 issue of *Population* is devoted to various aspects of France's population, including in particular the eighth in a series of general reviews (INED, 1979) and two reports on a survey of the use of contraception (Léridon and Sardon, 1979; Collomb and Charbit, 1979). Of a sample of women aged 20 to 44 who were interviewed in 1978, more than 96 percent of those who were fecund and did not want to become pregnant used some type of contraceptive method, including especially the pill and withdrawal. There were about a million one-parent families with children under 16, of whom well over half were illegitimate (Rallu, 1982); like other Western countries, France has witnessed the paradoxical combination of readier access to birth control with a larger number of presumably unwanted births outside of wedlock. The mean number of children per woman in the fecund age range was 2.0 in 1981, far from the lowest in Western Europe (Muñoz-Perez, 1982). Aging of the population has been slower than the low fertility would ordinarily indicate, for the cohorts moving into the higher ages are rather small. According to the 1975 census, 14.3 percent of the population (or 13.4 percent reckoned by exact age) were 65 years or over; seven other countries in Western Europe had higher percentages (Parant, 1981). France's economy has been dependent on immigration; the number of resident aliens rose from 1.6 million in 1954 to 3.4 million in 1975 (Tribalat-Brahimi, 1981). In a recent projection of France's population to the year 2075, various alternative levels of fertility and economic activity were considered, but the assumption was made throughout that the population is moving toward stability (LeBras and Tapinos, 1979).

In spite of the considerable international attention that France's population was given, few conclusions that one might have drawn from that country's experience were reflected in subsequent theory or practice. It has generally been assumed that fertility falls off after (or at the earliest, with) a rise in industry; the model fits England, where the birth rate started its decline about a century after that in France and the United States. That these first two democracies underwent the earliest decline in the birth rate at least suggests that political ideology may have more significance than it is generally accorded: seemingly the encouragement of upward social mobility included downward pressure on family size. In the country where before about 1914 some form of birth control was most practiced, the neo-Malthusian leagues were perhaps the weakest in Western Europe, but formal *family-planning programs are now widely perceived as crucial to any effort in less developed countries or elsewhere to reduce natality. That France was the first to go through the *fertility transition has not meant at all that it remained ahead of other countries, several of which have a lower fertility, a higher proportion of the aged, and a generally less favorable prospect of adjusting their population growth to the economy.

REFERENCES: Jean Bourgeois-Pichat, "France," Population Council, *Country Profiles* (New York, 1972). Gérard Calot, "Niveau de Vie et Nombre d'Enfants: Un Bilan de la Législation Familiale et Fiscale Française de 1978," *Population*, 35 (1980), 9-55. Philippe Collomb and Yves Charbit, "La Contraception en France en 1978: Une Enquête INED-INSEE, Différentielles Démographiques, Sociales et Culturelles," *Population*, 34 (1979), 1373-1390. Alain Girard, Louis Roussel, and Henri Bastide, "Natalité et Politique Familiale: Une Enquête d'Opinion," *Population*, 31 (1975), 355-377. Hans Harmsen, *Bevölkerungsprobleme Frankreichs unter Besonderer Berücksichtigung des Geburtenrückgangs* (Berlin-Grunewald: Vowinckel, 1927). Institut National d'Études Démographiques, "Huitième Rapport sur la Situation Démographique de la France," *Population*, 34 (1979), 1221-1289. John Knodel and Etienne van de Walle, "Lessons from the Past: Policy Implications of Historical Fertility Studies," *Population and Development Review*, 5 (1979), 217-245. Hervé LeBras and Georges Tapinos, "Perspectives à Long Terme de la Population Française et Leurs Implications Économiques," *Population*, 34 (1979), 1391-1451. Henri Léridon and Jean-Paul Sardon, "La Contraception en France en 1978: Une Enquête INED-INSEE, la Diffusion des Diverses Méthodes," *Population*, 34 (1979), 1349-1390. Francisco Muñoz-Perez, "L'Évolution de la Fécondité dans les Pays Industrialisés depuis 1971," *Population*, 37 (1982), 483-512. Alain Parant, "Les Personnes Âgées en France et Leurs Conditions d'Habitat," *Population*, 36 (1981), 577-605. Jean-Louis Rallu, "Les Enfants des Familles Monoparentales: Données de Recensement et d'État Civil," *Population*, 37 (1982), 51-74. Joseph J. Spengler, *France Faces Depopulation* (Durham, N.C.: Duke University Press, 1938). Michèle Tribalat-Brahimi, "Immigration en France en 1979 et Prévision d'Ici 1985," *Population*, 36 (1981), 147–161. Cicely Watson, "Birth Control and Abortion in France since 1939" and "Population Policy in France: Family Allowances and Other Benefits," *Population Studies*, 5 (1952), 261-286 and 8 (1954), 46-73.

France: Demographic Institutions

French demographic institutions differ from those of other Western nations in several respects. Though the country's universities have a large number of diverse research institutes, the most important in demography (INED, INSEE, ORSTOM) are all government-supported agencies or government bureaus. The distinction between the gathering of population statistics and demographic analysis, partly for this reason, is less sharp than elsewhere at, for instance, INSEE (see below).

The National Alliance against Depopulation was founded in 1896 by Jacques †Bertillon as the National Alliance for the Increase of the French Population. It subsequently changed its name to the National Alliance for a French Vital Force and then to its present designation. It was instrumental in obtaining passage of the Family Code, which includes various pronatalist provisions, and in obtaining state funding for the establishment of the National Institute of Demographic Studies (INED). Its main activity has been to encourage a popularized knowledge of population trends in France, in part through its own periodical, *Population et Avenir* (formerly *Vitalité Française*). Address: Alliance Nationale contre la Dépopulation, 35 rue Marbeuf, 75008 Paris. See also *France.

UNIVERSITY AND OTHER RESEARCH INSTITUTES

The Documentation Center for the Training of Migrant Laborers, of which Martine Charlot was director in 1980, collects data on migrations, minority groups, efforts to facilitate the economic assimilation of newcomers, and similar topics. Address: Centre de Documentation pour la Formation des Travailleurs Migrants, 4 rue de Stockholm, 75008 Paris.

The Documentation Center on Urbanism, established in 1967, was directed in 1980 by J. C. Daumas. It collects data on urbanization, city planning, and regional development. Address: Centre de Documentation sur l'Urbanisme, 2 avenue du Général Malleret-Joinville, 94110 Arcueil.

The Center of Urban Sociology, founded in 1901, was in 1980 headed by Georges Morlat, chairman. Its research, documentation, and publications pertain to housing policies, relations between metropolitan centers and their periphery, city planning, and other topics linked to population studies. Address: Centre de Sociologie Urbaine, 118 rue de la Tombe-Issoire, 75014 Paris.

The Interuniversity Center of Research and Documentation on Migrations, established in 1971, was directed in 1980 by René Duchac. It has focused on the migration and social adjustment of North Africans in France. Address: Centre Interuniversitaire de Recherche et de Documentation sur les Migrations, Université de Provence, 29 avenue Robert Schuman, 13100 Aix-en-Provence.

At the School of Advanced Studies in Social Sciences there is a Center of Social Mathematics, which includes statistical and biostatistical analysis in its training and research. Address: Centre de Mathématique Sociale, École des Hautes Études en Sciences Sociales, 54 boulevard Raspail, 75006 Paris Cédex 05.

The Urban Sociology Group, a private nonprofit organization in existence since 1967, had J. C. Borthez as its president in 1980. Its research and documentation pertain to population, migration, urbanization, and similar topics. Address: Groupe de Sociologie Urbaine, 102 rue Tronchet, 69006 Lyon.

The Demography Institute of Paris (IDP) is essentially a teaching unit with a small faculty under B. M. Grossat, which can be supplemented for particular functions from the staffs of ORSTOM, INSEE, and INED. It used to be called the Demography Institute of the University of Paris (IDUP), and it is still administratively and financially part of the Sorbonne. Address: Institut de Démographie de Paris, Université de Paris I, 26 rue des Cordelières, 75013 Paris.

The National Institute of Demographic Studies (INED), which in 1982 was under the direction of Gérard †Calot, was established with government support in 1945 and under Alfred †Sauvy as director became one of the world's major population research centers. It concentrates on the population of France, especially French fertility, but has studied such social problems as alcoholism, the demography of other countries, and population theory and policy. Its publications include: *Population*, a major bimonthly journal; *Population et Sociétés*, monthly; and *Travaux et Documents de l'INED*, occasional monographs. Address: Institut National d'Études Démographiques, 27 rue du Commandeur, 75675 Paris Cédex 14.

The Ministry of Labor has a Center of Employment Studies, of which Henri Chaffiotte was the director in the late 1970s. It has conducted studies of elderly workers in the Paris region, of the participation of women in the work force, and of other demographic topics related to its main function. Address: Centre d'Études de l'Emploi, Ministère du Travail et de la Participation, 51 rue de la Chaussée d'Antin, 75009 Paris.

The Bureau of Scientific and Technical Overseas Research (ORSTOM), a government agency, has a Demographic Section of which Pierre †Cantrelle was the scientific director in 1980. It analyzes the demography of population-economic relations of less developed countries, including especially the francophone countries of Africa. Address: Section de Démographie, Office de la Recherche Scientifique et Technique Outre-Mer, 24 rue Bayard, 75008 Paris.

The Society of Historical Demography reflects the importance of this subdiscipline in France, with 348 individuals and 33 firms as members. It publishes the *Annales de Démographie Historique*. Address: Société de Démographie Historique, 54 boulevard Raspail, 75006 Paris.

The University of Nancy has a teaching and research Institute of Demography, founded in 1954, of which J. N. Ray was director in 1980. Address: Institut de Démographie de l'Université de Nancy, 13 place Carnot, 54000 Nancy.

The University of Nice has an Institute of Interethnic and Intercultural Research, established in 1966 and directed in 1982 by M. Oriol. Its research, though reportedly worldwide, has focused on the migrants to France and their relations with the native population. Address: Institut d'Études et de Recherche Interéthniques et Interculturelles, Université de Nice, 34 rue Verdi, 06000 Nice.

At the University of Toulouse II there is an Interdisciplinary Center of Urban Research, founded in 1966 and directed in 1980 by Guy Jalabert. It deals with urbanization, city planning, and urban populations. Address: Centre Interdisciplinaire d'Études Urbaines, Université de Toulouse-le-Mirail, 109-bis rue Vauquelin, 31081 Toulouse Cédex.

GOVERNMENT STATISTICAL BUREAUS

The National Institute of Statistics and Economic Studies (INSEE) (formerly known as Statistique Générale de la France) is responsible for conducting the country's censuses, the most recent of which was in 1982. It also publishes an *Annuaire Statistique* and a *Bulletin Mensuel de Statistique*, both with the usual range of population data, as well as an occasional, more specific *Mouvement de la Population*. Two of its series, published irregularly, are *Démographie et Emploi*, on the population and the labor force, and *Ménages*, on households. Address: Institut National de la Statistique et des Études Économiques, 18 boulevard Adolphe Pinard, 75675 Paris Cédex 14.

INSEE also publishes the official statistical data on French territories overseas, including the following:

French Guiana, an *Annuaire Statistique*, a quarterly *Bulletin Trimestriel de Statistiques*, and a monthly *Bulletin de Statistiques*, all of which include population figures.

Guadeloupe, an *Annuaire Statistique* that includes general population data and a *Bulletin de Statistiques*, monthly and annual, with details on vital statistics and international migration.

Martinique, an *Annuaire Statistique* that includes population data and a monthly *Bulletin de Statistiques* with vital statistics and figures on international migration.

Réunion, an *Annuaire Statistique* with many population data; an irregular *Statistiques Démographiques* in two parts, *Mouvement Migratoire de la Population* and *Mouvement Naturel de la Population*.

INSEE has a demographic research section, which in 1980 was under the direction of Jacques †Boudoul and Solange †Hémery. It carries out analyses of France's population, coordinating them with national and regional plans.

The National Institute of Health and Medical Research (INSERM), founded in 1941 as the National Institute of Hygiene, was headed in 1980 by Philippe Laudat, general director. Among its regular publications is a series on *Statistiques de Morbidité et Mortalité*. It has sponsored or cosponsored a number of conferences on topics related to demography, including one on the biology of reproduction, reported in *Régulation de la Fécondité: Bilan et Perspective* (1979). Address: Institut National de la Santé et de la Recherche Médicale, 101 rue de Tolbiac, 75645 Paris Cédex 13.

frequency, the number of members of a given category or of the occurrences of a type of event, expressed either as an absolute figure or as a proportion of the total. A frequency distribution, which relates the frequencies to the values of the variables, can be represented either in tabular form or in a frequency curve.

fringe belt, in Britain a strip of mixed land uses at the edge of a built-up area, similar to what in the United States is commonly termed an *urban fringe.
REFERENCE: J.W.R. Whitehead, "Fringe Belts: A Neglected Aspect of Urban Geography," *Transactions of the Institute of British Geographers*, 41 (1967), 223–233.

frontier, a region or zone between two countries or at the edge of settled territory, is contrasted with a *boundary, a line dividing two countries. In Britain "the

Frontier" refers to the Northwest Frontier of India, presently between Pakistan and Afghanistan. In the United States the effect of the westward-moving frontier was the subject of a long scholarly debate; see Frederick Jackson †Turner.

REFERENCE: Ladis K. D. Kristof, "The Nature of Boundaries and Frontiers," *Annals of the Association of American Geographers*, 49 (1959), 269–282.

functional economic areas (FEAs), proposed regions of the United States that would include as components both *Metropolitan Statistical Areas and *state economic areas. All of the interstices presently left out would also be included, so that the sum of all FEAs would constitute the total area of the country. Each would be defined by its relative economic independence, as measured by the labor market, consumer purchases, and similar indicators.

REFERENCE: Karl A. Fox, *Social Indicators and Social Theory: Elements of an Operational System* (New York: Wiley, 1974), chap. 8.

Fundamentalism and **Modernism,** the two principal tendencies in American Protestantism, reflect conflicts manifested also in other Christian countries and, indeed, in other religions. Modernism was defined by Shailer Mathews, dean of the Divinity School of the University of Chicago and one of the principal defenders of the movement, as "the use of the methods of modern science to find, state, and use the permanent and central values of inherited orthodoxy in meeting the needs of a modern world. . . . Modernists are Christians who accept the results of scientific research as data with which to think religiously . . . [and] who adopt the methods of historical and literary science in the study of the Bible and religion" (Mathews, 1924, pp. 22–36). From the point of view of the more orthodox, such a compromise with science and biblical criticism was seen as the first step toward the abandonment of religion altogether. The name "Fundamentalist" came from *The Fundamentals*, a work in eleven volumes (1910–15) financed by two oil millionaires and edited successively by A. C. Dixon, Louis Meyer, and Reuben Torrey. In a modern restatement, the essence of Fundamentalism consists of "a very strong emphasis on the inerrancy of the Bible; . . . a strong hostility to modern theology and to the methods, results, and implications of modern critical study of the Bible; [and] an assurance that those who do not share their religious viewpoint are not really 'true Christians' at all" (Barr, 1977, p. 1; see also Marsden, 1980).

A movement that insisted on the literal interpretation of the Bible could not remain within the bounds of merely theological dispute. A central point at issue became the theory of *evolution, which contradicted the biblical account of how the universe was created. In 1925 Tennessee passed a law prohibiting the teaching of evolution in the state's public schools; and John Thomas Scopes, a substitute teacher of biology in a Dayton high school, was tried in a highly publicized contest between Fundamentalists and their opponents. After only ten minutes' deliberation, the jury convicted Scopes; the Tennessee Supreme Court, which heard the case on appeal, upheld the law but reversed Scopes's conviction on

the ground that he had improperly been fined $100. The case had wide reper-
cussions, aggravating the hostility between the two wings of American Protestantism. Journalists' attacks on the South as the country's benighted region led
eventually to the rise of the Agrarian literary movement, a group of distinguished
men of letters who defended the South and its conservative ways (cf. Garwood,
1969, chap. 6). On the specific issue of evolution, the Scopes trial was not
merely a provincial show, but one important stage in the controversy that started
with Charles Darwin and has continued to the present day; in 1983, the U.S.
Supreme Court declined to review a lower court's decision that Creationism is
not, as alleged by its supporters, an alternative scientific view that therefore
should be taught in public schools together with evolution.

Typically associated with differences about theology and evolution there have
been strongly held convictions about social practices. In the seven biographical
sketches of prominent Fundamentalists compiled by C. Allyn Russell (1976),
the opposition to what they saw as pernicious life-styles was as prominent as
their defense of orthodox doctrine. John Roach Straton, a Baptist minister whom
newspapers called the "Pope of Fundamentalism," joined even with Catholics
in denouncing birth control as an "artificial interference with the sources of
life," "race suicide." The heaviest broadsides of J. C. Massee, a revivalist
pastor who served as the first head of organized Fundamentalism, were concentrated on sexual "sins"—dancing, petting, birth control, and especially divorce.
Clarence E. Macartney, an eloquent and dignified Presbyterian minister, had a
longer list of personal "sins": dancing, drinking, attending movies, reading
comic sheets, sexual "irregularities," watching prizefights, birth control, and
desecrating the Sabbath. "Should the recommendations of many Protestant min-
isters today be followed," he wrote, "it will come to this: After a second or
third child has been brought into the home by a physician, the Protestant minister
will be summoned to strangle it, so that the firstborn will have a chance to go
to college." With deep roots particularly in millenarian doctrines of the nineteenth century, Fundamentalism deeply split the major Protestant denominations—Baptists both Northern and Southern, Methodists, Presbyterians,
Episcopalians, and Disciples of Christ. The bitter disputes in the 1920s and
1930s about such issues as contraception and divorce, though often pictured in
retrospect as only between Catholics and others, were largely an intra-Protestant
affair.

If such later movements as the Moral Majority are seen as a continuation of
Fundamentalism, the changes are as significant as the persistent characteristics.
Jerry L. Falwell, president of the Moral Majority, is a Baptist minister who for
a dozen years restricted his activities to preaching in his church in Lynchburg,
Virginia, a town that hardly fits the stereotype of the backward South. It is the
site of modern industrial plants and of two liberal women's colleges, Randolph-
Macon and Sweet Briar, and almost two-thirds of its high-school graduates go
on to college. Race relations are good, both generally and in Falwell's church.
He began to appear on television in 1971 and, with money collected from his

viewers, rapidly expanded to a nationwide audience. His social message is less sectarian than that of the Fundamentalists a half-century earlier. He opposes not drinking but "excessive" drinking, not dancing but pornography and the Equal Rights Amendment, not contraception but abortion, not irreligion generally so much as the ban on school prayers, not every symptom of "immorality" but specifically homosexuality, drugs, and violence on television (FitzGerald, 1981). Various surveys give the number of his supporters as anything between 400,000 and 67 million.

REFERENCES: James Barr, *Fundamentalism* (London: SCM Press, 1977). Frances FitzGerald, "A Disciplined Charging Army," *New Yorker* (May 18, 1981). Willard B. Garwood, Jr., ed., *Controversy in the Twenties: Fundamentalism, Modernism, and Evolution* (Nashville: Vanderbilt University Press, 1969). George M. Marsden, *Fundamentalism and American Culture: The Shaping of Twentieth-Century Evangelicalism, 1870–1925* (New York: Oxford University Press, 1980). Shailer Mathews, *The Faith of Modernism* (New York: Macmillan, 1924). C. Allyn Russell, *Voices of American Fundamentalism: Seven Biographical Studies* (Philadelphia: Westminster Press, 1976). Daniel Yankelovich, "Stepchildren of the Moral Majority," *Psychology Today*, 15 (November, 1981), 5–10.

G

Gabon: Demographic Institutions

The Bureau of Surveys and Demography collects and analyzes population data. It conducted a census in 1969–70, and one was planned for 1980. Address: Bureau des Enquêtes et de la Démographie, Direction de la Statistique et des Études Économiques, Ministère du Plan, du Développement et de la Statistique, Boîte Postale 2081, Libreville.

The ORSTOM Center (of the Bureau of Scientific and Technical Overseas Research, Paris) in Libreville carries out similar activities. Address: Centre ORSTOM (Office de la Recherche Scientifique et Technique Outre-Mer), Boîte Postale 3115, Libreville.

gainful worker, an economically active person, one who derives or tries to derive pay or profit from his work; loosely, a member of the *work force. In the United States the concept of gainful worker was supplanted by that of *labor force following the 1930 census; the principal difference is that the former has no time referent but pertains only to a person's "usual" means of earning a living. Since the period covered was indefinite, statistics on "gainful workers" could not be used to measure the number of unemployed, a datum that was of great significance especially during the depression of the 1930s.

Galton's problem, so called by anthropologists, is how to discriminate between "historical" and "functional" associations in cross-cultural surveys. In 1889, when Edward Tylor presented a paper on the evolution of marriage laws in various primitive societies, Francis †Galton pointed out that such traits often spread by borrowing or migration, and that unless this *diffusion could be systematically distinguished from independent development, one could not reliably interpret even a perfect correlation between traits. The dilemma hampers analysis in all the social sciences. For example, are W. W. Rostow's "stages of economic growth" (1960) independent of any influences from developed to less developed countries? Or, to what extent is the succession from one "stage" of the *demographic transition to the next inherent (as with a decline in infant mortality followed by a decline in fertility) and to what extent the consequence of diffusion (as a demand for Western consumer goods leading to smaller families, as was the case earlier in the West)? The resolution of the dilemma that Raoul †Naroll (1965) suggested, using relative propinquity to indicate the likelihood of diffusion, makes sense in the study of primitive societies, but hardly for international comparisons of countries the world over.

REFERENCES: Raoul Naroll, "Galton's Problem: The Logic of Cross-cultural Analysis," *Social Research*, 32 (1965), 428-451. W. W. Rostow, *The Stages of Economic Growth: A Non-Communist Manifesto* (Cambridge, England: Cambridge University Press, 1960).

Gambia: The Central Statistics Department conducts the country's censuses, the most recent of which was in 1973 (one was scheduled for 1983). Address: Ministry of Economic Planning and Industrial Development, Wellington Street, Banjul.

Gastarbeiter, German for "guest worker," is used also in other languages to designate an alien given a temporary work permit of varying duration. The term came into use after the end of World War II, when the great economic progress of Western Europe was combined with the far wider availability of welfare benefits, so that natives were usually unwilling to accept low-level jobs. Migrant laborers have typically moved from one of the Mediterranean countries to one of those in Northwestern Europe. Though juridically the foreigners were temporary, sociologically they were becoming part of the society in which they lived and demographically often a rapidly increasing one. The 15 million or so alien residents in the early 1970s comprised what was often called the tenth member of the Common Market, larger in total population than several of the member countries. With the recession of the mid-1970s, hostility to Gastarbeiter developed in several of the receiving countries, especially Switzerland, where the world-famous amity among language and religious groups was seriously damaged by the importation, proportionate to its population, of close to the largest number of foreign workers. *Überfremdung* (in French, *hyperxénie*; in a possible English translation, "hyperforeignization") became a major issue in several Swiss elections and resulted in some significant revisions in immigration law. See also *migration; *migration, international; *population abroad.

REFERENCE: Mark J. Miller and Philip L. Martin, *Administering Foreign-Worker Programs: Lessons from Europe* (Lexington, Mass.: Lexington Books, 1982).

gateway city, an urban place linking one region with another, especially one commanding the entrance to a hinterland. A good example of the way the concept is used is a paper on "gateway to the grasslands" (Silag, 1983).

REFERENCES: A. F. Burghardt, "A Hypothesis about Gateway Cities," *Annals of the Association of American Geographers*, 61 (1971), 269-285. William Silag, "Gateway to the Grasslands: Sioux City and the Missouri River Frontier," *Western Historical Quarterly*, 14 (1983), 397-414.

GBF/DIME is an acronym used by the U.S. Bureau of the Census for "geographic base file" and "dual independent map encoding"—respectively, a file of census maps and a technique for preparing such files and checking their accuracy. GBF/DIME Files are computerized versions of census maps, which in 1980 were prepared for each small urban part of the 277 Standard Metropolitan Statistical Areas. The data include police records, tax assessments, and various other statistics, all of which contain street addresses and can therefore be aggregated by such specified areas as census tracts, congressional districts, and wards. The easy combination of a wide assortment of data can give local administrators a much clearer view of whether neighborhoods are prospering or deteriorating, and, if the latter, which features demand special attention.

Gemeinschaft and **Gesellschaft,** sometimes translated as "Community" and "Society," were Ferdinand †Tönnies's terms for a polarity that, with some differences in meaning and particularly in emphasis, has been a familiar element of social analysis. A list of some of the other examples includes Henry Maine's society of status versus society of contract, Max †Weber's traditionalist versus rational authority, Émile †Durkheim's mechanical versus organic solidarity, Robert Redfield's folk versus urban society, Robert MacIver's culture versus civilization, David Riesman's tradition-directed versus other-directed character. All of these several pairs are ways of describing the changes in society loosely designated by *modernization, the cultural concomitant of a narrowly defined economic development. See also *folk society.

gender, derived from the French *genre* and thus closely associated with *genus*, has been used in modern English mainly as a grammatical term, to classify nouns into types more or less similar to male and female; see also *sex. In recent years many feminist spokespersons have used "gender" in place of "sex" in order to stress their allegation that most differences between men and women are culturally ascribed rather than biologically given. Indeed, differences between the sexes derive partly from biology, partly from roles that men and women traditionally play in society, and partly from beliefs and opinions concerning sex-linked attributes and behavior. All three are reflected in language, and in the abstract it would be useful to denote biological factors by one term (say, sex) and socio-cultural ones by another (say, gender); but actually the two are generally very difficult to distinguish in real life. Eschewing the word *sex* altogether and substituting *gender* in all cases, as in "gender chromosomes," for instance (Kessler and McKenna, 1978), is reminiscent of the effort to abolish the word *race and supplant it by "ethnic group" or some other supposedly innocuous equivalent. In both cases, the suggested change muddles the distinction among physiological, social, and cultural determinants of behavior. Like some other languages, English has no words to denote the two sexes only of human beings irrespective of age. In some countries, particularly where a lower status for women has been traditional, the equivalents of *male* and *female* refer mainly to other species and suggest a vulgar animality when applied to humans. In Spanish, for instance, two columns of age distributions beginning with the first year would be headed "Hombres" and "Mujeres," respectively; and a similar practice is seemingly beginning in English-language demography. In general speech, the "perverse" use of *woman* as an adjective (as H. W. Fowler termed it in *Modern English Usage*) has become common in phrases like "woman lawyer" and even "women lawyers." In 1984 France's Minister for Women's Rights, Yvette Roudy, appointed a committee to work out feminine forms of the designations of high-level positions and otherwise to reform the sexist proclivity of the French language (*Economist*, June 23, 1984).

REFERENCE: Suzanne J. Kessler and Wendy McKenna, *Gender: An Ethnomethodological Approach* (New York: Wiley-Interscience, 1978).

Genealogical Society of Utah, founded in 1894, is located in the headquarters building of the Church of Jesus Christ of Latter-day Saints (the Mormon church) and is wholly supported by church funds. The size of the society's operation is indicated by the fact that in 1981 it had about 600 full-time employees, plus a considerable number of trained volunteers. About a quarter of the employees work outside the United States, locating vital records of various types irrespective of whether they pertain to Mormons, obtaining permission to transfer them to microfilm, and arranging for their reproduction and shipment. The microfilm collection, growing at the annual rate of 40,000 rolls of film, each 100 feet long, comprised in 1981 over a billion pages of source materials, all available to any user with no restrictions beyond any that might have been imposed by the original source. Address: 50 East North Temple Street, Salt Lake City, Utah 84150.

The holdings include civil registration records; census schedules; parish registers; land, probate, and tax records; notarial records; and family and local histories. The largest collections are for the United States and some of the principal Western European countries of past emigration; but included are also records from such countries as the Philippines, Zimbabwe, Israel, Iceland, and much of Central and South America. The data have stimulated sociologists and historians at the University of Utah to initiate several studies in social and family history and in historical demography; some are described in a *Newsletter* of the Center for Historical Population Studies, of which the first number appeared in 1979. Since records from many places are available at a single site, the collection is especially suitable for comparative analyses. The main limitations of the microfilms reflect the sometimes dubious accuracy and legibility of the original, as well as the fact that the accumulation is a continuing process (cf. Bean et al., 1980).

A second set of records, pertaining only to *Mormons and their ancestors, reconstitutes three or more generations of particular families. Forms are filled out by a family member either from public records or from such private sources as a family Bible. Though limited to a particular population, these data are complete enough to provide a base for various types of study. Several demographers at the University of Utah have linked these genealogies with medical records in order to investigate the genetic transmission of disease entities (Bean et al., 1978).

In August 1980 the Genealogical Society sponsored a World Conference on Records, of which the proceedings are available either in toto or pertaining to particular countries or stocks. As might be expected, the conference was dominated by papers on genealogy and family history, but it also reflected a considerable interest in population records and their use in demographic analysis.

REFERENCES: Lee L. Bean, Dean L. May, and Mark Skolnick, "The Mormon Historical Demography Project," *Historical Methods*, 11 (1978), 45-53. Bean, Geraldine P. Mineau, Katherine A. Lynch, and J. Dennis Willigan, "The Genealogical Society of Utah as a Data Resource for Historical Demography," *Population Index*, 36 (1980), 6-19.

genealogy, an enumeration of a person's *ancestors and their *descendants in the natural order of succession, is pertinent to demographic analysis in several contexts. Most obviously, with genealogies one can follow hereditary characteristics over time, noting such properties of genes as dominance, recessiveness, expressivity, and penetrance, and observing the effects of differential fertility and mortality on the population (e.g., Sutter and Tabah, 1956). If genealogies are not known, they are often assumed. The race of a person in law or other social relations has often been specified by the race of a half, a quarter, or some other fraction of his forebears. But when the designated fraction is very small, a definition based on genealogy contradicts the evidence of one's senses. For example, the Five Civilized Tribes in Oklahoma included on the tribal rolls persons who are supposed to have been 1/256 Indian (Beale, 1958).

A second important link to population analysis is in the method of *family reconstitution developed by Louis †Henry as a tool of *historical demography and anthropology (see also *Genealogical Society of Utah). It is laborious to extract the maximum information out of the usually incomplete and not wholly accurate parish records of the past, and Henry's innovation consists essentially of filling in the gaps on the basis of the highest probabilities. A work on "genealogical demography" is a review of the use of the computer in ethnographic research (Dyke and Morrill, 1980).

REFERENCES: Robert C. Anderson, "The Genealogist and the Demographer," in World Conference on Records, *Lecture Papers*, no. 209 (Salt Lake City: Genealogical Society of Utah, 1980). Calvin L. Beale, "Census Problems of Racial Enumeration," in Edgar T. Thompson and Everett C. Hughes, eds., *Race: Individual and Collective Behavior* (New York: Free Press, 1958). Bennett Dyke and Warren T. Morrill, eds., *Genealogical Demography* (New York: Academic Press, 1980). Louis Henry, *Manuel de Démographie Historique* (2nd ed.; Paris: Librairie Droz, 1970). Jean Sutter and Léon Tabah, "Méthode Mécanographique pour Établir la Généalogie d'une Population: Application à l'Étude des Esquimaux Polaires," *Population*, 11 (1956), 507-530.

general fertility rate, the simplest of the *fertility measures specified by age and sex, is the number of births during a year per 1,000 women of fecund age in the midyear population. Whether the fecund period should be defined broadly or narrowly, to include all ages at which some females give birth or only those at which most births take place, is difficult to decide on principle (Kuczynski, 1928, pp. 102-103). Various ranges have been used, but the usual convention has become to define the childbearing period as 15 to 44 years. In that case:

$$\text{General Fertility Rate} = \frac{B}{P^f_{15-44}} \times 1,000$$

The general fertility rate relates the actual reproduction to the potential better than the crude birth rate, but it is less precise than an *age-specific rate, for the reproductive proclivity is not constant over the whole of the fecund period, however this is defined. The rate also conforms to the curious convention in demography that males are irrelevant to the process of family building; see *paternal fertility.

REFERENCE: R. R. Kuczynski, *The Balance of Births and Deaths* (Brookings Institution; New York: Macmillan, 1928).

generation, one stage in the succession of natural descent; all persons of the same genealogical rank. It is conventional in demography to set the length of a generation as the average age of mothers when they give birth to daughters. As with the *reproduction rates from which this concept of generation derives, one can take as an alternative figure the average age of fathers at the birth of their sons. Depending on the usual age at marriage and the size of families, the length of generations is typically between 23 and 33 years.

One of the principal limitations of the conventional reproduction rates is that they are based on annual data and thus fluctuate with merely temporary shifts just as much as the simpler and less pretentious crude birth rate. Several demographers, therefore, have devised methods of constructing generation reproduction rates either from vital statistics or from data on *children ever born (cf. Shryock and Siegel, 1971, pp. 537-539). Louis †Henry (1976, p. 70) uses the term generation rate in another sense, to denote the ratio of the total number of births during a generation to the number of women in the fecund age bracket.

Since *adolescence lies between the subservience of childhood and the independence of maturity, it is often marked by a rejection of parental authority, which in a social-political context can result in a rhythmic pattern (Elazar, 1978). Particularly in analyses of the student riots of the 1960s, the conflict of generations became a recurrent theme (but see Decter, 1975).

REFERENCES: Midge Decter, *Liberal Parents, Radical Children* (New York: Coward, McCann & Geoghegan, 1975). Daniel J. Elazar, ''The Generational Rhythm of American Politics,'' *American Politics Quarterly*, 6 (1978), 55-94. Henry, *Population*. Shryock and Siegel, *Methods and Materials of Demography*.

genocide was coined by the Polish Jewish lawyer Raphael Lemkin (1944, 1947). Shortly thereafter genocide was censured at the first session of the United Nations

General Assembly. The subsequent U.N. Genocide Convention of 1949, with no attempt to offer a precise legal definition, condemned not only the mass murder of those of a particular religion or ethnicity (the definition that one would assume from the word's etymology), but also causing grievous bodily or spiritual harm to members of such a group, deliberately enforcing group living conditions that could lead to the partial extermination of the inhabitants, measures designed to prevent births among group members, and the physical removal of children from one group to another. The text of the Convention is reprinted, among many other places, in *Hearings before a Subcommittee of the Committee on Foreign Relations*, United States Senate, 91st Congress, 2nd Session, 1970 (Washington, D.C.: U.S. Government Printing Office, 1970). In 1986, after many delays, the United States ratified the Convention with two reservations.

REFERENCES: Raphael Lemkin, *Axis Rule in Occupied Europe: Laws of Occupation, Analysis of Government, Proposals for Redress* (Washington, D.C.: Carnegie Endowment for International Peace, 1944); "Genocide as a Crime under International Law," *American Journal of International Law*, 41 (1947), 145-151.

gentrification, a term coined by the British urban analyst Ruth Glass, denotes a sharp rise in the status of an urban neighborhood's residents. In a misnamed "back-to-the-city" movement—cf. Laska and Spain, 1980—(few actually come from the suburbs), "renovators" do much of the work of rehabilitating old houses, either for their own families or as a commercial enterprise. In the United States between 1970 and 1980, the prior trend continued in the central cities of all Standard Metropolitan Statistical Areas considered together: the white population declined, and that of blacks increased substantially. The only central city where the proportion of whites increased was Washington, D.C., a prototype of gentrification. However, with race used as an index of social class, certain small areas of many other cities showed a remarkable shift during the intercensal decade (Spain, 1981). This reversal of the long deterioration has been opposed by some analysts because, they contended, it implied the displacement of the poor who had lived there. In fact, the pattern has varied considerably from city to city, with no necessary link between gentrification and the removal of earlier residents (Henig, 1980).

REFERENCES: Jeffrey R. Henig, "Gentrification and Displacement within Cities: A Comparative Analysis," *Social Science Quarterly*, 61 (1980), 638-652. Shirley Bradway Laska and Daphne Spain, eds., *Back to the City: Issues in Neighborhood Renovation* (Elmsford, N.Y.: Pergamon Press, 1980). Spain, "A Gentrification Scorecard," *American Demographics*, 3 (November, 1981), 14-19.

geographic code, in the usage of the U.S. Bureau of the Census, a set of letters and/or numbers assigned to specific geographic areas and used to represent them in a computer program, for instance. The assignment of such codes to the area is called *geocoding*.

geography, an ancient field of study with a lineage traceable to classical Greece, was concerned initially with describing the earth's surface and interpreting it in a human context. Indeed, this man-land relation may be said to be the distinguishing characteristic of the discipline. But as every survey of the field stresses (e.g., Taylor, 1958; Brown, 1980), in its modern phase geography has divided into more or less discrete subdisciplines, which can be roughly classified as those concerned with the natural world (physical geography, climatology, oceanography, etc.), methodological specialties (cartography, for instance), and those that fit under the rubric of the social sciences. Not only have practitioners of various schools developed separately but often their progress has been marked by mutual antagonisms between physical and social geographers or, more recently, between statistical and nonmathematical geographers. What to label the portion of the field related to the social disciplines is a problem, for the several designations also have particularist meanings. "Human geography," in one view, is concerned with people, their activities, and their spatial distributions; it is subdivided into social and economic geography, into urban and rural geography, historical and welfare or radical geography (Wilson, 1980). This use of "human geography" as the generic term, once common in Europe, is still followed also in the prestigious Lund Series in Geography, divided into physical, human, and general or mathematical geography. In the United States the term coined by Carl Sauer at the University of California, Berkeley—"cultural geography"—has hardly spread beyond his students and their followers; it relates to such matters as man's exploitation of his habitat, settlement patterns, and the origin and spread of culture (Price, 1968; Ley, 1981). "No generally accepted definition of social geography exists," and the range of topics included in it does not differentiate it sharply from "human" or "cultural" geography (Buttimer, 1968; cf. Jones, 1980). Virtually all of these subdisciplines are likely to include population as one important factor, but the overlap with demography is greatest with what has been termed "statistical geography" (Duncan et al., 1961; Berry, 1968)—except, of course, for those in the discipline who have taken to calling themselves population geographers.

What types of problems do social geographers, broadly defined, deal with that pertain to population? The first is the spatial distribution of people, both static (population density, urban-rural contrasts) and dynamic (migration). A second is how the inhabitants of a particular *region interact with its physical characteristics and develop a specific regional character. The relation between man and land, or more broadly between people and natural resources, underlies †Malthus's principle of population and is generally at least implicit in the distinction between developed and less developed countries that economic geographers especially are likely to study. Some of the techniques developed by geographers, finally, have been applied to studies related to population. The mathematical analysis of *diffusion, as one example, is used to trace the spread of attitudes toward family size and of the use of contraceptives. More generally, models to analyze spatial relations are used in very similar ways in the two disciplines. See also *International Geographical Union; *Association of American Geographers.

REFERENCES: Brian J. L. Berry, "Statistical Geography," in *International Encyclopedia of the Social Sciences*, 6, 145-151. E. H. Brown, ed., *Geography Yesterday and Tomorrow* (Oxford: Oxford University Press, 1980). Anne Buttimer, "Social Geography," in *International Encyclopedia of the Social Sciences*, 6, 134-142. Otis Dudley Duncan, Ray P. Cuzzort, and Beverly Duncan, *Statistical Geography: Problems in Analyzing Areal Data* (New York: Free Press, 1961). R. J. Johnston, ed., *Dictionary of Human Geography* (New York: Free Press, 1981). Emrys Jones, "Social Geography," in Brown, ed., *Geography Yesterday and Tomorrow*. David Ley, "Cultural/Humanistic Geography," *Progress in Human Geography*, 5 (1981), 249-257. Edward T. Price, "Cultural Geography," in *International Encyclopedia of the Social Sciences*, 6, 129-134. Griffith Taylor, ed., *Geography in the Twentieth Century: A Study of Growth, Fields, Techniques, Aims and Trends* (3rd ed.; New York: Philosophical Library, 1958). A. G. Wilson, "Theory in Human Geography: A Review Essay," in Brown, ed., *Geography Yesterday and Tomorrow*.

geometric progression, a series of which each item is a constant multiple of the preceding one; thus, x, ax, a^2x, ... a^nx. It is contrasted with an *arithmetic progression; see also *doubling time; *exponential growth; †Malthus.

geopolitics, coined by Rudolf †Kjellén following the precedent of Friedrich †Ratzel's *Politische Geographie*, was developed especially by Halford †Mackinder. It came into popular use during the period between the two world wars to denote the application of geography to serve expansionist national policies. Especially in Germany, Nazi geopoliticians were less concerned with explanations than with a justification of the Party's decisions. As conceived by Karl †Haushofer, nation-states are supra-individual organisms engaged in a perpetual struggle for space, "lebensraum," and thus for life.

REFERENCE: Edward Mead Earle, "Haushofer and the Geopoliticians," in Earle, Gordon A. Craig, and Felix Gilbert, eds., *Makers of Modern Strategy: Military Thought from Machiavelli to Hitler* (Princeton, N.J.: Princeton University Press, 1944).

Germany, East (German Democratic Republic): Demographic Institutions

In 1972 the economics faculty of Humboldt University in East Berlin established a chair in demography, held since then by Parviz †Khalatbari, an Iranian. The instructional program is focused on the demographic transition and problems associated with it in less developed countries, as well as the population of socialist countries. Address: Bereich Demographie, Sektion Wirtschaftswissenschaften, Humboldt-Universität Berlin, Spandauerstrasse 1, DDR-102 Berlin.

The State Administration of Statistics conducts the country's census, the most recent of which was in 1971 (one was scheduled for 1981). Since 1963, its head has been Arno †Donda. The Bureau publishes a *Bevölkerungsstatistisches Jahrbuch*, a more general *Statistisches Jahrbuch* with many population data, and a *Statistical Pocket Book* in various languages. Address: Staatliche Zentralverwaltung für Statistik, Hans-Beimler Strasse, 70-72, DDR-1026 Berlin.

Germany, West (Federal Republic of Germany): Demographic Institutions

The German Demographic Society, an autonomous association of about 200 individuals and five organizations, was founded in 1952. It sponsors an annual conference and publishes its proceedings. Address: Deutsche Gesellschaft für Bevölkerungswissenschaft, Postfach 5528, D-6200 Wiesbaden.

The Federal Ministry for Economic Cooperation began in 1969 to support family-planning programs in other countries. Most of its funding has been through the U.N. Development Program (UNDP), the U.N. Fund for Population Activities (UNFPA), and the Development Center Population Program of the Organization for Economic Cooperation and Development (OECD). The first bilateral aid was in a grant to the private agency, Pro Familia, in Tunisia. Address: Bundesministerium für Wirtschaftliche Zusammenarbeit, Karl-Marx-Strasse 4-6, D-5300 Bonn.

UNIVERSITY AND OTHER RESEARCH INSTITUTES

The Academy of Regional Research and Land Planning, established in 1946, in 1975 reported a membership of 55 plus 180 corresponding members. Its publications include the bimonthly *Raumforschung und Raumordnung*. Its *Regionale Aspekte der Bevölkerungsentwicklung unter den Bedingungen des Geburtenrückganges* (1983) is the report of a working group established in 1978 to analyze regional aspects of population change in West Germany. Address: Akademie für Raumforschung und Landesplanung, Hohenzollernstrasse 11, 3-Hannover.

The University of Bamberg established in 1980 West Germany's first chair in demography, held by Josef †Schmid, whose prior work was in population theory, among other fields. Address: Universität Bamberg, Hornthalsstrasse 2, D-8600 Bamberg.

The University of Bielefeld was in late 1980 in process of establishing an Institute of Population Research, with Franz-Xaver †Kaufmann as chairman of the planning committee. The prospective program was cast on broad interdisciplinary lines, in anticipation of cooperation with other units of the university. Address: Institut für Bevölkerungsforschung, Universität Bielefeld, Universitätsstrasse 24, D-4800 Bielefeld.

The Federal Institute of Population Research, a government institution established in 1973, has long been directed by Karl †Schwarz. In its function of developing knowledge useful to the government, it conducts research on population and family problems. It publishes the *Zeitschrift für Bevölkerungswissenschaft* and the *Schriftenreihe des Bundesinstituts für Bevölkerungsforschung*. Address: Bundesinstitut für Bevölkerungsforschung, Gustav-Stresemann-Ring 6, Postfach 5528, D-6200 Wiesbaden.

The Friedrich Meinecke Institute at the Free University of Berlin includes among its staff of historians Arthur E. †Imhof, who has conducted research on Germany's population from the sixteenth to the twentieth century and interpreted his findings in a broad interdisciplinary perspective. He has organized a series of international multidisciplinary symposia on historical-demographic themes. Address: Friedrich-Meinecke-Institut, Freie Universität Berlin, Habelschwerdter Allee 45, D-1000 Berlin (West) 33.

The Society for Social Progress has a work group under Karl Martin †Bolte to study population development and the rising generation—specifically how the prospective changes in West Germany's population will affect the life-style of the next generation. Address: Gesellschaft für Sozialen Fortschritt e.V., Arbeitskreis "Bevölkerungsentwicklung und Nachwachsende Generation," Münsterstrasse 17, D-5300 Bonn 1.

The University of Kiel has an Interdisciplinary Population Program, of which Hans W. †Jürgens has long been the director. It has concentrated its research on longitudinal studies of the social, economic, and psychological factors influencing fertility, including in particular relations between population and the family. Address: Interdisziplinäres Lehrfach für Bevölkerungswissenschaft an der Universität Kiel, Neue Universität, Olshausenstrasse 40-60, D-2300 Kiel 1.

The University of Kiel also had in its Institute of World Economics a Population Research Group, which until her retirement in 1980 was under the direction of Hilde †Wander. Its principal research topics were economic demography, migration, and the labor force; but as of this writing no plans to continue population research there have been announced. Address: Institut für Weltwirtschaft an der Universität Kiel, Düsternbrooker Weg 120-122, D-2300 Kiel 1.

At the University of Munich the Psychology Institute has organized a longitudinal study under Lutz von Rosenstiel on motives in fertility behavior. About 700 couples have been surveyed on what value the husband and the wife, separately and jointly, place on their having children. Address: Institut für Psychologie der Universität München, Bauerstrasse 28, D-8000 Munich.

Also at the University of Munich the department of sociology under Karl Martin Bolte includes population in its instruction and research programs, for instance on the attitude of young women toward family life and childbearing. Address: Lehrstuhl für Soziologie an der Universität München, Konradstrasse 6, D-8000 Munich 40.

At the Ruhr University, Bochum, the Institute for Development Research and Policy includes a Demography and Sociology Section, which has long been directed by Wolfgang †Köllmann. Its research program includes population history, the consequences of fertility decline, and population problems of less developed countries, in particular a comparative analysis of Singapore and Malaysia. Address: Sektion für Demographie und Soziologie, Institut für Entwicklungsforschung und Entwicklungspolitik, Ruhr-Universität Bochum, Universitätsstrasse 150, D-4630 Bochum 1.

Also at the Ruhr University, Bochum, the Department of Social and Economic History (also under Wolfgang Köllmann at the same address) includes in its instructional program population theory, history, and policy, and the population of less developed countries.

The Sociological Institute of the Technological University of Berlin has instituted a population instructional and research program under Rainer †Mackensen as managing director. Research is focused on migration and urbanization, regional differences in fertility behavior, and the formation and coordination of such social institutions as family, neighborhood, government. Address: Institut für Soziologie, Technische Universität Berlin, Dovestrasse 1/715, D-1000 Berlin (West) 10.

The Werner Reimers Foundation has a study group on population development with Rainer Mackensen as the coordinator. It has been analyzing the decline of Germany's fertility in the context of sociology, psychology, economics, history, and anthropology and studying such particulars as age and sex structure, social change, personality development, and regional differences in fertility behavior. Address: Studiengruppe Bevölkerungsentwicklung, Werner Reimers Stiftung, Am Wingertsberg 4, D-6380 Bad Homburg.

GOVERNMENT STATISTICAL BUREAUS

The Federal Statistical Bureau conducts the country's censuses, of which the most recent on which there are published data was in 1970 (one scheduled for 1981 was postponed). Among the regular series the bureau publishes are *Bevölkerung und Erwerbstätigkeit*, with data on the work force and employment, and *Bevölkerung und Kultur*, with statistics on education among other topics. Other series have annual compilations on aliens and nationality, causes of death, and various other subjects. In addition to the more general *Statistisches Jahrbuch*, the bureau publishes a very brief *Statistical Compass*, available in German, English, French, and Spanish. Address: Statistisches Bundesamt, Gustav-Stresemann-Ring 11, Postfach 5528, D-6200 Wiesbaden 1.

The Statistical Office of Berlin, the most important of the eleven provincial bureaus, publishes monthly a general *Berliner Statistik* and a more specific *Die Bevölkerungsentwicklung*. Its annual reports include a general *Statistisches Jahrbuch* and more specific *Bevölkerungsvorgänge, Die Sterbefälle nach Todesursachen*, and *Die Natürliche Bevölkerungsbewegung*. Migration is covered in *Die Wanderungen*, monthly, and in an annual compilation of naturalizations and renunciations of German citizenship, *Die Ausländer*. Address: Statistisches Landesamt Berlin, Fehrbelliner Platz 1, D-1000 Berlin (West) 31.

gerontology, the scientific study of the phenomena of *old age, has concentrated on the sector of the population most accessible to research—that is, those living in institutions (e.g., Caplow, 1974; Tobin and Lieberman, 1976). Of those aged 65 and over in the United States, however, only 3.8 percent were institutionalized in 1960, only 5.5 percent in 1970 (cf. U.S. Health Care Financing Administration, 1978). Not only is this a very small proportion of the elderly but presumably those living in institutions are generally less healthy and more dependent than persons of the same age residing among the general population. Of the various surveys designed to supplement census data, one by the National Council on

Aging (1974) is the most ambitious but also subject to similar criticisms (Henretta et al., 1977). One knows some general facts about the elderly (e.g., Bouvier et al., 1975), but too much research has been based on a social-welfare perspective to further our broader understanding either of the high proportion of aged in the society today or of the sizable increase that is anticipated over the next several decades. Some 70 percent of the aged population in the United States are healthy and moderately well-to-do home-owners, and a survey of 1,500 out of this more representative sector reached conclusions quite at variance with the usual, rather dismal picture of "the aged" (Rabushka and Jacobs, 1980).

REFERENCES: Leon F. Bouvier, Elinore Atlee, and Frank McVeigh, "The Elderly in America," *Population Bulletin*, 30 (1975). Theodore Caplow et al., *The Elderly in Old-Age Institutions* (Center for Program Effectiveness Studies; Charlottesville: University of Virginia Press, July, 1974). John C. Henretta, Richard T. Campbell, and Gloria Gardocki, "Survey Research in Aging: An Evaluation of the Harris Survey," *Gerontologist*, 17 (1977), 160-167. National Council on Aging, "The Myth and Reality of Aging" (Washington, D.C., 1974; mimeographed). Alvin Rabushka and Bruce Jacobs, *Old Folks at Home* (New York: Free Press, 1980). Sheldon S. Tobin and Morton A. Lieberman, *Last Home for the Aged* (San Francisco: Jossey-Bass, 1976). U.S. Health Care Financing Administration, *Selected Characteristics of the Living Arrangements and Institutionalization of the Elderly in the States, HEW Regions, and the United States— 1970 Census Data* (Washington, D.C.: U.S. Government Printing Office, 1978).

gerrymander, to draw the boundaries of a voting district so as to produce political results favorable to those arranging the redistricting; also, a district so drawn. Elbridge Gerry, the governor of Massachusetts, in 1811 signed a bill that favored Democrats at the expense of Federalists, who had won nearly two-thirds of the votes cast. Gilbert Stuart, the painter, fancied he saw a salamander in a map of the districts and called them a gerrymander (now pronounced with a soft g, though Gerry's name was with a hard one). The commonest mode of gerrymandering is to waste the votes of the opposition party, either by concentrating its adherents in a few districts, where they will have an overwhelming majority, or dispersing them over many districts, where they will constitute an ineffective minority. Another type is a bipartisan effort of incumbents to maintain themselves in power by arranging the *apportionment in their favor (cf. Heslop, 1980; Safire, 1978). Journalists have dubbed gerrymandered districts the "monkey wrench" (in Iowa), the "dumbbell" (in Pennsylvania), the "shoestring" (in Mississippi), and the "horseshoe" (in New York). New York State has been particularly rich in strangely shaped districts; in 1961 critics of Governor Nelson Rockefeller's reapportionment called the result "Rockymandering," but the name did not stick (cf. Wells, 1980).

In a series of decisions in the 1960s, the U.S. Supreme Court supported the principle of "one-man, one-vote," with orders to base elections to the U.S. House of Representatives and to both houses of all state legislatures on districts of substantially equal population (cf. O'Loughlin, 1982). This controversial reform did not end gerrymandering, and such groups as Common Cause, the self-styled citizens' lobby, have proposed laws to transfer the authority to re-district from state legislatures to "independent nonpartisan commissions"—a shift that in critics' views would do less to remove political influence from the process than to cloak it.

REFERENCES: Alan Heslop, "The Redistricting Tangle," *American Demographics*, 2 (May, 1980), 25-29. John O'Loughlin, "The Identification and Evaluation of Racial Gerrymandering," *Annals of the Association of American Geographers*, 72 (1982), 165-184. William Safire, *Safire's Political Dictionary* (New York: Random House, 1978). David I. Wells, "Statistical Surgery in N.Y.," *American Demographics*, 2 (May, 1980), 30-33.

Ghana: Demographic Institutions

For the U.N. Regional Institute for Population (RIPS), see the discussion under *United Nations.

At the University of Ghana, the Institute of Statistical, Social and Economic Research (ISSER), of which K. Twum-Barima was director in 1982, has a unit concerned with population studies. In collaboration with the University of North Carolina, Chapel Hill, it has undertaken research and training projects in demography. Address: P.O. Box 74, Legon, Accra.

In collaboration with the Division of Population, Family, and International Health in the School of Public Health, University of California, Los Angeles, the Department of Community Health in the Medical School, University of Ghana, conducted a project in the district of Danfa to seek effective ways of delivering both health and family-planning services to a rural population; see *The Danfa Comprehensive Rural Health and Family Planning Project, Ghana: Final Report* (Accra, 1979).

Also at the University of Ghana there is a Population Dynamics Program, which has issued a *Ghana Population Series* beginning in 1969. Address: P.O. Box 145, Legon, Accra.

The government's Central Bureau of Statistics (CBS) issues an annual report on international migration, a *Statistical Yearbook*, and a partly overlapping *Statistical Handbook*. These include some data on population as well as statistics on education, national income, and industry. Address: P.O. Box 1098, Accra.

CBS's Demographic and Social Statistics Division conducts population surveys and censuses, the most recent of the latter in 1982. Address: P.O. Box 1350, Accra.

Also in CBS is the Births and Deaths Registry, charged with civil registration. In 1981, the Registrar was Jacob Botwe †Assie. Address: P.O. Box M270, Accra.

ghetto may derive from the Venetian word for foundry; in 1516, the Jews of the city were expelled to a Venetian islet named Ghèto from the foundry situated there. The standard meaning is the residential and business quarter of particularly Russian cities to which Jews were confined. In an unfortunate extension, the word is now used to denote any area dominated by members of an ethnic group, whether they have been segregated there through discrimination or, as occurs in some instances, they live there by choice. See also *segregation; *slum.

REFERENCES: Amitai Etzioni, "The Ghetto—A Re-evaluation," *Social Forces*, 37 (1959), 255-262. Louis Wirth, *The Ghetto* (Chicago: University of Chicago Press, 1928).

Global 2000 is the usual short reference to a report prepared by the U.S. Council on Environmental Quality and the U.S. Department of State (1980). Its very pessimistic conclusions were reminiscent of those propounded some years earlier by the *Club of Rome (Meadows et al., 1972), partly because some of the same analysts were involved in both studies. According to *Global 2000*, "If present trends continue, the world in 2000 will be more crowded, more polluted, less stable ecologically, and more vulnerable to disruption than the world we live in now. . . . The outlook for food and other necessities will be no better. For many it will be worse." As earlier with the report of the Club of Rome, such asseverations were both denounced as irresponsible and vehemently defended (e.g., Gillman and Simon, 1981). In a book edited by Julian †Simon and Herman Kahn (1984), the authors made a point-by-point rejoinder to every prediction of gloom. As the editors noted, forecasts by government bureaucracies are likely to reflect the vested interest that every department has in predicting one course rather than another.

REFERENCES: Katherine Gillman, "Julian Simon's Cracked Crystal Ball," and Julian L. Simon, "False Bad News Is Truly Bad News," *Public Interest*, no. 65 (1981), 71-89. Donella H. Meadows, Dennis L. Meadows, Jørgen Randers, and William H. Behrens III, *The Limits to Growth: A Report for the Club of Rome's Project on the Predicament of Mankind* (New York: New American Library, 1972). Simon and Herman Kahn, eds., *The Resourceful Earth: A Response to Global 2000* (Oxford: Basil Blackwell, 1984). U.S. Council on Environmental Quality and U.S. Department of State, *The Global 2000 Report to the President: Entering the Twenty-First Century*, 3 vols. (Washington, D.C.: U.S. Government Printing Office, 1980).

goodness of fit, the relative agreement between a set of observed values and one derived from a hypothesis concerning them, as measured, for example, by the relation between two curves representing, respectively, a theoretical distribution and a *regression line.

gradient, a measure of change in a variable—for example, density, land value, proportion of the labor force in white-collar occupations—relative to distance from a selected point. Gradients are used in analyzing how population and land use are distributed in cities. For example, in the equation

$$y = Ae^{-bx}$$

y is the population per square mile, A is the theoretical density of population at the center, e is the base of natural logarithms, b is the rate of decline in density, and x is the distance in miles from the center of the city. See also *population density.

graduation, in statistics, means the smoothing of a curve made up of points representing an irregular series of observed values. Several methods are used, depending on the specific type and accuracy of the data (Shryock and Siegel, pp. 682-689). A more difficult problem, which cannot be solved by mere techniques, is whether converting the observed data represents an essential falsification, rather than filling in the unobserved points through interpolation. A well known example in demography pertains to the age distribution of populations in less developed countries (Keyfitz, 1965, 1966; van de Walle, 1966).

REFERENCES: Nathan Keyfitz, ''Age Distribution as a Challenge to Development,'' and ''Reply'' to Etienne van de Walle, *American Journal of Sociology*, 70 (1965), 659-668; 71 (1966), 556-557. Shryock and Siegel, *Methods and Materials of Demography*. Van de Walle, ''Some Characteristic Features of Census Age Distributions in Illiterate Populations,'' *American Journal of Sociology*, 71 (1966), 549-555.

graphic presentation of numerical data is an important skill in demography and in a number of other disciplines. As early as 1915, a committee representing seventeen American associations and agencies drew up a set of standards derived mainly from the experience of mechanical engineers but applicable far more widely. The best methods of what is termed graphic communication as they evolved from that beginning depend on a sound background in statistics, supplemented by a special expertise in representing statistical ideas in a readily understandable form. Even the simplest graph on rectilinear coordinates can be drawn so as to minimize or to exaggerate the motion either upward or to the right, and to compose a graph that represents accurately the actual trend requires an appreciation of how deceptive a graph can be. Beginning around 1955 computer graphics have undergone a phenomenal development, and ''during the early 1970s computer graphic technology progressed far more rapidly than many of its most ardent proponents had hoped was possible'' (Schweitzer, 1973). It is easier to read a well executed chart than a complex table, and for some uses a map is better than either. Some firms find it expedient, in spite of the initial cost, to base decisions concerning plant location on a computer-drawn map of an area, with overlays showing population density and growth, income levels, and other relevant data (Burke, 1981).

REFERENCES: Barbara Burke, ''Computer Mapping: Demographic Revolution,'' *American Demographics*, 3 (March, 1981), 27–29. Calvin F. Schmid, ''Graphic Presentation,'' *International Encyclopedia of Statistics*, 1, 425–435. Calvin F. Schmid and Stanton E. Schmid, *Handbook of Graphic Presentation* (2nd ed.; New York: Wiley, 1979). Richard H. Schweitzer, Jr., *Mapping Urban America with Automated Cartography* (Washington, D.C.: U.S. Government Printing Office, 1973). U.S. Bureau of the Census, *Graphic Presentation of Statistical Information*, Technical Paper 43 (Washington, D.C., 1978).

gravidity, pregnancy, or the number of pregnancies a woman has undergone. Also *gravida*, a pregnant woman, specified by order as gravida I or primigravida during the first pregnancy, gravida II or secundigravida during the second pregnancy, gravida III, gravida IV, and so on.

gravity model, which has been used to analyze distribution and flow patterns, is based on the assumption that movement or exchanges over distances are proportional to the product of the masses and inversely proportional to the distances separating the masses. For example, the flow of migrants from i to j is given by the equation:

$$F_{ij} = g \frac{P_i P_j}{d_{ij}^{\,2}}$$

where g is a constant (in the mechanical model the gravitational force), P_i and P_j are the population of the two places, and d_{ij} is the distance between them. See also *center of population; *median location; *population potential.

REFERENCES: John Q. Stewart, "Empirical Mathematical Rules concerning the Distribution and Equilibrium of Population," *Geographical Review*, 37 (1947), 461–485. T. R. Tocalis, "Changing Theoretical Foundations of the Gravity Concept of Human Interaction," in Brian J. L. Berry, ed., *The Nature of Change in Geographical Ideas* (DeKalb: Northern Illinois University Press, 1978). John K. Wright, "Some Measures of Distribution," *Annals of the Association of American Geographers*, 27 (1937), 177–211.

Greece: Demographic Institutions

The Center for Planning and Economic Research, a public nonprofit institute founded in 1961, was in 1983 under the direction of Reghinos D. Theocharis. Its research on the Greek economy touches on population peripherally. Address: 22 Hippokratous Street, Athens 144.

The University of Athens has a Center of Demographic Research in its Medical School; in 1980 the center was under the direction of Dimitrios †Trichopoulos. Research has been concentrated on abortion, prematurity, and similar factors affecting the development of population policy. Address: Goudi, Athens 609.

The University Center of Biometric and Demographic Research and Training, established in 1962 with Vasilios †Valaoras as director, functioned only until 1970. During that short period it conducted a fertility survey of Greece, with publications on contraception and abortion; a biometric survey of army conscripts; a study of the epidemiology of breast cancer; and the start of an analysis of air pollution in Greater Athens.

The Medical School of the University of Ioannina conducts biomedical research in its Department of Hygiene, of which the head in the late 1970s was Vasilios Katsouyannopoulos. Address: Ioannina.

The National Statistical Service of Greece, established in 1828, is both the country's principal statistical bureau and an important center of demographic analysis. Since 1860 it has conducted censuses at roughly ten-year intervals, the latest in 1981. A report on some of these is available in English, *Main Results of the Recent Censuses and Manpower Surveys in Greece* (1967). The Service has also compiled vital statistics, first from ecclesiastic registers and then, from 1920 on, from civil registers. Migration data have been compiled from census and from frontier-control statistics. The Population Division, which in 1981 was under the direction of George S. †Siampos, publishes detailed analyses of each census, a *Vital statistical yearbook* (in Greek), a *Statistical Yearbook* (in Greek and English), and a *Monthly Statistical Bulletin* (also in Greek and English). Address: Ethnikē Statistikē Hypēresia, 14 Lycourgou Street, Athens 12.

During the 1960s the Population Division and the University Center of Biometric and Demographic Research and Training of the University of Athens collaborated in producing a number of works on Greek life tables and population projections. Out of this cooperation there developed in 1972 another unit of the National Statistical Service, the Research Office, which issued its principal findings to date in *The population of Greece during the second half of the twentieth century* (in Greek; 1980).

green revolution, a common appellation for the spectacular increase in food production using new varieties of grains developed initially by the American biologist Norman Borlaug. When he first visited India in 1961, he predicted that with the new seeds the country could double its wheat production in a decade; actually, it took eight years (Sen, 1975, pp. 5–6). High-yielding varieties of rice set comparable records. Such results raised unreasonably high expectations, and probably fewer analysts have celebrated the undoubted successes than discounted them with accounts of new problems (e.g., Morgan, 1977). Since the superplants need more water and more fertilizer, the relatively well-to-do agriculturists could best take advantage of the opportunity they offered. Though the Indian government provided production loans to smallholders, the result of the new technology in some areas was to widen the economic gap between landlords and tenants and thus to sharpen political antagonisms. Just in those provinces that raised agricultural production most, three radical parties were busy organizing a different kind of revolution (Frankel, 1971). According to a later study, however, the effect of the increased production has been to lower prices of foods and thus to effect a more equitable distribution of consumption. Though landowners benefited more than laborers, even the latter would have been worse off without the new plants (Pray, 1981). Manifestly, one innovation, no matter how significant, has not effected a change in the social structure of less developed countries.

REFERENCES: Francine R. Frankel, *India's Green Revolution: Economic Gains and Political Costs* (Princeton, N.J.: Princeton University Press, 1971). W. B. Morgan, *Agriculture in the Third World: A Spatial Analysis* (London: G. Bell and Sons, 1977). Carl E. Pray, "The Green Revolution as a Case Study in Transfer of Technology," *Annals of the American Academy of Political and Social Science*, 458 (1981), 68–80. Sudhir Sen, *Reaping the Green Revolution: Food and Jobs for All* (Maryknoll, N.Y.: Orbis Books, 1975).

greenbelt (or green belt), a margin of agricultural land or land left in its natural state surrounding a town in order to give its inhabitants a sense of spaciousness and to protect them from the encroachment of unattractive land uses. As a planning concept, it was promoted in England by Ebenezer †Howard (1898) as one element of his "garden city." In the United States in the 1930s, Rexford Tugwell supervised the construction of three "greenbelt cities" or lower-class suburbs, which the federal government later had to auction off at under half their cost (Donaldson, 1969, chap. 2).

REFERENCES: Ebenezer Howard, *Garden Cities of Tomorrow* (first published 1898; Cambridge, Mass.: M.I.T. Press, 1965). Scott Donaldson, *The Suburban Myth* (New York: Columbia University Press, 1969).

grid pattern, a rectangular design of urban streets, has been widely used in the cities of both Western and non-Western societies. Dan Stanislawski (1946) hypothesized that the pattern spread by diffusion, but the economies of occupancy that the design affords would seem to argue for repeated independent inventions.

REFERENCE: Dan Stanislawski, "The Origin and Spread of the Grid-Pattern Town," *Geographical Review*, 36 (1946), 105–120.

grid sampling, a form of *cluster sampling, in which the clusters are defined as particular areas on a grid pattern.

GRIDS, an acronym for Grid Related Information Display System, is a computer graphics system that can convert data into maps with shading of various types to indicate differences in density or other values.

REFERENCE: U.S. Bureau of the Census, *Census Use Study: GRIDS, A Computer Mapping System* (Washington, D.C., n.d.).

gross, in statistical terminology, is frequently contrasted with *net*. Gross migration, for example, is the sum of movements into and out of a specified area; net migration is the difference between them. A gross reproduction rate is a measure of fertility, which when it is corrected for the mortality of women in the fecund ages is called the net reproduction rate. The Gross National Product of a country is the total monetary value of all goods and services produced during a year—termed the Net National Product when depreciation is deducted. In other words, the distinction is that some quantity is subtracted from a gross figure to yield a net one, and most of the pairs used in demography need no further explication.

Gross National Product (often abbreviated as GNP; in Britain, Gross Domestic Product) is the total flow in money terms of all goods and services that an economy produces during a specified period, calculated without duplication by excluding intermediate products and counting only the end products (e.g., only automobiles but not the steel used to make them). Each of the several methods of calculating the GNP should yield the same result, for the expenditures on goods and services should equal their sales value, which in turn should equal what firms pay out in wages, dividends, and so on, plus their undistributed profits. In fact, even in advanced countries difficulties in measurement lead to a range of equally defensible figures; and for less developed countries the estimates are so ambiguous that some experts doubt their usefulness altogether (cf. Kravis et al., 1978; United Nations, 1964). The term has become a rough equivalent of *national income.

The usual index of *economic development, GNP per capita, has been used to delineate the modern history of Western nations (e.g., Bairoch, 1976). In comparing the progress of presently less developed countries, the several fundamental deficiencies are greater not only in the data typically available but in the concepts underlying them. Much of less developed countries' produce is not marketed but consumed directly, and the food derived from hunting and fishing or grown in small private plots is either excluded from the GNP by definition or is brought in through the wildest of guesses. Since the extension of the market economy means precisely that an ever larger proportion of this household production is shifted to cash crops or paid work, a recorded increase in GNP can reflect either the transformation of the distribution system, a higher overall production, or both in an unknowable ratio. Moreover, the portion of the national product that goes into the market is typically converted into dollars at international exchange rates, but purchases in the village are at a markedly different rate. In what J. H. Boeke, the Dutch economist, called a *dual economy, this distinction is between "dualistic" and "village" money. For both these reasons, the figures cited for the GNP per capita of the poorest countries are well below the subsistence level and thus obviously false. The United Nations set up an International Comparison Project to work out methods by which own-currency prices could be converted into international ones without flouting economic realities. A more serviceable comparison can be calculated, according to one analyst, based on such social and economic indicators as literacy and per-capita energy consumption, from which it is possible to estimate GNP per capita without using the prices of commodities at all (Gilbert, 1980).

REFERENCES: Paul Bairoch, "Europe's Gross National Product, 1800–1975," *Journal of European Economic History*, 5 (1976), 273–340. C. L. Gilbert, "Statistical Methodology and the Use of Economic and Social Indicators in the Estimation of Per Capita GDP Levels for Developing Countries," *Oxford Bulletin of Economics and Statistics*, 42 (1980), 281–303. Irving B. Kravis, Alan W. Heston, and Robert Summers, "Real GDP Per Capita for More than One Hundred Countries," *Economic Journal*, 88 (1978), 215–242. U.N. Statistical Office, *National Accounting Practices in Sixty Countries*, Studies in Methods, Ser. F, no. 11 (New York, 1964).

group is often used loosely (as in *age group) to mean *category. More precisely it denotes a particular subpopulation whose individual members share not only certain characteristics but also a degree of internal coherence. A group, so defined, is midway between a sector and a *community.

group quarters, according to the usage of the U.S. Bureau of the Census, includes both *institutions and such composite residential units as rooming houses, college dormitories, military barracks, convents or monasteries, ships, and the like. The residents are classified as "secondary individuals"; see *primary individual.

Growth of American Families (GAF), two national surveys of fertility determinants in the United States (1955, 1960), were followed by a *National Fertility Study* (NFS) using similar techniques and premises (1965, 1970). GAF was planned as a longitudinal study, but in NFS the sample was expanded to include women aged 40 to 44, who were excluded from the first surveys, and the questionnaire was changed somewhat. The principal innovation was an attempt to probe the motivation for having children. In the GAF surveys respondents were asked the number of children they "expected," and in the NFS this query was expanded into four categories, though with so little differentiation as to make their usefulness doubtful. The 1965 averages were:

Expected fertility	3.36 children
Intended fertility	3.24
Desired fertility	3.29
Ideal fertility	3.29

The most consistent and significant difference found in the studies was between Catholic and Protestant couples—though this was partly due to the fact that most Fundamentalist Protestants were excluded from the samples. In any case, it proved to be a temporary factor, for American adherents of *Roman Catholicism rather quickly abandoned their church's teaching on contraception. The most thoroughgoing critique of the surveys was by one author of the NFS books (Ryder, 1973). He pointed to the useful findings of the studies but also to their limitations, some of which were built into the surveys from the inception of the project. Several of the categories most important in both analytical and policy terms were omitted—illegitimate births, blacks in the first two surveys, residents of urban slums. The data related to motivation were not to be trusted, for when women responded, for example, on whether they wanted to have babies already born, their replies were often rationalizations. No new theory emerged from the surveys, and the analysis by cross-tabulation was continued to the point where the numbers of cases in the cells were too small to justify any conclusions. See also Blake, 1966, 1967, 1974; Westoff et al., 1957.

REFERENCES: Judith Blake, "Ideal Family Size among White Americans: A Quarter Century's Evidence," *Demography*, 3 (1966), 154–173; "Family Size in the 1960s: A Baffling Fad?" *Eugenics Quarterly*, 14 (1967), 60–74; "Can We Believe Recent Data on Birth Expectations in the United States?" *Demography*, 11 (1974), 25–44. Ronald Freedman, Pascal K. Whelpton, and Arthur A. Campbell, *Family Planning, Sterility, and Population Growth* (New York: McGraw-Hill, 1959). Norman B. Ryder, "A Critique of the National Fertility Study," *Demography*, 10 (1973), 495–506. Ryder and Charles

F. Westoff, *Reproduction in the United States* (Princeton, N.J.: Princeton University Press, 1971). Westoff, E. G. Mishler, and E. Lowell Kelly, "Preferences in Size of Family and Eventual Fertility Twenty Years After," *American Journal of Sociology*, 62 (1957), 491–497. Westoff, Robert G. Potter, Jr., Philip C. Sagi, and Mishler, *Family Growth in Metropolitan America* (Princeton, N.J.: Princeton University Press, 1961). Whelpton, Campbell, and John E. Patterson, *Fertility and Family Planning in the United States* (Princeton, N.J.: Princeton University Press, 1966).

growth of the human body has become an important topic of physical anthropology (cf. Boyd, 1980; Garn, 1981). Like other physical characteristics, height, weight, and other body measurements reflect both genetic and environmental factors, either of which may influence such demographic variables as fecundity and mortality (cf. Steckel, 1983). In 1964 the International Council of Scientific Unions established an International Biological Program, which has collated studies of growth patterns in various sectors of the world's population. Irrespective of the environment, Northwest Europeans are the tallest and Asians are the shortest; but patterns especially in Africa are much affected by undernutrition and disease in the first few years of life and, therefore, range widely from such a norm as the measurements of upper-class Yoruba in Nigeria, for instance (Eveleth and Tanner, 1976).

REFERENCES: Edith Boyd, *Origins of the Study of Human Growth* (Portland: University of Oregon Health Sciences Center, 1980). Phyllis B. Eveleth and J. M. Tanner, *Worldwide Variation in Human Growth* (London: Cambridge University Press, 1976). Stanley M. Garn, "The Growth of Growth," *American Journal of Physical Anthropology*, 56 (1981), 521–530. Richard H. Steckel, "Height and Per Capita Income," *Historical Methods*, 16 (1983), 1–7.

growth pole is a concept that was developed first in France as *pôle de croissance*. It means a city, whether existent or planned, that will draw off some of the economic activity and population from a central metropolis regarded as too large and dominant; see also *primate city. Much of French city planning has been concerned with developing seven or eight regional "growth poles" designed to reduce the primacy of Paris. The same kinds of policy have been proposed or tried in countries as different as Britain (cf. *new town), the Soviet Union, and Japan.

REFERENCE: D. F. Darwent, "Growth Poles and Growth Centers in Regional Planning—A Review," *Environment and Planning*, 1 (1969), 5–31.

Guatemala: Demographic Institutions

San Carlos University of Guatemala has an Institute of Economic and Social Research, established in 1959 and in 1980 directed by J. A. Figueroa Galvez. Its training and research program relates to migration and urbanization, social-economic development, rural life, and similar topics. Address: Instituto de Investigaciones Económicas y Sociales, Universidad de San Carlos de Guatemala, Avenida la Reforma 0-63, Zona 10, Guatemala City.

In 1977 the University of Valle, a private institution, established a Center for

Research on Population, the Environment, and Natural Resources under the direction of Jorge †Arias. It carries out research on all aspects of the country's population. Address: Centro de Estudios de Población, Medio Ambiente y Recursos Naturales, Universidad del Valle de Guatemala, Vista Hermosa III, Zona 15, P.O. Box 82, Guatemala City.

The Department of Censuses and Surveys in the General Bureau of Statistics conducts the country's censuses, the most recent of which was in 1981. The bureau issues a statistical yearbook with population data from the last prior census; a semi-annual statistical bulletin and a statistical quarterly; and a weekly *Informador Estadístico*, which discusses a different topic in each issue. Address: Departamento de Censos y Encuestas, Dirección General de Estadística, 8a Calle 9-55, Zona 1, Guatemala City.

guilds (or, in the original spelling, gilds) were in the Germanic law of the Middle Ages associations of free men intended to supplement kin groups. Their common characteristics were an oath, drinking bouts, sometimes a common fund, and above all an obligation of mutual aid. According to the London ordinances, "For friendship as well as for vengeance, we shall remain united, come what may" (Bloch, 1962, pp. 419-420). Concerning the later medieval or early modern periods, the term has been more or less restricted to occupational groups, which typically closely regulated the conditions of work. Not only the family but also religion (each guild had its patron saint) and even magic were interwoven with economic activities. In particular, guilds generally inhibited marriage until after an apprentice had finished his training period and moved up to the next level; they acted, thus, as a significant curb on the fertility of the urban population. Certain of the regulations, though decaying, were still partly operative during the establishment of the factory system in England (e.g., Griffith, 1926).

REFERENCES: Marc Bloch, *Feudal Society* (2nd ed.; London: Routledge and Kegan Paul, 1962). G. Talbot Griffith, *Population Problems in the Age of Malthus* (Cambridge, England: Cambridge University Press, 1926).

Guinea: Demographic Institutions

The State Office of Scientific Research, directed in 1980 by Sidiki Kobele-Keita, conducts research in the social disciplines and publishes the journal *Recherches Africaines*. Address: Secrétariat d'État à la Recherche Scientifique, Boîte Postale 561, Conakry.

The Ministry of Planning and Cooperation includes a Statistical Office, whose staff in 1980 included Salion Bala Sow, an economist and demographer. Address: Direction Statistique, Ministère du Plan et de la Coopération, Boîte Postale 221, Conakry.

The Central Office of International Technical Cooperation issues a quarterly *Bulletin Spécial de Statistique*. Address: Division Centrale de Coopération Technique Internationale, Présidence de la République de Guinée, Boîte Postale 1210, Conakry.

Guinea-Bissau: Demographic Institutions

The Central Department of Census conducts the censuses, of which the latest was in 1979. Address: Departamento Central de Recenseamento, Bissau.

The Statistical Office publishes an annual *Anuário Estatístico*, which includes estimates of population. Address: Direcção de Estatística, C.P. 6, Bissau.

Gulag, the Soviet penal and forced-labor system, a Russian acronym for Chief Administration of Corrective Labor Camps. The term became familiar to the English-reading public through the translation of Aleksandr Solzhenitsyn's detailed depiction of the underside of a socialist planned economy. See also *Soviet society.

REFERENCE: Aleksandr I. Solzhenitsyn, *The Gulag Archipelago, 1918-1956: An Experiment in Literary Investigation*, 3 vols. (New York: Harper and Row, 1973-74).

Guyana: The government's Statistical Bureau publishes an annual *Statistical Abstract* that includes population data. Address: Ministry of Economic Development, P.O. Box 542, Georgetown.

Gypsies are the descendants of nomads who left India over a millennium ago and traveled westward, sojourning in Egypt long enough to give them their popular designation. They call themselves Rom and their language Romanes (pronounced ROM-a-nez), which is related both to classical Sanskrit and modern Hindi. The slang word "gyp" apparently derives from the common association of Gypsies with thievery, and the Rom have encountered hostility everywhere. The Nazis classed them on a par with Jews, to be killed off whenever they could be apprehended; and many of the countries where they live today have both a widespread prejudice and official discriminatory laws. How many Gypsies exist in the world no one knows, partly because they are as difficult to count as any other nomadic people, partly because the ethnic boundary is often vague. In 1970, according to a summary of census figures and prior estimates (Puxon, n.d.), there were just under 4 million in Europe, including 650,000 in Yugoslavia, 540,000 in Romania, 500,000 in Spain, 480,000 in Hungary, 414,000 in the Soviet Union, 363,000 in Bulgaria, and 300,000 in Czechoslovakia. Estimates for the United States have ranged between 100,000 and 300,000, as noted by Matt Salo (1979), but he believes that the Rom population is not more than 20,000.

REFERENCES: Gratton Puxon, *Rom: Europe's Gypsies* (London: Minority Rights Group, n.d.). Matt T. Salo, "Gypsy Ethnicity: Implications of Native Categories and Interaction for Ethnic Classification," *Ethnicity*, 6 (1979), 73-96.

H

habitat, in biology an organism's typical abode as defined by its physical characteristics alone; contrasted with its ecological *niche, which includes not only the physical space it occupies but its functional role in the community, and with its *environment, which may also include organic and social elements.

Haiti: Demographic Institutions
The Center of Family Hygiene, a government agency established in 1971, has tried to enhance family welfare by instilling responsible parenthood. It does research on family planning and trains the personnel of other programs related to the center's activities. Address: Centre d'Hygiène Familiale, 65 Turgeau, Port-au-Prince.

In 1968 the Haitian Center for Social Science Research (CHISS), a private organization, set up a section on population studies, of which the director in 1980 was Max Carre. It published a study reporting women's adherence to family-planning programs by the number of their children. Address: Section d'Études de Population, Centre Haïtien d'Investigation en Sciences Sociales, Boîte Postale 2497, Port-au-Prince.

The government's Haitian Statistical Institute conducts the country's censuses, the most recent of which was in 1982. It issues quarterly and annual statistical bulletins, as well as an irregular *Guide Économique*, all of which include population data. One of its subunits, the Division of Analysis and Demographic Research, conducted a national fertility survey in collaboration with the *World Fertility Survey. It also publishes information on housing and households. Address: Institut Haïtien de Statistique, Département des Finances et des Affaires Économiques, Port-au-Prince.

hamlet, a settlement too small to be called a village. It is officially designated as an incorporated place smaller than a village in some states of the United States. In England, a village generally has a church and a constable, a hamlet does not.

Hayflick limit, one of the biological factors that for any species determine its
*life span, the longest period that an individual can live. All the cells in a body
except the sex cells continually reproduce by splitting into two, so that as they
die off they are replaced by others. Leonard Hayflick (1968) found, however,
that normal cells in tissue cultures double only a finite number of times; as any
individual approaches the genetically fixed end of his life, more cells die than
the number of replacements. See also *age; *aging.

REFERENCE: Leonard Hayflick, "Human Cells and Aging," *Scientific American*,
218 (March, 1968), 32-37.

head of either a family or a household is defined, according to the recommendation of the United Nations, as the member so regarded by others in the group,
presumably on the basis of such characteristics as sex, age, and status (cf. Burch,
1980). Although a more suitable definition of a head of household might be the
person who bears the chief economic responsibility, the United Nations did not
recommend applying this definition because of the difficulty in collecting the
information (cf. Shryock and Siegel, 1971, pp. 299–300). Indeed, the concept
of head made full sense only so long as the typical family consisted of a husband-
father who went out to work, a wife-mother who kept the house, and minor
children. In developed countries, with both of the spouses working outside the
home and dividing household tasks between them, neither is likely to be seen
by the pair as the "head." The term "head of household" does not appear in
either the 1980 United States census schedule or Current Population Surveys
beginning from that year. The substitute term was *householder, the person in
whose name the home was owned or rented; he or she was listed first, and the
relationship to this "reference person" was noted in order to determine the
make-up of the family or other living group (cf. Glick and Norton, 1980).

REFERENCES: Thomas K. Burch, "The Index of Overall Headship: A Simple Measure of Household Complexity Standardized for Age and Sex," *Demography*, 17 (1980),
25-37. Paul C. Glick and Arthur J. Norton, "New Lifestyles Change Family Statistics,"
American Demographics, 2 (May, 1980), 20-23. Shryock and Siegel, *Methods and
Materials of Demography*.

headship rate is the ratio of the *heads of households, classified by sex, age,
and sometimes marital status, to the corresponding sectors of the population.
The rates are used as a tool in projecting the number of households, based on
the assumption either that the ratio will remain constant or that it will change
in a designated way. See also *householder.

health, seemingly a rather obvious concept, is extraordinarily difficult to pinpoint
precisely. According to a typical understanding of the past, health was a correlative of the death rate or life expectancy: a population in which relatively
fewer died was taken to be healthier. And this concept, of course, has not
disappeared. When the U.S. Surgeon General began his 1979 report, which he

entitled *Healthy People*, with the assertion, "The health of the American people has never been better," the principal evidence he offered was the decline of mortality. Life expectancy had increased from 47.3 years in 1900 to 73.8 years in 1979 and for blacks, the sector of the population that showed the greatest improvement, from 33 to 70 years. Rises of similar proportions took place in other industrial countries (see, as one example, Wilkins, 1980) and, more recently, also in less developed countries. But as mortality declined, the notion that everyone alive is by definition healthy became more and more unsatisfactory (cf. Pollard, 1980). Some diseases are disabling without affecting the death rate significantly. However, if health is defined as the absence of disease, and disease as a condition inconsistent with health, then some route is needed out of the circle. One supposed solution is to take "positive health" as the norm, as in the definition proposed by the World Health Organization (WHO): "Health is a state of complete physical, mental, and social well-being, and not merely the absence of disease or infirmity." Such a utopian goal, it needs no stressing, hardly relates to the actual problems of measurement.

In the real world it is useful first to make some elementary distinctions. Although "healthy" is commonly used in both an instrumental and an intrinsic sense, it is better to differentiate between an *unhealthful* food, habit, or environment (e.g., excessive sugar, smoking, polluted air) and the higher proportion of *unhealthy* persons that may be the result. Because disease entities vary considerably in their duration, it is usual to measure both their prevalence and their *incidence. Pain is not a reliable indicator of ill health: severe internal lesions may lack entirely any accompanying subjective distress, and such normal processes as teething, menstruation, and childbirth may be quite painful. Nor is it satisfactory to identify health as what some biologists call "Darwinian fitness," or a successful adaptation to a particular environment. That sickle-cell anemia developed in populations living in malarial areas and provided a partial protection against *malaria, for example, does not warrant our designating this adaptation as symptomatic of good health. More generally, a total absence of struggle with a consequent total lack of pain is incompatible with the life process of any species, including our own. See also *crowding.

*Morbidity data from existent medical records (as collected by physicians, clinics and hospitals, or health-insurance plans, for instance) depend on the existence of medical personnel and institutions, so that the more medical facilities available, the lower in general would be the indicated level of health. If the state of a population's health is to be measured independently of differential access to medical care, the index cannot be a by-product of existent records. In the 1977 Health Interview Survey conducted by the U.S. National Center for Health Statistics in cooperation with the Bureau of the Census, 87 percent of the sample responded to a question concerning the state of their health with "Excellent" or "Good," only 3 percent with "Poor" (cf. Lunde, 1981; U.S. National Center for Health Statistics, 1981). In any case, since a significant proportion of a survey sample typically refuse to subject themselves to the time and trouble of answering questionnaires on their health (not to say submitting to a physical examination), respondents are often nonrepresentative enough to cast doubt on any such study (see, for example, Chen and Cobb, 1958). Those who do participate generally are not reliable witnesses to their own medical histories (Cartwright, 1963).

To measure reasonably precisely the cost of illness and disability—that is, the economic value of national good health—requires a new combination of several types of noncomparable data: Gross National Product, attitude surveys, physicians' diagnoses, census classifications, sampling theory, and concepts specific to a health survey itself (cf. Mullner et al., 1983; Rice, 1983). In spite of the large body of writings in recent years (see Williams and Brook, 1978), no one has generated a full and overall definition of health. As Christopher Boorse (1977) pointed out, the health of each individual ought to be related to that of a class of which he is a member—as a minimum persons of one or the other sex and in a designated age range, possibly also those in particular races (with different genetic characteristics and living conditions) or nationalities (with various norms of what "good" health connotes). In each member of such a reference class, "normal functioning" means the performance of all statistically typical functions at efficiency levels within or above some chosen central region of the population distribution (Chrisman and Kleinman, 1980). See also *health care.

Such an "operational" or "instrumental" definition of health derives not from the supposed causes of morbidity or disability, but from the use that is to be made of the data—thus, on the effect of good or ill health on absenteeism or other specified types of behavior (for example, Patrick et al., 1973; Fuchs, 1976). The typical framework of analysis is based on the familiar foundation of economic choice, whether by the individual (should I forgo the pleasure of fattening foods in order to reduce the probability of heart disease?) or by society (should the community be provided with another expensive hospital in order to reduce ill health by so and so much?). When nations or communities are compared in such a context, the results hardly fit the usual preconceptions. Good health is usually shown to be highly correlated with education and only slightly correlated with medical care, and with no significant relation to per-capita income (Fuchs, 1976).

REFERENCES: Christopher Boorse, "Health as a Theoretical Concept," *Philosophy of Science*, 44 (1977), 542-573. Ann Cartwright, "Memory Errors in a Morbidity Survey," *Milbank Memorial Fund Quarterly*, 41 (1963), 5-24. Edith Chen and Sidney Cobb, "Nonparticipation Problems in a Morbidity Survey Involving Clinical Examination," *Journal of Chronic Diseases*, 7 (1958), 321-331. Noel J. Chrisman and Arthur Kleinman, "Health Beliefs and Practices," *Harvard Encyclopedia of American Ethnic Groups* (Cambridge, Mass., 1980). Victor R. Fuchs, "Concepts of Health—an Economist's Perspective," *Journal of Medicine and Philosophy*, 1 (1976), 229-237. Anders S. Lunde, "Health in the United States," *Annals of the American Academy of Political and Social Science*, 453 (1981), 28-69. Ross M. Mullner, Calvin S. Byre, and Cleve L. Killingsworth, "An Inventory of U.S. Health Care Data Bases," *Review of Public Data Use*, 11 (1983), 85-192. Donald L. Patrick, J. W. Bush, and Milton M. Chen, "Toward an Operational Definition of Health," *Journal of Health and Social Behavior*, 14 (1973), 6-24. A. H.

Pollard, "The Interaction between Morbidity and Mortality," *Journal of the Institute of Actuaries*, 107, Part 3 (1980), 233-313. Dorothy P. Rice, "Health Care Data in the United States," *Review of Public Data Use*, 11 (1983), 79-84. U.S. National Center for Health Statistics, *Current Estimates from the National Health Interview Survey: United States, 1980* (Washington, D.C., 1981). Russell Wilkins, *Health Status in Canada, 1926-1979* (Montreal: Institute for Research on Public Policy, 1980). Kathleen N. Williams and Robert H. Brook, "Quality Measurement and Assurance," *Health and Medical Care Services Review*, 1 (May-June, 1978), 1-32, as well as other issues of this bibliographic journal.

health care and **medical care,** sometimes used more or less synonymously, have gradually been differentiated as the end points of a continuum from a broad to a narrow range of components. In the traditional view of a physician's role, he studied the patient's symptoms, identified the ailment, and applied the appropriate therapy. The practice was most effective when the typical complaint was an infectious disease, but it became less so as the major causes of death shifted to heart diseases and cancers, of which the causes, generally not well understood, seem to be related to overall *life-style. Health care, then, consists of medical care in the older sense plus attention to general environmental and behavioral factors in illness. The shift in orientation was accompanied by an institutional one from a single practitioner working more or less on his own to a large and complex bureaucratic structure (Mechanic, 1976, 1981). A generation ago the training of American physicians began to include new elements of what was sometimes called "comprehensive medical care," by which the doctor assumed responsibility for the patient's "total health" (Hammond and Kern, 1959). With this broader perspective, doctors would be more cognizant of ethnic and class differences in diet, for instance, and of the way that various social groups define illness and react to treatment (e.g., Rosser and Mossberg, 1977). For example, in a comparison of the use of medical facilities in Chester, England; Burlington, Vermont; and Smederevo, Yugoslavia, the authors began with the "basic postulate" that "the use or nonuse of health services in a defined population varies with (1) perception of the symptoms and conditions or health situation for which use or nonuse occurs; (2) demographic characteristics, (3) the accessibility of physicians, nurses, other health workers, and hospital and nursing-home beds available to the population" (White and Murnaghan, 1969). The frequent concentration on the third factor as the only significant determinant of a population's *health is, by this view, mistaken.

REFERENCES: Kenneth A. Hammond and Fred Kern, *Teaching Comprehensive Medical Care: A Psychological Study of a Change in Medical Education* (Cambridge, Mass.: Harvard University Press, 1959). David Mechanic, *The Growth of Bureaucratic Medicine: An Inquiry into the Dynamics of Patient Behavior and the Organization of Medical Care* (New York: Wiley, 1976); "Some Dilemmas in Health Care Policy," *Milbank Memorial Fund Quarterly*, 59 (1981), 1-15. James M. Rosser and Howard E. Mossberg, *An Analysis of Health Care Delivery* (New York: Wiley, 1977). Kerr L. White and Jane H. Murnaghan,

"International Comparisons of Medical Care Utilization: A Feasibility Study," National Center for Health Statistics, *Vital and Health Statistics*, Ser. 2, no. 33 (1969).

Health Maintenance Organization (HMO), a term that came into use in the United States around 1970, means the particular type of group practice first developed in the 1930s by the Kaiser-Permanente Medical Care Program on the West Coast. The keynote is voluntary prepaid medical insurance. Doctors voluntarily band together into an HMO, optimally associated with a hospital, and groups of patients voluntarily join it in preference to using competing sources of health care. The total costs are divided among the members, so that all are protected against paying for catastrophic illnesses. Each visit to a physician or hospital incurs a small additional fee, enough to inhibit hypochondriacs. Doctors get a larger income, the healthier they keep their patients; and there is an incentive, contrary to the system in Medicare and Medicaid, to balance cost against utility.

REFERENCES: Nathan Glazer, "Perspectives on Health Care," *Public Interest*, no. 31 (1973), 110-125. Ernest W. Saward and Scott Fleming, "Health Maintenance Organizations," *Scientific American*, 243 (October, 1980), 47-53. Saward and Merwyn R. Greenlick, "Health Policy and the HMO," *Milbank Memorial Fund Quarterly*, 50 (1972), 147-176. Grady Wells, "Healthy Growth for HMOs," *American Demographics*, 6 (March, 1984), 34–38, 46–47.

heart disease, a lay term for various types of malfunctions that together with *cancers cause most deaths in industrial countries. Medical terminology may seem needlessly complex, with three words as apparent approximate synonyms— *heart* as an adjective; *cardiac*, the Latin equivalent; and *coronary*, which in fact means encircling in the manner of a crown. Note also *cardiovascular*, pertaining to the heart and the blood vessels, and *cardiovascular-renal* (CVR), pertaining to the heart, blood vessels, and kidney. The proportion of deaths in the United States ascribed to CVR diseases rose from a fifth in 1900 to well over half today. The main reason is that during this period fewer and fewer persons died of infectious diseases, and, with the rise in the average age of the population, degenerative diseases became proportionately more important as causes of death (cf. Handler et al., 1982).

The heart is a pump. When blood that has picked up oxygen in the lungs fills the left atrium and ventricle, the heart pumps it through the arteries and their tributaries throughout the body. After nourishment has been absorbed from the blood, the veins return it to the heart's right atrium and ventricle. The beating of the pump is measured by taking one's blood pressure, systolic (from *systole*, the period of the heart's contraction) when the left ventricle is pumping and diastolic (from *diastole*, the dilating of the heart) when the heart is filling. The normal ranges are 100 to 140 millimeters of mercury in the systolic phase and 60 to 90 in the diastolic, usually written as a fraction, such as 120/80. Hypertension (from *hyper-*, excessive; *tension*, the condition of being stretched or strained) is the term for blood pressure consistently above the normal range.

Ischemic heart disease (from *ischemia*, a deficiency of blood in a part of the body) is one of the more important broad categories (Cohen and Kleinman, 1979). A typical cause is atherosclerosis (one type of arteriosclerosis or "hardening of the arteries"), the deposit of fatty substances along the walls of blood vessels with a consequent reduction in the flow of blood through them or eventually an occlusion, or total blockage. In the United States the commonest fatal condition is atherosclerosis of the coronary arteries, which through their numerous branches supply the heart with fresh blood. The reduced flow there or elsewhere may be caused by an embolism, a blood clot (or *thrombus*, formed by a process termed *thrombosis*) that breaks loose from its original site, travels through the circulatory system, and eventually lodges in the heart or another organ. From any cause, reduced flow of blood to the heart can damage the heart muscle, resulting in heart failure, or myocardial infarction (from *myocardium*, the heart muscle; *infarct*, an area of body cells dying from coagulation). The back-up of blood from a blockage can cause such symptoms as angina pectoris (pain in the chest), paroxysms with a feeling of suffocation and impending death, pain or swelling in the arms or legs, and general fatigue (Alpert, 1978).

For a considerable period heart disease in the United States increased greatly both overall and as a cause of death, but recent advances in getting stricken patients to hospitals quickly have reduced the toll. The long-term trend cannot be described in full. *Mortality statistics have been available for the country only since the mid-1930s; and with the greater attention given to this type of malfunctioning, diagnostic precision has also grown, making data relatively incomparable over time and also from one locality or even one physician to another. The difficulties are exemplified by the inconclusive results of a 10-year $115-million study of the causes of heart disease sponsored by the U.S. National Heart, Lung, and Blood Institute (cf. *cholesterol). A Multiple Risk Factor Intervention Trial (MRFIT) was designed to determine whether men who reduced their blood cholesterol, blood pressure, and cigarette smoking would postpone their deaths, as they should have according to current medical beliefs. But the men who reduced these risk factors lived no longer on the average than those in a control group. The reason may have been that two common diuretics prescribed to the participants, hydrochlorothiazide and chlorthalidone, may be toxic in large doses.

Though demographic patterns vary somewhat by the particular ailment, some broad generalizations hold for most kinds of heart disease. Among males there is a markedly increased incidence with age, particularly after the middle years, and they are notably more susceptible than females. Deaths are—or have been in the recent past—proportionately more numerous among blacks than whites. In each color-age grouping, death rates are higher for obese persons than for those of normal weight, and for single than for married persons. Mortality fell in the 1970s, presumably because of better facilities for giving prompt care. And in general similar conclusions would be derived from the data of other industrial countries.

REFERENCES: Joseph S. Alpert, *The Heart Attack Handbook* (Boston: Little, Brown, 1978). Bruce B. Cohen and Joel C. Kleinman, "Death Rates from Ischemic Heart Disease and Other Related Diseases by Health Service Area, 1968-72," U.S. National Center for Health Statistics, *Statistical Notes for Health Planners*, no. 10 (1979). Frederick H. Epstein, "The Epidemiology of Coronary Heart Disease," *Journal of Chronic Diseases*, 18 (1965), 735-774. Philip Handler et al., "On Some Major Human Diseases," in National Research Council, *Outlook for Science and Technology: The Next Five Years* (San Francisco: W. H. Freeman, 1982). Edward A. Lew, "Some Implications of Mortality Statistics Relating to Coronary Heart Disease," *Journal of Chronic Diseases*, 6 (1957), 192-209. Iwao M. Moriyama, Dean E. Krueger, and Jeremiah Stamler, *Cardiovascular Diseases in the United States* (Cambridge, Mass.: Harvard University Press, 1971).

hearth tax was imposed at various places in medieval and early modern Europe. In England "hearth money" or "chimney money" of two shillings per hearth was imposed in 1662. It was so unpopular that in 1689 it was dropped and replaced by a window tax. The relevance to demography is that estimates of the number of households and thus of the population can sometimes be obtained from such tax records.

heredity, the transmission of parents' physical and psychic characteristics to their offspring, is throughout the natural world the mechanism by which the process of *evolution works; see also *population genetics. With respect to the human species, however, there has been a long and recurrent dispute between rigid proponents of opposed views concerning heredity *or* the environment, nature *or* nurture. The best of present-day theorists emphasize that it is the interaction of the learned and the instinctive that determines human behavior. In a recent paper in the *American Journal of Physical Anthropology*, William Pollitzer (1981) traced the development of papers in that journal on genetics and population studies from its founding in 1918, showing that there had been a trend from classification to process as the main emphasis. The relatively new discipline of psychogenetics is defined by P. L. Broadhurst (1968) as "that specialization which concerns itself with the interaction of heredity and environment, insofar as they affect behavior." Such an interaction has been typically very difficult to specify, however, for whenever children remain in the same social-economic situation as their parents—which is the usual case—a similarity in the two generations may be due to heredity, the continuing pressure of the unchanged environment, or both factors in proportions difficult to estimate. With the recently developed techniques of molecular biology, it should be possible to progress very much faster in rounding out our knowledge of inherited characteristics (Lewis, 1981).

The effect of genetic factors on demographic characteristics is also imperfectly known. The hereditary influence on fecundity, though still impossible to prove generally, is perceptible at the two extremes of the fecundity range. On the one hand, the physiological ability to have offspring can be impaired by any of a number of defects in the sexual organs, and a predisposition toward such a constitutional impediment can be inherited. The genetic transmission of a high level of fecundity, on the other hand, is suggested by the fact that the proportion of *multiple births, which seems to be correlated with general fertility, differs significantly from one family line and from one race to another (e.g., Pearl, 1939). For instance, the rate of twinning is several times higher among American blacks than among American whites; the difference, however, is only in the dizygotic twinning rate, not in the monozygotic, and it is believed that the inheritance is through the female line (Bulmer, 1970).

Long life also seems to depend to some degree on an inherited capacity (cf. Damon, 1969). When Louis †Dublin and his colleagues (1949, p. 117) wrote their classic work on mortality, they summed up earlier studies with the conclusion that a favorable ancestry would add 2 to 4 years to one's expectation of life from age 25. And in 1915 having long-lived parents supposedly had added 7 more years to one's expectation of life than the utmost that medical science could then achieve (Pearl, 1922, p. 165). According to more recent studies, such differences depend largely on the several thousand heritable conditions or diseases that have been identified. About a few of these—Down's syndrome as a prime example—medical knowledge has grown substantially; but many affect very small populations, often in ways elusive to earlier methods of genetic research. As a recent example of what is possible with molecular techniques, it has been hypothesized that a person's sodium metabolism is inherited, and thus also the effect of sodium in the diet on hypertension, one of the most important precursors of *heart disease (*Science*, 211, February 27, 1981, p. 911). Genetic factors have been plausibly cited also as a cause of at least some *cancers, as well as in such psychic ailments as depression and "hereditary alcoholism." In short, it is at least a hypothesis—and some experts would rank it higher—that some of the principal causes of death in advanced societies, including diseases of the heart, stroke, and cancers, develop partly as a consequence of an inherited susceptibility.

REFERENCES: P. L. Broadhurst, "Genetics and Behavior," *International Encyclopedia of the Social Sciences*, 6, 96-102. M. G. Bulmer, *The Biology of Twinning in Man* (Oxford: Clarendon Press, 1970). Albert Damon, "Race, Ethnic Group, and Disease," *Social Biology*, 16 (1969), 69-80. Louis I. Dublin, Alfred J. Lotka, and Mortimer Spiegelman, *Length of Life: A Study of the Life Table* (rev. ed.; New York: Ronald, 1949). Roger Lewis, "Jumping Genes Help Trace Inherited Diseases," *Science*, 211 (February 13, 1981), 690-692. Raymond Pearl, *The Biology of Death* (Philadelphia: Lippincott, 1922); *The Natural History of Population* (New York: Oxford University Press, 1939). William S. Pollitzer, "The Development of Genetics and Population Studies," *American Journal of Physical Anthropology*, 56 (1981), 483-489.

Hinduism, the principal religion of *India, has well over 400 million adherents in that country, Nepal, and Sri Lanka, as well as sizable numbers among emigrant Indians and Western converts. Orthodoxy is based on the texts of the four Vedas, dating from 1400 to 800 B.C., and the subsequent Upanishads. The first are largely allegorical and encourage a wide range of interpretation; the second fixed the *caste system and established the dominance of the priestly Brahmans in all social functions. The ascetic pessimism of Hinduism is exaggerated among heterodox Jainists, who trace their origins to a legendary pre-Vedic past and do not recognize the authority of the Vedas. Rishabha, the first Jaina, was born 100 billion *sagaras* ago; a *sagara* is 100 billion *palyas*, and a *palya* is the period needed to empty a well a mile deep filled with fine hairs if one hair is withdrawn every hundred years. Against such a perspective all human effort is completely beyond good and evil, proceeding through many lifetimes toward an absolutely transcendent purity and impassivity (Frazier, 1969).

Scholars dispute how Hinduism has affected Indian society. Some note the chasm between saintly goals and actual behavior, others emphasize characteristics ranging from the pervasive caste divisions to the cows that eat up scarce food. The religion's evolution during the past century or more has been by an interaction between reformers, who accommodated in various ways to Islamic and Christian influences, and revivalists, who tried to retain or reestablish Vedic doctrine in a pure form (cf. *child marriage). One type of amalgam that emerged was represented by M. K. †Gandhi, and it may be that the Indian nationalist drive for independence could not have succeeded without the unifying force of Hinduism. According to a survey of some 200 students at Andhra University, orthodoxy is still a powerful force among those studying physical or social sciences, as well as the humanities. True, well over half did not believe in "the traditional divisions of Hindu society and the code of conduct" prescribed by that caste tradition, but about as many affirmed their faith in astrology and/or palmistry, and 85 percent held that *dharma*, the divine moral order of Hinduism, applies to the modern world (Ashby, 1974).

The self-restraint imposed on pious Hindus includes a form of chastity. Among the most orthodox marital coitus is a semireligious rite; sex is permissible only for the procreation of the species, being otherwise considered vulgar if not sinful. Yet according to the Upanishads themselves, "Now the woman whom one desires [with the thought] 'may she not conceive,' after inserting the member in her, joining mouth to mouth, he should first inhale and then exhale and say, 'With power, with semen I reclaim the semen from you.' Thus she comes to be without semen." In short, the desire of the man to prevent conception is seen as licit, though we may question the efficacy of the method. There is a widespread belief that semen is a great source of strength and good health, and the many days when marital coitus is forbidden may be observed more faithfully than one might suppose (Nag, 1972).

REFERENCES: Philip H. Ashby, *Modern Trends in Hinduism* (New York: Columbia University Press, 1974). Allie M. Frazier, ed., *Hinduism* (Philadelphia: Westminster Press, 1969). Moni Nag, "Sex, Culture, and Human Fertility," *Current Anthropology*, 13 (1972), 231-237. Sarvepalli Radhakrishnan, *The Hindu View of Life* (Boston: Unwin Paperbacks, 1980).

hinterland, from the German for "land behind," has derived from this etymology the primary meaning of the accessible land behind a coastal settlement
or port. According to the so-called doctrine of the hinterland, in international
law it was once held that the occupation of the coast implied a right also to
occupy inland territories. As presently used in human ecology, the word has
come to mean the tributary area of a city.

Hispanics, or **Latinos,** an ethnic minority in the United States, have been
especially difficult to classify statistically. Before 1930 the U.S. Bureau of the
Census included those born in Mexico and those of Mexican or mixed parentage
in the foreign stock, treated in census documents just like nationalities originating
in European countries. In 1930 Mexican Americans were placed under the rubric
"other races," reflecting the high proportion of mestizos among them. The
classification became an occasion for protests from the Mexican government and
the U.S. Department of State, and it resulted in a sizable undercount of upper-
class persons of Mexican descent, many of whom were of light complexion. In
1940, by another shift, Mexican Americans were classified by their "mother
tongue," the language spoken in early childhood; but a high proportion of those
who by other criteria were "Mexican" reported this to be English.

In 1950 the classification became "white persons of Spanish surname." A
list of about 7,000 surnames had been prepared by the U.S. Immigration and
Naturalization Service, and it was subsequently supplemented occasionally by
specialists in Romance languages. With acculturation, however, some persons
may have changed their name from "Martinez," say, to "Martin," and women
marrying out of the Hispanic group would, according to this criterion, lose their
ethnic identity immediately. In 1980 the census schedule offered a choice among
various Hispanic options, including Mexican, Mexican-American, and Chicano.
Whether such casual self-identifications are more significant than the earlier
specifications can be doubted, and presumably most statistical compilations will
ignore the differentiation and report the sum of all these categories. In 1980
some 2.9 million persons, or 6.2 percent of the population, spoke Spanish at
home, and of these one-sixth could not speak English.

However identified, Hispanics comprise groups of great cultural differences:
descendants of the Spanish settlers in the Southwest; descendants of early immigrants from Mexico, many of whom have moved up into the middle class (cf.
*Hispano); recent immigrants from Mexico, mostly of the lower classes, in-
cluding many temporary or illegal sojourners whose status in the United States
(and thus in a census count) is difficult to fix (see also *migration, illegal); Cuban
refugees, mainly middle-class in origin and aspirations, presently distinguishable
geographically; Puerto Ricans, also set apart by the fact that they reside mainly
in the East; and a growing number of immigrants, legal and illegal, from Spain
and Central and South America. As a striking instance of the diversity among
Hispanics, when the Anheuser-Busch brewery translated "This Bud's for you"

into Spanish, it found it expedient to produce four versions of the jingle—a hot salsa beat for Puerto Ricans in New York, a chiranga style for Cubans in Florida, and two different mariachi arrangements, one for the Mexican population of Texas (who came mostly from the border regions) and the other for those in the rest of the Southwest (whose subculture derives more from the area of Mexico City). In 1980 the census enumerated a total of 14.6 million persons of Spanish origin, of whom 8.7 million were Mexican, 2.0 million Puerto Rican, and 0.8 million Cuban. About 2.1 million residents reported that they had been born in Mexico, which thus became the leading country of birth of immigrants, followed by Germany, Italy, and Canada.

REFERENCES: Robert W. Buechley, "A Reproducible Method of Counting Persons of Spanish Surname," *Journal of the American Statistical Association*, 56 (1961), 88-97. Edwin H. Carpenter and Larry G. Blackwood, "The Potential for Population Growth in the U.S. Counties that Border Mexico: El Paso to San Diego," *Natural Resources Journal*, 17 (1977), 545-569. Leo Grebler, Joan W. Moore, and Ralph C. Guzman, *The Mexican-American People: The Nation's Second Largest Minority* (New York: Free Press, 1970). José Hernández, Leo Estrada, and David Alvírez, "Census Data and the Problem of Conceptually Defining the Mexican American Population," *Social Science Quarterly*, 53 (1973), 671-687. A. J. Jaffe, Ruth M. Cullen, and Thomas D. Boswell, *The Changing Demography of Spanish Americans* (New York: Academic Press, 1980). David E. Lopez, "Chicano Language Loyalty in an Urban Setting," *Sociology and Social Research*, 62 (1978), 267-278. William E. Morton, "Demographic Redefinition of Hispanos," *Public Health Reports*, 85 (1970), 617-623. U.S. Bureau of the Census, "Persons of Spanish Ancestry," Supplementary Report, *1970 Census of Population*, PC(S1)-30, 1973.

Hispano, the designation preferred by the *Hispanics in the Southwest of the United States, mainly in New Mexico, whose forebears were inhabitants of that region when it was part of Mexico. When the U.S. Bureau of the Census established a classification of "Mexican" for the 1930 enumeration, one consequence was a gross undercount of Hispanos. Though about half of New Mexico's population, or some 200,000 people, would have been included among the Spanish-speaking sector, the census counted only 61,960 "Mexicans." Hispanos continue to insist on their discrete identity, but most works on Mexican Americans or Hispanics fail to make the distinction.

REFERENCE: A. J. Jaffe, Ruth M. Cullen, and Thomas D. Boswell, *The Changing Demography of Spanish Americans* (New York: Academic Press, 1980).

histogram, a bar graph that corresponds to a simple univariate frequency table. It consists of a set of columns, arranged side by side, of which the heights are proportional to the class frequencies and the widths to the size of the class intervals. Since data are usually classified into equal intervals, the width of the columns is ordinarily the same and only their height differs. A line connecting the midpoints of the tops of the columns describes what is called a "frequency polygon."

historical demography can be understood merely as the writing on population in a historical context—a special field of such men as Julius †Beloch (1886) on the ancient world, Ping-ti †Ho (1959) on China, or J. C. †Russell (1948) on Europe. These are competent works in what is sometimes termed "population history," or "demographic history," whose authors treated population data more or less like any other type of material: given a range of estimates from competing sources, they used their detailed knowledge of the whole social context to judge which is most likely to be correct—the process that the German historian Leopold von Ranke termed a *Quellenkritik*. Population differs, however, from other topics of historical analysis in that it is to some degree a self-contained process, no matter what the cultural context. Aging is continuous, and persons known to be x years old in a particular year can be assigned the age $x + 10$ a decade later. The population of any area, without migration in or out, is equal to that at an earlier date plus the intervening *natural increase. Since in any society infants and the elderly are more likely to die within a year than adolescents and young adults, and since childbearing is physiologically limited to females in the same favored age range, there is a necessary relation among mortality, fertility, and the age structure.

A revolution took place when men trained in mathematical techniques entered the field and converted "population history" to "historical demography" (Flinn, 1981, chap. 1). The pioneer internationally was Louis †Henry, whose analyses culminated in the authorship of a manual detailing the methods of *family reconstitution (Henry, 1970); he has also participated in the Société de Démographie Historique, which sponsors the *Annales de Démographie Historique*. France's so-called *Annales* School (associated with the journal *Annales: Économie, Société, Civilisations*) developed in part independently, in part through cooperation, as in the well known work on Crulai (cf. Louis †Henry). In Britain historical demography was fostered in part by David †Glass (see Glass and Eversley, 1965), in part by the Cambridge Group for the History of Population and Social Structure (see Wrigley, 1966, 1969; Wrigley and Schofield, 1981). In Italy the section in the population association devoted to historical demography developed into a separate organization, the Italian Society for Historical Demography; its successive annual meetings have probed the sources available and difficulties in using them (see, e.g., Santini, 1972). Counterparts in other countries have developed both independently and through international contacts—in Scandinavia (e.g., Matthiessen, 1970); Germany (Imhof, 1975); the Low Countries (cf. Petersen, 1960); Hungary (Horváth, 1981); Japan (cf. Hanley and Yamamura, 1977); and Latin America (cf. Arretx et al., 1983); see also the bibliographic essays by Etienne †van de Walle and Louise Kantrow (1974); International Committee of Historical Sciences et al. (1981). The American colonies and the United States that evolved from them have presented a special problem, since there the parish records on which European analyses are based are scanty or lacking (but see also *Genealogical Society of Utah). Even so, much work has been done during the past several decades, both on the colonies (e.g., Cassedy, 1969; Norton, 1971; Wells, 1971) and the period after the establishment of the Republic (e.g., Leet, 1976; Mott, 1972; Uhlenberg, 1969); see also the bibliography by Maris Vinovskis (1978) and the methodological manual by J. Dennis Willigan and Katherine Lynch (1982). Fundamental to such advances were analyses of vital registration (Gutman, 1959) and the censuses (Coale and Zelnik, 1963; Wells, 1975). In each of these countries, the work of historians writing about population in the framework of a *Quellenkritik* is being supplanted by analyses based on the physiological patterns of demographic factors. No one supposes that the historical expertise is dispensable, but few any longer doubt the superiority of the joint product (for good summaries, see Flinn, 1981; Willigan and Lynch, 1982).

An important achievement came with *The Population History of England, 1541-1871* (Wrigley and Schofield, 1981). Vital records were gathered by a team of volunteers from all over England, and these data were expanded into an estimate of the country's full experience over more than three centuries. Then, with a technique that the authors developed, the schedule of births, deaths, and marriages was converted into one including estimates of net migration and population size and structure. With these it was possible to trace the course of fertility and mortality, with the surprising conclusion that over this period mortality fluctuated around a norm that changed rather little, and that fertility rose significantly. This contradicts earlier analyses, as well as the imaginary history of the *demographic transition.

Overlapping with historical demography but following a partly separate course there has been a very considerable rise in *family history*, a "discovery of complexity," as Glen Elder (1981a) termed it. A major stimulus, again, came from France, with the work of Philippe †Ariès, *Centuries of Childhood* (1962), as well as the methodology of family reconstitution as developed by Louis Henry and others. The *American Journal of Family History* is international in its scope, as indicated by *Family and Sexuality in French History*, of which the journal's founder and editor was co-editor (Wheaton and Hareven, 1980). At Stanford University there is a Project on the History of Fertility Control (e.g., David and Sanderson, 1978). The Cambridge Group has traced the links between family form and fertility, especially but not exclusively in Britain (e.g., Laslett and Wall, 1972; Laslett et al., 1980; Smith, 1981). Something like the cohort analysis in demography has been taken over in studies of "the life course" (Elder, 1981b). A high point of interdisciplinary cooperation was reached in *Historical Studies of Changing Fertility* (Tilly, 1978), a composite work by economists, historians, and demographers who were able to penetrate one another's disciplines and achieve a coherent frame of reference though, indeed, with important differences in their conclusions.

REFERENCES: Philippe Ariès, *Centuries of Childhood: A Social History of Family Life* (New York: Knopf, 1962; French original, 1960). Carmen Arretx, Rolando Mellafe, and Jorge L. Somoza, *Demografía Historica en América Latina: Fuentes y Metodos* (San José, Costa Rica: Centro Latinoamericano de Demografía, 1983). Julius Beloch, *Die*

Bevölkerung der Griechisch-Römischen Welt (Leipzig: Duncker und Humblot, 1886). Cassedy, *Demography in Early America*. Ansley J. Coale and Melvin Zelnik, *New Estimates of Fertility and Population in the United States* (Princeton, N.J.: Princeton University Press, 1963). Paul A. David and Warren C. Sanderson, *The Effectiveness of Nineteenth-Century Contraceptive Practices: An Application of Microdemographic Modelling Approaches* (Stanford, Calif.: Stanford Project on the History of Fertility Control, 1978). Glen H. Elder, "History of the Family: The Discovery of Complexity," *Journal of Marriage and the Family*, 43 (1981a), 489-519; "History and the Life Course," in Daniel Bertaux, ed., *Biography and Society: The Life History Approach in the Social Sciences* (Beverly Hills, Calif.: Sage Publications, 1981b). Michael W. Flinn, *The European Demographic System, 1500-1820* (Baltimore, Md.: Johns Hopkins University Press, 1981). Glass and Eversley, *Population in History* (1965). Robert Gutman, *Birth and Death Registration in Massachusetts, 1639-1900* (New York: Milbank Memorial Fund, 1959). Susan B. Hanley and Kozo Yamamura, *Economic and Demographic Change in Preindustrial Japan, 1600-1868* (Princeton, N.J.: Princeton University Press, 1977). Louis Henry, *Manuel de Démographie Historique* (2nd ed.; Paris: Librairie Droz, 1970). Ping-ti Ho, *Studies on the Population of China, 1368–1953* (Cambridge, Mass.: Harvard University Press, 1959). Robert A. Horváth, "Le Développement des Remariages en Hongrie de 1890 à 1977," in Jacques Dupâquier et al., eds., *Marriage and Remarriage in Populations of the Past* (1981). Arthur E. Imhof, *Historische Demographie als Sozialgeschichte* (Darmstadt: Hessische Historische Kommission, 1975). International Committee of Historical Sciences, International Commission on Historical Demography (Lausanne); Société de Démographie Historique (Paris); and IUSSP, Committee on Historical Demography (Liège), "International Bibliography of Historical Demography, 1981," *Annales de Démographie Historique* (1981). Peter Laslett and Richard Wall, eds., *Household and Family in Past Time* (Cambridge, England: University Press, 1972); Laslett, Karla Oosterveen, and Richard M. Smith, *Bastardy and Its Comparative History* (Cambridge, Mass.: Harvard University Press, 1980). Don R. Leet, "The Determinants of the Fertility Transition in Antebellum Ohio," *Journal of Economic History*, 36 (1976), 359-378. Poul C. Matthiessen, *Some Aspects of the Demographic Transition in Denmark* (Copenhagen: Kobenhavns Universitets Fond, 1970). Frank L. Mott, "Portrait of an American Mill Town: Demographic Response in Mid-nineteenth Century Warren, Rhode Island," *Population Studies*, 26 (1972), 147-157. Susan L. Norton, "Population Growth in Colonial America: A Study of Ipswich, Massachusetts," *Population Studies*, 25 (1971), 433-452. William Petersen, "The Demographic Transition in the Netherlands," *American Sociological Review*, 25 (1960), 334-347. J. C. Russell, *British Medieval Population* (Albuquerque: University of New Mexico Press, 1948). Antonio Santini, "Techniques and Methods in Historical Demography (17th-18th Centuries)," *Journal of European Economic History*, 1 (1972), 459-469. Richard M. Smith, "Fertility, Economy, and Household Formation in England over Three Centuries," *Population and Development Review*, 7 (1981), 595-622. Charles Tilly, ed., *Historical Studies of Changing Fertility* (Princeton, N.J.: Princeton University Press, 1978). Peter R. Uhlenberg, "A Study of Cohort Life Cycles: Cohorts of Native-Born Massachusetts Women, 1830-1920," *Population Studies*, 23 (1969), 407-420. Etienne van de Walle and Louise Kantrow, "Historical Demography: A Bibliographical Essay," *Population Index*, 40 (1974), 611-622. Maris A. Vinovskis, "Recent Trends in American Historical Demography: Some Methodological and Conceptual Considerations," *Annual Review of Sociology*, 4 (1978), 603-627. Robert V. Wells, "Family Size and Fertility Control in Eighteenth-Century America:

A Study of Quaker Families," *Population Studies*, 25 (1971), 73-82; *The Population of the British Colonies before 1776: A Survey of Census Data* (Princeton, N.J.: Princeton University Press, 1975). Robert Wheaton and Tamara K. Hareven, eds., *Family and Sexuality in French History* (Philadelphia: University of Pennsylvania Press, 1980). J. Dennis Willigan and Katherine A. Lynch, *Sources and Methods of Historical Demography* (New York: Academic Press, 1982). E. A. Wrigley, *Population and History* (New York: McGraw-Hill, 1969); Wrigley, ed., *An Introduction to English Historical Demography from the Sixteenth to the Nineteenth Century* (New York: Basic Books, 1966); Wrigley and Roger Schofield, *The Population History of England, 1541-1871: A Reconstruction* (Cambridge, Mass.: Harvard University Press, 1981).

Hochelaga, a computer program of *family reconstitution first used with parish records of French Canada.

REFERENCE: Pierre Beauchamp, Hubert Charbonneau, and Yolande Lavoie, "Reconstitution Automatique des Familles par le Programme 'Hochelaga,' " *Population*, 28 (1973), 39-58.

holocaust, which derives from the Greek words for "whole" and "burnt," means generally a sacrificial offering to pagan gods of which the whole is consumed by fire. Recently "the Holocaust," with a definite article and a capital H, has been used to refer to the mass murder of European Jews in 1941-45, for which the Nazis used the euphemism *Endlösung*, or "final solution" of "the Jewish problem" (Fleischner, 1977). The number of Jews killed, usually estimated at 6 million, is hard to fix more precisely both because the records are difficult to interpret and because the key words "Jews" and "killed" are to some degree ambiguous. The *Nuremberg laws that Germany adopted in 1935 defined "Jews" by a racial criterion and thus included many who in their own estimation were Christians or agnostics. More than a third of the missing European Jews, and of German Jews perhaps as many as four-fifths, died from overwork, disease, hunger, and neglect. In probably the most conscientious attempt to estimate the totals, Raul Hilberg (1967) gives 3 million as the number annihilated in the killing centers, plus 1.4 million exterminated by the Einsatzgruppen (traveling murder squads operating in the areas of Eastern Europe under German control) and 700,000 "aggravated deaths" in the concentration camps into which Jews and others were herded. His total, thus, is 5.1 million Jews, to which must be added members of other "inferior" "races," political opponents of the Nazis, and bystanders. The long-run effects of this slaughter on Jewish populations have of course been marked (Eckardt and Eckardt, 1978; Shur and Littell, 1980). See also *anti-Semitism; *pogrom.

REFERENCES: Alice Eckardt and Roy Eckardt, "Studying the Holocaust's Impact Today: Some Dilemmas of Language and Method," *Judaism*, 27 (1978), 222-232. Eva Fleischner, "A Select Annotated Bibliography on the Holocaust," *Horizons*, 4 (1977), 61-83. Raul Hilberg, *The Destruction of the European Jews* (Chicago: Quadrangle, 1967). Irene G. Shur and Franklin H. Littell, eds., "Reflecting on the Holocaust: Historical, Philosophical and Educational Dimensions," *Annals of the American Academy of Political and Social Science*, 450 (1980), 1-255.

homeopathy, a system of therapy that is based on the thesis that one treats like with like (from the Greek *homoio–*, similar; *pathos*, suffering). It was developed by [Christian Friedrich] Samuel Hahnemann (1755-1843), a German physician, who contrasted it with *allopathy* (*allos*, other), the orthodox theory of medicine. According to Hahnemann, medical practitioners should not focus their attention on germs, for example, which constitute an essential part of the human equilibrium with the natural environment, but examine also the "terrain," or what today is called the *ecosystem. See also *Indian medicine.

homeostasis, in biology, maintenance of the steady state; the tendency of a living organism to hold to and, when necessary, to restore certain of its basic conditions. For example, if mutation results in a repeated addition of a harmful gene to a pool, the resultant defective organisms, with a lower rate of reproduction, will approximate a stable proportion of the whole. In the context of ecology homeostasis is often exemplified with the familiar relation between predators and their prey: when rabbits multiply, so do foxes, which by their larger numbers reduce the rate of rabbits' increase, and thus also that of foxes; and so on. Particularly by the stimulus of the American physiologist Walter B. Cannon (1963), the concept of homeostasis was transferred to social analysis, with often a strong implication that disruptive change is pathological. The term has been used in historical demography to denote a long-term tendency of fertility and mortality, for example, to balance out, as in the classic Malthusian model or, in an analysis of reconstitutions of European families, in the tendency for early marriage to be associated with lower marital fertility and higher child mortality.

REFERENCES: Walter B. Cannon, *The Wisdom of the Body* (2nd ed.; New York: Norton, 1963). Daniel Scott Smith, "A Homeostatic Demographic Regime: Patterns in West European Family Reconstitution Studies," in Ronald D. Lee, ed., *Population Patterns in the Past* (New York: Academic Press, 1977).

Homestead Act, passed by the U.S. Congress in 1862, culminated a long effort by the Republican Party, whose main strength was in the West, to stimulate the settlement of that region. Under its terms any family head over 21 years of age, a citizen or in the process of becoming one, could acquire 160 acres of unoccupied public land after 5 years of continuous residence and the payment of a nominal registration fee. However, far less of the land in the public domain was distributed under the act than was sold. There was also a Southern Homestead Act (1864), designed to provide 160-acre farms in five Southern states to freed slaves; by 1872, when the law was repealed, only 4,000 black families had received plots.

homicide, the killing of one person by another, is usually understood as what is more precisely termed felonious homicide, an act not justified by an excuse like self-defense. Legal codes differ according to national norms. Japan is harshest in punishing the killing of one's lineal descendant; Italy makes a special provision for a passionate defense of one's honor; negligence is more severely penalized in continental Europe than in Britain or the United States. According to Anglo-American jurisprudence, manslaughter is a homicide without malice, either "voluntary," when a provocation leads to a sudden heat of passion, or "involuntary," when the killing results from culpable negligence. Murder is killing with malice, either expressed or implied. In most jurisdictions of the United States, it is divided into two types: first-degree murder is deliberate and premeditated, or especially cruel, or committed while perpetrating another felony such as a burglary or rape; murder lacking such characteristics is of the second degree.

Homicide relates to demography in two ways (cf. Farley, 1980). As a cause of death, though statistically of minor importance in most populations, in some cases it is as significant as a major disease. Both murderers and their victims, on the other hand, are generally concentrated in particular age-sex-ethnic sectors. Since most murderers are young males, some analysts ascribed the rise in the murder rate of the United States during the past several decades to the fact that those born during the *baby boom were reaching adulthood. According to one study, however, the increase in the rate during the 1960s was more than ten times greater than it would have been merely from the change in age structure (Wilson, 1975, p. 17). Each year in the mid-1960s some 8,500 murders were reported in the United States, or only slightly fewer than the deaths from all forms of tuberculosis. The number of murders, as well as the already existent disparity between the United States and other industrial countries, rose subsequently. In the 1970s the perennial debate on whether capital punishment acts as a deterrent was renewed, with a notable shift in public opinion away from the liberal views of the 1950s and 1960s (Tittle and Rowe, 1974; Carrington, 1978).

The rate for nonwhite victims, both male and female, set this portion of the American population apart from groups of comparable size anywhere in the world. During the 1960s, when there was a substantial improvement in the civil rights, income, and general well-being of many blacks, the threat of murder— in the main by other blacks—increased. By 1977 homicide was the leading cause of death among black males aged 25 to 44 years; the rate of 125.2 per 100,000 in that color-age-sex group contrasted with one of 14.2 in the comparable white bracket. Indeed, there had been a decline in the difference since 1950, but mainly because the number of whites who were killed rose (Rice, 1980).

REFERENCES: Frank G. Carrington, *Neither Cruel Nor Unusual* (New Rochelle, N.Y.: Arlington House, 1978). Reynolds Farley, "Homicide in the United States," *Demography*, 17 (1980), 177-188. Dorothy P. Rice, "Homicide from the Perspective of NCHS Statistics on Blacks," *Public Health Reports*, 95 (1980), 550-552. Charles R. Tittle and Alan R. Rowe, "Certainty of Arrest and Crime Rates: A Further Test of the Deterrent Hypothesis," *Social Forces*, 52 (1974), 455-462. James Q. Wilson, *Thinking about Crime* (New York: Basic Books, 1975).

homosexuality can refer to either (1) erotic acts between persons of the same sex, sometimes only because of the absence of heterosexual opportunities, or

(2) a psychosocial proclivity, which may be entirely suppressed and never directly expressed in behavior. The age of the person involved should also be considered in any definition, for adolescence is often (or even generally) a period of transitional confusion about sexual identity. Yet neither opponents nor proponents of homosexuality necessarily make the distinction usual in legal and moral codes between the homosexuality of consenting adults and pedophilia, or the seduction of boys by homosexual men or of girls by lesbian women (cf. Schofield, 1965). A definition that takes these stipulations into account is given by Ruth Barnhouse (1977, p. 22): homosexuality is "an *adult* adaptation characterized by *preferential* sexual behavior between members of the same sex" (italics in the original).

Like a number of other behavior patterns, homosexuality has been characterized successively as a sin, a crime, a disease, and an alternative life-style. It is hardly necessary to elaborate on the facts that, by the Judeo-Christian norm as it has been traditionally interpreted, homosexual practices are an abomination, or that until very recently most Western jurisdictions prohibited them. Redefining the aberration as a disease was seen as a humanitarian reform. A crusade conducted mainly by physicians started in 1869 with a paper by Carl Westphal, a Berlin professor of psychiatry (cf. Bullough, 1976, 1977), and it developed strength through most of the next century. Sigmund Freud's influential view was that homosexual attachments, a sign of immaturity or of a regression to a childlike stage, can hardly ever be cured through psychoanalysis. In the most extensive study based on psychoanalytical premises, seventy-seven psychiatrists contributed detailed information on their male patients, a total of 106 homosexuals plus 100 heterosexuals used as a control. The data were analyzed in a book of which Irving Bieber (1962) was the principal author. Concerning the etiology of the "psychopathology," the study found that "the homosexual adaptation [is] an outcome of exposure to highly pathologic parent-child relationships and early life situations," especially an unhealthily intimate mother-son dyad. It was assumed that "every homosexual is a latent heterosexual," who with suitable treatment could be restored to the "biological norm." If this was the authoritative statement it seemed to be in 1962, the general view of American psychiatrists soon changed. In the first edition of its *Diagnostic and Statistical Manual, Mental Disorders* (1952), the American Psychiatric Association had characterized homosexuality as a "sociopathic personality disturbance," but in the 1968 revision this was softened to "non-psychotic mental disorder" (cf. Bayer, 1981, chap. 1).

Apart from psychologists and physicians, some of those in other disciplines offered evidence that homosexuality is too prevalent a state to be suitably characterized as a disease. Classicists collected references in the literature of ancient Greece that indicated or suggested both that homosexuality had been common there and that it was generally accepted. Arabists noted the pattern in the Middle East by which men married and produced a family but maintained love affairs with young boys. In the United States Alfred †Kinsey, perhaps the most influential proponent of tolerance in the late 1940s and early 1950s, viewed the

human species with the eyes of an entomologist. The surprisingly high proportions of males he found who had had some homosexual experiences or were
completely homosexual reflected an egregiously nonrepresentative sample: the
range of occupations of his male respondents, which included YMCA secretaries
and pimps, omitted the whole central core of mechanics and plumbers, book-
keepers and salesmen (Kinsey et al., 1948). In their survey of ethnographic data
on sexual behavior, Clellan †Ford and Frank Beach (1951, chap. 7) summed up
with the conclusion that "some homosexual behavior occurs in a great many
human societies, . . . more common in adolescence than in adulthood." That this
is so also among infrahuman primates they took to be additional evidence that
the behavior is "natural"—as though not only primitive tribes but also apes
were a suitable model for civilized men and women. One of the more important
studies of the period was by the American psychologist Evelyn Hooker (1958),
who administered projective tests to thirty homosexuals not undergoing psychiatric treatment and compared the results with tests given to a control group of
heterosexual men. There were few or no differences between the two groups.
But the Rorschach test she used cannot distinguish males from females, and that
the two small samples reacted similarly was interesting but not truly significant.

These works helped change opinions, but the decisive step was political. In
England pressure from advocates of greater tolerance resulted in the appointment
of a commission of inquiry, which recommended the repeal of all laws restricting
sex relations between consenting adults (Committee on Homosexual Offences,
1956). In the United States homosexual activists also succeeded in getting local
jurisdictions to make similar changes in their laws. From 1970 through 1972,
they disrupted some sessions of the American Psychiatric Association annual
meetings, demanding that it delete homosexuality from its list of diseases. When
the board of trustees of the APA acceded, some demanded that the issue be put
to a vote of the membership. Of those who participated in the vote, 58 percent
supported the board's stand and 37 percent opposed it (Bayer, 1981, chap. 4).
That the official professional body of psychiatrists split on whether to define a
set of behavior patterns as normal or pathological suggests how disruptive the
question had become.

In the early 1970s the over 800 male "gay" and lesbian-feminist organizations
in the United States began to win a greater tolerance of what is increasingly
defined as a legitimate alternative way of life, and, correlatively, sought and
sometimes obtained some of the legal rights once ascribed to such particular
classes as married persons, fathers or mothers of children, guardians of dependent
children, and others who were seen to be acting as agents of society (Boggan
et al., 1975). Some aberrant clerics have performed weddings for homosexual
couples, but the first court cases petitioning for full legal marital status have not
yet succeeded in any state. With the strong push for *zero population growth,
some analysts have argued that homosexual "families" would be a convenient
manner of helping to effect the necessary ecological adjustment.

Essentially homosexuality is a moral issue. For a period, in a manner typical of the nineteenth century, moral positions were half-disguised as scientific or medical findings. At the present time, ethical norms are more likely to be set through politics by skirmishes between a small but determined pressure group and the more or less indifferent general population.

REFERENCES: Ruth Tiffany Barnhouse, *Homosexuality: A Symbolic Confusion* (New York: Seabury Press, 1977). Ronald Bayer, *Homosexuality and American Psychiatry: The Politics of Diagnosis* (New York: Basic Books, 1981). Irving Bieber et al., *Homosexuality: A Psychoanalytic Study of Male Homosexuals* (Society of Medical Psychoanalysts; New York: Vintage, 1962). E. Carrington Boggan, Marilyn G. Haft, Charles Lister, and John P. Rupp, *The Rights of Gay People: The Basic ACLU Guide to a Gay Person's Rights* (New York: Avon Books, 1975). Vern L. Bullough, *Sexual Variance in Society and History* (New York: Wiley, 1976); "Challenges to Societal Attitudes toward Homosexuality in the Late Nineteenth and Early Twentieth Centuries," *Social Science Quarterly*, 58 (1977), 29-44. Committe on Homesexual Offences and Prostitution, *Report of the Committee*, John Wolfenden, chairman (London: H. M. Stationery Office, 1956. C. S. Ford and Frank A. Beach, *Patterns of Sexual Behavior* (New York: Harper, 1951). Evelyn Hooker, "Male Homosexuality in the Rorschach," *Journal of Projective Techniques*, 22 (1958), 33-54. Alfred C. Kinsey, Wardell B. Pomeroy, and Clyde E. Martin, *Sexual Behavior in the Human Male* (Philadelphia: Saunders, 1948). Michael Schofield, *Sociological Aspects of Homosexuality: A Comparative Study of Three Types of Homosexuals* (Boston: Little, Brown, 1965).

Honduras: Demographic Institutions

The Honduran Association of Family Planning (ASHONPLAFA) was founded in 1963. It conducts an educational program, in cooperation with personnel of the Ministries of Public Health and Education, covering such topics as the social-economic aspects of population growth, reproductive biology, and contraception. Through two pilot clinics it started to give assistance in contraceptive methods. Address: Asociación Hondureña de Planificación de la Familia, 2a Calle B, Casa no. 308, Colonia Palmira, Tegucigalpa, D.C.

The National Bureau of Statistics and Censuses (DGEC) administers the country's censuses, the most recent of which was in 1974 (one was scheduled for 1982); see the summary volume, *Censos de Población y Vivienda Levantados en Honduras de 1791 a 1974* (1977). The periodic reports on population and vital events that the bureau publishes include *Compendio Estadístico*, from 1966, and *Inventorio Estadístico Nacional*, from 1969. In cooperation with the Latin American Demographic Center (CELADE), DGEC carried out the Honduras portion of the World Fertility Survey, the results of which were published in *Encuesta Demográfica Nacional de Honduras (EDENH)*, 7 vols. (Santiago, Chile, 1975-1976). Address: Dirección General de Estadística y Censos, Secretaría de Economía, Tegucigalpa, D.C.

The Council of Economic Planning (CONSUPLANE) in 1979 established a Population Unit under the direction of Luz Estela de Sarmiento. Its purpose is to construct population projections and conduct demographic research that could contribute to economic planning. It publishes a *Boletín Bibliográfico*. There is also a Human Resources Planning Unit, which published *Diagnóstico de los*

Recursos Humanos, 1961-1974 (1976). Address: Unidad de Población and Unidad de Planificación de Recursos Humanos, Consejo Superior de Planificación Económica, Apartado Postal 1327, Tegucigalpa, D.C.

Hong Kong: Demographic Institutions

The Chinese University of Hong Kong has a Social Research Center, established in 1969 and in 1980 directed by R. P. Lee. It has published studies of family structure and fertility, public policy on housing, aging, ethnicity, and other topics related to the populations of Hong Kong and Communist China. Address: Shatin, New Territories, Hong Kong.

At the University of Hong Kong the Center of Asian Studies, established in 1968 and in 1980 under F. H. King as director, has conducted research on population and family planning in Southeast Asia, problems associated with urbanization, and human ecology. It publishes the *Journal of Oriental Studies*. Address: Pokfulam Road, Hong Kong.

Also at the University of Hong Kong the Department of Statistics, which in 1982 was headed by John Aitchison, has conducted demographic research on Hong Kong. It has published a general monograph on the country's population and a projection of it. Address: Pokfulam Road, Hong Kong.

The government's Census and Statistics Department conducts the country's censuses, the most recent of which was in 1981. It issues a *Monthly Digest of Statistics* and an *Annual Digest of Statistics*, both of which include basic population data. It also publishes irregularly *Births, Deaths, and Marriages* and *Social and Economic Trends*. Address: Kai Tak Commercial Building, 317 Des Voeux Road Central, Hong Kong.

The Immigration Department publishes annual reports by the director of immigration and the registrar general. Address: International Building, 141 Des Voeux Road Central, Hong Kong.

hormone, a substance that is secreted into the body fluids by one of the endocrine glands and regulates the behavior of other organs. The sex-related hormones are, respectively, androgenic (i.e., making more male) or estrogenic (i.e., making more female). Two important androgens are testosterone, formerly isolated from a bull's testes and now typically prepared synthetically, prescribed in order to maintain a male's secondary sex characteristics; and androsterone, excreted in the urine of both sexes, prescribed as an injection to counteract the ancillary effects of castration. Among the important estrogens are estriol and estrone, both obtainable from a female's urine during pregnancy and prescribed to treat conditions associated with estrogen deficiency, as during *menopause. Hormones injected into a woman's muscle or implanted under her skin have proved to be a highly effective type of *contraception; see *injectable progestational agents.

hospice once meant a house for the shelter and sustenance of travelers, especially one run by a religious order. The hospice movement of modern times has established clinics where an attempt is made to teach the terminally ill to face death without fear. These institutions are also one expression of a variegated effort to discontinue the inappropriate prolongation of life by "heroic" means—as another example, by redefining the legal meaning of *death. If the practice becomes general of allowing the terminally ill to die "naturally," one can expect that life expectancy will be cut appreciably, especially that from older ages.

REFERENCE: Sandol Stoddard, *The Hospice Movement: A Better Way of Caring for the Dying* (New York: Stein and Day, 1978).

hospital, an institution to provide *health care for the sick or injured, also in many cases to train *medical manpower. In the mid-1970s there were an estimated 100,000 hospitals in the world, of which about 7,500 were in the United States. In other countries most hospitals, except for a small remnant of religious institutions, are government-owned. American hospitals are run mainly by voluntary, nonprofit corporations or church-sponsored societies, only in some instances by local jurisdictions or such federal agencies as the Veterans Administration.

Although there were hospitals of some sort in the ancient world, the institution really developed during the Middle Ages in the Islamic East and the Christian West, both as an adjunct to military expeditions and as an expression of religious good works. As early as the fourteenth century European hospitals in cities were often administered by the municipality, though still with religious personnel. The small institution run by Herman Boerhave (1668-1738) in the Netherlands exemplifies the beginning trend toward teaching hospitals. During the eighteenth and early nineteenth centuries, especially in Britain, a large number of hospitals were established under a new principle, financed by subscriptions and bequests. However, until the nature of infection was understood and accepted, and until medical care consisted in more than the ministration of nostrums and bleeding, in any place where the sick were congregated it was as likely that a patient would die from contagion as that he would be cured.

For demography one important function of hospitals is as a source of data, and the records that all hospitals maintain are fundamental to the statistical analysis of disease. Since in the United States approval by the Joint Commission on Accreditation of Hospitals is largely based on these records, they are ordinarily carefully kept and retained for at least twenty-five years. According to the minimum basic data set recommended by the U.S. National Center for Health Statistics (1972), the record on each patient should include such personal characteristics as name and date of birth, as well as a unique number within the hospital's system; all physicians associated with the case, their diagnosis and treatment, with relevant dates; the disposition of the patient; and the expected principal source of payment for services. As intimated in a booklet by the same agency (1969), these data are useful for retrospective studies of cases, but for more intensive analyses it is necessary to use the person as a unit, linking case records in various localities or hospitals by the patient's name or, preferably, his social security number; see also *record linkage.

REFERENCES: U.S. National Center for Health Statistics, *Use of Hospital Data for Epidemiologic and Medical-Care Research* and *Uniform Hospital Abstract: Minimum Basic Data Set*, Ser. 4, nos. 11 and 14 (Washington, D.C., 1969 and 1972).

household was defined by the United Nations in its recommendations for the 1970 censuses as "either (a) a one-person household—that is, a person who makes provision for his own food...or (b) a multiperson household—that is, a group of two or more persons who make common provision for food or other essentials for living;...they may be related or unrelated persons, or a combination of both." The concept used in the United States censuses, however, differs fundamentally: all the persons who occupy a housing unit, which can be a house, an apartment, or a single room (cf. *head; *one-person household). Neither definition is especially appropriate for the main interests of demographers—to use statistics on households to judge the number and size of families. At least in modern Western countries the modal household consists of a nuclear *family (though lacking adult children, who typically form households of their own). For other periods and places, however, the overlap may be far less (Burch, 1979). What is called in the United States the *household population* of an area may give a false impression of the demographic characteristics of a state like Hawaii (with a high proportion of military) or a locality like Leavenworth County, Kansas (with both a federal prison and an army post). For most purposes the total *population, including the portion living in *group quarters, is the more pertinent datum.

One of the key problems in historical demography is to estimate the population of a locality from the number of households, for the latter datum is generally the only one available. For 1695, Gregory †King, for instance, estimated this multiplier to be 5.4 for the 97 London parishes within the walls down to 4.0 in villages and hamlets; and the range used by modern demographers has been greater (e.g., Glass, 1965). The issue has been little discussed, for there is not much to be said beyond the point that all computations depend on this estimate (but see Smith and Lewis, 1980, 1983). Even when other measures differ considerably, the annual growth rate may vary little with different estimates of the household size (cf. Eversley, 1966).

REFERENCES: Thomas K. Burch, "Household and Family Demography: A Bibliographic Essay," *Population Index*, 45 (1979), 173-201. D.E.C. Eversley, "Exploitation of Anglican Parish Records by Aggregative Analysis," in E. A. Wrigley, ed., *An Introduction to English Historical Demography* (New York: Basic Books, 1966). D. V. Glass, "Two Papers on Gregory King," in Glass and Eversley, eds., *Population in History* (1965). Stanley K. Smith and Bart B. Lewis, "Some New Techniques for Applying the Housing Unit Method of Local Population Estimation"; "Further Evidence," *Demography*, 17 (1980), 323-339; 20 (1983), 407-413.

household and family demography is the study with census and other population data of such topics as a trend in *family size; the change in typical variables over the course of the *life cycle; the interrelation between *household structure and fertility, mortality, and migration; and the use of *models to analyze these and other patterns.

REFERENCES: Thomas K. Burch, "Household and Family Demography," in *International Encyclopedia of Population*, 1, 299-307. Helmut V. Muhsam, "On the Demography of Families," *Journal of Comparative Family Studies*, 7 (1976), 133-146.

householder was substituted for the prior *"head of household" in the 1980 census of the United States. Either term means the member of a household in whose name the housing unit is owned or rented, or, if there is no such person, an approximate equivalent. The head or householder is the "reference person," and the relationship of all other members of the household to him/her is noted. For the first time in 1980 several additional relationships were identified in the long form: father/mother, brother/sister, partner/roommate, and paid employee.

housing, the collective term for dwelling quarters, is an important concept not only in demography but in anthropology, economics, and sociology. Every culture shows an intimate but complex relation between its family types and its *households (Madge, 1968). A recurrent theme in sociology has centered on problems associated with the *slum and *crowding. The number of housing starts, a sensitive economic indicator, both reflects demand and affects significantly such social-economic trends as employment, marriage, and fertility (Maisel, 1968). Of the population trends that affect housing demand, the most important are changes in age structure and thus in the number of marriageable persons, the tendency of young persons to marry later and live during some years in nonfamily households, the increasing difference between the sexes in life expectancy, and shifts in migration and settlement patterns (Morrison, 1976).

Not surprisingly, advanced countries generally collect a wide range of data on housing. In the United States housing statistics have been included since 1940 in the census, and during recent decades also in periodic surveys pertaining either to the residences themselves or to such related topics as construction. Housing censuses and surveys cover every housing unit, which is defined as one or more rooms occupied or intended for occupancy by a family or other group that lives and eats apart. Not included, thus, are transients' accommodations, military or workers' barracks, dormitories, and similar institutional quarters. From the number of rooms in the unit one can derive the number of persons per room, the usual index of crowding. Most of the items are intended to measure the level of living (whether the unit includes running water, a flush toilet, air conditioning, television, and other conveniences) and thus, cross-classified with other items, how conditions of life differ among ethnic groups or regions, and how they have changed over time. A longitudinal Annual Housing Survey, conducted since 1973 by the U.S. Bureau of the Census with funds from the U.S. Department of Housing and Urban Development and published in two series, H-150 and H-170, includes the same type of questions and also data on, for instance, how well household facilities work, how dependable services are, and how the respondents perceive certain aspects of the neighborhood (Riche, 1981; U.S. Bureau of the Census, 1978). It is possible to use the data on housing to derive various population estimates more expeditiously than from alternative sources (e.g., Smith and Lewis, 1980).

The more than 88 million housing units counted in 1980 in the United States census were almost 20 million more than in 1970. Over the decade the number of housing units rose by nearly 29 percent, the population by only 11 percent. About 23 percent of the respondents reported that they had moved into their residence during the preceding 15 months, and only one in six had lived in the present home for more than 20 years. Between 1970 and 1980, the proportion of married couples that owned their home rose from 70 to 80 percent; and even among those under age 35, the percentage rose from 49 to 62. This increase took place in spite of the fact that the median value of single-family homes rose from $17,000 in 1970 to $47,200 in 1980, or by 178 percent. This sharp rise in costs reflected the general inflation during the decade, but also a considerable improvement in housing quality. There was a substantial decline in the number of units with characteristics that had long been used to indicate inadequacy. Only 3 percent of the owner-occupied and only 7 percent of the renter-occupied units had more than one person per room (Young and Devaney, 1983).

REFERENCES: John Madge, "Housing, Social Aspects," and Sherman J. Maisel, "Housing, Economic Aspects," *International Encyclopedia of the Social Sciences*, 6, 516-526. Peter A. Morrison, "Demographic Trends that Will Shape Future Housing Demand," *Rand Paper Series*, no. P-5596 (February, 1976). Martha Farnsworth Riche, "The Annual Housing Survey," *American Demographics*, 3 (November, 1981), 42-44. Stanley K. Smith and Bart B. Lewis, "Some New Techniques for Applying the Housing Unit Method of Local Population Estimation," *Demography*, 17 (1980), 323-339. U.S. Bureau of the Census, *Reference Manual on Population and Housing Statistics from the Census Bureau* (Washington, D.C., 1978). Arthur F. Young and F. John Devaney, "What the 1980 Census Shows about Housing," *American Demographics*, 5 (January, 1983), 17-23.

human capital means inputs to a national economy through improvements in such characteristics of the work force as their education and health, or, more generally, an "investment in human beings." The term was introduced by Irving Fisher in *The Nature of Capital and Income* (1906) and brought into more recent discussions by a supplement to the October 1962 issue of the *Journal of Political Economy*. Much of the considerable body of writings is polemical, for it is repeatedly suggested that conventional economists—as well as demographers (see Schultz, 1980, chap. 2)—restrict their analyses to the quantity of population and ignore its quality. No one is really opposed to the improvement of the human lot. Those who, like Mark Blaug (1976), have taken "a slightly jaundiced view" of proposals concerning human capital are not sure that the seemingly most direct route to this end is really the fastest and most certain. Since investment funds are always limited, expenditures on schools or hospitals must be at least partly substituted for those on roads, factories, and power plants, which many development economists believe will improve human welfare faster.

Perhaps the main reason the debate has flourished is that "quality" is so elusive (e.g., Bowman, 1962). For example, *health is extraordinarily difficult to measure even in countries with good statistics. And if the analysts are correct who hold that the increased years of schooling in the United States have yielded a declining amount of *education, a cost-benefit equation based on the former variable is not likely to be very satisfactory (cf. Becker, 1975; Wood and Campbell, 1970). In the view of its proponents, investment in education has an additional important advantage in less developed countries, for it will bring about a reduction in *fertility (Sirageldin, 1979)—a conclusion hardly in accord with the ambiguous results of the many empirical studies.

REFERENCES: Gary S. Becker, *Human Capital: A Theoretical and Empirical Analysis with Special Reference to Education* (2nd ed.; New York: National Bureau of Economic Research, 1975). Mark Blaug, "The Empirical Status of Human Capital Theory: A Slightly Jaundiced View," *Journal of Economic Literature*, 14 (1976), 827-855. Mary Jean Bowman, "Human Capital: Concepts and Measures," U.S. Office of Education, *Bulletin*, no. 5 (1962), 69-92. Theodore W. Schultz, *Investing in People: The Economics of Population Quality* (Berkeley: University of California Press, 1980). Ismail A. Sirageldin, ed., *Research in Human Capital and Development* (Greenwich, Conn.: JAI Press, 1979). W. Donald Wood and H. F. Campbell, *Cost-Benefit Analysis and the Economics of Investment in Human Capital: An Annotated Bibliography* (Kingston, Ontario: Queen's University, Industrial Relations Center, 1970).

Human Life and Natural Family Planning Foundation was established in 1977 by the merger of the Human Life Foundation of America with the Natural Family Planning Federation of America, combining the research and educational activities of the two organizations. It encourages biomedical research on how to detect the timing of ovulation and other aspects of human reproduction, and it has developed materials for teachers and users of "natural" methods of contraception. See also *rhythm method. Address: 205 South Patrick Street, Alexandria, Va. 22314.

Human Relations Area Files (HRAF), a compilation of all the data deemed to be reliable on every culture in the world from the beginning of ethnographic work to today. It was the life work of C. S. †Ford and George P. Murdock, starting from a first draft in 1937 through the latter's *Outline of Cultural Materials* (4th ed., 1961) and the *Outline of World Cultures* (1975). One broad area of classifying criteria pertains to demography: population, population composition, birth statistics, morbidity, mortality, internal migration, immigration and emigration, and population policy. Two of the earliest books based on the files related, respectively, to family structure (Murdock, 1949) and fertility (Ford and Beach, 1951). Like any project on so broad a scale, it has been subjected to many criticisms related partly to the mode of classification, partly to details concerning particular cultures. Demographers are likely to find the compilations rather thin in their main areas of interest, for population structure and growth have not been close to the center of most works in anthropology.

REFERENCES: Erika Bourguignon and Lenora S. Greenbaum, *Diversity and Homogeneity in World Societies* (New Haven, Conn.: HRAF Press, 1973). C. S. Ford and Frank A. Beach, *Patterns of Sexual Behavior* (New York: Harper, 1951). George P. Murdock, *Social Structure* (New York: Macmillan, 1949).

human rights, in contrast to civil rights or *civil liberties, do not define the proper relation between a state and the individuals or groups that make up its population, but rather the ultimate natural or moral rights that according to some philosophers underlie just law (cf. Hart, 1955). In the eighteenth century such revolutionary societies as the United States and France sought to legitimize their new status by a Bill of Rights and a Declaration of the Rights of Man, respectively. According to the Universal Declaration of Human Rights, proclaimed by the United Nations in 1948, "everyone, as a member of society, has the right to social security" (Article 22) and "to a standard of living adequate for the health and well-being of himself and his family, including food, clothing, housing" (Article 25). Of course, these are not rights in the sense of imposing corresponding duties on the governments concerned, nor are they even canons of ideal political behavior by which states are typically judged.

In accordance with this basic document and a number of supplementary pronouncements, UNESCO published a volume entitled *Human Rights Aspects of Population Programmes* (1977). Such programs, it declared, should be viewed less as ends in themselves than as a means of securing basic human rights (p. 12). All persons have the right to work and to be free from hunger, with an adequate standard of living, including health and old-age insurance. The equality of men and women is guaranteed, and also that of legitimate and illegitimate children. The right to "adequate education and information on family-planning matters," as well as access to contraceptive means, follows the usual knowledge-attitude-practice (*KAP) of proponents of contraceptive programs. Everyone should have freedom of movement, freedom for privacy (cf. Barnett, 1978), freedom from environmental pollution. Freedom of conscience and of religion are human rights. The most important right, capping all the others, is to "the social, economic, and legal reforms necessary to ensure these [other] rights." Sometimes rights may be instituted by force, for "the use of coercive measures to further human rights is not necessarily incompatible with human rights principles" (p. 25). On the other hand, the right of everyone to "leave any country, including his own," is subject to whatever restrictive measures may be "necessary to protect national security, public order, public health or morals, or the rights and freedoms of others" (p. 77). Countries that signed the covenant guaranteeing the right of any person to leave have thus been offered a choice of excuses for denying that permission to virtually all in the country. For "governments are, of course, free to undertake additional programmes to further the goals of human rights, such as incentives and disincentives in a form which best suits the conditions of their countries'' (pp. 145-146).

REFERENCES: Larry D. Barnett, "Population Growth, Population Organization Participants, and the Right of Privacy," *Family Law Quarterly*, 12 (1978), 37-60. H.L.A. Hart, "Are There Any Natural Rights?" *Philosophical Review*, 64 (1955), 175-191. UNESCO, *Human Rights Aspects of Population Programmes with Special Reference to Human Rights Law* (Paris, 1977).

Humanae Vitae ("Of Human Life"), a papal encyclical issued in 1968, reaffirmed the Catholic Church's traditional opposition to contraception. Many Catholics had hoped that this stand would be changed, for a Papal Birth Control Commission (1966) had recommended an overall revision. The position paper of a majority of the commission condemned abortion but did not otherwise specify a licit method of contraception. The means of controlling family size, it held, should be selected by "the couple" on the basis of the following criteria: (1) "The whole meaning of the mutual giving and of human procreation [shall be] kept in a context of true love," and extramarital contraception is barred. (2) The method used shall have an appropriate "effectiveness." (3) There shall be the "least possible" number of negative side-effects, whether biological or psychological. (4) No absolute rules shall apply, for the best means may depend on the situation of "a certain couple." The commission submitted its majority and minority reports to Pope Paul VI on June 28, 1966, and the expectation that the church's position would follow the commission's recommendations was strengthened by an encyclical issued in March, 1967, *Populorum Progressio* ("Development of Peoples"), which stressed the need to control population growth in less developed countries, but with the means left indefinite.

According to *Humanae Vitae*, however: "Marriage and conjugal love are by their nature ordained toward the begetting and education of children.... In the task of transmitting life, therefore, [the parents] are not free to proceed completely at will... but must conform their activity to the creative intention of God.... Each and every marriage must remain open to the transmission of life.... Abortion, even if for therapeutic reasons, [is] absolutely excluded... [as are also] sterilization... [and] every action which, either in anticipation of the conjugal act or in its accomplishment, or in the development of the natural consequences, proposes, whether as an end or as a means, to render procreation impossible" (Liebard, 1978, pp. 331-347). The sanctioning of the *rhythm method was affirmed, provided it is used "for just motives" not further specified.

REFERENCES: Odile M. Liebard, ed., *Official Catholic Teachings: Love and Society* (Wilmington, N.C.: McGrath Publishing Co., 1978), pp. 331-347. Papal Birth Control Commission, "Schema for a Document on Responsible Parenthood," *National Catholic Reporter* (April 19, 1967).

Hungary: Demographic Institutions

Demography is taught at four universities:

Eötvös Loránd University, under Professor József †Kovacsics. Address: P.O.

Box 109, 1364 Budapest V. Also at the university, the Chair of Statistics publishes the bilingual *Historisch-Demographische Mitteilungen/Communications de Démographie Historique*. Address: Egyetem-tér 1-3, 1364 Budapest V.

Karl Marx University of Economic Sciences. Address: Dimitrov-tér 8, 1828 Budapest IX.

University of Pécs, under Professor István †Hoóz. Address: Rákoczi u. 80, 7622 Pécs.

Attila József University, under Professor Róbert †Horváth. Address: Dugonics-tér 13, H-6701 Szeged.

The Central Statistical Office conducts the country's censuses, the most recent of which was in 1980. It is the main agency for gathering and publishing statistical data. It publishes a statistical yearbook, in Hungarian with Russian and English table titles available separately; a demographic yearbook, in Hungarian with Russian and English table titles; and an annual *Statistical Pocket Book*, in Hungarian, Russian, English, and German editions. The head of its Population Statistics Department in 1982 was András †Klinger. Address: Központi Statisztikai Hivatal, Keleti Károly u. 5-7, 1525 Budapest II.

The Office has a Demographic Research Institute, of which István Monigl was director in 1982. It conducts both research and training on the population of Hungary and Eastern Europe, and publishes the quarterly journal *Demográfia*. Address: Népességtudományi Kutató Intézet, Veres Pálné u. 10, Budapest V.

The Hungarian Academy of Sciences has a Committee for Demography, whose members include many of the country's analysts of population. The Committee sponsors the publication of research monographs and other works. Address: Magyar Tudományos Akadémia, Roosevelt-tér 9, 1361 Budapest V.

hunting and gathering, a primitive mode of obtaining sustenance from whatever foodstuffs are available without the cultivation of plants or the domestication of animals. Archeological evidence indicates its prevalence in the prehistoric era. Among the few hunters and gatherers in the world today, prominent examples are the Pygmies of the Central African rain forest, the Bushmen of the Kalahari, and those Eskimos that still follow their traditional way of life. Only small groups can survive in so primitive an economy, and typically they must go where the game leads. Though the cultures are highly diverse in some respects, the social structure is generally simple, associated with a minimum division of labor or institutional differentiation.

REFERENCES: Ester T. Boserup, "Environment, Population, and Technology in Primitive Societies," *Population and Development Review*, 2 (1976), 21-36. L. T. Hobhouse, G. C. Wheeler, and Morris Ginsberg, *The Material Culture and Social Institutions of the Simpler Peoples: An Essay in Correlation* (London: Chapman and Hall, 1930). Moni Nag, "Anthropology and Population: Problems and Perspectives," *Population Studies*, 27 (1973), 59-68. Colin M. Turnbull, *The Forest People* (New York: Simon and Schuster, 1961).

Hutterites, a sect of Anabaptists that arose in South Germany and Switzerland in the sixteenth century. Persecuted by both Catholic and Protestant rulers, they emigrated eastward to Moravia, where Jakob Hutter, their leader, was publicly burned to death. They moved eventually to Russia and, in the late nineteenth century, to South Dakota. From this nucleus, daughter colonies were established in Canada and elsewhere in the United States. In America Hutterites have maintained a communal life, retaining the pacifist views and religious doctrines of the founder (Hostetler, 1974, chaps. 1-5).

Originally couples were matched by the sect's leaders in accordance with God's will. Presently marriage is by personal choice as influenced by group pressures. A man's status is enhanced when he marries; but a wife, living in her in-laws' colony and sometimes in their home, is isolated and vulnerable to their pressure to conform. With an average of more than ten children in a completed family, Hutterites have been taken as the measure of "man's capacity to reproduce," the title of a work by Joseph †Eaton and A. J. Mayer (1954; cf. Tietze, 1957; Sheps, 1965; Laing, 1980). In the measure called the *index of overall fertility, the age-specific fertility of Hutterites is taken to be the highest physiologically possible for a population, and that of other peoples is compared with this maximum. Though the number of conversions is minuscule (smaller even than the tiny number of defections), the Hutterites in the United States increased from 443 in 1880 to 21,521 in 1974, or by almost fifty times in not quite a century.

Analysts of mental health have also studied the sect. According to a notable work by Eaton and Robert J. Weil (1955), their simple and uncomplicated way of life, with each person assured security for life, has not reduced their susceptibility to mental disorders, in part because the strong religious commitment often generates strong guilt feelings. Since the group is inbred, some disorders may have a genetic base.

REFERENCES: Joseph W. Eaton and A. J. Mayer, *Man's Capacity to Reproduce: The Demography of a Unique Population* (Glencoe, Ill.: Free Press, 1954). Eaton and Robert J. Weil, *Culture and Mental Disorders* (Glencoe, Ill.: Free Press, 1955). John A. Hostetler, *Hutterite Society* (Baltimore: Johns Hopkins University Press, 1974). L. M. Laing, "Declining Fertility in a Religious Isolate: The Hutterite Population of Alberta, Canada, 1951-1971," *Human Biology*, 52 (1980), 288-310. Mindel C. Sheps, "An Analysis of Reproductive Patterns in an American Isolate," *Population Studies*, 19 (1965), 65–80. Christopher Tietze, "Reproductive Span and Rate of Reproduction among Hutterite Women," *Fertility and Sterility*, 8 (1957), 89–97.

hygiene derives from Greek for "health," which is also the root of Hygieia, the goddess of health and the daughter of Asclepius, the god of healing. It means a system of principles or regulations designed to promote the health of an individual or, more often, a community—similar to what used to be called "social medicine" and now is often termed "sanitary science." See also *public health.

hypergamy, in Hindu India the marriage of a man with a woman of lower caste. Such a union is generally countenanced, but *hypogamy*, the marriage of a woman to a man of lower caste, is almost universally condemned. Family sociologists have adopted the terms to denote interclass marriages in Western societies. See also *endogamy.

hysterectomy, the excision of the uterus or a part of it for medical rather than contraceptive reasons. The operation results in permanent sterility.

I

Iceland: The Statistical Bureau publishes three serials that include data on population, all in Icelandic: *Hagskýrslur Íslands: Mannfjöldaskýrslur* (statistics of Iceland: population and vital statistics), irregular; *Hagtídindi* (statistical bulletin), monthly; *Tølfraedihandbók* (statistical abstract), irregular. Address: Hagstofu Íslands, Reykjavík.

IE&C (or IEC), an acronym for "information, education, and communication," is used in relation to family-planning programs. In the budget of the U.N. Fund for Population Activities (UNFPA), an increasing proportion of the funds for IEC activities is used in programs of *population education, which encompass education in family planning within a broader context of population change.
  REFERENCES: Dae Woo Han, Chija Kim Cheong, and Kye Choon Ahn, eds., *Reducing Problem Groups in Family Planning IE&C Programs: A Secondary Analysis of Korean Surveys* (Seoul: Korean Institute of Family Planning, 1970). Gloria D. Feliciano, "What the IEC Task Is: Developing Culture-Based Strategies for Continued Contraceptive Use," and William O. Sweeney, "Communications Activities that Promote Behavior Change in Clients of Family-Planning Programs: Resources and Constraints," in Lyle Saunders, ed., *IEC Strategies: Their Role in Promoting Behavior Change in Family and Population Planning* (Honolulu: East-West Center, 1977).

illegitimacy, the opposite of *legitimacy, characterizes a conception or birth outside the lawful framework of marriage. Data vary greatly from one country or time period to another both in their probable accuracy and in their significance (cf. Hartley, 1975; Laslett et al., 1980). Trends are measured by an *illegitimacy ratio*, the number of illegitimate births per 1,000 live births, or the *illegitimacy rate*, the number of illegitimate births per 1,000 unmarried women in the fecund age range. When the data are available, the second measure is usually preferable, since it relates the phenomenon to the population at risk (cf. Berkov and Sklar, 1975).
  According to the once generally accepted theory, illegitimacy develops from "social disorganization"—the abandonment of a family norm by an aberrant

sector of the population released from traditional sanctions and subject to special pressures (cf. Teichman, 1982). A typical instance was the situation of rural in-migrants to the growing cities of countries undergoing industrialization. According to a survey by Edward Shorter (1973), "the years 1790-1860 were, in virtually every [European] society or community we know about, the peak period of illegitimacy." The characterization of bastardy as a social problem, however, led to what were seen eventually as discriminatory labels applied to both the mother and, according to this view, even more unjustly, the child. Sanctions were seen not as a defense of lawful marriage and childbearing but as social-class or racial prejudice.

Over the decade 1968-77 the U.S. Supreme Court considered fourteen cases involving illegitimacy. In each case a state or federal statute was challenged on the ground that it discriminated against illegitimate children; in ten instances the statutes were found to be unconstitutional. In 1968 each state had the right to promote family life by penalizing the children born of extramarital sexual re-lations. By 1977 this deterrent was condemned as "illogical and unjust" to the innocent children, whose constitutional rights had been ignored (Stenger, 1978). During the 1960s another shift in legal status gave American teenagers a greater degree of independence. The age of majority was reduced from 21 to 18 years, and 18-year-olds were given the right to vote. A woman of 18 years or over got the right to decide for herself on contraception and abortion, and in some instances similar changes were made with respect to girls under 18 (Paul et al., 1974).

In earlier years the U.S. Bureau of the Census had not posed direct questions about children born out of wedlock, for it was believed that the responses would not be sufficiently accurate to be useful. In the 1970 census, for the first time, unmarried women filling in the schedule themselves were asked how many children they had borne; those interviewed by an enumerator were asked the question only if children were present (cf. Grabill, 1976). Somewhat similarly, the 1970 census categorized one type of family as a "husband-wife family," changed in 1980 to a "married-couple family"—that is, what in a simpler era had been known as a "family." Since 1976 the annual overall Current Population Survey has included questions on the number of children borne and the expected number of additional births, both put to all women regardless of marital status (cf. O'Connell, 1980). According to a Current Population Survey of March 1978, there were 1,137,000 unmarried couples sharing living quarters (cf. Span-ier, 1983). The number had doubled from 1970 and increased by 19 percent in the single year from 1977. Just under one-quarter of these couples had one or more children living with them; but the 272,000 households with children had remained almost constant from 1960. The dramatic rise in unmarried cohabitation did not result, at least up to that date, in an increase in illegitimate births (Glick and Spanier, 1980).

Whether it is conceptually useful to define behavior as aberrant depends in part on the size of the deviant sector. There has been an interaction between moral/legal norm and the incidence of illegitimacy, with the change in each apparently reinforcing a trend in the other. So high a proportion of births in Scandinavia has been outside wedlock that one might say that a transition has been under way in changing the norm that once defined the illegitimacy (Kumar, 1969; Tomasson, 1976). This has been even more the case in Latin America, especially among lower-class blacks. Also in the United States, births to unmarried girls and women were once concentrated in the same sector of the population, but this is no longer the case. The shift began with an effort to justify the higher rates of illegitimacy among American blacks; this reflected, according to a new view, not a breakdown of middle-class norms but conformity to the different standards of a particular subgroup (cf. Freshnock and Cutright, 1979). Once having acquired a quasilegitimacy, premarital conceptions and births quickly spread to other sectors of American youth.

Wider knowledge about sex and significantly greater access to both contraception and abortion, paradoxically, resulted in what was termed an epidemic of teenage births, a high proportion of which were illegitimate. According to a report by the Planned Parenthood Federation (1977), in 1974 a tenth of all girls aged 15-19 years became pregnant. Two-thirds of the babies were conceived out of wedlock, and over a fifth were born illegitimate. Over a quarter were aborted. One in every four illegitimate children was born to a mother aged 17 or under (see also Chilman, 1980). By 1979 an estimated half of teenage girls resident in metropolitan areas were having sexual relations outside marriage, and illegitimate pregnancies continued to rise, increasing by two-fifths from 1973 to 1979 (Zelnik and Kantner, 1980). According to a survey of the clients of urban family-planning clinics, only 14 percent of the teenagers sought help before their first intercourse; more than a third came for the first time because they thought they might already be pregnant (Zabin and Clark, 1981). In Britain, as another example, illegitimate births doubled from 1977 to 1982, rising from one birth in ten to one in six. Teenagers as a group were having fewer babies than at any time since 1955, reflecting the general trend toward later marriage and childbearing. But between the same two dates, the number of births to unmarried teenagers doubled (*Economist*, June 16, 1984).

The new ethical standard concerning illegitimacy has given rise to an enormous body of analysis and commentary (cf. Thompson, 1983). One important theme has been to deny that there had been an increase in premarital sexual relations: the "myth of an abstinent past" was maintained only by widespread hypocrisy (Cutright, 1972; cf. Vinovskis, 1981). Two statistical facts, however, suggest that a genuine change of behavior took place—the rise of illegitimacy and the no less disturbing increase in *venereal disease. Perhaps the best study of teenage illegitimacy was made in California using data for the three years after legal abortion had become available and contraceptives were more accessible to teenagers than ever before. Yet the rate among black girls remained at its high level, and that among whites rose. The underlying reason, the authors concluded, was that social programs for unwed mothers had reduced the penalties incurred with illegitimacy (Sklar and Berkov, 1974). Social workers and family sociologists who had worked to remove the stigma challenged this conclusion, of course, and often held that the distinction between legitimate and illegitimate is itself a carry-over from obsolete norms. In a subsequent study the authors showed—what had once been taken for granted—that illegitimacy does indeed make a difference in the life chances of children, that one raised without a father or a responsible father substitute is handicapped. "Our data indicate that despite a decrease in the degree of stigma attached to illegitimacy and the proliferation of services and programs for illegitimate children and their mothers, these children do not begin life on an equal footing with legitimate children, and their handicaps persist beyond the hazards of infancy" (Berkov and Sklar, 1976).

REFERENCES: Beth Berkov and June Sklar, "Methodological Options in Measuring Illegitimacy and the Difference They Make," *Social Biology*, 22 (1975), 356-371; "Does Illegitimacy Make a Difference? A Study of the Life Chances of Illegitimate Children in California," *Population and Development Review*, 2 (1976), 201-217. Catherine S. Chilman, ed., *Adolescent Pregnancy and Childbearing: Findings from Research* (Washington, D.C.: U.S. Department of Health and Human Services, 1980). Phillips Cutright, "The Teenage Sexual Revolution and the Myth of an Abstinent Past," *Family Planning Perspectives*, 4 (1972), 24-31. Larry Freshnock and Cutright, "Models of Illegitimacy: United States, 1969," *Demography*, 16 (1979), 37-47. Paul C. Glick and Graham B. Spanier, "Married and Unmarried Cohabitation in the United States," *Journal of Marriage and the Family*, 42 (1980), 19-30. Wilson H. Grabill, "Premarital Fertility," *Current Population Reports*, Special Studies, Ser. P-23, no. 63 (1976). Shirley F. Hartley, *Illegitimacy* (Berkeley: University of California Press, 1975). Joginder Kumar, "Demographic Analysis of Data on Illegitimate Births," *Social Biology*, 16 (1969), 92-108. Peter Laslett, Karla Oosterveen, and Richard M. Smith, eds., *Bastardy and Its Comparative History: Studies in the History of Illegitimacy and Marital Nonconformity in Britain, France, Germany, Sweden, North America, Jamaica and Japan* (Cambridge, Mass.: Harvard University Press, 1980). Martin O'Connell, "Comparative Estimates of Teenage Illegitimacy in the United States, 1940-44 and 1970-74," *Demography*, 17 (1980), 13-23. Eve W. Paul, Harriet Pilpel, and Nancy F. Wechsler, "Pregnancy, Teenagers and the Law, 1974," *Family Planning Perspectives*, 6 (1974), 142-147. Planned Parenthood Federation of America, *Eleven Million Teenagers* (New York, 1977). Edward Shorter, "Illegitimacy, Sexual Revolution, and Social Change in Modern Europe," in Theodore K. Rabb and Robert I. Rotberg, eds., *The Family in History* (New York: Harper, 1973). Sklar and Berkov, "Teenage Family Formation in Postwar America," *Family Planning Perspectives*, 6 (1974), 80-90. Spanier, "Married and Unmarried Cohabitation in the United States, 1980," *Journal of Marriage and the Family*, 45 (1983), 277-288. Robert L. Stenger, "The Supreme Court and Illegitimacy: 1968-1977," *Family Law Quarterly*, 11 (1978), 365-405. Jenny Teichman, *Illegitimacy: A Philosophical Examination* (Oxford: Blackwell, 1982). Anthony P. Thompson, "Extramarital Sex: A Review of the Research Literature," *Journal of Sex Research*, 19 (1983), 1-22. Richard F. Tomasson, "Premarital Sexual Permissiveness and Illegitimacy in the Nordic Countries," *Comparative Studies in Society and History*, 18 (1976), 252-270. Maris A. Vinovskis, "An 'Epidemic' of Adolescent Pregnancy? Some Historical Considerations," *Journal of Family History*, 6 (1981), 205-230. Laurie Schwab Zabin and S. D. Clark, Jr., "Why They Delay: A Study of Teenage Family Planning Clinic Patients," *Family Planning Perspectives*, 13 (1981), 205-217. Melvin Zelnik and John F. Kantner, "Sexual Activity, Contraceptive Use and

Pregnancy among Metropolitan-Area Teenagers: 1971-1979,'' *Family Planning Perspectives*, 12 (1980), 230-237.

immunity is the power of an individual to resist or overcome an invasion of the body by specific pathogenic organisms. Some persons enjoy a natural immunity from birth and thus do not run the same risks as the rest of the population. Alternatively, immunity may be acquired, either "naturally" through the reaction of the body to such an invasion, or "artificially" by immunization. For example, a patient who has recovered from an attack of diphtheria is unlikely to have a second attack. The invader of the body, called an *antigen*, has stimulated the production of *antibodies*, which afford protection against that particular threat. The toxin of the diphtheria bacillus, when modified chemically and injected into a person, results in immunity without producing the disease. In immunology, one of the most active branches of biology, this distinction between "acquired" and "natural" is less important than in therapy. The essential subject of current research and practice is the immune system, how the body's whole set of mechanisms for defense works, and how it can become disordered and repaired. Antigens include many substances in addition to bacteria—red blood corpuscles, tissue extracts, pollens, dust, and so on. What is termed "immunological contraception" can be effected by stimulating antibodies against the reproductive process and thus producing a temporary sterility.

The importance of the immune system has been strikingly demonstrated by the rise of a new disease, called acquired immune deficiency syndrome or AIDS. The first established case was recorded in 1979, and from 1981 through 1985 there were 16,458 reported cases in the United States, of whom well over half had died. However, the disease is thought to have an incubation period of two to seven years, and no one knows how many more will start showing the symptoms. Apparently its cause is a virus (possibly a mutant form of an existent organism) that attacks the lymphocytes primarily responsible for conferring immunity. The principal route of contagion is by blood or another body fluid and the persons known to be at highest risk are promiscuous male homosexuals (apparently including Haitians, many of whom are reportedly homosexual), addicts who inject drugs into their blood stream, and hemophiliacs. The homosexual associations in California first tried to block any reports about AIDS in the news media and then, when this was no longer possible, campaigned against public authorities for not reacting more quickly (see Collier and Horowitz, 1983). Among those who acquire the disease, three out of four die within four years, either from an otherwise rare form of cancer, Kaposi's sarcoma, or from such infectious diseases as pneumonia, which the body is unable to combat.

REFERENCES: Peter Collier and David Horowitz, "Whitewash," *California Magazine*, 8 (July, 1983), 52-57. Robert A. Good and David W. Fisher, eds., *Immunobiology: Current Knowledge of Basic Concepts in Immunology and Their Clinical Applications* (Sunderland, Mass.: Sinauer Associates, 1971). "The AIDS Epidemic," *Harvard Medical School Health Letter*, 8:8 (June, 1983).

imperialism and **colonialism**, though in etymology seemingly correlative, are generally more or less synonymous pejorative designations of the social-political system by which a dominant people controls another nationality. Both words came into use in the nineteenth century. In the 1830s the French coined the word *impérialiste* to denote a partisan of Napoleon's former empire, and both French and English opponents of expansionist efforts developed "imperialist" into a term of abuse. For more recent writers such as Kwame Nkrumah (1965, p. ix), the president of Ghana, "neocolonialism" denotes the situation of a state with "all the outward trappings of international sovereignty" that is in fact a colony because "its economic system and thus its political system is [*sic*] directed from the outside." The common association of imperialism with capitalism, a link first made in 1902 by the English economist John A. Hobson (1858-1940), was picked up by a dozen Marxist writers and assiduously disseminated especially through †Lenin's *Imperialism: The Highest Stage of Capitalism* (1917). After it became obvious that some colonies brought the home countries no profits but often, on the contrary, drained off welfare funds, Marxists like the American economist Paul Sweezy (1942) held that the annexation of such areas is "strategic," "protective," or "anticipatory." In any case, the supposed link of imperialism to capitalism hardly helps in analyzing the great empires of the ancient world or, in our own day, the Soviet Union's recurrent *annexation of foreign territories inhabited by non-Russians (e.g., Kolarz, 1964). The word "imperialism" (as well as the word "colonialism," one might add) "has been corroded by overfrequent, emotional usage, but if overuse has blunted it as an intellectual tool, the resulting vagueness has certainly not diminished its potency as a political slogan" (Daalder, 1968).

A new variation on the same theme is *dependency*, or the lack of economic autonomy, the inability of one country to develop except in response to the expansion of another country's economy of which it is a subordinate adjunct. Since the term was coined by André Frank (1967; 1974) and Fernando Cardoso and Enzo Faletto (1969), there has been an explosive rise of commentary, such as the exchange between D.C.M. Platt (1980) and Stanley and Barbara Stein, and the full symposium in the first 1982 issue of *Latin American Research Review* (vol. 17, pp. 115-171). The dispute is partly a political one, partly one between historians and sociologists.

In the context of demography imperialism is important because it marked the usual original route for the dissemination of Western technology and social institutions to the rest of the world. The best data on the population changes accompanying economic development and modernization were all collected in colonies—by Japan in Taiwan, by Britain in India, and by France in some of its North African possessions. The life-saving techniques that underlie the population explosion in less developed countries appeared first in industrial nations, as also the birth-control ideology shaping the efforts to inhibit the growth of numbers. That family-planning programs have had the greatest success among *island populations, most of which are the small remnants of former colonies, has been plausibly explained by pointing out that culturally they are typically closer to the industrial West than the large less developed countries.

REFERENCES: Fernando Henrique Cardoso and Enzo Faletto, *Dependencia y Desarrollo en América Latina* (Mexico City: Siglo XXI, 1969), translated as *Dependency and Development in Latin America* (Berkeley: University of California Press, 1979). Hans Daalder, "Imperialism," *International Encyclopedia of the Social Sciences*, 7, 101-109. André Gunder Frank, *Capitalism and Underdevelopment in Latin America: Historical Studies of Chile and Brazil* (New York: Monthly Review Press, 1967); "Dependence Is Dead, Long Live Dependence and the Class Struggle: A Reply to Critics," *Latin American Perspectives*, 1 (1974), 87-106. Walter Kolarz, *Communism and Colonialism* (New York: St. Martins, 1964). Kwame Nkrumah, *Neo-colonialism: The Last Stage of Imperialism* (New York: International Publishers, 1965). D.C.M. Platt, "Dependency in Nineteenth-Century Latin America: An Historian Objects," with a "Comment" by Stanley J. Stein and Barbara H. Stein and a "Reply," *Latin American Research Review*, 15 (1980), 113-149. Paul M. Sweezy, *The Theory of Capitalist Development: Principles of Marxian Political Economy* (New York: Monthly Review Press, 1942).

implantation, or nidation, is the process by which the blastocyst (or the organism that develops from the fertilization of an ovum) penetrates the epithelium (or lining of the uterus) and is embedded in the endometrium (or the mucous membrane that lines the uterine cavity). Implantation is normally essential to the development of the *fetus. It occurs six to seven days after the fertilization of the ovum and is regarded by some as the moment of conception.

incest, defined broadly as sexual relations between persons who are not permitted to marry, is often interpreted more narrowly as cohabitation between any two members of the nuclear family apart from husband and wife. The taboo against the latter type, which comes close to being a cultural universal (but see Middleton, 1962), has therefore been subjected to much theorizing (Mead, 1968). As an important element of a broader *kinship structure, however, the incest taboo has little or no effect on any demographic variable. See also *ancestors; *marriage.

REFERENCES: Margaret Mead, "Incest," *International Encyclopedia of the Social Sciences*, 7, 115-122. Russell Middleton, "Brother-Sister and Father-Daughter Marriage in Ancient Egypt," *American Sociological Review*, 27 (1962), 603-611.

incidence, of a disease, the number of new cases during a specified period; also, the *incidence rate*, the incidence of a disease per unit of the midyear population. This is often preferable to the *prevalence rate*, or the number of persons diagnosed as having the disease on a given day (or other time period) per unit of the total population. Such an instantaneous count passes over the fact that disease is not an event but a process, so that those designated as ill at a particular time typically range from beginning cases to convalescents. The prevalence varies as the product of the incidence and the average duration from the disease's onset to its termination; that is, $P = I \times D$. In other words, a change in the prevalence may reflect a change in the incidence, the duration, or both.

income, the amount of money or its equivalent accruing over a specified period to an individual, family or household, firm, or nation. Precise definitions vary according to the context, whether economic theory, accounting practice, or statistical usage.

Apart from the United States and Canada, few countries collect data on personal income in their censuses, relying rather on such partial substitutes as sample surveys on household expenditures. The United States started to collect data on income in the 1940 census and, beginning in 1945, in the *Current Population Survey. Judging from the nonresponse rate (particularly in sample surveys, in which, unlike the census, a respondent may legally refuse to answer a question), queries on income are the most resented, and the data may therefore be less reliable than those on less touchy subjects. What each individual receives in money or such nonmonetary equivalents as food consumed on a farm, minus contributions for social insurance, is called *personal income*. The same calculation for members of a family living in the same household is called *family income*, and that for members of a household is called *household income*. The sum of the money or equivalent received by all income recipients in the country is called the *aggregate income*. When personal taxes and other payments to governments are subtracted from personal income, the balance is called *disposable personal income*. (*National income differs conceptually from other types; it is not derived from summing the incomes of individuals but is roughly the equivalent of *Gross National Product except that it excludes allowances for depreciation and indirect taxes.)

The calculation of income, however, is much more complex than these definitions might suggest. Most figures reported are gross money income, before deductions for taxes and generally with no provision for income in kind (cf. Browning, 1976). Since those with the highest incomes usually pay the most taxes, reporting their before-tax figures often exaggerates the amount the wealthy or well-to-do dispose of. A sizable proportion of the taxes they pay help fund such in-kind benefits as food stamps, housing subsidies, and Medicare and Medicaid (see *poverty), and when these components are left out, actual income of the beneficiaries is understated. The spread between the highest and the lowest incomes, thus, is increased by misleading reporting at both ends of the continuum.

Since the distribution of income is typically skewed, the conventional assumption is that a *median is a better index of centrality than a *mean. But sometimes a measure that is sensitive to extreme values may be more suitable. For example, if most incomes remain constant but the poor get poorer, the median will remain the same but the mean will reflect what could be an important change. In its annual ''Money Income of Households, Families, and Persons in the United States'' (*Current Population Reports*, Ser. P-60), the Bureau of the

Census provides both median and mean figures; and according to those estimates, the two measures of Americans' family income in current dollars were as follows:

	Median	Mean	Mean as a Percent of Median
1950	$ 3,319	$ 3,815	115%
1960	5,620	6,227	111
1970	9,867	11,106	113
1980	21,023	23,974	114

In other words, the usual practice of reporting the median reduces the figures by between 10 and 15 percent from the comparable mean. For either indicator, the denominator is taken to be the total number of persons who had any income at all during the report period. When large numbers of young people enter the labor market (for example, the cohorts of the *baby boom), or when many women seek only part-time jobs (as during the past several decades), the increased number of those with atypically small earnings reduces the average income for an essentially spurious reason.

During a period of rising prices income measured in "current" dollars (that is, not adjusted for inflation) can be quite deceptive, and the usual practice is to convert the figures into "constant" dollars of "real income." To do this, the Bureau of the Census uses the *Consumer Price Index as calculated by the Bureau of Labor Statistics. A superior deflator for the general population may be the sum of personal expenditures for consumption as given in the National Income and Product Accounts, which the Bureau of Economic Analysis compiles regularly. However, since both consumption patterns and prices vary greatly over the United States, it is hard to construct any index that reflects the typical relation between the two on a national basis.

The calculation of family income, or the sum of current family members' incomes during the previous calendar year, also involves difficulties. The many changes in what constitutes a *family affect the index—among others, the number of children, the age at which they leave home, the rise of *one-parent families. A person's status often differs between the report period and the time of the census or survey. For example, if a man who during the past year was the sole breadwinner leaves his wife and children in February, the March survey defines the abandoned group as a family with zero income. Similarly, if a pair of teenagers who had not been working in the previous year get married just before the survey, they also are denoted a family with zero income. One effect of the time lag, thus, can be to exaggerate the number of families living below the poverty line. With a growing population, the usual pattern is that more new families are formed than old ones dissolved, and the consequent overestimate of the number of families relative to the previous year's income means that the size of the mean family income is cut by another spurious factor.

Which of the various measures is best for any particular purpose is not easy to decide. As measured in constant dollars, from 1969 to 1979 median household income in the United States did not change, median family income rose by 5 percent, per-capita income by 18 percent, and aggregate income by 32 percent (Green and Coder, 1983). The first two measures are least suitable to indicate trends, for with the substantial decline in the sizes of families and households over the decade, measures related to either are not directly comparable. With per-capita income one avoids that false impression, but changes in the mix of working adults, children, and retired elderly affect household expenditures, and thus also the significance of personal income. Aggregate income rose most in regions where both per-capita income and population grew fastest—that is, in the South (by 54 percent) and the West (by 47 percent). The entity measured by all the indices is the annual income, but the more fundamental one is the lifetime income, which does not necessarily respond in the same way to changes in family structure, economically motivated migration, and other demographic influences.

Because data on income were known to be defective, in 1975 the Bureau of the Census established an Income Survey Development Program (ISDP) to seek ways of improving them. As part of this experiment, the bureau conducted six interviews three months apart with each member aged 16 years or over in a sample of 7,500 households. The results showed that prior data on income were indeed markedly deficient; when matched against comparable figures from the Current Population Survey, ISDP showed 56 percent more income from dividends, 32 percent more from interest, and 17 percent more from pensions. In October 1983 the bureau started a development from this trial, the Survey of Income and Program Participation (SIPP), in which persons in 20,000 American households answered a 47-page questionnaire. This is also a longitudinal survey, with each person in the sample to be interviewed eight times over two and a half years. With data collected on births and deaths, marriages and divorces, SIPP will provide detailed information on how household income is affected by such changes in family composition. Core questions are on participation in the labor force and on the amount of income from any of more than fifty types specified, including transfer payments and nonmonetary services from government sources. The first report will be cross-sectional, scheduled for publication in September 1984, and it is expected that subsequent publications will include both cross-sectional and longitudinal analyses (Riche, 1984).

REFERENCES: Edgar K. Browning, ''The Trend toward Equality in the Distribution of Net Income,'' *Southern Economic Journal*, 43 (1976), 912-923. Gordon Green and John Coder, ''Inside Income: 1980 Census Trends,'' *American Demographics*, 5 (June, 1983), 21-25. Martha Farnsworth Riche, ''Surveying Incomes,'' *American Demographics*, 6 (May, 1984), 42–44. Gerry B. Rodgers, ''Demographic Determinants and the Distribution of Income,'' *World Development*, 6 (1978), 305-318.

independence, as a characteristic of two events, means that the probability of one occurring is the same whether or not the other occurs. It can be shown, then, that the probability of their both occurring is equal to the product of the two separate probabilities.

independent variable, in a *regression analysis or other type of equation, is the variable that does not depend on the value of the other. For example, in the equation

$$y = a + x_1 + x_2 + \ldots + x_n$$

x is taken to be independent and y is the *dependent variable*.

index, an indicator, usually but not necessarily numerical, used to measure a more complex or less readily observable phenomenon. Sometimes a distinction is made between an indicator, based on a single measurement, and an index, composed of several indicators combined into one. An *index number* is a means of showing change (for example, over time) by relating subsequent values to that in a *base. Of the various methods of constructing such a comparison, the simplest is to assign 100 to the magnitude used as the base (e.g., the average of 1968-72 $=$ 100) and then to relate the subsequent magnitudes to it (e.g., 1973 $=$ 102; 1974 $=$ 110; etc.).

index of overall fertility, perhaps the most elegant of the *fertility measures, was devised by Ansley †Coale (1970) and used to good advantage in such a work, for example, as that by Ron †Lesthaeghe (1977). The measure is based on comparing the *total fertility rate of any population with the highest one ever recorded, which is taken to be unity. If a woman married at age 15 and, throughout her fecund period, had the same number of children that *Hutterites do in each age interval, she would bear an average of 12.6 children during her lifetime. If we take this to be the maximum physiological potential for a population (individual families have of course been larger), the reproduction of less prolific peoples can be related to this norm by the following equation:

$$I_f = \frac{B}{\Sigma W_i F_i}$$

where

I_f = the Index of Overall Fertility
B = the number of births to the subject population in a given year
W_i = the number of women in each 5-year age interval from age 15 to age 49
F_i = the marital fertility of Hutterite women in each age interval

The capital sigma indicates that one should sum the items following it. By breaking down the data, one can calculate in the same way separate rates of legitimate and illegitimate fertility. See also *rate.

REFERENCES: Ansley J. Coale, "The Decline of Fertility in Europe from the French Revolution to World War II," in S. J. Behrman et al., eds., *Fertility and Family Planning*

(Ann Arbor: University of Michigan Press, 1970). Ron J. Lesthaeghe, *The Decline of Belgian Fertility, 1800-1970* (Princeton, N.J.: Princeton University Press, 1977).

India, with a population of over 746 million in 1984, was after *China the most populous nation, with about 15.7 percent of the world's total population and 21 percent of that in less developed countries. Apart from its size, India is significant in the context of demography also for several other reasons. Beginning in 1881 the census administrators of British India compiled a surprisingly comprehensive set of data about a country at that economic level (cf. Davis, 1951). Since India became a sovereign republic in 1949, both Western and Indian demographers have analyzed its population and ancillary factors in an exceedingly large number of studies. Many of these have been related to *family-planning programs, which were initiated relatively early and proliferated with a variety of methods and incentives. In short, many of the issues that are studied in relation to less developed areas generally have been analyzed most intensively using Indian data (cf. Hofsten, 1982; Jain, 1980; Premi, 1982).

In some respects India is comparable not to one Western country but to all of Western Europe. In a monumental 19-volume *Linguistic Survey of India* (1903-28), George †Grierson listed 179 languages and 544 dialects in British India. After the separation of Pakistan, the Indian census of 1951 raised this to 1,652. In fact, of course, many of these are of little account; but Indians use fourteen or fifteen major languages in addition to English. Among the educated classes English was (and, to a large degree, remains) the major vehicle of formal communication; according to the 1961 census, although fewer than 30 million knew any Indian language in addition to their own, more than 11 million knew English (Das Gupta, 1970, chap. 2). Like other postcolonial states, independent India did not want to adopt formally the language of the imperialist era, no matter what its practical advantages might be. The choice of Hindi as the national language, however, exacerbated greatly the already strong regional rivalries (Harrison, 1960; Das Gupta, 1970).

Overriding this diversity of language is *Hinduism, but the degree of unity that it affords must be set against two countervailing factors. The partition between Muslim *Pakistan and Hindu India both reflected and aggravated religious antagonisms; mass disorders on either side of the border resulted in an estimated half million violent deaths. Hostility, which never subsided completely, flared up in renewed Indian-Pakistani wars in 1965 and 1971. The partition, however, did not really separate adherents of the two religions; compared with the 64 million Muslims that ended up in Pakistan, there were 36 million in India. This Muslim minority, most of whose political leaders had gone over to their new state, has been at a distinct disadvantage in India. But Hinduism also is hardly unitary, for the *caste system separates members of the religion not only by degree of purity and endogamous category but also into blocs of political antagonists (see also *child marriage; *purdah; *suttee). Very little that is written about "India" is true of all of this enormously variegated subcontinent.

The year 1921 marked a turning point in India's demographic history, as can be seen by comparing the average annual intercensal growth before and after that date (Visaria and Visaria, 1981, Table 2; cf. Choudhry, 1955):

1891-1901	0.30%
1901-11	0.56
1911-21	− 0.03
1921-31	1.06
1931-41	1.34
1941-51	1.26
1951-61	1.98
1961-71	2.20
1971-81	2.22

The increase in numbers, which had been slow or even negative, began its acceleration, and this was hardly interrupted by World War II and not initially slowed by the massive efforts to control fertility. In the last decades of British India famine was cut by improved irrigation and transportation to formerly isolated areas, and the devastation from some epidemic diseases was mitigated (Davis, 1951, chap. 6). In independent India the incidence of malaria was sharply reduced by the mass spraying of DDT, that of smallpox by mass vaccinations; but the major benefits of such measures have been garnered. In the early 1980s the principal causes of death were dysentery and diarrhea, tuberculosis and pneumonia, with chronic malnutrition as a frequent contributing factor. Over the past three generations the estimated crude death rate fell from 42.6 in 1911 to 14.0 in 1984 (cf. Chandrasekhar, 1975). In a paper that suggests how further improvement might be attained, Moni †Nag (1981) compared the mortality of two Indian states. Death rates have been lower in Kerala than in West Bengal since the beginning of the century, and the difference has recently widened. Yet most of the underlying factors usually cited to explain the level of mortality have favored West Bengal: among others, nutrition, income level and distribution, and industrialization. Apparently the crucial difference has long been that people in Kerala, particularly females, receive more schooling, with a significant effect on childrearing and other relevant behavior patterns (cf. Caldwell et al., 1983).

The population classified as urban increased from just under 11 percent in 1901 to 23.7 percent in 1981. As one would expect in such a highly stratified society, ethnic identity has affected migration patterns markedly (cf. Lewandowski, 1980). During the last intercensal decade, cities grew faster than had been anticipated, but most of the acceleration was not in the largest metropolises, where further increases would be most deleterious, but in the cities with populations between 100,000 and 400,000 (Crook and Dyson, 1982). In 1981 more than three-quarters of the people lived in the almost 600,000 villages, most of which had fewer than a thousand inhabitants, who in some cases were split into widely separated hamlets. One reason for the better educational, health, and family-planning facilities in Kerala has been that there most villages are settlements of more than 10,000, where the provision of services is less cumbersome and far cheaper.

The problems associated with population growth and urbanization were not initially deemed important by most of India's leaders, who perceived the country's poverty as a consequence of British maladministration. Mohandas K. †Gandhi's principled opposition to contraception influenced millions of his devoted followers (cf. Abraham †Stone). The autobiography of Jawaharlal †Nehru (1946), independent India's first prime minister, included a chapter entitled "The Problem of Population: Falling Birth Rates and National Decay," which set a continuing increase in numbers as a precondition to the new nation's greatness. Not surprisingly under such circumstances, the government's interest in controlling fertility began slowly and developed fitfully (cf. Samuel, 1966; Simmons, 1971). However, each recent census, as it marked the highly visible increase in population, stimulated the government anew. In one volume of the 1951 census, R. A. †Gopalaswami, writing officially as the registrar general, defined all childbirths above the third order as "improvident maternity," of which the incidence, 40 to 45 percent in that year, he believed had to be reduced to under 5 percent in 15 years. In the First Five-Year Plan (1951-56), a family-planning program was described as of "supreme" importance, but by the end of the Second Plan "India [had] not achieved any reduction of its birth rate, . . . and there [was] no sign that a downturn [would] occur in the next few years" (Gopalaswami, 1962). In the Third Plan (1962-67), following the unexpectedly high count in the 1961 census, federal allocations in a new decentralized program were spent through state projects, and the search for an appropriate means of contraception was hastened. In 1967, when Sripati †Chandrasekhar became minister of health and family planning, there was a new emphasis on sterilization, "of all the methods tried so far the only [one that] has yielded significant results" (Chandrasekhar, 1967). Not all agreed with that appraisal. According to one study of vasectomy in Maharashtra, men who had been sterilized averaged 39 to 40 years in age and had an average of 5.33 living children. "There appears . . . to be no possibility of vasectomy camps having a significant effect on the birth rate" (Dandekar, 1963).

How sterilization worked at the local level is suggested by a detailed analysis of one small area in rural Karnataka, 125 kilometers west of Bangalore. Among married couples with the wife under 50 years, a third were using some method of family limitation; and of those 70 percent of the husbands and 15 percent of the wives had been sterilized. One couple in four included a sterile partner by the time the wife was 26 years old, and half by the time she was 36. Sterilization was so widely used both because the poor were given little choice of method and because the practice of setting targets in the sterilization program implied some moral pressure.

The rural elites, always a little apprehensive of the growth of the large poor section of society, have been convinced of the need for fertility control, . . . [which] is often expressed by officials and village leaders in public places and on public occasions, while opposition or doubts are voiced only privately. . . . When the multipurpose health worker (previously the auxiliary nurse midwife) or the lady health visitor, a woman of above-average education and with an official position, suggests the operation for the first time to a young woman with two or three children, there is little overt pressure on her or her family, but rejecting such advice (which is sometimes supported by the doctor as well) perhaps twenty or thirty times over a two-year period is much more difficult. This is particularly so in the Hindu society with its concepts of elite leadership and of religious virtue arising from proper social behavior [Caldwell et al., 1982].

Population grew at a higher rate than ever before in the 1960s, and in the 1970s the increase accelerated still more. In 1971-73 men willing to undergo sterilization were paid 100 rupees (about $12), more than a month's salary of an unskilled worker, and the number of operations rose from 1.3 million in 1970-71 to 3.1 million in 1976, then fell to 0.9 million in 1977, when the incentives were abandoned because of a cut in program funds, administrative problems, and a number of adverse rumors. At the Bucharest world population conference in 1975, Karan Singh, the newly appointed minister for health and family planning, asserted that in order to achieve a birth rate of 25 by 1983-84 India might have to "think of the unthinkable"—a legal limitation on family size (cf. *compulsuation). A month later he wrote to Prime Minister Indira Gandhi that he saw "no alternative but to think in terms of introduction of some element of compulsion in the larger national interest" (quoted in Visaria and Visaria, 1981, p. 38). Then Sanjay Gandhi, the prime minister's son, took on birth control as his special province and, with no official position, attacked the problem with his characteristic combination of enthusiasm and bullying (Mehta, 1978, chap. 5). Civil servants were denied raises or transfers and sometimes even salaries until they had convinced a specified number of eligible parents to undergo sterilization. In some cities officials used the licensing of hotels, theaters, banks, airlines, and other businesses to force firms to induce their employees with three or more children to be sterilized. Opposition to the program was exacerbated by charges that the Hindu majority was using it to reduce the proportions of Untouchables and particularly of Muslims. A Muslim slum was cleared of its inhabitants at gun point and then razed; when the people were allowed back to where their homes had been, they were given ration cards, which would be renewed only if the men underwent an operation forbidden by their religion. Police and family planners were killed; in one ugly incident, according to seven opposition members of Parliament, several dozen protesters were shot down and 150 were wounded in antisterilization riots. This opposition was a significant reason for the fall of the Gandhi government in 1977. Under the Janata government, in office from 1977 to 1980, not only was such compulsion strongly condemned, but at least initially family planning was given scant attention. In short, the attempt to force the pace of birth control reduced for a period the efficiency of government programs, which had never been very high (cf. Petersen, 1982; Soni, 1983).

Once again, the 1981 census indicated that most analysts had been too opti- mistic in projecting a lower average rate of growth; the actual rate of 2.22 percent was virtually the same as during the prior decade. At the first National Conference of the Indian Association of Parliamentarians for Problems of Population and Development (May 25, 1981), Prime Minister Gandhi, again head of the gov- ernment, reacted to the census figure with a vigorous "total commitment to voluntary family planning." The Sixth Plan (1980-81 to 1984-85), she reported, had earmarked over 10,000 million rupees (about $1.15 billion) for the control of fertility. "Family planning must become a people's movement—of the people, by the people, for the people. . . . The work of motivation and spreading of the message cannot be confined to officials." The parliamentarians attending the conference responded with a strongly worded resolution (both the statement and the resolution are reproduced in *Population and Development Review*, 7, 1981, 557-563). A determined optimist might emphasize that the annual rate of increase did not continue to rise during the 1970s, but it can be doubted that the renewed call to greater efforts will achieve the targeted levels of fertility.

Apart from government programs and incentives, the key question according to the *wealth-flow theory is whether, on balance, it has become more profitable for the average Indian to have fewer rather than more children. In a comparison between one Bangladeshi village and three in India, Mead Cain (1981) showed that in the former children were an economic asset, in the latter not. However, while the Bangladeshi village was more or less representative of the whole country, "it would be folly to suggest that the findings are a reasonable char- acterization of India as a whole." For so large and heterogeneous a population, it is still extremely difficult even to guess in how large a proportion of the population the economic gain that parents have from their progeny has turned into a net monetary loss. If it proves possible to move faster toward economic development and modernization, eventually this will mean a shift to the small- family pattern. But over the short term modernization can also bring about increased fertility (Nag, 1982).

Even before the 1981 census, Robert Cassen and Tim Dyson (1976) concluded from a review of population projections that a very large increase in the number of Indians is a near certainty. By the end of the century, the population will be close to one billion—according to various projections, between 947 million and 1.02 billion (Visaria and Visaria, 1981, p. 48). See also *India: Demographic Institutions.

REFERENCES: Mead T. Cain, "Risk and Insurance: Perspectives on Fertility and Agrarian Change in India and Bangladesh," *Population and Development Review*, 7 (1981), 435-474. John C. Caldwell, P. H. Reddy, and Pat Caldwell, "The Causes of Demographic Change in Rural South India: A Micro Approach," *Population and De- velopment Review*, 8 (1982), 689-727; "The Social Component of Mortality Decline: An Investigation in South India Employing Alternative Methodologies," *Population Studies*, 37 (1983), 185-205. Robert Cassen and Tim Dyson, "New Population Projections for India," *Population and Development Review*, 2 (1976), 101-136. Sripati Chandrasekhar,

"India's Population: Fact, Problem and Policy," in Chandrasekhar, ed., *Asia's Population Problems* (London: Allen and Unwin, 1967); *Infant Mortality, Population Growth and Family Planning in India* (Chapel Hill: University of North Carolina Press, 1975). N. K. Choudhry, "A Note on the Dilemma of Planning Population in India," *Economic Development and Cultural Change*, 4 (1955), 68-81. Nigel Crook and Dyson, "Urbanization in India: Results of the 1981 Census," *Population and Development Review*, 8 (1982), 145-155. Kumudini V. Dandekar, "Vasectomy Camps in Maharashtra," *Population Studies*, 17 (1963), 147-154. Jyotirindra Das Gupta, *Language Conflict and National Development: Group Politics and National Language Policy in India* (Berkeley: University of California Press, 1970). Kingsley Davis, *The Population of India and Pakistan* (Princeton, N.J.: Princeton University Press, 1951). R. A. Gopalaswami, "Family Planning: Outlook for Government Action in India," in Clyde V. Kiser, ed., *Research in Family Planning* (Princeton, N.J.: Princeton University Press, 1962). Selig S. Harrison, *India: The Most Dangerous Decades* (Princeton, N.J.: Princeton University Press, 1960). Erland Hofsten, "Population Growth in India," *Statistisk Tidskrift*, 20 (1982), 24-30. S. P. Jain, "Demographic Models and Studies of Indian Fertility and Mortality," *Artha Vijñāña*, 22 (1980), 355-382. Susan J. Lewandowski, *Migration and Ethnicity in Urban India: Kerala Migrants in the City of Madras, 1870-1970* (New Delhi: Manohar, 1980). Ved Mehta, *The New India* (New York: Penguin Books, 1978). Moni Nag, "Impact of Social Development and Economic Development on Mortality: A Comparative Study of Kerala and West Bengal," and "Modernization and Its Impact on Fertility: The Indian Scene," Center for Population Studies, *Working Papers*, nos. 78 and 84 (New York: Population Council, 1981 and 1982). Jawaharlal Nehru, *The Discovery of India* (New York: Harper and Row, 1946). William Petersen, "The Social Roots of Hunger and Overpopulation," *Public Interest*, no. 68 (1982), 37-52. Mahendra K. Premi, *The Demographic Situation in India* (Honolulu: East-West Population Institute, 1982). T. J. Samuel, "The Development of India's Policy of Population Control," *Milbank Memorial Fund Quarterly*, 44 (1966), 49-67. George B. Simmons, *The Indian Investment in Family Planning* (New York: Population Council, 1971). Veena Soni, "Thirty Years of the Indian Family Planning Program: Past Performance, Future Prospects," *International Family Planning Perspectives*, 9 (1983), 35-45. Pravin M. Visaria and Leela Visaria, "India's Population: Second and Growing," *Population Bulletin*, 36 (October, 1981), 1-54.

India: Demographic Institutions

The Family Planning Association of India, a private nonprofit organization, was established in 1949 by such Indian activists as Lady Rama †Rau and Sripati †Chandrasekhar. Advocacy of its program is partly through its *Journal of Family Welfare*. Address: 1 Jeevan Udyog, Dadabhai Naoroji Road, Bombay 400 000.

The Gandhigram Rural Institute, a private organization, was directed in 1980 by L. Ramachandran. It has published a series of monographs related to family planning. Address: Gandhigram P.O., Madurai District, Tamil Nadu.

The Indian Institute for Population Studies was founded by Sripati Chandrasekhar, who still edits its *Population Review*. Address: Kodikanal, Tamil Nadu.

The Population Centers of the India Population Project of the *International Bank for Reconstruction and Development deal with family planning and report their activities in their *PopCen Newsletter*, Bangalore and Lucknow. In 1980 the directors were P. H. †Reddy and N. B. Lal. Addresses: Population Center, Bangalore 560 003; Population Center, Indira Nagar, Faizabad Road, Lucknow.

The Population Council of India, of which C. D. Deshmukh was president in 1975, has tried to stimulate support for antinatalist policy and family-planning programs. Address: 40 Lodi Estate, New Delhi 3.

UNIVERSITY AND OTHER RESEARCH INSTITUTES

The Anthropological Survey of India, an agency of the Government of India, has been in process since 1945. In 1980 it was directed by D. P. Mukherjee. It is compiling an ethnographic atlas, and its research relates also to such demographic factors as the changing role of women. Address: 27 Jawaharlal Nehru Road, Calcutta 16.

In 1967, the M.S. University of Baroda (for Maharaja Sayajirao) set up a Population Research Center, of which the co-director in 1980 was M. M. †Gandotra. It teaches demography at the graduate level and does research on such topics as fertility and family planning, rural health services, internal migration, and the relation between population growth and economic development. Address: Lokmanya Tilak Road, Baroda 390 002.

The University of Bombay's economics department, headed in the late 1970s by Dhansukhlal T. Lakdawala, has analyzed the social and economic implications of population trends. Address: C.S.T. Road, Kalina, Bombay 400 029.

The Gokhale Institute of Politics and Economics, which has been in existence since 1930, has established a solid reputation for research related to population, agricultural economics, historical demography, and related fields. In 1980 its director was Kumudini V. †Dandekar. The institute publishes the journal *Artha Vijnāña*, which includes many papers on population. The department of demography has conducted demographic and statistical research on India, especially pertaining to factors related to family planning. Address: Poona 411 004, Maharashtra.

The Indian Statistical Institute, founded by P. C. †Mahalanobis, has a Demographic Unit, which in 1980 was under the direction of B. P. Adhikari. It has conducted demographic research on India, including in particular a Calcutta Fertility Survey. It also includes a Family Planning Research Unit, with which Samir †Guha Roy and Anima †Sen Gupta were associated in the late 1970s. The institute publishes *Sankhyā: The Indian Journal of Statistics* in two series, one narrowly statistical and the other with papers on such applied fields as demography. Address: 203 Barrackpore Trunk Road, Calcutta 700 035.

The Institute of Economic Growth, a private center established in 1958, was directed in 1980 by P. B. †Desai. Its Demographic Research Center has conducted research on factors affecting fertility, mortality, migration, and urbanization. The institute publishes the journal *Demography India*. Address: University Enclave, Delhi 110 007.

The Institute of Social and Economic Change, established in 1972, was in

1980 directed by V.K.R.V. †Rao. Its demographic unit included among its research personnel P. H. Rayappa and K. S. †Srikantan. Address: Bangalore-Mysore Road, Bangalore 560 040.

International Institute for Population Studies, Bombay. See *United Nations.

In 1962 Jadavpur University established in its applied economics section a Demographic Research Unit, of which the director in 1980 was Ambica P. †Ghosh. It has constructed models, using long-term demographic and economic variables, for Calcutta and other areas of India. Address: Calcutta 700 032.

The J.S.S. Institute of Economic Research (for Janata Shikshana Samiti), a private research organization established in 1957, was directed in the 1970s by Balkrishna D. †Kale. Its Population Research Center has conducted demographic surveys and evaluated family-planning programs with a view to improving their efficacy. Address: Vidyagiri, Dharwar 580 004, Mysore State.

The Bureau of Economics and Statistics of the State Government of Kerala, of which G. N. Nair was director in 1980, has analyzed family-planning and vasectomy programs. Address: Trivandrum 695 001, Kerala.

The University of Kerala's department of statistics, under the direction in 1980 of Aleyamma †George, has conducted demographic and statistical research on fertility trends and behavior in Kerala State. The university's Bureau of Economics and Statistics has a population research center, with which R. S. †Kurup and P. S. Gopinathan †Nair were associated in 1980. The Family Planning Community Action Research Center in its department of sociology, of which the director in 1980 was P.K.B. †Nayar, has conducted *action-research on family planning. Address: Kariavattome P.O., Trivandrum 695 581, Kerala.

The University of Lucknow's department of economics includes a Demographic Research Center, which in 1980 was under the direction of N. N. Shrivastava. It has carried out research on age at marriage, family planning, fertility, and perinatal mortality in the Lucknow district, and on the relation between population and economic development. It has published a bibliography, *Demography and Development Digest*. Address: Lucknow 226 007, Uttar Pradesh.

The University of Mysore has an Institute of Development Studies, of which R. P. Misra was director in 1980. Its main focus of research has been on city and regional planning, human settlement, and other aspects of population geography. Address: Manasa Gangotri, Mysore 570 006.

The National Institute of Family Planning, a government agency, includes a Demography and Statistics Division of which the director in 1980 was B. R. †Kohli. It has conducted evaluation studies of various family-planning programs. Address: D-18 Green Park, New Delhi 110 016.

The National Institute of Health and Family Welfare, a unit of the Ministry of Health and Family Welfare, was directed by R. K. Sanyal in 1980. It conducts research projects and publishes the findings in its journal, *Health and Population: Perspectives and Issues*. Address: Near D.D.A. Flats, Munirka, New Delhi 110 067.

The National Institute of Rural Development, a government agency, was headed in 1980 by B. C. Muthayya, dean. Its research relates to, among other elements of rural life, population, health, and ethnicity. Address: Rajendranag, Hyderabad 500 030.

Operations Research Group, Baroda, is a private consulting and research firm that has done studies on family planning, health and nutrition, and rural and urban planning. For example, it conducted two all-India surveys of contraceptive users, and it evaluated the mass vasectomy camp in Gujarat. Address: Baroda 390 002.

The sociology department of Panjab University, of which Victor S. †D'Souza was chairman in 1980, concentrates in both its instruction and its research on urban and population studies. Topics typically pertain to the social correlates of population variables. Address: Chandigarh 160 014, Punjab.

The University of Patna has a Demographic Research Center, established in 1966 and in 1980 directed by D. N. Lal. It has evaluated rural-health and family-welfare programs, and made a study of the scheduled castes and tribes in Bihar. Address: Patna 800 005, Bihar.

Sri Venkateswara University has a Population Studies Center, where research has been announced on some demographic topics, and reports have been published, for example, on the sociology of fertility. Since 1978 the center has issued the *Indian Journal of Population Studies*. Address: Tirupati 517 502, Andhra Pradesh.

Utkal University has a Population Research Center, which L. K. Mahapatra directed in the late 1970s. It has undertaken studies of sterilization, infant and child mortality, and traditional family-planning methods. Address: Bhubaneswar 751 004, Orissa.

GOVERNMENT STATISTICAL BUREAUS

The Department of Statistics issues a *Monthly Abstract of Statistics* and a *Statistical Abstract* and a *Statistical Pocket Book*, both annual. All contain estimates of population, births, and deaths. Address: Ministry of Planning, Sardar Patal Bhavan, Parliament Street, New Delhi 110 001.

The Office of the Commissioner for Scheduled Castes and Scheduled Tribes issues an annual report on the "Untouchable" castes. Address: New Delhi.

The Office of the Registrar General conducts the country's censuses, the most recent of which was in 1981. It publishes the results, as well as annual compilations of *Vital Statistics* and *Causes of Death*. The value of the latter is diminished by the considerable underregistration and the delay in their publication. Address: Ministry of Home Affairs, 2-A Man Singh Road, New Delhi 110 011.

The National Sample Survey (NSS) is one of a series of surveys instituted by the Government of India in 1950 and continued at the rate of one or two "rounds" per year. Because registration data are lacking or poor in much of the country, the NSS has become a chief source of estimates on fertility and family planning, mortality and morbidity, and internal migration, as well as employment and unemployment, consumer expenditures, and other nondemographic topics. Informed opinion differs on how accurate these estimates probably are, though in some cases the fault is too great to be missed. As one example, the crude death rate for rural India supposedly fell from 19 in 1959 to 15 in 1960, a consequence of serious undercount in the latter round. The comparability of data from successive rounds is marred not only by sampling error but by frequent and sometimes significant changes in procedures. Probably the most satisfactory comparisons are not over time but rather between rural and urban populations or between other major sectors of the country. REFERENCE: Nitai C. Das and N. Bhattacharya, "National Sample Survey: An Appraisal of Demographic Data," in Ashish Bose et al., eds., *Population Statistics in India* (New Delhi: Vikas, 1977).

The Sample Registration System (SRS), based on a sample drawn from the 1961 census, was instituted in the mid-1960s and spread to the whole of the country over the following years. It is estimated that about 80 percent of births and deaths are registered of rural samples, somewhat less of urban samples. By and large the results are about the same as from the NSS, which includes questions on more topics but does not attempt a continuous survey specifically of fertility and mortality. REFERENCE: R. B. Lal and V. S. Swamy, "Vital Statistics: Sample Registration System," in Ashish Bose et al., eds., *Population Statistics in India* (New Delhi: Vikas, 1977).

Indian medicine of the traditional Hindu type is based on the Ayurveda, a work of one hundred chapters, each of one hundred stanzas, that was handed down by Brahma, creator of the universe. Over the centuries since Ayurveda practice originated, around 4000 B.C., commentaries and exegeses have accumulated, including, for example, hymns to cure specified diseases. The parallel Muslim Unani, as derived from ancient Greek physiology, is based on four qualities (hot, cold, wet, and dry), which in various combinations set the four humors of sanguine, phlegmatic, choleric, and melancholic (related, respectively, to blood, phlegm, yellow bile, and black bile). And as the last important ingredient, *homeopathy was added in the mid-nineteenth century by a German practitioner who had treated a maharaja successfully (Sanyal, 1964).

Aware of the long-term threat to their existence in British India, the native practitioners organized themselves into a professional body, which from the 1920s on received at least partial support from the Indian National Congress. A school of Indian medicine was established in Madras to teach a combination of Western medicine and Ayurveda stripped of what were seen as superstitious accretions. After India attained its independence the conflict between modernizers and defenders of tradition became sharper; repeated efforts to find a compromise by combining the two systems did not work, for in a joint environment with Western medicine Ayurveda tends to disappear. In 1952 a movement was started for Shuddha (pure) Ayurveda, purged of alien influences and essentially hostile to Western science. The nationalist opposition in less developed countries to the practices half-incorporated during the colonial period includes in this instance a rejection of what would seem to Westerners to be an obvious benefit. See also *Chinese medicine.

REFERENCES: Ralph C. Croizier, "Medicine, Modernization, and Cultural Crisis in China and India," *Comparative Studies in Society and History*, 12 (1970), 275-291. P. K. Sanyal, *A Story of Medicine and Pharmacy in India* (Calcutta: Sanyal, 1964).

Indianapolis Study, the usual designation of "Social and Psychological Factors Affecting Fertility," which was published in thirty-three articles in the *Milbank Memorial Fund Quarterly* and later bound in five volumes (1946, 1950, 1952, 1954, and 1958). The research, sponsored by the *Milbank Memorial Fund, was undertaken in order to explain why fertility had reached such low levels, but by the time it was completed, the *baby boom had reversed the prior long-term trend. The study was a pioneer effort to supplement conventional demographic data with a survey of attitudes of potential and actual parents. Even though the sample was quite homogeneous—relatively fecund native white Protestant couples in a Midwestern city—little evidence was found of how attitudes help determine family size. As Clyde V. †Kiser and P. K. †Whelpton, who jointly directed the project, stated in the final paper of the series, "Our measures of psychological characteristics probably were too crude to afford precise differentiations." Thus, "the chief lesson" from the study is that fertility is generally more closely related to "broad social factors (including the economic)" than to psychological.

REFERENCE: Clyde V. Kiser and P. K. Whelpton, "Social and Psychological Factors Affecting Fertility, XXIII: Summary of Chief Findings and Implications for Future Studies," *Milbank Memorial Fund Quarterly*, 36 (1958), 282-329.

Indonesia, with 161.6 million inhabitants in 1984, is the fifth most populous nation in the world, as well as one of the most heterogeneous. The country comprises an archipelago of five major islands—Sumatra, Java (with the adjacent small island of Madura), Kalimantan, Sulawesi, and Irian Jaya—and thousands of smaller ones, which sprawl over some 3,100 miles (5,000 kilometers). Within this vast area are many peoples, languages, and cultures, with ways of life ranging from the most civilized to the primitive. Land also varies from rich soils of volcanic origin to large areas of poor quality. The national motto, "Unity in Diversity," represents less a description than a goal. Islam is a unifying force, with 87 percent of the population as claimed adherents, though indeed of quite different degrees of orthodoxy. The national language, a variant of Malay called Bahasa Indonesia, may also help to bring the people together at some time in the future (Jones, 1982).

For several centuries most of Indonesia was ruled by the Dutch, first through the Dutch East India Company and then, after its liquidation in 1799, directly by the Netherlands government. Its rule was briefly interrupted during the Napoleonic wars (1811-15), when the British under Stamford Raffles occupied the islands. Raffles is important in this context because he administered what is regarded as the first census. The 4.6 million recorded in 1815, when combined with the much more accurate enumeration in 1930, implied a population that had grown very rapidly during the whole of the intervening 115 years. Recently a number of scholars have challenged this often cited datum as specious, based on a gross underenumeration in the earlier count (e.g., Nitisastro, 1970; Peper, 1970; McNicoll and Mamas, 1973). If these analysts are correct in raising the population to about double that listed in the 1815 census, then the subsequent growth was at an annual rate of something like 1.2 percent, rather than the anomalous 2.1 percent that the incomplete count indicated.

The first reliable census took place only in 1930, when the population was 60.7 million. During the years 1929-33 export income fell by nearly 70 percent. The Japanese, who occupied the islands from 1942 to 1945, used forced labor and imposed harsh sanctions on any who failed to produce the amount of food set in procurement quotas. Indonesia achieved its independence in a very destructive war (1945-49) with a significant loss of life. Thus, the next census, in 1961, took place long after a severe depression, an occupation by a hostile army, and a war of independence, each of which probably resulted in more deaths and fewer births. Over the more than three decades the population had risen to 97.0 million, or by an average of only 1.5 percent per year. It was expected that during the next decade, without such disturbances in growth patterns, the increase would be much faster; but the 1971 enumerated population of 119.2 million meant an average growth rate of between 2.1 and 2.2 percent, up by less than had been anticipated. The most recent census, in 1980, recorded a total of 148 million (cf. McNicoll, 1982). See also *Indonesia: Demographic Institutions.

One reason that growth remained slower than many projections was that normal mortality also was high. Writing in 1960, Justus van der Kroef cited estimates of death rates of 20 to 40 per thousand from malaria alone, "the highest infant mortality rate in the world," at least half the world's cases of yaws, 10-15 percent of the adult population of Java with venereal disease, and a diet so inadequate that kwashiorkor (malignant malnutrition) was regarded as possibly the most prevalent chronic disease of infants. From age data in 1971, it was possible to estimate an infant mortality rate—143 for the whole country but 133 in crowded Java and only 110 in Java's urban areas (McNicoll and Mamas, 1973, Table 3). Seemingly the negative effects of very high population density were more than compensated by Java's better health facilities and its more effective control of malaria and tuberculosis. In 1965 an attempted coup by the Communist Party was also centered in Java; and for months after its suppression, members of the Party and affiliated organizations, as well as, allegedly, ethnic Chinese with no political connections, were killed in undocumented numbers sometimes estimated in the hundreds of thousands (Mortimer, 1972). What the trend in normal mortality has been is impossible to state with any great assurance. In some parts of the country especially, malnutrition has remained a serious problem, and in Java at least public health measures, narrowly defined, would have less effect on the death rate than a rise in the level of living.

Since the 1930s, first the Dutch administration and then the Indonesian have tried to reduce population density by a program called *transmigration, or a mass redistribution of people to the outer islands (cf. Heeren, 1967). In 1964 President Sukarno enthusiastically endorsed the program: "If you exploit all the land in Indonesia you can feed 250 million, and I have only 103 million. . . . In my country, the more [children] the better" (quoted in Hull et al., 1977). Most evaluations of transmigration, however, have judged it to have been a complete failure, but it has not been abandoned. As part of the Third Five-Year Plan (1979-84), half a million households, or more than two million people, were to be moved from Java, Bali, and Lombok—a project that, if achieved, would draw off about a quarter of that area's natural increase. Road-building and other projects were planned on the outer islands, in the hope that these would also stimulate an independent movement. There is a good deal of migration within Java, much of it short-distance and short-term (Hugo, 1980; McNicoll and Mamas, 1973). The rapid increase of urban populations is regarded as a serious social and political problem, and in 1970 Jakarta was declared a "closed city."

For some decades transmigration was used as a substitute for a more direct check on Java's population growth. Several pioneer efforts led to the formation in 1957 of the Indonesian Planned Parenthood Association, an independent organization usually known by its Indonesian acronym, PKBI. After a gradual change in official policy, this was followed in 1970 by the establishment of the government's National Family Planning Coordinating Board (BKKBN), which oversees all family-planning services. Contraceptives were distributed through clinics—in fact, typically a few hours set aside each week in a local health center. Initially each worker in clinics or the field was paid for each new acceptor recruited into the program, but this system was abandoned after three years. Targets were set that stimulated—or overstimulated—local officials to find recruits. At least by its first results, the program was a seeming success in Java and Bali. The median number of living children at the time the woman accepted the service fell from 4.0 in mid-1971 to 2.6 in mid-1976. By the latter date more than a fifth of married women in the fecund age range were using some form of birth control. The total fertility rate, estimated in the late 1960s at about 5.2 children, may have fallen by about 15 percent in 1976. However, the declines estimated with various methods of calculation ranged between 6.8 and 19.7 percent in West Java, for example, and between 25.9 and 35.6 percent in Bali (Hull et al., 1977; cf. Surjaningrat et al., 1980; World Fertility Survey, 1978).

If 15 percent can be taken as a reasonable approximation of the decline in fertility, this was not due entirely to the family-planning program. The female age at marriage rose dramatically from 1971 to 1976, and divorce and separation were frequent. "Characteristics relevant in explaining the relatively low fertility in Central and East Java include an ancient and eclectic religio-cultural tradition, a long history of colonial exploitation, extremely dense agricultural populations, an intricate system of land tenure marked by an absence of large holdings, a truncated pattern of social stratification, and a nuclear family norm but with strong interfamily obligations within each village'' (McNicoll and Mamas, 1973, p. 37).

If fertility continues to fall rapidly—a far from certain alternative—Indonesia's projected population in the year 2000 will be of the order of 215 million, with 54 million school children, 96 million working or looking for work, and 58 million women in the fecund age range.

REFERENCES: Hendrik J. Heeren, *Internal Migration in Indonesia* (Meppel: Boom, 1967). Graeme J. Hugo, ''Circular Migration in Indonesia,'' *Population and Development Review*, 8 (1982), 59-83. Terence H. Hull, Valerie J. Hull, and Masri Singarimbun, ''Indonesia's Family Planning Story: Success and Challenge,'' *Population Bulletin*, 32 (November, 1977), 3-52. Gavin W. Jones, ''Indonesia,'' *International Encyclopedia of Population*, 1, 334-339. Geoffrey McNicoll, ''Recent Demographic Trends in Indonesia,'' *Population and Development Review*, 8 (1982), 811-819. McNicoll and Si Gde Made Mamas, *The Demographic Situation in Indonesia*, East-West Population Institute, Paper no. 28 (Honolulu, 1973). Rex Mortimer, *The Indonesian Communist Party and Land Reform, 1959-1965* (Melbourne: Center of Southeast Asian Studies, Monash University, 1972). Widjojo Nitisastro, *Population Trends in Indonesia* (Ithaca, N.Y.: Cornell University Press, 1970). Bram Peper, ''Population Growth in Java in the Nineteenth Century: A New Interpretation,'' *Population Studies*, 24 (1970), 71-84. Suwardjono Surjaningrat, R. Henry Pardoko, Peter Patta Sumbung, and M. Soedarmadi, ''East Asia Review, 1978-79: Indonesia,'' *Studies in Family Planning*, 11 (November, 1980), 320-324. Justus M. van der Kroef, ''Cultural Aspects of Indonesia's Demographic Problem,'' *Population Review*, 4 (1960), 27-39. World Fertility Survey, *The Indonesia Fertility Survey, 1976: A Summary of Findings* (London, 1978).

Indonesia: Demographic Institutions

The Indonesian Demographers' Association (IPADI), formed in 1973, sponsors an annual meeting and publishes, through the Demographic Institute of the University of Indonesia, the semi-annual bilingual *Journal of Indonesian Demography/Majalah Demografi Indonesia*, started in 1974.

The Indonesian Planned Parenthood Association (PKBI), an independent organization generally referred to by its Indonesian initials, was established in 1957. It trains workers and provides family-planning services, and undertakes research and evaluation of its program. Address: Jakarta.

The National Family Planning Coordinating Board (BKKBN), widely known by its Indonesian initials, was established in 1970 directly under the Office of the President. It oversees all government family-planning activities and has primary responsibility for developing the country's population policy. The board funds research by other agencies, and it has itself made various special studies of family-planning programs. Its Bureau for Coordination and Bureau of Research and Evaluation, the main units concerned with policy and program research, are in the board's Population Division, headed in 1981 by R. Henry †Pardoko. Address: P.O. Box 186, Jakarta.

UNIVERSITIES AND OTHER RESEARCH INSTITUTES

Gadjah Mada University, a public institution, in 1973 set up a Population Research and Study Center, an autonomous unit under Masri †Singarimbun as director. The center has had an intensive research program, mostly in the Yogyakarta region of Java, focused on microstudies of population growth and economic-anthropological research on population issues. For example, in 1982 several researchers from the center studied the results of a mobile tubectomy team that had operated in the region. It also conducts a training program to help develop staff for the population institutes at provincial universities. Included in its active publication program have been working papers, monographs, and books published through the Gadjah Mada University Press. Address: Universitas Gadjah Mada, Bulaksumur G-7, Yogyakarta.

The National Institute of Economic and Social Research (LEKNAS), a division of the Indonesian Institute of Sciences (LIPI), established a Population Studies Center in 1969. The center has focused its research on internal migration and the labor force. Its director in the late 1970s was †Suharso, succeeded in 1981 by Sukobandiono. Address: Jalan Gondangdia Lama 39, Jakarta.

The National Institute of Public Health, a government research unit under the Department of Health, conducts research on fertility and contraception as well as public health. Address: Jalan Indrapura 17, Surabaya.

The University of Indonesia, a public institution, established a Demographic Institute in its Faculty of Economics in 1964. The institute has undertaken research on population trends and problems in Indonesia, including the 1973 Fertility-Mortality Survey—a large-scale demographic study of Indonesia. It has also helped establish demographic institutes at provincial universities, in particular by providing much of the training of their professional staff. Its director from 1964 to 1967 and from 1969 to his death in 1979 was Nathanael †Iskandar, succeeded by Kartomo †Wirosuhardjo. Notable among the institute's publications are the reports of the 1973 Fertility-Mortality Survey, and the *Demographic Factbook of Indonesia*. Address: Universitas Indonesia, Jalan Salemba Raya 4, Jakarta.

During the 1970s many provincial universities set up demographic institutes or population studies centers. Most of these have been thinly staffed and local in their interests. Those active around 1980 were:

Population Studies Center, Andalas University, Jalan Perintis Kemerdekaan 77, Padang, West Sumatra.

Demographic Institute, Faculty of Economics, Brawijaya University, Jalan Mayjen. Haryono 169, Malang, East Java.

Population Studies Center, Diponegoro University, Jalan Imam Barjo 1, Semarang, Central Java.

Population Institute, Faculty of Economics, General Soedirman University, Kalibakal, Purwokerto, Central Java.

Population Institute, Hasanuddin University, Jalan Mesjid Raya, Ujung Pandang, South Sulawesi.

Demographic Institute, Faculty of Economics, Lambung Mangkurat University, Jalan Kayutangi, Banjarmasin, South Kalimantan.

Population Institute, University of North Sumatra, Jalan Prof. Ma'as 3, Medan, North Sumatra.

Population Studies Center, Padjadjaran State University, Jalan Dipati Ukur 35, Bandung, West Java.

Population Institute, Sam Ratulangi University, Kleak, Manado, North Sulawesi.

Demographic Institute, Faculty of Economics, Syiah Kuala University, Jalan Darusalam, Banda Aceh, Aceh.

Population Studies Center, Faculty of Medicine, Udayana University, Jalan Jendral Sudirman, P.O. Box 105, Denpasar, Bali.

GOVERNMENT STATISTICAL BUREAU

The Central Bureau of Statistics in 1982 was under the direction of Azwar Rasjid. It issues annually *The population of Indonesia* and *Characteristics of the population of Indonesia*, both in Indonesian, as well as a *Statistical Yearbook of Indonesia* and a *Statistical Pocketbook*, both in English as well as Indonesian. The bureau is also an important source of analytical reports. It published the two-volume principal report of the 1976 Indonesia Fertility Survey (the local component of the *World Fertility Survey), and in 1981 began issuing a series of reports of findings of the 1980 census. The head of the bureau's demographic analysis section in 1981 was Si Gde Made †Mamas. Address: Biro Pusat Statistik, Jalan Dr. Sutomo 8, Jakarta.

industrial revolution, often spelled Industrial Revolution, was used by French writers as early as the 1820s and by Arnold Toynbee, the English economist and social philosopher, in a very influential analysis published in 1882. The term designates the substitution of power-driven machines for hand tools, particularly in the textile industry, and the accompanying changes in Western Europe's agriculture, trade, and transportation. Many critics have pointed out that the usually designated period, from 1760 to 1840, is too precise, that the speed of the transformation varied from one industry to another, and that the social changes instituted by the factory system were more fundamental than those generally included in the term. Apart from such quibbles about precise details, all analysts agree that profound economic changes took place and that these facilitated the modernization of many social institutions and behavior patterns. The phrase has not only survived but has spawned a series of offspring: urban revolution, agricultural revolution, scientific revolution, and demographic revolution. As with many such journalistic metaphors, excessive use has robbed the term of whatever impact it once had.

industry is used in the social disciplines with an unfortunate double meaning. In such terms as "industrialization," "the industrial revolution," "industrial workers," and so on, there is at least an implied contrast between large-scale manufacturing and such other sectors of the economy as agriculture, mining, and commerce. In census classifications among many other contexts, however, industry is the generic term, designating any branch of economic activity. In its recommendations for the 1970 censuses, the United Nations defined industry as "the activity of the establishment in which an economically active person worked"—that is, the kind of goods or services produced. It was recommended that industries be grouped according to its "International Standard Industrial Classification of All Economic Activities" (ISIC), which the United Nations revises periodically. See also *labor force; *occupation; *work force.

In *The Conditions of Economic Progress* Colin †Clark introduced a classification, since widely imitated, among primary industry (agriculture, hunting and fishing, and forestry), secondary (manufacturing, construction, mining, and the production of electric power), and tertiary (commerce, transport, public administration, and personal and professional services). As expounded in a number of works, modern society has supposedly evolved through this series, with the greatest emphasis successively on subsistence, manufacturing, and services. As generally interpreted, an industrial or modern society uses mechanical sources of power and machine processes in large-scale production and distribution, all integrated under a single government, a single price system, and a comprehensive transportation and communication network. Related characteristics include a mechanized agriculture, a highly urban population, universal literacy, well controlled fertility and mortality, and often a stratification based largely on achievement. The nuclear family is far more important than extended kin, partly because some traditional family functions have been shifted to specialized agencies. In what various writers have termed a "post-industrial society," the dominance of the service sector is greater, with the rise of a new social class of professionals and technicians. Alternative designations of the same concept include "post-economic," "post-capitalist," "post-maturity."

Census data on industry can be exemplified by those collected on a sample basis in the United States enumeration in 1980. The questions, number 28 on the long form, were as follows:

a. For whom did this person work?
    _____ (Name of company, business, organization, or other employer)
b. What kind of business or industry was this? Describe the activity at location where employed.
    _____ (For example: Hospital, newspaper publishing, mail order house, auto engine manufacturing, breakfast cereal manufacturing)
c. Is this mainly—(Fill in one circle)
    ○ Manufacturing   ○ Retail trade
    ○ Wholesale trade   ○ Other (agriculture, construction, service, government, etc.)

Responses were coded into one of the 231 industry categories in the *Standard Industrial Classification* (SIC), which had been developed by the Office of Management and Budget and the Office of Federal Statistical Policy and Standards Directives.

REFERENCE: Colin Clark, *The Conditions of Economic Progress* (3rd ed.; London: Macmillan, 1957).

infancy, the earliest period of human life; babyhood. The word derives ultimately from Latin for "not speaking," which suggests the duration in its original meaning. In demography, the period is set arbitrarily as the first year of life. Thus, for any year the infant mortality rate is defined as the deaths during the first year of life per 1,000 births (see *mortality, infant).

infanticide, the killing of a recently born child, has been a common and often legal method of population control from time immemorial. In some of the ancient Greek city-states, the practice was not only permitted but under some conditions prescribed; in Rome it was limited by various legal restrictions and finally, in the fourth century A.D., made a capital offense. However great a sin by Christian precepts, infanticide was common in medieval and early modern Europe, according to the imprecise evidence available. It can be plausibly argued that the practice remained more than a minor aberration in Western Europe until the last quarter of the nineteenth century, when it was supplanted by contraception (Langer, 1974; see also Kellum, 1974; Trexler, 1974; Hoffer and Hull, 1981). And in present-day United States, once *child abuse was defined in law and thus recognized by the public, its prevalence was found to be astounding, and in many cases it verged on infanticide.

Moral compunctions aside, infanticide has the disadvantage of exposing the mother to the pain and risk of childbirth to no purpose, but where advanced medical techniques to determine the sex of a fetus do not exist, it has also been the only method of controlling family size that permits a selection among offspring. Wherever infanticide is practiced, female infanticide is the rule, supplemented by the elimination of defective and unhealthy children and those undesirable by reason of some magical (e.g., multiple births) or social (e.g., illegitimacy) factor. The killing of girls is associated with the higher valuation of males, as in a hunting society (Eskimos), among certain polyandrous peoples, and in many of the great agrarian civilizations (cf. Dickeman, 1975).

One of the best statistical records for a non-Western civilization pertains to the Jhareja, who live in Kathiawar (Gujarat) in western India. They were notorious for the proportion of their female infants that they killed, and to check on its success in ending the custom the British government collected a mass of data, which have been recently analyzed in an interesting paper. In 1817, at the time of the first comprehensive inquiry, the *sex ratio of this people was 235.8, and over the following decades it did fall off, though not to parity (Pakrasi and Sasmal, 1970; see also Miller, 1981).

In *Japan infanticide was euphemistically termed *mabiki* (literally, "thinning," as of rice seedlings when some are pulled up to encourage the growth of the remainder). Every account of late Tokugawa and early Meiji Japan notes the widespread prevalence of *mabiki*, and yet by the end of the nineteenth century it had disappeared except possibly from some isolated rural areas, without then being replaced by either abortion or contraception. In other words, as modern Japan adopted some of the ethical norms of the West, the children who would have been left to die were permitted to live—thus contributing to the country's probable increase in recorded fertility and its momentous population growth.

*China had a long tradition of female infanticide, which has recently been revivified by the policy of limiting family size, when feasible, to one child and, under all conditions, to two at the most. According to the statistics available, the sex ratio at birth in 1979 was close to the normal 106 males per 100 females, but by 1981 it had risen to 138, which means that roughly one female in four who might have been expected to live was drowned or abandoned (*Economist*, April 16, 1983). According to the *China Youth Daily*, in some localities the sex ratio of those who survived the first two years of life was as high as 150. Such appalling figures are given some implicit verification by the large number of high-level public officials who have condemned both the practice and the denigration of women who have given birth to female children (cf. Haupt, 1983).

REFERENCES: Mildred Dickeman, "Demographic Consequences of Infanticide in Man," in R. F. Johnston et al., eds., *Annual Review of Ecology and Systematics*, vol. 6 (1975). Arthur Haupt, "The Shadow of Female Infanticide," *Intercom*, 11 (January-February, 1983), 1, 13-14. Peter C. Hoffer and N.E.H. Hull, *Murdering Mothers: Infanticide in England and New England, 1558-1803* (New York: New York University Press, 1981). Barbara A. Kellum, "Infanticide in England in the Later Middle Ages," *History of Childhood Quarterly*, 1 (1974), 368–387. William L. Langer, "Infanticide: A Historical Survey," *History of Childhood Quarterly*, 1 (1974), 353-365. B. D. Miller, *The Endangered Sex: Neglect of Female Children in Rural North India* (Ithaca, N.Y.: Cornell University Press, 1981). Kanti B. Pakrasi and Bibhas Sasmal, "Effect of Infanticide on the Sex Ratio of an Indian Population," *Zeitschrift für Morphologie und Anthropologie*, 62 (1970), 214-230. Richard C. Trexler, "Infanticide in Florence: New Sources and First Results," *History of Childhood Quarterly*, 1 (1974), 98-116.

infertile and **infertility** are the antonyms, respectively, of fertile and *fertility. As applied to a person, a couple, or conceivably a population, the terms designate the failure, whether voluntary or involuntary, to have produced a live birth— whether at any time at all or, as in some empirical studies, during a particular one or more reproductive cycles. The differentiation between *fecundity and fertility—that is, between the physiological ability to have children and the actual reproduction—is not carried over: as ordinarily used, infertile is synonymous with either "infecund" or "subfecund." In one study (Mosher, 1982), infertility was operationally defined as a couple's failure to conceive after one year or more of continuous married life during which no contraceptives were used. In the sample the percentages of American wives aged 15-44 were as follows:

	1965	1976
Surgically sterile	15.8	28.2
Infertile for other reasons	11.2	10.3
Fecund	73.0	61.6

The sharp increase in the proportion that had undergone *sterilization reflected a trend particularly among women near the end of their fecund period. The slight decline in the proportion classified as infertile masked a substantial rise in particular sectors—in particular from 3.4 to 15.4 percent among black wives aged 20 to 24 years.

REFERENCE: William D. Mosher, "Infertility Trends among U.S. Couples, 1965-1976," *Family Planning Perspectives*, 14 (1982), 20-27.

informed consent, as applied to medical patients or subjects of a research project, connotes that the willingness to participate is based on knowledge of what the permission entails. The concept arose as an ethical and legal norm after World War II, largely as a reaction against the horrors of medical pseudoresearch under Nazi auspices. In the United States some physicians see informed consent as, at best, an unattainable ideal, for how can the average layman really understand the ramifications of any suggested therapy? However, courts have sometimes set the criterion in terms not of professional opinion but of the judgment of a "prudent person" in the patient's place (cf. Gray, 1978). Without proof that the patient agreed to a course of action, physicians and particularly certain types of specialists have been subject to malpractice suits, with extraordinarily high judgments in some cases. Insurance against such suits has greatly increased medical costs, both directly through rapidly rising premiums and indirectly by the self-protective practice of performing probably unnecessary diagnostic tests and seeking second opinions on any doubtful point.

In the social disciplines American research involving humans is subject to similar controls whenever a project is funded by a government agency. Professional associations set up ethics committees but generally have not instituted meaningful procedures to realize the abstract norms they issued. According to one study, introducing a questionnaire on such sensitive issues as drinking and sexual behavior with an informative and truthful statement about the survey's purpose did not reduce the response rate either to individual questions or over all (Singer, 1978). The most troublesome characteristic of informed consent is that it is still in the process of being defined precisely, so that physicians and researchers must cope with an impediment of large but unknown dimensions.

REFERENCES: Bradford H. Gray, "Complexities of Informed Consent," *Annals of the American Academy of Political and Social Science*, 437 (1978), 37-48. Eleanor Singer, "Informed Consent: Consequences for Response Rate and Response Quality in Social Surveys," *American Sociological Review*, 43 (1978), 144-162.

infrastructure was coined in England in the 1950s to denote the internal administrative apparatus of a political entity. After Winston Churchill remarked that the term had been introduced by intellectuals "anxious to impress British labor with the fact that they learned Latin at Winchester," it was less used for a while. Its principal current meaning is in the context of economic planning, to designate the transportation, communication, power, and other similar facilities that make up the services underlying industrial growth. In the latter sense it occurs frequently in analyses of the relation between economic development and population growth, particularly in discussions of subsidized industrialization that did not take such ancillary features into account.

in-group and **out-group**, coined by William Graham Sumner in his *Folkways* (1907), was used to differentiate particularly in primitive societies "between ourselves, the we-group, and everybody else, or the others-groups. The insiders in a we-group are in a relation of peace, order, law, government, and industry to each other. Their relation to all outsiders, or others-groups, is one of war and plunder, except so far as agreements have modified it." The terms have been adopted by analysts of ethnicity and other characteristics of complex societies and modified to fit the different context. See also *ethnocentrism.

REFERENCE: William Graham Sumner, *Folkways: A Study of the Sociological Importance of Usages, Manners, Customs, Mores, and Morals* (Boston: Ginn, 1907).

injectable progestational agents, a type of *contraception, were rated by Christopher †Tietze (1970) as among the most effective. One field study was made in Thailand, where every three to six months 2,863 women were given intramuscular injections of an estrogen supplement. The method proved to be "very popular, highly effective, and safe" (McDaniel, 1968). A similar type of contraceptive is called NORPLANT; implanted under the skin, it provides protection against pregnancy for five years or more and, if removed, permits an immediate return to normal fecundability. The active agent is levonorgestrel, a synthetic progestin widely used in combination oral contraceptives. Of 816 women enrolled in a test program, only five became pregnant after three years. Sizable proportions, however, dropped out of the program—15.8 per 100 acceptors because of menstrual problems and smaller percentages for other reasons (Sivin et al., 1982). See also the June-July 1983 issue of *Studies in Family Planning* (vol. 14, no. 6/7), all of which is on studies of NORPLANT as used by various populations.

REFERENCES: Edwin B. McDaniel, "Trial of a Long-Acting, Injectable Contraceptive as a Substitute for the IUCD and the Pill in a Remote Region of Thailand," *Demography*, 5 (1968), 699-701. Irving Sivin, Francisco Alvarez-Sanchez, Soledad Diaz, Olivia McDonald, Pentti Holma, Elsimar Coutinho, and Dale N. Robertson, "The NORPLANT Contraceptive Method: A Report on Three Years of Use," *Studies in Family Planning*, 13 (1982), 258-261. Christopher Tietze, "Ranking of Contraceptive Methods by Levels of Effectiveness," *Excerpta Medica*, International Congress Series, no. 224 (1970), 117-126.

injury, which derives from the Latin words for "not just," is still often used in the original legal sense. In medical terminology it is the most general term for any kind of hurt or wound. Each year in the United States some 75 million persons are injured severely enough to require medical attention or to restrict their activity. Most injuries result from *accidents, particularly those involving a motor vehicle. In the mid-1970s some 150,000 persons were fatally injured annually, including 20,000 victims of *homicide and more than 25,000 *suicides.

Age-specific rates are high for children under 5, teenagers, and those aged 75 and over. These high-risk groups are similar in that it is difficult, whether for physical or for cultural reasons, to induce individuals to adjust their behavior. Most of the reduction in injuries has been achieved by improving the environment—of the working place, for example, and to a lesser degree of the home; but violence and recklessness are far more difficult to control.

REFERENCES: Susan P. Baker and Park Elliott Dietz, "Injury Prevention," in *Healthy People: The Surgeon General's Report on Health Promotion and Disease Prevention, Background Papers* (Washington, D.C.: U.S. Government Printing Office, 1979). Donald D. Trunkey, "Trauma," *Scientific American*, 249 (August, 1983), 28-35.

inner city, a loose designation in the United States of a city center, usually characterized by *slum conditions and often inhabited by a particular ethnic or racial group (cf. *ghetto). It is a journalistic term for what was once called a zone in transition—that is, an area adjoining the central business district with delapidated homes converted into rooming houses, intermingled with commercial and industrial enterprises.

instantaneous rate means, with respect to any variable, the measure over a single instant of time or, in operational terms, the limit of the change in the variable as the period over which it takes place moves toward zero. Virtually any demographic rate can be calculated in this fashion, rather than by taking the estimated midyear population as the denominator. For example, the instantaneous rate of population growth is calculated by the following equation:

$$r(t) = \lim_{\Delta t \to 0} \frac{P(t + \Delta t) - P(t)}{\Delta(t)}$$

$r(t)$ is thus the derivative of $P(t)$, or in a closed population the difference between the instantaneous rates of fertility and mortality.

institution, a pattern of significant social interaction as set by the values or interests of a society or one of its sectors. Some analysts differentiate an "association" (e.g., the family) from supportive institutions (in that case, marriage, inheritance, etc.); other analysts would designate the family as an institution. As defined by the U.S. Bureau of the Census, institutions include jails, prisons, and reformatories; homes for orphans, the aged, or retired members of the armed forces; asylums and hospitals for the insane; other hospitals for tubercular and other chronic patients; nursing and convalescent homes, but not general hospitals or other dispensaries of medical care where the usual stay is only for a short period. Residents are separately classified as "inmates of institutions," but the deaths of such persons are often assigned on death certificates to the place of residence before institutionalization. See also *group quarters.

integration is sometimes used as a rough equivalent of *assimilation and is thus divided into "cultural integration" (which might be better termed *acculturation) and "social integration" (which in that case could dispense with the adjective). The various more or less synonymous terms are seldom used precisely and then generally only by one analyst. For Herbert †Spencer, integration was the process by which the manifold is compacted into the relatively simple and permanent—the correlative of "differentiation." Something of this idea is often present, usually restricted to economic, political, or societal factors rather than culture. Most recently the term has come to denote co-existence in a residential, educational, or business place with no necessary trend toward a commonality of values or behavior. Thus, in a racially integrated school or apartment complex all races are accepted for admission but usually subcultural behavior patterns continue to exist in separate cliques. At the 1974 World Population Conference in Bucharest, the term "integrated population activities" came into being, loosely referring to family-planning programs linked to economic development, health projects, or other of the state's policy-oriented activities (cf. Files, 1982).

REFERENCES: Laurel A Files, "A Reexamination of Integrated Population Activities," *Studies in Family Planning*, 13 (October, 1982), 297-302. Donald N. Levine, "Cultural Integration," and Robert Cooley Angell, "Social Integration," in *International Encyclopedia of the Social Sciences*, 7, 372-386.

intelligence can be loosely defined as efficiency in adapting to novel circumstances or in coping with abstractions. Psychologists and other professional analysts of intelligence have not been able to agree on a more precise definition. In most of the vast body of writings, the faculty is defined operationally as the intelligence quotient (IQ), or 100 times the ratio of "mental age" to chronological age. By definition, an IQ of 100 is the norm, and in a sizable population scores range from about 55 to about 145, with a distribution approximating a normal curve.

That individuals and groups differ in measured intelligence has insistently posed the question, why? Answers tend to cluster at two positions, those who emphasize the influence, respectively, of biological heredity and social environment. If the genetic factor in intelligence is significant, the negative correlation between social class and family size suggests that the average intelligence of Western populations may be declining. Many studies with various instruments testing diverse populations have consistently shown a significant correlation, usually around $-.2$ to $-.3$, between the number of siblings and the intelligence scores of school-age children (Duncan, 1952). One reason is that less intelligent women are presumably less competent in the use of contraceptives (Udry, 1978). One of the most impressive demonstrations was tests on all 11-year-old pupils in Scotland in 1932 and again in 1947. At both dates the expected negative correlation was found between family size and average IQ, but over the period the scores *rose* appreciably. Those conducting the tests had no full answer to the puzzle (Scottish Council for Research on Education, 1949; Thomson, 1950). See also Cyril †Burt.

The heated debate in Britain over the alleged association between social class and intelligence has been still sharper in the United States, where the issue was largely rephrased as the relation, if any, between race and inherited intelligence. The controversy was initiated anew with a paper by Arthur Jensen, a professor of psychology at the University of California, Berkeley, in the *Harvard Education Review* (1969), in which he suggested that large-scale efforts to raise the educational level of lower-class students, white or black, were failing because of the important genetic component in intelligence (see also Jensen, 1973). The journal also published a symposium in which seven psychologists rejected Jensen's thesis. The controversy was broadened when Richard Herrnstein, a psychologist at Harvard University, discussed the issue in *Atlantic Monthly* (1971) and the English psychologist Hans J. Eysenck published a book also aimed at a general audience (1971). It was alleged that from the very beginning of intelligence testing its practitioners helped install or perpetuate discriminatory practices, but the charge was supported with less than adequate historical research (e.g., Kamin, 1974; Samuelson, 1975). A welcome relief from the scholarly bickering is to be found in the book by the American psychologist Sandra Scarr (1981); in large part it is made up of previously published papers, together with comments by those who disagreed with them, and the book ends with overall critiques by psychologists at the two extremes of the controversy, Leon Kamin and Arthur Jensen, with a reply by Scarr (see also Block and Dworkin, 1976).

With our present knowledge, taking the views of all the experts in the field, we cannot state whether group differences in IQ scores do or do not reflect a significant genetic basis. It is disturbing that some scientists hold that it would be best to maintain this ignorance (e.g., Bodmer and Cavalli-Sforza, 1970; Kamin, 1981). The National Academy of Sciences (1969) voted down a proposal that it encourage the study of "hereditary aspects of our national human quality problems"; for "there is no scientific basis for a statement that there are or are not substantial hereditary differences in intelligence between Negro and white populations," and unless all aspects of the environment could be made equal, "answers to this question can hardly be more than reasonable guesses." Those few competent scholars who have continued to do research on this tabooed topic have been victimized by the academic community; in the preface to his book (1973), Herrnstein urbanely recounts the appalling experiences to which he was subjected (cf. Holden, 1973). Yet Herrnstein insists only that the evidence demonstrates that individual differences in intelligence are in part genetic; concerning racial or other group differences, he has maintained a scrupulous agnosticism.

Issues of importance in public life on which experts disagree are nevertheless decided, often by those far less qualified to set public policy. In the case of the IQ the most influential decision was made by a judge of the U.S. District Court for the Northern California District in the case of *Larry P.* versus *Wilson Riles et al.* (1981). In 1971 a class-action suit had been brought against various officials of San Francisco pertaining to the placement of school children in Educable Mentally Retarded (EMR) classes. These special classes, established for those "whose mental capabilities make it impossible for them to profit from the regular educational program,'' were designed to help them adjust socially and become economically independent. Children were selected for the classes in part by their IQ scores, but a written parental consent was also required, and the law meticulously specified various other substantive and due-process safeguards to prevent children from being placed inappropriately. Blacks were clearly overrepresented in the EMR classes, allegedly because the IQ test was culturally biased in favor of whites. In his decision the judge held that ''an unbiased test that measures ability or potential should yield the same pattern of scores when administered to different groups of people,'' and the defendants were therefore ordered to ''monitor and eliminate disproportionate placement of black children in California's EMR classes.'' The IQ test, which the judge did not bother to read, was designated an instrument of race discrimination and banned (Glazer, 1981).

It is perhaps unfortunate that the IQ tests were labeled measures of ''intelligence,'' for in fact they are useful devices to assess what Brigitte Berger (1978) terms ''modern consciousness.'' Admission to colleges based on criteria that include IQ as one important element generally has let in those who can pass and kept out those who would fail in any case. Economists who stress the importance of *human capital have proposed programs to improve health and education, but they are also concerned with intelligence in the sense of the ability to adapt usefully to a society undergoing modernization. Help to people going through this transformation is more likely to be effective if one differentiates between those more likely and those less likely to make good use of new opportunities.

REFERENCES: Brigitte Berger, ''A New Interpretation of the I.Q. Controversy,'' *Public Interest*, no. 50 (1978), 29-44. N. J. Block and Gerald Dworkin, eds., *The IQ Controversy: Critical Readings* (New York: Pantheon Books, 1976). Walter F. Bodmer and L. L. Cavalli-Sforza, ''Intelligence and Race,'' *Scientific American*, 223 (October, 1970), 19-29. Otis Dudley Duncan, ''Is the Intelligence of the General Population Declining?'' *American Sociological Review*, 17 (1952), 401–407. H. J. Eysenck, *The IQ Argument: Race, Intelligence and Education* (New York: Library Press, 1971). Nathan Glazer, ''IQ on Trial,'' *Commentary* (June, 1981), pp. 51-59. Richard J. Herrnstein, ''IQ,'' *Atlantic Magazine*, 228 (September, 1971), 44-64; *I.Q. in the Meritocracy* (New York: Atlantic Monthly Press, 1973). Constance Holden, ''R. L. Herrnstein: The Perils of Expounding Meritocracy,'' *Science*, 181 (July 6, 1973), 36-39. Arthur R. Jensen, ''How Much Can We Boost IQ and Scholastic Achievement?'' *Harvard Educational Review*, 39 (1969), 1-123; *Educability and Group Differences* (New York: Harper and Row, 1973). Leon J. Kamin, ''The Science and Politics of I.Q.,'' *Social Research*, 41 (1974), 387-425; ''Commentary,'' in Scarr, *Race, Social Class, and Individual Differences in IQ*, pp. 467-482. National Academy of Sciences, *News Report*, 19 (June-July, 1969), 11. Franz Samuelson, ''On the Science and Politics of the IQ,'' *Social Research*, 42 (1975), 467-492. Sandra Scarr, *Race, Social Class, and Individual Differences in IQ* (Hillsdale, N.J.: Lawrence Erlbaum Associates, 1981). Scottish Council for Research in Education, *The Trend of Scottish Intelligence: A Comparison of the 1947 and 1932 Surveys of the Intelligence of Eleven-Year-Old Pupils* (London: University of London Press, 1949). Godfrey H. Thomson, ''Intelligence and Fertility: The Scottish 1947 Survey,'' *Eugenics Review*, 41 (1950), 163-170. J. Richard Udry, ''Differential Fertility by Intelligence: The Role of Birth Planning,'' *Social Biology*, 25 (1978), 10-14.

Inter-American Statistical Institute (IASI), founded in 1940, in 1980 claimed a membership of 434 individuals and 48 institutions from nations that are members of the *Organization of American States (OAS). It tries to improve the collection, tabulation, analysis, and publication of both official and unofficial statistics in the Western Hemisphere. One of its committees actively prepared for the 1980 censuses in the Americas. Publications include: *Estadística*, quarterly; *Boletín Estadístico*, monthly; jointly with OAS: *América en Cifras*, biennial, and *Statistical Compendium of the Americas*. Addresses: 1725 I Street, N.W., Washington, D.C. 20006; Casilla 10015, Santiago, Chile.

interferon, one of several proteins that the body produces naturally in minute quantities as a protection against viral infections (cf. *immunity). In a very small number of cases interferon seemingly brought certain cancers under control and even effected cures. It has been very difficult to verify such conclusions, however, because of the extreme rarity of the substance and its consequent enormous cost. If efforts to synthesize interferon succeed, it may well prove to be an effective therapy for at least some cancers.

REFERENCE: Mike Edelhart, *Interferon: The New Hope for Cancer* (Reading, Mass.: Addison-Wesley, 1981).

Intergovernmental Committee for Migration (ICM) was established in 1951 by sixteen member countries as the Intergovernmental Committee for European Migration (ICEM) in order to facilitate the movement of refugees from Europe and, through selective migration, to promote the social-economic development of Latin America. Its activities gradually expanded from this original purpose, and in 1980 it changed its name to the present one. The number of member states has grown to thirty-two, plus ten observers, and ICM has offices and missions throughout the world. Though not part of the United Nations, it cooperates closely with several of the Specialized Agencies. Since 1952, according to its reports, it has assisted in the resettlement of 1.6 million refugees. It retains its principal original functions—to plan migration so as to meet the needs of less developed countries and to further the transfer of technical skills through migration. Publications: *International Migration*, quarterly in English, French, or Spanish; *People for Progress*; *News Information Bulletin*, irregular. Addresses: headquarters, 16 avenue Jean Trembley, Casse Postale 100, CH-1211 Geneva 19, Switzerland. U.S. offices: 1346 Connecticut Avenue, Washington, D.C. 20038, and 60 East 42 Street, New York, N.Y. 10017.

Intergovernmental Coordinating Committee for Population and Family Planning in Southeast Asia (IGCC; also known as the Southeast Asia Intergovernmental Coordinating Committee) was established in 1970 to help coordinate population and family-planning activities in the region. It set up study tours, training courses and workshops, and a center for the exchange of information. Address: P.O. Box 550, Kuala Lumpur, Malaysia.

intermarriage, sometimes termed "assortative marriage," is self-explanatory in the abstract, but it is very difficult to relate it to empirical data (cf. Cavan, 1971; Eckland, 1968). All peoples live by rules of *endogamy and exogamy, but in modern industrial societies these rules are embodied less in law than in constantly changing custom. It is probable that short persons usually marry other short persons, or—to take a more significant example—that most marriages are between persons of the same social class; but deviant cases are seldom studied, if only for lack of data. Analyses of intermarriage in the United States pertain to crosses over lines marked by *nationality, *religion, or *race (cf. Heer, 1980). In some cases, however, the definitions are muddled. Someone who converts to Catholicism in order to marry a Catholic, for instance, may follow the church's teaching only nominally or more precisely than those born in the faith. Among American Catholics, divisions by nationality are becoming less significant, with a consequent greater tendency toward interethnic marriages (Alba and Kessler, 1979). Protestants and Jews who intermarry are closer in their years of schooling than those who do not (Kobrin and Goldscheider, 1978, chap. 6). In short, what is termed intermarriage may be homogamous along the dimension that the two persons consider to be most important. Two agnostics, one labeled a Jew and the other a Protestant, may in fact agree on all the moral issues subsumed under religion. Race is not consistently defined anywhere, and interracial marriages therefore usually include a proportion that could be otherwise classified. If a marriage truly flouts the norms of both the society and the two partners, one would expect it to be more fragile than intragroup marriages; and the slight evidence available suggests that this is so, if only because normative pressures create strains with which the partners may find it difficult to cope. In a work that goes well beyond earlier theories, Robert Alan Johnson (1980) explains religious intermarriage in the United States by the proportions of the two faiths in the population, the "social distance" separating the two religions, and their intrinsic endogamous tendency. In a detailed analysis of Protestants, he not only considers the major denominations separately, but ranks them in order to specify his variable of "social distance." The generalizations seem to apply also to interethnic marriage in the United States (cf. Gurak and Kritz, 1978).

REFERENCES: Richard D. Alba and Ronald C. Kessler, "Patterns of Interethnic Marriage among American Catholics," *Social Forces*, 57 (1979), 1124-1140. Ruth S. Cavan, "Annotated Bibliography of Studies on Intermarriage in the United States, 1960-1970, Inclusive," *International Journal of Sociology and the Family*, 1 (1971), 157-165. Bruce K. Eckland, "Theories of Mate Selection," *Social Biology*, 29 (1968), 71-84. Douglas T. Gurak and Mary M. Kritz, "Intermarriage Patterns in the U.S.: Maximizing Information from the U.S. Census Public Use Samples," *Public Data Use*, 6 (1978), 33-43. David M. Heer, "Intermarriage," *Harvard Encyclopedia of American Ethnic Groups* (Cambridge, Mass., 1980), pp. 513-521. Robert Alan Johnson, *Religious Assortative Marriage in the United States* (New York: Academic Press, 1980). Frances E. Kobrin and Calvin Goldscheider, *The Ethnic Factor in Family Structure and Mobility* (Cambridge, Mass.: Ballinger, 1978).

International Bank for Reconstruction and Development (IBRD), commonly known as the World Bank, is a Specialized Agency of the *United Nations. It was established at the Bretton Woods Conference in 1944 and began operations in 1946. Its announced purpose was to further economic development by lending money and providing technical assistance and related services to member states. Under Robert S. McNamara as president (1968-81), however, it moved increasingly to support the development of the *human capital of less developed countries, supplementing its loans for construction and equipment with advances for education and health (cf. Baldwin et al., 1973; Crane and Finkle, 1981). Since 1968 IBRD has also funded population research and the training of family-planning operatives. The Population and Human Resources Division conducts research and supports policy-based activities related to population, health, nutrition, and education as it affects fertility behavior; the Population, Health, and Nutrition Department finances programs in family planning, health, and nutrition; and such IBRD activities as agricultural and rural development, environmental affairs, and urban development also relate to population. Since 1977 the bank has had an advisor on women and development, who monitors the impact of its loans and programs on the status of women.

In 1960 an affiliate of IBRD was established, the International Development Association (IDA), to supplement the activities of the World Bank "by providing financing on terms more flexible and bearing less heavily on the balance of payments of the recipient countries." Loans are for fifty years with no interest but only a service charge. IDA is a separately funded legal entity but with the same president, executive directors, board of governors, and address. By mid-1980 credits to sixty-eight member nations totaling $20.5 billion had been granted to help finance delivery of electric power, transportation, telecommunications, agricultural and rural development, industry, and municipal water supplies, as well as educational facilities and family-planning projects.

The World Bank's development reports often are a useful source of data and interpretation (cf. International Bank, 1980), far better than the farrago of national statistics that other agencies too often publish quite indiscriminately. Among its publications are: *World Bank Atlas* (1979), with basic population data for each country of one million inhabitants or more; *World Atlas of the Child* (1979), in English, French, and Spanish editions, with population and economic data supplemented with those on infant mortality, child labor, and similar topics; *World Tables* (1980), with a wide range of population statistics, including not only life expectancy and percent urban of the population but, for instance, the number of acceptors and users of family-planning services (Anon., 1980). Address: 1818 H Street, N.W., Washington, D.C. 20433.

REFERENCES: Anon., "International Bank for Reconstruction and Development," *Population Index*, 46 (1980), 619-620. George B. Baldwin, George C. Zaidan, and Peter C. Muncie, "The Population Work of the World Bank," *Studies in Family Planning*, 4 (1973), 293-304. Barbara B. Crane and Jason L. Finkle, "Organizational Impediments to Development Assistance: The World Bank's Population Program," *World Politics*, 33 (1981), 516-533. International Bank for Reconstruction and Development, *World Development Report, 1980* (London: Oxford University Press, 1980).

International Catholic Migration Commission (ICMC), founded in 1951, coordinates the activities in forty-six countries of Catholic organizations whose work is related to migrants and refugees. Publications: *ICMC Migration News*, quarterly; *ICMC Newsletter*, quarterly; *Migrations dans le Monde*, quarterly; *Menschen Unterwegs*, 2/year. Address: 65 rue de Lausanne, CH-1202 Geneva, Switzerland.

International Classification of Diseases, Injuries, and Causes of Death (ICD) evolved gradually over more than a century—from 1853, when the first International Statistical Congress commissioned two of its leading members to work up an improvement on the alphabetical list of causes of death then in general use, to January 1, 1979, when the Ninth Revision of the ICD went into effect (cf. Israel, 1978). The criteria on which the classification is based reflect gaps in medical understanding, compromises among the medical and statistical practices of various nations, and additional compromises among the public-health practitioner's interest in ultimate etiology, the clinician's in the symptoms requiring his care, the pathologist's in the disease process, and the anatomist's in the part of the body affected. Since 1946 the *World Health Organization (WHO) has prepared the revisions that appeared approximately decennially, and the first edition of the ICD under its auspices, the Sixth Revision, included both morbidity and mortality, as well as setting comprehensive rules for making subsequent changes and additions. Adaptations have been incorporated in order to make the ICD suitable for medical audit systems and the evaluation of medical care, and other proposed changes would make the classification useful for maintaining health insurance statistics. These extensions, which made for greater detail, were countered by the wider use of the ICD in less developed countries, where subtle distinctions are generally irrelevant.

The classification used in the ICD is first into a number of broad categories: infectious and parasitic diseases; neoplasms; mental disorders; diseases of the nervous, circulatory, respiratory, or other systems of the body; congenital anomalies; "symptoms, signs and ill defined conditions"; and injury and poisoning. This listing is supplemented by two others, the first of which notes several categories of external causes, including traffic accidents and homicide; and the second, factors influencing health status and contact with health services. Within each of these broad categories are several narrower classes, which are then divided into particular diseases, conditions, or sites, each identified by a three-digit number. Thus, cancers of the digestive organs are classified into malignant neoplasms, respectively, of the esophagus (150), stomach (151), small intestine (152), and so on. Number 150 then is subdivided by two subclassifications: $.0 - .2$, by anatomical description, and $.3 - .5$, by thirds; thus, 150.4 denotes a malignant neoplasm of the middle third of the esophagus. For use in the United States, a supplementary volume, *Ninth Revision, International Classification of Diseases, Clinical Modification*, gives further detail with a fifth digit. See also *cause of death, *death, and the more important diseases and other factors in morbidity and mortality.

REFERENCES: Robert A. Israel, "The International Classification of Diseases: Two Hundred Years of Development," *Public Health Reports*, 93 (1978), 150-152. Jacques Vallin, "Pour une Approche Démographique de la Classification des Causes de Décès," in Université Catholique de Louvain, Département de Démographie, *Morbidité et Mortalité aux Âges Adultes dans les Pays Développés* (Louvain-la-Neuve, Belgium, 1983). World Health Organization, *Manual of the International Statistical Classification of Diseases, Injuries, and Causes of Death*, 2 vols. (Geneva, 1977).

international conventional total, as defined by the United Nations in its recommendations for the 1960 censuses, comprised "the total number of persons present in the country at the time of the census, excluding foreign military, naval, and diplomatic personnel and their families located in the country but including military, naval, and diplomatic personnel of the country and their families located abroad and merchant seamen resident in the country but at sea at the time of the census. This is neither a de facto nor a de jure population." For the censuses a decade later, however, the United Nations changed its recommendation; see *population.

REFERENCE: Shryock and Siegel, *Methods and Materials of Demography*, pp. 92-93.

International Federation for Family Health (IFFH), an American organization established in 1977, was called until 1979 the International Federation of Family Health Research. In 1980 it coordinated the activities of eighteen national and international organizations in less developed countries, focusing on the delivery of maternal, child-health, and family-planning services, with funding mainly from the U.S. Agency for International Development and the U.N. Fund for Population Activities. Address: Triangle Drive and Highway 54, Research Triangle Park, N.C. 27709.

International Fertility Research Program (IFRP), an independent American organization established in 1971. In 1979 it reported a staff of 195 and a budget of $4.5 million, principally from the U.S. Agency for International Development (AID). Its purpose is to identify and evaluate new methods of regulating fertility and to make it possible for persons, especially in less developed countries, to choose among several methods. With data compiled from 267 clinical centers in 47 countries, it does research on contraceptive methods, sterilization, and the distribution of family-planning means, and it trains health-care personnel. Publications: *International Journal of Gynecology and Obstetrics*, bimonthly; *Network*, quarterly. Address: Triangle Drive and Highway 54, Research Triangle Park, N.C. 27709.

International Geographical Union (IGU), founded in 1923, in 1980 comprised research or academic bodies in eighty-six countries. Much of its work is conducted through commissions and working groups, of which several relate to population studies. The Commission on Population Geography, established in 1976, was chaired by Leszek A. †Kosiński, from Canada, who in 1980 was succeeded by John I. †Clarke, from the United Kingdom. It publishes an irregular newsletter on its activities, which have ranged over the whole world. Other related commissions and their chairmen in 1981 include: Environmental Problems, I. P. Gerasimov, U.S.S.R.; Man and Environment, Gilbert F. White, United States; Comparative Research in Food Systems of the World, Muhammad Shafi, India; Agricultural Productivity and World Food Supply, Jerzy Kostrowicki, Poland; Medical Geography, Andrew T. A. Learmonth, United Kingdom; Rural Development, György Enyedi, Hungary; National Settlement Systems, Kazimierz †Dziewoński, Poland; Regional Systems and Politics, Rameshwar P. Misra, with the United Nations in Japan. There is also a large number of working groups on topics of a smaller range, including those pertaining to spatial organization, land-use systems, rural-urban divisions, and energy resources. Address: Geographisches Institut, Universität Freiburg, D-7800 Freiburg, West Germany.

REFERENCE: International Geographical Union, *Orbis Geographicus, 1980/84: World Directory of Geography* (5th ed.; Wiesbaden: Franz Steiner Verlag GMBH, 1982).

International Institute for Applied Systems Analysis (IIASA) was founded in 1972 as a multidisciplinary international research organization. The original membership, the academies of science or equivalent associations of twelve nations, had grown by 1981 to seventeen nations: eight in Western Europe, six in the Communist bloc, plus the United States, Canada, and Japan. With a staff of ninety, IIASA has conducted policy-oriented research on energy systems, food and agriculture, management and technology, and other similarly large topics. The program most closely related to demography is Human Settlements and Services, in which about thirty scientists were enrolled in the early 1980s. Directed for a period by Andrei †Rogers, this project has done research on such topics as health-care systems, manpower analysis, urban change, and population and resources. IIASA sponsors specialized conferences and larger meetings; and its many publications range from journal papers or pamphlets through collections of articles to sizable books, including approximately one hundred research monographs a year; *Options*, quarterly newsletter; *IIASA Publications*, quarterly. Address: Schloss Laxenburg, A-2361 Laxenburg, Austria.

International Institute for Vital Registration and Statistics (IIVRS) provides a professional forum for the exchange of administrative and technical information relating to civil registration and vital statistics. Its series of *Technical Papers* includes short discussions on procedures in particular countries as well as reports from regional conferences. Publication: *Roster of Specialists in Civil Registra-*

tion, Vital Statistics, Population Registers (1979). Address: 9650 Rockville Pike, Bethesda, Md. 20014.

International Labor Organization (ILO), founded in 1919, is the only major international body that moved from the *League of Nations to the *United Nations, of which it is a Specialized Agency. It is run by the International Labor Office (also abbreviated as ILO), consisting of the director general and his staff, which carries out the general directions of an International Labor Conference and a smaller but still unwieldy Governing Body. The International Labor Organization is unique in its tripartite structure, with representatives from the 141 member nations (in 1980) and also from employers' and workers' associations. For example, the United States delegation is made up of representatives of the government, the National Association of Manufacturers and the U.S. Chamber of Commerce, and the AFL-CIO, the major federation of trade unions. In the case of the Communist countries, of course, this distinction has no significance, and they merely send a larger number of government representatives.

Though the move was opposed by both business and labor representatives of Western countries, a Soviet representative was appointed to the ILO directorate in 1970. Thereafter the ILO's ostensible purposes, to improve the conditions of workers in various ways, were increasingly sacrificed to the agency's growing politicization. Under pressure from the AFL-CIO, in 1977 the United States withdrew from the ILO, returning in 1980 (Galenson, 1981). With the resultant loss of much of its income in the interim, the agency was forced to reduce its political activities, and it softened its overt anti-American stance. For the first time in many years, the ILO began to comment adversely on the conditions of workers in Eastern Europe, criticizing specifically the use of slave labor to construct the Siberian gas pipeline, Czechoslovakia's suppression of human rights, and Poland's crushing of Solidarity, the independent trade union.

In its programs related to population and labor policies, the ILO conducts research on the interrelation among growth of employment, income distribution, and changes in population size, structure, and location; and on how data are used to set population policy. It also encourages *population education. Its World Employment Program has conducted or sponsored research on migration, population growth, and labor policy (cf. ILO, 1981). In recent years the agency has conducted research on social-economic factors influencing fertility, the provision of technical assistance for family planning, and the training of organizers and administrators of family-planning programs (Anon., 1978; ILO, 1976; Partan, 1973). The serial publications of ILO include: *International Labour Review*, bimonthly; *Bulletin of Labour Statistics*, quarterly; *Social and Labour Bulletin*, quarterly; *Yearbook of Labour Statistics*, in English, Spanish, and French; *Labour Force Projections*, in English, French, and Spanish, irregular; *Women at Work*, biannual. Addresses: 4 route des Morillons, CH-1211 Geneva 22, Switzerland. Washington branch: 1750 New York Avenue, N.W., Washington, D.C. 20006.

REFERENCES: Anon., "International Labour Organisation," *Population Index*, 44 (1978), 213-217. Walter Galenson, *The International Labor Organization: An American View* (Madison: University of Wisconsin Press, 1981). International Labor Organization, *The ILO Population and Labour Policies Programme* (Geneva, 1976); *Population and Development: A Progress Report on ILO Research on Population, Labour, Employment and Income Distribution* (3rd ed.; Geneva, 1981). Daniel G. Partan, *Population in the United Nations System* (Durham, N.C.: Rule of Law Press, 1973).

International Planned Parenthood Federation (IPPF), which coordinates the activities of private birth-control organizations in ninety-five countries, was founded at a conference in Bombay in 1952, following two preparatory meetings in Stockholm (1946) and London (1948). It has had to straddle two conflicting points of view—that population control is needed because of food shortages, poverty, and other global problems aggravated by high fertility; and that each individual has the right to control the size of his family irrespective of broad economic or political imperatives. Its publications include *People*, a popular quarterly in English, French, and Spanish; *IPPF News*, a bimonthly house organ for member organizations in English, French, Portuguese, Spanish, or Arabic; *IPPF Medical Bulletin*, bimonthly in English, French, or Spanish, alternately with *Research in Reproduction*, in English; *Family Planning in Five Continents*, in English, French, or Spanish. IPPF, with its headquarters in London, has regional offices in New York, Nairobi, Lomé, Tunis, Colombo, and Kuala Lumpur. Addresses: headquarters, 18-20 Lower Regent Street, London SW1Y 4PW, England. Western Hemisphere Office: 105 Madison Avenue, New York, N.Y. 10016.

International Projects Assistance Services (IPAS), an American organization founded in 1974, reports that it has helped establish abortion and sterilization programs or clinics in more than seventy-five countries. It is funded by private contributions and the sale of equipment. Address: 123 West Franklin, Chapel Hill, N.C. 27514.

International Review Group of Social Science Research on Population and Development (IRG) was established in 1976 with funding from the Ford and Rockefeller Foundations and the Population Council; the Norwegian Agency for International Development, the Swedish International Development Authority, and the United Kingdom Overseas Development Administration; the International Development Research Center, U.N. Fund for Population Activities (UNFPA), and International Bank for Reconstruction and Development (IBRD). Carmen A. †Miró served as IRG's president, and Joseph E. Potter as associate in the project's Secretariat, located at the College of Mexico. Other members of the group at its founding were: Bernard †Berelson, John C. †Caldwell, P. B. †Desai, José †Encarnación, Jr., Akin L. †Mabogunje, Riad B. †Tabbarah, and Raúl †Urzúa. Having completed its assigned task, the IRG published its findings in *Population Policy: Research Priorities in the Developing Countries* (1980).

REFERENCE: Carmen A. Miró and Joseph E. Potter, "Social Science and Development Policy: The Potential Impact of Population Research," *Population and Development Review*, 6 (1980), 421-440.

International Sociological Association (ISA), founded in 1949, comprises some 1,000 individuals in fifty-six countries, forty-three national associations, forty-four institutes and research centers, and seven regional groups. It organizes a convention every four years, and publishes *Current Sociology*, mainly bibliographic, three times a year. Address: P.O. Box 719, Station A, Montreal, Quebec H3C 2V2, Canada.

In 1972 the ISA established a Research Committee on Migration, directed by Hans-Joachim †Hoffmann-Nowotny, a Swiss sociologist and demographer, and located at the University of Waterloo, Waterloo, Ontario N2L 3G1, Canada. Its purpose is to encourage scholars to do more and better research on the sociology of migration, and to this end it has incorporated an International Newsletter on Migration into the quarterly journal, the *International Migration Review*.

International Statistical Institute (ISI), founded in 1885, is an autonomous organization of approximately 1,100 individuals "distinguished for contributions to the development or application of statistics." ISI includes four sections: the Bernoulli Society for Mathematical Statistics and Probability (formerly the International Association for Statistics in Physical Sciences); the International Association for Regional and Urban Statistics (formerly the International Association of Municipal Statisticians); the International Association for Statistical Computing; and the International Association of Survey Statisticians (IASS), established in 1971 "to promote the study and development of both theoretical and practical aspects of statistical censuses and surveys." IASS publishes *Survey Statistician*, semi-annual; it is located at 18 boulevard A. Pinard, F-75675, Paris 14, France.

There are many links between ISI and demography, of which two of the most important deserve mention. In 1950, in cooperation with the Indian Statistical Institute, ISI established an International Statistical Center in Calcutta under the joint auspices of UNESCO and the Government of India. In 1972, in cooperation with IUSSP and with the collaboration of the U.N. Fund for Population Activities, the U.S. Agency for International Development, and the United Kingdom's Overseas Development Administration, ISI undertook the *World Fertility Survey. Publications of ISI include dictionaries, directories, books, and periodicals, of which the most important are: *International Statistical Review*, three times a year since 1933; *Bulletin of the ISI*, proceedings of the biennial meetings; *Statistical Theory and Methods Abstracts*, quarterly. Address: 428 Prinses Beatrixlaan, NL-2270 AZ Voorburg, Netherlands.

International Union for the Scientific Study of Population (IUSSP) had a rather strange beginning. It derived indirectly from the first World Population

Conference, held in Geneva in 1927 and organized by Margaret †Sanger, already well known as an advocate of birth control. The statisticians, biologists, and economists who attended the meeting, however, deemed it inappropriate to establish a continuing organization linked to so controversial a topic as birth control and so outspoken an advocate as Mrs. Sanger. They met privately in Paris the following year, and the IUSSP was officially founded there, with Raymond †Pearl as its first president. On the other hand, IUSSP's first conference was designated the "2nd," in succession from the one that had preceded it.

The organization lapsed during the Second World War; and when it was reconstituted in 1947, the rather modest association of professionals in various demographic disciplines expanded its activities considerably. The IUSSP now tries to interest governments, national and international organizations, scientific bodies, and the general public in matters related to population; to stimulate research and foster the dissemination of research findings; and to facilitate contacts among those engaged in population studies. The criteria for membership still restrict the association to professionals in the field, but over the years 1976-79 members' dues made up an average of only 7.5 percent of the annual budget. The balance came from contributions by most Western governments, several units of the United Nations, a number of private American foundations, and miscellaneous sources. In other words, the IUSSP both is an international body of scholars and has—with all that that implies—consultative status with the U.N. Economic and Social Council and UNESCO.

The presidents of IUSSP from 1947 to 1981 have included some of the world's major demographic scholars, as follows:

Adolphe †Landry, France
Liebmann †Hersch, Switzerland
Giorgio †Mortara, Italy-Brazil
Frank †Lorimer, United States
Alfred †Sauvy, France
D. V. †Glass, England
Dolfe †Vogelnik, Yugoslavia
C. †Chandrasekaran, India
Carmen A. †Miró, Panama
Ansley J. †Coale, United States
Mercedes B. †Concepción, Philippines

Much of the work of the IUSSP takes place or is reported at its periodic conferences. Those convened during the interwar period, two of which met in Fascist Italy and Nazi Germany, could hardly avoid the political issues that their sites implied. Counting the one that antedates the founding of the IUSSP, there were five conferences, as follows:

Geneva, 1927: *Proceedings of the World Population Conference, Geneva, 1927*, ed. Margaret Sanger (London: Arnold, 1928).

London, 1931: *Problems of Population, Being the Report of the Proceedings of the 2nd General Assembly of the International Union for the Scientific Investigation of Population Problems*, ed. G.H.L.F. Pitt-Rivers (London, 1932), 1 vol.

Rome, 1931: International Congress for Studies on Population, *Proceedings*, ed. Corrado Gini (Rome, 1933-34), 10 vols.

Berlin, 1935: International Congress for Studies on Population, *Bevölkerungsfragen: Bericht des Internationalen Kongresses für Bevölkerungswissenschaft*, ed. Hans Harmsen and Franz Lohse (Munich, 1936), 972 pp. in 1 vol.

Paris, 1937: International Congress for Studies on Population, *Congrès International de la Population* (Paris, 1938), 8 vols.

The self-descriptive brochure that the IUSSP now distributes ignores these earlier meetings and begins the series following the rebirth of the organization in 1947 (cf. Dechesne, 1974). These postwar conferences were in some cases discrete, in some cases held in collaboration with the International Statistical Institute (ISI), and in two instances (Rome, 1954 and Belgrade, 1965, but not Bucharest, 1974) were part of the U.N. World Population Conferences. Presently meetings are held every four years, with often regional or special conferences in the interim. Proceedings are not consistently designated and, in many libraries, are catalogued in a confusing manner. (In this work the minor differences in titles have been ignored and references are cited uniformly as ''IUSSP, International Population Conference, location, year, *Contributed Papers* [year]'' and ''World Population Conference, location, year, *Proceedings* [year].)

The publications were as follows:

Washington, 1947: International Statistical Institute, *Proceedings of the International Statistical Conference*, 25th Session, vol. 2, pp. 215-235; vol. 3, Part B, pp. 597-857.

Bern, 1949: International Statistical Institute, ''Compte Rendu de la 26ᵉ Session,'' *Bulletin de l'Institut International de Statistique*, 32 (1950), vol. 1, pp. 150-165; vol. 2, pp. 117-124 and 315-440.

New Delhi and Calcutta, 1951: International Statistical Conference, India, 1951, *Bulletin of the International Statistical Institute*, 33 (1951), vol. 4, pp. 1-254.

Rome, 1953: International Statistical Institute, ''Actes de la 28ᵉ Session,'' *Bulletin de l'Institut International de Statistique*, 34 (1954), vol. 1, pp. 221-259; vol. 3, pp. 1-432.

Rome, 1954: *Proceedings of the World Population Conference, Rome, 1954* (New York: United Nations, 1956-57), 6 vols. with papers in the original languages; summary report in English, French, and Spanish.

Petropolis, Rio de Janeiro, 1955: International Statistical Institute, ''Actes de la 29ᵉ Session,'' *Bulletin de l'Institut International de Statistique*, 35 (1957), vol. 3, pp. 119-490.

Stockholm, 1957: International Statistical Institute, ''Actes de la 30ᵉ Session,'' *Bulletin de l'Institut International de Statistique*, 36 (1958-59), vol. 1, pp. 66-73, 105-110, 119-121, and 137-142; vol. 2, pp. 1-339.

Vienna, 1959: IUSSP, *International Population Conference, Proceedings* (729 pp.; Vienna, 1959) and *Discussions* (134 pp.; Vienna, 1962), also in German and French.

New York, 1961: IUSSP, *International Population Conference, New York, 1961* (London, 1963), 1,372 pp. in 2 vols., also in French.

Ottawa, 1963: IUSSP, *International Population Conference, Ottawa, 1963* (Liège: IUSSP, 1969), 468 pp. in 1 vol., also in French.

Belgrade, 1965: U.N. Department of Economic and Social Affairs, *Proceedings of the World Population Conference, Belgrade, 1965* (New York, 1966-67). Vol. 1, *Summary Report* (also in French, Spanish, and Russian); vol. 2, *Fertility, Family Planning, Mortality*; vol. 3, *Projections, Measurement of Population Trends*; vol. 4, *Migration, Urbanization, Economic Development* (vols. 2-4 also in French and Spanish).

Sydney, 1967 (a regional conference): IUSSP, Sydney Conference, Australia, 1967, *Contributed Papers* (1,099 pp.); *Population Change: Asia and Oceania*, ed. W. D. Borrie and Morag Cameron; *Proceedings* (Canberra: Department of Demography, Australian National University, 1969), 212 pp.

London, 1969: IUSSP, *International Population Conference, London, 1969* (Liège: IUSSP, 1971), 3,050 pp. in 4 vols., also in French.

Mexico City, 1970 (a regional conference): IUSSP, *Conferencia Regional Latinoamericana de Población, México, 1970* (Mexico City: Colegio de México, 1972), ed. Susana Lerner and Raúl de la Peña, 1,167 pp. in 2 vols.

Accra, 1971 (a regional conference): *Population in African Development*, ed. Pierre A. Cantrelle (Liège: IUSSP, 1974), 2 vols.

Liège, 1973: IUSSP, *International Population Conference, Liège, 1973* (Liège: IUSSP, 1973-74), 1,380 pp. in 3 vols., also in French.

Mexico City, 1977: IUSSP, *International Population Conference, Mexico, 1977* (Liège: IUSSP, 1977-78), 2,243 pp. in 4 vols., also in French.

Helsinki, 1978: IUSSP, *Proceedings of the Conference on Economic and Demographic Change: Issues for the 1980s* (Liège: IUSSP, 1978), 1,240 pp. in 3 vols., also in French.

Jakarta, 1981: *International Conference on Family Planning in the 1980s*, co-sponsored by the United Nations Fund for Population Activities, International Planned Parenthood Federation, and Population Council. At the time of writing, the proceedings were not yet published.

Manila, 1981: IUSSP, *International Population Conference*, Manila, 1981 (Liège: IUSSP, 1982, 1983), 5 vols.

Florence, 1985: IUSSP, *International Population Conference*, Florence, 1985 (Liège: IUSSP, 1985), 4 Vols.; papers are either English or French with an abstract in the other language.

One might say that, with the trend come full circle, Margaret Sanger was posthumously vindicated. Successors of the scholars who feared the contamination of birth control now hold conferences in conjunction with its advocates and on planned parenthood.

Beginning in 1974, the IUSSP has organized or cosponsored a number of meetings, seminars, or specialized conferences, which generally also resulted in a publication. There have been also a series of other papers or larger books, published by Ordina Editions (Dolhain, Belgium); some of these are narrowly methodological, others on such broad topics as, for instance, *Population Growth and Economic Development in the Third World*, ed. Léon Tabah (1975). One notable series is the *Multilingual Demographic Dictionary*, which has appeared successively in various languages:

French (1958); 2nd ed., ed. Louis Henry (1981).
English (1958); 2nd ed., ed. Etienne van de Walle (1983).
Spanish (1959).
Italian (1959), ed. Bernardo Colombo.
German (1960), ed. Wilhelm Winkler.
Swedish (1961), ed. Hannes Hyrenius.
Finnish (1962), ed. Gunnar Fougstedt, Jorma E. Hyppölä, Tapani Purola, and Aarno Strömmer.
Russian (1964).
Czechoslovak (1965), ed. Zdenék Pavlík, Jaromír Korčák, Vladimir Roubíček, and Vladimír Srb.
Polish (1966), ed. Edward Rosset.
Portuguese (1969).
Serbo-Croatian (1971).
Arabic (1971).
Dutch (1980).

Address: 34 rue des Augustins, 4000 Liège, Belgium.

REFERENCE: Jean-Louis Dechesne, *Bibliography of IUSSP Conference Proceedings from 1947 to 1973* (Liège: IUSSP, 1974).

International Union of Anthropological and Ethnological Sciences (IUAES), founded in 1948, in 1973 set up a Population Commission made up of fourteen anthropologists throughout the world with a strong interest in population research and the president and secretary general of the IUAES as ex-officio members. Moni †Nag, the commission chairman, undertook as one of his first tasks to compile *Population Anthropology: An International Directory of Contributors and Their Works* (1978), in which about 400 persons in the subdiscipline are listed. Since many of them are quite young, often in the process of completing their doctoral work, the number suggests not the present importance of population studies among anthropologists but possibly its potential. Neither the IUAES nor the commission has a permanent location, but the commission can be addressed care of its chairman: Dr. Moni Nag, Center for Policy Studies, Population Council, 1 Hammarskjold Plaza, New York, N.Y. 10017.

interpolation, the technique of estimating values of a distribution at points for which data are not reported but which can be estimated from prior and subsequent points. For example, an equation fitted to the trend of census figures from 1940 to 1980 might be used to estimate the population in 1945, 1955, and so on. By special techniques, it is possible to estimate not only population size but also such other variables as the levels of fertility and mortality (Preston, 1983). Interpolation is contrasted with *extrapolation*, the use of an equation based on a series of known values to estimate one beyond their range. For example, from the equation fitted to the trend of census figures from 1940 to 1980, one might estimate the population in 1990 and subsequent dates. In the nineteenth century the line was usually assumed to be linear, but later such more complex trends as a *logistic curve were used to forecast future populations, though generally not with much success. See also *graduation; *population projections.

REFERENCES: Samuel H. Preston, "An Integrated System for Demographic Estimation from Two Age Distributions," *Demography*, 20 (1983), 213-226. Shryock and Siegel, *Materials and Methods of Demography*, pp. 681-702, 875-878.

interval, a brief segment of a longer time period; or, more generally, a portion of any numerical or otherwise ordered sequence. The term is used with particular meanings in several disciplines. In statistics, a "confidence interval" (or confidence region) indicates the range of probable error in an estimate; for example, if between 53.5 and 54.5 percent of a population is estimated to have a certain characteristic, the usual convention is to write this as 54 ± 0.5 percent, thus indicating the interval over which the estimate is valid with a certain degree of probability. In learning theory, an "interval schedule" denotes the times between responses and their reinforcement by a supplementary stimulus. An ordinal scale in which the differences between the numbers correspond in some way to the differences in the property that the scale is used to measure is called an "interval scale"—for example, the degrees of temperature or the dates of a calendar. In demography, the commonest use of the word is probably in the phrase "age interval," or that between the two end points of an *age group. The French phrase "*intervalle à cheval*" recalls the posture of someone on horseback: it means an interval that straddles a central point, such as, for instance, a person's thirtieth birthday. In an analysis of fertility various intervals are important— such as those between marriage and the first birth, between marriage and the nth birth, between successive births, or between successive pregnancies. See also *open-end interval.

intervening variable, a term introduced by the American psychologist E. C. Tolman (1951), he defined as one of "a set of intermediating functional processes which interconnect between the initiating causes of behavior, on the one hand, and the final resulting behavior, on the other." As used by sociologists, however, "intervening variable" is often synonymous with test factor—a real and measurable variable used to stratify a population in order to determine whether a seeming relation holds. For example, according to one survey, married women working in a factory had a higher rate of absenteeism than single women. When tested by the amount of housework each category had to do, the difference was explained (Zeisel, 1968). In demography the term recalls especially an important paper by Kingsley †Davis and Judith †Blake (1956) in which the very loose relation between social structure and fertility, which had generally been discussed by citing contrasting cultural characteristics of developed and less developed countries, was sharpened by indicating a series of intermediate variables, as follows:

I. *Factors Affecting Exposure to Intercourse*
    A. Those governing the formation and dissolution of unions in the reproductive period.
        1. Age of entry into sexual unions.
        2. Permanent celibacy: the proportion of women never entering sexual unions.
        3. Amount of reproductive period spent after or between unions.
            a. When unions are broken by divorce, separation, or desertion.
            b. When unions are broken by death of husband.
    B. Those governing the exposure to intercourse within unions.
        4. Voluntary abstinence.
        5. Involuntary abstinence (from impotence, illness, unavoidable but temporary separations).
        6. Coital frequency (excluding periods of abstinence).
II. *Factors Affecting Exposure to Conception*
        7. Fecundity or infecundity, as affected by involuntary causes.
        8. Use or non-use of contraception.
            a. By mechanical and chemical means.
            b. By other means.
        9. Fecundity or infecundity, as affected by voluntary causes (sterilization, sub-incision, medical treatment, etc.).
III. *Factors Affecting Gestation and Successful Parturition*
        10. Fetal mortality from involuntary causes.
        11. Fetal mortality from voluntary causes.

Of these eleven factors, four explained 96 percent of the variance in total fertility rate in forty-one diverse populations—namely, proportion married, contraception, induced abortion, and postpartum infecundity. The other seven factors may be significant in particular instances but not generally (Bongaarts, 1982).

REFERENCES: John P. Bongaarts, "The Fertility-Inhibiting Effects of the Intermediate Fertility Variables," *Studies in Family Planning*, 13 (1982), 179-189. Kingsley Davis and Judith Blake, "Social Structure and Fertility: An Analytical Framework," *Economic Development and Cultural Change*, 4 (1956), 211-235. E. C. Tolman, "The Intervening Variable," in M. H. Marx, ed., *Psychological Theory* (New York: Macmillan, 1951). Hans Zeisel, *Say It with Figures* (5th ed.; New York: Harper and Row, 1968).

intra-uterine device (IUD), a small ring, loop, Y-shape, or other compressible device, made of copper, silkworm gut, or plastic, which when inserted into the uterus expands to its original shape and acts as a contraceptive. Since it was first developed in the 1920s by Ernst Gräfenberg, a Berlin physician, it has been used in a dozen variations all over the world. How the IUD prevents contraception is not known precisely; it may be by impeding the *implantation of the ovum on the uterus wall (Tatum, 1972).

A small proportion of users, differing according to the device used, have reported bleeding or other side-effects, and others have ejected the device, some-times without knowing it (cf. *Dalkon shield). As with many other contraceptives, efficacy depends in part on the competence of the physician and the sophistication of the user, but even in advanced countries the record is less good than was first anticipated. For various samples of British women, the net cumulative rates over twelve months per 100 users ranged between 4.2 and 8.1 who removed the IUD because of bleeding and pain, between 0.6 and 15.6 who expelled it, and between 2.8 and 4.4 who became pregnant (Snowden, 1975). In the mid-1970s an estimated 15 million IUDs were being used throughout the world, and serious complications associated with their use occurred at the rate of only 0.3 to 1.0 per 100 women-years of use (Huber et al., 1975). One reason for the wide range in such data may well be the inadequate methodology (cf. Jain and Sivin, 1977). Of the various IUDs in use, the least dangerous and most effective seems to be the Lippes loop, designed by the Buffalo physician Jack Lippes.

REFERENCES: Sallie Craig Huber, Phyllis T. Piotrow, F. Barbara Orlans, and Geary Kommer, "IUDs Reassessed—A Decade of Experience," *Population Reports*, Ser. B, no. 2 (1975). Anrudh K. Jain and Irving Sivin, "Life-Table Analysis of IUDs: Problems and Recommendations," *Studies in Family Planning*, 8 (1977), 25-47. Robert Snowden, "Recent Studies in Intrauterine Devices: A Reappraisal," *Journal of Biosocial Science*, 7 (1975), 367-375. Howard J. Tatum, "Intrauterine Contraception," *American Journal of Obstetrics and Gynecology*, 112 (1972), 1000-1023.

intrinsic rates of birth, death, and natural increase are those derived from a stable population—that is, one that would be reached eventually with fixed distributions by age of fertility and mortality. These "true" rates, thus, reflect a population's fertility and mortality apart from the influence of its age structure.

REFERENCE: Alfred J. Lotka, "The Geographic Distribution of Intrinsic Natural Increase in the United States, and an Examination of the Relation between Several Measures of Net Reproductivity," *Journal of the American Statistical Association*, 31 (1936), 273-294.

invasion, the usually forcible penetration en masse of an area by a population different from the initial inhabitants—either temporary, as in a military incursion, or permanent. In bio-ecology, the term is used metaphorically to indicate the movement of a species into a new habitat; for example, when American salt marsh grass was introduced into Britain, it crossed with the native species to produce a new one, which invaded formerly bare tidal flats (cf. *ecology). In human ecology the term denotes the movement of new occupants into an area, such as that of immigrants into a quarter of a city. It is the first step of a *succession.

inverse projection, a technique developed by Ronald †Lee (1974) for work in historical demography, begins with the series of birth and death totals available from parish records and uses these to estimate the underlying structures of fertility and mortality. In what they term an ''aggregative back projection,'' E. A. †Wrigley and Roger †Schofield (1981) adapted the technique to include also estimates of net migration.

REFERENCES: Ronald D. Lee, ''Estimating Series of Vital Rates and the Age Structures from Baptisms and Burials: A New Technique with Applications to Pre-industrial England,'' *Population Studies*, 28 (1974), 495-512. E. A. Wrigley and Roger Schofield, *The Population History of England, 1541-1871: A Reconstruction* (Cambridge, Mass.: Harvard University Press, 1981).

Iran: Demographic Institutions

The University of Shiraz (formerly Pahlevi University) has a Population Center that conducts research related to fertility, mortality, migration, population composition and projection, family planning and population policy, the status of women and the family. Address: Department of National Development and Sociology, University of Shiraz, Shiraz.

Several units of the University of Tehran conduct research related to population. The College of Social Sciences and Cooperative Studies, of which the director in 1982 was Mohammad †Mirzaee, conducts research related to social-economic development and migration. The Institute for Social Studies and Research, of which Parviz Amini was director in 1982, has published life tables for Iran and a monograph on women's roles; and work was under way on studies of fertility and mortality in Tehran, divorce, ethnicity, and similar topics. Address: Khiabane Danesharch Seraye Jaleh, P.O. Box 13.1155, Tehran.

The government's Statistical Center conducts the country's censuses, of which the last was in 1976. It has been issuing reports in Farsi and English on each *shahrestan* (or subregion) of the twenty-three *ostans* (or provinces), with a full range of demographic data. Address: Tehran.

The government's Plan and Budget Organization publishes a *Statistical Yearbook* in both Farsi and English editions. Its Population and Manpower Bureau prepares population projections and other aids to formulating policy. Address: Dr. Fatemi Avenue, Tehran.

Iraq: *The Agency for Census and Population Studies conducts the country's censuses, the most recent of which was in 1977. In 1981 its director was Widad Hamoudi Ahmed. The agency is a unit in the Central Statistical Organization, which publishes an *Annual Abstract of Statistics* in English and Arabic that includes population data. Address: Mudīrīyat al-Nufūs al-'Āmmah, Ministry of Planning, P.O. Box 8001, Baghdad.

Ireland has been a demographic anomaly for several centuries. After the introduction of the potato from America, the population increased at an almost unprecedented rate (Connell, 1950; Ó Gráda, 1979; Daultrey et al., 1981; Goldstrom and Clarkson, 1981), and after the potato blight in the 1840s the people suffered the only major *famine in modern Western history (MacArthur, 1957). The subsequent departure of millions made Ireland the prototypical country of emigration, with a far larger proportion of females leaving than in almost any other international movement. Postfamine fertility was controlled by the chaste postponement of marriage that †Malthus had recommended, plus the usual concomitant that many put off a family commitment so long that they saw no point in assuming it at all. As late as the 1930s, almost a century after the famine, of persons aged 45-54 about a third of the males and over a quarter of the females had never married—again more than in any other Western country (Kennedy, 1973). In the usual interpretation the main reason for Ireland's anomalous history has been Roman Catholicism, but it is easy to exaggerate the church's influence. One motive for becoming a priest or a nun, for example, was a prior decision to remain unmarried.

REFERENCES: K. H. Connell, *The Population of Ireland, 1750-1845* (Oxford: Clarendon, 1950). Stuart Daultrey, David Dickson, and Cormac Ó Gráda, "Eighteenth-Century Irish Population: New Perspectives from Old Sources," *Journal of Economic History*, 41 (1981), 601-628. J. M. Goldstrom and L. A. Clarkson, *Irish Population, Economy and Society: Essays in Honour of the Late K. H. Connell* (Oxford: Clarendon, 1981). Robert E. Kennedy, Jr., *The Irish: Emigration, Marriage, and Fertility* (Berkeley: University of California Press, 1973). William P. MacArthur, "Medical History of the Famine," in R. Dudley Edwards and T. Desmond Williams, eds., *The Great Famine: Studies in Irish History, 1845-52* (New York: New York University Press, 1957). Ó Gráda, "The Population of Ireland, 1700-1900: A Survey," *Annales de Démographie Historique* (1979).

Ireland: Demographic Institutions

The Economic and Social Research Institute, directed in 1981 by K. A. Kennedy, had on its staff J. G. Hughes, J. Sexton, and B. J. Whelan, who analyzed migration and population trends. The wide range of its research included such topics as housing and poverty, farm families, internal migration flows, engagement and marriage, and the elderly. Address: 4 Burlington Road, Dublin 4.

The Irish Productivity Center has a Human Sciences Committee, of which Charles McCarthy was chairman in 1980. Its research, focused on industrial relations, also includes such demographic topics as urbanization and the emigration of professionals. Address: 35-39 Shelbourne Road, Dublin 4.

The public Medico-Social Research Board, which in 1981 was under the direction of Geoffrey Dean, has studied the morbidity and mortality of the Irish population, including such social-medical topics as mental health, alcoholism, air pollution and smoking, and unmarried mothers. Address: 73 Lower Baggot Street, Dublin 2.

The government Central Statistics Office conducts the country's censuses, of which the last was in 1981. It also publishes each quarter a statistical bulletin and a vital statistics report, each year a statistical abstract and a vital statistics report. Address: Ardee Road, Rathmines, Dublin 6.

irredentism, the ideology of a nationalist movement to retake territory claimed on historical, linguistic, or cultural grounds. Prominent examples include Fascist Italy's demand for the Austrian Tyrol after World War I, or Nazi Germany's demand for the Sudetenland in Czechoslovakia in the 1940s, or, in the 1980s, Somalia's for portions of Ethiopia and Kenya. Sometimes the term is also used to refer to competing claims within a single country, as by the Flemish and Walloons in Belgium. Whenever such a competition exists, it becomes much more difficult to determine the relative size of the populations that would validate the claim of one side or the other.

irrigation, the artificial application of *water to agricultural land in order to assist in the growth of crops, is by flooding, canals or ditches, or spraying. The cost can vary from a relatively cheap diversion of a flowing stream through the digging of wells to the construction of a dam system; but when projects are paid for out of taxes, the price to the consumer is in any case well below the cost. The economic return depends, among other factors, on the relative availability of water, the type of soil and climate, how much moisture the particular crop requires, and the demand for the product. Hardly any part of the inhabited globe would have the same population potential lacking its man-made water supply (Clark, 1967). Once built, irrigation systems must be maintained, and they sometimes cause new problems. For example, in Egypt the damming of the Nile's flow at Aswan was first conceived in 1890, completed in 1902, greatly enhanced in 1912 and again in 1934. The far larger Aswan High Dam, the most momentous achievement during President Gamal Abdal Nasser's administration, generated problems on a new scale, especially the proliferation of the blood flukes that cause schistosomiasis (Heyneman, 1979); see also *Egypt.

The social effect of irrigation systems has been depicted most dramatically in Karl Wittfogel's concept (1957) of a "hydraulic society," in which the centralized political power developed in order to build the works is used thereafter for the despotic control of the state. According to the emendation proposed by several critics, in certain places and periods the development of an agriculture based on large-scale control of the water supply aggravated an already existent tendency toward the centralization of all governmental functions (Wheatley, 1971; Kappel, 1974; Hunt and Hunt, 1976).

REFERENCES: Colin Clark, *The Economics of Irrigation* (Oxford: Pergamon Press, 1967). Donald Heyneman, "Dams and Disease," *Human Nature* (February, 1979), pp. 50-57. Robert C. Hunt and Eva Hunt, "Canal Irrigation and Local Social Organization,"

Current Anthropology, 17 (1976), 389-411. Wayne Kappel, "Irrigation Development and Population Pressure," in Theodore E. Downing and McGuire Gibson, eds., *Irrigation's Impact on Society* (Tucson: University of Arizona Press, 1974). Paul Wheatley, *The Pivot of the Four Corners: A Preliminary Enquiry into Origins and Character of the Ancient Chinese City* (Chicago: Aldine, 1971). Karl A. Wittfogel, *Oriental Despotism: A Comparative Study of Total Power* (New Haven, Conn.: Yale University Press, 1957).

Islam, "the act of submitting to God," is the preferred designation of the religion founded by Mohammed (A.D. 570-632) and based on the Koran. The estimated half to three-quarter billion adherents are mainly in northern and tropical Africa, the Middle East, and such Asian countries as *Pakistan, *India, Malaysia, *Indonesia, and the Philippines. By Western standards Islam is less a religion than a unitary religion-state. The Koran, a body of law called the *shari'ah*, and particularly the supplementary exegesis set a *sunnah*, or customary behavior, for both civil and religious acts. Of the several rituals that used to distinguish Muslims, alms giving is virtually obsolete and the five daily prayers are often skimped, especially in towns. Fasting during the month of Ramadan, on the contrary, is strictly adhered to and functions as the main social cement of Muslim communities; and the conditional duty of a *hajj*, or pilgrimage to Mecca, still confers honor on the returned pilgrim. Though in principle the judges' consensus (*ijma*) has become a third type of revelation, parallel to the Koran and the *sunnah*, in fact Islam has been highly schismatic. The main competitor to Sunni, orthodox followers of the *sunnah*, are Shi'a, who are split into numerous sects and subsects and are especially strong in Iran and among other non-Arab Muslims (Levy, 1962).

The Arabic word for "family" is not found in the Koran with its present meaning; among Semites the basic social unit was the clan. With his judicial function, Mohammed gradually created a body of family law, based only in part on existent practices; and elements borrowed later from conquered peoples were incorporated into this Arabic base. Though sympathetic scholars frequently point out that Mohammed raised the status of women from the then current norm of the Middle East, judged by modern Western standards it is still very low. According to the Koran itself, "Men stand superior to women in that God hath preferred the one over the other. . . . Those whose perverseness ye fear, admonish them and remove them into bed-chambers and beat them; but if they submit to you do not seek a way against them" (cf. *feminism). As the orthodox interpret such injunctions today, women are unfit for public duties and have virtually no civic role; see also *purdah. Their proper function is familial.

Traditionally a marriage is contracted between the groom and the bride's *wali*, or guardian; thus, the consent of the groom is required but not necessarily that of the bride. Polygamy, sanctioned in the Koran, has been common in all Muslim countries except Turkey and Tunisia, where secularization included the prohibition of plural marriage. Divorce is of two types, the traditional one by which a husband can repudiate his wife by a simple declaration, and the annulment of a marriage (or any other) contract, as by the wife's *wali*. Muslim norms encourage marriage and procreation; according to a dictum ascribed to Mohammed, there is no monkery in Islam. By the conventional practice, wives and grown daughters are more or less restricted to the harem, the Turkish form of the Arabic word for the women's quarters, and when abroad must wear the veil. A barren wife is a hapless creature, who to this day may induce her husband to take a second spouse, either in the superstitious hope that she herself will then become fruitful, or with the simple desire to bring children into her home.

The stand of Islam on contraception in its essentials contrasts sharply with the Jewish and Christian traditions, but the varying interpretations by different authorities have made the issue more complex; see in particular the proceedings of a conference of Muslim clergy and scholars from various sects and countries, sponsored by the International Planned Parenthood Federation (International Islamic Conference, 1974). Basic doctrine pertains to coitus interruptus, the classic method of limiting births. A man's desire not to have a child, though in itself licit, should not conflict with the right of the woman to have both children and sexual satisfaction. With a wife who was a free woman, thus, withdrawal could be practiced only if she gave her consent in a manner specified differently in various sects. With a slave-concubine, that permission was obviously not required; and with a wife who was the slave of another man, the intermediate status resulted in different constraints. The use of contraceptives by women, typically some sort of suppository that blocked the "channel of conception," was generally held to be licit if the husband granted his permission (Mahmood, 1977; Musallam, 1974; Sodhy et al., 1980).

With this tradition to guide them, present-day Muslims either accept or reject the use of birth control depending largely on their social class, with most lower-class respondents in various interviews holding that their religion forbids the planning of families and many middle-class respondents holding the opposite. The birth-control movement considered it a great victory when in 1936 the mufti of Egypt issued a *fatwa* (a formal legal opinion on canon law) permitting the use of contraceptives, and subsequently his interpretation of the law has been repeated by other authorities (Haddad, 1978).

In various studies of the fertility of Muslim populations, analysts have found it expedient to divide them into subgroups. For example, in his study of a sample of Muslims in Kanput, the largest city of Uttar Pradesh, M. E. Khan (1979) consistently divided all his data between respondents with hereditary and non-hereditary occupations—roughly, an index of traditionalist and modernist ways of life. In spite of consistent contrasts in social-economic determinants, the difference in fertility was only between, respectively, 237 and 231 live births per 1,000 married women in the fecund age range. In his analysis of fertility in Lebanon, as another example, Joseph Chamie (1981) emphasized that a simple Muslim-Christian contrast is not particularly meaningful. From high to low, the ranking of period and cohort fertility was: Shi'a, Sunni, Druze and Catholic, and non-Catholic Christian. The Shi'a were distinct from all the others in that they wanted more children, were least knowledgeable about contraceptives, and used them least. In all groups, however, the higher the level of the wife's education, the lower the fertility. Following what Chamie termed the interaction hypothesis, fertility levels depend both on official religious doctrines and on the social-economic levels of the religious groups (cf. Nagi and Stockwell, 1982).

Islam has been preeminently an urban religion. For Mohammed the clearest sign that the desert tribes had accepted the new faith was their settlement in towns. *Hegira*, which primarily denotes the Prophet's journey to Medina from which the Muslim calendar starts, is used today by Arab sociologists to mean also an in-migration to cities, with overtones of spiritual improvement. As Islamic tradition developed, to return to the tribe from the city came to be considered almost a kind of apostasy; for only in a city—a settlement with a mosque for Friday service, a market, and preferably a public bath—can all the requirements of the faith be properly fulfilled (Grunebaum, 1954; but see also Bouhdiba and Chevallier, 1982).

The urban-religious link, anomalous by sociological theories developed from Western examples, is paralleled by the relation between religion and modernization. In some sectors of Muslim societies, contact with the West has brought about a considerable secularization, especially among women. But more generally the amazingly strong and widespread Islamic revival has been evident not only in superficial details but in basic institutions. For instance, Western-style courts of justice have given way to a reconstituted *shari'ah*, with punishments ranging from lashing as a common sentence to the 1975 beheading of the Saudi prince who had killed King Faisal. It is at least the intention of the rulers of some Islamic countries to combine this revivified religion with Western technology, to benefit from the modern world without succumbing to what are seen as its grave defects. Virtually all writing on modernization—a good compilation is Benjamin Rivlin and Joseph Szyliowicz (1965)—is based on an assumed contradiction between those two elements, tradition versus innovation, an assumption that earlier made the development of Japanese society so puzzling to Westerners (see *Japan).

REFERENCES: Abdelwahab Bouhdiba and Dominique Chevallier, eds., *La Ville Arabe dans l'Islam* (Tunis: University of Tunis, 1982). Joseph Chamie, *Religion and Fertility: Arab Christian-Muslim Differentials* (Cambridge, England: Cambridge University Press, 1981). Gustave E. von Grunebaum, *Medieval Islam: A Study in Cultural Orientation* (2nd ed.; Chicago: University of Chicago Press, 1954). William Haddad, "The Legal Provisions Governing the Status of Women in Some Arab Countries," *Population Bulletin of ECWA*, no. 14 (1978), 26-46. International Islamic Conference, Rabat, Morocco, 1971, *Islam and Family Planning: A Faithful Translation of the Arab Edition of the Proceedings of the International Islamic Conference Held in Rabat (Morocco), December, 1971*, 2 vols. (Beirut: International Planned Parenthood Federation, 1974). M. E. Khan, *Family Planning among Muslims in India: A Study of the Reproductive Behaviour of Muslims in an Urban Setting* (New Delhi: Manohar, 1979). Reuben Levy, *The Social Structure of Islam* (Cambridge, England: Cambridge University Press, 1962). Tahir Mahmood, *Family Planning: The Muslim Viewpoint* (New Delhi: Vikas Publishing House,

1977). Basim F. Musallam, "The Islamic Sanction of Contraception," in H. B. Parry, ed., *Population and Its Problems: A Plain Man's Guide* (Oxford: Clarendon, 1974). Mostafa H. Nagi and E. G. Stockwell, "Muslim Fertility: Recent Trends and Future Outlook," *Journal of South Asian and Middle Eastern Studies*, 6 (1982), 48-70. Benjamin Rivlin and Joseph S. Szyliowicz, eds., *The Contemporary Middle East: Tradition and Innovation* (New York: Random House, 1965). L. S. Sodhy, Gale A. Metcalf, and Joel S. Wallach, *Islam and Family Planning: Indonesia's Mohammadiyah* (Chestnut Hill, Mass.: Pathfinder Fund, 1980).

island populations are by definition relatively isolated, and sometimes this common characteristic has seemingly set similar trends in the demographic rates. In particular, many of the less developed countries where fertility fell most rapidly during the past two decades were either islands (*Taiwan, Mauritius, Sri Lanka, Fiji, Cuba, Barbados, Trinidad), predominantly islands (Hong Kong, Singapore), or what have been termed quasi-islands—that is, peninsulas or isthmuses (Malaysia, Honduras), portions of an island (Haiti), or littoral countries (Chile). In an attempt to account for the decline in the crude birth rates of ninety-four countries between 1965 and 1975, Parker †Mauldin and Bernard †Berelson (1978) suggested incidentally that their geography was one relevant factor. However, as John †Cleland and Susheela Singh (1980) pointed out in a more specific analysis, this relation does not hold in all cases. The insular setting may indeed induce a greater awareness of population pressure, sometimes leading to an earlier or apparently more successful family-planning program; but a simple geographic explanation is here, as in most instances, just too simple.

In an analysis of the populations of microstates, defined as those with a 1970 population of less than half a million, John †Caldwell et al. (1980) covered the same material (see also *nation). Of the seventy-seven places so identified, 79 percent were islands and 15 percent were coastal; and it was largely their isolation that kept the microstates independent, rather than being amalgamated into larger countries. Most of the island microstates, moreover, can be regarded as outposts of Western culture; 85 percent were predominantly Christian, 91 percent had an official language taken over from Europe. In almost three-quarters of all the microstates, and especially the westernized islands among them, the expectation of life at birth was 60 years or more, often in sharp contrast to the populations of adjacent mainlands. In short, the demography of insular microstates is distinctive, with lower death rates, lower birth rates, and a greater propensity to migrate to developed countries. The principal reason is that, as parts of a European maritime system from a time when the West lacked the strength to penetrate continental areas, they were parts of colonial empires for a longer period than most mainland components (cf. *imperialism). In short, they are intermediate between Western and non-Western in the cultural attributes that help determine demographic rates.

REFERENCES: John C. Caldwell, Graham E. Harrison, and Pat Quiggin, "The Demography of Micro-States," *World Development*, 8 (1980), 953-967. John G. Cleland and Susheela Singh, "Islands and the Demographic Transition," *World Development*, 8

(1980), 969-993. W. Parker Mauldin and Bernard Berelson, "Conditions of Fertility Decline in Developing Countries, 1965-75," *Studies in Family Planning*, vol. 9, no. 5 (May, 1978).

isolate, a concept used especially in population genetics, is defined as a population island lacking well defined geographic, social-economic, religious, ethnic, or cultural boundaries. The crucial factor is that persons in an isolate tend to intermarry; the consequent inbreeding in a static situation can be mitigated by migration.

REFERENCES: Francisco M. Salzano and Newton Freire-Maia, *Problems in Human Biology: A Study of Brazilian Populations* (Detroit: Wayne State University Press, 1970), chap. 5. Jean Sutter and Léon Tabah, "Les Notions d'Isolat et de Population Minimum," *Population*, 6 (1951), 481-498.

isolation can be understood as an extreme case of underpopulation or, more commonly, as the opposite of *crowding, with a greater emphasis on psychological consequences rather than social-economic determinants. Among some species of lower animals, a population below a certain small number seemingly results in excessive inbreeding and abnormal sexual behavior (and thus a decline in fertility) and in increased aggression (and thus a rise in mortality). Man is a much more adaptable species than many others, but underpopulation can have similar harmful effects (Galle and Gove, 1978). A small population living in isolation does not build up an immunity against infectious diseases, and thus their effect when contact is established can be devastating. The most deleterious consequences become manifest in a child brought up in more or less total isolation (Davis, 1940). Persons living alone are much more susceptible to particular causes of illness or death (Chen and Cobb, 1960). Three factors seem to be operating on such individuals: the absence of mutual care (influenza and pneumonia), sexual promiscuity and self-indulgence (venereal diseases, addictions, and cirrhosis of the liver), and social isolation (suicide and accidents). The sudden imposition of such social isolation can result in what has been termed the "mortality of bereavement": the risk of dying within one year of the death of a close relative was seven times that in a control group matched by age, sex, and marital status (Rees and Lutkins, 1967). That immigrants acculturate more readily to their new country if they are not too numerous relative to the native population is a truism, but aliens living in isolation are likely to suffer from neurotic symptoms and to acculturate very ineffectively (e.g., Mauco, 1932).

REFERENCES: Edith Chen and Sidney Cobb, "Family Structure in Relation to Health and Disease: A Review of the Literature," *Journal of Chronic Diseases*, 12 (1960), 544-567. Kingsley Davis, "Extreme Social Isolation of a Child," *American Journal of Sociology*, 45 (1940), 554-565. Omer R. Galle and Walter R. Gove, "Overcrowding, Isolation, and Human Behavior: Exploring the Extremes in Population Distribution," in Karl E. Taeuber et al., eds., *Social Demography* (New York: Academic Press, 1978). Georges Mauco, *Les Étrangers en France: Leur Rôle dans l'Activité Économique* (Paris:

Armand Colin, 1932). W. Dewi Rees and Sylvia G. Lutkins, "Mortality of Bereavement," *British Medical Journal*, 4 (1967), 13-16.

Israel is in several respects a unique country. Though the return to the ancient homeland had a vague religious underpinning, Zionism was essentially a product of European *anti-Semitism. Most of the early migrants to Palestine came from the Pale of Settlement, the provinces of Tsarist Russia to which most Jews in that country were restricted. Theodor Herzl (1860-1904) lost his faith in the possibility of Jewish assimilation during the two trials of Alfred Dreyfus, the French army captain who, as a Jew, was falsely accused of treason. The case divided France into two camps of which one was virulently hostile both to Dreyfus and to all *Jews, and Herzl wrote *The Jewish State* (1896), the most important statement of Zionist aims up to that date. The realization of Herzl's dream was largely a reaction to the Nazi *Holocaust. Each *aliyah* (Hebrew for "going up"; one of the five major migrations to Palestine before the founding of Israel) coincided with a wave of *pogroms or other anti-Jewish acts. These pioneer movements are now featured in every account of Israel (see also *kibbutz); but according to the census of 1922, of the population of 752,000 in Palestine, only 84,000 were Jews (Friedlander and Goldscheider, 1979, chap. 2).

From 1918 to 1948 Palestine was under the control of Great Britain, whose mandate the League of Nations validated in 1922. As a gesture of appreciation to Chaim Weizmann, a Jewish chemist whose new explosives had helped Britain's war effort, the Foreign Office issued a statement that became known as the Balfour Declaration (Sanders, 1983). Britain declared its intention "to facilitate...the establishment in Palestine of a National Home for the Jewish People," provided, however, that "nothing shall be done which may prejudice the civil and religious rights of existing non-Jewish communities in Palestine." Both Jews and Arabs criticized the implementation of this British policy—the Jews because the restrictions on immigration and on the purchase of land they interpreted as contrary to the encouragement and facilitation they had been promised, the Arabs because any steps toward the establishment of a national home for the Jews were seen as a threat (cf. Peretz, 1981). In 1937 a Royal Commission on Palestine (the Peel Commission) concluded that the Arab and Jewish positions were irreconcilable and recommended that Palestine be partitioned into two national states, with Britain retaining its mandate only over the area of Jerusalem and a corridor from it to the sea. After the war, Britain passed the problem over to the United Nations, a commission of which made a similar recommendation—separate political states within an economic union and with United Nations control of Jerusalem. Thus, even before the founding of the state of Israel on May 14, 1948, the issues that were to come up again and again had been raised with both sides given official support (Nyrop, 1979, chap. 1).

How many Arabs there were in the territory that became Israel is not known, and the figures offered by various analysts differ according to their partisan sympathies. Israel won its independence not by a mere declaration but by winning a war in 1947-48 against invading Arab armies. The new state included much more territory than it would have had under the United Nations plan. The Negev (later returned to Egypt) was Israeli; the Gaza strip was under the control of Egypt; and Transjordan (which became the Hashemite Kingdom of Jordan) formally annexed the West Bank and East Jerusalem (cf. Schmelz, 1981). Between 500,000 and 600,000 Arabs fled during the war and went to a number of camps in Jordan and other Arab countries; some later entered their work forces (cf. *United Nations Relief and Works Agency for Palestine Refugees in the Near East). On the other hand, there was a sizable Jewish influx, especially from camps on Cyprus, where European refugees had been detained by the British. In an incomplete census conducted in October 1948, some 156,000 Arabs were counted, or 19 percent of the total; they had changed from an overwhelming majority into a minority. Their natural increase, however, is extremely rapid: mortality is low, with an expectation of life of over 70 years, and fertility has remained very high. In 1982 the approximately 690,000 Israeli Arabs constituted about 17 percent of the total population, but they were growing by 4.0 percent per year, as against 1.7 percent for the Jewish population (Friedlander and Goldscheider, 1984, Table 2). The proportion of Jews has risen only because of immigration, and once that faltered the trend would be reversed.

Palestine had been a very backward area of Turkey, and the people who lived there had little or no sense of a separate identity. Palestinian nationalism, which started to develop under the British mandate, grew especially as a counter to the Jewish nationalism of Zionism. Paradoxically, a rise in the status and educational level of Israeli Arabs may well have led to a growing disaffection (cf. Garcia, 1980; Nakhleh, 1977; Tessler, 1980). One factor has been the age structure implicit in the rapid growth; adolescents and young men, the sectors from which the more extremist nationalists are recruited, are proportionately very numerous compared with the generally more traditional older age groups.

Israeli Arabs have benefited from the country's relatively efficient administration and economy. Whether they are presently well off depends on the benchmark against which they are compared—whether the Israeli Jew or the average Arab in other countries. The very fact that the country is defined as a ''Jewish state'' has meant that no attempt has been made to assimilate non-Jews (cf. Landau, 1969). Israeli Arabs of both sexes attend public schools, where they are taught in Arabic and also learn Hebrew. Even so, in the mid-1970s their median schooling was only 5.9 years, compared with 9.5 for Jews; the proportion illiterate was 24.4 percent, compared with 8.1 percent of Jews. Israeli Arabs participate in the country's democratic processes, voting and being elected to the Knesset (or parliament), writing sharply critical comments on the government in their own press. (They might have been more effective if they had been able to coalesce around a single Arab party, but because they were not, their de facto political organ has been the Communist Party, which most Israelis strongly oppose mainly for other reasons.) In no other Middle Eastern country has the general run of people had similar rights; the Arab countries have agreed that none of them should grant citizenship to Palestinian refugees, in order to ensure the maintenance of their separate identity (Mar'i, 1978, p. 118)—but also to avoid a potentially hostile bloc like the one in Jordan that fought a civil war. Whatever material and civil advantages Israeli Arabs enjoy relative to compatriots in other countries, however, they have resented—it would seem, increasingly with the years—living in a country where the professed pluralism is always subject to some degree of Jewish dominance.

Nothing changed more fundamentally with the establishment of the state than migration policy. In its Declaration of Independence, the new nation declared that "the State of Israel is open to Jewish immigration and the ingathering of Exiles," and the first order of the provisional government was to redefine illegal immigrants as legal residents. The Law of Return (1950) gave every Jew in the world, with minor health and security exceptions, the right to immigrate. This absence of barriers, moreover, was only the most visible of the measures to encourage the ingathering of Jews that was at least implicit in Zionist ideology. Dov †Friedlander and Calvin †Goldscheider (1979, chap. 4) classified Israel's immigration policy into four periods:

1948-51, mass immigration based in part on enthusiastic hopes for the new state, in part on the deplorable conditions of Jews in European camps and Middle Eastern countries. Relative to the size of the receiving population, the migration was the largest in world history. Accommodations were available in the houses abandoned by Arabs who had fled during the 1948 war, but eventually the crush of people against very limited resources became insupportable.

1951-54, loose restrictions set on the basis of potential immigrants' age, health, and occupation. The decline in the number arriving was also due, however, to the economic conditions under which earlier immigrants had had to live during a considerable period of integration.

1955-67, with an economic boom sufficient to attract large numbers of immigrants from North Africa, Levantine, or East European countries. Though quotas were set according to the estimated possibility of absorption, enough came to change drastically the ethnic composition of the Jewish population.

1968-75, following Israel's victory in the Six Day War (1967), was a period of political security and economic prosperity. Immigrants came in large numbers from Western countries and the Soviet Union, with much money and attention spent on assuring their successful integration. In a typical publication by the Israel Central Bureau of Statistics (1981), immigrants from Latin America were classified by such background characteristics as age, religious observance abroad, and membership in Jewish or Zionist organizations abroad, and then by such indices of integration as type of work, housing, language, and social contacts. During this period, particularly after the Yom Kippur War of 1973, the political and economic security deteriorated. Immigration all but ceased, and in the years since 1975 officials started to worry openly about the relatively large number of emigrants.

The right of every "Jew" in the world to immigrate to Israel brought to the fore the immemorial question, Who is a Jew? (cf. Kraines, 1976). During most of its existence Israel has been governed by a coalition dominated by secularist socialists but including also representatives of religious parties, whose cooperation was secured by giving them control over such matters as the definition of Jewishness. In over twenty cases, rabbinical courts have affirmed and specified in detail their own designation: an individual is a Jew who was born of a Jewish mother or who converted to Orthodox Judaism and did not profess another religion. Those who could fit under this rubric could become Israeli citizens automatically, while for others civil and political rights were granted, if at all, only after legal battles. Members of the Bene Israel, a Jewish sect in India, were denied full status in Israel until the Rabbinical Council yielded to the Knesset's entreaty to make an exception. Another sect, the Karaites, were forbidden to intermarry with other Jews. The Supreme Court denied automatic citizenship to Brother Daniel, born a Polish Jew and converted to Catholicism, who disguised as a Gestapo interpreter had heroically saved many Jewish lives. In the case of Mrs. Rina Eitani, born in Germany and after her immigration a political activist who served with distinction in the Israeli army, Israeli courts used Nazi records on "Aryan" and "non-Aryan" forebears to prove that she had a Jewish father but a Gentile mother (cf. Talmon, 1965). Perhaps the strangest pattern of discrimination is against practitioners of Conservative and Reform Judaism, the denominations that in the United States and other Western countries furnish most of the Jewish support for Israel.

Class differences by ethnic background became marked after the sizable immigration from African and Middle Eastern countries. Helmut †Muhsam (1965) noted the five social-economic strata that are generally recognized in Israel, as follows:

   I. Born in Europe or America, immigrated before 1948.
  II. Born in Israel.
 III. Born in Europe or America, immigrated in 1948 or after.
  IV. Born in Asia or Africa, immigrated before 1948.
   V. Born in Asia or Africa, immigrated in 1948 or after.

In later years, this list was sometimes extended by distinguishing between Israeli-born of European and of Oriental parentage (e.g., Friedlander and Goldscheider, 1978). These differences by social class are typically reflected in the amount of education, the type of occupation, the level of income, and the type of housing and personal possessions, as well as in the levels of mortality and fertility. In many surveys, with samples too small for so detailed a classification, the full range is collapsed into a contrast between "European" and "Oriental" Jews. Though a difference remains between those whose forebears came from Eastern Europe or from the Middle East, the cultural gap has often been exaggerated (cf. Elazar, 1983).

With the decline of all mortality, the disparity in family size has been the most striking demographic difference. The variegated effort to assimilate African and Asian Jews to the Western culture that the first immigrants established in Israel has included, but only implicitly, an inculcation of the small-family pattern. The arrangement of marriages by matchmakers has declined in importance (Matras, 1973). Ignorance of contraception has been dissipated to some degree (Friedlander, 1973). And the fertility of Oriental Jews has shown a downward trend, not by the action of official family-planning programs, of which there are none, but by the free access to contraceptives and a shift in values (Friedlander et al., 1980; Goldscheider and Friedlander, 1981). There are two ways, however, of lessening the gap in fertility between the two sectors of Israeli Jews, either by lowering that of Orientals or by raising that of Europeans.

Though the pronatalism in both *Judaism and Zionism was somewhat mitigated by the large immigration, as early as 1962 the government established a Natality Commission under Roberto †Bachi as chairman (Friedlander and Goldscheider, 1979, chaps. 5-6; Bachi, 1980). Eventually its report led to the establishment of a Demographic Center in the Office of the Prime Minister, but this was soon incorporated into the social-welfare program, reflecting the shift that some officials wanted from pronatalism to a greater emphasis on family planning for the lower classes. Apart from such disagreements among both demographers and the general public, experience in many countries suggests that pronatalist policies are difficult to implement, and particularly in such a country as this. Israel already had family assistance of various types as part of its extensive social welfare. To deny free access to contraceptives would be politically inconceivable, and the minor limitations on access to abortion probably had little or no effect on fertility. If any pronatalist measure was successful, moreover, it would probably not raise the family size of European Jews so much as maintain that of Oriental Jews and Muslims. Most fundamentally, the rapidly growing population that pronatalists believe is needed for the nation's security would require yet more support in addition to the massive funds presently donated by the United States government and by Western Jewish organizations. See also *Israel: Demographic Institutions.

REFERENCES: Roberto Bachi, "A Population Policy for Israel?" with a "Rejoinder" by Dov Friedlander and Calvin Goldscheider, *Jewish Journal of Sociology*, 22 (1980), 163-185. Daniel J. Elazar, "Israel's New Majority," *Commentary* (March, 1983), pp. 33-39. Friedlander, "Family Planning in Israel: Irrationality and Ignorance," *Journal of Marriage and the Family*, 35 (1973), 117-124. Friedlander and Goldscheider, "Immigration, Social Change and Cohort Fertility in Israel," *Population Studies*, 32 (1978), 299-317; *The Population of Israel* (New York: Columbia University Press, 1979); "Israel's Population: The Challenge of Pluralism," *Population Bulletin*, 39 (April, 1984), 1-39. Friedlander, Zvi Eisenbach, and Goldscheider, "Family-Size Limitation and Birth Spacing: The Fertility Transition of African and Asian Immigrants to Israel," *Population and Development Review*, 6 (1980), 581-593. Sandra Anderson Garcia, "Israeli Arabs: Partners in Pluralism or Ticking Time Bomb?" *Ethnicity*, 7 (1980), 15-26. Goldscheider and Friedlander, "Patterns of Jewish Fertility in Israel: A Review and Some Hypotheses," in Paul Ritterband, ed., *Modern Jewish Fertility* (Leiden: Brill, 1981). Israel Central Bureau of Statistics, *Immigrants from Latin America One Year and Three Years after Immigration*, Special Series, no. 652 (Jerusalem, 1981). Oscar Kraines, *The Impossible Dilemma: Who Is a Jew in the State of Israel* (New York: Bloch Publishing Co., 1976). Jacob M. Landau, *The Arabs in Israel: A Political Study* (New York: Oxford University Press, 1969). Sami Khalil Mar'i, *Arab Education in Israel* (Syracuse, N.Y.: Syracuse University Press, 1978). Judah Matras, "On Changing Matchmaking, Marriage, and Fertility in Israel," *American Journal of Sociology*, 79 (1973), 364-388. H. V. Muhsam, "Differential Mortality in Israel by Socioeconomic Status," *Eugenics Quarterly*, 12 (1965), 227-232. Khalil Nakhleh, "Anthropological and Sociological Studies on the Arabs in Israel: A Critique," *Journal of Palestine Studies*, 6 (1977), 41-70. Richard F. Nyrop, ed., *Israel: A Country Study* (Washington, D.C.: U.S. Government Printing Office, 1979). Don Peretz, "Israeli Jews and Arabs in the Ethnic Numbers Game," *Ethnicity*, 8 (1981), 233-255. Ronald Sanders, *The High Walls of Jerusalem: A History of the Balfour Declaration and the Birth of the British Mandate for Palestine* (New York: Holt, Rinehart and Winston, 1983). O. U. Schmelz, "Notes on the Demography of Jews, Muslims and Christians in Jerusalem," *Middle East Review*, 13 (1981), 62-68. J. L. Talmon, "Who Is a Jew?" *Commentary* (May, 1965), pp. 28-36. Mark Tessler, "Arabs in Israel," American Universities Field Staff, *Reports*, no. 1 (1980).

Israel: Demographic Institutions

The Association for Jewish Demography and Statistics is a learned society that promotes the scientific study of Jews throughout the world by means of data on population and other characteristics. It is located at the Institute of Contemporary Jewry.

The Department of Demography of the Hebrew University of Jerusalem, under the chairmanship in 1980 of Helmut V. †Muhsam, is Israel's principal academic unit of demographic research and teaching. The department offers programs at three levels—undergraduate, master's, and doctoral. Address: Jerusalem.

The Institute of Contemporary Jewry was chaired in 1980 jointly by Roberto †Bachi and Usiel O. †Schmelz. Concentrating on the demography of the Jewish diaspora, it has coordinated research on the numbers of Jews in all parts of the world, collected documents and publications related to demographic data on Jewish communities, and published bibliographic information on this subject. Address: Sprinzak Building, Hebrew University of Jerusalem, Jerusalem.

The Israel Institute of Applied Social Research, founded in 1947, is one of the world's best known centers of survey research. It was established by Louis Guttman, who remained as scientific director. Surveys have been conducted on many questions, including family-size preferences, attitudes toward abortion and contraception, integration of immigrant physicians, health behavior, and Jewish self-identity. Address: 19 George Washington Street, P.O. Box 7150, Jerusalem 91 070.

The private Maurice Falk Institute for Economic Research in Israel, of which Yoram †Ben-Porath was director in 1980, has done research on such topics as participation in the labor force and economic determinants of family size. Address: 17 Keren Hayesod Street, Jerusalem 94 188.

The Ministry of Labor and Social Affairs has a Demographic Center headed by Simon Yair. Its announced purpose is to strengthen the family and stimulate fertility, and it has undertaken research to that end. Address: Hakiria, Building 3, Jerusalem.

Tel-Aviv University has the David Horowitz Institute for the Research of Developing Countries, of which Zvi Y. Hershlag was director in 1980. It studies the relations between Israel and the Common Market, and economic factors, including population, in Southwest Asia. Address: Ramat-Aviv, Tel-Aviv.

The government's Central Bureau of Statistics conducts the country's censuses, the most recent of which was in 1983. Included in the bureau is a Demographic and Social Division, of which Usiel O. †Schmelz was director in 1980. It is responsible for the collection, processing, analysis, and publication of population data. Annual publications, all in Hebrew and English editions, include: *Causes of Death, Immigration to Israel, Statistical Abstract*, and *Vital Statistics*. Special surveys cover a wide range of Israeli society, including both such standard topics as cohort fertility and labor mobility and, more unusually, the absorption of immigrants, university graduates, television viewers, and victims of crimes. Address: ha-Lishkah ha-Merkazit li-Statistikah, P.O. Box 13015, Jerusalem.

Italy: Demographic Institutions

The Italian Committee for the Study of Population Problems (CISP), a professional society, was founded by Corrado †Gini in 1928 to foster research in demography and related disciplines. Its president in 1982 was Nora †Federici. It sponsors periodic meetings, of which several have been on demographic history, and publishes *Genus*, multilingual, with one or two issues a year. Address: Comitato Italiano per lo Studio dei Problemi della Popolazione, Via Nomentana 41, 00161 Rome.

The Italian Society of Economics, Demography, and Statistics, founded by Livio †Livi in 1938, has a membership of about 450 individuals, 80 firms, and 120 organizations. It maintains a library, organizes conferences, and publishes the *Rivista Italiana di Economia, Demografia e Statistica*, a quarterly. Address: Società Italiana di Economia, Demografia e Statistica, Via Boncompagni 16, 00187 Rome.

The Italian Society for Historical Demography (SIDES) was founded in 1977 with Athos †Bellettini as president. It developed out of the former Italian Committee for the Study of Historical Demography. Address: Società Italiana di Demografia Storica, c/o Lorenzo Del Panta, secretary, Dipartimento Statistico, Università di Firenze, Via Curtatone 1, 50123 Florence.

A National Conference on Emigration, organized by the government in 1975, was commissioned to assess the drain of manpower from the country and to make policy recommendations. Four volumes of preliminary documentation were published in 1974, and the following year the proceedings of the conference were issued in five volumes. Included in these works were discussions of Italy's economy and employment patterns, the political significance of the migration, and statements of diverse views on policy. Laws were subsequently enacted facilitating the participation from abroad in Italian politics and the remittance of money to Italy. REFERENCES: Conferenza Nazionale dell'Emigrazione, *Aspetti e Problemi dell'Emigrazione Italiana: Elementi di Documentazione Preliminare*, 4 vols. (Rome, 1974); *L'Emigrazione Italiana nelle Prospettive degli Anni Ottanta*, 5 vols. (Rome, 1975).

UNIVERSITY AND OTHER RESEARCH INSTITUTES

Many Italian universities have graduate programs related to population studies. Graduate degrees in the following disciplines may include training in demography, population economics, social demography, population theory, or another specialty:

ECONOMICS: Bari, Bologna, Cagliari, Catania, Catholic University of the Sacred Heart in Milan, Cosenza, Florence, Milan, Naples, Parma, Pisa, Rome, Venice.
STATISTICAL SCIENCES: Bari, Bologna, Messina, Padua, Palermo, Rome, Siena.
POLITICAL SCIENCES: Bari, Camerino, Milan, Milan Bocconi, Pavia, Perugia, Rome, Teramo, Trento.
BIOLOGICAL SCIENCES: Parma.

Details are given here concerning only the more important research institutes.

The state University of Bari has in its faculty of economics a Chair in Demography, held in 1980 by Giuseppe †Chiassino. Research under his direction has been on Bari's mortality, fertility, and nuptiality. Address: Facoltà di Economia e Commercio, Università di Bari, Largo Fraccacreta 2, 70121 Bari.

The state University of Bologna's department of statistics has a Demographic Section, which in 1980 was under the direction of Athos †Bellettini. It has focused its research on the historical demography of Bologna and its region. Address: Reparto di Demografia, Dipartimento di Statistica, Università di Bologna, Via Belle Arti 41, 40126 Bologna.

The Catholic University of the Sacred Heart has an Institute of Economic Sciences, of which Giancarlo Mazzocchi was the director in 1980. Its research has been on population-economic relations in Italy and Europe. Address: Istituto di Scienze Economiche dell'Università Cattolica del Sacro Cuore, Piazza San Ambrogio 9, 20100 Milan.

At the same university the Institute of Sociology, directed in 1980 by Guido Baglioni, studies population, urbanization, and the work force, among other topics, and publishes some of the results in its journal, *Studi di Sociologia*. Address: Istituto di Sociologia, Università Cattolica del Sacro Cuore, Largo A. Gemelli 1, 20100 Milan.

The demographers in the state University of Florence's Department of Statistics, which in 1980 was under the direction of Carlo A. †Corsini, have concentrated their research on the analysis of fertility and nuptiality, and on various aspects of historical demography. Address: Dipartimento Statistico, Università di Firenze, Via Curtatone 1, 50123 Florence.

An Institute of Anthropology at the same university, headed in 1980 by Brunetto Chiarelli, has concentrated its research on isolated Alpine populations. This type of anthropometry overlaps with demography as this has traditionally been defined in Italy. Address: Istituto di Antropologia ed Etnografia, Università di Firenze, Via Proconsolo 12, 50125 Florence.

The faculty of statistical, demographic, and actuarial sciences of the state University of Padua has an Institute of Statistics, which in 1980 was directed by Paolo De Sandre. The research of the institute's members, reflecting their diverse interests, includes mathematical analyses of Italy's population, a study of the ideologies behind population policies, nuptiality, and sources for the study of the family. Address: Istituto di Statistica, Facoltà di Scienze Statistiche, Demografiche ed Attuariali, Università di Padova, Via VIII Febbraio 9, 35100 Padua.

The state University of Palermo includes an Institute of Demographic Sciences, which had been under the direction of Stefano †Somogyi, who retired in 1980 and was succeeded by Giovanni †Cusimano. It has concentrated on biometry and factors affecting the mortality of Sicily. Address: Istituto di Scienze Demografiche, Università di Palermo, Viale delle Scienze, 90128 Palermo.

The state University of Pavia has in its Institute of Statistics a Center of Economic and Social Research, of which Pasquale Scaramozzino was secretary general in 1980. Its research has been on factors, including demographic ones, affecting social-economic development. Address: Centro di Ricerche Economiche e Sociali, Istituto di Statistica, Università di Pavia, Strada Nuova 65, 27100 Pavia.

The state University of Rome has an Institute of Demography, which in 1980 was under the direction of Antonio †Golini. Its research on the population of Italy has produced works on mortality, fertility and women's work, spatial distribution, and two Italian-language bibliographies of Italian demography: 1930-1965, by Antonio Golini, and 1966-1972 by Golini and Graziella †Caselli. Address: Istituto di Demografia, Facoltà di Scienze Statistiche, Demografiche ed Attuariali, Università di Roma, Via Nomentana 41, 00161 Rome.

The International Center for Family Studies, a private nonprofit documentation center established in 1973, was directed in 1980 by Charles G. Vella. It has published bibliographies on delinquency and stated an interest in family planning. Address: Centro Internazionale Studi Famiglia, Via Giotto 36, 20145 Milan.

The Italian Center of Biostatistics, a private organization of which Stefano †Somogyi was president in 1980, conducts research in demography and related disciplines and collaborates with other institutions in publishing its findings. Address: Centro Italiano di Biostatistica, Via Filippo Nicolai 49, 00136 Rome.

The Center for the Study of Emigration is a private nonprofit research, training, and documentation institute, of which G. B. Sacchetti was president in 1980. It publishes a journal, *Studi Emigrazione/Études Migrations*, and monographs on emigration and the integration of Italians in receiving countries. Address: Centro Studi Emigrazione—Roma, Via Calandrelli 11, 00153 Rome.

In 1980 the National Research Council of Italy, a government agency, set up an Institute of Population Research headed by Antonio Golini. Its announced purpose is to analyze trends in Italy's fertility, mortality, migration, aging, and population distribution. Address: Istituto di Ricerche sulla Popolazione, Via Nomentana 41, 00161 Rome.

The National Institute of Rural Sociology, a private research center, organizes conferences and publishes monographs on the relation between population and economy in rural Italy. Address: Istituto Nazionale di Sociologia Rurale, Via Boncompagni 16, 00187 Rome.

GOVERNMENT STATISTICAL BUREAUS

The Central Bureau of Statistics (ISTAT) is responsible for conducting the country's censuses, the most recent of which was in 1981. It issues an *Annuario di Statistiche Demografiche* on vital statistics; an *Annuario di Statistiche Sanitarie* on health statistics; a comprehensive *Annuario Statistico Italiano*; *Le Regioni in Cifre*; and *Popolazione e Movimento Anagrafico dei Comuni*, which summarizes the changes recorded in the population registers. Address: Istituto Centrale di Statistica, Via Cesare Balbo 16, 00100 Rome.

One unit of ISTAT, the Population Statistics and Studies Service, was headed by Marcello †Natale in 1980. It has published studies on fertility, infant mortality, population distribution by age and sex, and similar topics. Address: Servizio di Statistica Demografica e di Studi sulla Popolazione, Viale Liegi 13, 00198 Rome.

A National Committee on Population (Comitato Nazionale della Popolazione) was established by the Office of the Prime Minister in order to coordinate and stimulate the work of ministries and agencies concerned with population. In 1980 its president was a member of Parliament, Maria Eletta Martini.

Ivory Coast: Demographic Institutions

The National University of the Ivory Coast established in 1972 an Ivory Coast Center of Economic and Social Research (CIRES). In the late 1970s it was under the direction of Jacques Pégatienan Hiey. Intended to contribute to the country's economic development, the center's research has been focused on agricultural and industrial production and the labor market. Demographic research—for example, on fertility and infant mortality—has been supervised by Alfred Dittgen. The center publishes a quarterly, *Cahiers du CIRES*. Address: Centre Ivoirien de Recherches Économiques et Sociales, Université Nationale de la Côte d'Ivoire, Boîte Postale 08 1295, Abidjan 08.

Demography is taught at the College of Statistics of Abidjan, which also does some research. Beginning in 1980, it has issued together with the Ministry of the Economy a series of monographs, *Études et Recherches*; the first was on nuptiality, and the second on population growth and forecasts. Address: École de Statistique d'Abidjan, Boîte Postale 3, Abidjan 08.

The government's Statistical Bureau is responsible for conducting the country's censuses, the latest of which was in 1975. In cooperation with the French government's Bureau of Scientific and Technical Overseas Research (ORSTOM), which maintains an office in the Ivory Coast, it conducts demographic surveys, including the country's fertility survey. Addresses: Direction de la Statistique, Ministère de l'Économie, des Finances et du Plan, Boîte Postale V55, Abidjan 04; Office de la Recherche Scientifique et Technique Outre-Mer (ORSTOM), Boîte Postale 293, Abidjan 04.

The Ministry also includes a Development Studies Bureau, which collects data and prepares analyses on which the country's population policy is based. Address: Direction des Études de Développement, Ministère de l'Économie, des Finances et du Plan, Boîte Postale 649, Abidjan 04.

Demographic data are also available in the yearbook of the Ministry of Public Health and Population, *La Côte d'Ivoire en Chiffres*, published by its Documentation and Health Statistics Bureau. Address: Direction de la Documentation et des Statistiques Sanitaires, Ministère de la Santé Publique et de la Population, Boîte Postale 341, Abidjan 04.

J

Jamaica: Demographic Institutions

The Department of Sociology at the University of the West Indies has a Census Research Program, which in the mid-1970s was under the direction of George W. †Roberts. It has conducted research on the demography of English-speaking Caribbean areas, concentrating on the study of fertility. Address: Kingston 8.

At the same university the Institute of Social and Economic Research (ISER) publishes *Social and Economic Studies*, which often includes papers on population. Address: Mona, Kingston 7.

The most recent enumeration of which the results have been published was part of the Commonwealth Caribbean Census in 1970. A census of Jamaica, scheduled for 1981, was to be administered by the government Department of Statistics, which also conducted the Jamaica Fertility Survey of 1975-76. The department publishes annually a general *Statistical Yearbook*, a specific *Demographic Statistics*, and two shorter summaries, *Pocketbook of Statistics* and *Statistical Abstracts*. Address: 9 Swallowfield Road, Kingston 5.

Japan is in Western eyes full of contradictions. The first and most important non-Western country to industrialize, it has retained a culture in which traditions derived from *Confucianism and *Buddhism not only persist but proliferate. The contradictions exist, however, mainly because Japan does not follow the dictum of Western social analysts that tradition and progress are totally opposed, that the rise of Gesellschaft entails the demise of *Gemeinschaft (cf. *Islam). For from the standard interpretation of the French or the Russian Revolution, as well as of the industrial revolution, Westerners have come to expect that revolutionary change can come about only by the abandonment or destruction of all prior beliefs and institutions (cf. Ogawa and Suits, 1982).

The transformation that Japan carried out was more successful than in any other country. Since the Tokugawa regime (1603-1868) had cut off the country almost completely from alien influences, the modernization during the Meiji era (1868-1912) started from close to zero. It began with a "restoration" in the sense that the Emperor Meiji was given not only all his prior secular authority but, with the rise of Shinto, a new or enhanced status as a living god. Industry and the state were administered mainly by samurai, a seemingly obsolescent class of warrior knights. The workers in textile factories were often young rural girls transferred temporarily to the towns; they lived in factory dormitories and, after they had earned enough to pay their dowry, returned home to marry and raise their children. The system not only afforded cheap labor but avoided the urban disorganization accompanying the destruction of the rural family. While the government protected the country's social structure, Japan absorbed wholesale Western technology, education, legal codes, and political administration. Within a few decades the country's industry was competing successfully with England's, and in two wars Japan defeated China and, yet more amazingly, Russia, thus acquiring a series of colonies.

From 1875-79, shortly after the Meiji regime was installed, to 1915-19, when the initial phase of rapid industrialization was over, the population increased from about 35.1 million to about 55.5 million. From inadequate statistics, it seems that over this period the death rate remained constant at around 20, but the birth rate rose from 25 to well over 30. The natural increase thus began its stupendous acceleration—which, in later years with better records, would become world-famous—not from a decline in mortality, as posited in the theory of the *demographic transition, but from a rise in fertility (Taeuber, 1958, pp. 232-233).

The context of fertility was Japan's family, which retained to a remarkable degree its traditional hierarchical structure. The terms *oya* (parent) and *ko* (child) and the relation that they connote spread to such nonkin pairs as boss and worker, employer and employee, leader and follower (Passin, 1968). Many unrelated persons were brought into the family directly by *adoption, which has a much wider function in Japan than in the West. The gradual disappearance of *infanticide, which until the last decades of the nineteenth century was the standard lower-class means of family limitation, was one reason for the apparent rise in fertility. More fundamentally, when Japan adapted China's familistic culture to the straitened economy of the islands, the dominant goal was still to maintain continuity in the male line. But whereas in China this was realized in principle through a numerous progeny, Japan sacrificed numbers to quality (Taeuber, 1958, p. 31; see also Hanley, 1972, 1974; Eng and Smith, 1976).

After Japan's defeat in World War II, when some 6.3 million members of the armed forces and repatriated civilians returned to the homeland, population pressure became unbearable. Following the reunion of families, fertility rose, while mortality continued to decline. Under a 1948 law enacted originally for eugenic purposes, *abortion clinics were established throughout the country, and by 1958 the number of abortions rose to 1.1 million, or 682 per 1,000 live births (Muramatsu, 1960). The birth rate was halved in one decade, and eventually Japan's officials recommended policies that would avoid what was seen as an imminent labor shortage (Kurushima, 1970; Nizard, 1970).

Japan is a modern country but not a Western one. In 1890 an English scholar summed up his many years in Meiji Japan: "The national character persists intact, manifesting no change in essentials. Circumstances have deflected it into new channels" (Chamberlain, 1890, p. 6). And most Japanists would still agree with Herbert Passin (1968) that "it is still possible to say much the same thing today."

REFERENCES: Basil Hall Chamberlain, *Things Japanese: Being Notes on Various Subjects Connected with Japan, for the Use of Travellers and Others* (London: K. Paul, Trench, Trubner, 1890; 6th ed., 1939); reprinted as *Japanese Things*, with the same subtitle (Rutland, Vt.: Tuttle, 1971). Robert Y. Eng and Thomas C. Smith, "Peasant Families and Population Control in Eighteenth-Century Japan," *Journal of Interdisciplinary History*, 6 (1976), 417-445. Susan B. Hanley, "Toward an Analysis of Demographic and Economic Change in Tokugawa Japan: A Village Study," *Journal of Asian Studies*, 31 (1972), 515-537; "Fertility, Mortality, and Life Expectancy in Pre-modern Japan," *Population Studies*, 28 (1974), 127-142. Hidesaburo Kurushima, "An Opinion on the Reproductive Trends in Our Country," *Studies in Family Planning*, no. 56 (1970). Minoru Muramatsu, "Effect of Induced Abortion on the Reduction of Births in Japan," *Milbank Memorial Fund Quarterly*, 38 (1960), 153-166. Alfred Nizard, "Le Japon Vingt Ans après la Loi Eugénique," *Population*, 25 (1970), 1236-1262. Naohiro Ogawa and Daniel B. Suits, "Lessons on Population and Economic Change from the Japanese Meiji Experience," *Developing Economies*, 20 (1982), 196-219. Herbert Passin, "Japanese Society," *International Encyclopedia of the Social Sciences*, 8, 236-249. Taeuber, *The Population of Japan*.

Japan: Demographic Institutions

The Asian Statistical Institute operates, with funding from the U.N. Economic Commission for Asia and the Far East (ECAFE), to train statisticians in less developed countries of the region. Its headquarters is in the office of the Institute of Developing Economies.

The Japanese International Cooperation Agency, a government agency, was established in 1974 as successor to the Overseas Technical Cooperation Agency, which had funded family-planning programs abroad from 1969. The new agency has continued aid to the Philippines and Thailand, as well as to other less developed countries, through the U.N. Fund for Population Activities (UNFPA) and the International Planned Parenthood Federation (IPPF). Address: 2-1 Nishi-Shinjuku, Shinjuku-ku, Tokyo 162.

The Japanese Organization for International Cooperation in Family Planning, a private agency with some government funding, supports family-planning efforts in other countries. Address: c/o Hoken Kaikan, 2-1 Sadohara-cho, Ichigaya, Shinjuku-ku, Tokyo 162.

UNIVERSITY AND OTHER RESEARCH INSTITUTES

Hitotsubashi University has an Institute of Economic Research, founded in 1940 and directed in 1980 by Masakichi Ito. Its general research is narrowly focused on Japan's economy, but its documentation center is developing a data bank of Japanese historical statistics, including those on population. Address: 2-1 Naka, Kunitachi-shi, Tokyo 186.

The Institute of Developing Economies, a government agency, compiles and analyzes the population data of less developed countries, especially in its Statistics Department, headed in the late 1970s by Yamazaki Shigeru. Monographs have been published, in both Japanese and English editions, on the world's population structures and the work forces. The institute has an English-language journal, *The Developing Economies*. Address: 42 Honmura-cho, Ichigaya, Shinjuku-ku, Tokyo 162.

The Institute of Population Problems in the Ministry of Health and Welfare was under the direction of †Shinozaki Nobuo in 1980. It is the most active population research unit in the country and has undertaken since its inception in 1939 a large number of studies on both Japan and other countries. It regularly conducts fertility surveys and in 1978 published the results of the seventh in the series. Its mainly Japanese-language publications include: *Jinkō Mondai Kenkyū*, Journal of Population Problems, a quarterly; *Research series*, irregular; *English Pamphlet Series*, irregular; *Field survey report*, annual; *Selected demographic statistics*, semi-annual. Address: 2-2-1 Kasumigaseki, Chiyoda-ku, Tokyo 101.

Mainichi Newspapers has sponsored a Population Problems Research Council that, under the direction in the mid-1970s of †Mihara Shinichi, has surveyed public opinion on family planning every two years. Address: 1-1 Hitotsubashi, Chiyoda-ku, Tokyo 101.

In 1979 the private Nihon University set up a Population Research Institute headed by Ide Susumu. Its purpose is to carry out research on the relation between population growth and social-economic change, especially but not exclusively in Japan. Address: 2-6-16 Nishikanda, Chiyoda-ku, Tokyo 101.

GOVERNMENT STATISTICAL BUREAUS

The Ministry of Health and Welfare publishes annually in both Japanese and English editions a very full compilation of *Vital Statistics*. Address: 42 Ichigaya-Honmachi, Shinjuku-ku, Tokyo.

The Statistics Bureau of the Prime Minister's Office, headed in 1980 by Shimamura Shiro, is responsible for conducting the country's censuses, the latest of which was in 1980. Annual reports are published in both Japanese and English on current population estimates, population growth, and internal migration. The annual *Statistical Handbook* and *Statistical Yearbook* include basic population data. Address: 95 Wakamatsu-cho, Shinjuku-ku, Tokyo 162.

Japanese Americans, a small minority, are of general interest because some of their characteristics challenge theses based on more numerous nationalities. As Asian immigrants to a population predominantly of European origin, they were set apart by their religious beliefs, cultural attributes, and social organizations— as well as their race, under which all other attributes were often subsumed; see *population abroad. Like *Chinese Americans, they were barred for some decades from citizenship, the ownership of agricultural land, and many higher-level occupations. And Japanese Americans were also seen as representatives of an enemy country. During World War II, with hardly a facade of legal procedure or justification, all those residing in the Western states were incarcerated in concentration camps. In terms not of past history but of the actual experiences of living persons, the Japanese have been subjected to the worst discrimination, the greatest frustrations, of all American minorities. Ordinarily such treatment results in a pattern of poor education, low income, high crime rate, and unstable family life, with each of these comprising one component of a self-sustaining slum. Yet compared with all other identifiable ethnic groups, including native-born whites of native-born parents, Japanese Americans have the most years of schooling and probably the least crime. Their stable community life and remarkable upward mobility were realized, moreover, by their own unaided efforts.

Except for small numbers in New York City and Chicago, virtually all Japanese Americans live in the West, especially in California and Hawaii. Of the slightly more than 700,000 enumerated in 1980, 538,000 lived in the Pacific states. Apart from a few genetic ailments and perhaps some mental illnesses, they are typically healthier than the rest of the American population, and their age-specific mortality is significantly lower. Fertility is also low; this is probably for the same reason that *Jews have small families. Those trying to rise in social status typically reduce their family burdens; and if this upward mobility is impeded by discrimination focused on a particular ethnic group, then its fertility is likely to be depressed even more (Goldscheider and Uhlenberg, 1969).

REFERENCES: Calvin Goldscheider and Peter R. Uhlenberg, "Minority Group Status and Fertility," *American Journal of Sociology*, 74 (1969), 361-375. William Petersen, *Japanese Americans* (New York: Random House, 1971); "Chinese Americans and Japanese Americans," in Thomas Sowell, ed., *Essays and Data on American Ethnic Groups* (Washington, D.C.: Urban Institute, 1978).

Jews were once defined simply as a religious grouping, those who adhered to the tenets of *Judaism. They were so identified in Tsarist Russia, which can be taken as the main source of modern Jews' history; and for more than a century state and church officials there undertook to convert them to Christianity. In 1791 Catherine the Great instituted the "Pale of Settlement," an area in southern and western Russia to which Jews were henceforth restricted. Subsequently they were hindered in the practice of their religion, excluded from most public offices, required to serve in the army under harsher conditions and for longer terms (during the reign of Alexander I from the age of 12), and restricted to quotas as students in secondary and higher schools. These official acts were recurrently reinforced by quasi-official outbursts of looting and raping (cf. *pogrom). A high proportion of the 5.2 million Russian Jews enumerated in the census of 1897 had been driven into penury in their *ghettos. Isolation from the Gentile world reinforced the authority of Orthodoxy, which until the middle of the nineteenth century hardly anyone in Russia questioned. Persecution was not an effective means of conversion (Pakalns, 1961).

The challenge to Orthodoxy came from within, particularly in the movement known as *Haskalah*, or Enlightenment. This was a local version of eighteenth-century secularist philosophy, of which elements were translated into Hebrew and spread from Germany through large sectors of Eastern Europe (Zborowski and Herzog, 1952, pp. 161-164). Boys being trained in their religion, and sometimes their teachers as well, would surreptitiously read forbidden works—including, as a prominent later example, a popularization of †Darwin's theory of evolution. Secularist ideas led to the formation of political parties, of which the two main ones were "the Bund" (the General Jewish Workers' Bund of Russia and Poland, founded in 1897), which in ostensible accord with Marxist principles called for a socialist commonwealth in which Jews would enjoy "cultural autonomy" with Yiddish as their official native language, and Zionism, the largest of the Jewish movements, with some 300,000 adherents by 1917. Smaller parties tried to reconcile the two with a "proletarian Zionism," or by calling for the establishment of a Jewish state in a territory other than Palestine. All socialists defended Yiddish as the language of the masses, but they were attacked by Hebraists who denounced Yiddish as a debased and ugly amalgam. In short, before Russian Jews began to emigrate in their hundreds of thousands, a large majority had absorbed some portions of secular Western culture.

Most of the emigrants followed the lead of Jews already resident in the West and became assimilationists. A German, French, or American Jew, they held, is distinguished only by his religion or, in many cases, not even that. Only a diminishing minority of the Orthodox continued to defend traditional beliefs. For anti-Semites accustomed to attacking Jews as adherents of a false religion, this secularization posed a problem. In his memoirs Hellmut von Gerlach, a member of the Reichstag during the 1890s, noted that it failed to pass an anti-Jewish law because those in favor of such legislation could not agree on a workable definition of "Jew." Eventually the problem was solved by positing a continuity of Jewish identity as a *race. Thus, under *National Socialism a "Jew" was defined either as someone who practiced Judaism or as someone who was descended from three or four Jewish grandparents, and intermediate categories of *Mischlinge* of the first or second degree were stipulated as those with smaller proportions of Jewish forebears (Hilberg, 1961, chap. 4).

The extension of the concept of "Jew," whether from within or by anti-Semites, has not been consistent; there is no agreement on what genetic, linguistic, nationalist, or other characteristics are to be added to the historical-religious core. In *Israel ever since the founding of the state, the formal identity of nonreligious Jews has been a recurrent judicial issue (e.g., Rabi, 1971; Pelli, 1976); and the persistent ambiguity has been reflected in divergent answers elsewhere in the world to the central question of who is a Jew (e.g., Karp, 1976; Ellman, 1977).

The demography of Jews is of course crucially affected by this ambiguity (cf. Rosenthal, 1969; Schmelz, 1973). If in various countries or contexts Jews are defined or define themselves inconsistently, then the first query that demographers put to any set of data—how many people are there in this category?—is far less simple than it might seem. Since 1955 more than twenty Jewish communities in the United States have undertaken self-surveys, seeking to repair the gap left by the absence of official statistics, and a National Jewish Population Survey is compiling a profile for the whole Jewish minority (Sidney Goldstein, 1971; cf. Alice Goldstein, 1983). From the statistics available, it is manifest that in their demographic characteristics American Jews—like those in most other countries—differ strikingly from the rest of the population.

During the first century of the Republic's existence, the Jewish population of the United States was minuscule, rising from 1,200 in 1790 to still only 230,000 in 1880. With the subsequent enormous immigration, the proportion of Jews rose from 0.5 percent in 1880 to 3.7 percent in the mid-1930s. In the nineteenth century, when the typical European emigrant was a young unmarried male, Jews left Russia not only for economic reasons but because of persecution or actual pogroms; thus, the overseas migrants included a much larger proportion of females and children than among other nationalities (Hersch, 1931). Emigrants from Russia, unrepresentative of Russian Jewry, were almost entirely from the lower classes and not from the culturally advanced middle class (Halevy, 1978). With the later rise of totalitarian states and particularly Nazi Germany, economic motives for leaving were almost entirely supplanted; both the stimulus to family migration and the difficulties in realizing it increased.

As measured by various indices, most American Jews started low in the social structure, but they or their children often rose to the highest level. According to the 1950 census, for example, both foreign-born and second-generation "Russians" had the highest occupational rank among European nationalities (Nam, 1959); and surveys during the years 1963-72 depicted Jews as the best educated, with the greatest proportion of white-collar jobs, the highest occupational prestige, and the largest family income (Greeley, 1972). Concomitant with this remarkable upward mobility has been a characteristic settlement pattern; virtually all American Jews live in cities or suburbs and especially in the largest metropolitan areas.

Whether because of their typically middle-class way of life or other factors, American Jews' mortality patterns differ from those of other whites (Sidney Goldstein, 1966, 1971). According to a thesis developed by Calvin †Goldscheider (e.g., 1965, 1967), the generally lower fertility of Jews was a consequence of their social position. Like others trying to advance themselves, they reduced the burden of their family responsibilities; but since they moved up against the special barriers of anti-Semitism, the cut in family size had to be greater (cf. Della Pergola, 1980). The hypothesis has been generalized to include such other minorities as the *Japanese Americans, who also rose remarkably fast in spite of special impediments of a focused discrimination and, as a consequence, have a small average family size (Goldscheider and Uhlenberg, 1969).

REFERENCES: Sergio Della Pergola, "Patterns of American Jewish Fertility," *Demography*, 17 (1980), 261-273. Yisrael Ellman, "The Ethnic Awakening in the United States and Its Influence on Jews," *Ethnicity*, 4 (1977), 133-155. Calvin Goldscheider,

"Ideological Factors in Jewish Fertility Differentials," *Jewish Journal of Sociology*, 7 (1965), 92-105; "Fertility of Jews," *Demography*, 4 (1967), 196-209. Goldscheider and Peter R. Uhlenberg, "Minority Group Status and Fertility," *American Journal of Sociology*, 74 (1969), 361-372. Alice Goldstein, "The Coordinated Use of Data Sources in Research on the Demographic Characteristics and Behavior of Jewish Immigrants to the United States," *American Jewish History*, 72 (1983), 293-308. Sidney Goldstein, "Jewish Mortality and Survival Patterns: Providence, Rhode Island, 1962-1964," *Eugenics Quarterly*, 13 (1966), 48-61; "American Jewry, 1970: A Demographic Profile," *American Jewish Year Book*, 1971, pp. 3-88. Andrew M. Greeley, "The Demography of Ethnic Identification," unpublished, 1972. Zvi Halevy, "Were the Jewish Immigrants to the United States Representative of Russian Jews?" *International Migration*, 16 (1978), 60-73. Liebmann Hersch, "International Migration of the Jews," in Walter F. Willcox ed., *International Migrations* (New York: National Bureau of Economic Research, 1931). Raul Hilberg, *The Destruction of the European Jews* (Chicago: Quadrangle Paperbacks, 1961). Abraham J. Karp, "Ideology and Identity in Jewish Group Survival in America," *American Jewish History Quarterly*, 65 (1976), 310-334. Charles B. Nam, "Nationality Groups and Social Stratification in America," *Social Forces*, 34 (1959), 328-333. Karl Rudolf Pakalns, "Jews," in *Encyclopedia of Russia and the Soviet Union* (1961). Moshe Pelli, "Jewish Identity in Modern Hebrew Literature," *Judaism*, 25 (1976), 447-460. W. Rabi, "Modes et Indices d'Identification Juive," *Social Compass*, 18 (1971), 337-356. Erich Rosenthal, "Jewish Populations in General Decennial Population Censuses, 1955-61: A Bibliography," *Jewish Journal of Sociology*, 11 (1969), 31-39. U. O. Schmelz, Paul Glikson, and Sergio Della Pergola, eds., *Papers in Jewish Demography, 1969* (Jerusalem: Institute of Contemporary Jewry, 1973). Mark Zborowski and Elizabeth Herzog, *Life Is with the People: The Culture of the Shtetl* (New York: Schocken Books, 1952).

Jordan: Demographic Institutions

The University of Jordan includes a Population Studies Program of which Ahmad †Hammouda was director in 1982. Address: P.O. Box 1682, Amman.

The Demographic Section of the Department of Statistics conducts the country's censuses, the most recent of which was in 1979. It issues a *Statistical Yearbook* in English and Arabic editions. Address: P.O. Box 2015, Amman.

Judaism, the religion of *Jews, is considerably more important than their small numbers would suggest, since it was a significant source of both Christian and Islamic thought. The characteristic norms of Judaism are difficult to specify, however, since they have differed greatly from one period or denomination to another. Not even the basic law of the Torah (or Pentateuch) is stable, since it has been interpreted in successive layers of exegesis in the Talmud and other commentaries.

Jewish tradition has no counterpart to the Christian ambivalence concerning *sexual behavior: chastity denotes the avoidance not of sex but of illicit sex. There is at least an implicit prohibition of premarital relations, but for a married person intercourse does not need the justification of procreation; it is not only legitimate but a *mitzvah*, a good deed or, in this case, a duty to one's spouse.

The commandment to reproduce has been interpreted as having at least one son and one daughter. Extrapolating from the biblical prohibition of onanism, the Talmud inveighs against "bringing forth the seed in vain." Though permitted or even mandatory under some circumstances, in the Orthodox view contraception is not necessarily permitted as a general practice. According to many rabbinic interpretations during the past two centuries, urgent medical reasons are the only valid justification for a married woman to use birth control; male contraceptives and any controls outside marriage are never sanctioned.

Traditional Judaism flourished in the *ghettos, but many Jews living in the general community and particularly in the free societies of the West relaxed the restrictions on personal behavior. Reform Judaism, starting among German laity at the beginning of the nineteenth century, was developed by a new generation of rabbis several decades later and then spread to Britain and especially the United States. By 1880, of the roughly 200 American synagogues 180 were Reform. The strong tendency of Reform Judaism to imitate American Protestantism was countered, however, by the fact that those most inclined to acculturate fully shifted to entirely secular institutions, with a consequence that some of those remaining reverted to traditionalism, called "Conservative" in the United States and "Liberal" in Europe. Differing considerably from one grouping to another, this was essentially an attempt to adjust to the modern world without sacrificing the core of religious faith. *Israel represents a similar compromise, with traditional rabbis using state power to maintain their norms in a population of which a large proportion is hostile to Orthodox practice or even indifferent to religion (Smooha, 1978).

REFERENCES: Nathan Glazer, *American Judaism* (Chicago: University of Chicago Press, 1957). Sammy Smooha, *Israel: Pluralism and Conflict* (Berkeley: University of California Press, 1978).

jus sanguinis, literally "law of the blood," is the legal principle by which citizenship is determined by parentage rather than by jus soli, "law of the soil" or the place of birth. The basic norm in the United States is the second: according to the Fourteenth Amendment to the Constitution, all persons born in the United States (except children born to foreign diplomats, as one of several minor exceptions) are citizens of the United States. Jus sanguinis applies in only a few cases, principally when a child is born abroad to a couple of whom at least one is an American citizen. See also *dual citizenship.

K

Kampuchea (Cambodia): The government's National Bureau of Statistics and Economic Research issues irregularly an *Annuaire Statistique*, which includes basic data on the population. Address: Institut National de la Statistique et des Recherches Économiques, Ministère du Plan, Boîte Postale 105, Pnompenh, Kampuchea.

KAP, an acronym for knowledge-attitude-practice, is used to designate sample surveys, particularly in less developed countries, that presumably measure whether people know about various means of contraception, how they feel about using them, and whether they actually do use any (Mauldin, 1965). According to some studies, many of the responses are false. When Mahmood Mamdani (1972, chap. 2) reinterviewed the respondents in the earlier *Khanna study, some of them told him that, out of rapport with a field worker trying to inculcate family planning, they reported what he hoped to hear. "It is sometimes better to lie," one respondent remarked. "It stops you from hurting people, does you no harm, and might even help them" (cf. Stoeckel and Choudhury, 1969). Edward Herold and Marilyn Goodwin (1980) have developed a scale to predict continued use of a contraceptive method from attitudes concerning it. In another extension of the schema, attitudes were found to depend on effectiveness of the method, discretion, pleasure, legality, permanence, harmfulness, and cost (Kee and Darroch, 1981). In a longer study, in-depth interviews were used to trace attitudes of Bangladeshi women toward contraceptives from their religious and proto-scientific beliefs (Maloney et al., 1980).

REFERENCES: Edward S. Herold and Marilyn S. Goodwin, "Development of a Scale to Measure Attitudes toward Using Birth Control Pills," *Journal of Social Psychology*, 110 (1980), 115-122. Poo-kong Kee and Russell K. Darroch, "Perception of Methods of Contraception: A Semantic Differential Study," *Journal of Biosocial Science*, 13 (1981), 209-218. Clarence Maloney, K.M.A. Aziz, and Profulla C. Sarker, *Beliefs and Fertility in Bangladesh* (Rajshahi, Bangladesh: Rajshahi University, Institute of Bangladesh Studies, 1980). Mahmood Mamdani, *The Myth of Population Control: Family, Caste, and Class in an Indian Village* (New York: Monthly Review Press, 1972). W. Parker Mauldin, "Fertility Studies: Knowledge, Attitude, and Practice," *Studies in Fam-*

ily Planning, no. 7 (1965). John Edwin Stoeckel and Moqbul A. Choudhury, "Pakistan: Response Validity in a Kap Survey," *Studies in Family Planning*, no. 47 (1969).

Kenya: Demographic Institutions

In 1976 the University of Nairobi, a government institution, and the U.S. Agency for International Development (AID) jointly established on campus a Population Studies and Research Institute. Its director since 1977 has been Simeon H. †Ominde. Its research has focused on population trends and projections in Kenya, to a lesser degree in other countries of East Africa, and it has run seminars for government planning personnel. Address: P.O. Box 30197, Nairobi.

The government's Central Bureau of Statistics conducts the country's censuses, the last of which was in 1979. It also conducts a sample survey program, of which John Kekovole was in charge in 1980. The bureau issues a quarterly statistical digest, a more detailed annual abstract, and an irregular compilation of migration statistics. Address: Ministry of Economic Planning and Community Affairs, P.O. Box 30266, Nairobi.

Khanna study, the first major field study of birth control in India, was conducted in Punjabi villages over a period of six years at a cost of about one million dollars (Wyon and Gordon, 1971). Six villages on which family-planning efforts were focused were contrasted with six others as a control. A temporary decline in the birth rate began before the program got under way, continued at the same rate for a period, occurred among both the test and the control populations, and was due to a rise in the age at marriage rather than the increased use of contraceptives. The Khanna study, in short, was a failure in its professed aim of inducing a reduction in fertility, but this fact is known only because—quite atypically—an analysis of the results could be checked against a control. The Khanna study was also the only important family-planning program anywhere that was subjected to a detailed replication by an independent analyst, who challenged both the reported findings and the conclusions (Mamdani, 1972). See also *action-research; *KAP.

REFERENCES: Mahmood Mamdani, *The Myth of Population Control: Family, Caste, and Class in an Indian Village* (New York: Monthly Review Press, 1972). John B. Wyon and John E. Gordon, *The Khanna Study: Population Problems in the Rural Punjab* (Cambridge, Mass.: Harvard University Press, 1971).

kibbutz, Hebrew for "group" (plural, *kibbutzim*), denotes a collective farm in *Israel. Only a tiny fraction of the Israeli population actually live and work on such farms; around 1980 the approximately 250 settlements had a total membership estimated at only 100,000. Many of those who formally are members, moreover, live in cities and contribute a part of their income to the upkeep of the collective. Currently kibbutzim are significant in the life of the country mainly as a symbol, somewhat analogous to the ideology of rugged individualism on the American frontier. The kibbutz has been much studied as a community in which socialist and feminist aspirations were partly fulfilled on however small a scale. Though arrangements vary from one type of settlement to another, generally children have been reared at least in part through communal institutions, with a greater equality between the sexes as one proclaimed goal. The conclusions of the best studies have been disconcertingly varied. Melford Spiro, an American anthropologist, wrote analyses based on research separated by more than two decades. In the first two books (1955, 1958), though he noted the difficulties in realizing equality between men and women with different biologically determined roles, he believed that on balance the moral principles inculcated in children brought up in the kibbutz would eventually hold sway. "Gender" would become more important than sex. In the latest book (1979), however, he held that the earlier goal of equality between the sexes had given way to one of "equivalence," which he regarded as more realistic. According to another recent study (Tiger and Shepher, 1976), women had come to resent being "freed" of the "burden" of rearing their children. At the instigation of the mothers, care of the children in almost all kibbutzim has become more family-centered and private.

REFERENCES: Melford E. Spiro, *Kibbutz: Venture in Utopia* and *Children of the Kibbutz* (Cambridge, Mass.: Harvard University Press, 1955 and 1958); *Gender and Culture: Kibbutz Women Revisited* (Durham, N.C.: Duke University Press, 1979). Lionel Tiger and Joseph Shepher, *Women in the Kibbutz* (New York: Harcourt, Brace, 1976).

kinship, a system of relationships denoted by a specified set of kin terms with an associated set of behavior patterns and sometimes places of *residence, has been a dominant topic particularly of the British school of social anthropology. The four main criteria used to designate members of a kinship system are sex, generation, the distinction between consanguineal (or blood) and affinal (or marital) relatives, and the distinction between lineal and collateral descent. Some cultures also include such variables, among others, as the sex of the speaker (as well as that of the person spoken of), the relative age within the same generation, and whether a person is alive or dead. The task of arranging these variables into patterns has brought forth an elaborate vocabulary and method of diagraming, by which one can distinguish parallel from cross cousins, second cousins from cousins once removed, patrilineal from matrilineal descent or lineage, and other relationships (Schusky, 1972).

Kinship systems affect behavior mainly by specifying choices—which individuals may or must be avoided, granted respect, included in a joking relation, and so forth. Such early theorists as Lewis Henry Morgan tried to demonstrate a causal relation between kin terminology and marriage practices, but this thesis proved to be wrong or at best overstated. The marriage practices of all cultures are set in part by rules of *endogamy and exogamy and especially by the avoidance of *incest; but such rules, again, mainly specify choices among individuals rather than distinguishing overall behavior patterns. How much an interpretation can depend on the analyst's general orientation can be shown by contrasting the theories of George P. Murdock, Claude Lévi-Strauss, and Meyer †Fortes, all of whom wrote extensively on kinship (Barnes, 1971). For a demographer the most interesting question would be whether a particular kinship system seemingly induced a higher fertility, for instance. The answer is that, according to some analysts, particular types of *family structure encouraged a higher reproduction, but the effect of wider configurations on population variables is nil (cf. Mogey, 1976).

REFERENCES: J. A. Barnes, *Three Styles in the Study of Kinship* (Berkeley: University of California Press, 1971). John Mogey, "Residence, Family and Kinship: Some Recent Research," *Journal of Family History*, 1 (1976), 95-105. Ernest L. Schusky, *Manual for Kinship Analysis* (2nd ed.; New York: Holt, Rinehart and Winston, 1972).

Kiribati (formerly the Gilbert Islands): The Ministry of Home Affairs took the first census in 1978. Address: Tarawa.

Korea, South (Republic of Korea): Demographic Institutions

The Korean Institute for Population and Health, a quasigovernmental agency, was established in 1981 out of the Korean Institute for Family Planning and the Korean Health Development Institute. Its director in 1982 was Park Chan-Moo, M.D. Since 1968 the institute and its predecessors have conducted seven national surveys on fertility and family planning, including South Korea's World Fertility Survey, in coordination with the National Bureau of Statistics. It also trains government family-planning workers. Its publications include many reports of its studies and family-planning statistics, as well as the *Journal of Family Planning Studies* and the *Journal of Population and Health Studies*, both in Korean and English. Address: 115 Nokbun-dong, Sudaemon-ku, Seoul.

The Korean Institute for Research in the Behavioral Sciences, a private non-profit bureau funded in part by the World Health Organization (WHO), was directed in 1982 by Lee Sung-Jin. Among its research projects was an investigation of Korean attitudes toward birth control. Address: 163 Ankook-dong, Chongno-ku, Seoul.

The Planned Parenthood Federation of Korea is active in promoting family planning. It issued, in English, *New Population Policy in Korea: Social and Legal Support for Small Families* (1982), an analysis of the new government policy. Address: Seoul.

Dong-A University, a private institution, has a Population Research Center, of which the director in 1982 was Park Jae-Young. Address: 3-1 Dongdesin-dong, Seo-ku, Busan.

Seoul National University, a government institution, has a Population and Development Studies Center, directed in 1982 by †Kwon Tai-Hwan. It has undertaken demographic, sociological, and economic analyses of population growth, fertility, mortality, migration, and the labor force in Korea. It publishes the *Bulletin of the Population and Development Studies Center*, in Korean and English. Address: Gwan-ak Gu, Seoul.

Yonsei University, a private institution, has a Center for Population and Family Planning, of which the director in 1982 was †Yang Jae-Mo. It has a program of demographic research concentrated on Korean fertility. Address: P.O. Box 71, Seoul.

The National Bureau of Statistics of the Economic Planning Board is the central government's agency for coordinating Korea's statistical activities. It conducts quinquennial population and housing censuses, the most recent of which were in 1980. It also is a collection agency of other primary data, including vital-registration and other social-economic statistics. The Bureau publishes several annual reports in Korean and English: *Major Statistics of the Korean Economy, Statistical Handbook*, the more complete *Statistical Yearbook, Annual Report on the Economically Active Population Surveys*, and *Yearbook of Migration Statistics Based on Resident Registration*. Address: 90 Gyeongun-dong, Seoul.

Kurds, a people of the Middle East allegedly descended from the Medes, whom the Persians conquered in 550 B.C. For about three millennia they have continuously lived in a region they call Kurdistan, which has an area about the size of France. Population figures are dubious, for Kurdish nationalists are likely to exaggerate their numbers and the governments under which they live to minimize them. The range in printed sources is from 7 to 16.5 million. Splitting the difference more or less down the middle gives one a total of about 11 million, half of whom live in Turkey, about 3 million in Iran and 2 million in Iraq, with smaller numbers in Syria and the Soviet Union and a relatively tiny community of immigrants in Lebanon. Probably the Kurds constitute the world's largest coherent nation occupying a single territory that is divided among several alien states. Without question they are one important factor in the region's political instability.

REFERENCE: Martin Short and Anthony McDermott, *The Kurds* (London: Minority Rights Group, 1975).

Kuwait: The Central Statistical Office conducts the country's censuses, the latest of which was in 1980. It publishes an *Annual Statistical Abstract*, in English and Arabic, that includes population data. Address: Ministry of Planning, P.O. Box 15, Kuwait City.

L

labor force, sometimes used as equivalent to the generic terms "economically active population" or *work force, is preferably restricted to one specific designation of those who participate, or try to participate, in the production of a nation's economic goods and services. This narrower concept was developed in the United States during the 1930s and used in the 1940 and subsequent censuses, as well as in monthly sample surveys; and it was later imitated in a number of other countries. The earlier concept of the *gainfully occupied*, or gainful workers, related to the "usual" occupation; thus, the classification, less subject to short-term fluctuations caused by temporary circumstances, was more stable from one count to the next. For that portion of the population that was unemployed or did not really have a single occupational role, however, it was an improvement to ask what work each person was actually doing.

In the United States, data on the labor force are collected each month from a large sample of households. Everyone in each household aged 14 years or over is asked whether during the past week he was working or looking for work. Both the employed and the unemployed are in the labor force, classified according to the occupation in which they have or hope to have jobs. Many of the published data include only those aged 16 years or over, and in the more complete compilations the younger teenagers are usually classified separately (cf. Adams, 1981; Cain, 1978). See also *employment; *occupation.

Analysis of the work force, gainfully occupied, or labor force—depending on the type of measure used in a particular country—can begin with the *crude activity* (or participation) *rate*, the percentage of the total population that is economically active. The simplest refinement results in the *general activity rate*, the percentage of persons of working age that is economically active. Sometimes this is calculated for males only or, if for the whole population, by sex-specific activity rates (see also *women in the work force). For comparisons among populations with markedly different age structures, it may be useful to standardize for age or for both age and sex. How changes in the shape of the population pyramid affect the labor force can be assessed with either of two measures. A *replacement ratio*, calculated for each age group in the working population, is the number of entrants to the labor force during a specified period per 100 losses from death or retirement. The alternative measure of a *replacement rate* is, for each age group in the working population, the difference between the numbers of those entering and departing as a percentage of the total number at the beginning of the period. The most useful analytical instrument is a working-life table, an adaptation of the *multiple-decrement table developed by Seymour †Wolfbein (1949) and Stuart †Garfinkle (1955, 1956) to designate accession to and separation from the labor force, whether by retirement or by death (cf. Schoen and Woodrow, 1980).

REFERENCES: A. V. Adams, "The American Work Force in the Eighties: New Problems and Policy Interests Require Improved Labor Force Data," *Annals of the American Academy of Political and Social Science*, 453 (1981), 123-129. Glen G. Cain, *Labor Force Concepts and Definitions in View of Their Purposes* (Washington, D.C.: National Commission on Employment and Unemployment Statistics, 1978). John D. Durand, *The Labor Force in the United States, 1890-1960* (New York: Social Science Research Council, 1948). Stuart H. Garfinkle, "Changes in Working Life of Men, 1900-2000" and "Tables of Working Life for Women, 1950," *Monthly Labor Review*, 78 (1955), 297-300, and 79 (1956), 654-659. A. J. Jaffe and Charles D. Stewart, *Manpower Resources and Utilization: Principles of Working Force Analysis* (New York: Wiley, 1951). Robert Schoen and Karen Woodrow, "Labor Force Status Life Tables for the United States, 1972," *Demography*, 17 (1980), 297-322. Shryock and Siegel, *Methods and Materials of Demography*, chap. 12. S. L. Wolfbein, "The Length of Working Life," *Population Studies*, 3 (1949), 286-302.

labor mobility, a composite term for any change in economic activity, including entering or leaving the *work force; changing one's occupation, employer, industry, or status; moving from one geographical area to another. A comparison of the economic activity in two or more generations, typically of father and son, is called "intergenerational labor mobility" (see also *social mobility). In the abstract, labor migration is one important mechanism for bringing together the means of production and the workers who use them; but in fact people move, or fail to move, for varied and complex reasons. Even if one considers only economically motivated migrants (omitting, for example, those who move for family or political reasons), the choice of most persons concerned is restricted severely by the typical lack of information about possible options. According to a national sample in the United States, for instance, two-thirds of all migrants considered no other destination than the one they moved to, six out of ten relied on only one source of information about job opportunities in the new place, and information about openings came most frequently from friends or relatives (Lansing and Mueller, 1967; cf. Morrison, 1977). Even so obvious a supposition as that people move to improve their income has been amended; according to one study, a decision to migrate is typically based on expected and not current earnings (Nakosteen and Zimmer, 1980). The influence of education on the propensity to migrate for economic reasons is also complex. Since positions demanding a particular higher skill are likely to comprise only a small proportion of the local work force, those able to fill them may have to move greater distances (cf. Todaro, 1980). On the other hand, most migrants are generally close to the beginning of their career, when the young men and women have few or no accumulated benefits that they would have to give up and often minimal ties to their place of residence. See also *migration; *migration, internal; *urbanization.

REFERENCES: John B. Lansing and Eva Mueller, *The Geographic Mobility of Labor* (Ann Arbor, Mich.: Survey Research Center, 1967). Peter A. Morrison, "The Functions and Dynamics of the Migration Process," in Alan A. Brown and Egon Neuberger, *Internal Migration* (New York: Academic Press, 1977). Robert A. Nakosteen and Michael Zimmer, "Migration and Income: The Question of Self-Selection," *Southern Economic Journal*, 46 (1980), 840-851. Michael P. Todaro, "The Influence of Education on Migration and Fertility," in John Simmons, ed., *The Education Dilemma* (Oxford: Pergamon Press, 1980).

LABSTAT, a computer tape containing time-series data from U.S. Bureau of Labor Statistics surveys and programs. Some of the data included are characteristics of the labor force, consumer price index, labor turnover, employment and unemployment, hours and earnings, and international comparisons of labor and prices.

lactation, the secretion of milk from the mammary glands in the nursing of infants or young children at the breast. Until about 1900 virtually all infants throughout the world were breastfed, if not by the mother then by a wet nurse. Since then there has been a significant decline both in the proportion especially of urban women who nurse their children and in the period of nursing (Baer and Winikoff, 1981; Knodel and Nibhon, 1980). The shift to bottle-feeding, which has certain advantages in homes equipped with middle-class Western kitchens, can result in more frequent malnutrition, disease, and death without adequate knowledge, money, and care (cf. UNICEF, 1981). In the United States a return to breastfeeding has become a cause among young educated women; proponents claim that, if they avoid anxiety and follow a recommended regimen, virtually all women can nurse their babies, and that optimally mother's milk is nutritious, free of contagion, convenient, and cheap (Buchanan, 1975). It is alleged on the basis of partial evidence that a mother's immunity against certain diseases is transmitted with her milk and that, on the other hand, addictions of various types affect the milk adversely.

Lactation prolongs the period of relative infecundity following each birth, though by how much is not known (Parkes et al., 1977; Masnick, 1979). Carlo †Corsini (1979) collected all of the data then available, and if one accepts the figures at face value, breastfeeding explains about 77.4 percent of the variation in postpartum *amenorrhea. There are a number of problems with the figures, however. The length of amenorrhea varies according to the woman's age and state of health, which are not generally reported accurately. Whether a renewal of menstruation indicates a resumption of ovulation, as assumed, depends on how amenorrhea is defined. Similarly, "breastfeeding" and "lactation" are generally assumed to be congruous, but as the milk from the breast is gradually supplemented with other food, the physiological effect of lactation is diminished; and this variation in behavior may not be reported. Postpartum abstinence from sexual relations is usual for a period, varying from one culture to another (e.g., Saxton and Serwadda, 1969), and in some areas women have reportedly been readiest to accept contraceptives during their lactation. Even so, a number of field studies have reported that prolonged breastfeeding is consciously used to inhibit ovulation (e.g., Bleek, 1976; Page and Lesthaege, 1981). In societies with little or no birth control, the average birth interval ranges from barely more than two to nearly three years (Potter et al., 1965). If we were to grant that lactation accounts for the whole difference, it would hardly constitute an adequate control of family size.

REFERENCES: Edward C. Baer and Beverly Winikoff, eds., "Breastfeeding: Program, Policy, and Research Issues," *Studies in Family Planning*, 12 (1981), 123-206. Wolf Bleek, "Spacing of Children, Sexual Abstinence, and Breast-Feeding in Rural Ghana," *Social Science and Medicine*, 10 (1976), 225-230. Robert Buchanan, "Breast-Feeding: Aid to Infant Health and Fertility Control," George Washington University Medical Center, *Population Reports*, Ser. J, no. 4 (1975). Carlo A. Corsini, "Is the Fertility-Reducing Effect of Lactation Really Substantial?" in Henri Léridon and Jane Menken, eds., *Natural Fertility* (Liège: Ordina Editions, 1979). John Knodel and Nibhon Debavalya, "Breastfeeding in Thailand: Trends and Differentials, 1969-79," *Studies in Family Planning*, 11 (1980), 353-377. George S. Masnick, "The Demographic Impact of Breastfeeding: A Critical Review," *Human Biology*, 51 (1979), 109-125. Hilary J. Page and Ron Lesthaege, *Child-Spacing in Tropical Africa: Traditions and Change* (New York: Academic Press, 1981). Alan S. Parkes, Angus M. Thompson, Malcolm Potts, and Margaret A. Herbertson, eds., "Fertility Regulation during Human Lactation," *Journal of Biosocial Science*, Supplement no. 4 (1977). Robert G. Potter, Jr., Mary L. New, John B. Wyon, and John E. Gordon, "Applications of Field Studies to Research on the Physiology of Human Reproduction: Lactation and Its Effects upon Birth Intervals in Eleven Punjab Villages, India," *Journal of Chronic Diseases*, 18 (1965), 1125-1130. G. A. Saxton, Jr., and D. M. Serwadda, "Human Birth Interval in East Africa," *Journal of Reproduction and Fertility*, Supplement 6 (1969), 83-88. U.N. Children's Fund, "Breast-Feeding and Health," *Assignment Children*, no. 55/56 (1981).

lag, a regular difference in time between two related events. In many cases, a lag is implicit between a set of data and what one wants to measure, as the difference in time between a poor harvest and a consequent decline in the marriage rate, or one between a lower marriage rate and a fall in the number of legitimate first births. Many important causes of death, similarly, have a time lag between behavior patterns and their ultimate consequence—between smoking and cancer, for instance. In a *lag regression*, the values of the dependent variable are adjusted for a time difference with respect to one or more of the independent variables. *Cultural lag*, a term coined by the American sociologist William F. †Ogburn in his *Social Change*, means the period between an important invention or other major change and the subsequent adjustment in a related element of the culture.

The disequilibrium during the interim stimulates a reaction toward a new equilibrium.

REFERENCE: William F. Ogburn, *Social Change, with Respect to Culture and Original Nature* (rev. ed.; New York: Viking, 1950).

Lambeth Conferences of Bishops of the Anglican Communion have been convened approximately each ten years since 1867 by the Archbishop of Canterbury, who invites officials of the Church of England and associated churches. The effort to build a Pan-Anglican organization has been an ecclesiastical counterpart of the parallel construction of the British Commonweatlh of Nations, with the same theme of overall unity competing with the insistence of each unit on its full independence. In the context of demography the conferences from 1920 on were important in all Christian countries, however, because their increasingly permissive view of birth control influenced both Protestant and—more slowly—Catholic attitudes.

REFERENCES: John C. Bennett, "Protestant Ethics and Population Control," *Daedalus*, 88 (1959), 454-459. William Redmond Curtin, *The Lambeth Conferences: The Solution for Pan-Anglican Organization* (New York: AMS Press, 1968).

land, that portion of the earth's surface not covered by water, just under 30 percent of the total, can be classified along several dimensions. Natural regions range from ice cap or tundra through temperate forests and grasslands, steppes and deserts, to tropical rain forests. Economists designate land as excellent to possible for agriculture, good to poor for grazing or forestry, or suitable only for wildlife, watersheds, or recreation. By a very rough estimate, in the mid-1960s less than a quarter of the world's cultivable land was being used for any type of crop, but the potential expansion varied greatly—very small in Britain or India, very large in the United States and especially Canada (Stamp, 1968). Later estimates of such gross areas would not differ very much, but many analysts have emphasized rather the diversity of land use over a rather small space. W. B. Morgan (1977, pp. 191-192), for instance, cited a number of studies that delineated eight regions with different agricultural characteristics in Ghana; a patterning of plantation, mixed, or subsistence crops in southwestern Nigeria; and a similar zonation of horticulture, dairying, cereals, and cattle grazing in the very different environment of Uruguay. The new varieties of grains of the *green revolution have sometimes had a marked influence on land use; where production increased substantially, marginal plots were retired from agriculture.

Land tenure, the legal terms setting the period and conditions under which parcels of land are occupied and used, can affect greatly the amount and quality of produce. The transition from serfdom to villenage to tenantry of several types differed in various localities. Unless a leaseholder's interests are protected especially with reference to improvements that he makes, his uncertain tenure often results in neglect of the land and a long-term decline in productivity. In English law such improvements eventually came to entail responsibilities for both landlord and tenant. Tenancy law in the United States followed the English model, but as settlement moved westward it was repeatedly adapted to new conditions (Orwin and Peel, 1926; Harris, 1953). On a world scale several types of land tenure have been much studied, partly because they are often closely associated with political protest (cf. *peasantry). Latifundia, large landed estates worked by peons, have been common in Latin America, parts of southern Europe, and the Middle East. In the mid-1970s over three-quarters of Brazil's agricultural population, for example, were landless, and 4.5 percent of the landowners held 81 percent of the farmland. In southern Italy before the reform of 1950, 3 percent of the landowners possessed 60 percent of the land, and there were over two million landless workers. In Asia large holdings have generally been operated not as centrally managed units but in small holdings rented out, usually through intermediaries, to cultivators frequently in debt bondage to the owners and, in many instances, to moneylenders as well. Another type of holding, the *plantation, typically produces a single commercial crop under the management of a corporate owner, with wage laborers working on a seasonal basis (e.g., King, 1977, chap. 1).

Land reform, a recurrent program in less developed countries, differs according to the context. The most prevalent demand is that those who work the land should own it, and in such places as Japan and Taiwan the division of large holdings among the cultivators was highly successful. Often, however, the breakup of latifundia has resulted in a marked decline in overall productivity, with occasionally a reconcentration of the small holdings into very large units under state control (see *Soviet society). Plantations are a frequent target of reform, but to convert an economy based on monoculture into one with a diversity of crops is not easy. A prime instance is Cuba: one of Fidel Castro's main aims was to break the heavy dependence on one export commodity, but after a few years sugar was as dominant as before the revolution (cf. Draper, 1965, chap. 3).

The relation of a growing population to a fixed land area has been a matter of recurrent concern since †Malthus's first enunciation of the principle of population, or the subsequent application of the "law of diminishing returns" to agriculture. According to this generalization, however much agricultural techniques may improve, eventually increased amounts of labor and capital in agriculture will result in smaller increments in the product. In other words, the finite space will lead to "standing room only." That these dicta may be valid ultimately does not make them helpful guides to setting policy over the foreseeable future; see also *food; *population density. The symptom of Malthusian pressure is likely to be the growth of surplus labor in agriculture. In such a country as *Egypt, for instance, as much as a quarter of the agricultural work force has been classified as surplus—meaning that if one person in four was withdrawn, the total production would not decline. Under such circumstances, the conditions of rural life induce many to move to the cities, but the *urban policy of many countries is to inhibit such a flow or, in some cases, forcibly to reverse it.

If population and the land on which it must subsist are in imbalance, one seemingly obvious solution is to convert more of the earth's surface to agriculture; cf. *irrigation. The effect of land reclamation on such an imbalance, however, is complex, as can be indicated by two historical examples—the enclosure movement in England and the creation of polders in the Netherlands.

The whole mode of English agriculture was transformed in the second half of the eighteenth century. In a series of individual acts of Parliament, the common land of villages was transferred to the private ownership of families with some ancient title to it. Under a new type of managers, agrarian enterprises flourished. According to one classic source, "The age of enclosure was also the age of new methods of draining, drilling, sowing, manuring, breeding and feeding cattle, making of roads, rebuilding of farm premises, and a hundred other changes, all of them requiring capital" (Trevelyan, 1942, p. 376). Potatoes and other root crops became staples. Feed was grown that could be stored during the winter, and the prior custom of converting the major portion of a herd into salt meat was abandoned. During the eighteenth century about two million acres of waste land were brought under cultivation. Though it is hardly in question that the food supply improved enormously in both quantity and variety, scholars have differed fundamentally in their overall appraisal of the enclosures. According to the English socialist historians, J. L. and Barbara Hammond (1932, p. 73), another frequently cited source, "Enclosure was fatal to three classes: the small farmer, the cottager, and the squatter. To all of these classes their common rights were worth more than anything they received in return." However, those same classes were—according to a third basic work—the prime cause of agricultural backwardness: "Landlords and tenants were equally ignorant and sunken in routine. . . . Any spirit of enterprise, any undertaking that involved a considerable period for its completion, were out of the question. . . . The effect of backwardness was to make for more backwardness" (Mantoux, 1952, p. 162). On balance, most demographers have concluded that the increase in England's population during the decades of the enclosures was based essentially on an improved food supply, even among the poorest. By 1830 scurvy had become so rare that a well known physician was unable to diagnose it (Drummond and Wilbraham, 1957, p. 392; cf. McKeown et al., 1972). In the English case, one can reasonably conclude that land reclamation worked as it was supposed to, for it was part of a general improvement by which agriculture was brought under more effective management.

Though the Dutch have been reclaiming land from the sea for hundreds of years, the conversion of the Zuyder Sea into the fresh-water IJssel Lake, with a subsequent draining of that lake to create some 220,000 hectares (almost 90,000 acres) of new land, was a project on a new scale. From its first conception to its ultimate completion, the project will take more than a century, eventually adding about 8 percent to the country's arable land. In the early 1950s, when the second of the polders was being drained and settled, there was an intensive debate on how this new land would affect population pressure in the countryside. Aspirant settlers had to be young and healthy, for building a farm on newly reclaimed land is very hard work. They had to have a certificate of good behavior from their priest or minister, for the government wanted to build solid communities as soon as possible. And in order to relieve the rural population pressure in the rest of the country, they had to be farmers' sons without land of their own—that is, young men who were often unable to marry and raise a family before acquiring their new plot. Though this was not their purpose, these attributes favored a selection of new settlers with extremely high fertility. The birth rate on the polders on occasion rose to about 70 per thousand. Thus, according to one analysis, "the conversion of the former Zuyder Sea into agricultural land will in no way mitigate the problem of the surplus agrarian population. Of course, a number of today's farmers' sons are helped, but the problem as such does not disappear. It is even aggravated" (Groenman, 1952b; cf. Groenman, 1952a).

REFERENCES: Theodore Draper, *Castroism, Theory and Practice* (New York: Praeger, 1965). J. C. Drummond and Anne Wilbraham, *The Englishman's Food: A History of Five Centuries of English Diet* (rev. ed.; London: Cape, 1957). Sjoerd Groenman, "L'Assèchement du Zuiderzée et le Problème de la Population aux Pays-Bas," *Population*, 7 (1952a), 661–674; "Zuiderzeegronden en Sanering van de Kleine Boerenbedrijven," *Landbouwkundig Tijdschrift*, 64 (1952b), 5-14. J. L. Hammond and Barbara Hammond, *The Village Labourer, 1760-1832: A Study in the Government of England before the Reform Bill* (London: Longmans, Green, 1932). Marshall Harris, *Origin of the Land Tenure System in the United States* (Ames: Iowa State College Press, 1953). Russell King, *Land Reform: A World Survey* (London: Bell, 1977). Paul Mantoux, *The Industrial Revolution in the Eighteenth Century: An Outline of the Beginnings of the Modern Factory System in England* (rev. ed.; London: Cape, 1952). Thomas McKeown, R. G. Brown, and R. G. Record, "An Interpretation of the Modern Rise of Population in Europe," *Population Studies*, 26 (1972), 345-382. W. B. Morgan, *Agriculture in the Third World: A Spatial Analysis* (London: Bell, 1977). C. S. Orwin and W. R. Peel, *The Tenure of Agricultural Land* (2nd ed.; Cambridge, England: University Press, 1926). L. Dudley Stamp, "Land Classification," *International Encyclopedia of the Social Sciences*, 8, 556-562. G. M. Trevelyan, *English Social History: A Survey of Six Centuries, Chaucer to Queen Victoria* (London: Longmans, Green, 1942).

language is defined in a dictionary of linguistics as "a system of communication by sound, i.e., through the organs of speech and hearing, among human beings of a certain group or community, using vocal symbols possessing arbitrary conventional meanings" (Pei and Gaynor, 1954, p. 119). While accurate enough in its own terms, this definition vastly understates the difficulty in distinguishing, for example, between a language and a *dialect, the emotional energy with which such issues are often disputed, and the consequent problems in population counts of speech communities.

How many languages there are in the world, a datum specified with a re-markable variation, differs according to how one defines the term. The number of African languages, for instance, cannot be stated at all precisely, for not only is our knowledge often partial or of dubious quality, but the sometimes arbitrary distinction between language and a subordinate speech form is of course crucial. If one adds the estimates of two authorities, Joseph Greenberg's list of non-Bantu languages and Malcolm Guthrie's classification of Bantu, the total comes to 1,200. Pierre Alexandre (1972) cut this back to a conservative 800, from which he derived the highly artificial average of about 200,000 persons per language. How many people actually speak each depends largely on geography, with much fragmentation in mountainous or forest areas and the greatest range over savannahs. But only those widespread languages with a written form that is taught in schools (e.g., Swahili, Yoruba, Hausa) have a genuine unity, for the spoken dialects are so different that, according to Alexandre, "one hesitates to consider them as constituting single entities"—thus bringing one back close to the original 1,200. Of this total, however one specifies it, only fifty-two languages or sets of closely related dialects are each spoken by as many as a million people. Of the new states in black Africa, only four very small ones are linguistically homogeneous. Sometimes the numerically dominant language is strongly opposed by combined minorities; in other instances significant languages number from two in Togo to roughly a hundred in Cameroon (see also *African society; *bilingualism).

The number of languages, moreover, is everywhere in constant flux. It was once thought that with the spread of a few dominant civilizations the peoples absorbed in them would eventually all acculturate. For example, the last speaker of Dalmatian, a Romance language once spoken in what is now Yugoslavia, was killed in a mine explosion in 1898; in the late 1930s only two speakers were left of the American Indian languge Chitimacha. But whether modernization tends to reduce linguistic diversity is a disputed question (e.g., Lieberson, 1977; Lieberson et al., 1974, 1975; de Vries, 1977); for the process has also been accompanied by a tremendous surge of nationalist fervor. Languages seemingly on the road to extinction (like Erse or Welsh) have been revived; liturgical languages have taken on secular functions (Hebrew); dialects or compounds of dialects have been promoted to national status (Landsmål in Norway, Hindi in India). The two processes of consolidation and diversification can be exemplified from American history. At one time it was expected that immigrants to the United States would learn English as a minimum step toward full membership in the society, and generally no one followed this rule more enthusiastically than the immigrants themselves. Now Spanish is formally a second official language not only of New Mexico (as it always was) but of the whole country, and by the Voting Rights Act of 1975 even very small minorities must be given ballots and instructions in their own languages, whatever they may be (Hunter, 1976; cf. Kloss, 1971).

One process of diversification recently much studied has been through the rise of pidgins into creoles. Pidgin, originally an elliptical form of "pidgin English," a lingua franca used around the China Sea, derives from Chinese attempts to pronounce "business." In its generalized meaning, *pidgin* is a contact vernacular, used in trade or in employer-worker relations; typically it is a West European language stripped of grammatical niceties and with a sharply limited vocabulary often derived from several sources. The etymology of creole is from the Portuguese *crioulo*, which attached the diminutive suffix *-oulo* to a word derived from the Latin *creare*, "to breed"; a by-product, thus, of a particular genetic line, a creole meant originally a person of European descent born and raised in a tropical colony, later a native of such a colony whatever his race. As now used by linguists, a *creole* means a mother tongue that in many instances began as a pidgin but developed from a truncated second language into a fully rounded, though typically socially inferior, new one (Taylor, 1961; DeCamp, 1968).

A particularly interesting example of a one-time creole is Swahili (or Ki-Swahili), a Bantu language with a strong admixture of Arabic as well as bits of Hindustani, English, and Portuguese. It began as a pidgin of Arab slave traders and thus spread along eastern Africa as far inland as their nefarious business took them. Then in Zanzibar, a center of the slave trade, it developed into a rich language with a complex grammar and a written literature. In 1964, when Tanganyika and Zanzibar united to form Tanzania, it adopted Swahili as its official language; and a decade later, with far less basis in the speech of the population, Kenya followed suit (Harries, 1969, 1976). If the intent had been to foster cultural and economic relations with more advanced countries, the more rational choice in both cases would have been English, which was, however, tainted as the speech of imperialism; and the Kikuyu, the politically dominant group of Kenya, would have been resented even more if their language had been imposed on the rest of the country.

Diversification of langauges, often a symptom of nationalism, has sometimes been countered by the desire of the inhabitants of no matter what country to be able to communicate across national boundaries. Even distinctive alphabets are something of an impediment to business, cultural, or political relations. The gothic font in which most German works used to be printed was regarded by German nationalists as a valuable carry-over from the Nordic past, but in 1941 Hitler signed a decree supplanting it with the roman typeface. The Soviet Union followed a different pattern: in the 1930s, as one expression of extravagant Russian nationalism, the various Roman orthographies used for non-Russian languages were all replaced by cyrillic, and the difference between it and the roman alphabet has reinforced the political division between East and West. A language written without an alphabet impedes not only communication with foreigners but the acquisition of *literacy among native speakers. Such a language is harder to master, for there is little or no cumulation of knowledge from one character to the next. It is estimated, thus, that it takes some twenty years to acquire an ability to read and write the 50,000 characters that a person fully literate in Chinese must know. After the 1912 revolution the Nationalist government considered substituting for the Chinese script one of the roman orthographies that had been devised, but it is unlikely that this will ever be done. Chinese is not one language but a congeries of dialects, as different from one another as French and Italian, say, or German and Dutch. If these various "dialects" (or "languages") were written as they are pronounced, the linguistic unity of China would be lost. In 1958, the National People's Congress accepted for transliterations to other languages a system called pinyin (as clumsy as the Wade-Giles transliteration that, in Communist China, it replaced), but for political reasons the adoption of any alphabet within China was abandoned. In Kemal Ataturk's drive to modernize Turkey, on the contrary, one of his first acts after becoming president of the new republic in 1923 had been to substitute a roman alphabet for the Arabic script in which Turkish was written (Stubbs, 1980, chap. 4).

Population data on language are based on three types of queries: (a) mother tongue, or the language spoken in the respondent's home during his early childhood; (b) the language spoken, or most often spoken, in the respondent's present home; and (c) the ability of the respondent to speak one or more out of a list of designated languages. Why one or another form is used can be illustrated from the linguistic data on Europe, where ethnic differentiation is mainly based on language. Data on mother tongue, which are a generation old, favor minorities in the process of assimilation; in the protracted dispute about Brussels, a mainly French-speaking city with many in-migrants from Dutch-speaking Flanders, Flemish nationalists insist that that is how to collect the statistics. The "usual" language, on the other hand, favors the one currently dominant; in pre-1914 Austria it was used to the advantage of German. Question (c), knowledge of languages, also favors the country's dominant speech; in the British Isles the use of this criterion resulted in a maximum number of English speakers, including many bilingual Celts. Similar political purposes can be served by grouping languages into units one wants to aggrandize, or dividing others into smaller subunits. In the old Austrian censuses Yiddish speakers were classified as part of the German majority; in the censuses of Germany the two dialects Kaschub and Masurian were counted as separate from Polish, but German dialects were not distinguished. Linguistic statistics from an area with a dispute between language communities, as such examples show, cannot be accepted on faith (Kirk, 1946, pp. 224-226; cf. Kovács, 1928; Strassoldo, 1977).

In the United States the 1960 and 1970 censuses asked for the respondents' mother tongue whenever it was not English. In 1980 this question was dropped and supplanted by a query on the language(s) other than English currently spoken at home. Those who reported speaking another language were asked also to rate their ability to speak English: "very well," "well," "not well," or "not at all." One difficulty with such gradation is that each person may use a different criterion from his neighbor's, and to sum the two is thus a logically dubious procedure.

REFERENCES: Pierre Alexandre, *An Introduction to Languages and Language in Africa* (London: Heinemann, 1972). David DeCamp, "The Field of Creole Language Studies," *Latin American Research Review*, 3 (1968), 25-46. John de Vries, "Comment on 'The Course of Mother-Tongue Diversity in Nations,' " *American Journal of Sociology*, 83 (1977), 708-714. Lyndon Harries, "Language Policy in Tanzania," *Africa*, 39 (1969), 275-280; "The Nationalization of Swahili in Kenya," *Language in Society*, 5 (1976), 153-164. David H. Hunter, "The 1975 Voting Rights Act and Language Minorities," *Catholic University Law Review*, 25 (1976), 250-270. Dudley Kirk, *Europe's Population in the Interwar Years* (Princeton, N.J.: Princeton University Press, 1946). Heinz Kloss, "Language Rights of Immigrant Groups," *International Migration Review*, 2 (1971), 250-268. Aloÿse Kovács, "La Connaissance des Langues comme Contrôle de la Statistique des Nationalités," *Bulletin de l'Institut International de Statistique*, 23, Part 2 (1928), 246-346. Stanley Lieberson, "Response to de Vries's Comment," *American Journal of Sociology*, 83 (1977), 714-722. Lieberson, Guy Dalto, and Mary Ellen Johnston, "The Course of Mother-Tongue Diversity in Nations," *American Journal of Sociology*, 81 (1975), 34-61. Lieberson and Lynn K. Hansen, "National Development, Mother-Tongue Diversity, and the Comparative Study of Nations," *American Sociological Review*, 39 (1974), 523-541. Mario A. Pei and Frank Gaynor, *A Dictionary of Linguistics* (New York: Philosophical Library, 1954). Marzio Strassoldo, *Lingue e Nazionalità nelle Rilevazioni Demografiche*, Contributi e Ricerche Scienze Politiche Trieste, no. 8 (Trieste: CLUET, 1977). Michael Stubbs, *Language and Literacy: The Sociolinguistics of Reading and Writing* (London: Routledge and Kegan Paul, 1980). Douglas Taylor, "New Languages for Old in the West Indies," *Comparative Studies in Society and History*, 3 (1961), 277-288.

Laos: The National Statistical Service publishes an *Annuaire Statistique* and a semi-annual *Bulletin de Statistique*, both of which include population data. Address: Service National de la Statistique, Ministère du Plan et de la Coopération, Vientiane.

Latin America comprises (a) the countries of North and South America south of the United States, or (b) those in that region that speak a Romance language, including French, or (c) those that speak either Spanish or Portuguese, or (d) twenty independent republics, of which Spanish is the national language of eighteen, Portuguese of *Brazil, and French of Haiti. The *Organization of American States (OAS), finally, uses "Latin America" to denote (e) all of its total of thirty-one member states except the United States.

Most of the data in the United Nations *Demographic Yearbook* are by country, but in an overall survey the all-inclusive definition (a) is adopted. The region is divided into four subregions, with estimates as follows (*U.N. Demographic Yearbook, 1981*, p. 163; Population Reference Bureau, 1984; see also Sanchez-Albornoz, 1974):

	Population (millions)			Percent Annual Natural
	1950	**1975**	**1984**	**Increase, 1984**
Tropical South America	86	180	220	2.4
Middle America, mainland	36	79	102	2.8
Caribbean	17	27	31	1.8
Temperate South America	25	39	44	1.3
Latin America	164	324	397	2.4

Around 1984 estimated crude birth rates ranged from above 40 in Bolivia, Ecuador, Honduras, and Nicaragua to under 20 in Uruguay, Barbados, Cuba, Guadeloupe, and Martinique. At the same date the expectation of life ranged from 70 in Uruguay and Argentina to 50 in Bolivia (cf. Population Reference Bureau, 1984). Not only is the term "Latin America" ambiguous but the supposed homogeneity that it suggests is largely factitious (Martz, 1971).

Even in language, the criterion by which the several definitions are differentiated, a number of countries do not fit very well into the category. In Bolivia, for example, the Indians who speak Aymara or Quechua far outnumber the Spanish-speaking population; and there are considerable Indian minorities also in Mexico, Guatemala, Panama, Ecuador, Peru, and Brazil. Haiti's national language is French, but the patois spoken by most of the people would not be understood in Paris. The Italian minority of Argentina and the Italians, Germans, and Japanese in Brazil often speak their own languages, and they have affected greatly the official Spanish or Portuguese. In general, the high incidence of illiteracy means that everywhere standard speech competes with local dialects.

In genetic stock the populations combine three components—American Indian, white, and Negro—with sizable proportions of Asians in some areas. Negroes dominate in some of the islands of the Caribbean and around the northern coast of South America; and the people of three countries—Argentina, Uruguay, and Costa Rica—are mainly white. At one time administrators tried assiduously to identify the various mixtures; at present the dominant racial group in many of the countries is mestizo, or mixed Indian-white.

Among the major regions of the world, Latin America long had the highest fertility. At the earliest date to which the incomplete and inaccurate statistics take us (Chile in 1850-54), the estimated crude birth rate was 46.6, and in no country except Uruguay did it fall below 40 until after World War I (Collver, 1965). In the mid-1970s only Uruguay, Argentina, Chile, and Cuba had birth rates under 40; and some of the estimates indicate a slight upturn. Disturbingly, social-economic advance is not inducing the prompt decline in fertility that earlier theory had led demographers to anticipate. In 1975 the Mexican population was more than 72 percent literate and more than 60 percent urban; per-capita income had doubled over the prior two decades; the expectation of life at birth had risen to about 65 years and was still increasing. Even so, fertility in 1975 was, if anything, somewhat higher than it had been twenty years before (Coale, 1978). The official pronatalist policy, it is true, had been reversed, and unofficial estimates suggested that there had been a subsequent downturn in family size (Nagel, 1978). Whether the rapid population growth of Mexico and of many other countries of Latin America is really being stemmed, however, cannot yet be stated with assurance (cf. Goldman et al., 1983).

Much of the excess population moves from the rural areas to cities already unable to absorb their inhabitants into useful functions (for Colombia, see Martine, 1975). *Urbanization has not been, as during an earlier era in developed countries, by the movement of a self-selected sector especially well suited to take on urban tasks. In-migrants, pushed off the overcrowded land, have established squatters' settlements around each of the major cities; urban in location, many are still rural in their family-building orientation (e.g., concerning Peru, Mangin, 1967). Monterrey is a Mexican equivalent of Pittsburgh or Detroit, a large center of heavy industry; but according to a survey there in the mid-1960s, the wives of men aged 51-60 had had a mean of 6.03 live births, about one child more than the highest completed family size recorded in other Latin American studies (Zarate, 1967). Moreover, the antinatalist sentiment so evident in the commentaries of norteamericanos, though echoed in Latin America, is countered by an often stronger impetus to a larger population; traditional Roman Catholic views and, more importantly, those of Left nationalists combine into a vehement defense of a large and growing population (Stycos, 1965; McDonough and DeSouza, 1977). See also *consensual union; *machismo.

REFERENCES: Ansley J. Coale, "Population Growth and Economic Development: The Case of Mexico," *Foreign Affairs* (January, 1978), pp. 415-429. O. Andrew Collver, *Birth Rates in Latin America: New Estimates of Historical Trends and Fluctuations* (Berkeley: Institute of International Studies, University of California, 1965). Noreen Goldman, Anne R. Pebley, Charles F. Westoff, and Lois E. Paul, "Contraceptive Failure Rates in Latin America," *International Family Planning Perspectives*, 9 (1983), 50-57. William Mangin, "Latin American Squatter Settlements: A Problem and a Solution," *Latin American Research Review*, 2 (1967), 65-98. George Martine, "Volume, Characteristics and Consequences of Internal Migration in Colombia," *Demography*, 12 (1975), 193-208. John D. Martz, "Political Science and Latin American Studies: A Discipline in Search of a Region," *Latin American Research Review*, 6 (1971), 73-99. Peter McDonough and Amaury DeSouza, "Brazilian Elites and Population Policy," *Population and Development Review*, 3 (1977), 377-401. John S. Nagel, "Mexico's Population Policy Turnaround," *Population Bulletin*, 33:5 (December, 1978), 1-40. Population Council, Center for Policy Studies, "Population Brief: Latin America," *Population and Development Review*, 6 (1980), 126-152. Population Reference Bureau, *1984 World Population Data Sheet* (Washington, D.C., 1984). Nicolas Sanchez-Albornoz, *The Population of Latin America: A History* (Berkelely: University of California Press, 1974). J. Mayone Stycos, "Opinions of Latin-American Intellectuals on Population Problems and Birth Control," *Annals of the American Academy of Political and Social Science*, 360 (1965), 11-26. U.N. Economic Commission for Latin America, *Boletín Económico de*

América Latina, 7 (1962), Table 4. Alvan O. Zarate, "Differential Fertility in Monterrey, Mexico: Prelude to Transition?" *Milbank Memorial Fund Quarterly*, 45 (1967), 93-108.

Latin American Faculty of Social Sciences (FLACSO) was established in 1957 to further teaching, research, and cooperation among social scientists. Since 1978 FLACSO has had a postgraduate program in population studies for Latin Americans with a bachelor's degree in social sciences. In 1978-79 it had a joint program of research with the Latin American Demographic Center (CELADE). FLACSO has its headquarters in Buenos Aires and offices also in other Latin American countries. Address: Facultad Latinoamericana de Ciencias Sociales, Paraguay 577, Casilla 2490-c, Buenos Aires, Argentina.

Latin American Social Science Council (CLACSO) was established in 1967 with some eighty institutes in nineteen countries as members. The following year CLACSO set up a Commission on Population and Development, which initially focused its efforts on two priority areas, fertility and urbanization. In 1972 a program to formulate population policies was developed—Programa de Investigaciones Sociales sobre Problemas de Población Relevantes para Política de Población en América Latina, or *PISPAL. Publications: *Boletín CLACSO*, semi-annual; *Carta de CLACSO*, bimonthly. Address: Consejo Latinoamericano de Ciencias Sociales, Callao 875, 1023 Buenos Aires, Argentina.

League of Nations, the international organization set up after World War I in 1919, was mainly an attempt to avoid another destructive conflict. Like the United Nations that succeeded it in 1946, though on a far more modest scale, it also tried to intervene in various social, economic, or political matters related to population. According to a recent uncritical appraisal, the league's "efforts in the field of health, international labor legislation, refugee settlement, and international administration were invaluable" (Henig, 1973, p. 153). Article 25 of the league's Covenant committed it to "the improvement of health, the prevention of disease, and the mitigation of suffering throughout the world." Even on such noble purposes, it was difficult to reach enough agreement to form committees; but by the early 1930s "the position [was] hopeful for the future," for "the tools [were] in existence" (Greaves, 1931, chap. 4).

Under the prodding of Fridtjof †Nansen, the league established a bureau that supervised the repatriation of prisoners of war and the settlement of refugees from Russia, Asia Minor, the Balkans, and, following Hitler's accession to power, Germany. "In 1934," according to a highly sympathetic account, "refugee relief was apparently coming to an end" (Myers, 1935, p. 237)—a prognosis that reflected not only the league's irrepressible optimism but its highly artificial and limited conception of "refugee," defined so as to avoid affront to any of the member nations. The *International Labor Organization was the one significant component of the league that survived its demise. The Committee on Intellectual Cooperation, which became the International Institute of Intellectual

Cooperation, merged with UNESCO in 1945. During its period of activity the members of the committee or institute met once a year to discuss the causes of war and advocate moral disarmament; they proposed the establishment of an international university; they published an *International Code of Abbreviations for Titles of Periodicals* (1930; 2nd ed., 1932); and they drove the concept of optimum population, already hardly adamantine, into meaningless confusion with such pronouncements as, for instance, "Overpopulation may be said to exist, not so much in actual figures as in the consciousness of the country concerned" (Wright, 1939, p. 80). The *Statistical Year-Book* that the league published contained population data, but its usefulness to demographers is limited by the fact that the International Statistical Institute put out the more comprehensive irregular serial, *Aperçu de la Démographie des Divers Pays du Monde* (1922-39).

REFERENCES: H.R.G. Greaves, *The League Committees and World Order* (London: Oxford University Press, 1931). Ruth B. Henig, *The League of Nations* (New York: Barnes and Noble, 1973). Denys P. Myers, *Handbook of the League of Nations* (Boston: World Peace Foundation, 1935). Fergus Chalmers Wright, *Population and Peace: A Survey of International Opinion on Claims for Relief from Population Pressure* (Paris: International Institute of Intellectual Cooperation, 1939).

least squares, the most common method of determining *goodness of fit. A particular form is determined (straight line, parabola, etc.) approximating the points of a scatter diagram, and then the distances are measured parallel to the y axis between each empirical point and the point on the curve that has been chosen. When the sum of the squares of these distances is at a minimum, the best-fitting curve has been specified.

Lebanon: Demographic Institutions

The government Central Bureau of Statistics conducted a census in 1970; because of the rivalry among the country's ethnic and religious factions, it has not been possible to have another count. The bureau issues, in Arabic and French, a monthly statistical bulletin and an annual *Recueil de Statistiques Libanaises*. Address: Direction Centrale de la Statistique, Ministère du Plan, Bir Hassan, Beirut.

The Department of Vital and Health Statistics has published since 1957 an *Annual Report of Vital and Health Statistics*. Address: Service des Statistiques Sanitaires, Ministère de la Santé Publique, Beirut.

lebensraum, literally "living space," was used by German nationalists and geopoliticians, particularly during the Nazi period, to justify expansion in order to give the German people room to live in. See also *geopolitics; Karl †Haushofer; Friedrich †Ratzel.

Leges Julia et Papia-Poppaea, a series of pronatalist laws instituted by the Emperor Augustus in Rome between 18 B.C. and A.D. 10. Adultery and celibacy were punished, interclass marriages were discouraged, and fathers received various types of legal advantage. The laws had little or no effect and, after several revisions, were finally abrogated by Constantine, who was also influenced in this respect by Christian norms.

REFERENCE: Stangeland, *Pre-Malthusian Doctrines*, pp. 30-38.

legitimacy, the characteristic of a lawfully conceived child who is thus entitled to full filial rights. The specification of legitimacy and of legitimation is precise in law, but in family sociology the concepts have often been no more than the unanalyzed opposite of *illegitimacy. In the nuclear family there are strong physiological bonds between husband and wife and between mother and nursing infant; but the link between father and child is mainly cultural, what the British anthropologist Bronislaw Malinowski called ''the principle of legitimacy.'' In every society an adult male, usually but not necessarily the physiological begetter (the ''genitor''), is designated the social father (the ''pater''), responsible for the care and training of the children assigned to him by this rule. Malinowski distinguished sharply between freedom of intercourse, which is common in human societies, and freedom of conception outside marriage, which in his view is virtually always defined as an aberration. If the principle is clear, its application in practice is blurred by such intermediate types as the *consensual union, and by the reluctance of both participants and many analysts to denigrate a deviation from legitimate birth as inferior (see also *one-parent family). According to Peter †Laslett, for example, the principle of legitimacy is ''far too drastic for the historical record'' of bastardy, since in Malinowski's concept of functionalism it was a prerequisite to societal survival. ''In reality,'' in Laslett's view, ''it was the rules of respectability, of praise and blame for people's conduct, which were at play for the most part during the comparative history of bastardy, rather than rules for survival'' (Laslett et al., 1980, Introduction). In Jamaica, for example, where between 70 and 74 percent of all births are out of wedlock, the question really is whether so prevalent a lack of two-adult teams to rear children is a serious impediment not only to the individuals concerned but to the society as a whole (Hartley, 1975, chap. 1; 1980).

REFERENCES: Shirley F. Hartley, *Illegitimacy* (Berkeley: University of California Press, 1975). Peter Laslett, ''Introduction'' and Hartley, ''Illegitimacy in Jamaica,'' in Laslett et al., eds., *Bastardy and Its Comparative History* (Cambridge, Mass.: Harvard University Press, 1980). Bronislaw Malinowski, *Sex, Culture, and Myth* (New York: Harcourt, Brace and World, 1962).

legitimation, the formal conferring of the status and rights of *legitimacy to a person born illegitimately. Also, *legitimize*, to confer such a status.

Lesotho: The government's Central Bureau of Statistics conducts the country's censuses, the latest of which was in 1976. It publishes an *Annual Statistical Bulletin* that includes population data. The Demography and Social Statistics Division was headed in 1980 by Ariel Mokhachane Mpiti. Address: P.O. Box 455, Maseru 100.

less developed countries (LDCs) is the presently usual term for what used to be called "developing countries" (even though in many cases the change was nil or even retrogressive), "underdeveloped countries" (which was sometimes resented as a seemingly censorious contrast with "developed countries"), or simply "poor countries." By whatever name, LDCs are difficult to characterize precisely, for the statistics with which to set the boundary are typically inadequate or nonexistent. One criterion is the proportion of the work force in agriculture, with half or more used to define the country as less developed. Generally in such a country the use of nonhuman energy is sparse, much of the trade is by barter, many are illiterate, and fertility is high. In other words, the characteristics of LDCs relate to both *economic development, narrowly understood, and *modernization.

Increasingly the demarcation has also been political. Attempts to set apart a "Third World," with common interests different from both the Western and the Communist blocs, resulted in their frequent appellation as "nonaligned nations," but the supposed independence was undermined when Cuba became head of the loose alliance. The "Group of 77," sometimes shortened to "G-77," came from the number of countries represented at a U.N. Conference on Trade and Development that met in New Delhi in 1968. By 1981 the number of members had grown to 120, but the name was retained. A designation with both economic and political implications is "North-South," given wide currency by the report of the Independent Commission on International Development Issues (1980), usually called the Brandt Commission after Willy Brandt, the former West German chancellor, who was its chairman. If one draws a line along the southern borders of the United States, Europe, the Soviet Union, and Japan, with a swing down to include Australia and New Zealand, the developed countries are to the north and most of the less developed ones to the south. Of course, there are exceptions—Communist China and the Koreas, not to say Albania; but the short designation is felicitous and may gain greater currency.

In 1978 the total *Gross National Product for the whole world was estimated at $8.5 trillion, or an overall average per capita of just over $2,000. More than 80 percent of the total GNP was generated in the North, which contained just over a quarter of the world's population. Income per capita well exceeded $6,000 in the North but was less than $500 in the South. The contrast is likely to grow, mainly because of the sharp difference in the rates of population growth in the two areas. Economic development has been great in both sectors, but the increase in population betwen 1960 and 1980 was by 1.2 billion in the South, by less than 200 million in the North. Moreover, the rates of growth seem to be diverging farther, with momentous declines in the fertility of the North and an often sluggish adaptation to population pressure in the South (Demeny, 1981).

Manifestly, these overall statistics poorly reflect the actual state of the various countries (cf. Brenez and Seltzer, 1983). GNP is a much more accurate measure in developed than in less developed countries, for it omits much or all of what peasants produce for their own consumption. Contrasts are great not only within each sector but within each country. Development and modernization necessarily are initiated by an advanced portion of a country's population; and in the West's history cities were constantly renewed by those in rural areas best suited to take on urban occupations. In less developed countries today, however, people are often pushed out by rural overpopulation rather than pulled by urban opportunities, and in that case the innovative minority is overwhelmed by a flood of unassimilable humanity.

REFERENCES: J. P. Brenez and William Seltzer, "La Collecte des Informations Démographiques dans les Pays du Tiers Monde: Recensements et Enquêtes dans les Années 70 et 80," *Revue Tiers-Monde*, 24 (1983), 245-260. Paul Demeny, "The North-South Income Gap: A Demographic Perspective," *Population and Development Review*, 7 (1981), 297-310. Independent Commission on International Development Issues, *North-South: A Programme for Survival* (Cambridge, Mass.: M.I.T. Press, 1980); the portion of the report dealing with population is reprinted in *Population and Development Review*, 6 (1980), 335-343.

Lexis diagram, first developed by the German statistician Wilhelm †Lexis, has become a widely used tool in demography. On a grid of which the horizontal axis represents dates and the vertical axis ages, lines are drawn from the birth years of specified cohorts to their ages at successive dates (Pressat, 1972, chap. 2). In the illustrative diagram on page 514, the two age groups are compared, those aged 30-34 in 1960-64 and in 1970-74. These are the cohorts, labeled 1 and 2, born in 1930-34 and in 1940-44, respectively. From the diagram it is easy to reconstruct their two life histories. Up to the age of 10, Cohort 1 went through the Great Depression, and one would expect that age-specific deaths from childhood diseases affected it more than Cohort 2. Cohort 1 passed through the teens in the early 1950s, Cohort 2 in the much more tumultuous period of the early 1960s. Age-specific rates of migration varied from one year to the next and, with age-specific death rates, can be applied to each of such cohorts to derive the residual size at any given ages. The Lexis diagram can be used to represent not only birth cohorts but also any other. The two cohorts can be taken to be those that were married, or entered the labor force, or passed any other step in the life cycle between 1930 and 1934 and between 1940 and 1944, with the same convenience in analyzing how the events of such following years affected the members of the two cohorts.

REFERENCE: Roland Pressat, *Demographic Analysis: Methods, Results, Applications* (Chicago: Aldine, 1972).

LHRH, which stands for luteinizing hormone-releasing hormone, is a brain hormone that plays a crucial part in the physiology of reproduction. Man-made analogs of LHRH are said to be the most promising base for improving contraceptives for both males and females.

REFERENCE: John M. Benditt, "Current Contraceptive Research," *Family Planning Perspectives*, 12 (1980), 149-155.

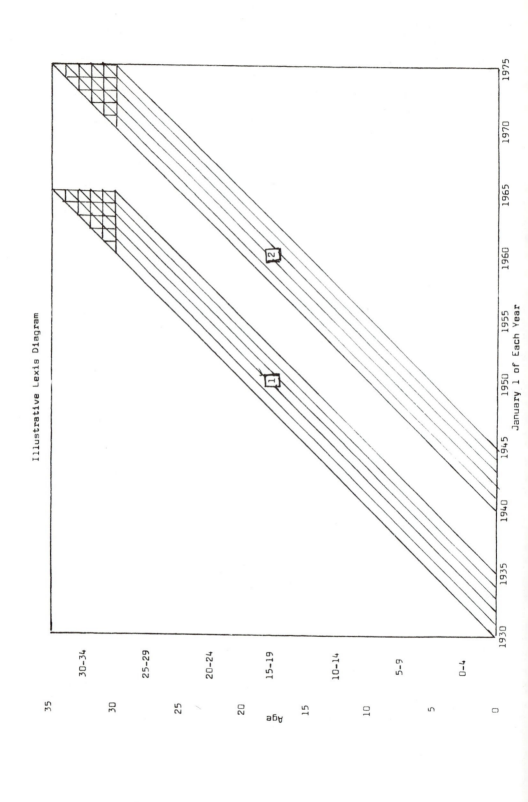

Illustrative Lexis Diagram

Liberia: Demographic Institutions

In 1973 the University of Liberia, a government institution, established a Demographic Unit, which in 1981 was under the direction of Mohan Lal †Srivastava. Its staff teaches demography both to university students and to employees of government bureaus. It has published studies on population growth in the capital, immigration and internal migration, fertility and mortality, and divorce. Address: P.O. Box 9020, Monrovia.

The Ministry of Planning and Economic Affairs has several units concerned with population. Its Bureau of Statistics issues an annual *Economic Survey of Liberia*, which includes basic data and estimates on population and vital events. The Manpower Division analyses statistical data on employment. The Population Division, established in 1969 and in 1980 under the direction of Abel Zuana †Massalee, is charged with providing the government with the population data needed for planning. It has analyzed the returns from the 1974 census and a 1978-79 sample survey. Address: P.O. Box 9016, Monrovia.

Libya: The government's Census and Statistics Department conducts the census, the most recent of which was in 1973. It publishes an annual *Vital statistics*, in Arabic with an English introduction, table of contents, and table titles, and an annual *Statistical Abstracts*, in English and Arabic, which includes population data. Address: Ministry of Planning and Development, Tripoli.

Liechtenstein: The Economics Office conducts the censuses, the most recent of which was in 1980. Among the office's serial publications are *Wohnbevölkerungsstatistik*, on housing; *Ausländerstatistik*, on aliens; and two more general annual series, *Statistisches Jahrbuch* and *Zivilstandsstatistik*, both of which contain data on population. Address: Amt für Statistik des Volkswirtschaft Liechtenstein, FL-9490 Vaduz.

life chances, a translation from the German *Lebenschancen*, was used by Max †Weber (1946) to denote the supply of goods, living conditions, and personal experiences—a particular specification of what is more generally termed level of living. An important element of life chances is what demographers analyze, differential morbidity and mortality by social class.

REFERENCE: H. H. Gerth and C. Wright Mills, eds., *From Max Weber: Essays in Sociology* (New York: Oxford University Press, 1946).

life cycle, the successive stages of married life, or of life more generally, as indicated by the timing of specific events. The concept is similar to that of a *rite of passage, facilitating the analysis of family or demographic variables in their relation to population structure. The stages of a family cycle can be measured by, for instance, the median ages at first marriage, at the births of the first and the last children, at the first marriage of the last child, or at the death of one spouse (Glick and Parke, 1965). Since the concept has spread from the United

States to Canada and Spain, for example, it can make comparative studies much more meaningful (Campo, 1980; Rodgers and Witney, 1981). It is almost routine now to mark the successive phases in studies of family history (e.g., Segalen, 1977). Or the model can be applied to such social-economic variables as the age at leaving school, at entering the labor market, at entering and leaving military service, and so on (Hogan, 1981; Winsborough, 1978). Or such social-economic variables can be joined with family ones to show how they interact (Oppenheimer, 1974). The family cycle, a construct of Paul †Glick, has proved to be a modest but most useful tool in a wide range of analyses.

REFERENCES: Salustiano del Campo, *El Ciclo Vital de la Familia Española* (Madrid: Real Academia de Ciencias Morales y Políticas, 1980). Paul C. Glick and Robert Parke, Jr., "New Approaches in Studying the Life Cycle of the Family," *Demography*, 2 (1965), 187-202. Dennis P. Hogan, *Transitions and Social Change: The Early Lives of American Men* (New York: Academic Press, 1981). Valerie K. Oppenheimer, "The Life-Cycle Sequence: The Interaction of Men's Occupational and Family Life Cycles," *Demography*, 11 (1974), 227-245. Roy H. Rodgers and Gail Witney, "The Family Cycle in Twentieth Century Canada," *Journal of Marriage and the Family*, 43 (1981), 727-740. Martin Segalen, "The Family Cycle and Household Structure: Five Generations in a French Village," *Journal of Family History*, 2 (1977), 223-236. Hal H. Winsborough, "Statistical Histories of the Life Cycle of Birth Cohorts: The Transition from Schoolboy to Adult Male," in Karl E. Taeuber et al., eds., *Social Demography* (New York: Academic Press, 1978).

life expectancy, the average number of years to be lived on the basis of mortality conditions expressed in a particular *life table (cf. Arriaga, 1984). Without specification, the term usually denotes the number of years to be lived from birth; more precisely, one can designate it from any age. This empirical measure is contrasted with the hypothetical one of *life span, the expectation of life that one can presume under the best of conditions conducive to good health.

The increase in life expectancy, or longevity, can be illustrated by data on the United States:

	1900–02	1974	1978	1985 (est.) Male	Female
From birth	49.2	71.9	73.3	71.3	78.8
From age 65	11.9	15.6	16.3	14.65	19.2
75	7.1	9.8	10.4 (75–80)	11.8 (70)	15.6 (70)
80	5.3	7.6	8.1 (80–85)	2.5 (100)	2.7 (100)

In other words, the remarkable reduction in mortality in this century pertained mostly to the deaths of infants and children, somewhat to those of young adults, but only marginally to those of the older population; see also *aging; *old age. Whether life expectations at older ages will increase faster over the coming years depends, of course, on controls of specific diseases. In the older population the leading causes of death are, in order, heart diseases (first by a considerable margin), cancers, and strokes, which together account for almost 60 percent of the deaths of Americans aged 65 and over. These diseases have a markedly different impact on the two sexes, and over the same almost eight decades from 1900-02 to 1978, the increased life expectation of 4.4 years at age 65 was only 2.5 years for white males but 6.2 for white females. According to the 1985 estimates, females retain a very slight advantage even at age 100 (Faber, 1982).

REFERENCES: Eduardo E. Arriaga. "Measuring and Explaining the Change in Life Expectancies," *Demography*, 21 (1984), 83-96. Joseph F. Faber, *Life Tables for the United States: 1900-2050*, Actuarial Study no. 87 (Washington, D.C.: U.S. Social Security Administration, 1982). U.S. National Center for Health Statistics, *Vital Statistics of the United States, 1978*, vol. II, Section 5, "Life Tables" (Washington, D.C., 1980).

life potential, a proposed new measure defined as the product of the number of individuals of a given age and the mean number of years they have to live, as applied to all ages. The concept is illustrated by A. Schobbens with data from Belgium.

REFERENCE: A. Schobbens, "Évolution du Potentiel Démographique de la Belgique 1930-1947-1961-1970-1975," *Bulletin de Statistique* (Brussels), 63 (1977), 1,155-1,184.

life sciences, the term often used in the United States to designate collectively all disciplines that deal with the classification, structure, or behavior of living beings—what is also called biological sciences or *biology in its broadest sense. Apparently the term (like *behavioral sciences and *earth sciences) came into use by the reorganization of university departments into larger units in an attempt to develop interdisciplinary linkages among closely related disciplines.

life span, the maximum duration of human life under optimum conditions, is of course not known precisely. It was once conventional to set it at about "fourscore and ten"; now it is estimated at 114 years (Fries and Crapo, 1981). In earlier times, however, it was sometimes set higher than at present; and the proportion of *centenarians in certain primitive cultures has been reportedly much higher than in industrial societies. As another example, both William †Godwin and A. N. de †Condorcet, the two *utopian philosophers that stimulated the first edition of †Malthus's *Essay*, speculated that with the best possible social organization the extension of life would continue beyond any assignable limit. Their fallacy consists of extrapolating the considerable past increase of *life expectancy into the indefinite future. The reduction of early deaths, however, has been by the control of infectious diseases, while the maximum duration of life is set by the deterioration of organic processes as a concomitant of *aging. If the human life span is fixed, and if the age at which the first serious infirmity occurs continues to rise, then the duration of infirmity will decrease.

REFERENCE: James F. Fries and Lawrence M. Crapo, *Vitality and Aging: Implications of the Rectangular Curve* (San Francisco: W. H. Freeman, 1981).

life-style, or style of life, has been used in several senses. Francis Chapin (1935) developed a Social Status Scale based on whether or not seventeen items were present in a person's living room, and William Sewell (1940) used a similar index specifically for farm families. Such applications of the concept imply that education, occupation, and income more or less determine the type and range of cultural behavior. In the 1920s, when immigration was a much debated political issue in the United States, nativist groups cited remnants of a European cuisine, for example, as a sign that acculturation was not progressing well.

Presently the usual meaning of the phrase is something akin to "any distinctive, and therefore recognizable, mode of living" (Sobel, 1981). Until rather recently most people in the United States or other developed countries had more or less fixed behavioral and consumption patterns set by their education, occupation, and income; and it was therefore possible to predict how under specified conditions members of broad social categories would act—what they would buy, how many children they would have, and so on. Beginning in the 1960s middle-class Americans were able to select individual patterns of consumption, something akin to what economists call "taste," or rather a set of tastes integrated into a personal unit (cf. Hirschman, 1982; Zablocki and Kanter, 1976). Those couples who, for example, have few or no children because they want to maintain their life-style operate, it is assumed, under no outside constraints—though parents who "choose" to have a small number of what Gary †Becker called "expensive" children generally accommodate to standards set by their social class and community; see *New Home Economics. With the far lesser importance of infectious diseases as causes of death, much of mortality has also come to depend on life-styles. That *smoking and other types of *addiction are linked to *cancer is now accepted as fact by virtually every authority. The association between elements of one's diet and *heart disease is more complex (see, for example, *cholesterol), but that there is a relation between the two is certain. Many automobile *accidents, the major cause of death of children and young adults, result from a readier tolerance of drunk drivers in the United States than in Western Europe—that is, from another facet of American life-style. In short, a further extension of life in Western countries must be largely based on successful efforts to induce individuals to live differently, not a task for which physicians have a special professional competence.

REFERENCES: Francis S. Chapin, *Contemporary American Institutions: A Sociological Analysis* (New York: Harper, 1935). Albert O. Hirschman, *Shifting Involvements* (Princeton, N.J.: Princeton University Press, 1982). William H. Sewell, *The Construction and Standardization of a Scale for the Measurement of Oklahoma Farm Families: Socioeconomic Status* (Stillwater: Oklahoma Agricultural and Mechanical College, 1940). Michael E. Sobel, *Lifestyle and Social Structure* (New York: Academic Press, 1981). Benjamin D. Zablocki and Rosabeth Moss Kanter, "A Differentiation of Life Styles," *Annual Review of Sociology*, 2 (1976), 269-298.

life table (sometimes called a mortality table) is a device for deriving from statistics on deaths a number of supplementary data useful in demography, life insurance, public health, and other contexts. In particular, it shows the probability of surviving from each age to any subsequent age, given the age-specific death rates prevailing at a particular time and place.

The history of the life table coincides with the development of demography as a scientific discipline (cf. Shryock and Siegel, chap. 15). The first one was devised by Edmund †Halley from registration data for 1687-91 in Breslau, Germany. The first table that conformed to modern standards of correctness was prepared by Joshua †Milne, based on the mortality in 1779-87 of two parishes of Carlisle, England. In the United States official complete life tables were prepared beginning in 1900-02 as an adjunct of the censuses, and an annual series of abridged tables has been continued since 1945. The *U.N. Demographic Yearbook* gives summary figures for those countries with usable life tables and periodically reviews them in detail. The most complete worldwide summary over a considerable time is in a book by Nathan †Keyfitz and William †Flieger (1968).

In a complete life table mortality is analyzed by single years of age; in an abridged life table such as in Table 1, it is by 5-year age brackets. In either case, however, the first year, a significant period in any schedule of deaths, is listed separately. This example is called a *current* or *period life table*, based on United States statistics for the year 1977 (U.S. National Center for Health Statistics, 1980, Table 5-1). In some cases, the base period is chosen as two or three successive years, in order to avoid selecting a single year with possibly atypical mortality. A *generation* or *cohort life table*, in contrast, is based on the experience of a particular birth *cohort. For example, the mortality of all persons born in the year 1880 would be recorded year by year until all of them die off.

In column 1 of Table 1, x to $x + n$, the figures giving the age are precise; that is, 0 is the date of birth, 1 is the date of the first birthday, and so on.

The figures in column 2, $_nq_x$, are *not* the usual age-specific death rates but so-called *mortality rates*, which indicate the proportion alive at the beginning of the indicated age interval who will die before reaching the end of that interval. For example, of every 1,000 persons alive on their 50th birthday, slightly more than 37 will die before reaching age 55. (Sometimes, as in this example but not in the life table, the figures in the $_nq_x$ column are multiplied by 1,000, in order to avoid the long series of decimals.) In other words, each figure in the column represents the probability of not surviving from one of the indicated ages to the other one. Thus, of those born, 1.42 percent do not survive to age 1; of those alive on their first birthday, 0.27 percent die before they reach precise age 5; and so on. The last figure in the $_nq_x$ column is always 1, which by the usual convention indicates absolute certainty. The conversion of age-specific rates into life-table mortality rates is the only element of the table's construction that involves more than elementary arithmetic, and the calculation of mortality rates can be by any of several formulas (e.g., Spiegelman, chap. 5). All the other columns are derived from this one.

Column 3, l_x, shows the number of persons living at the beginning of the age interval given in column 1. The convention is to begin with a cohort, called a

Table 1
Abridged Life Table, United States, 1977

AGE INTERVAL	PROPORTION DYING	OF 100,000 BORN ALIVE		STATIONARY POPULATION		AVERAGE REMAINING LIFETIME
PERIOD OF LIFE BETWEEN TWO EXACT AGES STATED IN YEARS	PROPORTION OF PERSONS ALIVE AT BEGINNING OF AGE INTERVAL DYING DURING INTERVAL	NUMBER LIVING AT BEGINNING OF AGE INTERVAL	NUMBER DYING DURING AGE INTERVAL	IN THE AGE INTERVAL	IN THIS AND ALL SUBSEQUENT AGE INTERVALS	AVERAGE NUMBER OF YEARS OF LIFE REMAINING AT BEGINNING OF AGE INTERVAL
(1)	(2)	(3)	(4)	(5)	(6)	(7)
x to $x+n$	$_n q_x$	l_x	$_n d_x$	$_n L_x$	T_x	$\overset{\circ}{e}_x$
0-1	0.0142	100,000	1,421	98,751	7,316,270	73.2
1-5	.0027	98,579	268	393,693	7,217,519	73.2
5-10	.0017	98,311	167	491,106	6,823,826	69.4
10-15	.0018	98,144	173	490,355	6,332,720	64.5
15-20	.0051	97,971	499	488,723	5,842,365	59.6
20-25	.0067	97,472	650	485,756	5,353,642	54.9
25-30	.0066	96,822	637	482,517	4,867,886	50.3
30-35	.0070	96,185	677	479,306	4,385,369	45.6
35-40	.0097	95,508	928	475,369	3,906,063	40.9
40-45	.0151	94,580	1,428	469,565	3,430,694	36.3
45-50	.0239	93,152	2,222	460,552	2,961,129	31.8
50-55	.0372	90,930	3,379	446,727	2,500,577	27.5
55-60	.0555	87,551	4,861	426,258	2,053,850	23.5
60-65	.0858	82,690	7,095	396,531	1,627,592	19.7
65-70	.1173	75,595	8,868	356,669	1,231,061	16.3
70-75	.1764	66,727	11,768	305,147	874,392	13.1
75-80	.2647	54,959	14,550	238,929	569,245	10.4
80-85	.3612	40,409	14,596	164,964	330,316	8.2
85 AND OVER	1.0000	25,813	25,813	165,352	165,352	6.4

Source: U.S. National Center for Health Statistics, *Vital Statistics of the United States, 1977*, vol. II: "Mortality," Section 5: "Life Tables" (Washington: U.S. Government Printing Office, 1980).

radix, of 100,000, all of whom are assumed to have been born on the same day; and their experience is followed until the last of the 100,000 dies. Each figure in the l_x column is obtained by subtracting from the one above it the number who died in the previous interval, obtained from column 4, $_nd_x$. Thus:

$$
\begin{aligned}
100,000 \; - \; 1,421 &= 98,579 \\
98,579 \; - \quad 268 &= 98,311 \\
98,311 \; - \quad 167 &= 98,144
\end{aligned}
$$

and so on.

Column 4, the number dying is ($_nd_x$) calculated for each row by multiplying the number that survived (l_x) by the proportion that die during the interval ($_nq_x$). Thus:

$$
\begin{aligned}
0.0142 \times 100,000 &= 1,421 \\
0.0027 \times \quad 98,579 &= \quad 268 \\
0.0018 \times \quad 98,144 &= \quad 173
\end{aligned}
$$

and so on. (Because the figures in the $_nq_x$ column are rounded, those in the $_nd_x$ column may not be precisely the products of the two figures as shown.)

Of the 100,000 persons that are born every year, the proportions dying in each age interval are those shown in column 2. It is assumed in the model that there is no migration in or out. The survivors would constitute what is called a life-table or *stationary population*, in which the number of persons in each age bracket is constant. For whenever a person either moves up into the next age bracket or dies, he is replaced by someone moving up from the next lower age bracket. The stationary population in Table 1 is given in columns 5 and 6 (see also *population, stable; *population, stationary).

Column 5, $_nL_x$, shows the number of persons in the stationary population in the indicated age interval. A census taken of a population based on the assumptions built into a life table and with age-specific deaths in accordance with column 2 would on any date show, say, 485,756 persons aged precisely 20 to 25 years. In a complete life table the figures in the $_nL_x$ column would be derived by subtracting from the number alive at the beginning of the age interval (l_x) the number that died during the interval ($_nd_x$); thus:

$$97,472 \; - \; 650 = 96,822.$$

In an abridged table like this one it is necessary to multiply by the number of years in the age interval, or in this case 5. The 96,822 who survived from age 20 to age 25 lived 5 years each, or a total of $96,822 \times 5 = 484,110$ person-years. The 650 who died during the age interval lived on the average slightly more than half as long, or a total of $650 \times 2.532 = 1,646$. The total number of person-years during the interval, then, is $484,110 + 1,646 = 485,756$. The calculation changes with the shape of the curve representing age-specific deaths, and for the first year there is always a greater bunching of the deaths in the first week or month (cf. *mortality, infant).

Column 6, T_x, gives the total number of years lived by the survivors in the year x and all subsequent years. It is derived from the L_x column by calculating a cumulative total, beginning with the highest age. For ages 85 and over, thus, the two columns have the same figure, 165,352, and successive figures are calculated as follows:

$$165,352 + 164,964 = 330,316$$
$$330,316 + 238,929 = 569,245$$

and so on.

Column 7, $\mathring{e}_x$, gives the average number of years of life remaining at the beginning of the age interval or, in the usual phrase, the *average life expectancy* from age x. The T_x column gives the total number of years to be lived by all the survivors, and the l_x column gives the number of survivors at each age. The average is calculated, then, by dividing the total years by the number of persons, thus:

$$7,316,270 \div 100,000 = 73.2$$
$$7,217,519 \div 98,579 = 73.2$$
$$6,823,826 \div 98,311 = 69.4$$

and so on. For many purposes this $\mathring{e}_x$ column is the most interesting one in the table; it measures mortality conditions independent of the effect of age structure. The first figure in the column, 73.2 years, the life expectancy at birth, is usually the best index of mortality whenever a crude death rate is not sufficiently accurate.

Since the average life expectancy at birth is based in part on the considerable proportion who die during the first year, it indicates a shorter life than at any subsequent age. Indeed, the figures following 73.2 in the $\mathring{e}_x$ column are generally smaller, but they indicate the expectation of life from year x, which of course increases for each row. Obviously, the total years lived is the sum of each figure in column 7 and the corresponding value of x. Thus:

$$73.2 + 0 = 73.2$$
$$73.2 + 1 = 74.2$$
$$69.4 + 5 = 74.4$$

and so on. The *median expectation of life* (or what is sometimes called the *probable lifetime*) is always greater than the average. It is the age to which a person has a 50-50 chance of living or, from birth, the age at which the original cohort of 100,000 will be reduced to 50,000. In the example, as can be seen from the l_x column, the median is slightly more than 80 years, compared with the average of 73.2 years.

The example shown in Table 1 is for the total population of the United States, and it is usual to calculate life tables also for sectors of the population that show significant differences from the total, in particular the two *sexes and the two colors (Table 2). In analyses of the population of the whole country, "All Other" can be taken as essentially equivalent to *blacks. Note that females have a

Table 2
Life Expectation from Designated Ages, by Sex and Color, United States, 1977

Color and Sex	Expectation of Life from Age—				
	0	5	30	65	75
Total	73.2	73.2	45.6	16.3	10.4
Male	69.3	69.4	42.2	13.9	8.7
Female	77.1	77.1	49.0	18.3	11.6
White	73.8	73.8	46.1	16.3	10.3
Male	70.0	70.0	42.7	13.9	8.6
Female	77.7	77.6	49.4	18.4	11.5
All Other	68.8	69.4	42.2	16.0	11.2
Male	64.6	65.2	38.6	14.0	9.7
Female	73.1	73.6	45.8	17.8	12.5

Source: U.S. National Center for Health Statistics, *Vital Statistics of the United States, 1977*, vol. II: "Mortality," Section 5: "Life Tables" (Washington, D.C.: U.S. Government Printing Office, 1980).

consistent advantage over males. The longer life expectation of whites compared with nonwhites is greatest at birth, decreases gradually with higher ages, and for the elderly is reversed (cf. *mortality crossover). In other words, life expectation from birth is a summary figure heavily influenced by the sometimes gross differences in infant mortality, which may exaggerate the relative advantage of particular adult age brackets.

Table 3 gives life expectations from birth for the same sectors of the population at each decade since the beginning of this century. Note that over the years the advantage of females over males generally increased, while the gap between whites and nonwhites is gradually closing. The early figures, which are based on statistics from the *registration area for deaths, are difficult to interpret. On the one hand, it may be that those sections of the country where adequate data were first compiled also had the best control of early mortality; but those same sections, on the other hand, included most of the country's large cities, where particularly the mortality of infants and children was high.

The life table is a means of analyzing the attrition of a population subject to a particular schedule of age-specific mortality. In what is termed a *multiple-decrement table, the model has been adapted to populations subject to attrition by several factors—marriages that may end, for example, by the death of either spouse or by a divorce or separation. Or, as a more imaginative extension of the model, Jacques Véron (1983) analyzed the "survival" of members of the French parliament in their elected positions.

REFERENCES: Nathan Keyfitz and William Flieger, *World Population: An Analysis of Vital Data* (Chicago: University of Chicago Press, 1968). Shryock and Siegel, *Methods and Materials of Demography*. Spiegelman, *Introduction to Demography*. U.S. National

Table 3
Life Expectation from Birth, United States, 1900–02 to 1977

Date	Male		Female	
	White	All Other	White	All Other
1900–02[a]	48.23	32.54	51.08	35.04
1909–11[a]	50.23	34.05	53.62	37.67
1919–21[a]	56.34	47.14	58.53	46.92
1929–31[a]	59.12	47.55	62.67	49.51
1939–41	62.81	52.33	67.29	55.51
1949–51	66.31	58.91	72.03	62.70
1959–61	67.55	61.48	74.19	66.47
1969–71[b]	67.9	60.9	75.4	69.0
1977[b]	70.0	64.6	77.7	73.1

[a]Death-registration states.
[b]Excludes deaths of nonresidents of the United States from 1970 on.
Sources: U.S. National Center for Health Statistics, *Vital Statistics of the United States, 1975*, vol. II: "Mortality," Part A; *Vital Statistics of the United States, 1977*, vol. II: "Mortality," Section 5 (Washington, D.C.: U.S. Government Printing Office, 1979 and 1980).

Center for Health Statistics, *Vital Statistics of the United States, 1977*, vol. II: "Mortality," Section 5: "Life Tables" (Washington, D.C.: U.S. Government Printing Office, 1980). Jacques Véron, "Démographie du Parlement Français de 1958 à 1980," *Population* 38 (1983), 553-564.

linear is used in many phrases to indicate a mathematical relation of the first degree, one that is represented on Cartesian coordinates by a straight line. The most general equation for such a relation is:

$$y = a + bx$$

where y is the dependent variable, x is the independent variable, and a and b are constants. In such an equation all variables have an understood exponent of 1 (that is, they are not squared or raised to a higher power), and they are combined only by addition or subtraction. The linear change of a population is computed, for example, by dividing the difference between two census figures by 10, the number of years between them. It is the average *amount* of increase, as contrasted with the *rate*. The linear extrapolation of a population trend, or the linear interpolation between the populations at two dates, is computed from an equation of the form shown, on the assumption that the rate of growth is constant through the period.

REFERENCE: Shryock and Siegel, *Methods and Materials of Demography*, chap. 23.

Lippes loop, an *intra-uterine device in the shape of a double S, first developed by Jack Lippes, a physician in Buffalo, N.Y.

literacy and **illiteracy** are not so much opposite categories as the end points of a continuum, whose characteristics, moreover, differ greatly according to the context. In anthropology a "literate" society is one with a written language and a small coterie of priest-scholars adept in using it—a smaller proportion, probably, than one that in a worldwide comparison today would define a country as "illiterate." The measurement of literacy in historical studies, similarly, has typically been basesd on the proportion of a local population able to sign their names to a marriage register or some other public document (e.g., Resnick and Resnick, 1977). In a modern society, however, an illiterate can hardly function effectively at anything but the lowest level, and the government of virtually every less developed country has recognized, at least in theory, the relation between education and development. But the sometimes grandiose projects to eliminate illiteracy have introduced another source of confusion, for few states are willing to admit publicly that the expenditure of so much money and effort has resulted in far less than the anticipated progress. How inadequate statistics are likely to be can be illustrated from France in 1931—that is, a modern Western country well into this century. According to marriage records, the proportion of grooms illiterate was only 0.5 percent; in a census the proportion of males 10 years and over who reported themselves as illiterate was 4.8 percent; and according to army records based on results of an examination, the figure was 8.5 percent (UNESCO, 1957, p. 22). In an international comparison of literacy, moreover, one important factor is the relative difficulty of the various *languages.

The UNESCO report, *World Illiteracy at Mid-Century* (1957), discusses both the presumed trend and what the figures signify. The definition of literacy it recommended, the ability to read and write, with understanding, a short simple statement on everyday life, is not followed in collecting most data. Probably the usual procedure by which an enumerator questions respondents always results in a higher proportion of literates than would a test of their ability. The age range included is important: where should the lower cutoff be set, and should very old people, whose ability generally reflects the usually poorer education of a generation or two back, be excluded? The recommendation was to include all persons of 15 years and over. What should be done with the sometimes high proportion who do not respond? The recommendation was that they be excluded from the calculation. Those able to read but not to write, sometimes called semiliterate, were included with the illiterates. More generally, literacy is sometimes transmitted much like any occupational skill, without formal schooling (in England, for instance, primary education was not compulsory until 1876), and the diffusion is both more complex and more difficult to pin down than one would suppose from directives for gathering statistics (Laqueur, 1976).

In 1950, according to the estimate by UNESCO, some 43 to 45 percent of the world's population aged 15 years and over could not read and write, with a range from 80-85 percent in Africa down to 1-2 percent in Northern and Western Europe. According to later figures furnished to UNESCO by member states, the proportion of the same age category classified as illiterate fell to 29 percent in

1980, and this was projected to 25.7 percent in 1990. Even so, because of the rise in the populations of those countries with the most illiterates, the number of persons in the world unable to read and write would increase from 742 million in 1970 to 884 million in 1990. Of the thirty-four countries where seven persons out of ten were illiterate in 1970, twenty-four were in Africa, nine in Asia, and one in the Americas. Well over half of the illiterates in 1980 were in eleven countries (omitting Communist China, where data were not accurate enough to be included): Afghanistan, Iran, Bangladesh, Pakistan, India, and Indonesia; Egypt, Sudan, Ethiopia, and Nigeria; and Brazil (UNESCO, 1980).

In the United States a question on literacy was included in every census from 1840 through 1930; in 1940 and the following censuses the question was rather on the number of years of schooling completed (cf. Folger and Nam, 1967, chap. 4). Questions on literacy essentially conforming to the United Nations recommendation were continued, however, in Current Population Surveys. Since one would expect a high correlation between the number of years of *education and the ability to read and write, those with four or five years of schooling or less came to be designated as functionally illiterate. In 1977, however, when the median years of schooling completed by persons aged 25 years or more was 12.4 (and for blacks 11.4), the U.S. Office of Education estimated that 21 percent of 17-year-old students (or 42 percent of blacks) were functionally illiterate (cf. Hunter and Harman, 1979). Even in a fully developed country like the United States, it has become quite misleading to deduce an ability to read and write from statistics on school attendance.

REFERENCES: John K. Folger and Charles B. Nam, *Education of the American Population* (Washington, D.C.: U.S. Bureau of the Census, 1967). Carman St. John Hunter and David Harman, *Adult Illiteracy in the United States: A Report to the Ford Foundation* (New York: McGraw-Hill, 1979). Thomas Laqueur, "The Cultural Origins of Popular Literacy in England, 1500-1850," *Oxford Review of Education*, 2 (1976), 255-275. Daniel P. Resnick and Lauren B. Resnick, "The Nature of Literacy: An Historical Exploration," *Harvard Educational Review*, 47 (1977), 370-385. UNESCO, *World Illiteracy at Mid-Century* (Paris, 1957); *Literacy, 1972-1976: Progress Achieved in Literacy throughout the World* (Paris, 1980).

locality, a population cluster whose inhabitants live in nearby houses, is a looser term than *place. A locality may not even have a name until it is given one to aid in a census count. The smallest civil divisions of a country, thus, are not equivalent to its localities. An urban-rural hierarchy is sometimes termed a classification by "size of locality," but the preferable term is "size of place."

location theory, a set of generalizations concerning firms' decisions on where to place their factories, and thus concerning the spatial distribution of industry resulting from the aggregate of those decisions, developed as a branch of economics; see J. H. von †Thünen; Alfred †Weber. Theories about the spatial distribution of residences developed independently as a branch of sociology, and the two have seldom been related, though a major factor in deciding where to live is the avoidance when possible of an industrial district.

lodger, an unrelated person living as one member of a household, euphemistically called a "paying guest." In contrast to a lessee, a lodger lacks tenancy rights; in contrast to a *boarder, he or she typically does not eat meals with the rest of the household.

logistic curve, used by Raymond †Pearl and Lowell †Reed, among many others (cf. Pierre-François †Verhulst), to predict the future growth of various populations, has the formula

$$y = \frac{k}{1 + e^{(a + bt)}}$$

in which k is the asymptote that a symmetical S-shaped curve approaches, e is the base of natural logarithms, a is constant, and bt is a function of time, called the logistic. The three stages of slow growth, rapid growth, and again slow growth of the *demographic transition are thus approximated in the shape of the curve, and this was undoubtedly why some forecasts based on it were initially successful. In spite of its poor record over several decades, the logistic curve has been recurrently reconsidered (e.g., Leach, 1981).

REFERENCES: Donald Leach, "Re-evaluation of the Logistic Curve for Human Populations," *Journal of the Royal Statistical Society*, Ser. A, 144, Part 1 (1981), 94-103. Raymond Pearl and Lowell J. Reed, "On the Rate of Growth of the Population of the United States since 1790 and Its Mathematical Representation," *Proceedings of the National Academy of Sciences*, 6 (1920), 275-288.

longevity is used, particularly in popular writings, to mean what its etymology suggests—a long duration of life. In demography it is more likely to be a loose synonym for the more precise term *life expectancy.

longitudinal registration, a system of collecting data on vital events by which a registrar moves periodically through the district of which he or she is an inhabitant and collects information from public officials and other community leaders.

longitudinal survey is one that makes up a long-term analysis based on repeated observations of either the same sample (called a *panel study) or new ones chosen at usually regular intervals. See also *cross-section analysis.

REFERENCES: Duane E. Leigh, "The National Longitudinal Surveys: A Selective Survey of Recent Evidence," *Review of Public Data Use*, 10 (1982), 185-201. Burton Singer and Seymour Spilerman, "Some Methodological Issues in the Analysis of Longitudinal Surveys," in Karl E. Taeuber et al., eds., *Social Demography* (New York: Academic Press, 1978).

Lorenz curve, a graphic presentation showing the degree of concentration of income, wealth, or a similar variable. It is described by plotting the cumulative percentage distribution of the variable against the cumulative percentage distribution of the number of individuals or areas with given amounts of the variable. Each point on the curve, then, can be read, "x percent of the population receive y percent of the income." The curve has been adapted for use in demography to show the degree of population density by area.

REFERENCE: M. O. Lorenz, "Methods of Measuring the Concentration of Wealth," *Quarterly Publications of the American Statistical Association*, 9:70 (1905), 209-219.

low-level equilibrium trap (Nelson, 1956) or **low-income equilibrium** (Leibenstein, 1957, chap. 3), a staple of development economics, is essentially a translation into modern economic language of the argument of †Malthus's principle of population. Most or all of any rise of per-capita income from a low level will be spent on necessities, and hence little will be left for capital formation. With a fall in mortality (the typical reason for an increase in population), growing numbers will, at least over the short run, absorb the rise in income. Rather than an improvement in well-being, there will be more people living at or close to subsistence. According to Julian †Simon (1980), however, though the model may have validly described the past, it does not apply to less developed countries today. The additional children induced by a short-run rise in income from the subsistence level, according to the evidence that he presents, are not enough to push the population down again to subsistence. Similarly, as Malthus developed his theory from its initial presentation, he arrived at the generalization that a rise in income generates a taste for better living and thus eventually can lead to a smaller family. See also *equilibrium.

REFERENCES: Harvey Leibenstein, *Economic Backwardness and Economic Growth: Studies in the Theory of Economic Development* (New York: Wiley, 1957). Richard R. Nelson, "A Theory of the Low-Level Equilibrium Trap in Underdeveloped Economies," *American Economic Review*, 46 (1956), 894-908. Julian L. Simon, "There Is No Low-Level Fertility and Development Trap," *Population Studies*, 34 (1980), 476-486.

Lutheranism, the doctrines associated with the German theologian Martin Luther (1483-1546), one of the important leaders of the Reformation. As a priest and a professor of the Bible at the University of Wittenberg, he opposed the sale of indulgences and then developed more basic differences from Roman Catholic doctrine. He denied the dualism in ethics, the inherent antagonism between the material and the spiritual, that had been reinforced by neo-Platonism; for the separation that sin causes in man is removed by redemption. In all matters of faith and life, man is responsible to God alone. In Luther's works, thus, the appeal is only to the authority of individual conscience; the power of the church inheres in the word of God and is exercised by the teaching of the Gospel, the sole religious authority. On the other hand, divine intervention is specified in an aphorism ascribed to Luther: "God makes children, and He will also see that they are nourished."

Since Luther's original opposition to the papacy centered on its alleged corruption, his social views tended to be stricter than those of Catholicism. Over the years, however, the strong schismatic bent in Lutheranism permitted the development of a wide range of opinion on questions related to population. In the United States more than a dozen denominations developed, of which the more important reunited in 1960 into the American Lutheran Church. Most American Lutherans are whites of German or Scandinavian forebears, living in the Middle West and attending church somewhat more regularly than the Protestant norm demands; they are close to the prototypes of small-town Americans, with average or slightly higher than average education, occupation, and income. According to a 1970 survey of 4,745 Lutherans aged 15 to 65 years, including both laymen and clergy, there were some differences by denomination or age but a fundamental adherence to conservative values. All respondents saw the family as a focal institution in their lives. Contraception was not mentioned in the survey, but in Lutheran circles a 1954 statement by the Augustana Lutheran Church was regarded as very liberal: "God does not expect a couple to produce offspring at the maximum biological capacity. The power to reproduce is His blessing, not a penalty upon the sexual relationship in marriage." On the other hand, even in that pioneer assertion, the complete avoidance of parenthood was denoted as "sinful."

REFERENCES: Merton P. Strommen et al., *A Study of Generations* (Minneapolis: Augsburg Publishing House, 1972). Altman K. Swihart, *Luther and the Lutheran Church, 1483-1960* (New York: Philosophical Library, 1960).

Luxembourg: Demographic Institutions

The International University Institute of Luxembourg, of which Norbert Kunitzki was the director in 1980, publishes two series, Études Économiques Luxembourgeoises and L'Économie Luxembourgeoise, both of which occasionally pertain to the Grand Duchy's population. Address: Institut Universitaire International de Luxembourg, 162A avenue de la Faiencerie, Luxembourg.

The Central Bureau of Statistics and Economic Studies (STATEC), a state agency of which Georges †Als was director in the late 1970s, conducts the censuses, the latest of which was in 1981. It issues annually a statistical yearbook, a compilation of population statistics, one of vital statistics, a more compact *Le Grand Duché de Luxembourg en Chiffres*, and a *Bulletin du STATEC* six times a year. It has published a few of its Cahiers Économiques on the Grand Duchy's population. Address: Service Central de la Statistique et des Études Économiques, 19-21 boulevard Royal, Boîte Postale 304, Luxembourg.

M

m, an index of family limitation that is independent of the level of fertility. It is calculated by comparing the pattern of marital fertility in the observed population with that derived from several populations whose members presumably used few or no contraceptives. As against the standard pattern, more children born at older ages implies a greater control of fertility at younger ages, indicated by higher values of *m*.

REFERENCES: Ansley J. Coale and T. James Trussell, ''Model Fertility Schedules: Variations in the Age Structure of Child Bearing in Human Populations'' and ''Technical Note: Finding the Two Parameters That Specify a Model Schedule of Marital Fertility,'' *Population Index*, 40 (1974), 185-258 and 44 (1978), 203-212.

''M'' IUD, an *intra-uterine device in the shape of the letter M, first developed by Marc Chaft.

machine-readable data files are computerized supplements to the usual printed statistics issued by government agencies, individual researchers, or private survey institutes. Typical examples are the *public-use sample of the U.S. Bureau of the Census and the National Longitudinal Surveys of Labor Market Experience, which were initiated by Herbert †Parnes. In many cases details of a census or survey that never appear in print are available for secondary analysis in machine-readable form. For instance, printed reports of a United States census include breakdowns for whites, blacks, and Hispanics, but the same information concerning European nationalities is available only on tape. An analyst, thus, can do much more than rework the variables already studied in the published volumes. The number of machine-readable data files that can be bought by the general public has been increasing very rapidly, and with the first 1980 issue *Population Index* began to cite any that are of interest to demographers. It also published a paper describing the use of such files and listing the most important sources around the world (Rowe, 1979). See also Data User Services Division and National Technical Information Service, both of which are described in the entry on *United States: Federal Agencies.

REFERENCES: Center for Human Resource Research, *The National Longitudinal Surveys Handbook* (Columbus: College of Administrative Science, Ohio State University, 1980). Judy S. Rowe, "Population Index to Cite Publicly Available Machine-Readable Data Files," *Population Index*, 45 (1979), 567-575.

machismo (from *macho*, Spanish for "male"), a grossly exaggerated virility, has been used by some analysts to explain the high fertility of Latin Americans or North American blacks (cf. Stycos, 1965; Wallace, 1979). Supposedly males are driven not only to have sexual relations with many women but to demonstrate their fecundity by fathering a child with each of them. Alternatively, machismo is analyzed as no more than an expression of lower-class braggadocio, an attempt to reverse the relative positions of social classes or of nations. For example, a Mexican folk song popular when General Pershing was trying to capture Pancho Villa went as follows:

> Qué pensarán los bolillos tan patones
> Que con cañones nos iban a asustar?
> Si ellos tienen aviones de a montanes,
> Aquí tenemos lo mero principal.

(What do those gringo bigfeet think, that they can scare us with cannon? If they have lots of airplanes, we have what really counts.) The deliberately vulgar sexual humor of the American frontier or of some present-day ethnic or racial groups, similarly, may reflect feelings of cultural inferiority. In some less developed countries this personal drive has been coalesced into a kind of ideological machismo, "the feeling on the part of the intellectual classes that to reduce or slow down the rate of population growth or the fertility of a nation is a kind of cultural castration" (Stycos, 1965).

REFERENCES: Américo Paredes, "The United States, Mexico, and Machismo," *Journal of the Folklore Institute*, 8 (1971), 17-37. J. Mayone Stycos, "Survey Research and Population Control in Latin America," in Minoru Muramatsu and Paul A. Harper, eds., *Population Dynamics* (Baltimore: Johns Hopkins Press, 1965). Michele Wallace, *Black Macho and the Myth of the Superwoman* (New York: Dial Press, 1979).

Maghrib Association for the Study of Population, a loose confederation of demographic societies in the Maghrib (Arabic for "the West"), the region of Northwest Africa comprising Tripolitania, Tunisia, Algeria, and Morocco. Maghribi, the dialect of Arabic common to the region, reflects the influence of Berber languages. The strong historical links to Spain and France set these populations somewhat apart from Egypt and Libya and especially from the other Arab countries of the Middle East. The association sponsored a series of colloquia, meeting in Tunis in 1969, Oran in 1975, and Tunis in 1978. Address: Association Maghrébine pour l'Étude de la Population, chez Office National du Planning Familial et de la Population, 42 avenue de Madrid, Tunis, Tunisia.

Majzlin spring, a spring-shaped *intra-uterine device developed by Gregory Majzlin.

Malagasy Republic (formerly Madagascar): **Demographic Institutions**

The University of Madagascar has a program in demography in its faculty of economics. In 1980 this was directed by Tovonanahary A. Rabetsitonta. Address: Université de Madagascar, Boîte Postale 566, Antananarivo.

In the Office of Population of the Ministry of Public Health there is a Department of Demography, which in 1980 was directed by Sylvain Kara, a physician. Address: Ministère de la Santé et de la Population, Direction de la Population, Service de la Démographie, Boîte Postale 88, Antananarivo.

The Central Bureau of Statistics conducts the country's censuses, the latest of which was in 1975. Reports were issued jointly with the National Bureau of Statistics and Economic Research. Address: Commission Nationale du Recensement Général de la Population, Bureau Central du Recensement, Antananarivo.

The National Bureau of Statistics and Economic Research publishes an annual compilation, *Population de Madagascar: Situation au 1ᵉʳ Janvier 19* . . . Address: Institut National de la Statistique et de la Recherche Économique, Ministère des Finances, Boîte Postale 485, Antananarivo.

malaria, an infectious disease caused by protozoa of the genus *Plasmodium*, which are transmitted by the bites of infected mosquitoes of the genus *Anopheles*. The word derives from the Italian *mala aria*, the "bad air" associated with the low-lying swampy areas where the mosquito can flourish. Over the centuries malaria has been one of the most prodigious killers, and until World War II it was the world's principal cause of infant mortality. Those infected in childhood that do not die acquire a degree of immunity, but the cost is a characteristic listlessness. Several writers have hypothesized that the spread of civilization brought with it plowed fields and other breeding grounds and thus, where the disease was present, helped the vectors proliferate (Wood, 1975; Laderman, 1976).

Quinine used to treat malarial patients was one of the few effective specifics developed before the twentieth century. In the most recent period a mass attack on the disease has been waged with insecticides to kill off the population of mosquitoes. Particularly in Ceylon, *DDT, an insecticide that had been developed during World War II, was sprayed over malarial areas and brought about what seemed at first a miraculous effect. The expectation of life at birth increased from 43 years in 1946 to 52 in 1947—a gain in one year that had taken half a century in most Western countries. Since this remarkable decline in mortality was accompanied by a probable rise in fertility, there was a momentous impetus to population growth, a considerable aggravation of economic problems, and a long debate about whether the eradication program had been responsible.

According to Peter †Newman (1965, p. 69), "The antimalaria campaign is estimated to have contributed 60 percent of the rise in the rate of [Ceylon's] population growth since the war, resulting in a population size that by the end of 1960 was a million larger than it otherwise would have been.'' This thesis, challenged by Harald †Frederiksen (1960, 1961), S. A. †Meegama (1967, 1969) and Alberto Palloni (1975), was defended by R. H. Gray (1974, 1975) and in several subsequent papers by Newman (1969, 1970, 1977). The issue was not whether malaria was virtually eliminated as a cause of death—it was; or whether this was effected in part by the spraying of DDT on malarial areas—it was. The debate has been about the relative effect of such other factors as the alleviation of the wartime food shortages and the improvement in available medical care. A resolution has been hampered by the primitive reporting of diseases in Ceylon/ Sri Lanka (cf. Padley, 1959; *cause of death). The debate has continued, more-over, because of its moral implications. As Ceylon exemplified strikingly, when a highly successful control of mortality markedly increases the growth of pop-ulation in an area already burdened with people, saving lives may not be the unambiguous good it once was.

From the successes in Ceylon and other malarial areas, some analysts predicted that the disease would be eradicated. But there was a marked resurgence in the 1970s; and in 1983, according to the estimates of the World Health Organization, the number of new cases was estimated at 7.5 million. Because of the higher prices of the petroleum-based insecticides, some governments cut back on their control programs. In any case, mosquitoes have developed a resistance to several of the insecticides widely used, and the malaria microorganisms are also be-coming resistant to the drug most often prescribed to treat the disease.

REFERENCES: Harald Frederiksen, "Malaria Control and Population Pressure in Ceylon" and "Determinants and Consequences of Mortality Trends in Ceylon," *Public Health Reports*, 75 (1960), 865-868 and 76 (1961), 659-663. R. H. Gray, "The Decline in Mortality in Ceylon and the Demographic Effects of Malaria Control" and "Reply to Palloni," *Population Studies*, 28 (1974), 205-229 and 29 (1975), 499-501. Carol Lad-erman, "Malaria and Progress: Some Historical and Ecological Considerations," *Social Science and Medicine*, 10 (1976), 1-8. S. A. Meegama, "Malaria Eradication and Its Effect on Mortality Levels," and "The Decline in Maternal and Infant Mortality and Its Relation to Malaria Eradication,"*Population Studies*, 21 (1967), 207-237 and 23 (1969), 289-302. Peter Newman, *Malaria Eradication and Population Growth, with Special Reference to Ceylon and British Guiana* (Ann Arbor: University of Michigan School of Public Health, 1965); "Malaria Eradication and Its Effect on Mortality Levels: A Com-ment," and "Rejoinder," *Population Studies*, 23 (1969), 285-288 and 303-305; "Malaria Control and Population Growth," *Journal of Development Studies*, 6 (1970), 133-158; "Malaria and Mortality," *Journal of the American Statistical Association*, 72 (1977), 257-263. Richard Padley, "Cause-of-Death Statements in Ceylon: A Study in Levels of Diagnostic Reporting," *Bulletin of the World Health Organization*, 20 (1959), 677-695. Alberto Palloni, "Comments on R. H. Gray . . . " *Population Studies*, 29 (1975), 497-499. Corinne Shear Wood, "New Evidence for a Late Introduction of Malaria into the New World," *Current Anthropology*, 16 (1975), 93-104.

Malawi: The government's National Statistical Office conducts the censuses, the latest of which was in 1977. In 1981 the Commissioner for Census and

Statistics was Enock Fabiano Ching'anda. The Office publishes an annual *Statistical Yearbook* that includes population data. Address: Office of the President and Cabinet, P.O. Box 333, Zomba.

Malaysia: Demographic Institutions

The National Family Planning Board was headed by Datin Nor Laily Aziz, director general, in 1982. In addition to operating the government's family-planning program, the board conducts training and research related to its main function. Address: UMNO Building, Jalan Tungku Abdul Rahman, Kuala Lumpur 02-11. REFERENCE: Datin Nor Laily Aziz, Boon Ann Tan, Ramli Othman, and Lin Chee Kuan, *Facts and Figures: Malaysia National Population and Family Development Programme* (Kuala Lumpur: National Family Planning Board, 1982).

The Malaysian Center for Development Studies, a government bureau set up in 1966, was in 1980 under E. M. Engku Wock Abdul Rahman, director general. In its policy-oriented research on the country's economy and work force, it deals with various population factors. Address: Prime Minister's Department, P.O. Box 2341, Kuala Lumpur.

The University of Malaya has a Population Studies Unit in its faculty of economics and administration. Address: Lembah Pantai, Kuala Lumpur 22-11.

The government's Department of Statistics includes a Census and Demography Division, which conducted the most recent population census in 1980. It was headed in the late 1970s by Khoo Teik Huat. The department issues, in Malay and English, an *Annual Statistical Bulletin*, a more comprehensive *Statistical Handbook of Peninsular Malaysia*, *Vital Statistics: Peninsular Malaysia*, and *Social Statistics Bulletin: Peninsular Malaysia*. Research papers are published on such topics as labor supply and utilization, household projections, and fertility differentials. Address: Jabatan Perangkaan, Jalan Young, Kuala Lumpur 10-01.

Maldives: The National Planning Agency conducted the first modern census in 1977 and issued the first volume reporting on it in 1981. Address: Male.

Mali: Demographic Institutions

As part of its work on the drought in the subregion, the Institute of the Sahel carries out demographic studies on mortality, morbidity, nutrition, migration, and nomadism. Address: Institut du Sahel, Boîte Postale 1530, Bamako.

The government's National Bureau of Statistics and Public Information publishes an *Annuaire Statistique* that includes population data. Its Central Bureau of the Census, headed in 1980 by Bory Sow †Hamady, conducts the country's censuses, the latest of which was in 1976. Address: Direction Nationale de la Statistique et de l'Informatique, and Bureau Central de Recensement, Ministère du Plan, Boîte Postale 12, Koulouba, Bamako.

Malta: The government's Central Office of Statistics conducts the censuses, of which the most recent with published data was in 1967 (one was scheduled for

1980). The office publishes a *Quarterly Digest of Statistics* and each year a *Statistical Handbook* and an *Annual Abstract of Statistics*, as well as a more detailed *Demographic Review of the Maltese Islands for the Year* . . . . Address: Auberge de Castille, Valletta.

Malthusian usually pertains not to the theories of †Malthus but rather to the movement that was partly inspired by them. The Malthusian (or, later Neo-Malthusian) Leagues established during the latter decades of the nineteenth century in several European countries were the first organized efforts to diffuse birth control. They were typically more ideological than practical, and the version of Malthus's principle of population that they propagated included none of the refinements that he made in later editions of the *Essay on the Principle of Population*; see also *contraception. Some analysts still use "Malthusian population" to designate one characterized by a widespread knowledge, acceptance, and practice of family limitation, as contrasted with a "non-Malthusian population," which lacks deliberate family planning. In other contexts, however, such phrases as "Malthusian pressure" or "Malthusian dilemma" refer to the problem of a growing population for which food is imminently inadequate.

manpower is used in both professional and journalistic contexts to mean two quite different entities. On the one hand, the term refers to the largest potential *work force of a nation, including all who are economically active plus the "labor reserve," defined by the U.S. Bureau of the Census as persons not presently in the labor force who had worked during the past ten years and presumably could generally again produce goods and services if they so chose and if there was a sufficient demand. Of the total population, thus, the manpower excludes only the youngest and the oldest, those physically or mentally incapacitated, and the minimum number of homemakers to provide for the work force. Alternative (and unambiguous) designations are *labor pool* and *labor potential*. On the other hand, manpower is used to designate the actual work force. This is the usual connotation of such phrases as "manpower needs," "manpower development," "medical manpower," and so on, which typically refer not to a pool of potential workers but to those who would be working under the specified conditions. Those who substitute *gender for *sex* are likely to insist on the differentiation designated in the neologism "womanpower."

Maori, the aborigines of New Zealand, exemplify the common tendency to exaggerate the population losses of primitives. The depopulation suffered in wars with the whites, from disease, and even from the sterility induced by the disintegration of Maori culture allegedly doomed the race to eventual extinction (e.g., McCreary, 1968). Two important factors are omitted from this list. Until after World War II, all demographic data were flawed by considerable undercounts of this flourishing minority, partly because of a persistent ambiguity about the group's boundaries. From the beginning of their contact, Maori and whites interbred freely, very often in formal marriages, and the considerable progeny of mixed blood are sometimes counted as whites, sometimes as Maori. Ian †Pool (1977) coined the term "interethnic migration" to denote the frequent shift in ethnic identity from one census to the next. See also *American Indians; *hunting and gathering; *population, primitive.

REFERENCES: J. R. McCreary, "Population Growth and Urbanisation," in Erik Schwimmer, ed., *The Maori People in the Nineteen-sixties* (Auckland: Blackwood and Janet Paul, 1968). D. Ian Pool, *The Maori Population of New Zealand, 1769-1971* (Auckland: Auckland University Press, 1977).

maps are used in every phase of a census—in planning the operation, during the count, and in presenting the data to users. In the United States, some two and a half years before the date of the census, the country is divided into administrative areas of various sizes, some identical with the political units by which the data will eventually be reported, and others set for the greatest convenience in the enumeration. Supervisors use maps of small areas and their estimated populations to allocate their budgets and personnel. For some two years after the count, maps to display census data in cartographic form are planned, drafted, drawn, checked, and published.

REFERENCE: U.S. Bureau of the Census, *Mapping for Censuses and Surveys*, Statistical Training Document, ISP-TR-3A (Washington, D.C., 1977).

margin and **marginal** are used in the social disciplines with three special meanings. In economics, a "marginal analysis" concentrates on the last person or firm or other entity, the one "at the margin" in a particular trend of utility, cost, product, propensity to save, or whatever. A marginal change in that sense, ordinarily a very small increment or decrement to the total, differs substantially from an average, however defined; but that seemingly unimportant change underlies the decisions of entrepreneurs, consumers, and other actors in the economy. In mathematical economics, thus, marginal analysis is an application of differential calculus to find particular maxima or minima, which are defined as the optima toward which a free market tends in its unhindered development.

In the works of Robert E. †Park and his students, "marginal man" was used to denote a person who moved out of one social world without finding a place in another—thus, in terms of demography, an incompletely assimilated immigrant. This seemingly pejorative characterization was attacked particularly by American Jews, who pointed out that life at the edge of two cultures could be not destructive but enriching, resulting in a greater creativity (see, for example, Goldberg, 1941; Riesman, 1954).

In a *cross-tabulation of two or more variables, the distribution of each is called the "marginals" or "margins" because they appear in the margins of the statistical tables. In a two-variable table, they are called, respectively, the horizontal and the vertical marginals. Much of "the logic of survey analysis" (a text by Morris Rosenberg) pertains to the manipulation in specified ways of these marginal figures.

REFERENCES: Milton M. Goldberg, "A Qualification of the Marginal Man Theory," *American Sociological Review*, 6 (1941), 52-58. David Riesman, "Marginality, Conformity, and Insight," in *Individualism Reconsidered* (Glencoe, Ill.: Free Press, 1954). Morris Rosenberg, *The Logic of Survey Analysis* (New York: Basic Books, 1968).

marijuana and its close analogues, consumed by an estimated 200 to 300 million persons throughout the world, constitute the most prevalent group of illicit drugs. Their use in the United States and other Western countries, anomalous until the late 1950s, has spread to high proportions of the countries' youth. That the subsequent large body of writings has been sharply divided was due in considerable part to ignorance of even the chemistry of "cannabanoids," a term coined in the 1960s to designate the C_{12} compounds typical of and present in *Cannabis sativa*, their carboxylic acids, analogues, and transformation products. Cannabis preparations vary greatly, especially between marijuana (dried cannabis flowering tops) and hashish, which is much richer in resin.

What the physiological and psychological effects of the various cannabanoids are, as consumed in a range of doses under different conditions by persons with varying susceptibility, cannot be stated with certainty. There are overlaps with the effects of anesthetics, alcohol, and epilepsy. Findings from many studies include temporal and spatial disorientation, depersonalization, hallucinatory and delusory phenomena, increased suggestibility, and changes in cognitive and motor functions. There have been strong psychotic responses to a single dose, and far more cases with schizophrenic symptoms from prolonged use. In almost no cases have users died from marijuana, and then only from intravenous injections. See also *addiction.

REFERENCE: Raphael Mechoulam, ed., *Marijuana: Chemistry, Pharmacology, Metabolism and Clinical Effects* (New York: Academic Press, 1973).

marital history, a record with dates of a person's marriage(s), separation(s) or divorce(s), and the death(s) of spouse(s). Except that the data are collected in current censuses or surveys, the term is similar to but narrower than the family reconstitution associated with Louis †Henry. See also *life cycle.

In the United States censuses of 1970 and 1980, persons aged 15 years and over who had ever been married were asked whether they had been married more than once and whether the first marriage had been terminated by the spouse's death. Together with the information given on the persons' current marital status, those responses enabled the Census Bureau to derive the numbers of persons who had been widowed, divorced, or widowed and divorced.

marital status, alternatively termed *civil* or *conjugal status*, denotes the place of an individual in the succession single-married-widowed (or divorced). This placement is complicated both by the ambiguity of the three or four categories and by the frequent reluctance of persons to place themselves in them. In its recommendations for the 1970 censuses, the United Nations tried to transgress the great variety of concepts of *marriage, but with only partial success. It proposed that the population beginning at age 15 (or under, if possible) be classified by sex and 5-year age categories and by the following marital statuses: single, married, widowed, divorced, separated, and not stated.

*Single persons, or *bachelors and spinsters, are those who have been in that status all their lives; to avoid misunderstanding, they are sometimes referred to as the "never married." All other categories, thus, are the "ever married." In the IUSSP *Multilingual Dictionary* "single" is defined without reference to age; but it is the usual practice, of course, to classify as such only that portion of a population that is of marriageable age. Those who remain single to ages 30-34 or, even more so, 45-49 are often analyzed in studies of natality, since they represent one important manner by which a country's fertility is reduced (see, for example, *Ireland).

Married persons may or may not include those living in *consensual unions or other quasilegal partnerships. If the distinction is maintained in the abstract, it may not be in practice, for generally many of those living de facto as man and wife report (or used to report) themselves as married. Analysis of fertility depends on age at first marriage as an important variable, but whether persons are in their first or a subsequent marriage is often not included in the available data.

Widowed persons are defined as those currently in that status, thus excluding persons who have remarried. Women with illegitimate children, or those who have been divorced, sometimes avoid (or used to avoid) the stigma associated with either status by reporting themselves as *widows. The distinction between legal separation and divorce depends in part on law and religion, in part, since divorces are more expensive, on the income of the persons concerned; and statistics on *divorce are complicated also by what are termed migratory divorces, granted by such jurisdictions as Nevada to temporary residents. Since 1949 all jurisdictions in the United States have permitted divorce, but laws still differ greatly and many persons find it more convenient to establish temporary residence in a state with more permissive conditions.

Marital fertility relates the number of legitimate births to the married women that bore them, rather than all births to all women. How much a marital fertility rate differs from the general (or age-specific) fertility rate depends, thus, on the proportion of births recorded as illegitimate. And this datum depends in turn on how "legitimacy" is interpreted in the particular culture and how willing un-married mothers are to declare themselves as such. See also *fertility measures.

Markov chain, named after the Russian mathematician A. A. Markov (1856-1922), is a random process of which one can predict the future just as accurately from a knowledge of the present state as from a knowledge of the present together with the entire past history. Alternatively, it represents a process in which the probability that a population will be in a given state in the $(t + 1)$st period depends only on its state in the tth period. The probability P_{ij} that the population will move from state *i* to state *j* is called the *transition probability*, and a transition matrix has as its elements such transition probabilities (Billingsley, 1968).

The Markov chain has been used in various ways related to demography, particularly in studies of social mobility (e.g., Bartholomew, 1973). For instance, if one takes a Markov chain constructed from empirical data as the norm, an improvement along a career line is defined as a deviation from that course (Hodge, 1966). An application of Markov chains to labor mobility, as another example, started diverse research efforts (Blumen et al., 1955; cf. Singer and Spilerman, 1978). The transitions of migrations have been analyzed in a similar way by a number of scholars (e.g., Alonso, 1978; Rogers, 1968).

REFERENCES: William Alonso, "Theory of Movements," in Niles M. Hansen, ed., *Human Settlement Systems* (Cambridge, Mass.: Ballinger, 1978). David J. Bartholomew, *Stochastic Models for Social Processes* (2nd ed.; New York: Wiley, 1973). Patrick Billingsley, "Markov Chains" in *International Encyclopedia of the Social Sciences*, 9, 581-585. Isadore Blumen, Marvin Kogan, and Philip J. McCarthy, *The Industrial Mobility of Labor as a Probability Process* (Ithaca, N.Y.: Cornell University, 1955). Robert W. Hodge, "Occupational Mobility as a Probability Process," *Demography*, 3 (1966), 19-34. Andrei Rogers, *Matrix Analysis of Interregional Population Growth and Distribution* (Berkeley: University of California Press, 1968). Burton Singer and Seymour Spilerman, "Some Methodological Issues in the Analysis of Longitudinal Surveys," in Karl E. Taeuber et al., eds., *Social Demography* (New York: Academic Press, 1978).

marriage, according to the definition recommended by the U.N. Statistical Commission, is a "legal union of persons of opposite sex. The legality of the union may be established by civil, religious, or other means as recognized by the laws of each country; and irrespective of the type of marriage, each should be reported for vital statistics purposes" (United Nations, 1955, p. 60). Like alternative definitions that other agencies have proposed, this one is ambiguous in several respects. Not only do such religions as *Roman Catholicism or *Islam define marriage differently, but in any case the distinction between legal and extralegal unions often cannot be sharply drawn even within a single cultural context. It may be that two persons who participate in a *betrothal thus indicate a merely tentative intention to wed at some future date or, under the rules of *Hinduism, become spouses in a virtually indissoluble *child marriage. The range of common-law marriages—that is, those not sanctioned by either a religious or a civil ceremony—merges into casual liaisons; but *consensual unions are so frequent, particularly in Latin America, that both ethically and statistically they are defined as one type of the conjugal state. See also *marital status.

With respect to demography the principal ambivalence pertains to how marriage relates to fertility. At one extreme, as under the norms of traditional *Confucianism, marriage is perceived as the joining of two family lines through the union of two of their young representatives; its purpose is unequivocally propagation, the continuation of the two lineages. In the modern West, at the other extreme, a marriage is increasingly defined as a personal arrangement between two individuals who themselves decide whether to have children and, if so, how many (or even, as in the homosexual "marriages" that some aberrant clergymen have formally sanctioned, cannot conceive children at all). The one-time function by which marriage bestowed *legitimacy on a union's offspring has also been eroded by softening the legal and other penalties of *illegitimacy. If a married couple can without pressure from anyone deliberately avoid having children, and if, with little or no differentiation, children can be brought into the society in or out of wedlock, then the relation between *family and fertility would seem almost to be vestigial (cf. Davis, 1983).

Data on marriages depend on their registration, which according to the United Nations (1955, p. 33) should everywhere be compulsory. Of course, it is not, if only because of the difficulties we have noted in defining the process. Like other vital statistics, those on marriage and divorce are collected, if at all, at the local level; and then they may be compiled by a central agency into national totals. In the United States, for instance, a federal agency has set standards of accuracy and completeness for various items included in vital statistics, and has established *registration areas comprising those states that collect adequate data (see the sample certificate). Since the marriage-registration area still is incomplete, the United States in fact has no national statistics even now, and earlier compilations were even less representative.

The important distinction between *bachelor or spinster, on the one hand, and widower or *widow, on the other, can be blurred in terms pertaining to the married state. *Single persons can be understood either as those who never had a spouse or as those who presently do not have one. The ambiguity is avoided by using the phrases "ever married" or "never married." It is important to distinguish between first and subsequent marriages, and *nuptiality is ordinarily computed with respect to first marriages, either only or at least separately (e.g., Henry, 1976, chap. 5).

The commonest measure is the crude marriage rate, or the number of marriages during a year per 1,000 persons in the midyear population. The effect of differences in the age structure can be corrected in a general marriage rate, with the population aged 15 years and over as the denominator or, better, the marriageable population—that is, the total of single, divorced, and widowed adults. Alternatively, one can control for age by *cohort analysis or by using the so-called singulate mean age (Hajnal, 1953; Winsborough, 1978). Other refinements include specifications by sex, age and sex, or, if endogamy is generally practiced, religion, race, or nationality (Shryock and Siegel, chap. 19). Persons with particular characteristics who lack suitable partners are faced with what has been termed a marriage squeeze (Akers, 1967; cf. Heer and Grossbard-Shechtman, 1981; Schoen, 1983). To calculate the probability of marrying from the trend in the age structure is easily done, but the forecast implies that the only factor limiting a person's finding a spouse is how old he or she is.

*Age at marriage varies considerably, and the norm can have a great influence on fertility (Coale, 1971; Durch, 1980). On a world scale the lowest age at marriage has been in India, the highest in Ireland (Agarwala, 1962; Kennedy,

U.S. STANDARD

LICENSE AND CERTIFICATE OF MARRIAGE

TYPE OR PRINT IN PERMANENT INK — SEE INSTRUCTIONS FOR HANDBOOK

LICENSE NUMBER

STATE FILE NUMBER

GROOM

GROOM—NAME: FIRST / MIDDLE / LAST
1.

AGE
2.

USUAL RESIDENCE—STREET AND NUMBER
3a.

CITY, TOWN OR LOCATION
3b.

COUNTY
3c.

STATE
3d.

DATE OF BIRTH (Mo., Day, Yr.)
5.

BIRTHPLACE (State or foreign country)
4.

FATHER—NAME
6a.

BIRTHPLACE (State or foreign country)
6b.

MOTHER—MAIDEN NAME
7a.

BIRTHPLACE (State or foreign country)
7b.

BRIDE

BRIDE—NAME: FIRST / MIDDLE / LAST
8a.

MAIDEN NAME (If different)
8b.

AGE
9.

USUAL RESIDENCE—STREET AND NUMBER
10a.

CITY, TOWN OR LOCATION
10b.

COUNTY
10c.

STATE
10d.

DATE OF BIRTH (Mo., Day, Yr.)
12.

BIRTHPLACE (State or foreign country)
11.

FATHER—NAME
13a.

BIRTHPLACE (State or foreign country)
13b.

MOTHER—MAIDEN NAME
14a.

BIRTHPLACE (State or foreign country)
14b.

WE HEREBY CERTIFY THAT THE INFORMATION PROVIDED IS CORRECT TO THE BEST OF OUR KNOWLEDGE AND BELIEF AND THAT WE ARE FREE TO MARRY UNDER THE LAWS OF THIS STATE.

GROOM'S SIGNATURE ▲
15.

BRIDE'S SIGNATURE ▲
16.

LICENSE TO MARRY

THIS LICENSE AUTHORIZES THE MARRIAGE IN THIS STATE OF THE PARTIES NAMED ABOVE BY ANY PERSON DULY AUTHORIZED TO PERFORM A MARRIAGE CEREMONY UNDER THE LAWS OF THE STATE OF _____

SUBSCRIBED TO AND SWORN TO BEFORE ME ON Month / Day / Year
17a.

SIGNATURE OF ISSUING OFFICER ▲
17b.

TITLE OF ISSUING OFFICER
17c.

CEREMONY

I certify that the above named persons were married on: Month / Day / Year
18a.

WHERE MARRIED—CITY
18b.

COUNTY
18c.

PERSON PERFORMING CEREMONY ▲ (Signature)
18d.

TITLE
18e.

TYPE OF CEREMONY (Religious or civil, specify)
18f.

WITNESS TO CEREMONY ▲ (Signature)
19a.

WITNESS TO CEREMONY ▲ (Signature)
19b.

LOCAL OFFICIAL

LOCAL OFFICIAL MAKING RETURN TO STATE HEALTH DEPARTMENT ▲ (Signature)
20a.

DATE RECEIVED BY LOCAL OFFICIAL (Mo., Day, Yr.)
20b.

INFORMATION FOR STATISTICAL PURPOSES ONLY

GROOM

RACE—GROOM — Specify (e.g., White, Black American Indian, etc.)
21.

NUMBER OF THIS MARRIAGE — Specify (First, second, etc.)
22.

IF PREVIOUSLY MARRIED, LAST MARRIAGE ENDED: BY DEATH, DIVORCE, DISSOLUTION OR ANNULMENT (Specify)
23a.

DATE (Mo., Day, Yr.)
23b.

EDUCATION (Specify only highest grade completed): Elementary or Secondary (0-12)
24.

College (1-4 or 5+)

BRIDE

RACE—BRIDE — Specify (e.g., White, Black American Indian, etc.)
25.

NUMBER OF THIS MARRIAGE — Specify (First, second, etc.)
26.

IF PREVIOUSLY MARRIED, LAST MARRIAGE ENDED: BY DEATH, DIVORCE, DISSOLUTION OR ANNULMENT (Specify)
27a.

DATE (Mo., Day, Yr.)
27b.

EDUCATION (Specify only highest grade completed): Elementary or Secondary (0-12)
28.

College (1-4 or 5+)

1973, chap. 7). A marriage brought to an end by the death of one spouse or by a *divorce may be followed, after a time that religious or cultural norms usually determine, by a *remarriage. The duration of the intervening period may affect the person's total fertility; and the promiscuity of unstable unions, contrary to what is often assumed, can therefore result in a smaller number of offspring (e.g., Blake, 1961, chap. 14).

The school of economists that developed a *New Home Economics to explain the level of fertility have applied the same principles to marriage. According to Gary †Becker (1973-74), for instance, marriage rates depend essentially on a disproportion of the two sexes in the prime ages plus levels of income (cf. Ermisch, 1981a, 1981b; Fulop, 1980). Sociologists are likely to consider a wider range of variables, particularly in the large body of writings on intermarriage (e.g., Murstein, 1980). In Western countries patterns have been changing fast enough to confound most theories, and in less developed countries the shift from traditional to modernist is sometimes very rapid (cf. Durch, 1980). In Chinese and some other societies, *adoption is so prevalent that it can act as a functional substitute for reproduction and thus can affect the propensity to marry (cf. Wolf and Huang, 1980). In any society the factors that determine the rate of marriage affect also the proportion of the population that does not marry—obviously a very important sector in relation to fertility (Dixon, 1978; Kain, 1980).

REFERENCES: S. N. Agarwala, *Age at Marriage in India* (Allahabad, India: Kitab Mahal, 1962). Donald S. Akers, "On Measuring the Marriage Squeeze," *Demography*, 4 (1967), 907-924. Gary S. Becker, "A Theory of Marriage, Parts I and II," *Journal of Political Economy*, 81 (1973), 813-846; 82 (1974), S11-S26. Judith Blake, *Family Structure in Jamaica: The Social Context of Reproduction* (New York: Free Press of Glencoe, 1961). Ansley J. Coale, "Age Patterns of Marriage," *Population Studies*, 25 (1971), 193-214. Kingsley Davis, "The Future of Marriage," *American Academy of Arts and Sciences Bulletin*, 36 (1983), 15-43. Ruth B. Dixon, "Late Marriage and Non-marriage as Demographic Responses: Are They Similar?" *Population Studies*, 32 (1978), 449-466. Jane S. Durch, *Nuptiality Patterns in Developing Countries: Implications for Fertility* (Washington, D.C.: Population Reference Bureau, 1980). J. F. Ermisch, "Economic Opportunities, Marriage Squeezes, and the Propensity to Marry: An Economic Analysis of Period Marriage Rates in England and Wales," *Population Studies*, 35 (1981a), 347-356; "An Economic Theory of Household Formation: Theory and Evidence from the General Household Survey," *Scottish Journal of Political Economy*, 28 (1981b), 1-19. Marcel Fulop, "A Brief Survey of the Literature on the Economic Analysis of Marriage and Divorce," *American Economist*, 24 (1980), 12-18. John Hajnal, "Age at Marriage and Proportions Marrying," *Population Studies*, 7 (1953), 111-132. David M. Heer and Amyra Grossbard-Shechtman, "The Impact of the Female Marriage Squeeze and the Contraceptive Revolution on Sex Roles and the Women's Liberation Movement in the United States, 1960 to 1975," *Journal of Marriage and the Family*, 43 (1981), 49-65. Henry, *Population*. Edward L. Kain, "The Never-Married in the United States," doctoral dissertation, University of North Carolina, 1980. Robert E. Kennedy, Jr., *The Irish: Emigration, Marriage, and Fertility* (Berkeley: University of California Press, 1973). Bernard I. Murstein, "Mate Selection in the 1970s," *Journal of Marriage and the Family*, 42 (1980), 777-792. Robert Schoen, "Measuring the Tightness of a Marriage

Squeeze," *Demography*, 20 (1983), 61-78. Shryock and Siegel, *Methods and Materials of Demography*. United Nations, *Handbook of Vital Statistics Methods*, Ser. F, no. 7 (New York, 1955). Hall H. Winsborough, "Statistical Histories of the Life Cycle of Birth Cohorts: The Transition from Schoolboy to Adult Male," in Karl E. Taeuber et al., eds., *Social Demography* (New York: Academic Press, 1978). Arthur P. Wolf and Chieh-shan Huang, *Marriage and Adoption in China, 1845-1945* (Stanford, Calif.: Stanford University Press, 1980).

marriageable, able to marry under the laws and customs of the person's country and religion. Most countries set a minimum age at puberty or somewhat above it, and regulations prohibit the formation of incestuous unions, variously defined. The marriageable population consists, thus, of adolescent and adult *bachelors and spinsters, *widows and widowers (except where, as among pious Hindus, the remarriage of widows is prohibited), and *divorced persons of either sex (except where a remarriage is prohibited, sometimes only for a certain period). The nonmarriageable population consists, apart from children, of those who are married or separated but not legally divorced.

masculine differs from male (as does *feminine* from female) in referring not only to the biological *sex but also to the associated cultural or psychic characteristics sometimes subsumed under *gender. In the jargon of demography, however, the *masculinity proportion* means the proportion of males in a population, and the *masculinity ratio* is an alternative designation of the sex ratio as this is usually computed in English-speaking countries.

Master Area Reference File (MARF), a computerized list that the U.S. Bureau of the Census maintained to control the operation of the 1980 enumeration. It contained records of all the geographic areas recognized in the census arranged hierarchically from state down to *enumeration district and *block group. The comparable file for the 1970 census was called the *Master Enumeration District List* (MEDList).

matching is used by the U.S. Bureau of the Census to designate the process of checking one set of population data against another, in the expectation that two imperfect sources will yield a better result than either one by itself. For example, vital statistics can be matched with a census count to see how many births were not registered and how many infants were not enumerated. Sample surveys designed for other purposes, such as to determine the characteristics of the labor force, are sometimes matched against the results of a census count. *Record linkage is one type of matching, as in the study of differential mortality by Lillian †Guralnick and Charles †Nam (Kitagawa and Hauser, 1973, Appendix A).

    In recent decades a census has often been followed by a post-enumeration survey conducted by a small number of carefully selected and specially trained interviewers. In 1950, for instance, about 3,500 small areas were recanvassed in order to gauge the number of households omitted in the census, and 22,000 households were visited in order to see how many persons had been miscounted. It was estimated that there had been an underenumeration of 3.4 million persons and an overenumeration of 1.3 million persons, or a net undercount equal to 1.4 percent of the total enumerated population. Errors were relatively more frequent in the South, in rural areas, and among nonwhites. Essentially similar procedures were followed in the next censuses, and also in other countries (e.g., Lahiri, 1958; U.S. Bureau of the Census, 1964; Heer, 1968).

How much variation is to be found in supposedly invariant characteristics as reported in two or more surveys or censuses? In a summary of a number of prior comparisons, E. M. Schreiber (1975-76) pointed out that the reported ages matched in only 83 to 95 percent of the cases, the occupation of the respondent's father in 70 percent, the respondent's education in 62 to 77 percent, and the respondent's income in 50 to 64 percent. In Schreiber's own research, he compared responses from the same persons in a panel study. In the data on sex and race, which depended on the interviewer's observation rather than the respondent's answer, there was a slippage of only 1 or 2 percent, presumably due mainly to errors in coding. Age was consistent in 86.1 to 97.8 percent of the responses, father's occupation in 66.2 to 74.4 percent. Apart from the slight error from coding, so large a difference may have been the consequence of inconsistent prevarication, particularly on items that reflect social status. Similarly, when a group of teenagers was given the same test twice, on a scale of 100 the consistency was 70 for background information, 49 on questions concerning their intentions on when to marry and other family-related decisions, and 36 on questions reflecting their attitudes toward population growth. For the whole of the questionnaire, the index of reliability was only 47 (Brackbill, 1974).

As one more example of the hidden flaws revealed in matching studies, one can take the ''obvious'' fact that every emigrant from one country is matched by the same person when he is counted as an immigrant to another country. In 1972 the U.N. Economic Commission for Europe (ECE) conducted an analysis of migration between pairs of ECE countries—that is, nations that maintain in general the best statistical records in the world. For the total movement along 342 paths, the number of immigrants was 57 percent greater than the number of emigrants. Part of the reason was a time lag, but the main ones were that the definitions of ''emigrant'' and ''immigrant'' were not consistent and that countries generally keep a better record of those coming in than of those leaving (United Nations, 1978). See also *census; *errors; *PGE/ERAD/ECP.

REFERENCES: Yvonne Brackbill, ''Test-Retest Reliability in Population Research,'' *Studies in Family Planning*, 5 (1974), 261-266. David M. Heer, ed., *Social Statistics and the City* (Cambridge, Mass.: Harvard University Press, 1968). Evelyn M. Kitagawa and Philip M. Hauser, *Differential Mortality in the United States: A Study in Socioeconomic Epidemiology* (Cambridge, Mass.: Harvard University Press, 1973). Debabrata Lahiri, ''Recent Developments in the Use of Techniques for Assessment of Errors in

Nation-wide Surveys in India,'' *Bulletin de l'Institut International de Statistique*, 36 (1958), 71-93. E. M. Schreiber, ''Dirty Data in Britain and the USA: The Reliability of 'Invariant' Characteristics Reported in Surveys,'' *Public Opinion Quarterly*, 39 (1975-76), 493-506. United Nations, *Demographic Yearbook, 1977* (New York, 1978). U.S. Bureau of the Census, *Evaluation and Research Program of the U.S. Censuses of Population and Housing, 1960: Accuracy of Data on Population Characteristics as Measured by CPS-Census Match* (Washington, D.C., 1964).

mate, a rough equivalent of *spouse, sometimes in any type of sexual union apart from a formal *marriage, sometimes including partners in a consensual union.

maternal mortality, according to the definition recommended by the World Health Organization (WHO), comprises deaths of women while pregnant or within forty-two days of the pregnancy's termination from any cause related to or aggravated by the pregnancy or its management. Direct obstetric deaths are those resulting from complications of pregnancy, labor, or puerperium; indirect obstetric deaths are those resulting from a prior disease or one that developed during pregnancy but was not due to direct obstetric causes. In one study using data from Georgia for the years 1975-76, when death certificates were matched with corresponding birth certificates, maternal mortality increased by 27 percent over the figure derived from the death certificates alone (Rubin et al., 1981). Such an underestimate may be common, since it derived largely from the misclassification of deaths not immediately after the birth but still within the specified period of forty-two days. See also *reproductive mortality.

REFERENCE: George L. Rubin, Brian McCarthy, James Shelton, and Roger W. Rochat, ''The Risk of Childbearing Re-evaluated,'' *American Journal of Public Health*, 71 (1981), 712-716.

mathematical demography may be said to have originated with demography itself—in such works as those by John †Graunt (1662), the pioneer actuaries, and Leonhard †Euler (1760). From these beginnings the field has ramified greatly, particularly in the most recent period. In a very useful bibliographic essay, Nathan †Keyfitz (1976) noted works on *animal populations (for example, how the number of predators affects the number of their prey, and vice versa), spatial theory, *diffusion and *urbanization, and a number of other topics that are discussed elsewhere in this work. Some of the main steps marking the rise of mathematical demography were gathered into a convenient compendium with short prefatory notes (Smith and Keyfitz, 1977); and in introductions to the field, Keyfitz (1968, 1977) led the reader through the principal current applications (see also Feichtinger, 1979). In fact, however, though discussions of population phenomena are typically numerical, only a few of the questions that demographers pose can be analyzed mathematically. In only some cases is it possible to formulate the relevant variables and the relations among them in mathematical symbols and, once so formulated, to analyze them rigorously. At least for the time being, many of the important issues in demography can be usefully expressed and developed only in words.

In this century the most important pioneer was Alfred J. †Lotka, who over a long professional career raised some of the most pertinent questions and provided tools for answering them (e.g., Lotka, 1925). He devised and solved the *renewal equation, in which the numbers of births in two successive generations are related. Much of his effort was devoted to finding a "true" or *intrinsic rate of increase of nonstable populations. High fertility in the past results in an age structure favorable to a continuing high birth rate; and when fertility began to fall in Western countries, there were more births and a higher crude birth rate than the reduced age-specific fertility rates would imply. Behind the facade of a continuing increase in population there was an ultimate cessation of growth if the age-specific rates remained unchanged, as a number of analysts in several Western countries pointed out—Richard †Böckh (1890), Ladislaus von †Bortkiewicz (1893), Edwin †Cannan (1895), Louis †Dublin and Alfred Lotka (1925), R. R. †Kuczynski (1928, 1932); and Lotka (1936). Each of these analysts developed a concept of population replacement in a stationary population. A population can be said to replace itself, for example, when each female has produced a baby girl in the next generation or, almost equivalently, when to each couple in the adult population there are born approximately 2.3 children (with the precise number dependent on mortality and marriage rates). The argument is of some importance at the present time. Though in the early 1980s the United States had approximately 3.5 million births and only 2.0 million deaths annually, the birth rate was well below "replacement" as defined by those analysts; for if the age-specific birth and death rates were to continue for several generations without change, the annual number of births would fall to below the number of deaths.

The notion that immanent in every population there is a stable population toward which the present one is tending was linked to new methods of projecting growth. Indeed, the *reproduction rates that Kuczynski devised were often interpreted, sometimes even by professional demographers, as reflections of current reality, rather than of the future under specified transitional conditions. Eventually, however, the search for a *logistic curve (or other analytic curve) largely gave way to such summary measures, which in turn were superseded for some purposes by *model tables, such as those developed by the United Nations (1955), Sully †Ledermann and Jean Breas (1959), Ansley †Coale and Paul †Demeny (1966), and Coale, Demeny, and Barbara Vaughan (1983), among others. Model tables have also been developed for births (Coale and Trussell, 1974) and marriages (Coale and McNeil, 1972). William †Brass (e.g., 1974, 1975) has used a single standard table on which he superimposed a two-parameter function matched to a particular investigation of mortality. Though the concept of *generation is rather more complex, that of *cohort was developed only later, especially in the use of birth cohorts to analyze trends in fertility (Whelpton, 1946, 1954; Ryder, 1964).

Mathematical statistics remained a separate discipline, but various elements of its remarkable development influenced demography greatly. The theory of probability made it possible to substitute for data collected from a whole population, often for another purpose than demographic analysis, a sample *survey with questions focused precisely on the points at issue. Since the new methodology developed together with a growing concern about population growth, surveys have been used especially to study fertility and its control. Indeed, perhaps the most prominent new development in mathematical techniques has been in the analysis of the populations of less developed countries with relatively poor data (e.g., Coale, 1963; Coale and Demeny, 1967). Among others, Brass (1963) showed how from the number of children born to women and the number surviving until the date of a survey, one could derive usable estimates of infant mortality (cf. Matthiessen, 1972). Similarly, asking a sample of women of various ages whether their mothers are alive affords the possibility of estimating the mortality of older people. Leo †Goodman (1967) developed many aspects of stable-population theory—for instance, continuing the work of Ronald †Fisher (1930) and P. H. Leslie (1945) on reproductive values.

The techniques noted thus far pertain to a closed population. A succession of migrants can be viewed as differing from one of births only in that all births are at age zero and migrants are spread over a distribution with a certain usual range and central point (see also *Markov chain). The transitions of migration—say, among the fifty states of the United States—are formally the same as those among the various civil statuses (single, married, widowed, divorced) or occupational statuses (employed, unemployed, not in the labor force); and the same methods can be used to analyze any of them. The mathematical analysis of migration has been concentrated in particular research institutes, often linked to geography departments; among the many individuals engaged in such work, Andrei †Rogers (e.g., 1968) has been one of the most productive. William †Alonso (1978, 1980) has written a general theory of migration based on a number of his earlier works.

Much of the work in mathematical demography from its inception has been concerned with graduation over the various age categories of a population's births, deaths, migrants, or whatever. Not only does one want the material in compact form—with two or three parameters rather than the information on a hundred separate ages, or even twenty 5-year age groups—but filling in gaps in the data, or forecasting, or any other operation can be carried out more satisfactorily with a compact presentation. Efforts to find an analytic curve that would represent the incidence of mortality by age, which started with Benjamin †Gompertz in 1825, was continued in the works of D. R. Brillinger (1961) and John H. †Pollard (1973), among others.

Much of the mathematics in the work noted so far is elementary, depending only on symbolic representation of the variables and their algebraic manipulation. Repeatedly, however, mathematicians have been attracted to two or three genuinely difficult problems, including especially the conditions under which ergodicity is attained, the so-called *two-sex problem, and stochastic variation.

Like a number of other terms used in mathematical demography, ergodicity is borrowed from physics and engineering. From *erg*, the unit of energy or work, there developed such terms as *ergodic*, the path followed by energy; *ergonomics*, the study of the physical relation between man and a machine that he uses; and *ergodicity*, a property of a system that developed through time according to probabilistic laws, or, specifically in demography, the path by which the components of population growth interact to produce a particular result. For example, how does a population with fixed rates reach stability (Parlett, 1970); or, in what is termed weak ergodicity, how much can a population be said to forget its past by the action of varying rates?

All of the theory noted so far concerns essentially one sex (almost always the female one), with the other one brought in only as a proportion of the sex that is analyzed. Developing a genuine two-sex model, attempted by Leo Goodman (1953) among others, has remained beyond a full solution.

Although there is much talk of probability in everyday demography, most work is deterministic in the sense that, for instance, if the probability of death for an individual is .01, this is taken to mean that among 1,000,000 individuals there will be 10,000 deaths. But if each individual is independently subject to that probability, the number of deaths is a random variable. The second interpretation raises the level of mathematical difficulty, but not impossibly high, as David Kendall (1949) and a number of subsequent analysts have shown (cf. also Lotka, 1939). With the second interpretation demography becomes part of the analysis of *stochastic processes, an extensive field of mathematics, and shows an affinity to population genetics. The intractability of many stochastic formulations has led to an extensive use of *simulation (e.g., Hammel et al., 1976). With computers that now can draw millions of random numbers per hour, the work is no longer restricted by the limits of machine computation, as that of early pioneers seemed to be (e.g., Orcutt et al., 1961). The number of analysts using simulation to work on problems in demography is now very large (cf. Mode, 1975).

The effect of contraception on childbearing has been studied mathematically by, among others, Robert †Potter (1970) and Mindel †Sheps and Jane †Menken (1973). Though it is not possible to give straightforward answers to such questions as how much a given rate of abortion reduces the birth rate, or how effective the distribution of IUDs or contraceptive pills is, with certain reasonable assumptions that Potter and others have proposed, one can arrive at acceptable approximations.

In spite of all these recent developments, what one means by the term "mathematical demography" is not sharply delineated. The use of mathematical symbols is not the point; Samuel Karlin, the founder of the journal *Theoretical Population Biology*, has actively sought contributions offering new theoretical insights in straight prose. And what is deemed to be mathematical by whatever criterion can often be classified either in demography or in actuarial science, statistics, biology, genetics, epidemiology, or one of the other related disciplines.

REFERENCES: William Alonso, "Theory of Movements," in Niles M. Hansen, ed., *Human Settlement Systems* (Cambridge, Mass.: Ballinger, 1978), with a "Comment" by A. G. Wilson and "Reply," *Environment and Planning A*, 12 (1980), 727-733. Richard Böckh, "Die Statistische Messung der Ehelichen Fruchtbarkeit," *Bulletin de l'Institut International de Statistique*, 5 (1890), 159-187. Ladislaus von Bortkiewicz, *Die Mittlere Lebensdauer: Die Methoden Ihrer Bestimmung und Ihr Verhältnis zur Sterblichkeitsmessung* (Jena: Fischer, 1893). William Brass, "The Construction of Life Tables from Child Survivorship Ratios," in IUSSP, International Population Conference, New York, 1961, *Contributed Papers*, 1 (London: IUSSP, 1963), 294-301; "Perspectives in Population Prediction: Illustrated by the Statistics of England and Wales," *Journal of the Royal Statistical Society*, Ser. A, 137 (1974), 532-583; *Methods for Estimating Fertility and Mortality from Limited and Defective Data* (Chapel Hill: University of North Carolina, 1975). D. R. Brillinger, "A Justification of Some Common Laws of Mortality," *Transactions of the Society of Actuaries*, 13 (1961), 116-119. Edwin Cannan, "The Probability of a Cessation of the Growth of Population in England and Wales during the Next Century," *Economic Journal*, 5 (1895), 505-515. Ansley J. Coale, "Estimates of Various Demographic Measures through the Quasi-stable Age Distribution," in Milbank Memorial Fund, *Emerging Techniques in Population Research* (New York, 1963), pp. 175-193. Coale and Paul Demeny, *Regional Model Life Tables and Stable Populations* (Princeton, N.J.: Princeton University Press, 1966); with Barbara Vaughan (2nd ed.; New York: Academic Press, 1983). Coale and Demeny, *Methods of Estimating Basic Demographic Measures from Incomplete Data*, U.N. Department of Economic and Social Affairs, Population Studies, no. 42 (New York, 1967). Coale and D. R. McNeil, "Distribition by Age of the Frequency of First Marriage in a Female Cohort," *Journal of the American Statistical Association*, 67 (1972), 743-749. Coale and T. James Trussell, "Model Fertility Schedules: Variations in the Age Structure of Childbearing in Human Populations," *Population Index*, 40 (1974), 184-258. Louis I. Dublin and Alfred J. Lotka, "On the True Rate of Natural Increase," *Journal of the American Statistical Association*, 20 (1925), 305-339. Leonhard Euler, "Recherches Générales sur la Mortalité et la Multiplication," *Mémoires de l'Académie Royale des Sciences et Belles Lettres*, 16 (1760), 144-164; translated by Nathan Keyfitz and Beatrice Keyfitz in *Theoretical Population Biology*, 1 (1970), 307-314. Gustav Feichtinger, "Formale Demographie—Wohin? Entwicklungstendenzen der Bevölkerungsmathematik," *Mitteilungsblatt der Österreichischen Gesellschaft für Statistik und Informatik*, 9 (June, 1979), 1-14. Ronald A. Fisher, *The General Theory of Natural Selection* (1930; reprinted, New York: Dover Publications, 1958). Leo A. Goodman, "Population Growth of the Sexes," *Biometrics*, 9 (1953), 212-225; "On the Age-Sex Composition of the Population that Would Result from Given Fertility and Mortality Conditions," *Demography*, 4 (1967), 423-441. John Graunt, "Natural and Political Observations Mentioned in a Following Index, and Made upon the Bills of Mortality ..." (1662; reprinted in *Journal of the Institute of Actuaries*, 90, Part 1, 1964, 4-61). Eugene A. Hammel, David W. Hutchinson, K. W. Wachter, R. T. Lundy, et al., *The Socsim: A Demographic-Sociological Microsimulation Program* (Berkeley: Institute for International Studies, University of California, 1976). David Kendall, "Stochastic Processes and Population Growth," *Journal of the Royal Statistical Society*, Ser. B, 11 (1949), 230-264. Nathan Keyfitz, *Introduction to the Mathematics of Population* (Reading, Mass.: Addison-Wesley, 1968); "Mathematical Demography: A Bibliographic Essay," *Population Index*, 42 (1976), 9-38; *Applied Mathematical Demography* (New York: Wiley, 1977); "Mathematical Demography," in *International*

Encyclopedia of Population, 2, 437-443. R. R. Kuczynski, *The Balance of Births and Deaths* (New York: Macmillan, 1928); *Fertility and Reproduction: Methods of Measuring the Balance of Births and Deaths* (New York: Falcon, 1932). Sully Ledermann and Jean Breas, "Les Dimensions de la Mortalité," *Population*, 14 (1959), 637-682. P. H. Leslie, "On the Use of Matrices in Certain Population Mathematics," *Biometrika*, 33 (1945), 183-212. Alfred J. Lotka, "The Stability of the Normal Age Distribution," *Proceedings of the National Academy of Sciences*, 8 (1922), 339-345; *Elements of Physical Biology* (Baltimore: Williams and Wilkins, 1925; reprinted, New York: Dover Publications, 1956); "The Geographic Distribution of Intrinsic Natural Increase in the United States, and an Examination of the Relation between Several Measures of Net Reproductivity," *Journal of the American Statistical Association*, 31 (1936), 273-294; "Analyse Démographique avec Application Particulière à l'Espèce Humaine," in Georges Teissier, ed., *Théorie Analytique des Associations Biologiques*, XII, part 2 (Paris: Hermann, 1939). Poul C. Matthiessen, "Application of the Brass-Sullivan Method to Historical Data," *Population Index*, 38 (1972), 403-409. Charles J. Mode, "Perspectives in Stochastic Models of Human Reproduction: A Review and Analysis," *Theoretical Population Biology*, 8 (1975), 247-291. Guy H. Orcutt et al., *Microanalysis of Socioeconomic Systems: A Simulation Study* (New York: Harper and Brothers, 1961). Beresford N. Parlett, "Ergodic Properties of Populations, I: The One-Sex Model," *Theoretical Population Biology*, 1 (1970), 191-207. John H. Pollard, *Mathematical Models for the Growth of Human Populations* (New York: Cambridge University Press, 1973). Robert G. Potter, Jr., "Births Averted by Contraception: An Approach through Renewal Theory," *Theoretical Population Biology*, 1 (1970), 251-272. Andrei Rogers, *Matrix Analysis of Interregional Population Growth and Distribution* (Berkeley: University of California Press, 1968). Norman B. Ryder, "The Process of Demographic Translation," *Demography*, 1 (1964), 74-82. Mindel C. Sheps and Jane A. Menken, *Mathematical Models of Conception and Birth* (Chicago: University of Chicago Press, 1973). David P. Smith and Nathan Keyfitz, eds., *Mathematical Demography: Selected Papers* (New York: Springer, 1977). United Nations, *Age and Sex Patterns of Mortality: Model Life Tables for Underdeveloped Countries* (New York, 1955). P. K. Whelpton, "Reproduction Rates Adjusted for Age, Parity, Fecundity, and Marriage," *Journal of the American Statistical Association*, 41 (1946), 501-516; *Cohort Fertility: Native White Women in the United States* (Princeton, N.J.: Princeton University Press, 1954).

matrix, in mathematics, is a set of elements, finite in number and arranged in rows and columns, such that, if A_{ij} and B_{ij} are elements in the ith row and jth column of two such arrays, these arrays combine to form a product with the elements $C_{ij} = \Sigma A_{ik} B_{kj}$. The manipulation of such matrices, a branch of mathematics called matrix algebra, has a wide range of applications in the social sciences. In economics it is used to express linkages and flows among industries, and in demography it has been adapted to analyze interregional movements and to project population growth. The method permits one to distinguish the process of migration from the population that is undergoing it. Data on internal migration are typically poor, and the matrix form can be used also to estimate movements less crudely than from the *residuals of a *balancing equation.

REFERENCES: Nathan Keyfitz, "The Population Projection as a Matrix Operator," *Demography*, 1 (1964), 56-73. Andrei Rogers, *Matrix Analysis of Interregional Population Growth and Distribution* (Berkeley: University of California Press, 1968).

maturation, an individual's development following an innate tendency, rather than as a consequence of learning. During the 1920s, when the term became prominent among American psychologists, it served to retain a small hereditary potential at a time when extreme environmentalism flourished. One of the key issues related to demography is how early, apart from environmental influences, sexuality develops; see also *adolescence.

REFERENCE: Arnold L. Gesell, "Maturation and the Patterning of Behavior," *Psychological Review*, 36 (1929), 307-319.

Mauritania: The government's Bureau of Statistics and Economic Research publishes an *Annuaire Statistique* that includes population data. Its Central Bureau of Population Censuses was directed in 1980 by Mohamed El-Mokhtar Zamel. Address: Direction de la Statistique et des Études Économiques and Bureau Central du Recensement de la Population, Ministère de la Planification, Boîte Postale 240, Nouakchott.

Mauritius: Demographic Institutions

Action Familiale, a Catholic organization, and the Mauritius Family Planning Association provide family-planning services. Address: Port Louis.

The *Annual Report on the Registrar General's Department* includes vital statistics and other population data. Address: Registrar General's Department, Port Louis.

The Ministry of Health includes a Family Planning/Maternal and Child Health Division (FP/MCH). Its evaluation unit, which in 1980 included Vakil Rajacoomar as principal demographer, conducted a 1978 survey of fertility among a sample of 800 women; see *Survey on Fertility Patterns among Women Aged under 25 Years in the Island of Mauritius* (1980). Address: Port Louis.

The Central Statistical Office conducts the island's censuses, of which the most recent with published data was in 1972 (one was scheduled for 1982). The *Bi-annual Digest of Statistics* that it publishes includes population data. Address: Ministry of Economic Planning and Development, Rose Hill.

MCH, in the jargon of family-planning programmers, an abbreviation for "maternal/child health" services, which are sometimes used also to provide contraceptives.

mean, the sum of a set of values divided by their number, also referred to as an "arithmetic mean" or, loosely, as an "average." It is represented by a bar; for example, the mean of $x_1, x_2, \ldots x_n$ is written $\bar{x}$.

mean deviation, a measure of *dispersion, the average of absolute (that is, without regard to algebraic sign) differences between observations and some central value, such as the *mean or the *median.

measurement in the most general sense means the assignment of numbers to specified entities according to a particular rule. Measurement is thus a way of standardizing; for example, the weight of all things, no matter how diverse, can be compared using the single unit of a pound (or kilogram, or whatever). A prerequisite to measurement in its simplest sense, then, is that such a constant unit either exists in nature (persons in the count of a population) or can be arbitrarily designated (a foot or centimeter as a unit of length). The measurement of entities arranges them in an asymmetrical order; thus, if A is longer than B, B cannot be longer than A. The order is also transitive; that is, if A is longer than B and B is longer than C, then A is longer than C.

Because measurement transforms properties into quantitative and comparable symbols, permitting one to use mathematical techniques in an analysis, repeated efforts have been made to quantify qualitative characteristics. As Norman Campbell (1921) noted, it was a big step forward in physics when density (which cannot be measured according to the basic rules) was defined as the quotient of a body's weight and its volume (both of which follow these rules). This derived measure was first widely used only in the eighteenth century, a product not of common sense but of deliberate investigation. A different kind of extension is made when the numerals (or symbolic representations of numbers) used to designate an ordinal series are used as though they represented numbers in the normal sense (see *scale).

The fundamental unit of demography, the person, need not be contrived as is income in economics, power in political science, or community in sociology. The existence of this natural unit is a great advantage in measurement; and it was partly for this reason that in their early stages demography and statistics developed together. The *population of a country, however, depends also on arbitrary rules of *residence (de jure or de facto, for instance), as well as on whether or not certain sectors are excluded by definition (as were untaxed Indians in the United States before 1890). There is thus no single answer to such a question as what is the population of Country A or what is the largest city in the world. In much of demographic analysis, moreover, the subunits are defined by attributes that can be quantified only with the same kinds of compromise as in other social disciplines—*employment status or *occupation, *nationality or *race, and so on. In short, in population studies measurement may seem to be simpler than it ordinarily is.

REFERENCES: Norman Robert Campbell, "Measurement" (1921), in Newman, *The World of Mathematics*, 3, 1797-1813. Abraham Kaplan, *The Conduct of Inquiry: Methodology for Behavioral Sciences* (San Francisco: Chandler, 1964), chaps. 20-21.

median, that value of a variable that divides the total distribution into two halves, one higher and one lower than the median figure. This indicator of centrality is usually considered to be more suitable when the distribution is skewed (but see *income).

median location, a point in a state, district, town, or other areal unit at the intersection of two perpendicular lines, each of which divides the unit's population into two equal parts.

REFERENCE: James A. Quinn, *Human Ecology* (New York: Prentice-Hall, 1950), pp. 61-63.

medical manpower, or health personnel, comprise all who contribute professionally to *health care. According to one study, the three occupations that American convention so specified in 1910—physician, nurse, and nurse's aide—rose to 450 by 1974 and 600 by 1977 (Goldstein and Horowitz, 1977). The stupendous proliferation followed the growth of specialization among physicians, so-called allied health professions, and many lower-level jobs. Federal expenditures on programs to train New Health Practitioners (NHPs) rose from $1 million in 1969 to $21 million in 1979, by which date about 22,100 NHPs had been certified by a National Commission on the Certification of Physicians' Assistants. Substituting NHPs without loss in the quality of care is measured against the productivity of an average medical doctor; thus, 0.5 means that the productivity of the NHP is half that of a physician, and that the substitution would be cost-effective only if the cost of the NHP were less than half of that of an M.D. In the mid-1970s the annual earnings of primary-care physicians averaged about $50,000, and those of NPHs about $14,000; but both figures rose rapidly over the following years (Record et al., 1980). In short, though with lags imposed by licensing and hiring standards, American medical practice has been approaching that in many European countries, with the highly trained and expensive doctor working at the top of a variegated team rather than with only one or two assistants.

This differentiation has complicated the already difficult task of balancing the supply of physicians against the need for them. The ratio of physicians to the population, which is often used to measure the adequacy of health care, can be quite misleading. In 1873, when the pioneer Max von †Pettenkofer compared 33, the death rate of his home city of Munich, with the 22 in London, he ascribed the difference to the Londoners' living conditions—their more and better food, superior housing, and warm clothing. Without controls for factors of this kind, the American public have clamored for more physicians, and additional training facilities were supplied lavishly. An egregious example is the state of Ohio, where the three medical schools (at Ohio State University, the University of Cincinnati, and Case Western Reserve University) were being doubled in the 1960s and 1970s, with a new medical school at Toledo, an osteopathic school at Ohio University, and two consortia in the northeast and the west of the state. Yet as early as the 1950s competent studies were projecting a surplus of physicians (Lave et al., 1975; cf. Tarlov, 1983).

Somewhat belatedly the federal government, through which most of the funding flowed, also recognized the imbalance. The Health Professions Educational Assistance Act of 1976, which went into effect in 1978, shifted the emphasis from expanding training facilities to alleviating the geographic maldistribution and the shortage of primary-care practitioners—that is, specialists in family medicine, internal medicine, and pediatrics. From 1963 to 1978, more than $6 billion had been spent in the construction of new facilities, including medical and osteopathic schools, thus more than doubling the annual output both of physicians and of nurses. According to the U.S. Bureau of Health Manpower (1978), the projected supply and need were as follows:

	Thousands of Physicians	
Date	**Supply**	**High Estimate of Requirements**
1980	444	427
1985	519	492
1990	594	571

Though the generalization that less developed countries lack medical manpower is much better based, the issue in such a setting is also far more complex than is ordinarily assumed, as was highlighted in three studies—in Peru, Taiwan, and Turkey—undertaken through the Department of International Health at Johns Hopkins University. Each analyst tried to estimate the number and quality of medical personnel, the actual and effective demand for their services, the institutional setting and how this affected the delivery of services, and the consequent balance between current and projected supply and demand. The health of the population did not depend on whether physicians were in short supply, a state that in any case was impossible to gauge at all precisely (cf. Badgley et al., 1970). In the mid-1960s perhaps the healthiest town in Ethiopia was Harar, where each night packs of hyenas roamed the streets and picked them clean. One can conclude that teachers are probably as important to the furtherance of health as doctors, for often the key problem is sanitation (Torrey, 1967).

REFERENCES: Robin F. Badgley, John M. Last, and Raul Paredes, "Health Manpower in International Perspective," *Milbank Memorial Fund Quarterly*, 48:2, part 1 (1970), 204-237. Harold Goldstein and Morris Horowitz, *Health Personnel: Meeting the Explosive Demand for Medical Care; Entry-Level Health Occupations: Development and Future* (Boston: Center for Manpower Studies, Northeastern University, 1977). Judith R. Lave, Lester B. Lave, and Samuel Leinhardt, "Medical Manpower Models: Need, Demand, and Supply," *Inquiry*, 12 (1975), 97-125. Jane Cassels Record, Michael McCally, Stuart O. Schweitzer, Robert M. Blomquist, and Benjamin D. Berger, "New Health Professions after a Decade and a Half: Delegation, Productivity, and Costs of Primary Care," *Journal of Health Politics, Policy, and Law*, 5 (1980), 470-497. Alvin R. Tarlov, "The Increasing Supply of Physicians, the Changing Structure of the Health-Services System, and the Future Practice of Medicine," *New England Journal of Medicine*, 308 (May 19, 1983), 1235-1244. E. Fuller Torrey, "Health Services in Ethiopia," *Milbank*

Memorial Fund Quarterly, 45 (1967), 275-285. U.S. Bureau of Health Manpower, *Manpower: A Change in Course* (Washington, D.C., 1978).

medical sociology is so new a specialty that its practitioners are still attempting to define its scope (e.g., Hollingshead, 1973; Gill and Twaddle, 1977; Murcott, 1977; Pflanz and Keupp, 1977). In the United States the subdiscipline came into being by the coalescence of several diverse research fields into a body of material that sociologists taught to student nurses, for example, or used as members of a public-health team (cf. Straus, 1957). At its broadest compass medical sociology brings in bits from psychology (psychosomatic illnesses, "the sick role," mental disorders, and the interaction of patient and physician); anthropology (how sickness is defined especially in some primitive cultures); epidemiology (some idea of how diseases are classified); statistics (the basic concepts and procedures only); labor-force analysis (how physicians, nurses, and other health personnel are recruited and trained); economics (cost-benefit analyses of competing systems of health care); sociology of institutions (particularly hospitals); political science (health policy); and demography (especially the effect of the increased proportion of aged on medical care). How much of such materials is included varies, of course, according to each person's background and interests.

REFERENCES: Howard E. Freeman, Sol Levine, and Leo G. Reeder, eds., *Handbook of Medical Sociology* (3rd ed.; Englewood Cliffs, N.J.: Prentice-Hall, 1979). Derek G. Gill and Andrew C. Twaddle, "Medical Sociology: What's in a Name?" *International Social Science Journal*, 29 (1977), 369-385. August B. Hollingshead, "Medical Sociology: A Brief Review," *Milbank Memorial Fund Quarterly*, 51 (1973), 531-542. Anne Murcott, "Blind Alleys and Blinkers: The Scope of Medical Sociology," *Scottish Journal of Sociology*, 1 (1977), 155-171. Manfred Pflanz and Heinrich Keupp, "A Sociological Perspective on Concepts of Disease," *International Social Science Journal*, 29 (1977), 386-396. Robert Straus, "The Nature and Status of Medical Sociology," *American Sociological Review*, 22 (1957), 200-204.

megalopolis, a term coined by the French urban geographer Jean †Gottmann to designate an extensive metropolitan aggregate with a "nebulous structure" but incomparable economic, political, and cultural power. The prototype is the region in the United States from Boston to Washington, D.C.

REFERENCE: Jean Gottmann, *Megalopolis: The Urbanized Northeastern Seaboard of the United States* (New York: Twentieth Century Fund, 1961).

menarche (pronounced me-NAR-ke), the first menstrual flow; the usual indicator of *puberty in the female. Several international surveys of the age at menarche indicate that *maturation is faster with a better diet. Thus, there is a typical difference according to the level of social development: in Western countries the average is below 14 years, in African countries above 14 years, and in Asia somewhere between the two. Similarly—though there is some controversy about the trend—an improved level of living seemingly has resulted in a decline in the average age in developed countries. In Norway, the country with the longest record, it fell from above 17 years in 1844 to 13.2 years in the early 1950s.

REFERENCE: Grace Wyshak and Rose E. Frisch, "Evidence for a Secular Trend in Age of Menarche," *New England Journal of Medicine*, 306 (1982), 1033-1035.

menopause, the female climacteric, marked by a cessation of menstruation; the end of a woman's fecund period. In a fertility rate (the number of births per 1,000 fecund women), the upper limit of the category is conventionally set at either 45 or 50 years. According to a survey of American women, the first age is on the low side, the second on the high side (MacMahon and Worcester, 1966). In any case, there is a gradual decline in fecundity, analogous to its gradual development during *adolescence, from early middle age to its cessation at menopause. The potency of males also falls off with age, but more gradually and apparently with a greater variation among individuals.

REFERENCES: Marcha Flint, "Is There A Secular Trend in Age of Menopause?" *Maturitas*, 1 (1978), 133-140. Brian MacMahon and Jane Worcester, *Age at Menopause, United States, 1960-1962* (U.S. National Center for Health Statistics, Ser. 11, no. 19, 1966).

menstruation, the periodic bleeding from the uterus that, in the absence of pregnancy, normally recurs every lunar month during the fecund period of a human female. The beginning of this cyclical flow, called the *menarche, marks a female's puberty, and its gradual cessation during her *menopause sets the end of her reproductive period. During each month, while the ova are developing, the wall of the uterus swells, preparatory to receiving a fertilized ovum. If no fertilization takes place, the ova and the wall of the uterus disintegrate, discharging blood through the vagina. There is thus a menstrual cycle of about the same length as the recurrent ovulation, with each of the menses spaced about halfway between two ovulations. The fact that females are fecund during only a short fraction of each month means that they can avoid conceiving by abstaining from intercourse during that period. The flaw in the *rhythm method of contraception based on the menstrual cycle is that neither it nor the ovulation cycle is completely regular. According to a study that Louis †Henry (1976, p. 236) cites, for example, a quarter of the women in the sample menstruated every 28 days, 81 percent between 26 and 30 days, but the remainder between 22 and 34 days. To be effective, periodic abstinence must be based on such a concurrent index of ovulation as a change in either the body temperature or the chemical composition of vaginal mucus.

REFERENCE: Henry, *Population*.

mental disorders comprise psychotic or neurotic diseases or conditions with different causes, symptoms, and effects. Six etiological principles have been identified, using models labeled genetic, developmental, neurophysiological, internal environment, learning, and ecological (Zubin and Spring, 1977). Not only has the recurrent hope always proved false that all types of "mental illness" could be cured, but it would be a significant improvement in understanding if a consensus could be achieved on diagnosis, not to speak of therapy or prevention. In the *International Classification of Diseases "mental disorders" are divided between psychoses (290-299) and neuroses, personality disorders, and other nonpsychotic mental disorders (300-309). In the mid-1970s patients admitted to American hospitals for any of these ailments accounted for almost 30 percent of the total hospital-days, or more than any other major disease category; and the cost, including the loss of production, was estimated at an annual total of almost $20 billion (Rice et al., 1976). About one-third of severe *mental deficiency* (operationally defined as with an IQ of less than 50) results from Down's syndrome or mongolism, a genetic disease more likely to occur in children born to older mothers. An affected fetus can be detected before birth, and in recent years the incidence has been reduced by differential abortions. The overall prevalence of subnormality, however, has been rising in the United States because of the better control of infections and improved surgery to correct congenital anomalies (Eisenberg and Parron, 1979).

Given the general condition of statistics on mental disorders, one should not expect those on demographic characteristics to be satisfactory. There is so little confidence in surveys that some have been undertaken not to determine the correlates of mental diseases but to test the instruments themselves (e.g., Gaitz and Scott, 1972). Improvements in the American record date from the passage in 1946 of the National Mental Health Act, which led to an extensive nation-wide program to collect and analyze data on the care of the mentally ill. Since 1954 the federal government has annually compiled data from hospitals and outpatient psychiatric clinics, not only on diagnoses and the outcomes of terminated cases but also on age, sex, and other characteristics (cf. Kramer, 1969). For many disorders females show a higher incidence than males, but some analysts argue that the difference is due to biased reporting (Clancy and Gove, 1974; Dohrenwend and Dohrenwend, 1976, with a comment by Gove and Tudor and reply, 1977). An inverse correlation is typical between social class or education and rates of schizophrenia, but the interpretation of this datum varies (e.g., Kohn, 1972; Eaton, 1974).

The relation between migration and mental illness has been studied intensively enough to suggest the difficulties in establishing any such connection. According to a monograph based on age-standardized first admissions to New York State mental institutions, in-migrants were represented in much higher proportion than those born in the state (Malzberg and Lee, 1956). Many patients were admitted so soon after arrival that they must have been ill before moving, and this suggests that perhaps the mentally ill tend to migrate in greater proportion. But the difference between in-migrants and native residents was greater after the passage of some years, suggesting that in some cases the strains of adjusting to the new environment triggered the onset of the disease. Or, as a third possible cause, the contrast may be partly spurious: since the standards of institutional care were relatively good in New York State, the incidence of the mentally ill outside hospitals was probably higher elsewhere in the country, particularly in the South and among Negroes (Lee, 1963). See also *addiction; *alcoholism.

REFERENCES: Kevin Clancy and Walter R. Gove, "Sex Differences in Mental Illness: An Analysis of Response Bias in Self-Reports," *American Journal of Sociology*, 80 (1974), 205-216. Bruce P. Dohrenwend and Barbara Snell Dohrenwend, "Sex Differences and Psychiatric Disorders" and "Reply," *American Journal of Sociology*, 81 (1976), 1447-1459, and 82 (1977), 1336-1345. William W. Eaton, Jr., "Residence, Social Class, and Schizophrenia," *Journal of Health and Social Behavior*, 15 (1974), 289-299. Leon Eisenberg and Delores Parron, "Strategies for the Prevention of Mental Disorders," in *Healthy People: The Surgeon General's Report on Health Promotion and Disease Prevention* (Washington, D.C., 1979), 2, 135-155. Charles M. Gaitz and Judith Scott, "Age and the Measurement of Mental Health," *Journal of Health and Social Behavior*, 12 (1972), 55-67. Gove and Jeanette Tudor, "Sex Differences in Mental Illness: A Comment on Dohrenwend and Dohrenwend," *American Journal of Sociology*, 82 (1977), 1327-1336. Melvin L. Kohn, "Class, Family, and Schizophrenia: A Reformulation," *Social Forces*, 50 (1972), 295-313. Morton Kramer, "Statistics of Mental Disorders in the United States: Current Status, Some Urgent Needs and Suggested Solutions," *Journal of the Royal Statistical Society*, Ser. A, 132, Part 3 (1969), 353-407. Everett S. Lee, "Socio-economic and Migration Differentials in Mental Disease, New York State, 1949-51," *Milbank Memorial Fund Quarterly*, 41 (1963), 259-268. Benjamin Malzberg and Lee, *Migration and Mental Disease: A Study of First Admissions to Hospitals for Mental Disease, New York, 1939-1941* (New York: Social Science Research Council, 1956). Dorothy P. Rice, Jacob J. Feldman, and Kerr L. White, *The Current Burden of Illness in the United States* (Washington, D.C.: National Academy of Sciences, Institute of Medicine, 1976). Joseph Zubin and Bonnie Spring, "Vulnerability—A New View of Schizophrenia," *Journal of Abnormal Psychology*, 86 (1977), 103-126.

mercantilism, or what Adam †Smith called the mercantile system, is the label commonly given to the doctrines and practices that dominated European economic-political trends from roughly the fifteenth to the eighteenth centuries. The word is a modern one, first used by German writers in the 1860s as *Merkantilismus*, but is now standard in all Western languages. The basic premise of mercantilism was that any nation-state could prosper only at the cost of others; each, therefore, hoarded gold and people in order to augment its economic, political, and military power. The lower classes existed in order to produce at a subsistence level for the greater power of the state; in William †Petty's words, a worker need be able only to "live, labor, and generate."

The points of view varied somewhat from one country or period to another, but over all writers and statesmen were remarkably consistent in their almost fanatical espousal of population increase. In France, for example, Jean-Baptiste †Colbert instituted such pronatalist measures as an exemption from certain taxes for men who married early and pensions to fathers of ten or more living legitimate children. Indeed, it was continually noted that "overcrowding" resulted in vagrancy and crime; but in the mercantilist outlook the solution of this problem was to send any surplus population to colonies, where the power of the state could be aggrandized in another quarter of the globe. Young women were shipped from France by the boatload, and the military discipline of soldiers overseas included the duty to marry them; in the correspondence back and forth, the breeding of cattle and of humans was pictured as essentially equivalent. The interest in the number of its subjects, on the other hand, led representatives of each mercantilist state to initiate modern censuses and fumble toward the first beginnings of demography.

REFERENCES: Eli F. Heckscher, *Mercantilism*, 2 vols. (London: Allen and Unwin, 1935). Stangeland, *Pre-Malthusian Doctrines*, pp. 118-184.

metropolis, literally the mother city, referred initially to the relation between ancient Athens and its colonies. The derivative noun *metropolitan* meant originally an inhabitant of the metropolis; later, an ecclesiastical official. In its commonest present usage, a metropolis is a large urban center containing a region's principal cultural, commercial, and administrative institutions, all of which reflect its dominance over a tributary area. In this last sense, the term ''metropolitan area,'' or specifically in the usage of the United States, (Standard) *Metropolitan Statistical Area or *Urbanized Area, is often substituted.

The definitions of ''metropolitan'' in various countries vary so much that international comparisons are all but meaningless. In an attempt to lay a basis for cross-cultural analysis, Kingsley †Davis (1970-72) constructed an alternative set of data. He limited his perspective to urban or metropolitan agglomerations with a minimum population of 100,000, which he termed ''Cities,'' thus passing over a considerable proportion of the world's population that is considered urban by more inclusive criteria. The most important difference from other statistics, however, is his exclusive use of a demographic criterion to define a City—rather than also an administrative function or economic or cultural characteristics.

Metropolitan areas, however one defines them, are typically large enough to have a complex structure. The nucleus becomes the *central city of a larger region, to which portions of the population moved once mass transit systems made commuting possible—first trolley cars and then automobiles and good roads, electric railroads, and a telephone network (McKelvey, 1963, chap. 5; Hawley, 1956). Some of the smaller towns around the center developed out of industrial parks into half-independent economic units; others became prototypical *suburbs, residential units that in Britain are called *dormitory towns. There is a strong tendency to retain the concept of *dominance in ecological writings even when one can question its continued existence. In the United States many central cities are in economic and cultural decline, and their populations are maintained in considerable part out of tax funds paid by the well-to-do sector living either in suburbs or in smaller cities (but see also *gentrification).

REFERENCES: Kingsley Davis, *World Urbanization, 1950-1970*, 2 vols. (Berkeley: University of California, Institute of International Studies, 1970-72). Amos H. Hawley, *The Changing Shape of Metropolitan America: Deconcentration since 1920* (Glencoe,

Ill.: Free Press, 1956). Blake McKelvey, *The Urbanization of America (1860-1915)* (New Brunswick, N.J.: Rutgers University Press, 1963).

metropolitan economic area, a Standard *Metropolitan Statistical Area (SMSA) plus adjoining counties associated with it by a minimum level of commuting, so defined by Brian J. L. †Berry in a proposed revision of the SMSA. With commuting used as the sole criterion, rather than as one of several, the proposed new units were considerably larger than the 1960 SMSAs and also, it was argued, economically and socially better integrated, since they reflected self-contained labor markets based on daily journeys to work. See also *functional economic area.

REFERENCE: U.S. Bureau of the Census, *Metropolitan Area Definition: A Re-evaluation of Concept and Statistical Practice*, Working Paper no. 28 (Washington, D.C., 1969).

Metropolitan Life Insurance Company, incorporated in 1868, is one of the largest American firms in its field. In 1982 it had $57.9 million in life insurance policies and paid out $1.5 million in death benefits. Louis †Dublin joined the company in 1909 and, with such associates as Alfred J. †Lotka and Mortimer †Spiegelman, developed a notable statistical bureau that has analyzed not only mortality but population trends generally. It has published some of the results in a widely distributed *Statistical Bulletin*. Address: 340 Park Avenue South, New York, N.Y. 10010.

REFERENCE: Louis I. Dublin, *After Eighty Years: The Impact of Life Insurance on the Public Health* (Gainesville: University of Florida Press, 1966).

Metropolitan Statistical Area (MSA), an areal unit of the United States designated under that name in 1983 (cf. Forstall and González, 1984). Before that date the name of a similar unit was Standard Metropolitan Statistical Area (SMSA). It was defined as a county with a central city (or two or more closely situated cities) with a population of 50,000 or more, plus all contiguous counties having a generally metropolitan character based on their social and economic integration with the central city (Shryock, 1957). The concept was continually redefined, and the number and size of SMSAs changed periodically (cf. U.S. Federal Committee on Standard Metropolitan Statistical Areas, 1980). In 1981, following the results of the 1980 census, the U.S. Office of Management and Budget designated thirty-six new SMSAs and deleted one (Rapid City, N.D.) from the earlier list. This brought the total number of SMSAs to 323, including five in Puerto Rico. The people living in them numbered more than 169 million, or some 75 percent of the American population (U.S. Bureau of the Census, 1981). A useful "1980 Guide to Metropolitan Areas" is given in *American Demographics* (December, 1981, pp. 25-42). For the hundred largest SMSAs, ranked in order of size in 1980, a table gives for each central city and the suburbs the population and the number of households, with the percent change from 1970, and the number of whites, blacks, and Hispanics. In a second table the 1980 population and number of households are given for each of the constituent counties.

Under the somewhat revised criteria defining an MSA, the minimum population is either a city of at least 50,000 or an *Urbanized Area of at least 50,000 as part of a total metropolitan population of at least 100,000 (75,000 in New England). Counties with at least half of their population within the Urbanized Area qualify as the "central core" of the MSA. Outlying counties with a generally "metropolitan character" are included if at least 15 percent of their work force commutes to the center, or if, with lower population densities, higher proportions commute. Since MSAs are made up of whole counties, they may contain rural sections at the periphery, but if these portions are too large the counties are excluded. The central city is also defined by the number of commuters coming to it (see *metropolitan economic area, the areal unit proposed earlier, with commuting as the principal criterion used to set its boundaries). Most of the areas with a population of a million or more (what is often called a "greater" metropolitan area) are labeled Consolidated Metropolitan Statistical Areas (CMSAs), and each major unit within a CMSA is called a Primary Metropolitan Statistical Area (PMSA). On the basis of these new definitions, more than three Americans out of four live in the 350 areas that were specified, with populations ranging from 62,000 to 17.5 million.

In principle the Office of Management and Budget sets the number and size of the MSAs, but in some instances it depends on what people in the locality prefer. For example, Monroe County, Michigan, with slightly more commuters to Toledo than to Detroit, decided nevertheless to transfer to the Detroit MSA. If two cities are each of sufficient size to rank as MSAs, they may combine into one if they are within 25 miles of each other, and several pairs chose to do so. New PMSAs are not established unless there is strong local support for such separate recognition. That all of the units are labeled "statistical" indicates their primary purpose, but some federal agencies distribute funds according to whether a place has acquired the status of an MSA. For example, the Department of Housing and Urban Development allocates its Community Development Block Grants only to places designated as the central cities of MSAs.

REFERENCES: Richard L. Forstall and María Elena González, "Twenty Questions: What You Should Know about the New Metropolitan Areas," *American Demographics*, 6 (April, 1984), 22-31, 43-48. Henry S. Shryock, Jr., "The Natural History of Standard Metropolitan Areas," *American Journal of Sociology*, 63 (1957), 163-170. U.S. Bureau of the Census, *Data User News* (July, 1981), pp. 3-4. U.S. Federal Committee on Standard Metropolitan Statistical Areas, "Documents Relating to the Metropolitan Statistical Classification for the 1980s," *Statistical Reporter*, no. 80-11 (1980).

METROSIM, a simulation model of the urban system of the United States, based on data for the twenty SMSAs (Standard *Metropolitan Statistical Areas) with more than 250,000 inhabitants from the 1950, 1960, and 1970 censuses.

REFERENCE: Philip R. O'Connor, *METROSIM: A Computer Simulation Model of U.S. Urban Systems*, 2 vols. (Evanston, Ill.: Northwestern University, 1979).

Mexico: Demographic Institutions

The Association for Maternal Health was established in 1959 to promote family planning. It carries out biological research in its own laboratories and conducts social-cultural and psychological studies. In 1965 it instituted a training program on population and family planning for any interested persons. Address: Asociación Pro-Salud Maternal, A.C., San Luis Potosí no. 101, Colonia Roma, México 7, D.F.

The National Population Council (CONAPO) was established by the government in 1974 to aid in formulating policy and planning the requisite organization. The range of its charge went well beyond the usual economic impact of population growth and family-planning programs, including such topics as the status of women in society and the biology of reproduction. In 1980 it published a review of the country's population growth in the twentieth century—*México Demográfico: Breviario 1979*. Address: Consejo Nacional de Población, Avenida Juarez 92, México 1, D.F.

UNIVERSITY AND OTHER RESEARCH INSTITUTES

In 1964 the College of Mexico, a private institution, established a Center of Economic and Demographic Studies (CEED), of which the director until his death in 1981 was Luis †Unikel S. It publishes *Demografía y Economía*, the country's main population journal. Research of its staff has ranged over most areas of demography, while concentrating on the relation between population and economic development. Address: Centro de Estudios Económicos y Demográficos, El Colegio de México, Camino al Ajusco, México 20, D.F.

Also at the College of Mexico there is a Center of Sociological Studies, of which Claudio †Stern was director in 1982. In connection with its studies on social change and mobility, it has undertaken analyses of internal migration. Address: Centro de Estudios Sociológicos de Colegio del México, Camino al Ajusco, México 20, D.F.

The National Autonomous University of Mexico, a state institution, established in 1960 a Section on the Sociology of Population and Demography in its Institute of Social Research. In 1980 its director was Julio Labastida Martín del Campo. It administered the local component of the *World Fertility Survey, and it has done research on mortality and internal migration. Some of the results are published in its *Revista Mexicana de Sociología*. Address: Área Sociología de la Población y Demografía, Instituto de Investigaciones Sociales, Universidad Nacional Autónoma de México, Torre de Humanidades 70, Ciudad Universitaria, México 20, D.F.

The Autonomous University of Nueva Léon, a private institution, established in 1960 a Center of Economic Research, of which L. Durandeau Palma was director in 1980. Its research deals with human resources and economic development in Mexico. Address: Centro de Investigaciones Económicas, Universidad Autónoma de Nueva Léon, Loma Redonda 1515, Monterrey.

In 1960 the Mexican Institute of Social Studies, a private research organization, established a Family and Population Section, of which the director in 1980 was Luis †Leñero Otero. Its research has been focused on the family, bringing together sociological and demographic themes. Address: Instituto Mexicano de Estudios Sociales, Avenida Cuahtémoc 1486, México 13, D.F.

GOVERNMENT STATISTICAL BUREAU

The National Statistics Office (DGE) conducts the country's censuses, of which the latest was in 1980. It issues three annual yearbooks, an *Agenda Estadística*, an *Anuario Estadístico*, and an *Anuario Estadístico Compendiado*, of which the second is the most comprehensive. It also publishes a quarterly, *Revista de Estadística*, which includes basic population figures. Address: Dirección General de Estadística, Insurgentes Sur 795, México 18, D.F.

microcensus, sometimes called a minicensus, is a count of something less than the full population of the specified area. It generally has a larger population base than a sample *survey, collects more basic data, and is periodic. On the other hand, a microcensus usually has a smaller population base than the samples attached to a complete *census and lacks the financial support and political underpinning that the latter has. What has been termed a *rotating census* might be a monthly survey of a 1:120 sample of *enumeration districts or areas, with a different sample in each periodic survey.

REFERENCE: Leslie Kish, "Rotating Samples Instead of Censuses," *Asian and Pacific Census Forum*, 6 (August, 1979), 1ff.

microdata, in the jargon of the U.S. Bureau of the Census, unaggregated records concerning individual respondents or other reporting units. The basic record tapes with this information may be used only by bureau employees who have sworn to maintain the *confidentiality of records that is required by law. When it is possible to do so without divulging information about individuals, portions of census microdata may be made available as "public-use microdata samples."

microdemography is used in two related but distinct senses. It can mean the analysis of the population-related behavior of individuals or couples, especially the way that they reach decisions about whether or not to have a (or another) child; see *decision-making. Or it can mean the analysis of populations that are relatively small compared with the national units or other sizable aggregates that are usually studied. In analyzing smaller entities, the random distribution of characteristics cannot be assumed. The smaller the populations, in general the greater the variation in age and sex, and often the crude rates of a small population reflect the age-sex structure more than the actual levels of fertility and mortality.

Small populations are of three major types: the relatively tiny peoples that anthropologists have traditionally studied, modern nations below a certain arbitrary limit (cf. Roberts, 1976), and subpopulations of larger nations (e.g., Swanson, 1978). As a conclusion from one kind of ethnological study, the proportion of marriageable males for whom cross-cousin females are available depends mainly on a random variation in the numbers of sons and daughters in the relevant families and relatively little on the expected number of children (Kunstadter et al., 1963). Since in any society of whatever size the pool out of which marriage partners are generally chosen is bounded by social class, ethnicity, religion, and other factors, the patterning analyzed in social anthropology relates also to a study of family formation (cf. Sheps, 1963). Or, as another example of microdemography applied to sizable populations, migration is usually a behavior pattern of only a small fraction of either the sending or the receiving population, and migrants are usually skewed in their age and sex distribution (cf. Pryor, 1976; Prothero, 1976). The commonest instance is the study of *small-area populations—that is, those living in administrative divisions that are used in the analysis of *voting, for example, or of many types of social interaction at the local level (cf. Kosiński, 1976).

REFERENCES: A useful collection of papers, including a bibliography, is given in Leszek A. Kosiński and John W. Webb, eds., *Population at Microscale* (Hamilton, N.Z.: New Zealand Geographical Society, 1976). Included in this work are the following cited papers: Kosiński, "Impact of Administrative Divisions upon Availability of Demographic Data: East-Central Europe"; R. Mansell Prothero, "Microscale Studies of Population Mobility in Tropical Africa: Some Problems and Possibilities"; Robin J. Pryor, "Conceptualising Migration Behaviour—A Problem in Microdemographic Analysis"; and George W. Roberts, "Some Issues in the Study of Small Populations." Peter Kunstadter, Roald Buhler, Frederick F. Stephan, and Charles F. Westoff, "Demographic Variability and Preferential Marriage Patterns," *American Journal of Physical Anthropology*, N.S. 21 (1963), 511-519. Mindel C. Sheps, "Effects on Family Size and Sex Ratio of Preferences Regarding the Sex of Children," *Population Studies*, 17 (1963), 66-72. David A. Swanson, "An Evaluation of 'Ratio' and 'Difference' Regression Methods for Estimating Small, Highly Concentrated Populations: The Case of Ethnic Groups," *Public Data Use*, 6 (July, 1978), 18-27.

middleman minority, an ethnic group that finds a place as small traders between the upper and lower classes of a (usually) multi-ethnic society. Examples include Jews in Europe, Chinese in Southeast Asia, Indians in East Africa, and Arabs in West Africa. In this role they generally excite resentment and hostility from both above and below.

REFERENCES: Howard Becker, "Middleman Trading Peoples," in *Man in Reciprocity* (New York: Praeger, 1956). Jonathan H. Turner and Edna Bonacich, "Toward a Composite Theory of Middleman Minorities," *Ethnicity*, 7 (1980), 144-158.

midwife, a woman who assists other women in childbirth, was once the only obstetrical professional. The shift from births at home supervised by midwives to births in hospitals under an obstetrician's care was not smooth. The debate over the role of the two began in the United States about 1900, continued for several decades, and ended with the complete victory of licensed physicians, who could point to a significant decline in maternal and infant mortality. With the recent rise of a new feminist movement, however, the arguments are being reviewed again, sometimes with contrary conclusions (e.g., Litoff, 1978). In the mean time a new category developed, called the *nurse-midwife*, who is assigned to each case by a physician and works under his control and, if necessary, supervision. The nurse-midwife advises the patient during her pregnancy, manages a normal labor and conducts a normal delivery, and gives routine examinations to the mother and infant in the postpartum period—always with a physician on call in case of need (Thomas, 1965). See also *nurse.

REFERENCES: Judy Barrett Litoff, ''Forgotten Women: American Midwives at the Turn of the Twentieth Century,'' *Historian*, 40 (1978), 235-251. Margaret W. Thomas, *The Practice of Nurse-Midwifery in the United States* (Washington, D.C.: U.S. Children's Bureau, 1965).

midyear population, the denominator of many demographic rates, is the estimated number of people in the relevant unit on June 30 or July 1. Even in a census year, however, this figure must be based on an extrapolation from the date of the count. The figure in the numerator, moreover, must generally be adjusted for an undercount or other flaw in the basic data. This means that the commonest measures, the crude birth and death rates, involve more computation than the simple division that is indicated in the formulas.

migration, the relatively permanent movement of persons over a significant distance, is inherently imprecise. For by this definition or any paraphrase of it, the concept cannot be applied to any set of data until the most important terms (''permanent,'' ''significant'') have been specified. A person who goes to another country and remains there for the rest of his life, we say, is a migrant; and one who pays a two-hour visit to the nearest town is not. Between such two extremes lies a bewildering array of intermediate instances, which can be distinguished only by more or less arbitrary criteria (Lacroix, 1949). Because a migration, unlike a birth or a death, is not a discrete natural event, this third large sector of demographic analysis differs fundamentally from fertility and mortality (cf. Goldscheider, 1971, chap. 3). See also *mobility.

The most general distinction made in the concept is between movements within the boundaries of one country and those between two countries (see *migration, internal; *migration, international). However, there are many instances where the line is hard to draw between a self-governing territory and a separate region of the same state. Is the movement from Puerto Rico to the mainland of the United States or, within the confines of a single city, that between East and West Berlin ''internal'' or ''international''? In fact, depending on the purposes of the data to be gathered, such movements can be considered to be one or the other; juridically, Puerto Rico is part of the United States, but in many respects Puerto Rican migrants are like aliens, with the same kinds of difficulties in acculturating as those from other Latin American areas. In the usual analysis the differentiation between internal and international is maintained mainly because two sets of statistics that are ordinarily collected separately would be difficult to combine into a single series. Implicitly the distinction is based also on the assumption that a nation is culturally homogeneous, with a less significant variation among its subunits than any that sets it off from other nations. Though this is sometimes the case, it need not be so. A native of Toronto, for instance, who moves to San Francisco would in any but a juridical sense find it easier to acculturate than a migrant from, say, a Kentucky village. And in an area like West Africa, where tribal cultures very often extend over several of the newly established countries, this anomaly is the generality; sociologically, the significant move is from one tribal area to another, rather than from one state to another. Yet, however artificial, the distinction can be crucial. According to the definition used by United Nations agencies, an African fleeing from war and terrorism who happens to resettle on the same side of an international boundary is not a *refugee, though he or she may have lost just as much in tribal rights and personal property and, in the continent's multilingual states, have ended up among an alien and usually hostile people.

In the system of classification that the bibliographic journal *Population Index* adopted in 1972, the distinction is retained between internal and international migration only for citations where it is clearly pertinent, but otherwise all works on migration are listed under one heading. In many cases the type of migration is incidental to the purpose of the author, who may be using a particular set of data in order to exemplify generic features common to movements of all kinds. Sources of data, however, are remarkably diverse and scattered (Della Cava, 1979).

Within an area that is homogeneous with respect to factors that affect the propensity to move, the number of migrations will supposedly vary with the distance covered. This most general thesis can be expressed in the equation

$$M = aX/D^b$$

where M is the number of migrants
   D is the distance over the shortest transportation route
   X is any other relevant factor
   a and b are constants, usually set at unity.

In one version of this equation (Zipf, 1949, pp. 386-409), the so-called P_1P_2/D hypothesis, the populations at the end points of the movement are taken as the X factor. Another variation is the familiar proposition that "the number of persons going a given distance is directly proportional to the number of [employment] opportunities at that distance and inversely proportional to the number of intervening opportunities" (Stouffer, 1940).

Any proposition about migration between only two points is too simplistic, however, to be a useful building block for more elaborate theories. These have in general started from other premises. An important example is the three-volume study of *Population Redistribution and Economic Growth: United States, 1870-1950* (Kuznets, 1957-64), in which the available data concerning the regional distribution of the developing American economy and data concerning internal migration were combined into a unified analysis of the interaction between the two. According to several studies of the transatlantic movement, if conditions in the home country build up a pressure to emigrate, the volume, direction, and timing of the movement are set largely by the business cycle in the receiving country (e.g., D. S. Thomas, 1941). According to another interpretation, within a unified "Atlantic economy" push factors were more important (Brinley Thomas, 1972).

Push and pull factors do not exert their force equally. The process by which migrants differentiate themselves from the sedentary population is called *migratory selection* (e.g., D. S. Thomas, 1938). In both internal and international movements adolescents and young adults predominate; for not only do the young adapt more easily, but since they are close to the beginning of their working life, they can more readily take advantage of new opportunities. One of the famous "laws" of E. G. †Ravenstein (1885, 1889) was that "females are more migratory than males," but he noted that this was truer of short distances than of longer ones. Two characteristic types that Ravenstein was considering, male overseas migrants and farm girls who moved to cities to become domestic servants, were single young adults. Family migration, however, is now much more common, particularly when the motivation is political rather than economic, or, for different reasons, within the United States. According to a survey by the U.S. Bureau of the Census (1979), during the 1970s children made up almost as high a proportion of those moving as men or women in their twenties. Indeed, not only do married couples migrate but they often do so for reasons associated with their family life—in order to have a larger house for an increasing number of children, or to live close to a better school, and so on (e.g., Rossi, 1955).

A count of the number of migrants depends, of course, on how the phenomenon is defined. If one omits refugees and others who are politically motivated, it is easy to conclude that the others, most of whom are impelled to move for economic reasons, follow certain laws. In fact, there are no "laws" of migration in the sense of universal generalizations; the highest level of abstraction possible is the contrast of various types of migrants, whose similar characteristics motivate them to respond in the same way to particular economic, political, or other factors (Petersen, 1958). In a general typology, one can distinguish most fundamentally between innovating and conservative migrants—between those who seek the new and those who move in response to a change in their circumstances, hoping to preserve their old way of life in a new place. An ecological push impels a primitive migration; a state bureaucracy, a forced migration or a flow of refugees; a search for novelty, a free migration, which by its own impetus can mushroom into a mass migration. Under each set of circumstances, a different proportion of the population with different characteristics moves from one location to another, and the consequences for the sending and receiving areas therefore also differ.

The special concepts and measures that are used to analyze migration are sometimes confusing. One reason is that some words are used in several senses. "Migrant" is often a generic term, but the U.S. Bureau of the Census contrasts it with "mover." In what is called a mover-stayer analysis, however, "mover" is the generic concept. Sometimes, on the other hand, essentially equivalent ideas are given two or more designations. For example, a number of analysts have distinguished between those who themselves respond to push and pull factors and those who go along with a head of the family or move in order to join him. In various studies these two types of migrants are labeled, respectively, as "primary" and "secondary," "independent" and "dependent," or "resultant" and "epiphenomenal."

Migration involves at least two places. Every move is out of a country (or other area, place, or whatever) of origin and into a country (or some alternative) of destination. An international migrant is called an *emigrant* when he leaves and an *immigrant* when he arrives; the analogous terms for a migrant within a country are *out-migrant* and *in-migrant*. The related collective nouns—*emigration, immigration, out-migration,* and *in-migration*—are distinguished in the same way. The sum of movements in both direction is called the *gross migration* or the *turnover* for a designated area; the difference between them, the *net migration*. The latter term may have the equivalent of an algebraic sign, as either *net immigration* (or *net in-migration)* or *net emigration* (or *net out-migration*). The ratio of net migration to the turnover is sometimes called the *effectiveness* of the migration—that is the relative number of moves required to bring about a given population distribution. Movement back to the place of origin is called *return migration* or *remigration* (cf. Rhoades, 1979); those who participate in it are *return migrants* or *remigrants*. Similarly, a *migration stream*, which arises when the propensity to leave develops into a mass movement, may generate a *counterstream* (or reverse stream) in the opposite direction. Note, however, that there is no such creature as a "net migrant," and the sum of all remigrants need not be the same as the total remigration as inferred from the movements in both directions.

In principle migration rates are constructed like any other, by calculating the number who migrate per unit of the population at *risk. But the base population changes over the period of the migration. Should one take the number at the beginning of the period under consideration, that at the end, an average of the two, or some other figure? Rates of influx are even more difficult to set, for not only the time period but also the area must be decided on more or less arbitrarily (Thomlinson, 1962; Hamilton, 1965). Usage has not been consistent, for arguments for any procedure are not conclusive.

REFERENCES: Olha Della Cava, "Human Migration: A Survey of Information Sources," *Special Libraries*, 70 (1979), 311-319. Calvin Goldscheider, *Population, Mod-*

ernization, and Social Structure (Boston: Little, Brown, 1971). C. Horace Hamilton, "Practical and Mathematical Considerations in the Formulation and Selection of Migration Rates," *Demography*, 2 (1965), 429-443. Simon Kuznets, ed., *Population Redistribution and Economic Growth: United States, 1870-1950*, Memoirs 45, 51, 61 (Philadelphia: American Philosophical Society, 1957-64); summarized in Kuznets and Dorothy Swaine Thomas, "Internal Migration and Economic Growth," in Milbank Memorial Fund, *Selected Studies of Migration since World War II* (New York, 1958). Max Lacroix, "Problems of Collection and Comparison of Migration Statistics," in Milbank Memorial Fund, *Problems in the Collection and Comparability of International Statistics* (New York, 1949). William Petersen, "A General Typology of Migration," *American Sociological Review*, 23 (1958), 256-266. E. G. Ravenstein, "The Laws of Migration," *Journal of the Royal Statistical Society*, 48 (1885), 167-235; 52 (1889), 241-305. Robert E. Rhoades, ed., "The Anthropology of Return Migration," *Papers in Anthropology*, vol. 20 (1979). Peter H. Rossi, *Why Families Move: A Study in the Social Psychology of Urban Residential Mobility* (New York: Free Press, 1955). Samuel A. Stouffer, "Intervening Opportunities: A Theory Relating Mobility and Distance," *American Sociological Review*, 5 (1940), 845-867. Brinley Thomas, *Migration and Economic Growth: A Study of Great Britain and the Atlantic Economy* (2nd ed.; Cambridge, England: Cambridge University Press, 1973). Dorothy Swaine Thomas, *Social and Economic Aspects of Swedish Population Movements, 1750-1933* (New York: Macmillan, 1941); ed., *Research Memorandum on Migration Differentials* (New York: Social Science Research Council, 1938). Ralph Thomlinson, "The Determinants of a Base Population for Computing Migration Rates," *Milbank Memorial Fund Quarterly*, 40 (1962), 356-366. U. S. Bureau of the Census, "Population Profile of the United States: 1978," *Current Population Reports*, Ser. P-20, no. 336 (Washington, D.C., 1979). George K. Zipf, *Human Behavior and the Principle of Least Effort: An Introduction to Human Ecology* (Reading, Mass.: Addison-Wesley, 1949).

migration, illegal, the movement that takes place wherever there is a bar to the free passage of people—that is, at virtually every international border and within the many countries that restrict internal migration as well. One consequence of the increasing state supervision of *migration is a greater propensity to evade controls, especially but not exclusively when the contrast is sharp between conditions on either side of a border. The *Berlin wall is a striking symbol. But clandestine movements are not merely from totalitarian countries (Houdaille and Sauvy, 1974; Johnson and Williams, 1981). The *Intergovernmental Committee for Migration (ICM) devoted a study period to the issue and published some of its findings, together with a bibliography covering the whole world, a review of policies on illegal employment and public assistance, and a list of other bibliographies (*International Migration*, 21, 1983, B1-B47). According to a working estimate used in the late 1970s, one-tenth of the alien workers in Common Market countries, or a total of some 600,000 persons, were illegal. Following the decision of an international commission, any who knowingly organized illegal movements or employed illegal immigrants were to be subject to a punishment to be specified by each member country (*Economist*, November 13, 1976). Such controls are hampered by a typical ambivalence of the citizenry toward illegal aliens and often by an ambiguity of the illegality itself. Britain, for example, reacted to the large inflow of unskilled former colonials by imposing new controls—without, however, entirely abandoning the prior goal of free migration within the whole of the Commonwealth.

A somewhat similar situation developed in the region of the United States bordering on Mexico, where the distinction between "legal" and "illegal" immigrant, often ignored, became so fluid and blunted that some analysts prefer the term "undocumented" (e.g., Bustamante, 1977; García y Griego, 1980). Though formally the Western Hemisphere was not mentioned in the Immigration Acts adopted in the 1920s, consuls in Mexico were instructed to enforce rigorously the existent laws limiting visas to literate persons who would not engage in contract labor or become public charges, thus cutting the movement by about three-quarters in one year (Reisler, 1976). But over the longer run the influx of Mexicans continued to respond to the demand for agricultural labor in the Southwest, with the difference made up by more or less illegal migrants (Samora et al., 1971; Corwin, 1972, 1982; Frisbie, 1975; Spaulding, 1983). According to one projection up to the year 2000, the demand for labor will exceed the supply in the United States, and the contrary will be the case in Mexico; thus, increased immigration could have important advantages for both economies (Reynolds, 1979). More generally the intermittent debate on the issue of "wetbacks" (those who had evaded controls by swimming the Rio Grande) has been consistently between the same two camps, with the migrants themselves, their American employers (Stoddard, 1976), and Mexican officials (Mumme, 1978) generally in favor of a free movement, while opposed to it in the United States were trade unions, xenophobes hostile to all immigrants and often especially to Mexicans, and such restrictionists as the advocates of a zero population growth. That the migrants, the Mexican economy, and the American consumer benefit from the influx is virtually beyond dispute. The arguments in opposition are mainly three: that illegal aliens allegedly displace American workers, that the lower cost of producing foodstuffs is cancelled by the "social costs" of Mexican aliens, and that most illegal migrants allegedly settle permanently in the United States (Cornelius, 1977).

By definition, the number of illegal migrants is unknown, and guesses vary with the political stance of the person offering the figure, the stringency of control measures, and other spurious factors (Keely, 1977). The number of illegal Mexicans apprehended and/or deported rose very slowly from a few thousand in the mid-1920s to well over a million in 1954, then fell to several tens of thousands in the following decade, rising again from under 100,000 in 1966 to over 500,000 in 1973 (Briggs, 1975). How tenuous all estimates are is suggested by the table on page 572, which summarizes several studies. Note that some figures pertain to migration (or net migration) over a particular period, others to the accumulated population illegally resident in the United States. In addition to the many estimates of numbers, a few studies attempt to give some notion of the migrants' characteristics (e.g., Houstoun, 1983; Ranney and Kossoudji, 1983).

Estimates of Illegal Immigration or of Aliens Illegally Residing in the United States, Various Dates

Date of Estimate	Estimate (-000,000)	Comment	Source
1970	1.6	Mexican-origin population only	Goldberg (1974)
1973	3.9 (2.9 - 5.7)	Ages 18 to 44 only. The numbers in parenthesis represent rough 68-percent confidence limits.	Lancaster and Scheuren (1978)
1975	8.2	The figure includes an estimated 5.2 million of Mexican origin.	Lesko Associates (1975)
1975	0.6 - 4.7	White male population, ages 20 to 44 only	Robinson (1980)
1975	0.4 - 1.2	Net illegal immigration of Mexican-origin population, 1970-75.	Heer (1979)
1976	6		Chapman, INS* (1976)
1977	0.5 - 1.2	Mexican-origin population only.	García y Griego (1979)
1977	0.7 - 2.2	Mexican-origin population only; a re-estimation of García y Griego (1979).	U.S. Bureau of the Census
1978	3 - 6		Castillo, INS* (1978)
1978	1.1 - 4.1	Total population, ages 20 to 44	Robinson (1980)
Dec. 1978- Jan. 1979	0.4	Mexican nationals over 15 years of age working or looking for work, without regard to legal status, based on a National Survey of Emigration	Zazueta and Corona (1979)
1978-79	3.5 - 6	Total illegal alien population, based on methodological assessment of other studies listed	Siegel, Passel, and Robinson (1980)
1979	1.1 - 1.2	Based on a difference between legal entrants and alien population	Warren and Passel (1983)

*U.S. Immigration and Naturalization Service.
Sources: Siegel et al., (1980). Warren (1982).

REFERENCES: V. M. Briggs, Jr., "Mexican Workers in the United States Labour Market: A Contemporary Dilemma," *International Labour Review*, 12 (1975), 351-368. Jorge A. Bustamante F., "Undocumented Immigration from Mexico: Research Report," *International Migration Review*, 11 (1977), 149-177. Leonel Castillo, Statement before the House Select Committee on Population, U.S. House of Representatives, Ninety-fifth Congress, Second Session, Washington, D.C., April 6, 1978. Leonard F. Chapman, Statement before the Subcommittee on Immigration and Naturalization of the Committee on the Judiciary, U.S. Senate, Ninety-fourth Congress, Second Session, Washington, D.C., March 17, 1976. W. A. Cornelius, "When the Door Is Closed to Illegal Aliens, Who Pays?" *New York Times* (June 1, 1977), p. 27. Arthur F. Corwin, "Historia de la Emigración Mexicana, 1900-1970: Literatura e Investigación," *Historia Mexicana*, 22 (1972), 188-220; "The Numbers Game: Estimates of Illegal Aliens in the United States,

1970-1981," *Law and Contemporary Problems*, 45 (1982), 223-297. W. Parker Frisbie, "Illegal Migration from Mexico to the United States: A Longitudinal Analysis," *International Migration Review*, 9 (1975), 3-13. Manual García y Griego, *El Volumen de la Migración de Mexicanos No Documentados a los Estados Unidos (Nuevas Hipotesis)* (Mexico City: Centro Nacional de Información y Estadísticas del Trabajo, 1979). Howard Goldberg, *Estimates of Emigration from Mexico and Illegal Entry into the United States, 1960-1970, by the Residual Method* (Washington, D.C.: Georgetown University, Center for Population Research, 1974). David M. Heer, "What Is the Annual Net Flow of Undocumented Mexican Immigrants to the United States?" *Demography*, 16 (1979), 417-423. Jacques Houdaille and Alfred Sauvy, "L'Immigration Clandestine dans le Monde," *Population*, 29 (1974), 725-742. Marion F. Houstoun, "Aliens in Irregular Status in the United States: A Review of Their Numbers, Characteristics, and Role in the U.S. Labor Market," *International Migration*, 21 (1983), 372-413. Kenneth F. Johnson and Miles W. Williams, *Illegal Aliens in the Western Hemisphere: Political and Economic Factors* (New York: Praeger, 1981). Charles B. Keely, "Counting the Uncountable: Estimates of Undocumented Aliens in the United States," *Population and Development Review*, 3 (1977), 473-481. Clarice Lancaster and Frederick J. Scheuren, "Counting the Uncountable Illegals: Some Initial Statistical Speculations Employing Capture-Recapture Techniques," in American Statistical Association, *Proceedings of the Social Statistics Section, 1977* (1978), pp. 530-535. Lesko Associates, *Final Report: Basic Data and Guidance Required to Implement a Major Illegal Alien Study during Fiscal Year 1976*, prepared for the Office of Planning and Evaluation, U.S. Immigration and Naturalization Service (Washington, D.C., 1975). Stephen P. Mumme, "Mexican Politics and the Prospects for Emigration Policy: A Policy Perspective," *Inter-American Economic Affairs*, 32 (1978), 67-94. Susan Ranney and Sherrie Kossoudji, "Profiles of Temporary Mexican Labor Migrants to the United States," *Population and Development Review*, 9 (1983), 475-493. Mark Reisler, *By the Sweat of Their Brow: Mexican Immigrant Labor in the United States, 1900-1940* (Westport, Conn.: Greenwood Press, 1976). Clark W. Reynolds, "Labor Market Projections for the United States and Mexico and Current Migration Controversies," *Food Research Institute Studies*, 17 (1979), 121-155. J. Gregory Robinson, "Estimating the Approximate Size of the Illegal Alien Population in the United States by the Comparative Trend Analysis of Age-Specific Death Rates," *Demography*, 17 (1980), 159-176. Julian Samora, Bustamante, and Gilbert Cardenas, *Los Mojados: The Wetback Story* (Notre Dame, Ind.: University of Notre Dame Press, 1971). Jacob S. Siegel, Jeffrey S. Passel, and Robinson, "Preliminary Review of Existing Studies of the Number of Illegal Residents in the United States," in *U.S. Immigration Policy and the National Interest: The Staff Report of the Select Commission on Immigration and Refugee Policy* (Washington, D.C., 1980), Appendix E. Rose Spaulding, "Mexican Immigration: A Historical Perspective," *Latin American Research Review*, 18 (1983), 201-209. Ellwyn R. Stoddard, "A Conceptual Analysis of the 'Alien Invasion': Institutionalized Support of Illegal Mexican Aliens in the U.S.," *International Migration Review*, 10 (1976), 157-189. Robert Warren and Jeffrey S. Passel, *Estimates of Illegal Aliens from Mexico Counted in the 1980 U.S. Census* (Washington, D.C.: U.S. Bureau of the Census, 1983). Carlos H. Zazueta and Rodolfo Corona, *Los Trabajadores Mexicanos en los Estados Unidos: Primeros Resultados de la Encuesta Nacional de Emigración* (Mexico City: Centro Nacional de Información y Estadísticas del Trabajo, 1979).

migration, internal, or movement within the boundaries of a single country, overlaps conceptually and analytically with international migration, or movement between countries. The difference between the two is mainly political or juridical: citizens have the legal right to settle wherever they please within Western countries; and even the bars that states like the Soviet Union impose on the free movement within their borders are usually less restrictive than those regulating moves into or out of such totalitarian countries. In the context of demography, the most important distinction between the two types of migration is that the data collected on country-to-country flows are an adjunct of their control, but that statistics on within-country movements are collected by different agencies for different purposes, with a consequent difference in the problems of interpretation (cf. United Nations, 1978). According to the usual convention, those moving within a country are termed *out-migrants* and *in-migrants* (rather than emigrants and immigrants), and the collective nouns are *out-migration* and *in-migration* (rather than emigration and immigration). See also *migration; *migration, international; *migration policies and controls.

The fact that internal migration does not involve a significant event comparable to the crossing of the boundary between two countries means that its specification is problematic. Many shifts in residence are within the same neighborhood, perhaps only across the same street; others, to an adjacent town, may still be within an identical social environment. Three kinds of criteria are used to define an internal migrant. If a farmer's son moves to a city, or if in Belgium a Dutch-speaking Fleming moves to French-speaking Brussels, or generally if culturally or socially a person moves to an area where he is defined—and defines himself—as a stranger, this is a genuine migration. Second, the greater the distance, the more likely it is that the person will cross such a cultural-social boundary. And, third, one can take as an operational indicator the crossing of successive subnational units as an approximation of increasing distance. Thus, by the usage of the U.S. Bureau of the Census the *mobile population*, defined as those who reside in different houses within the United States on two specified dates, is classified first between *movers* within a single county and *migrants* from one county to another. The latter category is further divided according to whether the migration was within the same state, to a contiguous state, or to a noncontiguous state.

The data from which such estimates are made consist in responses to questions on where the person was born and on where he was living a certain number of years earlier. If the birthplace and the current place of residence are different, the movement between them is termed a *lifetime migration*. And if the respondent lived in a different location so and so many years before the survey or census, it is assumed that he moved once from that prior residence to his current one. All such deductions, of course, are subject to serious error. In what is called a *progressive migration*, a person may have moved a dozen times between his birth and the date of the census, and if the latest move happened to be back to his native place he would not be recorded as a migrant at all (DaVanzo and Morrison, 1982; for a discussion of the phenomenon in Indonesia, see Hugo,

1982). Another method, based on the *balancing equation, is to estimate the natural increase from vital statistics and subtract this from the growth in population. In such a calculation, however, whatever errors exist in recorded fertility, mortality, and population size are included in estimating merely the net movement— that is, what is left after possibly significant but undetected flows cancel each other out (cf. Shryock, 1964).

More satisfactory data can be obtained from sample surveys that include questions not only on where and when the moves were made but on why (cf. Bilsborrow and Akin, 1982; Isserman et al., 1982; Sell, 1983). Most so-called *primary migrants* move in order to change their job or to search for a new one (e.g., Greenwood, 1975). However, they are often accompanied or followed by members of their family, the *secondary migrants* who respond to economic opportunities only indirectly. Both kinds of motivation set the usual distribution by age and sex. According to two surveys by the U.S. Bureau of the Census (1979, 1981), though most migrants within the country are young adults, the proportion of young children is almost as high, for family migration is far more significant than a generation or two ago (cf. Long and Hansen, 1979). Though the populations of some retirement areas are growing very fast, the persons who move to them are only a relatively small proportion of the country's older people (cf. McCarthy, 1983). From 1965 to 1978, there was a net movement of 1.4 million persons out of the Northeast and the North Central regions to the South and West (but see also Masnick, 1981); that is, the historic westward movement continued, but the migration out of the South was reversed. This combination is typically explained as a drift to "the Sun Belt," but Southern and Southwestern states are also attractive because of their relatively favorable attitude toward business and their frequently lower taxes.

Migration within other industrial countries usually does not differ from that within the United States in its essential features. The Scandinavian and Low Countries maintain population registers from which a count of migrants can be made more expeditiously than from a periodic census or survey. Though the nations of Western Europe are generally no larger than American states, since regions within the countries are often quite distinct, migration can represent a highly meaningful shift. Geographic units are often quite heterogeneous, and a movement from one *Land* to another in West Germany, or one canton to another in Switzerland, is as difficult to interpret as one from one American state to another. The dominant shift over all has been from rural to urban; in Norway and Sweden, even the virtually empty northern regions lost population to the cities in the south. Several countries attempted to slow or reverse this *urbanization, and France especially was successful in building up regional centers that now compete with Paris (cf. *growth pole). More generally, the significance of internal migration per se became far less in the countries of the European Economic Community that signed a treaty guaranteeing the "free movement of labor" among them (Fielding, 1975). A United Nations report on labor migration in Europe included, as one would expect, both internal and international movements

(U.N. Economic Commission for Europe, 1979). A recent analysis of migration in Japan showed that the rate declines with age and distance and increases with education—a finding that might have been duplicated in almost any Western country (Inoki and Suruga, 1981).

The number of studies of internal migration in less developed countries, though smaller, has been growing rapidly (cf. Yap, 1975; Richmond and Kubat, 1976). Somewhat paradoxically, two major themes have been the contribution of migration to economic development and the excessive growth of cities from the large rural-urban movement. One reason for such contradictory conclusions is that the data are generally even less satisfactory than statistics on internal migration in industrial nations. The sample surveys from which many of the data are drawn very frequently have unspecified analytical frameworks and poor sample designs, and census results are applied inappropriately to issues that can be adequately tested only with more detailed responses. Sidney †Goldstein and Alice Goldstein (1981) have sifted through a mass of such studies, noted their lacks, and suggested procedures to improve future analyses.

Studies of internal migration vary greatly according to the discipline of the analyst (cf. Berliner, 1977; Neuberger, 1977). Demographic and geographic works have generally followed the example of E. G. †Ravenstein (1885, 1889) and noted the differential rates by population characteristics, often with little attempt at interpretation. Economists have concentrated on *labor mobility. Anthropologists, sociologists, and geographers have noted the diffusion of culture with migrants and their process of acculturation in the new setting. Political scientists have focused on policy, meaning principally how to avoid the rapid growth of large urban centers. Not only is there little communication across disciplines, but many of the studies pertain only incidentally to internal migration and could equally well apply to that between countries.

REFERENCES: Joseph S. Berliner, "Internal Migration: A Comparative Disciplinary View," in Brown and Neuberger (1977). Richard S. Bilsborrow and John S. Akin, "Data Availability versus Data Needs for Analyzing the Determinants and Consequences of Internal Migration: An Evaluation of U.S. Survey Data," *Review of Public Data Use*, 10 (1982), 261-284. Alan A. Brown and Egon Neuberger, eds., *Internal Migration: A Comparative Perspective* (New York: Academic Press, 1977). Julie S. DaVanzo and Peter A. Morrison, *Migration Sequences: Who Moves Back and Who Moves On?* (Santa Monica, Calif.: Rand Corporation, 1982). A. J. Fielding, "Internal Migration in Western Europe," in Leszek A. Kosiński and R. Mansell Prothero, eds., *People on the Move: Studies on Internal Migration* (London: Methuen, 1975). Sidney Goldstein and Alice Goldstein, *Surveys of Migration in Developing Countries: A Methodological Review* (Honolulu: East-West Population Institute, 1981). Michael J. Greenwood, "Research on Internal Migration in the United States: A Survey," *Journal of Economic Literature*, 13 (1975), 397-433. Graeme J. Hugo, "Circular Migration in Indonesia," *Population and Development Review*, 8 (1982), 59-83. Takenori Inoki and Terukazu Suruga, "Migration, Age, and Education: A Cross-Sectional Analysis of Geographic Labor Mobility in Japan," *Journal of Regional Science*, 21 (1981), 507-517. Andrew M. Isserman, David A. Plane, and David B. McMillen, "Internal Migration in the United States: An Evaluation of

Federal Data,'' *Review of Public Data Use*, 10 (1982), 285-311. Larry H. Long and Kristin A. Hansen, ''Reasons for Interstate Migration: Jobs, Retirement, Climate, and Other Influences,'' *Current Population Reports*, Special Studies, Ser. P-23, no. 81 (1979). George S. Masnick, ''Demographhic Influences on the Labor Force in New England,'' in John C. Hoy and Melvin H. Bernstein, eds., *New England's Vital Resource: The Labor Force* (Washington, D.C.: American Council on Education, 1981). Kevin F. McCarthy, *The Elderly Population's Changing Spatial Distribution: Patterns of Change since 1960* (Santa Monica, Calif.: Rand Corporation, 1983). Neuberger, ''Internal Migration: A Comparative Systemic View,'' in Brown and Neuberger (1977). E. G. Ravenstein, ''The Laws of Migration,'' *Journal of the Royal Statistical Society*, 48 (1885), 167–235; 52 (1889), 241–305. Anthony H. Richmond and Daniel Kubat, eds., *Internal Migration: The New World and the Third World* (Beverly Hills, Calif.: Sage Publications, 1976). Ralph R. Sell, ''Analyzing Migration Decisions: The First Step—Whose Decisions?'' *Demography*, 20 (1983), 299-311. Henry S. Shryock, Jr., *Population Mobility within the United States* (Chicago: University of Chicago, Community and Family Study Center, 1964). U. N. Department of International Economic and Social Affairs, Statistical Office, *Statistics of Internal Migration: A Technical Report*, Studies in Methods, Ser. F, no. 23 (1978). U.N. Economic Commission for Europe, *Economic Survey of Europe in 1977: Labour Supply and Migration in Europe, Demographic Dimensions 1950-1975 and Perspectives* (New York, 1979). U.S. Bureau of the Census, ''Geographical Mobility: March 1975 to March 1980''; ''Population Profile of the United States: 1978,'' *Current Population Reports*, Ser. P-20, no. 336 (1979); no. 368 (1981). L.Y.L. Yap. *Internal Migration in Less Developed Countries: A Survey of the Literature* (Washington, D.C.: International Bank for Reconstruction and Development, 1975).

migration, international, defined in principle by the crossing of a border between nations, is thus distinguished from movements within countries, though in many respects the two processes can be analyzed in similar ways (see *migration; *migration, internal). The differentiation is reflected in the convention that international migrants are termed *emigrants* when they leave and *immigrants* when they arrive (rather than out-migrants and in-migrants), and that the processes are termed *emigration* and *immigration* (rather than out-migration and in-migration).

Sometimes the distinction is ambiguous between an independent state and a quasi-independent colony, or between a temporary visitor or transient and a permanent migrant. But in general it would seem that the clear-cut criterion of crossing a border between two countries would delineate international migration more sharply than movement within a single country. In fact, however, the recording of international movements is far less simple than it might seem. According to the influential United Nations publication *The Determinants and Consequences of Population Trends* (1953, p. 98), '' 'migration' excludes population transfers, . . . deportations, refugee movements, and the movement of 'displaced persons.' '' Later analysts have also omitted those who cross international borders without permission (see *migration, illegal). Such a delimitation of the term leaves out a probable majority of those who have crossed international borders since World War II, as well as a significant proportion of those who did so during the prior generation (Petersen, 1978). The reasons for these amazing omissions are mainly two. Many of the members of the United Nations themselves generate *refugee flows, and it is understandable that the international body would not examine too closely the conditions that lead to politically motivated migrations. In any case, the movements of refugees, illegal migrants, and other supposedly anomalous types are often not recorded, if only because the concepts are imprecise.

A restriction of an analysis to economically motivated migrants does not eliminate problems with the data. Each year the U.N. *Demographic Yearbook* supplements a general review of population statistics with a more detailed survey of one particular topic; and in 1977, for the first time, the featured subject was international migration. As one example of how dubious many of the statistics are, the *Yearbook* cited a 1972 study by the U.N. Economic Commission for Europe (ECE) in which migrants within that region were counted at both ends of the 342 paths between any two ECE countries. The discussion was based in part on replies to a questionnaire that the United Nations agency had distributed, but only 116 countries responded to the basic request for their definition of "immigrant" and 96 for that of "emigrant." The number of recorded immigrants was 57 percent greater than that of emigrants, partly because of time lags but mainly because "emigrant" and "immigrant" are not counted consistently. The fact that data on international movements are an adjunct of state control means that national concerns largely determine the statistics; in this case, the countries' far lesser interest in those departing than in those arriving meant that the expected parity between the two figures was not even approximated. With that much inaccuracy in the documentation of *legal* migration within the region with the world's best population statistics, one must be very wary of conclusions about other categories or about recorded movements anywhere else.

According to the recommendations in a United Nations publication called *International Migration Statistics* (1953), the data compiled as an adjunct to border control are supposed to follow the schema shown on page 579 for those moving in one direction. From the totals entering or leaving a country, called *arrivals* and *departures*, there are first subtracted persons who continually move back and forth, usually with special cards rather than passports and visas. The residual category is divided according to whether or not the travelers are "permanent," depending on statements concerning their intention to remain for at least one year. Those who are not permanent are classified between *visitors* (e.g., tourists), who may not work for pay, and *temporary immigrants* (e.g., businessmen), who may. The *permanent immigrants*, finally, are classified between those who are and are not returning after a year abroad. This schema, complicated as it is, still does not include such special classes as diplomatic personnel, students, and refugees, who generally migrate under particular legal provisions. Most countries follow only some of these recommended classifications (for the

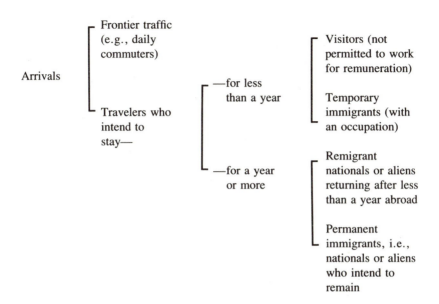

United States, see Riche, 1983). Statistics compiled as part of a border control, moreover, usually do not agree with those from such other sources as lists of passports or of ship or plane passengers, or from the replies to questions in censuses, sample surveys, or population registers.

During the modern era the great international migrations resulted in the spread of Europeans, Africans, and such Asians as Chinese and Japanese to different continents. Presently emigration is largely from the world's less developed areas (cf. Kritz et al., 1981). According to the *Demographic Yearbook* already cited, in mid-1974 an estimated 9.5 million emigrants from those countries were residents of Northwestern Europe, Northern America, and Australia and New Zealand. Latin America, which once had been second only to the United States as a target of immigration, has become a region of net emigration. Between 1960 and 1974, the international migration from Asia more than tripled. The reasons for these shifts were partly a change of legislation in the United States, which is still a significant country of immigration (see *migration policies and controls). But a more significant cause is the rapid population growth of less developed countries, combined with the rising aspirations of a sizable proportion of their inhabitants.

REFERENCES: Mary M. Kritz, Charles B. Keely, and Silvano M. Tomasi, eds., *Global Trends in Migration: Theory and Research on International Population Movements* (New York: Center for Migration Studies, 1981). William Petersen, "International Migration," *Annual Review of Sociology*, 4 (1978), 533-575. Martha Farnsworth Riche, "Immigration Statistics," *American Demographics*, 5 (October, 1983), 38-39. United

Nations, *International Migration Statistics*, Statistical Papers, Ser. M, no. 20 (1953); *The Determinants and Consequences of Population Trends*, Population Studies, no. 17 (1953); *Demographic Yearbook, 1977* (1978).

migration policies and controls have developed together in the modern period (but see also *mercantilism). As recently as the nineteenth century, there was little speculation about the ideal distribution of people and, therefore, hardly any attempt to effect what might have been seen as an optimum. Travelers could cross international borders without any papers except from such countries as the Ottoman Empire, whose demand for a passport was regarded as an indication of their backwardness. Today many countries try to control movement even within their own borders, especially in an effort to inhibit *urbanization (see *urban policy). And virtually all nations set limits of various kinds to the number and kind of immigrants to be admitted from abroad. See also *migration, internal; *migration, international; *population policy.

The trend can be illustrated by the legislative history of the United States, for more than a century the principal receiving country (Hutchinson, 1981). Up to the First World War, the federal governent set no controls at all, and various states along the Eastern seaboard that tried to do so had their laws excluding criminals and other manifest undesirables declared unconstitutional. From about 1880 the number of immigrants rose greatly, eventually to well over a million a year; and their source gradually shifted from Northwestern to Southern and Eastern Europe. The growing movement to exclude those from Italy and Russia did not at first directly challenge the right of any country's nationals to come to the United States but proposed instead that admission should be denied to illiterates. Of the two dozen such bills introduced into Congress, four were passed, to be vetoed successively by Presidents Cleveland, Taft, and Wilson. A more specific law was passed in 1921, seen as a stopgap measure until the problems could be studied; it limited European immigration to 3 percent of the number of foreign-born of each nationality residing in the United States at the time of the last available census, in 1910. A second law, passed in 1924, set another temporary check, which was more restrictive in two respects than its predecessor: the 3 percent quota was reduced to 2 percent, and the base population was changed from the 1910 to the 1890 census, when the proportions from Southern and Eastern Europe were smaller. Ultimately it was planned to regulate immigration according to the "national origins" of the American population—that is, "the number of inhabitants in continental United States in 1920 whose origin by birth or ancestry is attributable to [each] geographical area" designated in immigration statistics as a separate country. The committee that undertook to divide up the heterogeneous American gene pool admitted that there was a "considerable element of uncertainty" in such a classification; and even small discrepancies in 1790, the date of the first census, when increased geometrically from that year until 1920, made a substantial difference in the quota each country was allowed. To this base were added immigration figures, such as they were, and—for lack of a breakdown by ethnic group—an overall rate of natural increase (U.S. Senate, 1928).

These restrictive laws, renewed in the Immigration Act of 1952, achieved the goal of their sponsors. The total immigration from Europe—8.1 million in 1901-10 and 4.4 million in 1911-20 (the latter figure would have been larger but for the war)—was cut down to a decennial quota of about 1.5 million. And the so-called Old Immigration from Northwestern Europe, which had made up only about a quarter of the gross movement during the last 25 years of unrestricted influx, was assigned approximately 85 percent of the European quotas, or roughly the same proportion as in the immigration around 1880. The two purposes of numerical and qualitative restriction had been realized, but opposition to the national-quota system grew, and the principle was gradually eroded in a series of ad hoc laws that permitted *refugees and others to immigrate outside the quota limitations.

National quotas were abandoned in the Immigration and Nationality Act of 1965, which went into effect in mid-1968. As amended over the following years, this set a top limit on the number of immigrants admitted each year and gave preference to such categories as relatives of citizens, refugees, and persons in particular occupations; but the prior preference given to those from Northwestern Europe was not maintained. The earlier bar to permanent immigration from Asia was also relaxed, and in the subsequent period a sizable proportion of immigrants to the United States came from countries in what had been the "barred zone." The almost annual amendments to the law can be reviewed conveniently in a regular section of the *International Migration Review* devoted to both legislative and judicial developments, usually compiled by Austin I. Fragomen, Jr. Revisions in American immigration law changed greatly the nationality and occupation of the modal newcomer (e.g., F. S. Abrams, 1982; Elliott Abrams and F. S. Abrams, 1975; Keely, 1971, 1975). To some degree, however, policy and law have become almost irrelevant, for the dominant issue in the 1970s became how to control the flow of illegal migrants, especially but far from exclusively from Mexico (see *migration, illegal).

In sum, the immigration policy of the United States has vacillated between two contradictory goals—to reflect the country's democratic insititutions in a relatively open admission and to maintain more or less intact the size and ethnic make-up of the current population. Moreover, after the laws of the 1920s had been repealed, the dilemma returned in full force. The number legally admitted in 1980 (including refugees, who are not counted until their status has been adjusted to that of legal immigrants) was estimated at about 800,000, which together with a sizable illegal migration brings the total close to that during the first two decades of this century. But at least in the abstract, the proponents of zero population growth need not bother about immigration; for if the net reproduction rate of the base population is below replacement, the trend toward a stationary population will not be prevented by a constant number of immigrants with a fixed age distribution (Espenshade et al., 1982). There has also been a parallel shift in the source countries. By 1979, fewer than 6 percent of the legal immigrants came from Northwestern Europe, and over 80 percent from Latin America, the Caribbean, and Asia. In short, as in 1920 immigration levels are very high, and the race or ethnicity of most of those entering the country differs markedly from that of the native-born (cf. Bouvier, 1981).

The United Kingdom has had to face a similar dilemma, also based on the operation of contradictory policies. In the aftermath of the Second World War, Britain's far-flung empire broke up into independent countries that became, at least initially, new members of the Commonwealth. In 1948 the country enacted the British Nationality Act, which affirmed the right of all citizens of Commonwealth countries to enter Britain freely, to settle there, and to obtain a job. As a direct consequence the country acquired a nonwhite minority. Of the population of 49 million in 1951, 0.2 percent was nonwhite; and of the 54 million in 1981, about 4 percent was nonwhite. The 947,000 male immigrant workers in Britain in 1971 came from the following countries or areas (*Economist*, April 17, 1982):

Old Commonwealth	2%	
Irish Republic	27	
Other countries of the EEC	8	
Other European countries	13	
New Commonwealth	41	
West Indies		12%
India		12
Pakistan		8
Africa		4
Other		5
Elsewhere	9	

Though all the immigrant workers together made up only about 6 percent of the male work force, the purported competition for jobs and housing became sharp political issues. In 1962 the country had passed the Commonwealth Immigrants Act, which restricted entry to those holding work permits (relatively easy to obtain) or who were close kin of residents. Like the first restrictive laws in the United States, this represented an attempt to maintain the open policy in name while cutting back on the numbers who took advantage of it. The Commonwealth Immigrants Act of 1968, which the Labor government rushed through Parliament in three days, denied entry to British subjects of Asian descent—specifically Indians who were threatened with expulsion from Kenya. As with the United States laws of the 1920s, many in Britain regarded this as racist. The Immigration Act of 1971 maintained the preference for white immigrants but worded it more circumspectly. It coined the concept "patrial"—namely, a person with at least one British grandparent, or who had been naturalized or had lived in Britain for five years—who was permitted to enter freely, like citizens of any European

Economic Community country and Ireland. All others—whether holding British, Commonwealth, or foreign passports—needed entry permits. In sum, the intention to permit entry to any citizen of the British Commonwealth proved to be inoperable in practice, and the effort to cut back from that policy resulted in a series of compromises that fully satisfied neither side.

The typical desire in receiving countries for social-cultural homogeneity has often brought about another dilemma, for those willing to accept low-level jobs are likely to differ markedly from the typical natives of industrial nations or from the upper class of less developed ones. For years the elitist rulers of many South American countries encouraged the immigration of *brazos* (literally "arms"—that is, manual workers or hands), but impeded or prohibited the entry of the industrial entrepreneurs who might develop the economy but also compete for political power. An interesting modern example is the five small oil-producing states that line the Persian Gulf, which have had to import two-thirds of their work force. In spite of public statements to the contrary, the countries' rulers prefer non-Arabs, since Palestinians or others would make greater demands and perhaps threaten the states' political stability. The optimum immigrants are from India, hired with temporary work permits and obliged to leave the country if they are revoked for any reason. The policy leads not to assimilation but to a rigid separation between economic and social-cultural-political roles. The governments provide substantially fewer benefits to foreign workers than to the local populations, and neither the migrants themselves nor the government of India is in a position to raise objections (Weiner, 1982).

This policy is a variant of the institution of *Gastarbeiter that developed in Europe during the economic boom of the post-1945 decades. Men from Italy, Greece, Turkey, and other Mediterranean countries were hired to fill jobs in Germany, Switzerland, and the rest of Northern Europe. They came not as permanent settlers but with work permits of limited duration, bringing benefits to themselves and to the economies of both countries. Some "guest workers," however, brought in their families and settled—even if ostensibly temporarily— in such large congregations that they changed the culture of particular neighborhoods or even of cities. In some of the receiving countries laws were passed under which the immigrants received the same wages and social benefits as natives, thus negating one of the plan's original purposes. And what was seen as a threat to the native culture resulted, especially in Switzerland, in a xenophobic movement that brought about a sharp reversal in that country's admission policy. In any case, the recession of the late 1970s meant that Gastarbeiter, the first to lose their jobs, were cut back. From 1975 to 1980 their number in eight northern countries of Continental Europe fell by some 700,000—but still totaled 5.2 million. In 1977 France started offering repatriation grants (usually air fare plus up to $5,000) to encourage migrants to go home—an offer that over 90,000 accepted over the following several years (cf. DeLey, 1983). The Netherlands and Austria banned the recruitment abroad of new workers, and West Germany required companies to demonstrate that their labor demands could not be filled from the domestic work force. In other words, with some resistance and lags, the main purpose of providing a supply of temporary workers without permanent civil status was fulfilled, and some in the United States proposed that the policy be adopted there as a means of coping with the illegal movement from Mexico.

Indeed, according to an aberrant interpretation of past immigration to the United States, this always had elements of the Gastarbeiter pattern. What most analysts have denoted a free migration, according to Michael Piore (1979), was largely stimulated by industrialists' recruitment. Most migrants, he argued, have been *sojourners, and permanent settlement was usually evidence of their failure. Once migrants partly acculturated and no longer accepted the low-level jobs that initially attracted them, they became competitors rather than complements to the native work force; and the succession of new nationalities brought in at the bottom was made necessary by the upward mobility of each prior one. When immigration from Europe was sharply reduced first by World War I and then by the restrictive laws of the 1920s, company managers sought unskilled laborers in the American South; and in spite of wide differences in pay and personal security, sizable numbers of Negroes started to move out of the South only in the 1920s. This revisionist view can be seen, perhaps, as a useful exaggeration of a factor that has generally been understated or ignored in the standard histories of American immigration.

Thus far the discussion of migration policies has referred only to immigration, which is the more prevalent concern of nations. In many instances, however, countries have either deported certain portions of their populations or, on the contrary, tried to impede the emigration of those in other sectors (cf. United Nations, 1982). Both types of control have been common in tropical Africa. As the former colonies acquired independent status, they had to designate anew how membership in the new states was to be defined; and in virtually every case, citizenship was based on blood ties rather than birthplace. This meant, for instance, that the Indians long resident in East Africa, even those who opted for citizenship in the new states, were expelled—and, as has been noted, were also not accepted in Britain. It meant also that, as one example in West Africa, some 200,000 newly designated aliens were deported from Ghana (Peil, 1974); these were not of European or Asian stock but members of African tribes that could conveniently be penalized in the "indigenization" movement. In Nigeria, similarly, the Indigenization Program Decree of 1972 (revised in 1977) restricted foreigners to certain types of economic activities and set quotas on the employment of aliens in any type of work (Adepoju, 1981). Many of the refugees in Africa have had to flee from war, persecution, or natural disasters, but many others were ousted from their jobs by such rulings (cf. Gould, 1974). Those expelled or denied entry were in many instances persons with skills that the economy needed; thus, the policy of favoring a particular sector of composite populations aggravated labor shortages. On the other hand, when natives trained abroad failed to return—a typical example of *brain drain—officials of less developed countries complained that it was precisely their skills that their countries needed. The emigration of skilled laborers is not generally barred under the laws of African countries, but those intending to emigrate usually require an exit visa, which may be difficult to acquire if their work is judged to be useful for the national economy.

This combination of generating refugee streams and impeding the free movement of others, which can be interpreted as a marginal phenomenon in tropical Africa, is the typical pattern of totalitarian countries. From its founding in 1917, the Soviet Union has impelled millions to seek refuge outside its borders (cf. Kulischer, 1948). And especially in recent decades it has also impeded the emigration of those who wanted to leave. This latter policy received wide publicity in the West as a consequence of the Jewish Freedom Movement, which was organized around the single issue of the right to emigration, ostensibly guaranteed both under the Soviet Constitution and various international treaties to which the Soviet Union was a party. The OVIR, or Visa and Alien Registration Division, Ministry of Internal Affairs, often acts capriciously in granting or withholding permission to leave. In a 1971 amendment to its nationality law, Israel granted Israeli citizenship to any Jew otherwise eligible whose immigration to that country was prevented. In part because of such pressures, several thousand Jews were granted exit visas during 1971; and, paradoxically, in this respect they thus became one of the most favored of Soviet minorities, granted a right that was denied virtually all the others (cf. Knisbacher, 1973; Robin, 1979; Schroeter, 1974).

REFERENCES: Elliott Abrams and Franklin S. Abrams, "Immigration Policy—Who Gets in and Why?" *Public Interest*, no. 38 (1975), 3-29. Franklin S. Abrams, "American Immigration Policy: How Strait the Gate?" *Law and Contemporary Problems*, 45 (1982), 107-135. Aderanti Adepoju, "Military Rule and Population Issues in Nigeria," *African Affairs*, 80 (1981), 29-47. Leon F. Bouvier, "Immigration at the Crossroads," *American Demographics*, 3 (October, 1981), 17-21. Margo DeLey, "French Immigration Policy since May 1981," *International Migration Review*, 17 (1983), 196-211. Thomas J. Espenshade, Bouvier, and W. Brian Arthur, "Immigration and the Stable Population Model," *Demography*, 19 (1982), 125-133. W.T.S. Gould, "Refugees in Tropical Africa," *International Migration Review*, 8 (1974), 413-430. E. P. Hutchinson, *Legislative History of American Immigration Policy* (Philadelphia: University of Pennsylvania Press, 1981). Charles B. Keely, "Effects of the Immigration Act of 1965 on Selected Population Characteristics of Immigrants to the United States," *Demography*, 8 (1971), 157-169; "Effects of U.S. Immigration Law on Manpower Characteristics of Immigrants," *Demography*, 12 (1975), 179-191. Mitchell Knisbacher, "Aliyah of Soviet Jews: Protection of the Right of Emigration under International Law," *Harvard International Law Journal*, 14 (1973), 89-110. Eugene M. Kulischer, *Europe on the Move: War and Population Changes, 1917-47* (New York: Columbia University Press, 1948). Margaret Peil, "Ghana's Aliens," *International Migration Review*, 8 (1974), 367-381. Michael J. Piore, *Birds of Passage: Migrant Labor and Industrial Societies* (Cambridge, England: Cambridge University Press, 1979). Mark A. Robin, "Soviet Emigration Law and International Obligations under United Nations Instruments," *Journal of International Law and Economics*, 13 (1979), 403-431. Leonard Schroeter, "The Jewish Freedom Movement in the Soviet Union: Confrontation Tactics in a Totalitarian Society," *Civil Liberties Review*,

1 (Summer, 1974), 98-115. United Nations, Department of International Economic and Social Affairs, *International Migration Policies and Programmes: A World Survey* (New York, 1982). U.S. Senate, "Immigration Quotas on the Basis of National Origin," *Miscellaneous Documents 8870*, vol. 1, no. 65, 70th Congress, 1st Session (Washington, D.C., 1928). Myron Weiner, "International Migration and Development: Indians in the Persian Gulf," *Population and Development Review*, 8 (1982), 1-36.

migration, stepwise, usually means a movement from a rural birthplace first to a local village, then to a small town, and eventually to a major city. However, the term is not always so simple and unambiguous. Sometimes it refers to an individual or family making successive moves over one lifetime, sometimes to a mass movement over several generations. Other authors use the term to refer both to either of these types of movements and also to the process by which in-migrants from still more remote rural districts fill the gaps in the population left by prior out-migrants.

REFERENCE: Dennis Conway, "Step-wise Migration: Toward a Clarification of the Mechanism," *International Migration Review*, 14 (1980), 3-14.

Milbank Memorial Fund, an American foundation focused on public health broadly defined, including demography. Its predecessor was organized in 1905 by Mrs. Elizabeth Milbank Anderson, whose philanthropy had already been expressed in several expensive efforts to reduce mortality among the poor. The fund's essential difference from earlier types of support was that it conducted research to check on the effects of its attempts to do good. From 1922 to 1936 the main activity—in Cattaraugus County, a rural area of New York State; Syracuse, a middle-sized city; and the Bellevue-Yorkville district of New York City—was intended to show that under appropriate health departments tuber-culosis could be controlled and good health promoted in three diverse areas. A statistical advisory committee was established under the chairmanship of Walter F. †Willcox with such members as Robert E. †Chaddock and Louis †Dublin. The surveys were directed by Edgar †Sydenstricker, who extended the fund's research to population and family planning and converted a house organ into an excellent scientific journal, the *Milbank Memorial Fund Quarterly* (presently called *Health and Society*). He was followed as executive director by Frank Boudreau, who broadened the fund's research activities to include nutrition and housing. The continuing interest in demography was reflected in help given to establish the IUSSP (*International Union for the Scientific Study of Population). In cooperation with the U.S. Bureau of the Census, the fund conducted the first comprehensive study in the United States on differential fertility. This was followed some years later by the *Indianapolis Study of the social and psycho-logical factors that influence fertility, the first large-scale demographic analysis based on survey data. In 1936 the fund helped establish the Office of Population Research at Princeton University. Under Boudreau's successor, however, the division of research was abolished and the fund reverted to its original principal focus on medical care, maintaining only a peripheral interest in population. Address: 1 East 75 Street, New York, N.Y. 10021.

REFERENCE: Clyde V. Kiser, *The Milbank Memorial Fund: Its Leaders and Its Work, 1905-1974* (New York: Milbank Memorial Fund, 1975).

military records are often a useful supplement to standard demographic statistics. In the past soldiers were sometimes counted when no other part of the population was; and by applying a suitable multiplier to this sector, historians have estimated the population of India in the seventeenth century, for example, and that of China during the Chou dynasty (Hollingsworth, 1969, chap. 7). In early modern Europe the army records of several countries showed that the average height of soldiers increased significantly, suggesting a gradual improvement in the level of living of the populations from which they were drawn.

In the United States the statistics collected on the armed forces have provided a data base concerning a very large and highly homogeneous population. The Army maintains in Washington a Center of Military History, but its records are consulted mainly for such personal uses as to validate a widow's claim. The more general studies exemplified here have been made mainly by the Army itself. During World War I, when intelligence tests were used to screen and classify Army personnel, this was the first large-scale application of this tool (Yerkes, 1921). Those who might be in combat were tested, of course, also for their physical condition (cf. Love and Davenport, 1920). Following World War II, the statistical compendium of more than 18 million individual medical records included both battle and nonbattle injuries and diseases, with death rates classified by cause (Lada and Reister, 1975). The men drafted for military service in subsequent years were generally not a random sample of their age group, since they did not include volunteers who were accepted and those deferred on grounds other than health; but, even so, the results were often disturbing. In 1965, for instance, almost two-thirds were disqualified: 46.8 percent failed to pass the test of mental abilities, 12.8 percent were in poor physical health, 4.5 percent failed for both mental and physical reasons, and 1.8 percent were excluded for "administrative" reasons (Office of the U.S. Surgeon General, 1966).

Demographers have used the register of drafted men to check the completeness of census counts. In 1940, according to such a comparison, all males aged 21 to 35 were underenumerated by about 3 percent, and Negroes by about 13 percent (Price, 1947; Myers, 1948); but later comparisons showed a considerable improvement in the census count (Zelnik, 1968; Siegel and Irwin, 1969). See also *matching; *paleodemography.

REFERENCES: T. H. Hollingsworth, *Historical Demography* (London: Hodder and Stoughton, 1969). John Lada and Frank A. Reister, *Medical Statistics in World War II* (Washington, D.C.: Office of the U.S. Surgeon General, 1975). Albert G. Love and Charles B. Davenport, *Defects Found in Drafted Men* (Washington, D.C.: War Department, 1920). Robert J. Myers, "Underenumeration in the Census as Indicated by Selective Service Data," *American Sociological Review*, 13 (1948), 320-325. Office of the U.S. Surgeon General, "Results of the Examination of Youths for Military Service, 1965,"

Supplement, *Health of the Army*, 21 (July, 1966), 25. Daniel O. Price, "A Check on Underenumeration in the 1940 Census," *American Sociological Review*, 12 (1947), 44-49. Jacob S. Siegel and Richard Irwin, "Annual Comparisons of Census and Selective Data, 1949-1968," *Social Biology*, 16 (1969), 109-114. Robert M. Yerkes, ed., "Psychological Examining in the United States Army," National Academy of Sciences, *Memoirs*, vol. 15 (Washington, D.C.: U.S. Government Printing Office, 1921). Melvin Zelnik, "The Census and Selective Service," *Eugenics Quarterly*, 15 (1968), 173-176.

mingle, a recently coined term in the jargon of the American housing industry, two or more unrelated "singles" who buy or share a home. Builders of condominiums have responded to the demand with "dual masters"—homes with two master bedrooms and baths, separated by a common kitchen and living area. In mid-1982 some sixty firms nationwide were in the business of matching potential mingles.

minor, a person below the legally defined age of adulthood. The concept is based on the premise that before a specified age a person is not wholly responsible for his acts and needs special protection against others, including even his or her parents (cf. *child abuse). The age, however, varies with the context. In the United States the voting age was lowered in 1971 from 21 to 18 years, and there has been a move to apply this new age of majority generally. Minors who commit crimes or misdemeanors are usually tried in juvenile courts, where the emphasis is on rehabilitation and where, paradoxically, the usual legal guarantees are lacking. Traditionally minors require parental consent to marry, but how minority is defined for this purpose varies greatly from one jurisdiction to another and in any case has been eroded, even formally, in the general permissive trend of the last several decades. In the United States debates raged over whether parents must give consent, or be informed, if their under-age daughter acquires contraceptives or has an abortion through federally funded facilities, and over whether persons under 21 should be permitted to drink alcoholic beverages.

minor civil division (MCD), in the United States a political and administrative subdivision of a *county. The commonest designation of an MCD is *township, but in some states it is termed, for instance, a town or a magisterial district. For the 1980 enumeration the U.S. Bureau of the Census regarded the MCDs in only twenty-nine states as suitable for reporting census statistics, and in twenty other states the bureau itself established more or less equivalent census county divisions. In Alaska the population was classified by census subareas, in the District of Columbia by quadrants, and in Puerto Rico by ciudades, pueblos, and barrios.

Minority Rights Group (MRG), an international research and information unit founded in 1967 that publishes irregular reports on racial or ethnic minorities about whom accurate data are not readily available elsewhere—for example, religious minorities in the Soviet Union, Basques, Biharis in Bangladesh, European Gypsies, American Indians in South America, and so on. Address: Benjamin Franklin House, 36 Craven Street, London WC2N 5NG, England.

mobility, a generic term for movement, is used in the social disciplines with several meanings or connotations. When it means movement up or down the hierarchy of social classes, it can be specified as "social" or "occupational mobility," which are distinguished from "geographical" or "spatial mobility." "Population mobility," as ordinarily understood, includes both moves from one residence to another and such temporary moves as *commuting; it is of interest in the analysis of particular consumer markets, for instance, or to relate population distribution to civil defense. Data from censuses or surveys are typically gathered in response to questions like, "Where did you live x years ago?" The number of years so designated is called the *mobility period* (or *interval*); a classification of the population into those who did or did not change their residences over that period is called its *mobility status*. The *mobility rate* is ordinarily defined as the number of migrants per 1,000 in the population, but this is not a very satisfactory measure for several reasons (Thomlinson, 1962; Hamilton, 1965). See also *migration; *migration, internal.

REFERENCES: C. Horace Hamilton, "Practical and Mathematical Considerations in the Formulation and Selection of Migration Rates," *Demography*, 2 (1965), 429-443. Ralph Thomlinson, "The Determination of a Base Population for Computing Migration Rates," *Milbank Memorial Fund Quarterly*, 40 (1962), 356-366.

MOD-Series, a library of computer programs developed by Data Use and Access Laboratories (DUALabs) for work with the summary tapes of the 1970 United States census. The possibilities of retrieval, computation, and aggregation vary with each of the several programs. See also *data processing.

mode, a measure of central tendency of a variable—namely, the point or class with the largest number of values; thus, in a frequency curve, the highest point. Also, *modal*, pertaining to the mode; *bimodal*, pertaining to a distribution with two high points.

models, as used increasingly in all the social disciplines, are of several types. Their general characteristic is that certain interrelated variables, stripped of ancillary associations, are expressed in mathematical terms in order to determine how the pattern designated by the equation, table, or graph changes under specified conditions. What models are used in demography depends in part on how broadly one defines the discipline. In the simplest case one might designate as a model a closed population (that is, one lacking migration in either direction that therefore changes only by its natural increase), since it omits from consideration one usual element of reality. Most models, however, are a good deal more complex (cf. Menken, 1982; Shryock and Siegel, pp. 717-719; *mathematical demography).

In the mathematical expression of a model, the assumptions underlying it may be expressed with fixed values or, in what is termed a *stochastic model, as probabilistic distributions. Population projections, for example, are usually deterministic: alternative assumptions, from "high" to "low," concerning fertility, mortality, and sometimes migration produce population sizes and structures at specified future dates; but the U.S. Bureau of the Census, as one instance, carefully avoids the implication that any particular series is more or less probable. If several sets of assumptions, either fixed or probabilistic, are fed into a computer, the resultant *simulation can resemble a controlled experiment in the physical sciences. One can feed in probabilities, say, of *fecundability as related to *pregnancy loss, expected lengths of pregnancy and postpartum *amenorrhea, *parity, duration of marriage, desired *family size and spacing of births, and effectiveness of *contraception—all yielding a table that shows the proportions of a beginning *cohort of women who each month conceive, miscarry, have a stillbirth, or produce a live-born child (Potter and Sakoda, 1966).

The most important models used in demography are the *life table and the stable population (see Coale, 1972). In the "model life tables" that Ansley †Coale and Paul †Demeny (1966) devised, an assumed expectation of life at birth (which for females ranges by 2.5-year intervals from 20 to 77.5) sets the rest of the functions. They used over 300 life tables to indicate patterns the world over, and certain regional deviations were developed separately. Each of the four resultant sets contains twenty-four tables, calculated separately for the two sexes (see also Coale, Demeny, and Vaughan, 1983; Petrioli, 1982). Obviously any estimation from model life tables can be only approximate, but their advantages must be measured in the context of their typical use—with a country more or less totally lacking such statistics. With only a hint of some population variables, an analyst can use the tables to arrive at a reasonable estimate of many others. In an optimistic forecast of the prospects in demography, Hal †Winsborough (1978) held that those in the field would have larger amounts of data to analyze and would do this with the constructuion of new models of increased scope and complexity. See also *population, stable.

REFERENCES: Ansley J. Coale, *The Growth and Structure of Human Populations* (Princeton, N.J.: Princeton University Press, 1972). Coale and Paul Demeny, *Regional Model Life Tables and Stable Populations* (Princeton, N.J.: Princeton University Press, 1966); Coale, Demeny, and Barbara Vaughan, *Regional Model Life Tables and Stable Populations* (2nd ed.; New York: Academic Press, 1983). Jane A. Menken, "Reproduction Models," *International Encyclopedia of Population*, 2, 583-585. Luciano Petrioli, *Nouvelles Tables-types de Mortalité: Application et Population Stable* (Siena: Università di Siena, Facoltà di Scienze Economiche e Bancarie, 1982). Robert G. Potter, Jr., and James M. Sakoda, "A Computer Model of Family Building Based on Expected Values," *Demography*, 3 (1966), 450-461. Shryock and Siegel, *Methods and Materials of Demography*. Hal H. Winsborough, "Organization of Demographic Research: Problems of the Next Decade," in Karl E. Taeuber et al., eds., *Social Demography* (New York: Academic Press, 1978).

modernization, the all-encompassing social change by which less developed countries acquire modernity, is generally a rather loose term. In works by economists, modernization is often synonymous with industrialization or *economic development, a process that, for example, is accelerated by capital investment and is measured by an index like output per capita. When such narrowly economic criteria were applied to non-Western countries, however, the conventional assumption that all social-cultural factors remained constant often passed over too many significant changes. In a distinction suggested in many writings but not yet general, modernization denotes the development of the economy, narrowly defined, plus such associated shifts as a rise in literacy, a decline in extended-family ties, and a lesser impact of religion on secular activities (Peel, 1973; Schnaiberg, 1970). There are two major difficulties with the concept: "traditionalism" and "modernity" are not necessarily mutually exclusive systems, and neither end of the supposed polarity is always consistent and homogeneous (Bendix, 1967; Gusfield, 1967; Goldscheider, 1971).

The three stages of the *demographic transition are linked by the thesis, usually implicit, that the changes in population growth that accompany modernization are essentially the same wherever and whenever they occur. In fact, however, the fall in mortality has been far faster in less developed countries than in the historic West, and the spread of a small-family system has been far more urgently advocated but possibly slower in India or Egypt than in nineteenth-century Britain or France. The growth of numbers associated with Stage II of the demographic transition has been expressed in a rapid *urbanization, but not necessarily of the same type. Most of those who migrated to Western cities of the past were seeking jobs in which they could apply potential industrial capabilities; but many, perhaps most, of the new city dwellers of less developed countries have constituted only an overflow from rapidly expanding rural populations, a mass of persons without either urban skills or sometimes even the aspiration to acquire them. As these examples suggest, modernization resembles the demographic transition in that, by classifying widely divergent phenomena under broad rubrics, analysts apply history simplistically to present societies, thus often reaching false prognoses. As an important example, though modernization is ordinarily interpreted as an overall cause of a decline in family size, it can also bring about a rise in fertility (Heer, 1966; Nag, 1980, 1982).

REFERENCES: Reinhard Bendix, "Tradition and Modernity Reconsidered," *Comparative Studies in Society and History*, 9 (1967), 292-346. Calvin Goldscheider, *Population, Modernization, and Social Structure* (Boston: Little, Brown, 1971). Joseph R. Gusfield, "Tradition and Modernity: Misplaced Polarities in the Study of Social Change," *American Journal of Sociology*, 72 (1967), 351-362. David M. Heer, "Economic Development and Fertility," *Demography*, 3 (1966), 423-444. Moni Nag, "How Modernization Can Also Increase Fertility," *Current Anthropology*, 21 (1980), 571-587; "Modernization and Its Impact on Fertility: The Indian Scene," Center for Policy Studies, *Working Papers*, no. 84 (New York: Population Council, 1982). J.D.Y. Peel, "Cultural

Factors in the Contemporary Theory of Development," *European Journal of Sociology*, 14 (1973), 283-303. Allan Schnaiberg, "Measuring Modernism: Theoretical and Empirical Explorations," *American Journal of Sociology*, 76 (1970), 399-425.

momentum in physics means the property of a moving body that determines how long it will take to come to rest. As adapted to demography, momentum means the property of a population moving toward stability that sets a relatively smooth rate of change (see *population, stable). For example, if a large cohort of women produce only two children each, the small families will be numerous enough to ensure a continued increase of the population for several generations. The same relation between size of cohort and size of family works also in reverse: a small proportion of mothers each of whom has a relatively large family will not necessarily raise fertility above the replacement level.

REFERENCES: Tomas Frejka, "The Prospects for a Stationary World Population," *Scientific American*, 228 (March, 1973), 15-23. Nathan Keyfitz, "On the Momentum of Population Growth," *Demography*, 8 (1971), 71-90.

Monaco: The Census Commission conducted an enumeration in 1975 and published the results in 1977; the most recent census was in 1982. Address: Commission du Recensement, Monaco.

monogamy, which etymologically derives from the Greek for "one wife," is ordinarily understood as a system of *marriage under which each person of either sex is legally permitted only one spouse at a time. The contravention of that law is known as *bigamy*, even if several wives (or husbands) are involved. Marriage after the death of the first spouse (or, by extension, after a divorce) is sometimes called *deuterogamy* or *digamy*. With respect to a legal system that sanctions multiple marriages, the institution is called **polygamy* or, respectively, *polygyny*, one in which the husband is permitted to have more than one wife, and *polyandry*, where the wife may have more than one husband.

Montserrat: The government's Statistics Office conducts the country's censuses, the latest of which was in 1980. It publishes an annual *Statistical Digest* that includes population data, and an annual *Vital Statistics Report*. Address: P.O. Box 292, Plymouth.

moral statistics, a nineteenth-century term more common in French and German but sometimes used also in English. It means the statistics (or the statistical analysis) of social factors, or roughly what is today called quantitative sociology. For example, in his *Essai sur la Statistique Morale de la France* (1833), André Michel †Guerry analyzed the relation between level of education and the crime rate.

morbidity, the opposite of *health, has something of the same ambiguous range. The ultimate root of the word is *mors*, Latin for "death," and the link persists

between the study of morbidity, or sickness in the broadest sense, and that of
*mortality, one consequence of ill health. The concept is a central one in *ep-
idemiology, and it has been analyzed in the context of demography by such
institutions as the statistical units of the insurance companies and the *Milbank
Memorial Fund (e.g., Lew and Seltzer, 1970; Starfield, 1974).

Two types of criteria underlie morbidity statistics, the often temporary distinction between the ill and the healthy (see *disease), and the relatively permanent one between the disabled and the fit (see *disability). However, the data
can vary depending on such spurious factors as their purpose, the population
included in surveys, and the professional interest or bias of analysts. Most records
are kept on a case basis, though the medical history of persons would be more
illuminating for many purposes; see *record linkage. In professional writings
the important difference between *incidence and prevalence is maintained, but
the two are often confounded in popular discussions. Two obvious points suggest
the complexities of interpreting the morbidity data of populations. In an area
without medical facilities no one is formally recorded as being sick; and as
hospitals are built and doctors become available, the data show an increasing
amount of morbidity. Many medical improvements, moreover, have the same
effect. The use of insulin to treat diabetics has increased greatly the prevalence
of the disease—by keeping alive persons who formerly would have died.

Most analyses of how morbidity relates to mortality have been based on either
medical records or longitudinal studies of volunteer respondents. First visits to
a doctor were classified by cause of illness and then related to subsequent deaths
(Damiani, 1977). In the well known *Framingham Study, an attempt was made
to identify risks of heart disease and determine their incidence. One active area
of research has been whether and how such personal habits or group customs
as diet (see *nutrition), *smoking, and other types of *addiction result in ill
health or mortality. See also *aging.

REFERENCES: Paul Damiani, "Mesure de la Morbidité: Liaison avec la Mortalité,"
International Statistical Review, 45 (1977), 39-50. Edward A. Lew and Frederic Seltzer,
"Uses of the Life Table in Public Health," *Milbank Memorial Fund Quarterly*, 48, Part
2 (1970), 15-37. Barbara Starfield, "Measurement of Outcome: A Proposed Scheme,"
Milbank Memorial Fund Quarterly, 52 (1974), 39-50.

Mormons, or, more formally, members of the Church of Jesus Christ of Latter-
Day Saints, constitute in several respects a unique phenomenon. They began as
one of a dozen small religious sects that arose during the nineteenth century in
New York State and the Midwest. Because they practiced *polygamy, they were
subjected to official persecution and mob violence, from which they fled in a
series of westward migrations. This "Exodus" is featured in Mormon histories
as prominently as the Great Trek of the Boers or the Long March of Chinese
Communists; in all cases, accounts of the hardships of their forebears help unite
the present generation. Eventually they settled in "Deseret," which comprised
virtually the whole of Utah and Nevada, plus two-thirds of Arizona, half of

Colorado, and portions of southern California, New Mexico, Wyoming, Idaho, and Oregon. From this vast area the Territory of Utah was created in 1850, and thereafter "foreign" representatives of the federal government administered the affairs of a generally hostile population. Even after the church abandoned polygamy, outsiders—lumped together as "Gentiles"—opposed what they saw as a theocracy. For since Mormons used their democratic rights to elect officers of the church, the supposedly secular government reflected (and, to a lesser degree, still reflects) the religious values of the numerically dominant group. After the Utah War of 1857-58, Mormons won a moral victory, being widely regarded as martyrs who risked everything for religious freedom (Creer, 1929, chap. 8). In 1896, almost five decades after the first application, Utah was finally admitted to the Union.

No other Christian denomination has followed more literally the biblical command to "be fruitful and multiply." As no less a leader than Brigham Young put it, "It is the duty of every righteous man and woman to prepare tabernacles [that is, receptacles for the "pure and holy spirits" awaiting them] for all the spirits they can" (quoted in Kimball Young, 1954, p. 189). Like Roman Catholic doctrine as it was once interpreted, but much more explicitly, the Mormon view is that a numerous progeny is a religious duty, for the more children born on earth the more there will be to people the heavens. The hierarchy in Mormon heaven has each place determined almost entirely by the earthling's marital status and reproduction. Those who entered an everlasting covenant with their spouses become the rulers of the afterlife, where only they are able to continue to have children. No ecological problems will arise. "As soon as each God has begotten many millions of male and female spirits, and his Heavenly inheritance becomes too small to comfortably accommodate his great family, he in connection with his sons organizes a new world, after a similar order to the one which we now inhabit" (quoted in Kern, 1981, p. 148). Not surprisingly, birth control has always been officially taboo. Women reportedly have stretched the interval between births by breastfeeding, but if it extends beyond two years or so, the community begins to exert moral pressure on the delinquent wife. Before the abolition of polygamy, the women in many plural families engaged in "a friendly race among the wives to see who could have the most children. To surpass another wife in such matters enhanced one's prestige, rhetorically called 'adding jewels to one's crown of glory in the hereafter' " (Young, 1954, p. 190).

Mormon society still retains an ideology of rugged capitalist individualism, together with its strong family life, the banning of coffee, tea, tobacco, and liquor, and the possibility of excommunication for those who break the church's rules. Members are expected to donate a tenth of their before-tax income to the church, as well as to serve as missionaries and to work on church-owned farms that feed the needy (cf. May, 1980). Population grew from both a high natural increase and the immigration of European converts. Settlements of Mormons exist throughout the original Deseret, as well as in portions of Mexico and Canada. During the past several decades, this out-migration from the center has been reversed by a movement to Utah's cities, so that the state's Mormons increased from 56 percent of the population in 1920 to 72 percent in 1970. Since the end of World War II, worldwide membership in the church rose by four times, to the present total of about 4 million.

In recent years the genealogical records of Mormons have become available to demographers. Data on 170,000 "family group sheets," an estimated 80 to 90 percent of all the families that trekked to Utah, have been put on computer tape. As the first result, a report was published on the ages at marriage and fertility of more than 20,000 once-married Mormon couples from 1820 to 1920. Over this century, the number of children ever born fell from 9.00 to 5.02 for women married before age 20, from 7.07 to 4.57 for those married at ages 20-24, and from 5.67 to 3.83 for those married at age 25 and over. The 1870-80 decade was a watershed, after which the members' isolation was reduced by increasing numbers of non-Mormons moving into the area; but some of the group's persistent distinctiveness is still reflected in its demographic record (Skolnick et al., 1978; cf. Anderton et al., 1983). See also *Genealogical Society of Utah.

REFERENCES: Douglas L. Anderton, Joseph Conaty, and Thomas W. Pullum, "Population Estimates from Longitudinal Records in Otherwise Data-Deficient Settings," *Demography*, 20 (1983), 273-284. Leland H. Creer, *Utah and the Nation* (Seattle: University of Washington Press, 1929). Louis J. Kern, *An Ordered Love: Sex Roles and Sexuality in Victorian Utopias—the Shakers, the Mormons, and the Oneida Community* (Chapel Hill: University of North Carolina Press, 1981). Dean L. May, "Mormons," in *Harvard Encyclopedia of American Ethnic Groups* (Cambridge, Mass., 1980), pp. 730-731. Mark Skolnick, Lee L. Bean, May, V. Arbon et al., "Mormon Demographic History: I; Nuptiality and Fertility of Once-Married Couples," *Population Studies*, 32 (1978), 5-19. Kimball Young, *Isn't One Wife Enough?* (New York: Holt, 1954; reprinted, Westport, Conn.: Greenwood Press, 1970).

Morocco: Demographic Institutions

The National Institute of Statistics and Applied Economics (INSEA), established in the Ministry of Planning and Regional Development in 1961, was directed in the late 1970s by Chaouki Benazzou. Its research, concerned mainly with the country's economy and population, is reported in monographs and in the *Revue de l'Institut National de Statistique et d'Économie Appliquée*. Address: Institut National de Statistique et d'Économie Appliquée, Secrétariat d'État au Plan et au Développement Régional, Boîte Postale 406, Rabat.

The Statistical Office of the same ministry issues a statistical yearbook in Arabic and French and a partly overlapping *Maroc en Chiffres*. Its Bureau of Demographic and Social Research and Censuses, headed in 1980 by Abdelhamid †Abouchouker, conducts the country's censuses. The results of the 1971 count were published in 1976, and there was another census in 1981. In 1981 the Population Division was headed by Abdelaziz El-Ghazaili, and the Center of Demographic Research and Studies (CERED) by Housni El-Arbi. Address: Direction de la Statistique, Service des Enquêtes et des Recensements Démographiques et Sociaux, Division de la Population, and Centre de Recherche et d'Études Démographiques, Boîte Postale 178, Rabat.

The Central Health Statistics Bureau in the Ministry of Public Health also publishes statistics on population. Address: Service Central des Statistiques Sanitaires, Ministère de la Santé Publique, Rabat.

mortality, the aggregate of *deaths at a given time and place, was the first element of population to be subjected to detailed analysis, and formal demography began with the development of the *life table. Long after this start, however, the necessary data have often been incomplete, even in countries with acceptable censuses. It was only since 1933 that throughout the United States the statistics on deaths were supposedly at least 90 percent complete; see *registration areas. In many less developed countries the registration of deaths is still not attempted for sizable portions of the population, and the partial record sometimes includes statements on the *cause of death, for instance, that are totally useless.

As later with fertility, the mystery of death has been probed principally through a differential analysis: under various specified conditions, which social groups die in greater proportion? Differentials by age and sex, which combine biological and cultural determinants of mortality, are the most significant (cf. Preston, 1982). Where modern death control is lacking, there is a high risk during infancy and early childhood, and the relatively low one during adolescence and early adulthood continues until the start of significant senescence (cf. *mortality, infant; *old age; *senility). The typical graph of age-specific death rates, thus, is a U-shaped curve. In societies that have benefited from the momentous success in combatting infectious diseases, whose victims had been mainly the very young, this graph has a shortened left arm in the form of a J.

Except during the childbearing years, females generally have lower age-specific death rates than males (Heligman, 1983; Tabutin, 1978), and in modern Western societies this rule holds without the exception. Some of the difference is innate. Of the much larger proportion of fertilized ova that develop into male fetuses, more die during gestation, resulting in a typical *sex ratio at birth of about 105. Male infants also are more susceptible to many causes of death. For adults it is difficult to distinguish biological from environmental influences; but a comparison of two Catholic teaching orders, one of monks and the other of nuns, showed that, under their more or less equivalent conditions of life, females lived longer on the average (Madigan, 1957). The differential, moreover, has been widening during the past several decades. Since declines in maternal mortality were more or less matched by the falling risks associated with male *occupations, most of the growing female advantage is at higher ages, the consequence mainly of lower death rates from heart diseases and cancers (but see also *accidents). More males than females smoke cigarettes (though the pattern has been changing); and the diagnosis and cure of cancers frequent among females (breast and uterus) improved faster than of those more frequent among males (digestive system and lungs) (Hetzel, 1983; Preston, 1970; Retherford, 1975; Waldron,

1976). The most puzzling trend of the recent past is that in most advanced countries the mortality of middle-aged and elderly men has *risen* (Klebba, 1971). The older the age bracket, therefore, the higher the usual proportion of females; in 1980 the sex ratio of Americans ranged from 104.7 for those under 5 years to 67.6 for those 65 and over.

Morbidity and mortality differ by family status. With respect to alcoholism and drug addiction, for example, the cause–effect relation probably works in both directions: the addict's family withdraws from him, and a person isolated from strong personal bonds is more likely to become addicted. More generally, three factors seem to be operating: the absence of mutual care outside a family setting (resulting in higher incidence of influenza and pneumonia), sexual promiscuity and self-indulgence (venereal diseases and addictions), and social isolation (suicide and accidents) (Chen and Cobb, 1960). According to one study, the risk of mortality within a year of the death of a spouse or other close relative was seven times that of a control group matched by age, sex, and marital status (Rees and Lutkins, 1967). However, the family is sometimes a dangerous environment, resulting in battered children and wives (see *child abuse).

In the past there was almost always an inverse correlation between social class and mortality (e.g., Antonovsky, 1967; Kitagawa and Hauser, 1973). Those at the upper levels of society had less dangerous occupations, lived under more healthful conditions, and could more easily afford medical attention when it was necessary. But free clinics, group health insurance, Medicare and Medicaid, and similar institutions provided good medical care much more widely; and the decline of infectious diseases raised the relative influence on mortality of the style of life, especially such habits as *smoking, lack of exercise, overeating, and overrich diets (Preston, 1977). Various bits of evidence suggest that class differentials are becoming smaller or even disappearing (Antonovsky, 1968; cf. Crimmins, 1981; Weatherby et al., 1983), and it is very important to keep this chronology in mind and note the date of any statistics on class differences. To the degree that the lower classes of Western societies still have higher rates of mortality, moreover, this can be ascribed less often to a differential access to medical facilities than to such other factors as the effect of a poorer education on diet and childrearing patterns (Lerner, 1968; Lefcowitz, 1973; Stern, 1983).

The most remarkable change in mortality worldwide has been the precipitous decline over the past half century of the death rates of less developed countries (cf. U.N. and WHO, 1982). Following World War II life-saving medicines, techniques, institutions, and personnel were made available on a broad scale to populations that, in many cases, had until then made do with relatively ineffective traditional therapies. The sizable gap in mortality between the industrial West and the beneficiaries of its therapeutic services narrowed considerably—and then held constant. According to several analysts viewing data from quite different parts of the world, the application of effective health care can be continued only if the people who are affected become sufficiently well educated to use the means available (see also Arriaga, 1981). At an international conference on mortality

(U.N. and WHO, 1979), John †Caldwell used Nigerian data to show that, independent of other factors, a mother's education had a significant effect on the incidence of infant and child mortality; and he argued that the same relation would be found elsewhere. In a detailed comparison of death rates in two densely populated states of India, Moni †Nag (1981) showed that the most probable reason why Kerala has had a consistently better record than West Bengal is the higher literacy in Kerala, particularly among females. Perhaps the most striking evidence is a table showing the relation between mothers' education and the probability of their children dying during the first two years of life. For each of a series of Latin American countries, for which the total values of $_2q_0$ differed considerably, there was a marked decline as the years of schooling rose from zero to ten or more (Hugo Behm and Domingo Primante, *Notas de Población*, 33, no. 3, 1978; cited in Palloni, 1981), see *life table.

The simplest measure of mortality is the crude death *rate, the number of deaths during a year per 1,000 in the midyear population. Because of their wide variation along several dimensions, death rates are often computed specific to age groups, sex, some index of social class, or a combination of such factors. American life tables, which by definition differentiate by age, are often computed separately for the two sexes, whites and nonwhites, and the various regions of the country. *Standardization is frequently used to compare the mortality of populations with different age structures. By applying age-specific death rates to the distribution by age in a standard population, one obtains the "expected" number of deaths in each age bracket. The ratio of actual to expected deaths has been called the "standard mortality schedule" (Pressat, 1972, pp. 104-106) or the "comparative mortality index" (Henry, 1976, p. 125). Three of the commonest measures of mortality—the crude death rate, the standardized death rate, and the life-table death rate—are all what has been termed "aggregative"; that is, they are ratios of aggregate numbers of deaths and persons. Rather than a measure based on age distributions of deaths, which sometimes vary so little that they are difficult to analyze, one can use one based on death rates, namely, *"del," or the geometric mean of the age-specific death rates (Schoen, 1970, 1976).

REFERENCES: Aaron Antonovsky, "Social Class, Life Expectancy and Overall Mortality," *Milbank Memorial Fund Quarterly*, 45 (1967), 31-73; "Social Class and the Major Cardiovascular Diseases," *Journal of Chronic Diseases*, 21 (1968), 65-106. Eduardo E. Arriaga, "The Deceleration of the Decline of Mortality in LDCs: The Case of Latin America," in IUSSP, International Population Conference, Manila, 1981, *Solicited Papers* (Liège, 1981). Edith Chen and Sidney Cobb, "Family Structure in Relation to Health and Diseases: A Review of the Literature," *Journal of Chronic Diseases*, 12 (1960), 544-567. Eileen M. Crimmins, "The Changing Pattern of American Mortality Decline, 1940-77, and Its Implications for the Future," *Population and Development Review*, 7 (1981), 229-254. Larry Heligman, "Patterns of Sex Differentials in Mortality in Less Developed Countries," in Alan D. Lopez and Lado T. Ruzicka, eds., *Sex Differentials in Mortality* (Canberra: Australian National University, Department of Demography, 1983). Henry, *Population*. Basil S. Hetzel, "Life Style Factors in Sex Differentials in Mortality in Developed Countries," in Lopez and Ruzicka, eds., *Sex Differentials in Mortality*. (1983). Evelyn M. Kitagawa and Philip M. Hauser, *Differential Mortality in the United States: A Study in Socioeconomic Epidemiology* (Cambridge, Mass.: Harvard University Press, 1973). A. Joan Klebba, *Leading Components of the Upturn in Mortality for Men, United States, 1952-67*, U.S. National Center for Health Statistics, Ser. 20, no. 11 (Washington, D.C., 1971). Myron J. Lefcowitz, "Poverty and Health: A Re-examination," *Inquiry*, 10 (1973), 3-13. Monroe Lerner, "The Level of Physical Health of the Poverty Population: A Conceptual Reappraisal of Structural Factors," *Medical Care*, 6 (1968), 355-367. Francis C. Madigan, "Are Sex Mortality Differentials Biologically Caused?" *Milbank Memorial Fund Quarterly*, 35 (1957), 202-223. Moni Nag, "Impact of Social Development and Economic Development on Mortality: A Comparative Study of Kerala and West Bengal," Center for Policy Studies, *Working Papers*, no. 78 (New York: Population Council, 1981). Alberto Palloni, "Mortality in Latin America: Emerging Patterns," *Population and Development Review*, 7 (1981), 623-649. Roland Pressat, *Demographic Analysis: Methods, Results, Applications* (Chicago: Aldine, 1972). Samuel H. Preston, "An International Comparison of Excessive Adult Mortality," *Population Studies*, 24 (1970), 5-20; "Mortality Trends," *Annual Review of Sociology*, 3 (1977), 163-178; ed., *Biological and Social Aspects of Mortality and the Length of Life* (Liège: IUSSP, 1982). W. Dewi Rees and Sylvia G. Lutkins, "Mortality of Bereavement," *British Medical Journal*, 4 (1967), 13-16. Robert D. Retherford, *The Changing Sex Differential in Mortality* (Westport, Conn.: Greenwood Press, 1975). Robert Schoen, "The Geometric Mean of the Age-Specific Death Rates as a Summary Index of Mortality," *Demography*, 7 (1970), 317-324; "Measuring Mortality Trends and Differentials," *Social Biology*, 23 (1976), 235-243. Jon Stern, "Social Mobility and the Interpretation of Social Class Mortality Differentials," *Journal of Social Policy*, 12 (1983), 27-49. Dominique J. Tabutin, "La Surmortalité Féminine en Europe avant 1940," *Population*, 33 (1978), 121-148. United Nations and World Health Organization, *Proceedings of the Meeting on Socioeconomic Determinants and Consequences of Mortality* (New York, 1979); *Levels and Trends of Mortality since 1950* (New York, 1982). Ingrid Waldron, "Why Do Women Live Longer than Men?" *Social Science and Medicine*, 10 (1976), 349-362. Norman L. Weatherby, Charles B. Nam, and Larry W. Isaac, "Development, Inequality, Health Care, and Mortality at the Older Ages: A Cross-National Analysis," *Demography*, 20 (1983), 27-43.

mortality, bills of, compilations from parish registrations of deaths, published in many European cities and often used as a prime source in *historical demography.

REFERENCE: T. H. Hollingsworth, *Historical Demography* (London: Hodder and Stoughton, 1969), pp. 145-148.

mortality crisis has been defined as a short-term disturbance in the normal trend of mortality (with "normal" specified according to the deaths to be expected in that society at that time), such that the affected generation cannot be certain of reproducing itself even with the full expression of its recuperative capacity. So defined, the concept relates not merely to deaths but to the deaths of those that are or will be in the fecund ages—by a simplifying postulate, persons aged less than 15 years (Livi Bacci, 1978, pp. 9-10). From the plague to cholera, epidemic diseases affect various ages markedly differently. See also *disaster.

REFERENCE: Massimo Livi Bacci, *La Société Italienne devant les Crises de Mortalité* (Florence: Department of Statistics, University of Florence, 1978).

mortality crossover refers to a graph of age-specific death rates of two populations, one of which has higher mortality up to a particular age and lower mortality thereafter. For example, the rates of American blacks are higher than those of whites up to about age 75 and lower when older populations are compared. The crossover is not merely an artifact of differential reporting, and no alternative explanation that has been offered is altogether convincing. If there is a survival of the fittest among older blacks, this is an anomalous pattern.

REFERENCES: Kenneth G. Manton, Sharon Sandomirsky Poss, and Stephen Wing, "The Black/White Mortality Crossover: Investigation from the Perspective of the Components of Aging," *Gerontologist*, 19 (1979), 291-300. Charles B. Nam, Norman L. Weatherby, and Kathleen A. Ockay, "Causes of Death Which Contribute to the Mortality Crossover Effect," *Social Biology*, 25 (1978), 306-314.

mortality, infant, the aggregate of *deaths during the first year of life, constitutes so large a proportion of the total that it is typically analyzed separately. Infant mortality, moreover, used to be a sensitive index of general welfare, with high correlations between it and measures of literacy or industrialization, for instance. "No fact is better established," the English statistician Arthur †Newsholme wrote in 1910, "than that the death rate, and especially the death rate among children, is higher in inverse proportion to the social status of the population" (quoted in Antonovsky and Bernstein, 1977). In the more recent period the significant reduction in differentials by social class within advanced countries was the consequence mainly of social welfare and sanitation, rather than the inculcation of more healthful personal and family norms (cf. Chase, 1977). In less developed countries, similarly, a tremendous decline in mortality at early ages was effected less through their own development than by the importation of death-control techniques and personnel (see also *mortality). During the years 1958-68, four indicators of social level (economic-industrial development, newspaper circulation, population per physician, and urbanization) accounted for only 15 percent of the change in the infant mortality of less developed countries (Shin, 1975). If deaths of infants are generally as underrecorded as Alberto Palloni (1981) found in a sample of less developed countries, any correlation between mortality and other factors, of course, is less meaningful.

Whatever the accuracy of death statistics in a particular time or place, the data on infant mortality are generally the worst. The death of an adult is more likely to be recorded than that of a newborn; in the traditional Chinese culture, for instance, even to mention their deceased siblings is a bad omen for living children. The *infant mortality rate* of any year, or the number of deaths up to age 1 year per 1,000 live births during that year, is also flawed. The ratio does not indicate the risk of dying before one's first birthday, for some of the children born in any calendar year that do not survive the twelve months will die during the following year. If fertility is at a constant rate, the discrepancy is relatively unimportant, but a large and rapid change in the numbers born can introduce a sizable error. Converting the conventional infant mortality rate into a genuine probability, the ratio of deaths to the population at risk, involves mathematical manipulations based on a number of assumptions (see *separation).

According to a summary of sixteen ethnographic studies in various parts of the world, the proportion recorded as dying under 1 year of age ranged in these primitive societies between 10 and 35 percent, that under 5 years between 30 and 70 percent (Polunin, 1967). In Europe of the seventeenth and eighteenth centuries, studies suggest that typically one child in four died during its first year, with greater proportions among the first-born and children of high parities (Cohen, 1975; cf. Biraben, 1981). By the beginning of the twentieth century the international range was great, with infant mortality rates around 100 in advanced Western countries, and rates well over 200 in the worst of those less developed countries that had usable statistics (Chandrasekhar, 1959, p. 92). For the most recent period the difference is wider—below 30 in countries with the best records, and probably still well over 200 in those with least control but also the poorest data (Vallin, 1976; cf. Farah and Preston, 1982).

Infant mortality is high relative to that at other ages for two reasons—because a baby, if barely born alive, may not be able to remain so very long, and because any baby, even if born healthy, is especially susceptible to disease and accident. These two causes of infant mortality have been termed, respectively, *endogenous*, referring to what might be considered a postponed *fetal death, and *exogenous*, referring to a death that differs from general mortality only in the age of the person affected. Causes of death in the first category include immaturity, birth injuries, congenital malformations, and "ill defined diseases peculiar to early infancy" (in the words of the *International Classification of Diseases*); and those in the second category include certain parasitic diseases; pneumonia, influenza, and other infectious diseases; gastroenteritis and diarrhea; and accidents. The same distinction is made approximately by dividing the deaths of infants between *neonatal mortality*, or that during the first month of life, and *post-neonatal mortality*, or that during the rest of the first year. Until a few years ago neonatal mortality was regarded as the irreducible minimum; more recently, marked improvements in obstetrics have cut the critical period down to the first week, or the first day, or even the first hours of life (see also *birth weight).

The classification of some early mortality as endogenous implies that deaths shortly before and shortly after birth may not differ in principle. The two types are classified together as *perinatal mortality*, meaning the aggregate of deaths between the time when the fetus becomes viable to the time after birth when prenatal causes of death are relatively inoperative—or, by the convention recommended by the World Health Organization (WHO), between the twenty-eighth complete week of gestation and the first six days of life. The *perinatal mortality ratio* is defined as the number of deaths just before and just after birth (however specified) per 1,000 live births during the year. In the abstract it makes better sense to approximate the total number of viable fetuses as the base; and what is termed the *perinatal mortality rate* has as its denominator the number of births plus the number of late fetal deaths (see Shryock and Siegel, pp. 425-426).

The principles underlying this array of alternative measures are less confusing than the definitions. From the time of conception, one can distinguish three main stages of development: (1) a viable fetus, (2) birth, and (3) a time after birth when endogenous causes of death are no longer significant. The precise timing of the three stages must be somewhat arbitrary, in part because they depend on how advanced medical practice has become. In any case, the best measure in theory is often not the most practical to use, given the limited data particularly on fetal deaths.

REFERENCES: Aaron Antonovsky and Judith Bernstein, "Social Class and Infant Mortality," *Social Science and Medicine*, 11 (1977), 453-470. Jean-Noël Biraben, "Les Aspects Médico-écologiques de la Mortalité Différentielle des Enfants aux 18ème et 19ème Siècles," in IUSSP, International Population Conference, Manila, 1981, *Solicited Papers* (Liège, 1981). Sripati Chandrasekhar, *Infant Mortality in India, 1901-55: A Matter of Life and Death* (London: Allen and Unwin, 1959). Helen C. Chase, "Infant Mortality and Its Concomitants, 1960-72," *Medical Care*, 15 (1977), 662-674. Joel E. Cohen, "Childhood Mortality, Family Size and Birth Order in Pre-industrial Europe," *Demography*, 12 (1975), 35-55. Abdul-Aziz Farah and Samuel H. Preston, "Child Mortality Differentials in Sudan," *Population and Development Review*, 8 (1982), 365-383. Alberto Palloni, "A Review of Infant Mortality Trends in Selected Underdeveloped Countries: Some New Estimates," *Population Studies*, 35 (1981), 100-119. Ivan V. Polunin, "Health and Disease in Contemporary Primitive Societies," in Don Brothwell and A. T. Sandison, eds., *Diseases in Antiquity: A Survey of the Diseases, Injuries and Surgery of Early Populations* (Springfield, Ill.: Thomas, 1967). Eui Hang Shin, "Economic and Social Correlates of Infant Mortality: A Cross-sectional and Longitudinal Analysis of 63 Selected Countries," *Social Biology*, 22 (1975), 315-325. Shryock and Siegel, *Methods and Materials of Demography*. Jacques Vallin, "La Mortalité Infantile dans le Monde: Évolution depuis 1950," *Population*, 31 (1976), 801-838.

mortality ratio denotes the number of deaths in a designated sector of a population as related to those in the whole population. One frequent specification is the number of deaths from a particular cause per 100 (or 1,000) deaths from all causes; another is the number of deaths after reaching some age (say, 50 or over) per 100 total deaths. The ratio can be deceptive, for it typically varies greatly with the age structure. Usually, therefore, analysts standardize for age, and a standard (or standardized) mortality ratio, usually designated SMR, is a useful measure for comparing mortality characteristics.

REFERENCE: Spiegelman, *Introduction to Demography*, pp. 86-87.

motivators, in the jargon of birth-control programs, persons hired to persuade members of the *target population to participate in the program. An alternative designation is outreach personnel.

Mozambique: The government's National Statistics Office conducts the country's censuses, the most recent of which was in 1980. It publishes the *Anuário Estatístico*, an annual statistical yearbook in French and Portuguese that includes population data, as does the monthly *Boletim Mensal de Estatística*, in Portuguese with French table of contents and table titles. Address: Direção Nacional de Estatística, C.P. 493, Maputo.

MTP, an acronym for "medical termination of pregnancy," an alternative designation common especially in India for legally induced abortion.

multigravida, a pregnant woman who has been pregnant at least once before; alternatively, a woman pregnant for the third (or later) time. A more precise notation is also more convenient: Gravida II, III, IV, and so on.

multipara (or Para II, III, etc.), a woman who has had two or more pregnancies resulting in viable offspring, whether or not born alive. Also *multiparity*, the condition of being a multipara, or the production of more than one offspring in a single gestation; *multiparous*, having had two or more pregnancies that resulted in viable offspring, or producing several offspring at one time.

multiple births are relatively rare in the human species. Data are based on live births and fetal deaths in multiple deliveries, and this convention can raise some problems in interpretation. Twins are of two types, popularly called identical or fraternal, in scientific usage monozygotic or dizygotic (from *zygote*, a fertilized ovum), depending on whether one ovum split in two or two ova were fertilized separately. Triplets can be monozygotic, dizygotic, or trizygotic, and similarly for higher multiple births. Apparently dizygotic twinning, but not monozygotic, is governed by heredity, varying by both family line and race. All monozygotic twins have the same father, obviously. But if over a short period the mother had sexual relations with two men, dizygotic twins may have different fathers, and in one recorded case the two children were even of different races.

Since all monozygotic twins are of the same sex and dizygotic twins (like siblings generally) are divided roughly equally between the two sexes, one can calculate the twinning rate for each type as follows:

$$m = \frac{(L - U)}{n} \times 1,000 \text{ and } d = \frac{2U}{n} \times 1,000$$

where L and U are the numbers of like-sexed and unlike-sexed twins in a total sample of n deliveries. Over the fecund period of the mother, the value of m rises from about 3.5 to 4; the value of d rises from under 2 in the youngest mothers to above 15 at age 35 and then falls rapidly to the initial rate at menopause. Since there is an obvious relation between age of mother and parity of child, there is a similar curve for d by parity.

REFERENCE: M. G. Bulmer, *The Biology of Twinning in Man* (Oxford: Clarendon, 1970).

multiple-decrement table, an adaptation of the *life table to a population that is subject to attrition not only by mortality but also by other factors. So understood, the life table has acquired an extraordinary versatility (Spiegelman, 1957). In a marriage or nuptiality table, for instance, there are two columns comparable to the q_x column, in which are listed, per 1,000 alive and single at the beginning of each year of age, the numbers respectively that marry or that die while single; and the analysis is carried through to the final column, corresponding to $\mathring{e}_x$, that gives the average number of years before either first marriage or death (Jacobson, 1959, Tables 34-37). In a working-life table, as another example, from the percent of the population of each age above childhood in the work force, one can develop the proportions that leave it due to retirement, death, or all causes (Krishnan, 1977; Shryock and Siegel, pp. 456-458). In a table of school life, one can move from the percent in each school age that is enrolled to the proportion that die, drop out, graduate, or leave the school population for all causes (Stockwell and Nam, 1963).

Nathan †Keyfitz (1977, p. 53) has summed up such adaptations of the life table as follows:

> Associated single-decrement tables, classified by age and with a single mode of egress:
>   Cause of death
>   Leaving school
>   Entering labor force
> Multiple-decrement tables, classified by age and with two or more modes of egress:
>   Death by cause
>   Labor force and death
>   First marriage and death
>   Dropping contraceptive or becoming pregnant
> Combined table following an individual through successive contingencies:
>   Migration
>   Labor force with unemployment and retirement
>   Successive grades at school with dropouts and re-entry
>   Single population, nuptiality, and the married population
>   Successive parities.

REFERENCES: Paul H. Jacobson, *American Marriage and Divorce* (New York: Rinehart, 1959). Nathan Keyfitz, *Applied Mathematical Demography* (New York: Wiley, 1977). Parameswara Krishnan, "The Length of Working Life: India, 1971," *Journal of the Royal Statistical Society*, Ser. A, 140, Part 3 (1977), 359-365. Shryock and Siegel, *Methods and Materials of Demography*. Mortimer Spiegelman, "The Versatility of the Life Table," *American Journal of Public Health*, 47 (1957), 297-304. E. G. Stockwell and Charles B. Nam, "Illustrative Tables of School Life," *Journal of the American Statistical Association*, 58 (1963), 1113-1124.

multipurpose worker (MPW), a designation in India for a person assigned to tasks related to both public health and family planning.

REFERENCE: P. V. Kumas and B. D. Misra, "Some Aspects of the Implementation of the MPW Scheme in Andhra Pradesh," *Journal of Family Welfare*, 27 (June, 1981), 13-30.

multi-round survey, the repeated interviewing of the same respondents in order to obtain data suitable for a longitudinal analysis; an alternative designation of a *panel study. The term multi-round survey developed in relation to a common practice in Africa. In Senegal, for instance, the demographic section of the French agency ORSTOM (Bureau of Scientific and Technical Overseas Research) supervised eight annual surveys of the entire populations of two villages. The method has been criticized as too expensive and, in any case, as unlikely to develop adequate data because the surveyors and the respondents both became tired from the repetition.

REFERENCES: Francis A. H. Gendreau and Jacques Vaugelade, "A Population Laboratory in Senegal," and Étienne van de Walle, "The Role of Multi-round Surveys in the Strategy of Demographic Research," in Pierre A. Cantrelle, ed., *Population in African Development* (Dolhain, Belgium: Ordina Editions, 1974), 1, 231-236 and 301-308.

multivariate analysis in the language of statistics is one that includes more than one characteristic of each unit—for example, such so-called demographic variables as age, sex, education, and income. Typically such variables are interrelated even when they may seem to be independent. For instance, since age-specific death rates are not the same for males and females, in any population there is a relation between age and sex. The general purpose of a multivariate analysis is to uncover patterns of interrelation and to apply this knowledge in estimation, classification, and prediction. Various methods of achieving this have constituted a very active branch of mathematical statistics, and the bibliography of recent works is large (see Anderson et al., 1972; van de Geer, 1971).

REFERENCES: T. W. Anderson, Somesh Das Gupta, and George P. H. Styan, *A Bibliography of Multivariate Statistical Analysis* (New York: Halsted, 1972). John P. van de Geer, *Introduction to Multivariate Analysis for the Social Sciences* (San Francisco: Freeman, 1971).

municipality can mean a *town, *city, or other administrative urban unit having the powers of local self-government. In that sense, it is related to *municipium*, one of the cities of Roman Italy whose citizens had the same rights as those in Rome itself. The Spanish cognate *municipio*, however, is not an urban unit but the equivalent of a county or a township. More generally, "municipality" is not a useful generic term for the areal classification of populations; for like such other designations as "town," "city," or "borough," it is ambiguous. See also *urbanization.

Mysore Population Study, a large-scale survey of fertility conducted under the auspices of the United Nations in Mysore, a state of southern India. The study is notable for a comprehensive discussion of methodology and for the range of social and economic variables related to marriage, fertility, mortality, and family planning.

REFERENCE: United Nations, *The Mysore Population Study* (New York, 1961).